Communication Interventions for Individuals with Severe Disabilities

Communication Interventions for Individuals with Severe Disabilities

Exploring Research Challenges and Opportunities

by

Rose A. Sevcik, Ph.D.
Georgia State University

and

MaryAnn Romski, Ph.D.
Georgia State University

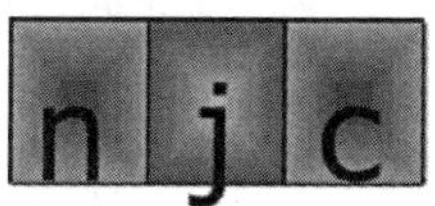

Baltimore • London • Sydney

Paul H. Brookes Publishing Co.
Post Office Box 10624
Baltimore, Maryland 21285-0624
USA

www.brookespublishing.com

The individuals described in this book are composites or real people whose situations are masked and are based on the authors' experiences. In all instances, names and identifying details have been changed to protect confidentiality.

The NJC conference was funded by an R13 conference grant (DC-011495) from the National Institute on Deafness and other Communication Disorders.

Library of Congress Cataloging-in-Publication Data

Sevcik, Rose A., editor. | Romski, Mary Ann, 1952- editor.

Communication interventions for individuals with severe disabilities: exploring research challenges and opportunities / edited by Rose A. Sevcik, Ph.D., Georgia State University, Atlanta, and MaryAnn Romski, Ph.D., Georgia State University, Atlanta ; with invited contributors.

Baltimore : Paul H. Brookes Publishing Co., [2016] | Includes bibliographical references and index.

LCCN 2015043861 (print) | LCCN 2016002494 (ebook) | ISBN 9781598573633 (paperback) | ISBN 9781681250878 (pdf) | ISBN 9781681250892 (epub)

LCSH: Children with mental disabilities—Language. | Children with mental disabilities—Education. | Developmentally disabled children—Language. | Developmentally disabled children—Education. | Developmentally disabled—Means of communication. | Communicative disorders—Treatment. | Facilitated communication. | Speech therapy. | EDUCATION / Special Education / Communicative Disorders.

Classification: LCC LC4616 .C66 2016 (print) | LCC LC4616 (ebook) | DDC 371.9—dc23

LC record available at http://lccn.loc.gov/2015043861

British Library Cataloguing in Publication data are available from the British Library.

2020 2019 2018 2017 2016

10 9 8 7 6 5 4 3 2 1

Contents

About the Editors

Rose A. Sevcik, Ph.D., Distinguished University Professor, Department of Psychology, Georgia State University, Post Office Box 5010, Atlanta, Georgia 30302

Dr. Sevcik is Distinguished Professor of Psychology and Chair of the Developmental Psychology Doctoral Program. She is the founding co-director of the university's Area of Focus: Research on the Challenges to Acquiring Language and Literacy and a founding member of the Center for Research on Atypical Development and Learning. She has made significant contributions to the field of developmental and learning disabilities and language and reading intervention research through more than 100 peer-reviewed publications, chapters, and books and numerous presentations at national and international conferences. She has been an investigator on 12 federally funded projects (National Institutes of Health, Institute of Education Sciences) with a long history of working with schools. Dr. Sevcik is a Fellow of the American Speech-Language-Hearing Association (ASHA), Association for Psychological Science and the International Society of Augmentative and Alternative Communication (ISAAC). She also is Fellow of the American Association on Intellectual and Developmental Disabilities (AAIDD) and past president of its Communication Disorders Division. A member of the National Joint Committee on the Communication Needs of Persons with Severe Disabilities, she is also on the Board of Directors for the United States Society for Augmentative and Alternative Communication.

MaryAnn Romski, Ph.D., Regents Professor of Communication, Psychology, and Communication Disorders and Associate Dean for Research and Graduate Studies, College of Arts and Sciences, Georgia State University, Post Office Box 4038, Atlanta, Georgia 30302-4038

Dr. Romski is Regents Professor of Communication, Psychology, and Communication Disorders at Georgia State University and the Associate Dean for Research and Graduate Studies in the College of Arts and Sciences. She is Director of the Center for Research on Atypical Development and Learning and a founding member of the university's Area of Focus: Research on the Challenges to Acquiring Language and Literacy. Dr. Romski is a certified speech-language pathologist with more than 4 decades of clinical experience and holds the Honors of the American Speech-Language-Hearing Association (ASHA). She is Fellow of the American Association of Intellectual and Developmental Disabilities (AAIDD), ASHA, and the International Society for Augmentative and Alternative Communication (ISAAC). Her continuously funded research program focuses on the communication development of children with developmental disorders who encounter difficulty speaking, particularly the development and evaluation of communication interventions that incorporate speech generating devices. Dr. Romski has published three books, more than 100 articles and chapters, and has given numerous national and international presentations. She is extending her research in South Africa and China. She serves as Associate Editor for *Augmentative and Alternative Communication* and *Infants and Young Children* and is the past chair of the National Joint Committee on the Communication Needs of Individuals with Severe Disabilities (1993–2000) and remains AAIDD's representative.

About the Contributors

Roger Bakeman, Ph.D., Professor Emeritus, Department of Psychology, Georgia State University, Post Office Box 5010, Atlanta, Georgia 30302

Dr. Roger Bakeman is Professor Emeritus in the Psychology Department at Georgia State University. A graduate of Antioch College, Bakeman earned his doctoral degree from the University of Texas at Austin in 1973. He has consulted widely, primarily on matters of methodology and statistical analysis as related to infant and child typical and atypical development. He is also coauthor with John M. Gottman of *Observing Interaction: An Introduction to Sequential Analysis* and with Vicenç Quera of *Sequential Analysis and Observational Methods for the Behavioral Sciences.*

R. Michael Barker, Ph.D., Assistant Professor, Department of Communication Sciences and Disorders, University of South Florida, 4202 East Fowler Avenue, PCD 1017, Tampa, Florida 33620

Dr. Michael Barker is Assistant Professor in the Department of Communication Sciences and Disorders at the University of South Florida in Tampa. He teaches classes on language disorders, augmentative and alternative communication (AAC), and research methodology. His research focuses on assessment and instruction of phonological awareness and literacy in children who use AAC.

Andrea Barton-Hulsey, M.A., CCC-SLP, Speech-Language Pathologist, Department of Psychology, Georgia State University, Post Office Box 5010, Atlanta, Georgia 30302

Ms. Andrea Barton-Hulsey is a doctoral student in developmental psychology and a Language and Literacy Fellow at Georgia State University. She has clinical and research experience working with children with developmental disabilities. Her work has focused on providing augmentative and alternative communication services and supports to facilitate language and reading development in children.

Nancy C. Brady, Ph.D., Associate Professor, Department of Speech-Language-Hearing Sciences and Disorders, University of Kansas, 1000 Sunnyside Avenue, Lawrence, Kansas 66045

Dr. Nancy C. Brady conducts research on early language and communication development in children and adults with severe disabilities, including individuals with autism, fragile X syndrome, and deafblindness. Her research focuses on stages of prelinguistic development, assessing communication, teaching beginning augmentative and alternative communication, and pragmatic aspects of early communication.

Mo Chen, M.A., Doctoral Candidate, Department of Educational Psychology, University of Minnesota, 250 Educational Sciences Building, 56 East River Road, Minneapolis, Minnesota 55455

Ms. Mo Chen is currently completing her doctoral degree in the special education track of the Department of Educational Psychology at the University of Minnesota. She has worked with children with developmental disabilities both in the

United States and China. Her research interests include function-based interventions for addressing problem behavior and conditional communication.

Curtis K. Deutsch, Ph.D., Associate Professor, *Eunice Kennedy Shriver* Center and Department of Psychiatry, University of Massachusetts Medical School, 55 Lake Avenue North, Worcester Massachusetts 01655

Dr. Curtis K. Deutsch is an investigator at the *Eunice Kennedy Shriver* Center and a member of a National Institute of Child Health and Human Development-supported Intellectual and Developmental Disabilities Research Center (IDDRC). His research program specializes in psychobiology and medical genetics. Within the IDDRC, he is co-principle investigator on a quantitative methods core that supports the survey of small *n* and single-subject analytic methods reviewed in this book.

Marc E. Fey, Ph.D., Professor, Hearing and Speech Department, University of Kansas Medical Center, Mailstop 3039, 3901 Rainbow Boulevard, HC Miller Building, Kansas City, Kansas 66160

Dr. Marc E. Fey is Professor of Hearing and Speech at the University of Kansas Medical Center. He received his doctoral degree from the Department of Audiology and Speech Sciences at Purdue University in 1981. Along with his articles, chapters, and software programs, Dr. Fey has published three books on language intervention. He holds distinguished alumnus status from the University of Georgia, Purdue University, and Wichita State University, as well as the Honors of the American Speech-Language-Hearing Association.

David J. Francis, Ph.D., Hugh Roy and Lillie Cranz Cullen Distinguished University Chair, Department of Psychology, University of Houston, 4811 Calhoun Road, 3rd Floor, Houston, Texas 77204

Dr. David J. Francis is the Hugh Roy and Lillie Cranz Cullen Distinguished Chair of Quantitative Methods and former Chairman of the Department of Psychology (2002–2014) at the University of Houston, where he also serves as Director of the Texas Institute for Measurement, Evaluation, and Statistics. He was a recipient of the 2006 Albert J. Harris Award from the International Reading Association and has received the University of Houston's Teaching Excellence Award and the Excellence in Research and Scholarship Award. In 2008, he received the Esther Farfel Award, which recognizes career accomplishments in research, teaching, and service and is the highest award given to faculty members at the University of Houston.

Howard Goldstein, Ph.D., Associate Dean of Research, College of Behavioral and Community Sciences, and Professor, Department of Communication Sciences and Disorders, University of South Florida, 13301 Bruce B. Downs Boulevard, MHC 1121, Tampa, Florida 33612

Dr. Howard Goldstein is Associate Dean for Research and Professor of Communication Sciences and Disorders in the College of Behavioral and Community Sciences at University of South Florida in Tampa. His research has focused on improving the communication and social skills of children with autism and other developmental disabilities. He is the author of two books and more than 100 scholarly journal articles and book chapters and is a nationally known scholar for his research in the field of child language intervention.

Lauren H. Hampton, M.Ed., BCBA, Doctoral Student, Department of Special Education, Peabody College, Vanderbilt University, Nashville, Tennessee 37203

Ms. Lauren Hampton is a doctoral candidate at the Peabody College of Vanderbilt University. Her research focuses on early communication interventions, parent training interventions, and classroom interventions for children with autism. She has more than 10 years of experience implementing early interventions for children with autism and their families.

Anne-Therese Hunt, Sc.D., Consultant, Intellectual and Developmental Disabilities Research Center, University of Massachusetts Medical School, Shriver Center, 55 North Lake Avenue, Worcester, Massachusetts 01655

Dr. Anne-Therese Hunt, owner of Hunt Consulting Associates and former faculty member at Harvard University, provides statistical and epidemiologic consulting services to the Boston area medical research community. She also serves as a biostatistician providing quantitative services and mentorship to members of the National Institute of Child Health and Human Development–supported Intellectual and Developmental Disabilities Research Center.

Ann P. Kaiser, Ph.D., Susan W. Gray Professor of Education and Human Development, Department of Special Education, Peabody College, Vanderbilt University, Nashville, Tennessee 37203

Dr. Ann P. Kaiser is the Susan W. Gray Professor of Education and Human Development at Peabody College of Vanderbilt University. Dr. Kaiser's research focuses on early language interventions for children with developmental disabilities and children at risk due to poverty. She has developed and researched an early communication program to improve the language outcomes for young children with intellectual and developmental disabilities, children with autism, and children at risk due to behavior problems.

Connie Kasari, Ph.D., Professor, Human Development and Psychology, Center for Autism Research and Treatment, University of California Los Angeles, 68-268 Semel Institute, 760 Westwood Plaza, Los Angeles, California 90024

Dr. Connie Kasari is Professor of Human Development and Psychology at UCLA with a joint appointment in the Department of Psychiatry. Since 1990, she has been on the faculty at UCLA where she teaches both graduate and undergraduate courses and has been the primary advisor to more than 40 doctoral students. Her research projects include targeted interventions for early social-communication development in infants, toddlers, and preschoolers with autism who are at risk and peer relationships for school-age children with autism. She is on the science advisory board of the Autism Speaks Foundation and regularly presents to both academic and practitioner audiences locally, nationally, and internationally.

Joanne B. Kledaras, M.A., Senior Research Scientist, Praxis, Inc., 69 West Street, Belmont, Massachusetts 02478

Ms. Joanne B. Kledaras received her bachelor of arts degree in special education from the University of Connecticut and her master's degree in applied behavior analysis from Northeastern University. Throughout her career, she has pursued parallel clinical and research activities, primarily in private and public special education settings. She is presently working on projects aimed at applying recent research findings and technology to develop more effective methods for teaching behavioral prerequisites for augmentative and alternative communication and rudimentary reading.

William J. McIlvane, Ph.D., Professor, Psychiatry and Pediatrics, University of Massachusetts Medical School, 333 South Street, Shrewsbury, Massachusetts 01545

Dr. William McIlvane directs a research program that addresses a number of topics relevant to understanding and perhaps correcting behavior deficits of people with neurodevelopmental disorders. His primary foci are procedures to encourage rapid learning of behaviors involved in symbolic communication and relevant assistive technologies to support efforts of clinicians and special educators. Methods developed in his research are now being applied to teach functional skills in general and special education in the United States and internationally, especially via a long-term collaboration with a large university network in Brazil.

Lee K. McLean, Ph.D., Professor Emeritus, School of Medicine, Department of Allied Health Sciences, University of North Carolina, Chapel Hill, North Carolina 27599

Prior to her retirement in 2013, Dr. Lee K. McLean served as Chair/Associate Dean of the Department of Allied Health Sciences/School of Medicine at the University of North Carolina. Prior to that position, she and her husband, James McLean, worked at Kansas University where they conducted research and training related to communication needs of people with severe disabilities. Dr. Lee is an American Speech-Language-Hearing Association Fellow and served as Chair of the National Joint Committee on the Communication Needs of Persons with Severe Disabilities from 2000–2007.

Beth A. Mineo, Ph.D., Associate Professor, School of Education, and Center Director, Center for Disabilities Studies, University of Delaware, 461 Wyoming Road, Newark, Delaware 19716

Dr. Beth A. Mineo is Director of the Center for Disabilities Studies, Director of the Assistive Technology Unit at the Center, and Associate Professor in the School of Education at the University of Delaware. Trained as a speech-language pathologist and specializing in supports for individuals with significant learning and communication disabilities, she has extensive experience in project design and implementation, services for individuals with disabilities, and assistive technology development, utilization, and policy. She currently conducts research and implementation projects focusing on accessible instructional materials, language representation, and utilization of assistive technology with children birth to 5 years.

Billy T. Ogletree, Ph.D., Professor and Head, Department of Communication Sciences and Disorders, Western Carolina University, 4121 Little Savannah Road, 158A HHSB, Cullowhee, North Carolina 28723

Dr. Billy T. Ogletree is Professor and Head of the Department of Communication Sciences and Disorders at Western Carolina University. His research interests include the communication abilities and needs of individuals with severe intellectual disabilities, including autism. Dr. Ogletree chairs the National Joint Committee for the Communicative Needs of Persons with Severe Disabilities.

Amy T. Parker, Ed.D., Assistant Fellow, Teaching Research Institute, Western Oregon University, 345 Monmouth Avenue North, Monmouth, Oregon 97361

Dr. Amy T. Parker has 20 years of experience working with people who are deafblind as an employment specialist, independent living teacher, in-home parent trainer, and advocate. She received her doctoral degree in special education with an emphasis in deafblindness and a certification in orientation and mobility in 2009 through a U.S. Department of Education, Office of Special Education-funded leadership and enrichment fellowship. She is interested in single-subject research as a means of validating intervention practices and has collaborated in participatory action research with colleagues to empower consumers and families in systems.

Diane Paul, Ph.D., Director, Clinical Issues in Speech-Language Pathology, American Speech-Language-Hearing Association, 2200 Research Boulevard, Rockville, Maryland 20850

Dr. Diane Paul is Director of Clinical Issues in Speech-Language Pathology for the American Speech-Language-Hearing Association (ASHA) and an ASHA Fellow. Dr. Paul provides professional consultation, develops education programs and products, and creates speech-language pathology practice resources. Dr. Paul is coauthor of the *Quality of Communication Life Scale, Talking on the Go,* and *RTI in Action.* She serves as ex officio to the National Joint Committee for the Communication Needs of Persons with Severe Disabilities.

Christine Regiec, Research Laboratory Manager, The Pennsylvania State University, 308 Ford Building, University Park, Pennsylvania 16802

Christine Regiec received her bachelor of science degree in Communication Sciences and Disorders from The Pennsylvania State University, where for 2 years she worked as Dr. Krista Wilkinson's Research Laboratory Manager on the study of visual supports in communication and education. She is attending Western Carolina University to pursue her master of science degree in Communication Sciences and Disorders.

Joe Reichle, Ph.D., Professor, Speech-Language-Hearing Sciences, 115 Shevlin Hall, 164 Pillsbury Drive Southeast, University of Minnesota, Minneapolis, Minnesota 55455

Dr. Joe Reichle holds appointments in the Departments of Speech-Language-Hearing Sciences and Educational Psychology at the University of Minnesota. He is an internationally recognized expert in the areas of augmentative and alternative communication and communication intervention for people with significant developmental disabilities and has written more than 100 articles and chapters. Dr. Reichle has coedited 10 books focused on his areas of expertise. He has served as a coeditor of the flagship journal of the American Speech-Language-Hearing Association (*Journal of Speech-Language-Hearing Research*). Dr. Reichle was former Associate Chair of the Department of Speech-Language-Hearing Sciences. During his 33-year career, he has served as a principle investigator, co-principle investigator, and investigator on numerous federally funded projects. Currently, he is Director of the University of Minnesota's Leadership Training Program in Neurodevelopmental Disabilities.

Katherine T. Rhodes, M.A., Graduate Research Assistant, Department of Psychology, Georgia State University, Post Office Box 5010, Atlanta, Georgia 30302

Ms. Katherine T. Rhodes is currently completing her dissertation in Developmental Psychology at Georgia State University. Her research focuses on mathematics cognition and measurement, especially for children who are linguistic minorities in the United States.

Megan Y. Roberts, Ph.D., CCC-SLP, Jane Steiner Hoffman and Michael Hoffman Assistant Professor, Department of Communication Sciences and Disorders, Northwestern University, 2240 Campus Drive, Evanston, Illinois 60208

Dr. Megan Y. Roberts is an assistant professor in the Roxelyn and Richard Pepper Department of Communication Sciences and Disorders. Her work focuses on family-centered early communication interventions for young children with language delays. This clinically based line of research examines different variations of parent-implemented communication interventions specifically tailored for different populations of children with language delays. Her research has been funded by the National Institute on Deafness and Other Communication Disorders and the Institute of Education Sciences.

Charity Mary Rowland, Ph.D., Professor, Institute on Disability and Development, Oregon Health and Science University, 707 Southwest Gaines Street, Portland, Oregon 97239

Dr. Charity Rowland directs the Design to Learn Projects at Oregon Health and Science University in Portland. Trained in developmental and experimental psychology, she has conducted extensive research related to communication and cognitive development in individuals with complex communication needs. She is the author of *The Communication Matrix.*

Richard W. Serna, Ph.D., Assistant Professor of Psychology, Department of Psychology, University of Massachusetts-Lowell, 113 Wilder Street, Suite 300, Lowell, Massachusetts 01854

Dr. Richard W. Serna received his doctoral degree in Psychology from Utah State University in 1987. He has held faculty positions in the Department of Psychology at Illinois Wesleyan University and the Department of Psychiatry at University of Massachusetts Medical School. Dr. Serna's career-long research interest has been in the area of stimulus control and discrimination learning—both visual and auditory—in individuals with neurodevelopmental disabilities. His research has been funded through grant support from the *Eunice Kennedy Shriver* National Institute of Child Health and Human Development.

Stephanie Yoshiko Shire, Ph.D., Post-Doctoral Fellow, University of California Los Angeles, 67-446, 760 Westwood Plaza, Los Angeles, California, 90024

Dr. Stephanie Y. Shire is a Post-Doctoral Fellow in the Department of Psychiatry at the University of California Los Angeles focusing on community-based interventions and supports for children with autism spectrum disorder.

Ellin B. Siegel, Ph.D., Associate Professor, Department of Special Education and Communication Disorders, University of Nebraska-Lincoln, 301 Barkley Memorial Center, Post Office Box 830738, Lincoln, Nebraska 68583

Dr. Ellin B. Siegel coordinates the graduate training programs in autism spectrum disorders (ASDs) and severe disabilities and teaches the coursework in these areas on campus and via distance education. Dr. Siegel has conducted research in natural school and home settings for children and youth with severe disabilities and ASDs. Her research focus has included identifying communication and environmental variables between individuals who do not use speech and their communication partners and validating teaching and assessment strategies.

Ashlyn L. Smith, Ph.D., Associate Clinical Researcher, Hussman Institute for Autism, 5521 Research Park Drive, Catonsville, Maryland 21228

Dr. Ashlyn L. Smith is an associate clinical researcher at the Hussman Institute for Autism. Her research focuses on issues related to language development and intervention for families of children with intellectual and developmental disabilities. Specifically, she investigates the role augmentative and alternative communication (AAC) can play in facilitating language development for children at risk for not developing speech, the involvement of parents in implementing AAC strategies, and collateral effects this may have on the family system.

Martha E. Snell, Ph.D., Professor Emeritus, Special Education, Curry School of Education, University of Virginia, 405 Emmet Street, Charlottesville Virginia 22904

Dr. Martha Snell is Professor Emeritus of Special Education at the Curry School of Education, University of Virginia where she directed the teacher preparation program in severe disabilities for 30 years. She has coauthored a number of books on teaching methods and the definition of intellectual disability and has been an active member of TASH and the American Association for Individuals with Intellectual and Developmental Disabilities. She directed both federal and state grants directed toward the preparation of teachers and research with individuals having intellectual disability and autism and their teachers; more recently her research has concerned Head Start classrooms and young children at risk. Her research topics have encompassed the inclusion of students with disabilities in general education classrooms, effective teaching strategies, communication intervention, and positive behavior interventions and supports for problem behavior.

Lorraine Sylvester, Ph.D., PT, Clinical Assistant Professor, Lee Mitchener Tolbert Center for Developmental Disabilities, Department of Rehabilitation Sciences, University of Oklahoma, 1200 North Stonewall Avenue, Room 1133, Oklahoma City, Oklahoma 73117

Dr. Lorraine Sylvester teaches physical and occupational therapy students in the preprofessional DPT and MOT programs, respectively. She provides consultative services to individuals with developmental disabilities, their family members, and other support personnel across Oklahoma.

Steven F. Warren, Ph.D., Professor, Speech-Language-Hearing Sciences and Disorders, Dole Human Development Center, University of Kansas, 1000 Sunnyside Avenue, #3045, Lawrence, Kansas 66045

Dr. Steven F. Warren's research has focused on communication and language development and intervention. Working with various colleagues, Dr. Warren has contributed to the creation of prelinguistic and milieu intervention approaches. Much of his research has focused on the effect of these intervention approaches and on the role of parenting on moderating the impact of developmental disorders, such as Down syndrome and fragile X syndrome.

Julie A. Washington, Ph.D., Professor, Special Education and Communication Disorders, Department of Educational Psychology, Special Education, and Communication Disorders, Georgia State University, 30 Pryor Street, Atlanta, Georgia 30303

Dr. Julie A. Washington is Professor in the Department of Educational Psychology, Special Education and Communication Disorders at Georgia State University. Her research focuses on improving understanding of the relationship between language variation and literacy learning in African American children growing up in poverty.

Krista M. Wilkinson, Ph.D., Professor, Department of Communication Sciences and Disorders, The Pennsylvania State University, 308 Ford Building, University Park, Pennsylvania, 16802

Dr. Krista M. Wilkinson is Professor at the Pennsylvania State University and editor of the American Journal of Speech-Language Pathology (2014–2016). Dr. Wilkinson's research applies the tools of neuroscience to understand visual and cognitive processing of individuals with severe disabilities in order to optimize visual augmentative and alternative communication interventions used to support their communication functioning.

Tiffany G. Woynaroski, Ph.D., Professor, Hearing and Speech Sciences, Vanderbilt, Department of Hearing and Speech Sciences, Vanderbilt University School of Medicine, 1215 21st Avenue South, Nashville, Tennessee 37232

Dr. Tiffany G. Woynaroski is Research Assistant Professor of Hearing and Speech Sciences at Vanderbilt University Medical Center. She received her master of science and doctoral degrees in speech-language pathology from Vanderbilt University. Her research focuses on identifying factors that 1) explain individual differences, 2) predict who will respond to treatment and treatment variations, and 3) help us understand how treatments work in young children with developmental disabilities and children with language impairments.

Paul J. Yoder, Ph.D., Professor, Department of Special Education, Peabody College, Vanderbilt University, Nashville, Tennessee 37203

Dr. Paul J. Yoder has been studying the transition from prelinguistic to linguistic communication in multiple populations with disabilities for more than two decades. He is a codesigner of Milieu Communication Teaching and has contributed to several studies examining the efficacy of this treatment. He teaches methods and measurement at Vanderbilt University.

Foreword

Let me begin with the bottom line. This edited collection is exciting to read and has the potential to help transform the field of treatment research related to communication interventions for individuals with severe disabilities and, therefore, to substantially improve the lives of such individuals.

This volume is the result of a meeting held in 2011 and sponsored by the National Joint Committee (NJC), which has as its charge advocacy for individuals who have intellectual disabilities and significant communication needs. The NJC includes representatives from virtually all major professional associations that in some way provide clinical services to people with significant intellectual disabilities, from speech-language clinicians and applied behavior analysts to occupational therapists and physical therapists. This disciplinary breadth was well represented at the meeting and interdisciplinarity pervades virtually every chapter of this volume. The range of disorders is also diverse, with some chapters focusing on particular etiologies (e.g., Down syndrome) or particular comorbid conditions (e.g., sensory impairment) and others parsing the heterogeneity of intellectual disabilities in terms of other individual characteristics, such as level of adaptive functioning or degree of challenging behavior. The range of methodological approaches is also diverse, including single-subject designs, randomized control trials, and secondary analyses of large datasets comprised of naturally occurring treatment outcomes. There is a balance as well between attention to verbal language as a target of intervention and to augmentative and alternative communication approaches. In addition, the chapters in this volume have all been updated since the meeting and so represent the most current approaches to communication intervention in this population. Thus, readers of this volume will truly come away understanding the breadth of the field and range of approaches that must be brought to bear to optimize communication functioning in people with significant intellectual disabilities and limited verbal language.

This volume certainly delivers as well in terms of presenting the state of the field. Readers will gain a deep understanding of the very best evidence-based practices available to clinical providers, as well as understanding the empirical data forming the evidence base and how those data were generated. Readers also will learn where there are knowledge gap practice limitations. In short, even nonscientists will come away from the volume being more informed "consumers" of information about clinical practices and, perhaps, be more willing to ask pointed questions about what should constitute evidence in the first place.

Perhaps the most important contributions of this volume, however, arise from the authors' and editors' willingness to critically evaluate their own fields in terms of assumptions, methods, and measurement of efficacy. Such critical examination is a prerequisite to innovation, and the authors and editors are to be commended on this point. Importantly, there also are a variety of innovative solutions offered in terms of design strategies, analytical approaches, and, especially, outcome measures. As a result, researchers reading this volume will be better positioned to conduct the "next generation" of treatment studies, which, of course, will benefit not only the field but, more importantly, people with intellectual disabilities and their families.

Lastly, it is worth noting that the authors of the chapters in this volume are true leaders in their fields. Many are senior scholars who have made decades-long contributions to communication intervention research. Other authors, however, are more junior but are already making their marks. Thus, there is a sense of continuity of thinking in this volume and recognition of the history of the field. This set of authors, and this volume, will continue to shape future research on communication intervention for many years to come.

One cannot come away from this volume without feeling that although there is much work to be done, we are on the verge of exciting and powerful innovation in communication intervention research.

Leonard Abbeduto

Preface

This edited volume grew out of the National Joint Committee (NJC) Conference on Research Challenges and Future Directions in Evidence-Based Communication Interventions for Individuals with Severe Disabilities, which was funded by the National Institute on Deafness and Other Communication Disorders (NIDCD) and held at Georgia State University in Atlanta, Georgia, on June 9–11, 2011.

The goals of the conference were 1) to examine the current state of interdisciplinary evidence, along with measurement and design challenges, that confront researchers seeking to evaluate the effectiveness of communication interventions for individuals with severe disabilities and 2) to create an integrated summary of research strengths and identify areas of need for future research. The NJC on the Communication Needs of Persons with Severe Disabilities spearheaded the development of this conference because the committee felt that there was too little recognition of research about communication interventions on the national agenda and it wanted to bring together a range of scholars who study aspects of communication interventions to examine the issues. The NJC consists of member professional organizations and their representatives at the time of the conference are listed in the box below. The NJC's web site (www.asha.org/njc) provides up-to-date information about its members, activities, and products.

2011 Members of the NJC

Nancy Brady (Chair), Krista Wilkinson, and Diane Paul (ex officio), American Speech-Language-Hearing Association

Beth A. Mineo, Association of Assistive Technology Act Programs

Billy T. Ogletree, Division for Communicative Disabilities and Deafness–Council for Exceptional Children

MaryAnn Romski, American Association on Intellectual and Developmental Disabilities

Judith Schoonover, American Occupational Therapy Association

Rose A. Sevcik, United States Society for Augmentative and Alternative Communication

Martha Snell and Ellin B. Seigel, TASH

Lorraine Sylvester, American Physical Therapy Association

The conference format consisted of seven 30-minute presentations on Day 1, followed by focused discussions specifically related to the presentations and general discussions cutting across presentations. Each presenter was asked to provide a brief summary of the research studies completed on his or her topic and then discuss research design challenges, measurement issues, and future areas of research exploration, including unique challenges to future advances. On Day 2, there were two panels that addressed specific issues related to 1) the design and methods used in communication intervention research and 2) measurement challenges followed by focused and general discussions. The second day concluded with breakout groups of speakers and participants whose goal was to synthesize the information presented and articulate the main research issues that should be brought forward to advance the field. The speakers, and the subsequent authors, were a mix of researchers who work in the area of communication and language intervention with individuals with severe disabilities as well as experts in related areas that extended the discussion and included research design and methods as well as measurement issues.

Focused discussion was a critical component of the meeting. Discussion summary chapters are included in this volume to reflect the richness of the specific discussions that took place during these 2 days. In addition to the invited presenters, there was an audience of researchers, clinicians, family members, and graduate students. The discussion chapters in this volume are authored by members of the NJC who participated in the conference and include the contributions of the broader audience. Conference participants are listed below.

Chapters in Section I are contributed by the conference speakers and their colleagues. The authors utilized a common framework that includes five sections: 1) brief summary of the research studies reported in this topic area, 2) research design challenges, 3) measurement issues, 4) future areas of research/exploration, including unique challenges to future advances, and 5) clinical and educational recommendations. Brady, Snell, and McLean provide a brief overview of the NJC's history and a systematic overview of the evidence about communication interventions in Chapter 1. Chapter 2 is written by Woynaroski, Fey, Warren, and Yoder and focuses on prelinguistic communication interventions for children with intellectual disabilities at the very beginning stages of communication development.

List of Conference Speakers

Roger Bakeman
Nancy Brady
Peg Burchinal
David Francis
Howard Goldstein
Ann Kaiser
Connie Kasari
Bill McIlvane
Billy Ogletree
Joe Reichle
MaryAnn Romski
Charity Rowland
Richard Serna
Rose Sevcik
Martha Snell
Steve Warren
Julie Washington

List of Participants

Erna Alant
R. Michael Barker
Andrea Barton-Hulsey
Cathy Binger
Jennifer Brown
Susan Bruce
Jessica Dykstra
Matt Foster
Peggy Gallagher
Gailynn Gluth
Amy Goldman
Ann Grossniklaus
Brittany Hess
Ayanna Howard
Jennifer Kent-Walsh
Lee McLean
Lyle L. Lloyd
John Lutzker
Emily Marturana
Michael McSheehan
Nancy Morrissey
Twyla Perryman
Stephen Plocher
Kathy Rhodes
Eric Sanders
Marie Simmons
Ashlyn Smith
Jeannie Visootsak
Virginia Walker
Ani Whitmore
David Yoder

It includes an extensive consideration of issues in current intervention research designs with particular attention to treatment intensity in the context of milieu communication teaching. Reichle and Chen present an overview of communicative alternatives as an intervention for problem behavior as part of a positive behavior support plan in Chapter 3. Rowland and Parker use national census data to provide a comprehensive survey of children and youth who are deafblind in Chapter 4. The Communication Matrix characterizes the early communication skills of these children. They conclude by examining communication interventions for this group of individuals from tangible symbols to speech-generating devices. In Chapter 5, Shire and Kasari examine targeted and comprehensive intervention programs focused on social-communication and spoken language for children with autism spectrum disorder and children with Down syndrome who have limited expressive language skills. Chapter 6 by Smith, Barker, Barton-Hulsey, Romski, and Sevcik provides a historical summary along with a contemporary review of the empirical research base for augmented language interventions for children with severe disabilities. In Chapter 7, Kaiser, Hampton, and Roberts review work on parents' roles in naturalistic language intervention, with particular emphasis on enhanced milieu teaching. Finally, in Chapter 8, Siegel, Paul, and Sylvester offer an overview of the discussions that emerged from the seven papers delivered on communication interventions.

The focus shifts explicitly in Section II to issues about research designs and methods in communication intervention research. In Chapter 9, McIlvane, Hunt, Kledaras, and Deutsch discuss integrating single-case and small *n* group designs to develop effective communication interventions. Barker and Francis examine randomized control trials and their applicability as a type of research design for communication intervention studies with individuals with severe disabilities in Chapter 10. They also suggest alternative models of design for consideration. In Chapter 11, Bakeman addresses the issue of small sample size in communication intervention research and offers several options to address small samples, yet advance the empirical data base.

The chapters in Section III address measurement issues related to communication intervention research. As an example of experimental assessment tools, Serna explores recent innovations in the assessment of auditory discrimination abilities of individuals who are not speaking in Chapter 12. Rhodes and Washington highlight often overlooked areas in communication intervention research and underscore the important role of cultural, ethnic, and linguistic factors in Chapter 13. Chapter 14 is written by Ogletree and reviews the literature on communication and language assessment for individuals with severe disabilities and characterizes measurement challenges. New directions for assessment are proposed. Goldstein explores social validity in Chapter 15, an underutilized construct for judging the success of communication interventions. Finally, Chapter 16, written by Wilkinson, Mineo, Paul, and Regiec, provides a synthesis of the discussions that occurred following the two panel presentations and highlights common themes.

Section IV looks to the future. Sevcik and Romski consider the papers and discussions and integrate them into five overall themes for future research and practice directions in Chapter 17.

In summary, we hope this volume provides the reader with a synthesis of the complex issues facing the field related to communication intervention and severe disabilities. The authors are encouraged by the advances evidenced in the research presented and are optimistic about the research and practice endeavors that will emerge in the future.

Acknowledgments

The research conference was supported by an R13 conference grant (DC-011495) from the National Institute on Deafness and Other Communication Disorders and a Scholarly Conference Grant from the Georgia State University Research Foundation. Additional sponsors included Brookes Publishing Co. and the Association of University Centers on Developmental Disabilities, Georgia State University's Area of Focus Initiative on Research on the Challenges of Acquiring Language and Literacy, Center for Research on Atypical Development and Learning, and College of Arts and Sciences, the University of Kansas Schiefelbusch Institute for Lifespan Studies, and the National Joint Committee on the Communication Needs of Persons with Severe Disabilities.

To the founding scholars in this area of study:
James E. McLean, David E. Yoder, and Richard L. Schiefelbusch.
Together, their vision and concern for the communication needs of people with severe disabilities laid the groundwork for what we know today.

I

Communication Interventions for Individuals with Severe Disabilities

What Is the Evidence?

1

What Is the State of the Evidence?

Nancy C. Brady, Martha E. Snell, and Lee K. McLean

Research is urgently needed to promote identification and implementation of effective communication interventions for individuals with severe intellectual and developmental disabilities (IDD). One of the long-standing goals of the National Joint Committee (NJC) for the Communication Needs of Persons with Severe Disabilities has been to promote research that will lead to additional communication resources. This chapter summarizes events leading up to this conference and the current state of the evidence regarding communication practices for individuals with severe intellectual and developmental disability (IDD).

BACKGROUND

In 1984, the Council of Language, Speech, and Hearing Consultants in State Education Agencies initiated efforts to develop national guidelines for developing and implementing educational programs to meet the needs of children and youth with severe communication disabilities. These efforts culminated in a national symposium, Children and Youth with Severe Handicaps: Effective Communication that was jointly sponsored by the U.S. Department of Education's Office of Special Education Programs (OSEP) and the Technical Assistance Development System (TADS) of Chapel Hill, North Carolina. This symposium was held August 19–21, 1985, in Washington, D.C. and involved professionals from state and local education agencies and universities across the nation—most of whom were directly involved in developing or implementing communication intervention programs for children and youth with severe disabilities.

The product of this symposium consisted of 33 consensus statements that put forth basic assumptions and recommendations to the planning and provision of appropriate services to meet the communication needs of children with severe disabilities. Some of these consensus statements reiterated philosophical and action statements in the Education for All Handicapped Children Act of 1975 (PL 94-142); others added texture and specifics to actions detailed in the law. The symposium participants recognized the need for interdisciplinary efforts in this overall service domain. One of the symposium recommendations was that the American

Speech-Language-Hearing Association (ASHA) and The Association for Persons with Severe Handicaps (TASH) coordinate an interagency task force for the preparation and dissemination of statements that set forth the parameters for the development and enhancement of functional communication for severely handicapped children and youth (terminology used in original documents). In 1986, ASHA and TASH organized a joint committee to focus on the communicative needs of children and adults with severe disabilities and issued invitations to other organizations to appoint representatives to this new NJC for the Communication Needs of Persons with Severe Disabilities.

The purpose of the NJC is to advocate for individuals with significant communication support needs resulting from intellectual disability and often coexisting with autism and sensory and/or motor limitations. The committee consists of representatives from ASHA, American Association on Intellectual and Developmental Disabilities (AAIDD), American Occupational Therapy Association (AOTA), American Physical Therapy Association (APTA), Association of Assistive Technology Act Programs (AATAP), Council for Exceptional Children Division for Communicative Disabilities and Deafness (CEC-DCDD), Rehabilitation Engineering and Assistive Technology Society of North America (RESNA), TASH, and the United States Society for Augmentative and Alternative Communication (USSAAC). The interdisciplinary composition of this committee reflects the pervasive importance of communication in all spheres of human functioning and across traditional boundaries. The shared commitment to promoting effective communication by people with severe disabilities provides a common ground on which the disciplines represented by the member organizations can unite in their efforts to improve the quality of life for all.

The first task of the NJC was to translate basic assumptions and recommendations reflected in the consensus statements issued by the OSEP/TADS 1985 symposium into a set of practice guidelines. The NJC identified the specific focus of these guidelines as pertaining to all people with severe disabilities, including people with severe to profound intellectual disabilities, autism, and other disorders, that result in severe socio-communicative and cognitive-communicative impairments. Representatives from all the constituent associations of the NJC met and worked together for several years to arrive at meaningful guidelines that reflected the 1985 consensus statements, including current values, intervention practices, and knowledge bases specific to the treatment of communicative impairments among people with severe disabilities. The practice recommendations presented in these guidelines reflected what were then considered best or recommended practices. The resulting document was then submitted to all constituent organizations for review (including widespread peer review by their members). After review and endorsement by all members, these guidelines were published in 1992 (ASHA, 1992) and has recently been updated (Brady et al., in press). The NJC included a Communication Bill of Rights, which has since been disseminated as a free-standing and powerful statement used by individuals and organizations to advocate for communication rights and services, as a part of these guidelines (see Box 1.1). The Communication Bill of Rights also has been updated (Brady et al., in press).

The committee underscored the need for such guidelines by stating that there were approximately 2 million Americans who were unable to speak or who demonstrated severe communication impairments. That figure would climb to more than

Box 1.1. Communication Bill of Rights

All people with a disability of any extent or severity have a basic right to affect, through communication, the conditions of their existence. All people have the following specific communication rights in their daily interactions. Each person has the right to

- Request desired objects, actions, events, and people
- Refuse undesired objects, actions, or events
- Express personal preferences and feelings
- Be offered choices and alternatives
- Reject offered choices
- Request and receive another person's attention and interaction
- Ask for and receive information about changes in routine and environment
- Receive intervention to improve communication skills
- Receive a response to any communication, whether or not the responder can fulfill the request
- Have access to augmentative and alternative communication (AAC) and other assistive technology (AT) services and devices at all times
- Have AAC and other AT devices that function properly at all times
- Be in environments that promote one's communication as a full partner with other people, including peers
- Be spoken to with respect and courtesy
- Be spoken to directly and not be spoken for or talked about in the third person while present
- Have clear, meaningful, and culturally and linguistically appropriate communications

From the National Joint Committee for the Communicative Needs of Persons with Severe Disabilities. (1992). Guidelines for meeting the communication needs of persons with severe disabilities. *Asha, 34(Suppl. 7)*, 2–3.

3 million based on estimates of 1% of the population having this degree of impairment. In light of this steady increase in population, there is a shortage of trained personnel to serve individuals with complex communication needs. Few personnel preparation programs address the communication needs of people with severe disabilities (Costigan & Light, 2010).

Materials to help guide instruction on assessments and interventions for people with severe IDD are needed, even when training programs exist. One of the goals for the NJC has been to develop tools that can help support interventions that reflect the NJC guidelines. After a 1992 OSEP symposium on effective communication for children and youth with severe disabilities, the NJC recognized the need to translate its guidelines into a functional tool—a communication supports checklist that programs could use to improve communication supports and services for people with severe disabilities (McCarthy et al., 1998). Although out of print, the communication supports checklist was used by many teachers and therapists to identify and implement interventions that reflected the NJC guidelines. The NJC developed additional educational materials that included conference presentations and an ASHA videoconference promoting communication assessments and interventions. Members of the NJC presented a webinar specifically about working with communication partners to promote communication (http://www.asha.org/Events/aac-conf/default). The organization's web site also contains a section on topics under the themes of Accessing Services and Intervention Issues and Practices (http://www.asha.org/njc).

The NJC also addressed inappropriate practices by publishing a position paper and discussion paper refuting restrictive eligibility policies and practices (NJC, 2003; Snell et al., 2003). The NJC made clear that there is no evidence to support restricting communication services based on achieving either cognitive or language milestones. Rather, it is the view of the NJC that evidence supports providing communication services based on communication needs. If an individual demonstrates a need to improve communication in order to improve his or her functioning within current and likely future environments, then he or she should be considered eligible to receive services.

Most of the materials presented were based on ideals and a limited set of research studies, usually based on small numbers of participants. Since the mid-2000s, numerous calls for increased use of evidence-based practices have been issued across all types of communication disorders (Dollaghan, 2007; Nippold, 2011; Whitmire, Rivers, Mele-McCarthy, & Staskowski, 2014). These reports described how to document or demonstrate that interventions met standards of evidence-based practices (e.g., Kratochwill et al., 2013), with a goal of facilitating practitioners' abilities to identify evidence-based practices in the literature and then implement these interventions in practice. Like all areas of communication intervention, there is a need to identify and promote evidence-based practices for individuals with severe disabilities. In addition, it is necessary to consider innovative research strategies to provide this evidence because of the extremely low incidence of the most severe IDD (which, in turn, makes it more difficult to find sufficient participants for most formal analyses). Members of the NJC realized that an examination of the existing research was necessary in order to strengthen its positions regarding services for individuals with severe ID and promote innovative research strategies.

EVIDENCE SUPPORTING INTERVENTIONS FOR PEOPLE WITH SEVERE INTELLECTUAL AND DEVELOPMENTAL DISABILITIES

The NJC published an article in 2010 that summarized intervention research completed over the previous 20 years with individuals with severe IDD (Snell et al., 2010). The committee members applied six criteria in conducting the literature search; articles that qualified 1) were published in peer-reviewed journals between 1987 and 2007, 2) were written in English, 3) had participants with severe IDD, 4) constituted intervention studies addressing language or literacy outcomes, 5) contained original data, and 6) were not case studies. The authors used four steps to locate research articles meeting these six criteria. The initial step used 13 electronic databases, and 31 search terms were applied to locate articles with a general focus on intervention, participants with severe disabilities, and treatment addressing communication performance. Next, the authors created and applied 47 expanded search terms with the same focus. Third, the authors searched the reference lists of relevant articles, scanning for additional studies. Fourth, authors searched publications authored by NJC committee members. The search yielded a pool of 269 potentially relevant articles.

Data Entry Instrument

The NJC developed a research evaluation instrument that consisted of four sections—reviewer and article information, the criteria for including a study in the review (see following section), description of study, and evaluation of the quality of evidence—in order to summarize the characteristics of research identified in the review. During the development process, NJC members read and coded randomly selected articles from the search, compared ratings, discussed differences, and made decisions about improving the instrument. This read-code-and-compare process was repeated three times by different subsets of the NJC at meetings and by conference call until all committee members were satisfied with the instrument and its informal reliability. The final version of the instrument had 39 coding items in four sections, 32 of which concerned the content of the research: 1) article/reviewer information (2 items), 2) inclusion criteria (5 items), 3) study description and characteristics (29 items), and 4) summary of evidence quality (3 items). The latter items made use of a rating system developed by the National Research Council (2001) that addressed internal validity, external validity, and generalization. Reviewers were required to make a single choice on slightly more than half of the items, whereas 44% of the items asked that reviewers check all of the 4–8 options that were relevant to a given study. Although the instrument had 32 items addressing content, the items with multiple options meant that each study was coded on 104 items. Committee members then converted the instrument into an electronic version and placed it on a web-based survey platform (http://www.zoomerang.com) so that the six NJC members who conducted coding could efficiently code and compare articles without physically being in the same location.

Three inclusion criteria against which committee members judged all 269 articles yielded by the search procedure were that articles 1) presented results from an intervention study, 2) included one or more participants with severe disabilities, and 3) applied an intervention addressing one or more areas of communication performance. Committee members determined that 116 studies of the 269 potentially relevant articles (43%) met all inclusion criteria; this group constituted the qualified database that received additional review on the 32 content items.

Interrater Agreement

The NJC committee members conducted interrater agreement at two levels—inclusion criteria and content items. *Inclusion criteria* reflected agreement about which articles met our criteria to be included in the review, and *content criteria* reflected agreement for answers to the 32 content-related questions.

Inclusion Criteria First, the committee assessed members' reliability in determining whether to include an article in the analysis. Only articles that included participants with severe disabilities and that focused on communication were included. Members used a broad definition of severe disability that included several characteristics. If an IQ score was provided, then a cutoff of 44 or below was needed; if no IQ scores were given, then a description of "severe disabilities" sufficed. If there was no IQ or severe disabilities label, then members used language-age guidelines aligned with chronological age to judge whether participants had severe disabilities. A language age that was half the chronological age or less was required for participants who were 5 years old or younger; a language age of 30 months or less was required for those older than 5 years (receptive or expressive language age, or both). The criterion for communication focus required that the research outcomes include one of the following:

> learning to understand and/or produce communication messages to a communication partner, using any mode (graphic, natural gestures, sign language, speech, picture symbols, etc.), and addressing one of the following functions: requesting, commenting, protesting, conveying social niceties, answering questions, repairing after a breakdown." (Snell et al., 2010, p. 367)

Committee members calculated agreement on the inclusion criteria by comparing two coders' independent ratings of a group of 71 articles (26.4%) randomly selected from the 269 potentially relevant articles identified in the search. Ratings were compared on a point-by-point basis and scored for agreement or disagreement; members used the following formula to obtain an agreement percentage—total agreements divided by the total number of agreements plus disagreements and multiplied by 100. Interrater agreement on each inclusion criterion was 1) 84.5%: investigator(s) includes one of more participants with severe disabilities; and 2) 81.7%: treatment addresses one or more areas of communication performance.

Content Items The committee used different procedures to assess reliability for the 32 content-related questions. The committee first randomly selected 35 studies from the qualified database of 116 studies that met inclusion criteria. This sample of qualified studies was independently rated by two reviewers on both inclusion criteria items and content items; ratings were compared using the same interrater reliability formula that was used with the inclusion criteria. Agreement was moderate to strong for most of the content items (81.3%- 95.8%) However, 12 subitems on the content-related questions fell below 70% agreement and were omitted from additional analysis; only information from the items with greater than 70% agreement was included in the committee's findings.

Findings

The information gleaned from this literature review is comprehensively described in the original research report (Snell et al., 2010) but will be summarized here in two sections—characteristics of the research and nature and quality of the evidence. Overall, the findings from this systematic examination of 20 years of communication intervention research with individuals having severe disabilities showed that "positive changes in some aspects of communication were reported in nearly all of the studies in the database" (p. 373). Naturally, this data set is susceptible to publication bias because interventions that fail to work are seldom reported.

The committee's aim, however, was to point out the many successes that have been demonstrated.

Characteristics of the Research The qualified database of 116 studies contained a total of 460 individuals with severe IDD; of this group, 62% were males and 38% were females. The 116 studies included a mean of four participants with severe disabilities, while the range varied from 1 to 41. The participants were categorized into five chronological age groups: 44% were between 0 and 5 years, 36.2% were between 6 and 11 years, 28.4% were between 12 and 17 years, 19.8% were between 18 and 20 years, and 25% were 21 years or older. Disabilities identified in participants included intellectual disability (79.3%), autism (45.7%), multiple disabilities (34.5%), cerebral palsy (18.1%), a specific syndrome (16.4%), sensory impairment (13.8%), and behavior disorder (7.8%).

A majority of the participants (66.4%) were described prior to intervention as having prelinguistic abilities, in that they had no real words in any mode and/or had expressive language ages of less than 18 months; 51.7% were described as having emergent communication (e.g., language age between 18 and 30 months); only 6% were considered to use multiple, nonecholalic words; and 9.5% were identified as being echolalic. Participants' communication mode prior to intervention was reported as speech (49.1%), augmentative and alternative communication (AAC) (30.1%) (unaided [17.2%], aided [8.6%], aided with speech output [4.3%]), gestures/vocalizations (59.5%), and other (21.6%), which included problem behavior. Finally, most researchers did not report on participants' receptive communication ability or give their receptive language age (RLA; 53.4%). When reported, this ability was minimal—not responsive (RLA 9 months or younger), simple directions (RLA 9–18 months), single words (RLA 18–30 months), and grammar/syntax (older than 30 months).

Dependent Variables Improvement in expressive communication (81%) was the most frequently targeted outcome variable, followed by progress in interaction or conversation (23.3%). Speech was the most commonly targeted mode for communication (41.4%) in these studies, followed in frequency by AAC device with no speech output (36.2%), AAC device with speech output (25%), and unaided AAC (21.6%). More than one mode was measured in 43.5% of the studies, with a range from 1 to 4 modes. For the most part, researchers neither targeted nor measured receptive communication in any mode as an outcome of intervention. But researchers who assessed receptive abilities focused on how well participants came to understand a partner's spoken speech. Regulating the behavior of others (53.4%) (e.g., requesting and/or rejecting objects or events) was the communication function that was most frequently targeted in this database. Eighteen percent of studies targeted multiple communication functions. The interaction or conversation targets addressed in these studies included turn-taking (11.2%), joint engagement (9.5%), and imitation (6.9%). Participants' challenging behavior was measured before and during intervention and reported in addition to communication outcomes in 10.8% of the studies.

Independent Variables Committee members assessed each study for its specific intervention characteristics, including context for the intervention, instructional methods, and who delivered the intervention. Interventions often took place in multiple contexts; thus, the following percentages add to more than 100. Intervention in most of the 116 studies took place in the classroom (44%). Other settings included therapy or experimental rooms (34.5%), other school contexts (e.g., playground, cafeteria, empty classroom; 29.9%), home (27.6%), and community (5.2%). Close to 33% of the research used more than one of these settings.

Most research provided intervention on a one-to-one basis, although group intervention occurred in 10% of the studies. Teaching trials were distributed across sessions or activities in 45.7% of the studies, rather than massed into a short time period. Intervention was provided in decontextualized settings in 39.6% of the reviewed studies; that is, settings that were removed from natural communication environments and that had conditions (e.g., time, setting, individuals present) that were intentionally manipulated. More than one individual provided intervention to participants in 35.3% of the studies. An experimenter delivered intervention in a majority of the studies (51.7%), but others also participated as interventionists, including teachers (35.3%), others (e.g., graduate student, occupational therapist, unspecified; 19.8%), parents (16.4%), paraprofessionals (12.1%), peers (9.5%), and speech-language pathologists (6%).

Nature and Quality of the Evidence Not surprisingly, because only published studies were reviewed, the committee members determined that 95.7% of the studies reported both positive and immediate results in the target skill after intervention. Multiple criteria were used in making these determinations. For example, committee members visually examined graphs in single-subject design studies. Committee members relied on significant tests and effect sizes (ES) for the small number of group studies.

There were numerous intervention approaches represented in the articles reviewed (e.g., functional communication training, Picture Exchange Communication System [PECS], systematic social interactive training). Committee members could not compare the relative effectiveness or efficiency of these different intervention approaches due to the wide variability in the variables reported, participant characteristics, and outcome measures. Instead, they focused on summarizing the available evidence supporting currently recommended practices and identified gaps in that evidence base to be addressed in future intervention research. As previously noted, the published studies that were reviewed reported positive outcomes with at least some participants. Several areas were identified, however, that needed further research to provide more reliable, valid, and replicable evidence regarding the effectiveness of specific intervention approaches to achieve important outcomes that will contribute to improved communication functioning for participants outside of the intervention context. These gaps and needs are discussed later in this chapter.

Quality Indicators of the Research The database was also judged by experimental design, validity, and intervention effectiveness. In terms of design, 67.2% of the studies used experimental single-subject research designs, whereas 19% used quasi-experimental design, 9.5% used qualitative designs, and 3.4% used experimental group design. When the database was examined for its measurement of stimulus or response generalization, slightly more than half of the research (51.3%) used some measure of skill generalization, such as transfer to new partners or settings. Stimulus generalization appears to have been facilitated by the fact that intervention was frequently delivered by more than a single person and in more than a single setting, and the classroom was the most commonly used setting for intervention. By contrast, the studies less often reported any information on skill maintenance postintervention. Only 25.2% of the researchers measured maintenance of effects 3 or more months after intervention was ended.

In terms of reliability, 89.5% studies reported interrater agreement, whereas only 2.6% reported measuring intrarater agreement (i.e., measurement of consistency in raters over time). Fidelity of treatment, or the evidence that the experimental conditions were implemented as described, was measured in 32.2% of the research. Social validity, or any measure of social acceptability or benefit of the intervention from the perspective of experts or users, was assessed only in 16.8% of the studies.

Of the four characteristics of quality research (generalization, maintenance, fidelity of treatment, social validity), only 2.6% of the studies measured all four characteristics, whereas any three of these were measured only 7.8% of the time, and any two of the four were measured 32.8% of the time, with the assessment of generalization and treatment fidelity being the most frequently assessed.

Implications for Future Research

As previously described, the state of the evidence base in severe disabilities is a case of the glass being viewed as half full or half empty. Although it is important to recognize that there is a substantial amount of published research that demonstrates positive effects for numerous communication outcomes, it is equally important to acknowledge the need for new research that will strengthen and expand the existing evidence base.

The committee members' aim was to document positive outcomes across a number of different interventions without comparing results across different interventions. Indeed, it is difficult to compare approaches when they are represented by only a few studies, most with small numbers of participants. A few studies, however, have directly compared different interventions. For example, Tincani (2004) compared the effects of PECS and sign language training for two children with autism. The outcome measures in this study were independent demands (requests/protests) and vocalizations. Interestingly, one child showed more gains with sign language and the other child showed greater gains with PECS. In a similar study, Beck, Stoner, Bock, and Parton (2008) compared PECS to use of a speech-generating device (SGD) in terms of ease of learning and effects on verbalizations. Again, the results varied by child and outcome. These studies illustrate how difficult it can be to compare effects across children when there is so much individual variability within this very low incidence population. The most feasible approach to comparison may be to conduct meta-analyses within specific intervention types (e.g., Flippin, Reszka, & Watson, 2010) and then compare ES across different meta-analyses. Such a meta-analysis is difficult, however, given the great variability found in how investigators conduct, evaluate, and report their intervention research. Specific areas to improve on in future research were identified in the articles that were reviewed. These areas are reliability, treatment fidelity, generalization and maintenance data, and procedural detail—including participant descriptions. Greater consistency in reporting these details is essential to conduct meta-analyses across multiple studies on the effectiveness of particular interventions and research on implementation of the interventions in real-world environments. The following sections offer some suggestions for moving the science forward by addressing these needs.

Reliability and Validity The committee members' review noted that interobserver reliability is frequently addressed and intraobserver reliability is sometimes addressed, but procedural reliability, also called fidelity of implementation, was seldom addressed. It is critical for intervention research that researchers indicate how accurately and consistently an intervention is administered. It is recommended that an objective rater who is not one of the experimenters document the fidelity with which the intervention procedures are followed. For example, Romski and colleagues (2010) implemented a treatment fidelity checklist that was completed by independent observers in their randomized control group study demonstrating vocabulary gains with AAC. Important steps for the intervention were listed, and the observers documented whether each of these steps was followed. Similar procedures were used by Tincani and colleagues in their single-subject research on PECS (Tincani, Crozier, & Alazetta, 2006). Regarding validity, the greatest need identified was in the area of social validity. Only one sixth of the articles reviewed included a social validity measure. There is a need to include information about how consumers—including family members, community members, and friends—evaluate communication changes following treatment. This information is extremely valuable for evaluating the overall effectiveness of an intervention. For example, Stanton-Chapman and Snell (2011) evaluated the social validity of a social-communication intervention by asking preschool teachers who were not affiliated with their research to indicate if the intervention procedures were acceptable and if the behavior changes being reported were socially important. The preschool teachers watched videotapes of participants at baseline and after the intervention in order to make these determinations.

Generalization and Maintenance Effective interventions have meaningful outcomes outside of the immediate treatment context; therefore, it is necessary to measure outcomes in different contexts and with different communication partners. This statement is true for all of communication research (Whitmire et al., 2014) but even more true for research with individuals with severe IDD. People with severe IDD frequently struggle with generalization (Snell, Lih-Yuan, & Hoover, 2006). Although the importance of measuring and teaching generalization and maintenance of communication behaviors has been recognized for decades, the committee members' review still found that generalization was assessed in only half of the articles, and maintenance was only measured less than 25% of the time. Teaching communication partners to carry out part or all of the intervention is one strategy that has been implemented to increase generalization. For example, parent responsiveness is often included as part of an intervention package to promote generalization of communication skills in parent–child interactions (Paul, Campbell, Gilbert, & Tsiouri, 2013; Warren, Yoder, & Leew, 2002). Teaching within the natural environment is another strategy. To illustrate, Schmidt, Drasgow, Halle, Martin, and Bliss (2014) taught three individuals with severe IDD to use functional communication behaviors as replacements for challenging behaviors within natural contexts. Additional probes indicated that two of the individuals also generalized their communication to other natural contexts and maintained their new communication skills over at least three additional sessions past the end of treatment.

Identify Specific Effects of Intensities and Durations The intensity and duration of an intervention are variables that are likely to influence outcomes and affect the ability to implement interventions across natural environments. Several articles have examined the key components to consider in terms of treatment intensity (Fey et al., 2013; Warren, Fey, & Yoder, 2007; Yoder, Fey, & Warren, 2012). For example, the frequency with which interventions are applied (dose frequency), as well as spacing of teaching episodes, interact with child characteristics to influence results (Yoder et al., 2012). Complex models are needed to adequately interpret these interactions, usually requiring data from large numbers of participants. Thus, creative new approaches to examining the effects of different intensities and durations within and across studies with these participants are needed.

CONCLUSION

The suggestions presented for improving the evidence base in severe IDD are not all new and include the need for more consistency in how intervention research is conducted and reported if the goal is to evaluate and demonstrate treatment effectiveness through comparative effectiveness research and meta-analyses. The fact that better research methods were suggested, despite the fact that most of these studies were completed by capable individuals, attests to the difficulties faced when conducting intervention research. Trying to maintain experimental controls while operating in the real world poses numerous logistic and ethical challenges. One purpose of the research conference was to convene experts in severe IDD with methodological experts in order to openly discuss better methods to advance the science in communication research for individuals with severe IDD. The remaining chapters further elaborate on how to address many of the identified needs for improved research on communication interventions for individuals with severe IDD.

REFERENCES

ASHA (1992). Guidelines for meeting the communication needs of persons with severe disabilities. http://www.asha.org/policy/GL1992-00201/

Beck, A.R., Stoner, J.B., Bock, S.J., & Parton, T. (2008). Comparison of PECS and the use of a VOCA: A replication. *Education and Training in Developmental Disabilities*, 198–216.

Brady, N.C., Bruce, S., Goldman, A., Erickson, K., Mineo, B., Ogletree, B.T.,... Wilkinson, K. (in press). Communication services and supports for individuals with severe disabilities: Guidance for assessment and intervention. *American Journal on Intellectual and Developmental Disabilities*.

Costigan, F.A., & Light, J. (2010). A review of preservice training in augmentative and alternative communication for speech-language pathologists, special education teachers, and occupational therapists. *Assistive Technology®, 22*(4), 200–212.

Dollaghan, C.A. (2007). *The handbook for evidence-based practice in communication disorders*. Baltimore, MD: Paul H. Brookes Publishing Co.

Education for All Handicapped Children Act of 1975 (PL 94-142), 20 U.S.C. §§ 1400 *et seq.*

Fey, M.E., Yoder, P.J., Warren, S.F., Bredin-Oja, S.L., Oetting, J., & Crais, E. (2013). Is more better? Milieu communication teaching in toddlers with intellectual disabilities. *Journal of Speech, Language, and Hearing Research, 56*(2), 679–693. doi: 10.1044/1092-4388(2012/12-0061)

Flippin, M., Reszka, S., & Watson, L. (2010). Effectiveness of the Picture Exchange Communication System (PECS) on communication and speech for children with autism spectrum disorders: A metanalysis. *American Journal of Speech-Language Pathology, 19*, 178–195.

Kratochwill, T.R., Hitchcock, J.H., Horner, R.H., Levin, J.R., Odom, S.L., Rindskopf,

D.M., & Shadish, W.R. (2013). Single-case intervention research design standards. *Remedial and Special Education, 34*(1), 26–38. doi: 10.1177/0741932512452794

McCarthy, C., McLean, L., Miller, J.F., Paul-Brown, D., Romskiy, M., Rourk, J.D., & Yoder, D. (1998). *Communication supports checklist for programs serving individuals with severe disabilities.* Baltimore, MD: Paul H. Brookes Publishing Co.

National Joint Committee. (2003). *Position statement on access to communication services and supports: Concerns regarding the application of restrictive "eligibility" policies* [Position statement].

National Joint Committee for the Communicative Needs of Persons with Severe Disabilities. (1992). Guidelines for meeting the communication needs of persons with severe disabilities. *Asha, 34(Suppl.* 7), 2–3.

National Research Council. (2001). *Educating children with autism.* Washington, DC: National Academies Press.

Nippold, M.A. (2011). How to be a critical consumer of treatment studies. *Language, Speech, and Hearing Services in Schools, 42*(3), 239–240. doi: 10.1044/0161-1461(2011/ed-03)

Paul, R., Campbell, D., Gilbert, K., & Tsiouri, I. (2013). Comparing spoken language treatments for minimally verbal preschoolers with autism spectrum disorders. *Journal of Autism and Developmental Disorders, 43*(2), 418–431. doi: 10.1007/s10803-012-1583-z

Romski, M., Sevcik, R., Adamson, L., Cheslock, M., Smith, A., Barker, R.M., & Bakeman, R. (2010). Randomized comparison of augmented and nonaugmented language interventions for toddlers with developmental delays and their parents. *Journal of Speech, Language, and Hearing Research, 53,* 350–364.

Schmidt, J.D., Drasgow, E., Halle, J.W., Martin, C.A., & Bliss, S.A. (2014). Discrete-trial functional analysis and functional communication training with three individuals with autism and severe problem behavior. *Journal of Positive Behavior Interventions, 16*(1), 44–55. doi: 10.1177/1098300712470519

Snell, M., Brady, N., McLean, L., Ogletree, B., Siegel, E., Sylvester, L., Sevcik, R. (2010). Twenty years of communication intervention research with individuals who have severe intellectual and developmental disabilities. *American Journal on Intellectual and Developmental Disabilities, 115*(5), 364–380. doi: 10.1352/1944-7558-115-5.364

Snell, M., Caves, K., McLean, L., Mollica, B. M., Mirenda, P., Paul-Brown, D., Yoder, P. (2003). Concerns regarding the application of restrictive eligibility policies to individuals who need communication services and supports: A response by the National Joint Committee for the Communication Needs of Persons with Severe Disabilities. *Research and Practice for Persons with Severe Disabilities, 28*(2), 70–78.

Snell, M., Lih-Yuan, C., & Hoover, K. (2006). Teaching augmentative and alternative communication to students with severe disabilities: A review of intervention research 1997–2003. *Research and Practice for Persons with Severe Disabilities, 31*(3), 203–214.

Stanton-Chapman, T.L., & Snell, M. (2011). Promoting turn-taking skills in preschool children with disabilities: The effects of a peer-based social communication intervention. *Early Childhood Research Quarterly, 26*(3), 303–319. doi: http://dx.doi.org/10.1016/j.ecresq.2010.11.002

Tincani, M. (2004). Comparing the Picture Exchange Communication System and sign language training for children with autism. *Focus on Autism and Other Developmental Disabilities, 19*(3), 152–163. doi: 10.1177/10883576040190030301

Tincani, M., Crozier, S., & Alazetta, L. (2006). The Picture Exchange Communication System: Effects on manding and speech development for school-aged children with autism. *Education and Training in Developmental Disabilities, 41,* 177–184.

Warren, S., Yoder, P., & Leew, S. (2002). Promoting social-communicative development in infants and toddlers. In H. Goldstein, L. Kaczmarek, & K. English (Eds.), *Promoting social communication: Children with developmental disabilities from birth to adolescence* (pp. 121–150). Baltimore, MD: Paul H. Brookes Publishing Co.

Warren, S.F., Fey, M.E., & Yoder, P.J. (2007). Differential treatment intensity research: A missing link to creating optimally effective communication interventions. *Mental Retardation and Developmental Disabilities Research Reviews, 13*(1), 70–77. doi: 10.1002/mrdd.20139

Whitmire, K.A., Rivers, K.O., Mele-McCarthy, J.A., & Staskowski, M. (2014). Building an evidence base for speech-language services in the schools: Challenges and recommendations. *Communication Disorders Quarterly, 35*(2), 84–92. doi: 10.1177/1525740113507316

Yoder, P., Fey, M.E., & Warren, S.F. (2012). Studying the impact of intensity is important but complicated. *International Journal of Speech-Language Pathology, 14*(5), 410–413. doi: 10.3109/17549507.2012.685890

2

Prelinguistic Communication Intervention for Young Children with Intellectual Disabilities

A Focus on Treatment Intensity

Tiffany G. Woynaroski, Marc E. Fey, Steven F. Warren, and Paul J. Yoder

Consider two different toddlers with intellectual disabilities (ID). Both are prelinguistic communicators (i.e., they rely on nonverbal means, such as eye gaze, gestures, and vocalizations, rather than spoken words, to communicate).

Sara and Daniel

The first child is Sara, a 30-month-old girl with ID of unknown etiology who rarely attempts to intentionally communicate and who has not acquired any conventional spoken words at the time she enters treatment. She has numerous schemes for playing with objects, however, and plays with most developmentally appropriate toys in their intended manner. The second child, Daniel, is a 26-month-old boy with Down syndrome (DS). Daniel shows similar communication and language delays to Sara but is limited in his interest in, and ability to play meaningfully with, different objects. Instead, he tends to ignore, mouth, or indiscriminately throw toys.

INTENSITY AS AN IMPORTANT CONSIDERATION IN TREATMENT PLANNING

A planning team must make many decisions in developing a treatment plan for these two toddlers who are not yet talking (McCauley & Fey, 2006). For example, they must determine which goals to target (e.g., prelinguistic or linguistic skills) and which modality to utilize (e.g., spoken language, sign, speech-generating device). They must also decide which treatment procedures (e.g., imitative prompts, recasts, reinforcers) to adopt and which activities provide the most desirable contexts in which to use them. The team must determine who is going to deliver the intervention—a speech-language pathologist (SLP), a caregiver, a teacher, or some combination of these and other options. Although we lack a complete understanding of precisely how these variables interact to influence the effects of intervention, few would disagree that decisions in these areas can have profound influences on treatment outcomes. This chapter focuses on another intervention variable that most assume can significantly affect treatment outcomes but that has received far less investigative attention than the aforementioned intervention variables—treatment intensity.

A CONCEPTUAL FRAMEWORK FOR CONSIDERATION OF TREATMENT INTENSITY

Warren, Fey, and Yoder (2007) noted that intensity had been inconsistently defined and inadequately studied in the literature on speech-language therapy in general, and in early intervention in particular. Accordingly, Warren and colleagues called for systematic investigation of intensity within established treatments as a necessary next step for creating optimally effective early communication interventions. They also proposed a conceptual framework, borrowed from pharmacology, which captured critical aspects of the intensity concept, to promote a common terminology and facilitate future investigation within the field. Within the proposed model, *dose* represents the length of a standard session and the number or rate of teaching episodes administered during such a session. *Dose form* reflects the type of activity within which teaching episodes are executed, such as massed drill versus a play-based approach or individual versus group treatment. *Dose frequency* refers to the rate per day, per week, or per month with which a dose is delivered, and *duration* indicates the total length of the treatment period. *Cumulative intervention intensity*, or the total number of intervention episodes experienced, is thus the product of dose, dose frequency, and total intervention duration. There is far from universal agreement with this model (Hoffman, 2009; Kamhi, 2012), and it clearly works better with some communication and language objectives than others. It is useful, however, as a point of departure in discussing issues related to intensity of treatment, so it is used throughout this chapter.

MILIEU COMMUNICATION TEACHING AS AN EARLY COMMUNICATION INTERVENTION FOR CHILDREN WITH INTELLECTUAL DISABILITIES

Presume that the planning teams for the case examples introduced at the beginning of the chapter elect to target spoken language using Milieu Communication Teaching (MCT). As it is currently conceptualized, MCT is composed of three key components—Prelinguistic Milieu Teaching (Yoder & Warren, 1999a, 1999b), Milieu Language Teaching (Hancock & Kaiser, 2006), and Responsivity Education (Yoder & Warren, 2002). Prelinguistic Milieu Teaching is a play-based treatment approach employed to establish foundational prelinguistic skills in children who enter treatment with limited communication and play skills. Once children have surpassed a threshold for mastery of prelinguistic skills (i.e., more than two intentional communication acts per minute or more than five functional words or signs during 20-minute treatment sessions or communication samples; Fey et al., 2006), Milieu Language Teaching is utilized to directly target spoken language skill. Responsivity Education is a parent education program component that is designed to increase parental responsivity to child communication to foster growth and generalization across settings, interaction partners, activities, materials, and interaction styles (Yoder & Warren, 1999b, 2001a, 2001b).

Two decades of systematic development make MCT, the treatment package or dose form that the planning team elected to use with Sara and Daniel, one of the most thoroughly researched options for early communication intervention in young children with ID. The first randomized trials of MCT produced effects that were positive, but only under certain conditions within and across samples of children with ID (Yoder & Warren, 1999a, 2001b, 2002). For example, Yoder and Warren's (1999a) first study observed a significant effect of Prelinguistic Milieu Teaching, but this effect was restricted to children whose mothers either were well educated and/or were highly responsive to their children's communicative efforts. This finding led to the incorporation of Responsivity Education to the treatment protocol. A subsequent randomized controlled trial (RCT; Yoder & Warren, 2002) similarly found that the combination of Responsivity Education and Prelinguistic Milieu Teaching (REPMT) favorably affected several communication skills, but only in a conditional manner. For example, greater gains in commenting were observed with REPMT only for those children who entered treatment with below average performance on this skill. In addition, REPMT facilitated growth in rate of requesting behavior, but only for toddlers with ID not due to DS (Yoder & Warren, 2002). These results prompted additional modifications to the treatment, including incorporation of milieu language teaching for children who demonstrated proficiency for prelinguistic communication targets at the onset of treatment.

Following fine-tuning of the treatment protocol, Fey and colleagues (2006) found unconditional, moderately sized main effects in favor of MCT versus a business-as-usual control group on a prelinguistic communication outcome (i.e., frequency of spontaneous intentional communication) in young children with ID with and without DS. Thus, MCT appeared to be a promising treatment option for children with ID, at least when the primary treatment target was prelinguistic ability. Unfortunately, there were no significant effects of MCT on linguistic skills at either the 6- or 12-month posttreatment follow-up periods, suggesting that prelinguistic gains may not have been sufficiently robust to yield anticipated improvements in subsequent spoken language (Warren et al., 2008). This is a problem if the overarching objective for Sara and Daniel is the development of spoken language.

This result led our research group to hypothesize that the failure to find effects of MCT on spoken language skills of children with ID could have been due to the relatively low intensity of intervention employed in previous work (Warren et al., 2008). The service delivery model employed in prior studies of MCT and its precursors had generally involved only three to four 20-minute treatment sessions per week over a total duration of 6 months. It was possible that this amount of treatment was insufficient to fully solidify foundational prelinguistic skills and transfer to later linguistic gains in children with ID, such as Sara and Daniel. Thus, the team considered whether more intensive treatment might lead to more optimal spoken language outcomes for these children.

A CONSIDERATION OF WHETHER MORE INTENSIVE TREATMENT MIGHT BE BETTER

Is more treatment always better? There are several logical reasons to presume that more intervention may be better for children who have language delays and ID, such as Sara and Daniel. More intensive treatment means that children experience more teaching episodes incorporating the procedures hypothesized to facilitate learning and get more practice in the use of target communication acts (Rogers & Dawson, 2010). As children with language impairments require greater exposure to acquire linguistic targets (Gray, 2003; Oetting, Rice, & Swank, 1995; Rice, Oetting, Marquis, Bode, & Pae, 1994), more experience may naturally be expected to produce greater developmental gains. In addition, increased time allotted to interaction with families means more opportunities to collaborate with parents regarding the goals of treatment and to help parents master their roles in the intervention program. Finally, more treatment may yield desirable indirect effects, such as greater familiarity with children, stronger relationships with families, and increased consistency and coherence in intervention routines, all of which may enhance the children's attention and compliance in and out of intervention, ultimately enhancing acquisition of communication skills (Warren et al., 2007).

Yet, more treatment may not always be better. More treatment may not yield better results for all children with ID, particularly if the intervention selected simply does not provide the type of input that is best suited for the child's profile. This is important to consider because more treatment comes at a cost to both interventionists and families in time and money. Attending more frequent or longer sessions may be stressful for families who are already juggling a heavy load of family obligations and time commitments. In addition, caregivers who commit to more intensive intervention schedules may be less likely to utilize strategies outside of treatment as a result of either fatigue from long or frequent appointments or a feeling that their child has received sufficient exposure to treatment targets in scheduled sessions. Furthermore, more intensive treatment may diminish engagement or induce boredom, fatigue, or frustration in young children, particularly if they are not developmentally ready to engage in longer or more frequent intervention.

INCONCLUSIVE FINDINGS FOR EFFECTS OF TREATMENT INTENSITY IN THE EXTANT LITERATURE

When Warren et al. (2007) were considering the potential impact of increased MCT intensity on spoken language outcomes of children with ID, only a handful of studies had examined the effects of intensity manipulations on language and literacy outcomes. Compounding the issue, no clear trend in conclusions had emerged across the studies that had been conducted. Some studies suggested that more treatment may lead to better outcomes (Al Otaiba, Schatschneider, & Silverman, 2005; Barratt, Littlejohns, & Thompson, 1992), but other investigations indicated that more intensive intervention may not always be warranted (Denton et al., 2011; Proctor-Williams & Fey, 2007; Ukrainetz, Ross, & Harm, 2009). Yet, other results suggested that more may be better to a degree, but increasing treatment intensity would at some point yield diminishing returns (McGinty, Breit-Smith, Fan, Justice, & Kaderavek, 2011).

To further complicate the matter, methodological differences within the extant literature made it difficult to draw conclusions about the effects of specific intensity manipulations. For example, some studies compared the effects of two or more aspects of intensity, such as the number of treatment sessions per week (i.e., dose frequency) and the total length of the treatment period (i.e., duration), within an intervention while equalizing the total number of teaching episodes that participants experienced across conditions (e.g., Ukrainetz et al., 2009). Such studies are interesting and important, but they do not reveal effects of manipulations of individual intensity components, nor do they contrast conditions that differ in cumulative intensity. Other investigations intended to manipulate one aspect of intensity, such as the number of treatment sessions per week, but failed to control for other key components of intensity, such as the rate of teaching episodes within sessions (Breit-Smith, Justice, McGinty, & Kaderavek, 2009). Still other studies confounded the investigation of intensity by simultaneously contrasting treatments that differed in both type and amount of treatment (e.g., Howard, Sparkman, Cohen, Green, & Stanislaw, 2005). As a result, it was difficult to parse out the impact of intervention intensity on outcomes, especially for early developmental communication interventions, an area in which treatment intensity had been the topic of a great deal of speculation, but to our knowledge the focus of no controlled investigations.

LESS THAN OPTIMAL APPROACHES TO PRESCRIBING TREATMENT INTENSITY

Without clear logical or empirical direction regarding how much treatment is best under specified conditions, interventionists currently base decisions about intervention intensity on a number of factors that are somewhat arbitrary or are most expedient (Brandel & Loeb, 2011). For example, decisions may be made in accordance with written or unwritten institutional protocols or even the interventionist's personally favored model. In these instances, a child's treatment intensity may be selected from a limited number of relatively standard programming options (e.g., a single 1-hour session per week, two 20-minute sessions per week) in a fairly indiscriminate manner. Treatment intensity determinations may also be influenced by caregiver input or clinical intuition regarding how much treatment is best for a given child. Unfortunately, even though interventionists attempt to personalize treatment planning according to child factors, such as severity of delay or disorder (Brandel & Loeb, 2011), there is insufficient evidence to guide such efforts. Finally, caseload demands may necessitate service delivery on a certain schedule (e.g., an individual appointment is available on Fridays from 4:00 p.m. to 5:00 p.m., the group best suited for this child's profile meets on Tuesdays and Thursdays from 12:00 p.m. to 12:30 p.m.). Of course, in some settings the amount of treatment prescribed may also be constrained by cost and reimbursement issues. There is nearly always a limit to how much treatment third-party payers are willing to fund and/or families are able to afford. Still, there is value in knowing whether societies should strive toward reallocating resources. Determining whether providing more treatment would lead to more optimal child language outcomes is the necessary first step in considering whether a reallocation of resources is warranted.

A RANDOMIZED CONTROLLED TRIAL OF TREATMENT INTENSITY IN TODDLERS WITH INTELLECTUAL DISABILITIES

Thus, Warren, Yoder, & Fey proposed a study to examine whether more intensive MCT might lead to more optimal spoken language outcomes for toddlers who have ID and who are not yet talking, such as Sara and Daniel. The participant sample for this study (Fey, Yoder, Warren, & Bredin-Oja, 2013; Yoder, Woynaroski, Fey, and Warren, 2014) included 64 prelinguistic toddlers (chronological age 18–27 months) with ID who were randomly assigned to receive MCT at either a high dose frequency (HDF; $n = 33$) or a low dose frequency (LDF; $n = 31$). Approximately half of the children within each dose frequency group were diagnosed with DS (HDF $n = 19$; LDF $n = 16$) and half presented with ID not due to DS (NDS; HDF $n = 14$; LDF $n = 15$). Comparisons on 34 pretreatment variables of interest confirmed that randomization successfully resulted in dose frequency groups and diagnostic groups that were highly similar at the pretreatment period.

All participants received MCT comprising Prelinguistic Milieu Teaching and/or Milieu Language Teaching, according to their communication and spoken language skill at the outset of treatment, over a period of 9 months. The HDF group received five 1-hour sessions per week, whereas the LDF group received only one 1-hour session per week. Interventionists administered teaching episodes within the treatment sessions at a rate of approximately one teaching episode per minute, for a total target dose of 60 episodes per session. In addition, caregivers completed nine sessions of Responsivity Education based on the Hanen Centre's *It Takes Two to Talk* program (Pepper & Weitzman, 2004) over the first 3 months of the treatment period. Thus, dose form (MCT), dose (60 teaching episodes per 1-hour session), and total treatment duration (9 months) were controlled to isolate the effects of the MCT dose frequency (and thus, cumulative intensity) manipulation on outcomes. Careful monitoring of treatment fidelity confirmed that dose and duration did not differ significantly between the subgroups defined by dose frequency assignment and DS diagnosis, and demonstrated that the difference in dose frequency translated to a nearly five-fold contrast in cumulative treatment intensity between the HDF and LDF groups.

Children's communication and language skills were assessed at five time points across the study—at entry, following 3 months of treatment, following 6 months of treatment, after completion of the entire 9-month treatment protocol, and 6 months after completing their prescribed dose frequency regimen. Outcomes of interest included three prelinguistic communication behaviors aggregated across communication sampling contexts, as well as three linguistic variables derived from the MacArthur-Bates Communicative Development Inventories: Words and Gestures checklist (MB-CDI; Fenson et al., 2006; i.e., the number of words understood, the number of words spoken, and the number of words signed and/or spoken).

Examiners for this study were either practicing SLPs or project staff who had many years of experience in administering standardized tests and engaging children in play interactions. Coders for this project were graduate students in speech-language pathology who completed a training protocol including a) a review of the coding manual, b) practice coding communication samples, and c) coding of three consecutive samples with 80% accuracy or higher. Although individual coders generally worked on this project for only 1 or 2 years, the coding supervisor who did all of the training and who supervised the reliability protocol was the same SLP over the course of the entire study. Caregivers, who completed the MB-CDI checklists, knew the dose frequency of their own children. With this exception, examiners and coders were blind to children's dose frequency assignment.

Each communication sample was coded by a primary coder, and approximately 20% of the samples were randomly selected for independent transcription and analysis by a secondary coder. After recording the reliability data of the two coders, the coding supervisor reviewed primary and secondary transcripts to identify any potential threats to reliability and resolve any discrepancies. The coding supervisor regularly corresponded with both primary and secondary coders regarding any concerns. Intraclass correlation coefficients confirmed that there was excellent agreement between observers for all variables of interest.

Although the investigators put forth no specific predictions for the results, several possible effects of MCT dose frequency on children's communication and language growth were anticipated. First, it was possible that dose frequency would exert a main effect on outcomes—that more intensive treatment would result in more favorable growth and outcomes on average across all children with ID. The failure of other investigators to find effects in favor of increased treatment intensity in several previous studies (Denton et al., 2011; Proctor-Williams & Fey, 2007; Ukrainetz et al., 2009), however, precluded a strong prediction of a main effect in favor of the HDF.

Fey and colleagues (2013) were also attentive to the possibility that MCT dose frequency could differentially affect subgroups of young children with ID. Previous findings led them to examine four variables as potential moderators of the effects of dose frequency on spoken language outcomes: a) object interest, or functional object play skills (Carter et al., 2011; Yoder & Stone, 2006; Yoder, Warren, & Hull, 1995); b) diagnosis of DS (e.g., Warren et al., 2008; Yoder & Warren, 2002, 2004); c) parent responsivity (Yoder & Warren, 1999a); and d) level of parental stress (Osborne, McHugh, Saunders, & Reed, 2008). In addition, the research team considered whether several factors could mediate, or explain, the effects of HDF on children's spoken language outcomes.

Fey and colleagues (Fey et al., 2013; Yoder, Woynaroski et al., 2014) used growth curve analyses to evaluate the effects of MCT dose frequency manipulations on child growth on prelinguistic and linguistic outcome measures after 9 months of treatment and after the 6-month maintenance period. Although there were significant gains observed over the treatment and maintenance periods, there were no main effects of treatment dose frequency on any of the outcomes at the posttreatment or follow-up periods. Evaluations of the hypothesized moderators, however, revealed several conditional effects with respect to gains in comprehension and production of words, as measured by the MB-CDI (Fenson et al., 2006).

First, children with ID who exhibited high object interest by playing functionally with nine or more toys during a 15-minute play assessment at entry to treatment showed significantly greater gains in spoken vocabulary if they received the HDF rather than the LDF intervention, regardless of whether or not their ID was due to DS (Fey et al., 2013). This moderated effect of the dose frequency of MCT, which is illustrated in Figure 2.1, was observed for lexical comprehension and production as measured both immediately postintervention and following the 6-month maintenance period. Second, children with DS exhibited less growth in spoken vocabulary on average relative to children without DS over the intervention period, regardless of the frequency of intervention they received. Children with DS who received HDF MCT exhibited greater growth in spoken vocabulary, as well as receptive vocabulary, however, compared with children with DS who received LDF MCT (see Figure 2.2) (Yoder, Woynaroski et al., 2014; Yoder, Woynaroski, Fey, Warren, & Gardner, 2015).

It was somewhat surprising that, following completion of the 9 month treatment protocol, significant effects were found for lexical measures, which included words not targeted in intervention, but were not found for any of the prelinguistic

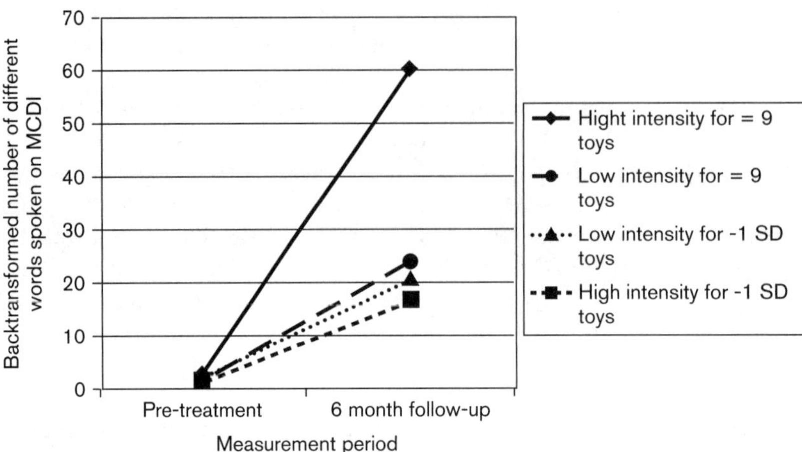

Figure 2.1. Growth curves for number of words said for four prototypical children who vary by intensity level (i.e., low dose frequency, high dose frequency) and initial object interest (i.e., number of objects chosen for functional play). MCDI = MacArthur-Bates Communicative Development Inventories. (Republished with permission of American Speech-Language-Hearing Association, from Is more better? Milieu communication teaching in toddlers with intellectual disabilities, Fey, Warren, Yoder & Bredin-Oja, 56, 2, 2013; permission conveyed through Copyright Clearance Center, Inc.)

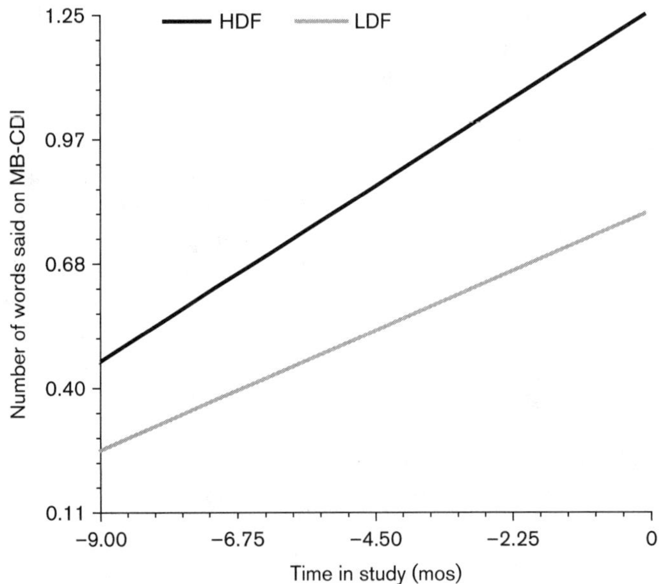

Figure 2.2. Effects of dose frequency on spoken vocabulary growth controlling for Bayley III Cognitive Composite standard score (IQ) in children with Down syndrome. Y-axis reflects log10 transformed values (log10 [x+1]) for the number of words children were reported to say on the MacArthur-Bates Communicative Development Inventories. X-axis denotes time in study (in months) centered at posttreatment (completion of the 9-month treatment protocol). *Key:* (MB-CDI) LDF = low dose frequency; HDF = high dose frequency.

Note: Controlling for Time 1 number of words said did not affect the interpretation of the dose frequency effects. (Republished with permission of American Association on Intellectual and Developmental Disabilities, from Effects of dose frequency on spoken vocabulary growth controlling for Bayley III Cognitive Composite standard score (IQ) in children with Down syndrome, Yoder, Woynaroski, Fey & Warren, 119, 1, 2013; permission conveyed through Copyright Clearance Center, Inc.)

communication outcomes, which were addressed directly in treatment for most children (Fey et al., 2013; Yoder, Woynaroski et al., 2014). Based on prior studies of MCT (Fey et al., 2006; Warren et al., 2008), as well as general trends within the literature (Yoder, Bottema-Beutel, Woynaroski, Chandrasekhar, & Sandbank, 2014), one might have hypothesized that MCT intensity effects were more likely to be found for more proximal prelinguistic communication skills and less likely to be observed on more distal linguistic skills. This led Fey and colleagues to consider whether the lack of dose frequency effects for the prelinguistic communication outcomes at the posttreatment period may be due, in part, to participants in one or both intervention groups reaching a ceiling for some outcome measures of interest. This possibility led to a reanalysis of the dataset for additional dose frequency effects earlier in the treatment period.

Canonical syllabic communication was one outcome variable of special interest because there is replicated evidence that it predicts later spoken vocabulary in preschoolers with ID (Yoder & Warren, 2004; Yoder, Warren, & McCathren, 1998). Canonical syllabic communication was operationalized as the proportion of child communication acts that were accompanied by a canonical syllable. Canonical syllables include a vowel and at least one consonant produced with a rapid, speech-like transition. We found that children in the HDF MCT group showed increased canonical syllabic communication relative to the LDF group at our 3-month assessment period (Woynaroski, Yoder, Fey, & Warren, 2014). This main effect of more intensive MCT is illustrated in Figure 2.3. Thus, a main effect on this particular prelinguistic skill was evident before effects on spoken vocabulary could be detected for subgroups of children with ID. We subsequently discovered that this early effect of dose frequency on canonical syllabic communication, as well as an early effect of dose frequency on receptive vocabulary growth, partially mediated the later effect of MCT dose frequency on spoken vocabulary growth and outcomes in children with DS (Yoder et al., 2015).

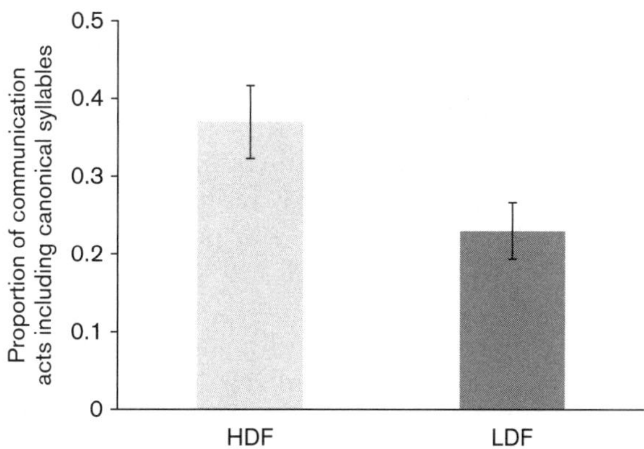

Figure 2.3. Main effect of dose frequency on canonical syllabic communication. High dose frequency (HDF) treatment (five, 1-hour sessions per week) increased canonical syllabic communication more than low dose frequency (LDF) treatment (one, 1-hour session per week) ($p < .05$). Error bars represent standard error of the mean. (Republished with permission of American Speech-Language-Hearing Association, from Woynaroski, Yoder, Fey & Warren, 57, 5, 2014; permission conveyed through Copyright Clearance Center, Inc.)

In summary, the first RCT that manipulated an isolated aspect of treatment intensity within an early communication intervention indicated that an increase in the dose frequency and cumulative intensity of MCT treatment from weekly to daily 1-hour sessions yielded an early effect on an important prelinguistic skill—canonical syllabic communication—for all children with ID. More frequent treatment, however, only led to better spoken language use after 9 months of treatment for some children with ID; specifically, children who entered treatment with above-average functional play skills and children with DS. This information has significant implications for the two case examples that were presented at the beginning of the chapter—Sara, the 30-month-old girl with ID of unknown etiology and good functional play skills, and Daniel, the 26-month-old boy with DS and few established schemas for functional or symbolic play. In many ways, these children were quite similar. They were close in chronological age. They both showed language and communication delays secondary to more global intellectual impairments. Prior to the MCT dose frequency investigation, there would have been no empirical basis for presuming that more frequent MCT might yield more optimal effects on prelinguistic or linguistic development for these two toddlers. Now there is reason, however, to expect that increasing the dose frequency of their early communication intervention to five, 1-hour doses per week would result in increased canonical syllabic communication for both toddlers after only a few months of treatment.

The evidence also suggests that such a boost in the intensity of intervention over a more extended treatment period of approximately 9 months would result in better spoken vocabulary outcomes for Daniel because he has DS and for Sara because her play skills are strong. The results of this study, however, suggest that other children with ID would not experience similar effects for spoken vocabulary with more intensive MCT. Thus, highly intensive MCT should be prescribed only for children whose profiles suggest that they will benefit from the additional time in intervention. The results of our research provide some insight into how research on the intensity of early communication intervention may pave the way toward more informed treatment planning for young children with ID.

RESEARCH DESIGN CHALLENGES

As the first systematic investigation of treatment intensity for an established early communication intervention, the MCT study reported by Fey et al. (2013), Yoder et al. (2014), and Woynaroski et al. (2014) also provides important insights into *when* and *how* intensity should be explored. Fey and Finestack (2009) proposed a progression for establishment of communication interventions from early pilot and feasibility studies to later efficacy and, ultimately, effectiveness investigations. Development of MCT to date has essentially evolved according to this model—from early single case, observational, and correlational studies to more recent RCTs examining the effects of the refined approach under controlled conditions. It is at these later stages, after a treatment has been observed to produce at least some therapeutic effects at a standard intensity, that experimental evaluation of treatment intensity is most warranted.

Furthermore, the study designs associated with the final phases of intervention development are most useful for investigations of treatment intensity.

Single-subject studies will be appropriate for pilot and feasibility studies on treatment intensity, and quasi-experimental studies may be useful in early studies on the effects of treatment intensity. Large-scale RCTs, however, are best suited to testing the effects of intensity variations within an intervention. Participants in RCTs can be randomly assigned to conditions in which one or more focal aspects of treatment intensity (e.g., dose frequency, cumulative treatment intensity) are manipulated while other variables (e.g., dose, dose form, total intervention duration) are measured or, ideally, kept constant. Researchers can experimentally and/or statistically control for potentially confounding variables to increase their confidence that effects observed are due to effects of treatment intensity manipulations. Other research designs afford experimental controls. RCTs tend to better control threats to interval validity, however, when the outcome variable of interest is a generalized skill (Yoder, Bottema-Beutel et al., 2014).

RCTs will also be useful for evaluating conditional effects of treatment intensity. Although single-subject designs can be effectively used to identify participant characteristics by which intensity manipulations vary, RCTs will have more utility for most dependent variables, treatments, and putative moderators (Yoder & Woynaroski, 2015). Randomly assigning large numbers of participants with predetermined characteristics (e.g., ID due to DS, ID not due to DS, good functional play skills, rather poor functional play skills) to treatment intensity conditions allows researchers to explore conditional or moderated effects of treatment on outcomes. Results from the reviewed work on MCT dose frequency suggest that all children will not derive equal benefit from boosts in intensity for all outcomes. Therefore, investigators must carefully consider who is likely to show improvements on outcomes of interest with more treatment. Developing a priori hypotheses about child and family factors apt to affect intervention outcomes will permit planning for formal measurement of putative moderators prior to the onset of treatment.

Investigators must also determine which types of intensity manipulations are most likely to improve growth and outcomes. Many possible configurations need to be considered because intensity comprises several distinct components (Warren et al., 2007). For example, one could opt to manipulate dose (in one or more of several ways), dose frequency, or treatment duration to intensify treatment. The combination of components most likely to optimize outcomes will depend on the treatment approach, the objectives of intervention, and the particular population that is the focus of investigation. A treatment condition comprising 30-minute doses delivered at a dose frequency of 3 times per day, 5 days per week may be especially problematic for a clinic-based treatment but completely manageable within a home-based, parent-mediated intervention. Ultimately, because of the enormous costs involved in this type of study, researchers must attempt to select for comparison intensity conditions that strike a balance between what is manageable and what will likely lead to a meaningful difference in outcomes.

Once apparently ideal contrasts have been determined, investigators must consider how best to control (or at least account for) other critical components of treatment intensity. Controlling the dose form, dose, and duration of treatment in the MCT study allowed Fey et al. (2013) to isolate the effect of the dose frequency comparison while making cumulative intensity greater in the more intensive condition as a natural consequence of more frequent delivery of the same treatment dose. Varying several aspects of intensity simultaneously (or simply allowing some aspect(s) to fluctuate naturally) will make it difficult to interpret which particular aspects of treatment intensity are responsible for differences on outcomes, which in turn will make it difficult to act on the findings. Admittedly, maintaining control of some aspects of intensity is arduous. For example, maintaining the rate of teaching episodes requires interventionists to respond to some external pacing cues or keep a constant count, and adhering to a strict dose frequency schedule requires both flexibility for the family's schedule and some insistence on prompt rescheduling of missed sessions.

Intensity investigations will come with a unique set of possible confounds. For example, families faced with the demands of a particularly high-intensity intervention condition may more often fail to comply with their treatment regimen or withdraw early from a study. Differential attrition according to dose frequency group was not observed in the reviewed MCT study. One can imagine, however, that this could occur as boosts in treatment intensity become more challenging for families to manage. For example, families may be less likely to comply with their prescribed treatment protocol if they are assigned to a condition involving 25-plus hours per week, which is the level of intensity recommended for children with autism spectrum disorder (ASD) by a group of professionals and researchers (National Research Council, 2001).

Furthermore, families assigned to low-intensity treatment conditions may attempt to compensate for their assignment by procuring nonproject intervention at a higher rate. The MCT study controlled for this potential problem by regularly monitoring participants' attendance to outside treatments. Acquiring frequent reports regarding both the type and amount of community-based services children receive is currently thought to allow researchers to gauge whether group differences in this area may be contributing to (or confounding detection of) differences between treatment groups. Most treatment providers and researchers, however, know that the quality of nonproject intervention matters as well. Measuring the quality of intervention is one of the great challenges facing the field. Nonetheless, researchers must carefully consider what factors may pose a threat to the internal validity of their investigation based on the specifics of their study (e.g., population, intensity conditions, potential parental response to their treatment assignment) and attempt to control accordingly for anticipated confounds.

MEASUREMENT AND ANALYSIS ISSUES

The MCT study (Fey et al., 2013; Yoder, Woynaroski et al., 2014) also has important implications for measurement and analysis in subsequent investigations of treatment intensity. Based on the series of reports on MCT dose frequency manipulations, it appears that the manner in which growth is measured and modeled may determine whether intensity effects are detected (Fey et al., 2013; Yoder, Woynaroski et al., 2014).

First, the findings suggest that investigators need to think critically about which types of measures will be sensitive to change when treatment is provided at a higher intensity than has routinely been studied. Fey and colleagues (2013) indexed growth of children with ID via preverbal and verbal dependent variables that varied in proximity to the treatment targets. This measurement approach permitted the team to a) detect early main effects of increased MCT dose frequency on proximal prelinguistic targets of MCT, b) detect later conditional effects of more frequent MCT on more distal linguistic targets, and c) confirm that early effects accounted for later effects of increased MCT treatment intensity for at least some children with ID. More intensive treatment may be expected to result in greater consolidation and integration of targeted skills, as well as translation to more distal developmental achievements (Guralnick, 1997). Thus, future studies need to similarly select measures that will be sensitive to growth over a wider developmental range than may typically be evaluated, taking into account the intensity of treatment (i.e., dose, dose frequency, duration), the time frame for measurement (e.g., immediate posttreatment, short-term follow-up, long-term follow-up), and the potential trajectories of growth, given the specific skill set and population of interest.

Second, the MCT results indicate that different types of growth models may be necessary to detect various effects of interest (Fey et al., 2013; Yoder, Woynaroski et al., 2014). In the first round of analyses, Fey et al. (2013) employed models that assessed the statistical interactions between putative moderators and dose frequency assignment across etiological subgroups. This approach to modeling led to the finding that dose frequency effects varied according to children's object interest at entry to the study. Thus, the across-etiology model was useful for evaluating a conditional effect of dose frequency that was consistent across children with ID, irrespective of diagnosis. The model that was inclusive of both DS and NDS subgroups, however, did not permit detection of differential dose frequency effects related to DS etiology.

Instead, predictive models conducted separately for etiological subgroups were necessary to confirm that dose frequency effects varied according to DS etiology in children with ID (i.e., that dose frequency affected outcomes for the DS subgroup but not for the NDS subgroup). These models revealed critical differences between the DS and NDS subgroups in both a) patterns of growth across the treatment period and b) responses to dose frequency contrasts. Toddlers with DS displayed significant individual differences in their outcomes and mean rates of spoken vocabulary growth across the treatment period that varied systematically according to the severity of their ID as well as their treatment intensity assignment. In contrast, though children in the NDS subgroup showed significant individual differences in their outcomes, rates of growth at posttreatment, and changes in rate of growth over the treatment period, none of the variation could be explained by children's dose frequency assignment or general cognitive ability. Consequently, when modeling was conducted across etiological subgroups, lack of a dose frequency effect in the NDS subgroup apparently masked the effect of dose frequency present within the DS subgroup. This result indicates that high levels of heterogeneity may hamper the detection of intensity effects with growth models. Therefore, researchers may need to employ models within more homogeneous groups, such as the etiological subgroups utilized in the MCT follow-up report (Yoder, Woynaroski et al., 2014), to determine who benefits from more intense treatment. Such analyses, however, will undoubtedly be limited, in large part by the relatively low prevalence of (and thus access to) many populations of interest.

AREAS FOR FUTURE RESEARCH

The findings from the reviewed work underscore the need for researchers to expand the systematic investigation of treatment intensity in an effort to maximize the benefits of interventions previously observed to have at least some favorable effect on outcomes when offered at a low intensity. Increased treatment intensity may yield important main effects across children with ID for some outcomes of interest. It cannot be assumed, however, that more treatment is always better for all children for all outcomes. Scarce resources necessitate determining whether the effects likely to be observed with increasing treatment intensity warrant more intense early communication intervention for children with ID. Results from the MCT intensity study suggest that increased intensity may, at least in certain instances, yield only effects that must be qualified by child or family factors.

Thus, it is also important that future research further consider the moderators already identified, as well as other variables that may moderate the effects of intensity manipulations. The reviewed work on MCT dose frequency found that effects for spoken vocabulary outcomes varied according to participants' diagnoses and functional play skills. Subsequent studies should consider child factors, such as etiology and other characteristics that may interact with intensity manipulations to affect outcomes. Furthermore, family factors may also induce differential response to intensity manipulations, at least for some treatments. For example, caregivers who are in a state of heightened stress at entry to treatment may respond positively to a relatively low-intensity, interventionist-implemented treatment regimen, but respond adversely to an intervention protocol that places higher demands on parental time and involvement. Although we did not detect moderation related to parental stress or caregiver responsivity in the investigation of MCT dose frequency (Fey et al., 2013), a previous study did find an interaction between parental stress and treatment intensity in children with ASD who received a variety of community-based interventions that varied according to type (i.e., reinforcement based, special nursery, speech-language therapy, parent education programs), service delivery model (i.e., one to one, group), and interventionist (i.e., teacher, tutor, parents) (Osborne et al., 2008). Thus, moderators of treatment intensity may be specific to the intervention and the population of interest.

Furthermore, not all children are likely to experience the same benefits in terms of spoken language outcomes with amplified treatment intensity, at least when it involves more of the same intervention in the same form, so researchers must seek to evaluate alternative program modifications for children who do not benefit from more of the same. Modification of the treatment protocol in accordance with the child (or family) characteristics influencing the response to more intense treatment is one possibility that researchers should consider when outcomes do not improve across all participants. For example, Fey and colleagues (2013) could address the finding of a differential effect of MCT dose frequency on spoken vocabulary outcomes according to child object interest by incorporating functional and/or symbolic play as a treatment target in future studies. Boosting play skill across the board, but in particular in the subgroup of children that is below average in this area, may lead to more optimal outcomes for all participants with ID.

Targeting some child characteristics associated with response to intensity manipulations in treatment will not be an option. This is certainly the case for moderators of treatment response, such as presence or absence of DS, that are simply not malleable. Consideration of a different response modality is another potential option for children who do not respond favorably to receiving more of a certain intervention. For example, children with ID who are not likely to achieve optimal spoken language outcomes with more MCT may display greater gains with an augmentative and alternative communication approach. This might also be considered when inflexible family factors are identified as moderators of treatment intensity manipulations. Hypothetically, if signs of parental depression predicted poor response to amplified parent-mediated treatment, then it would be appropriate for future research to consider whether such nonresponding parent–child dyads might show improved outcomes with an interventionist-implemented approach that placed fewer demands directly on the family.

Of course, failure to induce sizeable and unconditional effects on some communication and/or language outcomes may indicate that the ideal treatment intensity was just not identified in the investigation. Consideration of additional intensity configurations could be called for in this instance. For example, the conditional effects on spoken language outcomes that were observed with amplified MCT were only moderate in magnitude. One could speculate the relatively high-intensity condition (five 1-hour treatment sessions per week) was not high enough to produce optimal spoken vocabulary outcomes, even for responders. Five hours of treatment per week is far less than the recommended treatment intensity for some populations, such as children with ASD, for whom, as previously mentioned, intensities of 25 hours or more of instructional programming per week have been prescribed (American Speech-Language-Hearing Association, 2006; National Research Council, 2001). Although some intensive treatment approaches have been found experimentally to be efficacious in some instances (Dawson et al., 2010; Lovaas, 1987), recommendations for such intensive programs may be premature considering the paucity of research directly comparing the effects of promising interventions delivered at different intensities within treatment in children with developmental disorders. The need for this type of research is clear.

In light of the societal constraints on recommending more treatment (e.g., time, money, potential parental stress, feasibility for families), we should also consider whether we might boost intensity just as effectively, when warranted, without necessitating more hours in intervention. Different aspects of intensity may be manipulated to yield more treatment in a number of ways, many of which would not require more time in treatment. For example, one may intensify treatment by increasing the number or rate of teaching episodes per session (i.e., boosting the dose), rather than requiring families to spend more hours per visit in intervention. Ramping up the dose delivered per session is ultimately more efficient for families and interventionists than raising the dose frequency of treatment, and there is some evidence to suggest that the former may be as effective as the latter, at least in some instances when the increase in dosage corresponds with a decrease in dose frequency (McGinty et al., 2011).

Of course, increasing the rate of teaching episodes could induce fatigue or frustration at some point for both the interventionist and the child and, thus, become counterproductive (Hancock & Kaiser, 2006). Increasing the rate of teaching episodes per session could also compromise some essential elements of treatment. For example, it may be difficult or impossible to deliver teaching episodes at a high rate when employing an approach like MCT that rests on principles such as following the child's lead and providing minimally intrusive prompts for communication. One must take into account how potential compositions of intensity components may affect key ingredients of intervention. Unfortunately, there is still a long way to go in understanding how treatments affect child outcomes. That is to say, the essential elements of treatment are still unknown.

Few studies have sought to confirm active ingredients of early communication interventions through formal tests of treatment mediation (see Aldred, Green, Emsley, & McConachie, 2012). Moving forward, similar analyses will be important for determining which factors mediate the effects of intensity manipulations. For example, if parental responsivity mediates the relationship between treatment as offered in a standard form and communication outcomes (as in Aldred et al., 2012), then does more intensive treatment also boost outcomes as a result of changes in child–caregiver synchronicity? Child, caregiver, and even interventionist variables are important to bear in mind in attempting to explain why at least some children improve with more treatment.

CONCLUSION

We have come quite a long way in the development of prelinguistic and early language intervention options for young children with developmental delays and disorders. Programmatic research has led to the establishment of several approaches that show promise for treating language and communication impairments in this population (e.g., Brady, Bredin-Oja, & Warren, 2008; Fey et al., 2006; Girolametto, Pearce, & Weitzman, 1996; Rogers & Dawson, 2010; Romski et al., 2010; Tannock, Girolametto, & Siegel, 1992). The first systematic study of treatment intensity within an established intervention, MCT, represents an important next step for the field. The potential for MCT to affect prelinguistic and linguistic skills of young children with ID would not have been realized without research into its effect at various intensities. Through the manipulation of MCT dose frequency, it became apparent that some key communication skills of all children with ID and spoken language outcomes of some children with ID—those with DS and those with above average functional play skills—could be improved with more MCT than one might routinely prescribe. These findings emphasize the need for a sustained focus on treatment intensity to maximize the effects of established early communication interventions. Although challenging in many respects, such research will ultimately ensure that children receive the amount of treatment they need to achieve optimal outcomes

REFERENCES

Al Otaiba, S., Schatschneider, C., & Silverman, E. (2005). Tutor-assisted intensive learning strategies in kindergarten: How much is enough? *Exceptionality, 13*(4), 195–208. doi: 10.1207/s15327035ex1304_2

Aldred, C., Green, J., Emsley, R., & McConachie, H. (2012). Brief report: Mediation of treatment effect in a communication intervention for pre-school children with autism. *Journal of Autism and Developmental Disorders, 42*(3), 447–454. doi: 10.1007/s10803-011-1248-3

American Speech-Language-Hearing Association. (2006). Guidelines for speech-language pathologists in diagnosis, assessment, and treatment of autism spectrum disorders across the life span. Retrieved from www.asha.org/policy

Barratt, J., Littlejohns, P., & Thompson, J. (1992). Trial of intensive compared with weekly speech therapy in preschool children. *Archives of Disease in Childhood, 67*(1), 106–108. doi: 10.1136/adc.67.1.106

Brady, N.C., Bredin-Oja, S.L., & Warren, S.F. (2008). Prelinguistic and early language interventions for children with Down syndrome or fragile X syndrome. In J.E. Roberts, R.S. Chapman, & S.F. Warren (Eds.), *Speech and language development and intervention in Down syndrome and fragile X syndrome* (pp. 173–192). Baltimore, MD: Paul H. Brookes Publishing Co.

Brandel, J., & Loeb, D.F. (2011). Program intensity and service delivery models in the schools: SLP survey results. *Language, Speech, and Hearing Services in the Schools, 42*(4), 461–490. doi: 10.1044/0161-1461(2011/10-0019)

Breit-Smith, A., Justice, L.M., McGinty, A.S., & Kaderavek, J. (2009). How often and how much?: Intensity of print referencing intervention. *Topics in Language Disorders, 29*(4), 360–369 doi: 10.1097/TLD.0b013e3181c29db0

Carter, A.S., Messinger, D.S., Stone, W.L., Celimli, S., Nahmias, A.S., & Yoder, P. (2011). A randomized controlled trial of Hanen's "More Than Words" in toddlers with early autism symptoms. *Journal of Child Psychology and Psychiatry, 52*(7), 741–752. doi: 10.1111/j.1469-7610.2011.02395.x

Dawson, G., Rogers, S., Munson, J., Smith, M., Winter, J., Greenson, J., Varley, J. (2010). Randomized, controlled trial of an intervention for toddlers with autism: The Early Start Denver Model. *Pediatrics, 125*(1), e17–e23. doi: 10.1542/peds.2009-0958

Denton, C.A., Cirino, P.T., Barth, A.E., Romain, M., Vaughn, S., Wexler, J., Fletcher, J.M. (2011). An experimental study of scheduling and duration of tier 2 first-grade reading intervention. *Journal of Research on Educational Effectiveness, 4*(3), 208–230. doi: 10.1080/19345747.2010.530127

Fenson, L., Marchman, V.A., Thal, D.J., Dale, P.S., Reznick, J.S., & Bates, E. (2006). *MacArthur-Bates Communicative Development Inventories: User's guide and technical manual, Second Edition.* Baltimore, MD: Paul H. Brookes Publishing Co.

Fey, M.E., & Finestack, L.H. (2009). Research and development in child language intervention: A five-phase model. In R.G. Schwartz (Ed.), *Handbook of child language disorders* (pp. 513–529). New York, NY: Psychology Press.

Fey, M.E., Warren, S.F., Brady, N., Finestack, L.H., Bredin-Oja, S.L., Fairchild, M., Yoder, P.J. (2006). Early effects of responsivity education/prelinguistic milieu teaching for children with developmental delays and their parents. *Journal of Speech, Language, and Hearing Research, 49*(3), 526–547. doi: 10.1044/1092-4388(2006/039)

Fey, M.E., Yoder, P.J., Warren, S.F., & Bredin-Oja, S. (2013). Is more better? Milieu communication teaching in toddlers with intellectual disabilities. *Journal of Speech, Language, and Hearing Research, 56*(2), 679–693. doi: DOE:10.1044/1092-4388(2012/12-0081)

Girolametto, L., Pearce, P.S., & Weitzman, E. (1996). Interactive focused stimulation for toddlers with expressive vocabulary delays. *Journal of Speech, Language, and Hearing Research, 39*(6), 1274–1283.

Gray, S. (2003). Word-learning by preschoolers with specific language impairment: What predicts success? *Journal of Speech, Language, and Hearing Research, 46*(1), 56–67. doi: 10.1044/1092-4388(2003/005)

Guralnick, M.J. (1997). Effectiveness of early intervention for vulnerable children: A developmental perspective. *American Journal on Mental Retardation, 102*(4), 319–345. doi:10.1352/0895-8017(1998)102<0319:eoeifv>2.0.co;2

Hancock, T.B., & Kaiser, A.P. (2006). Enhanced milieu teaching. In R.J. McCauley & M.E. Fey (Eds.), *Treatment of language disorders in children* (pp. 203–236). Baltimore, MD: Paul H. Brookes Publishing Co.

Hoffman, L.M. (2009). Narrative language intervention intensity and dosage: Telling the whole story. *Topics in Language Disorders, 29*(4), 329–343. 310.1097/TLD.1090b1013e3181c1029d1095f.

Howard, J.S., Sparkman, C.R., Cohen, H.G., Green, G., & Stanislaw, H. (2005). A comparison of intensive behavior analytic and eclectic treatments for young children with autism. *Research in Developmental Disabilities, 26*(4), 359–383. doi: http://dx.doi.org/10.1016/j.ridd.2004.09.005

Kamhi, A.G. (2012). Pharmacological dosage concepts: How useful are they for educators and speech-language pathologists? *International Journal of Speech-Language Pathology, 14*(5), 414–418. doi: doi:10.3109/17549507.2012.685889

Lovaas, O.I. (1987). Behavioral treatment and normal educational and intellectual functioning in young autistic children. *Journal of Consulting and Clinical Psychology, 55*(1), 3–9.

McCauley, R.J., & Fey, M.E. (2006). *Treatment of language disorders in children.* Baltimore, MD: Paul H. Brookes Publishing Co.

McGinty, A.S., Breit-Smith, A., Fan, X., Justice, L.M., & Kaderavek, J.N. (2011). Does intensity matter? Preschoolers' print knowledge development within a classroom-based intervention. *Early Childhood Research Quarterly, 26*(3), 255–267. doi: 10.1016/j.ecresq.2011.02.002

National Research Council. (2001). *Educating children with autism.* Washington, DC: National Academies Press.

Oetting, J.B., Rice, M.L., & Swank, L.K. (1995). Quick incidental learning (QUIL) of words by school-age children with and without SLI. *Journal of Speech, Language, and Hearing Research, 38*(2), 434–445.

Osborne, L., McHugh, L., Saunders, J., & Reed, P. (2008). Parenting stress reduces the effectiveness of early teaching interventions for autistic spectrum disorders. *Journal of Autism and Developmental Disorders, 38*(6), 1092–1103. doi: 10.1007/s10803-007-0497-7

Pepper, J., & Weitzman, E. (2004). *It takes two to talk.* Toronto, Ontario, Canada: The Hanen Centre.

Proctor-Williams, K., & Fey, M.E. (2007). Recast density and acquisition of novel irregular past tense verbs. *Journal of Speech, Language, and Hearing Research, 50*(4), 1029–1047. doi: 10.1044/1092-4388(2007/072)

Rice, M.L., Oetting, J.B., Marquis, J., Bode, J., & Pae, S. (1994). Frequency of input effects on word comprehension of children with specific language impairment. *Journal of Speech, Language, and Hearing Research, 37*(1), 106-122.

Rogers, S., & Dawson, G. (2010). *Early Start Denver Model for young children with autism: Promoting language learning and engagement.* New York, NY: Guilford Press.

Romski, M., Sevcik, R.A., Adamson, L.B., Cheslock, M., Smith, A., Barker, R.M., & Bakeman, R. (2010). Randomized comparison of augmented and nonaugmented language interventions for toddlers with developmental delays and their parents. *Journal of Speech, Language, and Hearing Research, 53*(2), 350–364. doi: 10.1044/1092-4388(2009/08-0156)

Tannock, R., Girolametto, L., & Siegel, L.S. (1992). Language intervention with children who have developmental delays: effects of an interactive approach. *American Journal on Mental Retardation, 97*(2), 145–160.

Ukrainetz, T.A., Ross, C.L., & Harm, H.M. (2009). An investigation of treatment scheduling for phonemic awareness with kindergartners who are at risk for reading difficulties. *Language, Speech, and Hearing Services in the Schools, 40*(1), 86–100. doi: 10.1044/0161-1461(2008/07-0077)

Warren, S.F., Fey, M.E., Finestack, L.H., Brady, N.C., Bredin-Oja, S.L., & Fleming, K.K. (2008). A randomized trial of longitudinal effects of low-intensity responsivity education/prelinguistic milieu teaching. *Journal of Speech, Language, and Hearing Research, 51*(2), 451–470. doi: 10.1044/1092-4388(2008/033)

Warren, S.F., Fey, M.E., & Yoder, P.J. (2007). Differential treatment intensity research: A missing link to creating optimally effective communication interventions. *Mental Retardation and Developmental Disabililities Research Reviews, 13*(1), 70–77. doi: 10.1002/mrdd.20139

Woynaroski, T., Yoder, P., Fey, M., & Warren, S. (2014). A transactional model of spoken vocabulary variation in toddlers with intellectual disabilities. *Journal of Speech, Language, and Hearing Research, 57*(5), 1754–1763.

Yoder, P.J., Bottema-Beutel, K., Woynaroski, T., Chandrasekhar, R., & Sandbank, M. (2014). Social communication intervention effects vary by dependent variable type in preschoolers with autism spectrum disorders. *Evidence-Based Communication Assessment and Intervention, 7*(4), 150–174.

Yoder, P.J., & Stone, W.L. (2006). A randomized comparison of the effect of two prelinguistic communication interventions on the acquisition of spoken communication in preschoolers with ASD. *Journal of Speech, Language, and Hearing Research, 49*(4), 698–711. doi: 10.1044/1092-4388(2006/051)

Yoder, P.J., & Warren, S.F. (1999a). Facilitating self-initiated proto-declaratives and proto-imperatives in prelinguistic children with developmental disabilities. *Journal of Early Intervention, 22*(4), 337–354. doi: 10.1177/105381519902200408

Yoder, P.J., & Warren, S.F. (1999b). Maternal responsivity mediates the relationship between prelinguistic intentional communication and later language. *Journal of Early Intervention, 22*(2), 126–136. doi: 10.1177/105381519902200205

Yoder, P.J., & Warren, S.F. (2001a). Intentional communication elicits language-facilitating maternal responses in dyads with children who have developmental disabilities. *American Journal on Mental Retardation, 106*(4), 327–335. doi: 10.1352/0895-8017(2001)106<0327:icelfm>2.0.co;2

Yoder, P.J., & Warren, S.F. (2001b). Relative treatment effects of two prelinguistic communication interventions on language development in toddlers with developmental delays vary by maternal characteristics. *Journal of Speech, Language, and Hearing Research, 44*(1), 224–237.

Yoder, P.J., & Warren, S.F. (2002). Effects of prelinguistic milieu teaching and parent responsivity education on dyads involving children with intellectual disabilities. *Journal of Speech, Language, and Hearing Research, 45*(6), 1158–1174. doi: 10.1044/1092-4388(2002/094)

Yoder, P.J., & Warren, S.F. (2004). Early predictors of language in children with and without Down syndrome. *American Journal on Mental Retardation, 109*(4), 285-–00. doi: 10.1352/0895-8017(2004)109<285:epolic>2.0.co;2

Yoder, P.J., Warren, S.F., & Hull, L. (1995). Predicting children's response to prelinguistic communication intervention. *Journal of Early Intervention, 19*(1), 74–84. doi: 10.1177/105381519501900107

Yoder, P.J., Warren, S.F., & McCathren, R.B. (1998). Determining spoken language prognosis in children with developmental disabilities. *American Journal of Speech-Language Pathology, 7*(4), 77–87.

Yoder, P.J., & Woynaroski, T. (2015). How to study the influence of intensity of treatment on generalized skills and knowledge acquisition in students with disabilities. *Journal of Behavioral Education, 24*(1), 152–166.

Yoder, P.J., Woynaroski, T., Fey, M., & Warren, S. (2014). Effects of dose frequency of early communication intervention in young children with and without Down syndrome. *American Journal on Intellectual and Developmental Disabilities, 119*(1), 17–32.

Yoder, P.J., Woynaroski, T., Fey, M., Warren, S., & Gardner, E. (2015). Why dose frequency affects spoken vocabulary in preschoolers with Down syndrome. *American Journal on Intellectual and Developmental Disabilities, 120*(4), 302–314.

3

Challenging Behavior and Communicative Alternatives

Joe Reichle and Mo Chen

This chapter provides an overview of advances that have been made in providing communicative alternatives to challenging behavior. In the context of this discussion, the chapter also discuss how communicative alternatives fit into the bigger picture of schoolwide positive behavior support (SWPBS). Finally, in addition to advances, it addresses some current challenges and potential areas of focus for future applied research advancing knowledge and practice in the area of communicative alternatives to challenging behavior.

Rob

Rob is an 8-year-old with severe intellectual delay and autism spectrum disorder (ASD). Although Rob enjoys some parts of his daily routine, he does not enjoy physical education. One of the physical education activities involves going for a half-mile walk. During a typical walk, Rob begins to slow down at about the half-way mark. If he is not allowed to stop and play, then he engages in a severe tantrum that sometimes culminates in head banging on any available hard surface. Alternatively, the walk goes smoothly without tantrums or head banging when three or four stops are made so he can sit and play with toy cars. After replicating the outcomes of these two scenarios, his educators conclude that Rob's behavior is maintained escape (or postponement) from his walk.

Like Rob, many of his typically developing peers are not particularly fond of the half-mile walks. They, however, typically travel approximately two thirds of the half mile prior to politely requesting a break, which is always allowed by the physical education instructor. Rob unfortunately engages in tantrums (and sometimes head banging) to request a break because he does not have a socially acceptable method of requesting a break. Educators examine the point at which Rob most often starts to lag behind in the walk in order to provide behavioral support for him. They place a small stop sign at that point on the running path prior to the beginning of the walk. As soon as Rob approaches the sign, he is prompted to request a break. The prompts to request a break are faded after several successful opportunities, and the distance of the sign from the starting point is increased. Supporting prompts as Rob nears the time for the alarm to sound (e.g., "We are almost there") are paired with this strategy. Within 3 weeks, Rob has doubled his walking distance prior to a break with no challenging behavior.

This chapter discusses the role that socially acceptable communicative behavior plays in the support of individuals who engage in challenging behavior to make their wants and needs known. This chapter's position, which is supported by overwhelming evidence, is that communicative alternatives to challenging behavior can be a viable component of a comprehensive positive behavior interventions and supports (PBIS) plan. Since the early 1990s, professionals have learned that creating a PBIS plan requires that an interdisciplinary approach focus on a variety of intervention components, including 1) enhancing communicative alternatives, 2) strengthening self-regulatory skills, 3) withholding reinforcement from challenging behavior, and 4) modifying contextual features that involve communicative partners and other aspects of the environment (Bambara & Kern, 2005). This chapter focuses on enhancing communicative alternatives, although all components collectively must be addressed to fully support an individual with challenging behavior.

SUMMARY OF THE RESEARCH ADDRESSING CHALLENGING BEHAVIOR AND COMMUNICATIVE ALTERNATIVES

This section describes the prevalence of challenging behavior and the importance of addressing it. Subsequently, it delineates a framework to examine the purposes served by socially maintained challenging behavior (i.e., functional behavioral assessment [FBA]) and summarizes the research evidence in the field of functional communication training.

Prevalence and Significance of Challenging Behavior

Challenging behavior consistently ranks as one of the top problems reported by educators (Horner, Diemer, & Brazeau, 1992; Horner et al., 2005). Challenging behavior is more prevalent among individuals who experience severe and multiple developmental disabilities (Harvey, Boer, Meyer, & Evans, 2009). Overall, epidemiological estimates suggest that 15%–20% of individuals with intellectual and developmental disabilities (IDD) exhibit one or more forms of challenging behavior (Emerson, 2003; Lowe et al., 2007). Assessing challenging behavior in very young children is complicated by the knowledge that most children, regardless of their disability status, engage in some challenging behavior as they develop. For example, Patterson (1986) reported that approximately half of interactions among 2-year-olds involved challenging behavior. Challenging behavior for some children, however, is not naturally replaced with gains in socially acceptable communicative alternatives and social skill advances that foster greater self-regulatory competence. Challenging behavior can represent a significant problem for these children (Campbell, 2002; Johnston, Reichle, Feeley, & Jones, 2012; Sampers, Anderson, Hartung, & Scambler, 2001), yet one that is diagnostically challenging. Chronic and persistent challenging behavior is associated with greater risk for lower educational achievement (Campbell, 2002). In addition, Campbell (2004) reported that 18% of preschoolers with early onset moderate to high levels of aggression have been associated with a progressive worsening of challenging behavior. Campbell (2006) also reported that by the mid to late elementary years, these children displayed poorer academic and inferior social skills when compared with their peers. Several investigators (e.g., Loeber, Farrington, & Petechuk, 2003; Miller & Prinz, 1990) reported a strong correlation between chronic antisocial behavior in childhood and psychopathology and criminality in adolescence and adulthood. It has also repeatedly been demonstrated that challenging behavior becomes increasingly more likely among individuals who experience severe and multiple developmental disabilities (Emerson, 2003; Harvey et al., 2009; Murphy et al., 2005).

Significant early educational challenges may begin a cycle in which instruction becomes increasingly aversive for some children. As failure and corresponding escape attempts increase, interactions with educators become more punitive with a decrement in learning (Scott, Nelson, & Liaupsin, 2001). As with coercive parenting, challenging behavior can become negatively reinforced for the child as well as for the educator (Gunter, Jack, DePaepe, Reed, & Harrison, 1994; Maag, 2001). As a result, children who communicate by using challenging behavior rather than more conventional communicative forms may receive less positive attention from educators (Carr, Taylor, & Robinson, 1991; Fry, 1983; Luczynski & Hanley, 2013; Reichle, 1990; Rimm-Kaufman, Pianta, & Cox, 2000). The cost of challenging behavior to public schools is substantial. It can result in restricted school placements, restricted residential placements, and considerable stress for all of the involved stakeholders (Lauderdale-Littin, Howell, & Blacher, 2013; O'Neill, Vaughn, & Dunlap, 1998; Rishel, Morris, Colyer, & Gurley-Calvez, 2014; Sedlak & McPherson, 2010; Sinclair, Christenson, Evelo, & Hurley, 1998; Sinclair, Christenson, & Thurlow, 2005).

The integration of PBIS within the greater context of response to intervention (RTI; discussed later in this chapter) provides incremental levels of support in academics with a goal of preventing a learner from needing more intensive individualized instruction to the greatest degree possible. RTI has steadily gained popularity in the academic community. PBIS embraces the same preventative view of behavioral support (Bambara & Kern, 2005; Bayat, Mindes, & Covitt, 2010; Crosland & Dunlap, 2012; Kern, Gallagher, Starosta, Hickman, & George, 2006; Noltemeyer & Sansosti, 2012). Both approaches assume that a relatively small proportion of learners will require more intensive specialized intervention, even when provided with high-quality preventative measures (Batsche et al., 2006; Fuchs, Mock, Morgan, & Young, 2003; Klingner & Edwards, 2006). Recent SWPBS initiatives (Fallon, McCarthy, & Sanetti, 2014; Goh & Bambara, 2012; Kelm & McIntosh, 2012; McIntosh, Filter, Bennett, Ryan, & Sugai, 2010; Solomon, Klein, Hintze, Cressey, & Peller, 2012; Sugai, O'Keeffe, & Fallon, 2012; Vincent & Tobin, 2011) have yielded a framework of proactive social objectives that utilize the systematic delivery of more consistent and dense schedules of positive reinforcement for desired social behavior paired with consistent consequences for challenging behavior for all learners. The goal of comprehensive SWPBS in the preceding context is to prevent challenging behavior among the general population and to produce rapid, durable, and generalized reduction in challenging behaviors while improving the children's opportunities for educational success (Horner & Carr, 1997). Intervention procedures utilized within a PBIS framework include any combination of strategies that involve reinforcement contingencies, new curricula/activity schedule, promotion of self-regulatory skills, enhancement of personnel skills, modification of instructional delivery, functional communication training, and a host of antecedent focused strategies (e.g., tolerance for delay of reinforcement, contingent attention, choice making) (Carr et al., 1994; Durand, 1990; Facon, Beghin, & Rivière, 2007; Fenerty & Tiger, 2010; Hong et al., 2015; Johnston et al., 2012; Reichle et al., 1996; Reichle, Johnson, Monn, & Harris, 2010; Sellers et al., 2013; Sparks & Cote, 2012).

Efforts to validate SWPBS (Janney, Umbreit, Ferro, Liaupsin, & Lane, 2013; Kern, Choutka, & Sokol, 2002; Luiselli, Dunn, & Pace, 2005; Pace, Dunn, Luiselli, Cochran, & Skowron, 2005; Reinke, Herman, & Stormont, 2013; Sadler & Sugai, 2009; Simonsen, Britton, & Young, 2010; Spaulding et al., 2010; Turtura, Anderson, & Boyd, 2014) have involved the development of a framework of proactive social objectives paired with schedules of positive reinforcement for desired social behavior with consistent consequences for challenging behavior for all learners. To a great extent, SWPBS and the RTI framework embrace a very similar framework. Both approaches offer a three-tiered system of support (see Table 3.1).

Not surprisingly, the research design and support methodologies used to validate SWPBS, to a great extent, has been more commensurate with larger group design research that may have a propensity to give it a higher level of credibility in terms of external validity among policy decision makers (even though in some instances this work demonstrates poorer internal validity than high-quality replicated single-case design research examining strategies implemented in the tertiary tier of a PBIS model of service delivery). Indicators often utilized in measuring the

Table 3.1. Three tiers of a schoolwide positive behavior support framework

Level of tier	Description
Tier I	Tier I consists of universal interventions as the primary prevention. Universal interventions provide the foundation to positive and respectful environments for all learners, including learners with disabilities. The universal interventions are aimed to 1) teach schoolwide positive behavior expectations and procedures, 2) provide positive reinforcement for all learners, 3) provide consistent consequences for problem behavior, 4) implement effective procedures and supervision in nonclassroom areas, and 5) implement effective instruction and classroom management. Universal interventions work for approximately 80% of learners in the school.
Tier II	Tier II consists of targeted interventions as the secondary prevention. Targeted interventions use a function-based planning process to develop interventions and supports for learners at risk of increasingly restrictive responses (e.g., referral to special education, suspension, alternative school placement) due to behavioral concerns. A school-based team uses a variety of information-gathering tools and intervention options (e.g., check-in systems, social skill training) to address the underlying cause(s) of chronic problem behavior and emphasize the development of social and self-regulatory skills that will promote success across school settings. Targeted interventions work for approximately 15% of learners in the school.
Tier III	Tier III consists of intensive individualized interventions as the tertiary prevention. Individualized interventions are designed to provide the learners with individualized function-based interventions systematically implemented across the school day. Implementation of individualized interventions emphasizes 1) functional behavioral assessment and individualized behavior plans, 2) parent collaboration and education, 3) collaboration with learner's physician or mental health professional, and 4) intensive academic support. Individualized interventions work for approximately 5% of learners in the school (e.g., Solomon, Klein, Hintze, Cressey, & Peller, 2012; Sugai & Horner, 2006).

effectiveness of a SWPBS include changes in rates of office discipline referrals, attendance, suspensions, and expulsions (Irvin, Tobin, Sprague, Sugai, & Vincent, 2004) and learners' improvement in academic performance (Watson, 2003) in addition to measures on teacher, learner, and parent perceptions that may provide more socially valid information about the efficacy of SWPBS (see Bambara & Kern, 2005).

Describing a Framework to Discover Why Individuals Engage in Challenging Behavior

Events that maintain challenging behavior can be either nonsocial (the behavior is maintained by reinforcers that do not require the mediation of other people) or social (the behavior is maintained by a reinforcer whose delivery is mediated by other people). An example of behavior that is nonsocially maintained might involve an injury or health issue (e.g., ear infection, severe flu, urinary tract infection). An example of a challenging behavior maintained by a social event might be an offer of a cup of coffee subsequent to a learner throwing a cup at a social partner. With respect to social events maintaining challenging behavior, many researchers and practitioners have described classes of social consequences have been shown to maintain challenging behavior, including 1) attention seeking/maintaining, 2) tangible seeking/maintaining, and 3) escape/avoidance maintaining. By the early to mid-1980s, researchers were focusing on intervention strategies that directly addressed socially maintained challenging behavior as a member of one or more of these groups of maintaining variables (Reichle & Wacker, 1993).

FBA is designed to discover the reasons or variables that maintain (or reinforce learners for producing) challenging behavior. Assessment tools often used involve interview, direct observation, and (in a number of instances) a functional analysis. With respect to functional analyses, a number of early investigators (e.g., Carr, Newsom, & Binkoff, 1976, 1980; Iwata, Dorsey, Slifer, Bauman, & Richman, 1982/1994) demonstrated the efficacy of manipulating consequences in an experimental evaluation to determine social functions associated with challenging behavior. Functional analyses are distinguished from functional assessment in that they allow for a determination of causal relationships between challenging behavior and the circumstances that influence its occurrence and maintenance over time, rather than simply addressing correlative relationships between the challenging behavior and a social function that had been common in the applied literature. Although functional analyses may more quickly identify maintaining variables for challenging behavior (particularly with behavior that occurs relatively often), direct observation strategies such as ABC analysis (in which a practitioner carefully records the form of the challenging behavior along with the events that occurred prior to and immediately following the episode) can be very helpful. Subsequently, ABC assessment recordings are summarized to identify patterns of antecedents and consequences that appear to be associated with the challenging behavior. Numerous studies have demonstrated the efficacy of FBA (less intensive than the experimental functional analysis) paired with PBIS in reducing challenging behavior (e.g., Carr & Carlson, 1993; Carr et al., 2002; Durand, 1990; Kemp & Carr, 1995; Loman & Horner, 2014; Mace, Lalli, & Lalli, 1991; McIntosh et al., 2009; McLaren & Nelson, 2009).

This chapter discusses the current status of communication intervention as it relates to addressing the needs of individuals with severe developmental disabilities who engage in challenging behavior. The discussion will focus on strategies that have been reported as highly individualized intervention support plans for people already identified with significant challenging behavior because this is where the largest base of experimentally based evidence lies that supports the needs of people with severe disabilities. Highly preventative strategies can and should be implemented with the learner's peer community, including learners with severe disabilities, in a SWPBS or community-based model of support. Subsequently, research design and measurement challenges that face researchers working to develop intervention protocols focused on meeting the needs of people with severe disabilities who engage in challenging behavior are also addressed. Finally, this chapter culminates with some suggested priority for future research.

Summary of the Research Studies Reported in the Topic Area

It may be prudent to briefly trace the roots of functional communication intervention prior to summarizing evidence on functional communication intervention designed to address the relationship between challenging behavior and communication intervention.

Early Procedures of Differential Reinforcement and Punishment Between 1960 and 1980, interventions relied heavily on attempting to overpower challenging behavior with positive, tangible reinforcers for nonengagement in the challenging behavior and/or punishment procedures implemented immediately following challenging behavior. Many applications of these procedures were not designed to address the function or reasons for the learner engaging in the challenging behavior (Reichle & Wacker, 1993). Differential reinforcement procedures during this period became the standard to carefully address defined challenging behavior topographies. At the same time, the literature was replete with the application of punishment procedures, including time-out, overcorrection, and response cost (Azrin, Holz, & Hake, 1963; D'Andrea, 1971; Dardano, 1974; Kazdin, 1971; Murphy, 1978). Several aspects of these strategies were not particularly satisfying. First, they could be difficult to implement for several reasons delineated in detail by Sulzer-Azaroff and Mayer (1977). Punishment procedures increasingly met with complaints that they 1) modeled undesirable behavior, 2) were increasingly against school policies, 3) were subject to adaptation (Learners became sufficiently familiar with the procedures that they no longer were sufficiently punishing. This, in turn, resulted in having to increase them to an unacceptable level to continue the desired effect.), 4) tended to result in minimal performance (much like getting a speeding ticket results in future minimal compliance with the speed limit), 5) often resulted in brief periods of escalated behavior and 6) were labor intensive to implement. Furthermore, many of these procedures did not treat challenging behavior as potentially serving as a learner's method of communicating wants and needs. As such, the cause or reason for the challenging behavior often was never really adequately addressed.

Describing Functional Behavioral Assessment and Subsequent Functional Communication Training To a great extent, early evidence related to communicative alternatives for challenging behavior can be traced to highly individualized intervention strategies reported by Carr and Durand (1985), Wacker,

Wiggins, Fowler, and Berg (1988), and Wacker et al. (1990). These investigators described intervention procedures that involved differential reinforcement of communicative behavior (DRC) and contained differential consequences for a socially acceptable communicative alternative and challenging behavior. In addition, investigators began to surmise that the interventionist controls when the intervention opportunities occur in most differential consequences. The learner, however, was able to initiate instructional opportunities in a DRC. Durand and Carr (1992) examined the effect that implementing DRC could have compared with an interventionist-initiated intervention procedure (time-out) when the learner encountered interventionists who were not privy to the intervention procedures that had been implemented during acquisition. When the learner encountered a new interventionist who was not familiar with either intervention, DRC allowed learners to prompt the interventionist to provide a consequence that preempted the need for challenging behavior. Yet, learners who originally received the time-out intervention failed to maintain the gains because no procedures were implemented when the learners encountered novel interventionists who were not privy to the procedures, and learners began reverting to challenging behavior. Children who received DRC and encountered novel interventionists were able to prompt the interventionists to differentially reinforce desirable behavior.

The term *functional communication training* (FCT) was initially used to describe intervention procedures that were designed to establish functionally equivalent and socially acceptable communicative alternatives to challenging behavior. Successful use of functional communication resulted in a corresponding collateral decrease in challenging behavior (e.g., Carr & Durand, 1985; Wacker et al., 1990). Traditionally, these procedures have been deeply rooted in the behavioral perspective (e.g., Carr & Durand, 1985; Doss & Reichle, 1989; Durand & Carr, 1991, 1992; Reichle & Wacker, 1993; Wacker et al., 1990). FCT typically consists of several distinct phases that include a) an FBA to determine the function(s) associated with a challenging behavior, which is followed by b) the implementation of intervention that is directly matched to the function(s) of the challenging behavior.

Functional Behavioral Assessment Specific conditions are compared with the social function(s) of the targeted challenging behavior(s) during FBA. Social functions of challenging behavior have included attention seeking/maintaining, tangible seeking/maintaining, and escape/avoidance. By the early to mid-1980s, researchers were focusing squarely on intervention strategies that treated challenging behavior as a member of a response class that could have a social outcome. A number of early investigators demonstrated the efficacy of manipulating consequences in an experimental evaluation to determine social functions associated with challenging behavior (Carr et al., 1976, 1980; Iwata et al., 1982/1994; Lovaas, Freitag, Gold, & Kassorla, 1965; Lovaas & Simmons, 1969; Pinkston, Reese, LeBlanc, & Baer, 1973; Sailor, Guess, Rutherford, & Baer, 1968; Thomas, Becker, & Armstrong, 1968). As previously mentioned, functional analysis allows an assessment of causal relationships between challenging behavior and its purpose.

The standard applications of functional assessment in applied research today involve the inclusion of a functional analysis examining a manipulation of consequences that may influence challenging behavior. Antecedent-based manipulations (in which suspected triggers for challenging behavior are manipulated) have been used in a more limited number of investigations (e.g., see Reichle & McComas, 2004). In addition, in applied settings, investigators have used a multielement brief analysis of challenging behavior made popular by Wacker and his colleagues at the University of Iowa (Derby et al., 1992, 1994; Harding et al., 1999; Millard et al., 1993; Richman, Wacker, Asmus, & Casey, 1998). Brief analyses allow the flexibility of using a multielement experimental design rather than a more traditional reversal or strict alternating treatment design to establish experimental control and replication.

Some investigators have relied on out-of-context experimental manipulations that are sometimes referred to as *analog assessments* when implementing experimentally controlled assessments to determine social functions associated with challenging behavior. These assessments have a standard set of conditions related to common social functions associated with challenging behavior (Iwata et al., 1982/1994). Analog assessments have been useful when a functional analysis cannot be performed with sufficient internal validity in the authentic situation that has been maintaining the challenging behavior. As previously mentioned, controlled manipulations can be further categorized into antecedent-focused and consequence-focused manipulations. An antecedent comparison of variables (e.g., a structured descriptive assessment) (see Anderson & Long, 2002) manipulates functionally relevant antecedent events, whereas consequence manipulations compare two or more consequences delivered subsequent to the emission of challenging behavior (Dolezal & Kurtz, 2010). Both approaches have yielded impressive outcomes in demonstrating the efficacy of FBA followed by PBIS in reducing challenging behavior (e.g., Bopp, Brown, & Mirenda, 2004; Carr & Carlson, 1993; Carr et al., 2002; Chandler, Dahlquist, Repp, & Feltz, 1999; Durand, 1990; Hodgdon, 1996, 1999; Horner, O'Neill, & Flannery, 1993; Kemp & Carr, 1995; Mace et al., 1991; McClannahan & Krantz, 1999).

Linking Assessment to Intervention Carr and Durand (1985) were among the first to clearly demonstrate the importance of directly linking information gleaned through an FBA with the pragmatic function of the communicative act chosen for intervention. They showed that by selecting a communicative alternative that served the same social function as challenging behavior, they were able to teach the alternative and obtain collateral decreases in challenging behavior (see Doss & Reichle, 1989; Durand, 1990; Durand & Carr, 1987, 1991). Alternatively, selecting and teaching a nonmatching communicative alternative did not result in a corresponding collateral decrease of challenging behavior. Thus, communicative alternatives to challenging behavior require functional equivalence between the new alternative and the challenging behavior.

Establishing functional equivalence by matching one of the general major social functions (i.e., escape, obtain/maintain access to goods and services, obtain/maintain attention) of a particular challenging behavior to establish functional equivalence may not be sufficient to adequately link assessment outcomes to intervention. Determining that a behavior is reinforced by being able to escape or postpone engagement in an activity may not be sufficient to inform the interventionist's choice of a functionally equivalent communicative alternative. For example, suppose that an individual escaped an activity because it is unusually long. Although the function of this behavior is escape, the communicative alternative can be more narrowly pinpointed. Requesting a break might be the best matching communicative alternative in this case. Yet, if the learner escaped because an activity was excessively difficult, then requesting assistance may be the best option. Simply knowing that a behavior served an escape function would not be sufficient to allow a selection of a functionally equivalent communicative alternative (Reichle, Drager, & Davis, 2002; Reichle & Wacker, 2014).

An interventionist can design and implement an intervention once a learner's challenging behavior has been matched to a functionally equivalent and socially acceptable behavior. The majority of experimental investigations addressing communication intervention involving populations with severe developmental disabilities have involved the implementation of formats fairly commensurate with discrete trial intervention. Discrete trial instruction is a highly structured teaching technique that often involves an interventionist working one to one with a learner in a distraction-free setting. Repeated opportunities per session are typically conducted with a small interval between teaching opportunities. In contrast to the discrete trial instruction, delivery of instruction in authentic and less controlled contexts has been referred to as *natural or milieu intervention.* A blended instructional framework combines the characteristics of both discrete trial instruction and naturalistic instruction in the intervention. In spite of the diverse options of instruction format, the approach of discrete trial instruction often has been adopted in the experimental evidence associated with FCT interventions. Functional communication interventions have been implemented in home, school, and community environments. The former two environments, however, have most frequently been reported in applied research. Third, the majority of studies have been implemented by parents and practitioners using somewhat of an expert model. That is, rarely has contextual fit been thoroughly addressed when implemented by an interventionist other than the experimenter in a setting in which the learner typically has access. With this as a backdrop, the effectiveness of FCT is discussed. Subsequently, a more extended discussion of a variety of variables that represent current areas of interest in improving FCT is provided.

Is Functional Communication Training Intervention Effective? There is substantial and a rapidly growing evidence base addressing the effectiveness of FCT for various social functions of challenging behavior among individuals with a variety of disabilities (Chen, 2011). Moreover, FCT has been implemented in a wide variety of settings including inpatient hospitals, outpatient clinics, classrooms, homes, and a variety of diverse community settings (Derby et al., 1997; Durand, 1999; Hagopian, Fisher, Sullivan, Acquisto, & LeBlanc, 1998; Lalli, Casey, & Kates, 1995). The bulk of experimental evidence attesting to the effectiveness of FCT has utilized single-case design with a few demonstrations that have utilized larger group experimental designs (e.g., Durand & Carr, 1992; Hagopian et al., 1998; Reeve & Carr, 2000).

The success of communication intervention for many individuals who engage in challenging behavior has been impressive. The following paragraphs elaborate on the recipients of FCT and the settings in which it has been delivered. Subsequently, they address some of the variables that have been demonstrated to influence the success of interventions to establish communicative alternatives to challenging behavior.

Who Have Been the Recipients of Functional Communication Training? Chen (2011) systematically reviewed FCT implemented in school settings since the mid-2000s and reported that the mean age of the participants was approximately 8 years old (range: 2.75–19 years old). Seventy-six percent of these participants were male. The most common diagnoses for these recipients were ASD and IDD. The most common forms of challenging behavior were aggression, tantrum, and self-injury. In addition, most recipients of FCT produced very limited language. In the review by Chen, approximately 42% of the participants were nonverbal, whereas 32.26% used only single words. Fifty-four percent of the participants were taught to use verbal language as an alternative to challenging behavior, whereas 46% of them were taught to use pictures, gestures, signs, or speech-generating devices (SGDs) as the alternative to challenging behavior.

Where Is Functional Communication Training Implemented? Chen (2011) reported that of 50 participants in 17 studies reviewed, 52% of the participants received FCT in the settings outside of the environments in which they would be expected to use their functional communication skills (e.g., clinic). Twenty-two percent received intervention in their general education classroom, 20% in their special education classroom, 2% in both the general and special education classroom, and 4% with unspecified intervention settings.

Who Are the Interventionists? Almost 53% of the intervention procedures were implemented by trained experimenters. Approximately 18% were implemented by classroom educators, including teachers and paraprofessionals. The smallest percentage of interventions was implemented via the collective efforts from research assistants, teachers, and parents.

How Are Communicative Forms and Communicative Modes Selected? Matching law (Baum, 1974; Herrnstein, 1961) suggests that when learners have several behaviors that can be used for the same purpose, the behavior that is selected and emitted by a learner is the one with the most attractive reinforcement (making the behavior produce the most efficiency from the learner's perspective). Parameters of response efficiency typically include 1) the immediacy with which the response is desirably consequated, 2) the amount of physical or cognitive effort to produce each of the responses, 3) the response-to-reinforcement ratio (how long or how often must the response be produced to obtain a desired outcome), and 4) the relative quality of the reinforcement when comparing response options.

Exemplary of studies examining competing responses and their efficiency was an early investigation by Horner and Day (1991). These investigators examined response efficiency in the context of FCT. Each of three nonverbal participants with challenging behaviors was taught with a socially appropriate alternative response. For example, when a new alternative such as requesting help for a behavior maintained by escape was taught, it replaced the challenging behavior until requesting help resulted in obtaining more immediate assistance. For some learners, failing to address the immediacy of obtaining assistance could result in failure to establish a communicative alternative to challenging behavior. The preceding example also underscores the importance of a natural maintaining contingency for appropriate alternative behavior. For example, if an assistance request is likely to be consequated 30–60 seconds after it is produced, then the interventionist must ensure that it is the contingency that is in place prior to considering the new alternative behavior mastered.

Reichle and McComas (2004) suggested that identifying a basic social function that maintains challenging behavior may not be sufficient to select a communicative alternative. In working with a 10-year-old with significant escape who maintained challenging behavior that included property destruction and tantrumming, they demonstrated that the learner's challenging behavior resulted from encountering difficult problems. They chose requesting assistance as a communicative alternative after demonstrating that offering free assistance when the learner encountered difficult problems served to decelerate challenging behavior. Johnston et al. (2012) argued that the efficiency of the communicative alternative being taught is jeopardized without such a specificity of match between the communicative alternative and function maintaining challenging behavior.

Many learners served in the extant literature describing FCT were candidates for an augmentative and alternative communication mode. By and large, the selection of communicative mode utilized in implementing communicative alternatives appears to have been selected somewhat arbitrarily. In the review by Chen (2011), approximately 76% of the identified studies did not specifically describe the basis for the choice of the particular alternative communicative mode(s) that was/were selected to compete with challenging behavior.

Reichle, York, and Sigafoos (1991) and Johnston et al. (2012) suggested sampling communicative modalities and comparing learner acquisition, maintenance, and generalization rates in both graphic and gestural modes. Several investigators have used a form of modality sampling (e.g., Adkins & Axelrod, 2001; Anderson, 2002; Chambers & Rehfeldt, 2003; Hyppa-Martin, Reichle, Dimian, & Chen, 2013; Tincani, 2004). In most cases, the investigation resulted in mode selection unique to the individual participant. In the bulk of the available FCT literature, however, the focus of the investigation did not pursued the basis for a learner performing better in a particular communicative mode. Modality sampling originally described by Reichle et al. (1991) rarely has been utilized in authentic educational environments as a strategy to consider in selecting the most efficient communicative mode (Johnston et al., 2012).

What Prompting Procedures Have Been Used in Implementing Functional Communication Training? Prompts are generally used to increase the likelihood that a student will provide a desired response (Alberto & Troutman, 2003). Notably, a most-to-least prompt hierarchy refers to a technique of providing a high level of prompting when teaching a new skill and then systematically fading down to lower levels of prompting as the learner masters the skill. Conversely, a least-to-most prompt hierarchy refers to a technique of providing levels of prompting that proceed from least to most amounts of assistance as the learner gets to master a skill (Alberto & Troutman, 2003). Results from Chen (2011) suggested that more than half of interventionists utilized a most-to-least prompt hierarchy. A most-to-least prompt hierarchy presumably minimizes the time between prompt delivery and reinforcement for many learners and also minimizes the probability that after producing the alternative behavior the learner might engage in challenging behavior before the desired outcome could be delivered. Prompting the learner to produce a communicative alternative before the emission of challenging behavior has been emphasized in several studies (Braithwaite & Richdale, 2000; Drasgow, Halle, Michaelene, & Harbers, 1996; Johnston et al., 2012; Reichle & McComas, 2004). The rationale is to interrupt the association of a specific context with the production of challenging behavior. In other studies, however, prompting the new alternative behavior has been contingent on the challenging behavior or less serious precursor behavior (Najdowski, Wallace, Ellsworth, MacAleese, & Cleveland, 2008; Reeve & Carr, 2000). Reichle and Wacker (2014) suggested that most-to-least prompting hierarchies may tend to allow the interventionist to prompt the desired alternative prior to the challenging behavior. This, in turn, may help prevent a chain of behavior from developing in which the learner first produces challenging behavior and if it does not produce the desired effect, then the learner engages in the new communicative alternative being taught. Thus, when interventionists wait until challenging behavior occurs prior to prompting the desired alternative, the probability of reinforcing a behavioral chain (the learner first produces challenging behavior and then the desired alternative) is increased.

What Are Common Dependent Measures Used in Functional Communication Training? A large majority (94%) of studies reviewed by Chen (2011) reported dependent measures describing the participants' performance of both challenging behavior and functional communicative behavior as dependent variables. In addition to measuring challenging behavior and communicative alternative, an increasing trend in FCT research has been to include a dependent measure that shows the learner's moderated use of the communicative alternative over time. Doing so represents a rudimentary effort to begin monitoring the conditional use of newly established communicative alternatives for challenging behavior (not only monitoring situations where newly taught communication skills should be used, but also monitoring to ensure that they are not overused).

Reichle and McComas (2004) monitored attempts to do math problems and the number of math problems completed independently. The logic for measuring learner engagement and task completion is obvious in the case of a communicative act such as requests for assistance. For example, each time the learner produces a request for assistance, the interventionist has an opportunity to prompt engagement. If these prompts are faded over time, then it is reasonable to view the original requests for assistance by the learner as a prompt directing the interventionist to deliver a response prompt to enable completion of the task (that would otherwise be associated with challenging behavior), which over time will teach the learner to become more independent in completing the task. If a learner becomes more independent, then one would expect to see a diminished level of assistance requests with that task. Interestingly, few researchers have directly explored the area just described.

What Variations Have Been Used in Sequencing the Components of Functional Communication Training? Two approaches to sequencing the two major components of FCT exist. One approach is the concurrent implementation of intervention to decelerate challenging behavior and establish desired alternative behavior. A number of investigators demonstrated that it can be important to simultaneously reduce the efficiency of challenging behavior as one implements an intervention to establish a more socially acceptable communicative alternative (Fisher et al., 1993; Fisher, Kuhn, & Thompson, 1998; Hagopian et al., 1998; Hanley, Piazza, Fisher, Contrucci, & Maglieri, 1997; Kahng, Iwata, DeLeon, & Worsdell, 1997; Shirley, Iwata, Kahng, Mazaleski, & Lerman, 1997; Wacker et al., 1990). A common experimental strategy in demonstrating the importance of different contingencies for challenging behavior and the communicative alternative is demonstrated by comparing two conditions. In one, only the functional communicative alternative is the focus of intervention. This phase is compared with a condition in which communicative alternative emissions are reinforced while at the same time challenging behavior is subject to a different contingency (e.g., extinction in instances where challenging behavior is maintained by attention). A number of investigators have addressed this issue (see Buckley & Newchok, 2005; Durand & Carr, 1992; Najdowski et al., 2008; O'Neill & Sweetland-Baker, 2001; Wacker et al., 1990). The logic is compelling, dual contingencies maximize the contrast in outcomes (discriminability) associated with each of the two available response options. Available evidence supporting the concurrent establishment of a communicative alternative with a mildly punishing (e.g., matched to the function served by the challenging behavior) consequence is compelling. This is often unpopular with educators because they do not make a distinction between the connotation of aversive and the operational definition of procedures designed to minimize reinforcement for challenging behavior.

The other approach is the sequential implementation of intervention on challenging behavior after establishing alternative response in contexts not associated with challenging behavior. Johnston et al. (2012) suggested that challenging behavior in some situations should first be decelerated and then followed by the implementation of a communicative alternative. The underlying logic supporting this option lies in that engaging in a severe behavior problem would make it difficult to prompt the new communicative alternative. To boost participants' performance during FCT, some interventionists have taught participants the targeted communicative alternative in contexts in which there is no or little challenging behavior prior to the implementation of the intervention (Carr & Durand, 1985; Durand, 1999; Frea, Arnold, & Vittimberga, 2001; Schindler & Horner, 2005; Volkert, Lerman, Call, & Trosclair-Lasserre, 2009). While this is being done, approaches are implemented in the context of the challenging behavior to increase self-regulatory skills (see Reichle et al., 2010). On the basis of the limited work that has been completed related to the sequencing options that have been discussed, it is clear that concurrently placing a contingency on challenging behavior while reinforcing a communication alternative appears to enhance intervention effects.

Reichle and Wacker (2014) suggested first quickly teaching the new communicative alternative in a context not associated with challenging behavior. This newly taught behavior is subsequently implemented in contexts associated with challenging behavior. For example, assume that the learner is taught to produce a "no" response when asked if he or she would like additional milk at lunch, even though challenging behavior is not associated with this event. Once mastered, the response is introduced as a communicative alternative in escape situations associated with challenging behavior. The logic associated with this option is that fewer response prompts will be required, which, in turn, may enhance the efficiency of the new alternative from the learner's perspective, making "no" easier to compete with an existing repertoire of challenging behavior.

To What Extent Has Functional Communication Training Maintenance Been Considered? Only a handful of studies reviewed by Chen (2011) systematically investigated long-term maintenance. For example, Durand and Carr (1991) demonstrated that FCT intervention gains could be maintained across 2 years, most likely due to the natural maintaining contingencies. Hetzroni and Roth (2003) reported that the reduction in the amount of challenging behavior remained steady during the follow-up sessions probed several months later for all learners. Maintenance is more commonly addressed in anecdotal observations such as those made by Buckley and Newchok (2005), who indicated that the participant in their investigation sustained the reduction of aggression in his classroom over the next 2 months after successful implementation of FCT.

In their classic article, Stokes and Baer (1977) discussed the importance of considering natural maintaining contingencies (mentioned earlier) for newly established behavior. For example, assume that an individual is taught to request assistance with immediate assistance provided. If it is probable that the learner will need to wait 30–60 seconds prior to obtaining assistance in the environments where the he or she is expected to use the newly established behavior, then it may be difficult for the learner to maintain the newly taught behavior.

Investigators have begun using the term *resurgence* to frame maintenance issues associated with communicative alternatives to challenging behavior (Volkert et al., 2009). Participants included five children between 5 and 9 years old who had been diagnosed with ASD or other significant developmental disabilities and had been referred for the assessment and treatment of self-injury, aggression, or disruption. Three of the participants' challenging behavior was maintained by negative reinforcement (escape from demands). Another participant's challenging behavior was maintained by positive reinforcement (access to attention and tangibles). The final participant's challenging behavior was maintained by both positive reinforcement (obtaining tangibles) and negative reinforcement (escape).

Participants were taught to request the functional reinforcer using the alternative communicative behavior during the first experiment. The procedures during an extinction period were similar to those during FCT maintenance, except that the functional reinforcer was no longer provided for either challenging behavior or the alternative communicative response. This condition lasted for 10 sessions and was used to look for resurgence of challenging behavior. Three individuals participated in a second experiment. An ABCABC design was used, including baseline, FCT and FCT maintenance, and intermittent reinforcement of the alternative communicative behavior. Experimental conditions were the same as those for the first experiment, except that the appropriate communicative alternative was subject to a thin reinforcement schedule rather than extinction during the intermittent reinforcement condition. Results showed that challenging behavior reemerged for 4 of 5 participants when the socially acceptable communicative act was placed on extinction. This also occurred when the schedule of reinforcement was thinned.

The authors concluded that results from both of the experiments demonstrated a robust recovery of challenging behavior during resurgence tests. The high rate of reemergence of challenging behavior should be a concern in translational settings. Resurgence of challenging behavior is particularly concerning when one considers that some communicative alternatives must be used conditionally (e.g., one can politely reject an offer of a beverage rather than scream, but one cannot reject the offer of seizure-control medication). To date, limited research has explored this area. Future researchers may wish to consider evaluating a range of thinned reinforcement conditions to better pinpoint the ease with which a threshold of reinforcement is necessary to maintain effects (although this may, in fact, be somewhat learner specific).

What Collateral Gains Have Resulted from Functional Communication Training Implementation? Teaching functional communication skills may result in collateral gains that were not the original focus of an intervention procedure (e.g., affect improvement, longer on-task behavior, improved academic performance, greater levels of social initiation and engagement, an increase of peer play) (see Braithwaite & Richdale, 2000; Derby et al., 1997; Frea et al., 2001; Hetzroni & Roth, 2003; Lalli et al., 1995). For example, Derby et al. evaluated the short- and long-term effects of FCT on challenging behavior, target requests, and collateral behaviors. Results showed that positive social behavior (first-occurrence and ongoing social and toy play behaviors) emerged in all four participants while effective suppression of aberrant behavior was achieved. Frea et al. found that peer play increased in the targeted child following the intervention. Braithwaite and Richdale reported on a participant who was more inclined to persevere with tasks subsequent to FCT intervention. Others have reported the improved production of spoken language with learners who were verbally imitative at the outset of intervention, as well as gains in comprehension of spoken language (e.g., Mirenda, 1997; Yoder & Layton, 1988; also see Millar, 2009). Initial communicative ability that has been described as an important pivotal skill plays a critical role in selecting developmentally appropriate alternative behaviors and then implementing FCT.

Some attention has been given to the influence that FCT has on collateral behavior emissions. Winborn, Wacker, Richman, Asmus, and Geier (2002) evaluated the effects of teaching novel and existing requests during FCT with two 2-year-old children who experienced developmental delays. They found that the children used existing request forms more than novel requests when reinforcement for either request was concurrently available. The latter, however, was associated with higher levels of challenging behavior. One possible explanation is that challenging behavior and existing mands may have been reinforced in the children's daily lives. Therefore, it is important to avoid the possibility of chaining challenging behavior and alternative appropriate behavior (which appears to have happened relatively easily). Studies such as those by Winborn et al. (2002) not only speak to the importance of selecting target behaviors but also speak to the importance of considering sequencing relationships established between challenging behavior and the communicative alternative.

To What Extent and How Has Generalization Been Addressed in Functional Communication Training? Some studies addressing generalization provided anecdotal reports of relatively positive results. For instance, Carr and Durand (1985) mentioned that children performed consistently in conditions with different interventionists and settings. Several studies empirically demonstrated that participants' performance generalized across interventionists (Durand & Carr, 1991; Wacker et al., 1990), settings (Durand, 1999; Schindler & Horner, 2005), and tasks (O'Neill & Sweetland-Baker, 2001). O'Neill and Sweetland-Baker indicated that most, but not all, probes across untaught tasks showed some reduction in disruptive behavior and increases in unprompted break requests that was the focus of their original intervention procedures.

Yet, other investigators have reported limited generalization. Drasgow et al. (1996) reported a lack of generalized use of a protest sign in the untaught situations in spite of the adequate generalization of sign approximations used to produce requests. Learners were taught to use a more conventional communicative request in a classroom setting in Drasgow, Halle, and Ostrosky (1998). Generalization probes implemented in the home suggested no generalization. Rather than implementing the entire teaching procedure at home, they instead placed an extinction contingency on the challenging behavior that was occurring at home. Two of the three learners almost immediately began using the more conventional communicative symbol at home. A plausible explanation for the lack of generalization to children's home environment is provided by more closely examining response reinforcement contingencies in home and school. Challenging behavior was likely still reinforced at home while only the new communicative alternative was reinforced at school. Thus, challenging behavior at home resulted in the desired outcome so there was no reason to use a different form. The new alternative at school was more efficient than the challenging behavior, which resulted in a switch by the learner. This speaks to the importance of intervening with both challenging behavior and the new communicative behavior. Generalized use did occur in the case of participants in this investigation, but it was contingent on making the older, less socially acceptable communicative form more inefficient than the new communicative alternative that had been taught at school.

Reichle et al. (2002) explored the generalizability of the communicative alternative of requesting assistance across social contexts that involved positive as well as negative reinforcement. Sam was a 32-year-old man with severe disabilities whose challenging behavior was demonstrated (via functional analysis) to serve either a tangible or escape function. Interventionists chose a requesting assistance communicative act to replace challenging behavior. They attempted to determine whether it was necessary to select teaching examples that included both highly preferred but difficult to access items (positive reinforcers) and nonpreferred difficult activities (negative reinforcers) in order to obtain well-generalized use of requests for assistance. A multiple-probe design that consisted of three "legs" was implemented. Interventionists initially implemented intervention with a set of nonpreferred/difficult activities. Concurrently, a second set of comparable nonpreferred/difficult activities remained in baseline along with a third set of preferred/but difficult-to-access activities that were associated with the same form of challenging behavior that remained in baseline. Interventionists hypothesized that Sam would generalize a new request assistance symbol to the second set of nonpreferred/difficult activities but fail to generalize his newly acquired request for assistance to the group of preferred/but difficult-to-access activities that represented a different maintaining variable for the challenging behavior.

Requesting assistance served as a functionally equivalent and efficient alternative for challenging behavior maintained by both escape and object acquisition. Sam, however, generalized his new requesting assistance skill only to previously untaught situations involving nonpreferred and difficult activities (the same function that was addressed during intervention). He did not generalize assistance requests to situations that involved positive reinforcement (gaining access to preferred activities). In Sam's case, it appeared as if the generalization observed occurred primarily within a class of activities associated with negative reinforcement. Generalization was not observed, even though several activities associated with positive reinforcement were delivered in the same setting and were topographically similar to a teaching example involving negative reinforcement. It is possible that Sam's narrow boundary of generalization was that he engaged in a conditional discrimination in which a competing response (challenging behavior) was a more efficient response than a request for assistance in situations that involved positive reinforcement. Although a preliminary investigation, results suggested that generalization boundaries may be influenced by the social function associated with a particular communicative act. Yet, if Sam was producing different forms of challenging behavior that were specific to each of the social functions, then he may not have generalized because there was no intervention history that involved him being able to directly compare the efficiency of the new communicative alternative with the forms of challenging behavior associated with positive reinforcement.

Considering the Relationship Between Generalization and Conditional Use The bulk of investigations teaching communicative alternatives to challenging behavior have treated generalization as a phenomenon that occurs after acquisition. O'Neill and Reichle (1993) described a general-case instructional strategy that was designed to ensure that a sufficient range of teaching examples had been implemented to result in well-generalized, yet well-discriminated use of communicative acts. In general-case instruction, the interventionist carefully identifies a range of situations that call for the production of the communicative behavior being taught (positive teaching examples). Alternatively, the interventionist identifies situations that call for the learner to refrain from using the targeted communication behavior (negative teaching examples). A sufficient range of positive and negative teaching examples should maximize the discriminative use of the new skill while at the same time maximizing desired generalization. It is possible that failure to generalize may be the result of a volitional choice not to use a new behavior in a certain situation because it is not as efficient as the challenging behavior. A general-case instructional format emphasizes both appropriate and inappropriate generalization. Attending both to where one should and should not use a newly taught behavior ensure that the learner will begin to use communicative alternatives conditionally provides the best option to extend instruction if needed to establish conditional use. Conditional use helps to ensure that the learner does not overuse or underuse a newly taught behavior.

It would have been easy to conclude that learners failed to generalize in the Drasgow et al. (1998) study previously discussed. What one tends to think of as generalization, however, might involve more than the cognitive ability to associate an existing response form with a new stimulus situation. Learners may realize that a new behavior could be used in a new context but actively decide not to use it because an old behavior is more efficient. Thus, it may be difficult to consider issues involved in the conditional use of a newly taught behavior without also considering the relative efficiency of other behavior forms (e.g., challenging behavior) that can be used to obtain the same outcome. Horner and Day (1991) provided a potential example of response efficiency by comparing the effectiveness of an FCT package when the participant was required to sign a full sentence (high effort) versus one word (low effort). Results indicated that low rates of challenging behavior maintained by negative reinforcement occurred only with the low-effort mand, which can be more easily emitted for reinforcement in natural settings. Thus, if one related this study to an example, then one might consider an acceptable communicative alternative as the high-effort response and challenging behavior as the low-effort response. It is unlikely that a learner will generalize a newly taught communicative alternative as long as the low-effort response continues to work in a new context.

Considering Other Intervention Components to Combine with Functional Communication Training If one selects a single social function maintained by challenging behavior (e.g., escape), then it is reasonable to assume that some of the activities from which one wishes to escape may be escapable, contingent on the production of a more desirable communicative alternative. At the same time, other activities from which the individual may want to escape may not be escapable (e.g., taking seizure control medication). If this is the case, then it seems as though a concurrent implementation of two different intervention strategies may be needed to address a single social function associated with challenging behavior. In spite of this likelihood, there are relatively limited experimental reports of the concurrent implementation of procedures to simultaneously address situations in which 1) the behavioral form cannot be reinforced but the function of the behavior can or 2) neither the behavioral form nor the function of the behavior can be reinforced. In spite of the logic for the concurrent implementation of self-regulation and alternative response interventions, it is unclear whether this logic has been an influence in many of the multi-intervention packages that have been implemented. A number of authors have provided detailed discussions addressing a wide range of strategies that can be combined in a PBIS package to address when the function of challenging behavior can be reinforced and other contexts in which it cannot be reinforced (see Bambara & Kern, 2005). Examining the effect of these strategies in maximizing desired generalization while minimizing undesired generalization (e.g., overuse), however, has rarely been systematically explored.

From the standpoint of matching theory (Herrnstein, 1961) that was previously addressed, conditional discriminations can be thought of as matching a particular response to a particular situation in order to maximize one's gain. Conditional discriminations represent a necessity in teaching learners to moderate their use of newly established communicative alternatives to challenging behavior. Engaging in a conditional discrimination requires that the recipient of intervention learn when they can use a communicative alternative and when they should not use it. Reichle and McComas (2004) reported on Timothy, a 12-year-old third grader being served in a general elementary school classroom. His teacher reported that he engaged in high rates of challenging behavior to escape/avoid task demands associated with difficult work. Interventionists taught Timothy to request assistance. Although intervention procedures to teach requests for assistance were successful, the intervention protocol was unsuccessful in establishing improved independent performance in solving more difficult math problems. Interventionists hypothesized that Timothy had requested assistance on every teaching opportunity because doing so was easier than solving problems on his own. From a theoretical standpoint, because Timothy received a prompt as a result of his request that was faded over time, he should have begun to more independently solve the problems that were originally the focus of teaching assistance requests. Timothy began to use his requests conditionally (solving less difficult problems and requesting assistance with difficult ones) when interventionists implemented a competing response (independent problem solution) with a schedule of reinforcement that earned a greater value of reinforcer than the reinforcer associated with the original assistance request. Using a newly established communicative alternative conditionally requires that the learner balance discrimination and generalization skills.

In summary, the goal of any interventionist is to enable a learner to sufficiently generalize a newly taught behavior yet engage in its use discriminatively when it comes to making judgments about when it is acceptable and unacceptable to use the newly taught form. Relatively little research has directly focused on this coordinated use of newly taught communicative alternatives. Up to this point the chapter has dealt with communicative alternatives as one type of intervention strategy among many that comprise PBIS. It is impossible, however, to consider communicative alternatives as an intervention strategy without considering others that can be used concurrently with communicative alternatives. The next section briefly expands on this topic.

Functional Communication Training in the Context of Schoolwide Positive Behavior Interventions and Supports PBIS should be implemented at a systemic level in order to be effective. Much of the earliest intervention in the area of behavioral support occurred with only the individual who engaged in challenging behavior. Challenging behavior used for communicative purposes involves the totality of the environment. Consequently, one must consider FCT in the total framework of PBIS. Therefore, the tiers of systemic support provided in PBIS require brief discussion.

Three tiers of intervention have commonly been considered in SWPBS (see Table 3.1). The goal in systemic support for individuals engaging in challenging behavior is to affect the totality of the environment in which the learner and other stakeholders operate. Fewer intensive interventions directed at specific learners should occur when the environment is better prepared. This, in turn, facilitates more and higher quality opportunities for participation in inclusive settings.

When a three-tier SWPBS model is used, the needs of approximately 80% of the learners can be met in the primary tier, 15% of the learners will require a specialized group system at the secondary level, and 5% will require individualized supports at the tertiary level (Lewis, 2007). With the overview of three tiers in mind, the following section focuses on probing into the potential challenges faced by researchers working with learners having severe disabilities who are at risk for or with challenging behavior.

Tier I Intervention: Support for All Learners Universal supports within a SWPBS are characterized by 1) school expectations taught to all learners and acknowledged often with a schoolwide incentive system, 2) consistent reinforcement of expected behavior, 3) consistent consequences for inappropriate behavior, 4) monitoring of learners' behavior in all school settings, and 5) an SWPBS team making data-based decisions according to learners' support needs (Sailor, Dunlap, Sugai, & Horner, 2009; Sugai & Horner, 2006). Although Tier I interventions provide the least intensive supports, a growing body of literature demonstrated that the universal intervention delivered to every learner is effective in producing positive outcomes, mainly including reduced office discipline referral rates (Bohanon et al., 2006; Bradshaw, Mitchell, O'Brennan, & Leaf, 2010; Galloway, Panyan, Smith, & Wessendorf, 2008), increased safety of the school setting (Horner et al., 2009), and improved learner academic achievement (Ervin, Schaughency, Goodman, McGlinchey, & Matthews, 2006; Horner et al., 2009; Sadler & Sugai, 2009).

Tier II Intervention: Assistance for Learners Who Need Support but Do Not Require an Individualized Program Tier II interventions are standardized practices and systems designed to meet the needs of learners who are not responsive to Tier I intervention and require more intensive supports than what are available on Tier I and prevent the need for most of the intensive individualized supports on Tier III. Tier II interventions are typically delivered in a small-group format for learners with similar challenging behaviors. Crone, Hawken, and Horner (2010) pointed out that Tier II interventions are characterized by 1) consistent, standardized implementation across learners, 2) easy accessibility (e.g., within a few days of referral), 3) continuous availability, 4) the implementation by all school staff, and 5) being consistent with schoolwide expectations and interventions. So far relatively little attention has been devoted to Tier II interventions compared with a substantive amount of literature documenting the effectiveness of primary and tertiary intervention of SWPBS (Hawken, Adolphson, MacLeod, & Schumann, 2009).

Although a variety of intervention strategies can be implemented in Tier II, there is a relative paucity of empirical research that has been conducted with the application of these strategies within a tiered continuum of behavioral supports for learners at risk for severe challenging behavior. Anderson and Borgmeier (2010) summarized examples of intervention packages or strategies that can be implemented on Tier II, including check-in/check-out (Fairbanks, Sugai, Guardino, & Lathrop, 2007; Filter et al., 2007; Todd, Campbell, Meyer, & Horner, 2008), check and connect (e.g., Anderson, Christenson, Sinclair, & Lehr, 2004; Lehr, Sinclair, & Christenson, 2004), first step to success (Carter & Horner, 2007; Filter et al., 2007), activity schedules (e.g., Bryan & Gast, 2000; O'Reilly, Sigafoos, Lancioni, Edrisinha, & Andrews, 2005), group contingencies (e.g., Bushell, Wrobel, & Michaelis, 1968; Embry, 2002), increased supervision (Atkins et al., 1998; Lewis, Colvin, & Sugai, 2000), and social skills programs (e.g., Cook et al., 2008 for a review of social skills training; Gresham, Cook, Crews, & Kern, 2004). Although a review of each of the interventions aforementioned is beyond the scope of the current chapter, other investigators have provided more in-depth discussions (see Hawken & Horner, 2003; Hawken, MacLeod, & Rawlings, 2007; March & Horner, 2002; McIntosh et al., 2009; Todd et al., 2008).

Tier III Intervention: Support for Learners Who Require Individualized Support Tier III interventions represent highly customized intervention strategies designed to meet the needs of a specific learner. Much of this chapter's discussion has focused primarily on the use of tertiary intervention (Tier III) interventions for challenging behavior (i.e., FCT), and a brief description of major primary and secondary supports for challenging behavior was offered in the preceding section.

MEASUREMENT CHALLENGES FACED BY RESEARCHERS IN IMPLEMENTING COMMUNICATIVE ALTERNATIVE TO CHALLENGING BEHAVIOR WITHIN THE SCHOOLWIDE POSITIVE BEHAVIOR SUPPORT MODEL

This section is based on the summary of the research studies into the field of challenging behavior and communicative alternatives and describes some measurement challenges faced by researchers and practitioners in this area. The challenges mainly involve how to measure social validity or contextual fit, procedural reliability of treatment fidelity, and setting events or establishing operations. Each of these challenges are further delineated in the following sections.

Social Validity/Contextual Fit

Social validity (Wolf, 1978) refers to a stakeholder's satisfaction with a treatment and the feasibility of carrying out the treatment (Schwartz & Baer, 1991). Similarly, contextual fit requires that intervention procedures be consistent with the values, skills, resources, and administrative support of those who must implement the plan (Carr, 1997). Generally speaking, social validity for behavioral interventions has been investigated mainly through the use of questionnaires or informal observation (Machalicek, O'Reilly, Beretvas, Sigafoos, & Lancioni, 2007; see Chapter 15). Lucyshyn, Horner, Dunlap, Albin, and Ben (2002) emphasized the importance of working with families while delivering intervention in the context of important family activities. These investigators successfully used a family assessment of settings, values, and beliefs to inform intervention. In addition, Carr (2006), Horner and Sugai (2000, 2001, 2005), and others have advanced knowledge in this area by investigating approaches for sustainable use of intervention procedures within the SWPBS framework.

Considering contextual fit does not happen with great frequency, however, in the FCT literature addressing the needs of individuals with severe disabilities. For example, school districts select curricula and intervention strategies hoping that educators will adhere to a rigorous implementation of manualized procedures. Contextual fit is one variable that may influence implementation fidelity. Schindler and Horner (2005) described an approach for enhancing the contextual fit of intervention strategies within the three-tier SWPBS model. They conducted FCT with three 4- to 5-year-old children with ASD using high-effort intervention in one primary setting and low-effort intervention in two secondary settings. High- and low-effort interventions shared the equivalent controlling antecedents and consequences but varied in their implementation intensity. Results revealed that low-effort intervention in the secondary settings were not effective when implemented alone. After the implementation of high-effort intervention in the primary setting, however, the reintroduction of low-effort intervention in secondary settings brought about desired reduction of challenging behavior. The investigators provided parents and teachers/assistants with a 6-point Likert-like scale to assess their perceived effort of implementation and feasibility of FCT under high- and low-effort intervention conditions, respectively. With higher contextual fit reported for low-effort condition, this study highlighted the importance of designing interventions based not only on the evidence supporting an intervention but also on contextual fit variables that may affect whether an intervention will be implemented with fidelity in an applied context and generalized by interventionists to other untaught settings. Furthermore, this study also suggested that after a child receives high-effort intervention on the Tier 3 level and makes sufficient progress, he or she can be moved to a Tier 2 intervention that requires comparatively less effort but yields higher social acceptability as well as satisfactory outcomes.

Procedural Reliability/Treatment Integrity

The overwhelming majority of studies implementing FCT outcomes report relatively high response reliability (i.e., how well two or more independent observers can record the dependent measure). Alternatively, the previously referred to literature review by Chen (2011) revealed that only 6 of 17 investigations conducted procedural fidelity checks. Unless one can consistently implement the intervention plan as it was designed, it is less likely that the learner will benefit. Failure to report data addressing treatment integrity may have significant implications for translational research in applied settings. Johnson, Reichle, and Monn (2009) examined the fidelity with which PBIS strategies were implemented by educators in preschool environments. They reported that educators in their control group exhibited 38% fidelity while implementing PBIS strategies. A treatment group that had received longitudinal mentoring and on-site technical assistance exhibited 80% fidelity. These data suggest that obtaining treatment fidelity may represent an important activity not only for researchers but also practitioners. There are often a number of interventionists in school settings. Varied levels of fidelity across interventionists could directly influence intervention from the standpoint of the learner receiving the treatment dosage (intensity) that is required for behavior change. Data offered by Johnson et al. (2009) also suggested that a viable area of research exploration may involve examining the degree to which implementation fidelity can be degraded with a significant intervention outcome still being achieved. The study of treatment intensity provides a way to break down components of an intervention to obtain controlled examinations of the relative contributions of a variety of parameters that could contribute to an overall examination of the degree to which an interventionist's implementation of a program adheres to an established protocol and the effect that specified variations have on learner acquisition, maintenance, and generalization.

Treatment Intensity

Warren, Fey, and Yoder (2007) delineated a set of treatment intensity parameters that included dose, dose form, dose frequency, total intervention duration, and cumulative intervention intensity. *Dose* refers to the number of properly administered treatment episodes during a single intervention period. Here, a treatment episode contains one or more interventionist acts hypothesized to lead/push the child/adult toward a treatment goal. Dose form means the task/activity/context within which a treatment episode occurs. Dose frequency is the number of times that a dose of intervention is provided per day or week (e.g., once a week, 1-hour session of one teaching episode per minute—60 episodes in total). The *total intervention duration* refers to the total time period over which an intervention is delivered (e.g., weekly for 6 months). Finally, cumulative intervention frequency equals to the product of dose, dose frequency, and total intervention duration, which provides a useful general indicator of overall intervention intensity. For instance, a child might receive a 30-week intervention that includes 60 defined treatment episodes per hour for 1 hour per week, which yields 1,800 treatment episodes cumulatively.

Systematically examining treatment intensity represents an important tool in attempting to objectify intervention strategies implemented across a number of investigations. Intervention outcomes across studies often are difficult to compare because treatment dosage may have differed, even though the intervention strategy content may have been the same in two studies. This, in turn, makes it more difficult to determine whether the two studies can actually be thought of as implementing the same intervention protocol. There have been few systematic attempts to evaluate intervention parameters that comprise treatment intensity regardless of the intervention approach. One exception is the study by Parker-McGowan et al. (2014). These investigators applied the dosage framework proposed by Warren et al. (2007) to milieu language teaching interventions for learners with developmental disabilities ages birth to 23 years to examine how each of the dosage parameters (i.e., dose, dose form, dose frequency, total duration, cumulative intervention intensity) was reported in this area. Results demonstrated that only approximately one third of the studies located through systematic searches clearly defined treatment intensity and reported all of the dosage parameters (making it difficult, if not impossible, to compare results across studies). All of the studies that did report all dosage parameters were single-case design. Treatment dosage represents a viable line of measurement-based research for investigators to pursue. See Chapter 2 for a more in-depth discussion of treatment intensity.

Assessment of Setting Events/Establishing Operations

Setting events refer to past or present physiological, social, or environmental conditions that can influence the likelihood of challenging behavior (Conroy & Fox, 1994). Suppose that Johnny sees Tommy spit on his sandwich. He sees a teacher enter the lunch room just as he prepares to hit Tommy. Johnny strategically decides not to hit Tommy and defers the hit until later. He hits Tommy on the playground 2 hours later. The teacher explains in the incidence report that the hitting occurred with no provoking stimulus. As a field, investigators are not very good at assessing displaced events that may be associated with challenging behavior. There are investigators who have done an excellent job with longitudinal observational data looking at statistical correlations between antecedent behaviors and consequences. This methodology, however, is beyond the typical educators' resources and capability. Other investigators have reported on the use of setting event checklists. Again, knowing what to follow as setting events seems a bit hit or miss.

Setting event interventions have become increasingly appreciated as a critical component of PBIS for individuals with severe disabilities (see Bambara & Kern, 2005). For example, consider a learner who is significantly more apt to engage in challenging behavior to escape an activity in a very warm room compared with working in a cooler environment. Lowering the temperature of the room prior to the activity would represent a preventative action by the interventionist. Because setting event interventions are implemented prior to the emission of challenging behavior, they preempt the need for the learner to engage in challenging behavior. They can be particularly effective when combined with a communicative alternative. For example, a learner can be taught to ask for relief from the heat when a room is too warm. Doing so acts as a prompt to a communicative partner to act. Therefore, how to accurately pinpoint settings events (e.g., biological setting events) associated with socially motivated challenging behavior would be an important area for researchers to probe. In addition to the measurement challenges previously described, researchers in this field also face some methodological challenges, which are further described in the next section.

METHODOLOGICAL AND RESEARCH DESIGN CHALLENGES FACED BY RESEARCHERS WITHIN THE SCHOOLWIDE POSITIVE BEHAVIOR SUPPORT MODEL

The methodological and research design challenges for the area of challenging behavior and communicative alternatives have emerged as a critical issue given the call for better adherence to evidence-based practices. The National Professional Development Center on Autism Spectrum Disorders (2014) identified criteria for evidence-based practices and concluded that efficacy must be established through peer-reviewed research in scientific journals to be considered an evidence-based practice for individuals with ASD using the following.

- *Randomized or quasi-experimental design studies.* Two high-quality experimental or quasi-experimental group design studies.
- *Single-subject design studies.* Three different investigators or research groups conducting five high-quality, single-subject design studies.
- *Combination of evidence.* One high-quality randomized or quasi-experimental group design study and three high-quality, single-subject design studies conducted by at least three different investigators or research groups (across the group and single-subject design studies).

Therefore, high-quality experimental or quasi-experimental group design studies and single-case design studies are highly underscored in the evaluation and accumulation of evidence-based practices. Specifically, high-quality randomized or quasi-experimental design applications do not have critical design flaws that create confounds to the studies, and design features allow readers/consumers to rule out competing hypotheses for study findings. Instead, high quality in single-case design studies are reflected by 1) the absence of critical design flaws that create confounds and 2) the demonstration of experimental control at least three times in each study (see Horner & Sugai, 2005; Nathan & Gorman, 2002; Odom et al., 2004; Rogers & Vismara, 2008).

In addition to the requirement of high quality in group design as well as single-case design studies, meta-analyses are playing an increasingly important role in contributing to evidence-based practice, especially in terms of aggregating high-quality group design and/or single-case design studies (Jenson, Clark, Kircher, & Kristjansson, 2007; Odom, 2009). Meta-analyses are challenging, however, for applied research areas such as challenging behavior and communicative alternatives due to the large reliance on single-case designs and the difficulty of selecting agreed-on effect size (ES) metric(s) for quantifying outcomes (Lipsey & Wilson, 2001; Shadish, Hedges, Pustejovsky, 2014).

Challenges in Implementing Single-Case Designs

The popularity of single-case designs for the field of challenging behavior and communicative alternatives is understandable given some of its prominent strengths. Single-case designs allow for a high degree of internal validity along with the flexibility to adapt the design to troubleshooting needs of the intervention being implemented without sacrificing experimental control, although external validity is significantly limited in single-case designs. Good internal validity is typically the hallmark of single-case studies. In addition, learners with severe disabilities are a very low incidence and highly heterogeneous population that also lends itself well to single-case designs.

Chen (2011) reported that approximately 47% of investigations addressing FCT during the past 10 years utilized multiple, baseline, or probe design across subjects (17.66%), settings (11.76%), behavior (5.88%), or behavioral functions (11.76%). Approximately one quarter (23.54%) of studies examined used a reversal design, and one study (5.88%) used an alternating treatment design. In addition, several studies combined two types of research designs, such as group experimental design with multiple baseline design across subjects (11.76%), multiple baseline across subjects with a within-subject multiple probe design (5.88%), and concurrent multiple baseline across settings with nonconcurrent multiple baseline across subjects (5.88%).

Reversal designs in applied settings can have a distinct disadvantage in that they force the researcher to stop implementing a potentially effective intervention that is likely to also result in the reemergence of challenging behavior. Doing so can be particularly troublesome for interventionists and stakeholders in the learner's well-being. Consequently, reversal designs are often extremely brief during the return to a baseline condition. A brief reversal period sets the bar high for researchers in that the level of the learner's performance must shift dramatically in a relatively brief period of time toward baseline performance to demonstrate experimental control. Multiple baseline designs across settings, interventionists, or other intervention-relevant variables can be problematic in that the interventionist is placed in the situation of hoping that generalization does not occur to retain the integrity of the experimental design. Consequently, increasingly multiple baseline designs have been executed across participants rather than across settings or materials.

Because single-case design continues to be used extensively in experimental investigations of challenging behavior among people with severe and multiple developmental disabilities, it is important to consider their role in creating a sound evidence base and how they represent a component of the big picture in creating a sound evidence base (see Byiers, Reichle, & Symons, 2012, for additional discussion of strengths and weaknesses of single-case design). One of those areas involves delineating desirable ways of using ES to quantify outcomes from single-case design studies.

Challenges in Evaluating Effect Size in Single-Case Design Studies

The American Psychiatric Association (APA) emphasized that "complete reporting of all tested hypotheses and estimates of appropriate effect sizes and confidence intervals are the minimum expectations for all APA journals. It is almost always necessary to include some index of effect size or strength of relationship" (2013, p. 35). Therefore, calculating and reporting ES has become an important requirement in the field of contemporary social sciences research. Consequently, calculating and reporting ES represents a potentially important requirement in contemporary social sciences research. ES is viewed as a robust measurement of the magnitude of change following an intervention or manipulation of an independent variable (Manolov & Solanas, 2008). ES not only contribute to the understanding of the magnitude of behavior change in empirical intervention studies, but are also necessary for researchers to conduct a comprehensive meta-analysis.

Although the convention of reporting ES for group design research has been well established, several controversies regarding the application of ES exist for single-case design research (Campbell, 2004). First, the presence of autocorrelation in single-case design research data violates the basic statistical assumption of independent observations and so undermines the basis for many statistical strategies or procedures. Second, the tendency for trend(s) in time-series data would misestimate treatment ES (West & Hepworth, 1991). This challenge is compounded by a variety of ES that can be applied in the evaluation of treatment effects in single-subject studies paired with conclusive lack of consensus as to which type(s) of ES should be the standard.

In general, there are two major approaches to quantifying intervention effects in single-case design studies and nonparametric and parametric approaches. Nonparametric approaches include but are not limited to Mean Baseline Difference (MBD; Campbell, 2003), Percentage of Nonoverlapping Data (PND; Scruggs, Mastropieri, & Casto, 1987), Percentage of Zero Data (PZD; Scotti, Evans, Meyer, & Walker, 1991), Percent of Data Exceeding the Median of Baseline (PEM; Ma, 2006), Improvement Rate Difference (IRD; Parker & Hagan-Burke, 2007), Percentage of All Non-Overlapping Data (PAND) and Phi derived from PAND (Parker, Hagan-Burke, & Vannest, 2007), Nonoverlap of All Pairs (NAP; Parker & Vannest, 2009), and $\text{Tau}_{\text{novlap}}$ (Parker, Vannest, Davis, & Sauber, 2011). The parametric approaches consist of Standardized Mean Difference (SMD; Busk & Serlin, 1992), Regression-Based Standardized Mean Difference (d_{REG}; Allison & Gorman, 1993), and ANOVA-based Cohen's *d*, Hedges's *g*, and Pearson *r* or r^2 (Rosenthal, 1991). Chen (2014) compared seven nonparametric ES metrics (i.e., PEM, PND, IRD, PAND, Phi, NAP, $\text{Tau}_{\text{novlap}}$) using a data sample systematically extracted from communication interventions involving the use of SGDs for individuals with moderate to profound IDD. The extracted data consisted of 258 AB data sets. Her investigation revealed that PAND, Phi, IRD, and PND were more effective in quantifying intervention effects for the data sample. Although this is by no means a comprehensive evaluation of ES metrics for single-case design studies, it suggests that the field has not yet established a definitive gold standard even though ES measurement is a requirement in evidence-based studies. Significant additional work is required in this area.

CHALLENGES IN GROWING THE EVIDENCE BASE OF PRACTICES AND FUTURE DIRECTIONS

Major methodological challenges will be briefly summarized in this section, along with some general directions for future research and practice based on what is known and perceived. Numerous challenges need to be addressed as the field of communicative approaches in managing challenging behavior continues to grow (see Table 3.2). The following section briefly discusses some of these challenges.

Table 3.2. Challenges arising in the field of problem behavior and communicative alternatives and some relevant examples

Challenges	Examples
Linking outcomes of functional analysis and communicative alternative	Simply identifying a behavior function may not be sufficient for determining an appropriate communicative alternative (e.g., escaping from the tasks may be due to the fact that the tasks are long or they are difficult).
Developing methodologies to consider low-dose interventions	Limited knowledge has been accumulated about how to best program treatment intensity for most cost-effective intervention outcomes.
Considering criteria for the selection of communicative mode and specific communicative form to implement in replacing problem behavior	Modality sampling as a promising approach to selecting communicative mode has received relatively little attention so far in the area of functional communication training (FCT). A systematic approach to selecting specific communicative form with functional equivalence and response efficiency has not been fully considered.
Examining mediators and moderators of collateral behavior	Little evidence has been accumulated to inform interventionists of how participant characteristics (e.g., preintervention communication ability, IQ), environmental characteristics (e.g., family socioeconomic status), and intervention characteristics (e.g., intensity) may affect the acquisition of collateral appropriate behavior in FCT.
Carefully considering contextual fit	The measurement of contextual fit as well as social validity continues to be an issue that has not been fully addressed.
Validating instructional procedures in translational settings	More efforts are needed to investigate the idiosyncratic contingencies that provoke or maintain the problem behavior, such as setting events or establishing operations displaced in time.
Examining strategies to promote conditional use of newly taught communication skills resulting from FCT	It is important to start systematically documenting generalization errors, such as over- or undergeneralization. More research is needed to examine how to best program instruction to enhance the generalization and conditional use of newly taught communicative skills in FCT, especially from the perspective of general-case instruction.
Implementing in the context of a schoolwide positive behavior support (SWPBS) and response to intervention (RTI) framework	A lack of evidence exists on how to implement FCT across the three tiers of SWPBS and RTI framework.

Linking Outcomes of Functional Analysis to Communicative Alternative

Assessing the potential function(s) of challenging behavior and developing a PBIS plan are often viewed as two completely separate activities that are not related. Interventionists frequently see support plans that do not match the maintaining variables that were identified during the assessment process. Careful study of the degree to which FBA outcomes are directly linked to related PBIS strategies is needed.

Developing Methodologies to Better Address Applied Implementation Considerations

In addition to the importance of linking the results from FBA to the development and implementation of communicative alternatives, the field faces several challenges in developing scientifically validated methodologies to enhance applied implementation of FCT interventions.

Low-Dose Interventions Ensuring appropriate maintenance and generalized use for a number of FCT interventions will require that interventionists continue to implement the interventions across activities and settings. Many interventionists in some of these settings will not have had extensive training in the implementation of the interventions that are needed to address the needs of people who engage in challenging behavior. Consequently, interventions designed to maintain and generalize new behavior will have to be as straightforward as possible. It is likely that the rigor used to establish a behavior may not need to be as rigorously implemented to maintain or generalize the behavior for many learners. There is a paucity of evidence-based literature in this area, however.

Procedural Fidelity Relatively little is known about implementation fidelity in authentic environments. This chapter provides some evidence suggesting that fidelity may be far lower than in the evidence-based demonstrations that comprise the available literature. If this is a pervasive feature of service delivery, then it is important to find out why. Is it a lack of contextual fit? Alternatively, is it because many evidence-based procedures were not developed in authentic educational or home settings and the interventionists were highly trained research assistants rather than practitioners? Was it because the contextual variables surrounding the intervention were different? The effect of lower fidelity on intervention outcomes is one potentially important area to explore. Relatively little is known about the interaction of learner characteristics and the level of fidelity required to obtain desired treatment effects.

Contextual Fit There appears to be widespread agreement that contextual fit requires careful consideration. The science suggesting how to better ensure contextual fit between curricula and interventionists, however, has received limited attention beyond acknowledgement of its importance. Our experience suggests that often supervisors and administrative staff often select curricula and service delivery models with relatively limited inclusion of those who will actually serve as implementers. Furthermore, we suspect that interventionists often cannot explain the logic that supports the intervention that they are implementing. It is important that those charged with implementing interventions understand (and suppo logic behind them.

Considering the Selection Criteria for Communicative Mode and Specific Communicative Form to Implement in Replacing Challenging Behavior Very few investigators have systematically implemented individualized longitudinal assessment strategies to make evidence-based decisions in selecting which communication modes to implement in establishing FCT. This is an important issue (particularly with young beginning communicators) that involves a consideration of contextual fit as well as efficiency of the form of the behavior being taught from the learner's perspective.

Better Examination of Contextual Variables that May Influence Intervention Effectiveness The importance of what was previously described as setting events among learners who engage in challenging behavior has been well established. However, there is limited evidence addressing practitioners' ability to systematically identify and design intervention strategies to eliminate or ameliorate them. Setting event assessment and subsequent intervention are critical areas in extending the ability to anticipate situations associated with challenging behavior and to act more proactively. This area is particularly fertile ground for the next generation of strategies to support individuals who have a propensity to engage in challenging behavior.

Validating Instructional Procedures in Translational Settings Although information addressing the environments in which interventions were implemented and the people who served as the interventionist can be somewhat spotty in the existing literature, many of the current evidence-based intervention strategies have not been extensively implemented in authentic settings. For example, a substantial number of FCT strategies that have experimental validation have relied on the implementation of instructional protocols during one-to-one instruction with researchers as the interventionist in highly controlled settings.

Examining Strategies to Promote Conditional Use of Newly Taught Communication Skills Resulting from Functional Communication Training Virtually all of the FCT literature has focused on teaching learners when to use the communicative alternative. Very little evidence exists that explores the parameters of undesired generalization of functional communicative alternatives. Overuse from the available literature and from the reports of interventionists in the field can be a problem. Additional work needs to focus on instructional approaches such as general case instruction to make appropriate generalized use part of acquisition procedures. In addition, with learners who engage in significant repertoires of challenging behavior, it is important to consider combining FCT procedures with other interventions that are aimed at enhancing the learner's self-regulatory skills in situations in which it is not acceptable to use new communicative alternatives.

Collateral Gains Resulting from Communicative Alternatives for Challenging Behavior Finally, there have been a number of investigations reporting the emergence of collateral behavior as a byproduct of the implementation of FCT procedures (e.g., vocal/verbal gains from graphic/gesture production, play, comprehension, activity engagement, skill improvement). Unfortunately, more needs to be known about variables that may influence the probability of obtaining collateral outcomes.

Integrating Preservice and In-service Training Approaches This chapter has provided virtually no discussion of how professionals and paraprofessionals at the preservice and in-service levels are prepared. Bambara, Nonnemacher, and Kern (2009) summarized three major factors that may affect the sustainability of evidence-based practices, including 1) practitioners' beliefs and attitudes about intervention effectiveness (aspects of contextual fit), 2) opportunities for practitioners to integrate their experiential knowledge with research-based practices and acquire a deep understanding of research-based practices (understanding and adapting evidence-based practices), and 3) contextual or systems variables that place demands on practitioners' daily functioning in school, such as school policies, schedules, organization, and resources.

Each of these has great importance and requires a systems approach on the part of future applied researchers and practitioners. Enhancing the sustained use of the evidence-based practices needs to continue if the information can be embraced for its contextual fit and if practitioners have time to practice what researchers preach about well-coordinated intervention, data monitoring, and coordinated decision making among stakeholders that is based on the outcome of data monitoring.

Exerting a greater effort in the coordination of preservice and in-service professional development for educators is one possible approach that has received little attention (Begeny & Martens, 2006; Myers & Holland, 2000). For example, preservice training programs may place a greater emphasis on training cohorts of professionals across key disciplines that often share responsibility for implementing FCT in authentic educational settings. In our opinion, it makes little sense to train professionals in isolation and then expect them to know how to work collaboratively once they participate in the work force.

CONCLUSION

Improving the application of empirically supported interventions in addressing challenging behaviors is an unquestioned research and service delivery priority (Hemmeter, Fox, Jack, Broyles, & Doubet, 2007). This chapter outlined a number of areas that require additional attention from the applied research community and also from those who provide preservice and in-service preparation for professionals. In spite of what may seem to be overwhelming needs, it is equally important to attend to the impressive changes in the approaches and procedures that have emerged since the mid-1990s. A well-documented technology of assessment and intervention strategies to address the needs of learners who engage in challenging behavior is maintained as the result of socially mediated consequences. Schoolwide approaches for developing support systems for learners who engage in challenging behavior are being implemented. Although challenges in improving evidence-based instructional technology exist, perhaps the greatest need is to increase the application of the instructional technology that is available in authentic environments. That is, much of what has been developed and has been discussed in this chapter is not being deployed in many applied settings where it would benefit large numbers of students. The reasons for this are many and have not been systematically addressed. Thus, the biggest current need is to address the implementation of what interventionists already know how to do.

The field of communication intervention for people who experience challenging behavior has made spectacular advances in the past several decades. Stakeholders should revel in these accomplishments; however, they should also not lose sight of the number of challenges ahead.

REFERENCES

Adkins, T., & Axelrod, S. (2001). Topography- versus selection-based responding: Comparison of mand acquisitions in each modality. *Behavior Analyst Today, 2,* 259–266.

Alberto, A.A., & Troutman, A.C. (2003). *Applied behavior analysis for teacher* (6th ed.). Upper Saddle River, NJ: Merrill Prentice Hall.

Allison, D.B., & Gorman, B.S. (1993). Calculating effect sizes for meta-analysis: The case of the single case. *Behavior Research and Therapy, 31,* 621–631.

American Psychiatric Association. (2013). *Diagnostic and statistical manual of mental disorders* (5th ed.). Washington, D.C. Author.

Anderson, A.E. (2002). *Augmentative communication and autism: A comparison of sign language and the Picture Exchange Communication System* (Doctoral dissertation). *Dissertation Abstracts International, 62*(9-B), 4269.

Anderson, A.R., Christenson, S.L., Sinclair, M.F., & Lehr, C.A. (2004). Check and Connect: The importance of relationships for promoting engagement with school. *Journal of School Psychology, 42,* 95–113.

Anderson, C.M., & Borgmeier, C. (2010). Tier II interventions within the framework of school-wide positive behavior support: Essential features for design, implementation, and maintenance. *Behavior Analysis in Practice, 3*(1), 33–45.

Anderson, C.M., & Long, E.S. (2002). Use of a structured descriptive assessment methodology to identify variables affecting problem behavior. *Journal of Applied Behavior Analysis, 35,* 137–154.

Atkins, M.S., McKay, M.M., Arvanitis, P., London, L., Madison, S., Costigan, C., Webster, D. (1998). An ecological model for school-based mental health services for urban low-income aggressive children. *Journal of Behavioral Health Services and Research, 25,* 64–75.

Azrin, N.H., Holz, W.C., & Hake, D.F. (1963). Fixed-ratio punishment. *Journal of the Experimental Analysis of Behavior, 6,* 141–148.

Bambara, L.M., & Kern, L. (2005). *Individualized supports for students with problem behaviors.* New York, NY: Guilford Press.

Bambara, L., Nonnemacher, S., & Kern, L. (2009). Sustaining school-based individualized Positive Behavior Support: Perceived barriers and enablers. *Journal of Positive Behavior Interventions, 11,* 161–178.

Batsche, G., Elliott, J., Graden, J., Grimes, J., Kovaleski, J., Prasse, D., & Tilly, W.D. (2006). *Response to intervention: Policy considerations and implementation* (4th ed.). Alexandria, VA: National Association of State Directors of Special Education.

Baum, W.M. (1974). On two types of deviation from the matching law: Bias and undermatching. *Journal of the Experimental Analysis of Behavior, 22,* 231–242.

Bayat, M., Mindes, G., & Covitt, S. (2010). What does RTI (response to intervention) look like in preschool? *Early Childhood Education Journal, 37*(6), 493–500.

Begeny, J.C., & Martens, B.K. (2006). Assisting low-performing readers with a group-based reading fluency intervention. *School Psychology Review, 35,* 91–107.

Bohanon, H., Fenning, P., Carney, K.L., Minnis-Kim, M.J., Anderson-Harriss, S., Moroz, K., Pigott, T.D. (2006). School-wide application of positive behavior support in an urban high school. *Journal of Positive Behavior Interventions, 8*(3), 131–145.

Bopp, K., Brown, K., & Mirenda, P. (2004). Speech-language pathologists' roles in the delivery of positive behavior support for individuals with developmental disabilities. *American Journal of Speech-Language Pathology, 13,* 5–19.

Bradshaw, C.P., Mitchell, M.M., O'Brennan, L.M., & Leaf, P.J. (2010). Multilevel exploration of factors contributing to the overrepresentation of black students in office disciplinary referrals. *Journal of Educational Psychology, 102*(2), 508–520.

Braithwaite, K.L., & Richdale, A.L. (2000). Functional communication training to replace challenging behaviors across two behavioral outcomes. *Behavioral Interventions, 15,* 21–36.

Bryan, L.C., & Gast, D.L. (2000). Teaching on-task and on-schedule behaviors to high-functioning children with autism via picture activity schedules. *Journal of Autism and Developmental Disorders, 30,* 553–567.

Buckley, S.D., & Newchok, D.K. (2005). Differential impact of response effort within a response chain on use of mands in a student with autism. *Research in Developmental Disabilities, 26*(1), 77–85.

Bushell, J.D., Wrobel, P.A., & Michaelis, M.L. (1968). Applying "group" contingencies to the classroom study behavior of preschool children. *Journal of Applied Behavior Analysis, 1*(1), 55–61.

Busk, P.L., & Serlin, R.C. (1992). Meta-analysis for single-case research. In T.R. Kratochwill & J.R. Levin (Eds.), *Single-case research designs and analysis: New directions for psychology and education* (pp. 159–185). Mahwah, NJ: Lawrence Erlbaum Associates.

Byiers, B.J., Reichle, J., & Symons, F.J. (2012). Single-subject experimental design for evidence-based practice. *American Journal of Speech-Language Pathology, 21*(4), 397–414.

Campbell, J.M. (2003). Efficacy of behavioral intervention for reducing problematic behaviors in persons with autism: A quantitative synthesis of single subject research. *Research in Developmental Disabilities, 24,* 120–138.

Campbell, J.M. (2004). Statistical comparison of four effect sizes for single-subject designs. *Behavior Modification, 28,* 234–246.

Campbell, S.B. (2002). *Behavior problems in preschool children: Clinical and developmental issues* (2nd ed.). New York, NY: Guilford Press.

Campbell, S.B. (2004, October). *Symposium on new developments in ADHD in preschool children.* Symposium conducted at American Academy of Child and Adolescent Psychiatry, Washington, DC.

Campbell, S.B. (2006). Maladjustment in preschool children: A developmental psychopathology perspective. In K. McCartney & D. Phillips (Eds.), *The Blackwell handbook of early childhood development* (pp. 358–378). London, England: Blackwell.

Carr, E.G. (1997). The evolution of applied behavior analysis into positive behavior support. *Journal of The Association for Persons with Severe Handicaps, 22,* 208–209.

Carr, E.G. (2006). SWPBS: The greatest good for the greatest number, or the needs of the majority trump the needs of the minority? *Research and Practice for Persons with Severe Disabilities, 31*(1), 54–56.

Carr, E.G., & Carlson, J.I. (1993). Reduction of severe behavior problems in the community using a multicomponent treatment approach. *Journal of Applied Behavior Analysis, 26,* 157–172.

Carr, E.G., Dunlap, G., Horner, R.H., Koegel, R.L., Turnbull, A.P., Sailor, W., Fox, L. (2002). Positive behavior support: Evolution of an applied science. *Journal of Positive Behavior Interventions, 4,* 4–16, 20.

Carr, E.G., & Durand, V.M. (1985). Reducing behavior problems through functional communication training. *Journal of Applied Behavior Analysis, 18,* 111–126.

Carr, E.G., Levin, L., McConnachie, G., Carlson, J.I., Kemp, D.C., & Smith, C.E. (1994). *Communication-based intervention for problem behavior: A user's guide for producing positive change.* Baltimore, MD: Paul H. Brookes Publishing Co.

Carr, E.G., Newsom, C.D., & Binkoff, J.A. (1976). Stimulus control of self-destructive behavior in a psychotic child. *Journal of Abnormal Child Psychology, 4,* 139–153.

Carr, E.G., Newsom, C.D., & Binkoff, J.A. (1980). Escape as a factor in the aggressive behavior of two retarded children. *Journal of Applied Behavior Analysis, 13,* 101–117.

Carr, E., Taylor, J., & Robinson, S. (1991). The effects of severe behavior problems in children on the teaching behavior of adults. *Journal of Applied Behavior Analysis, 24*(3), 523–535.

Carter, D.R., & Horner, R.H. (2007). Adding functional behavioral assessment to first step to success: A case study. *Journal of Positive Behavior Interventions, 9,* 229–238.

Chambers, M., & Rehfeldt, R.A. (2003). Assessing the acquisition and generalization of two mand forms with adults with severe developmental disabilities. *Research in Developmental Disabilities, 24*(4), 265–280.

Chandler, L.K., Dahlquist, C.M., Repp, A.C., & Feltz, C. (1999). The effects of team-based functional assessment on the behavior of students in classroom settings. *Exceptional Children, 66,* 1, 101–122.

Chen, M. (2011). *Functional communication training for challenging behavior in school setting: A review.* Unpublished manuscript, Department of Educational Psychology, University of Minnesota, Minneapolis.

Chen, M. (2014). *Evidence-based practice and single case designs: Evaluating seven effect size metrics involving speech-generating device intervention studies.* Manuscript in preparation, Department of Educational Psychology, University of Minnesota, Minneapolis.

Conroy, M.A., & Fox, J.J. (1994). Setting events and challenging behaviors in the classroom. *Preventing School Failure, 38*(3), 29–34.

Cook, C.R., Gresham, F.M., Kern, L., Barreras, R.B., Thornton, S., & Crews, S.D. (2008). Social skills training for secondary students with emotional and/or behavioral disorders: A review and analysis of the meta-analytic literature. *Journal of Emotional and Behavioral Disorders, 16,* 131–144.

Crone, D.A., Hawken, L., & Horner, L. (2010). *Responding to problem behavior in schools: The Behavior Education Program* (2nd ed.). New York, NY: Guilford Press.

Crosland, K., & Dunlap, G. (2012). Effective strategies for the inclusion of children with autism in general education classrooms. *Behavior Modification, 36*(3), 251–269.

D'Andrea, T. (1971). Avoidance of timeout from response-independent reinforcement. *Journal of the Experimental Analysis of Behavior, 15,* 319–325.

Dardano, J.F. (1974). Response timeouts under a progressive-ratio schedule with a punished reset option. *Journal of the Experimental Analysis of Behavior, 22,* 103–113.

Derby, K.M., Wacker, D.P., Berg, W., DeRaad, A., Ulrich, S., Asmus, J., Stoner, E.A. (1997). The long-term effects of functional communication training in home setting. *Journal of Applied Behavior Analysis, 30,* 507–531.

Derby, K.M., Wacker, D.P., Peck, S., Sasso, G., DeRaad, A., Berg, W., Ulrich, S. (1994). Functional analysis of separate topographies of aberrant behavior. *Journal of Applied Behavior Analysis, 27*(2), 267–278.

Derby, K.M., Wacker, D.P., Sasso, G., Steege, M., Northup, J., Cigrand, K., & Asmus, J. (1992). Brief functional assessment techniques to evaluate aberrant behavior in an outpatient setting: A summary of 79 cases. *Journal of Applied Behavior Analysis, 25*(3), 713–721.

Dolezal, D.N., & Kurtz, P.F. (2010). Evaluation of combined-antecedent variables on functional analysis results and treatment of problem behavior in a school setting. *Journal of Applied Behavior Analysis, 43*(2), 309–314.

Doss, S., & Reichle, J. (1989). Establishing communicative alternatives to the emission of socially motivated excess behavior: A review. *Journal of The Association for Persons with Severe Handicaps, 14,* 101–112.

Drasgow, E., Halle, J.W., Michaelene, M.O., & Harbers, H.M. (1996). Using behavioral indication and functional communication training to establish an initial sign repertoire with a young child with severe disabilities. *Topics in Early Childhood Special Education, 16,* 500–521.

Drasgow, E., Halle, J.W., & Ostrosky, M.M. (1998). Effects of differential reinforcement on the generalization of a replacement mand in three children with severe language delays. *Journal of Applied Behavior Analysis, 31,* 357–374.

Durand, V.M. (1990). *Severe behavior problems: A functional communication training approach.* New York, NY: Guilford Press.

Durand, V.M. (1999). Functional communication training using assistive devices: Recruiting natural communities of reinforcement. *Journal of Applied Behavior Analysis, 31,* 247–267.

Durand, V.M., & Carr, E.G. (1987). Social influences on "self-stimulatory" behavior: Analysis and treatment application. *Journal of Applied Behavior Analysis, 20,* 119–132.

Durand, V.M., & Carr, E.G. (1991). Functional communication training to reduce challenging behavior: Maintenance and application in new settings. *Journal of Applied Behavior Analysis, 24,* 251–264.

Durand, V.M., & Carr, E.G. (1992). An analysis of maintenance following functional communication training. *Journal of Applied Behavior Analysis, 25,* 777–794.

Embry, D.D. (2002). The good behavior game: A best practice candidate as a universal behavioral vaccine. *Clinical Child and Family Psychology Review, 5,* 273–297.

Emerson, E. (2003). Prevalence of psychiatric disorders in children and adolescents with and without intellectual disabilities. *Journal of Intellectual Disability Research, 47,* 51–58.

Ervin, R.A., Schaughency, E., Goodman, S.D., McGlinchey, M.T., & Matthews, A.

(2006). Merging research and practice agendas to address reading and behavior school-wide. *School Psychology Review, 35,* 198–223.

Facon, B., Beghin, M., & Rivière, V. (2007). The reinforcing effect of contingent attention on verbal perseverations of two children with severe visual impairment. *Journal of Behavior Therapy and Experimental Psychiatry, 38*(1), 23–28.

Fairbanks, S., Sugai, G., Guardino, D., & Lathrop, M. (2007). Response to intervention: Examining classroom behavior support in second grade. *Exceptional Children, 73*(3), 288–310.

Fallon, L.M., McCarthy, S.R., & Sanetti, L.M.H. (2014). School-wide positive behavior support (SWPBS) in the classroom: Assessing perceived challenges to consistent implementation in Connecticut schools. *Education and Treatment of Children, 37*(1), 1–24.

Fenerty, K.A., & Tiger, J.H. (2010). Determining preschoolers' preferences for choice-making opportunities: Choice of task versus choice of consequence. *Journal of Applied Behavior Analysis, 43,* 503–507.

Filter, K.J., McKenna, M.K., Benedict, E.A., Horner, R.H., Todd, A., & Watson, J. (2007). Check in/check out: A post-hoc evaluation of an efficient, secondary-level targeted intervention for reducing problem behaviors in schools. *Education and Treatment of Children, 30,* 69–84.

Fisher, W.W., Kuhn, D.E., & Thompson, R.H. (1998). Establishing discriminative control of responding using functional and alternative reinforcers during functional communication training. *Journal of Applied Behavior Analysis, 31,* 543–560.

Fisher, W., Piazza, C., Cataldo, M., Harrel, R., Jefferson, G., & Conner, R. (1993). Functional communication training with and without extinction and punishment. *Journal of Applied Behavior Analysis, 26,* 23–36.

Frea, W.D., Arnold, C.L., & Vittimberga, G.L. (2001). A demonstration of the effects of augmentative communication on the extreme aggressive behavior of a child with autism within an integrated preschool setting. *Journal of Positive Behavior Interventions, 3*(4), 194–198.

Fry, P.S. (1983). Process measures of problem and non-problem children's classroom behavior: The influence of teacher behavior variables. *British Journal of Educational Psychology, 53,* 79–88.

Fuchs, D., Mock, D., Morgan, P.L., & Young, C.L. (2003). Responsiveness-to-intervention: Definitions, evidence, and implications for the learning disabilities construct. *Learning Disabilities Research and Practice, 18*(3), 157–171.

Galloway, R.L., Panyan, M.V., Smith, C.R., & Wessendorf, S. (2008). Systems change with school-wide positive behavior supports: Iowa's work in progress. *Journal of Positive Behavior Interventions, 10*(2), 129–135.

Goh, A.E., & Bambara, L.M. (2012). Individualized positive behavior support in school settings: A meta analysis. *Remedial and Special Education, 33*(5), 271–286.

Gresham, F.M., Cook, C.R., Crews, S.D., & Kern, L. (2004). Social skills training for children and youth with emotional and behavioral disorders: Validity considerations and future directions. *Behavioral Disorders, 30,* 2–46.

Gunter, P.L., Jack, S.L., DePaepe, P., Reed, T.M., & Harrison, J. (1994). Effects of challenging behaviors of students with emotional and behavioral disorders on teacher instructional behavior. *Preventing School Failure, 38,* 35–39.

Hagopian, L.P., Fisher, W.W., Sullivan, M.T., Acquisto, J., & LeBlanc, L.A. (1998). Effectiveness of functional communication training with and without extinction and punishment: A summary of 21 inpatient cases. *Journal of Applied Behavior Analysis, 31,* 211–235.

Hanley, G.P., Piazza, C.C., Fisher, W.W., Contrucci, S.A., & Maglieri, K.A. (1997). Evaluation of client preference for function-based treatment packages. *Journal of Applied Behavior Analysis, 30,* 459–473.

Harding, J., Wacker, D.P., Cooper, L.J., Asmus, J., Jensen-Kovalan, P., & Grisolano, L.A. (1999). Combining descriptive and experimental analyses of young children with behavior problems in preschool settings. *Behavior Modifications, 23*(2), 316–333.

Harvey, S.T., Boer, D., Meyer, L.H., & Evans, I.M. (2009). Updating a meta-analysis of intervention research with challenging behavior: Treatment validity and standards of practice. *Journal of Intellectual and Developmental Disability, 34*(1), 67–80.

Hawken, L.S., Adolphson, S.L., MacLeod, K.S., & Schumann, J. (2009). Secondary-tier interventions and supports. In W. Sailor, G. Dunlap, G. Sugai, & R. Horner (Eds.), *Handbook of positive behavior*

intervention and support (pp. 395–420). New York, NY: Springer.
Hawken, L., & Horner, R. (2003). Evaluation of a targeted group intervention within a school-wide system of behavior support. *Journal of Behavioral Education, 12,* 225–240.
Hawken, L.S., MacLeod, K.S., & Rawlings, L. (2007). Effects of the Behavior Education Program (BEP) on problem behavior with elementary school students. *Journal of Positive Behavior Interventions, 9,* 94–101.
Hemmeter, M.L., Fox, L., Jack, S., Broyles, L., & Doubet, S. (2007). A program-wide model of positive behavior support in early childhood settings. *Journal of Early Intervention, 29,* 337–355.
Herrnstein, R.J. (1961). Relative and absolute strength of response as a function of frequency of reinforcement. *Journal of the Experimental Analysis of Behavior, 4,* 267–272.
Hetzroni, O.E., & Roth, T. (2003). Effects of a positive support approach to enhance communicative behaviors of children with mental retardation who have challenging behavior. *Education and Training in Developmental Disabilities, 38*(1), 95–105.
Hodgdon, L.A. (1996). *Visual strategies for improving communication: Practical supports for school and home.* Troy, MI: Quirk Roberts Publishing.
Hodgon, L.A. (1999). *Solving behavior problems in autism: Improving communication with visual strategies.* Troy, MI: Quirk Roberts Publishing.
Hong, E.R., Neely, L., Rispoli, M.J., Trepinski, T.M., Gregori, E., & Davis, T. (2015). A comparison of general and explicit delay cues to reinforcement for tangible-maintained challenging behavior. *Developmental Neurorehabilitation, 24,* 1–7. doi: 10.3109/17518423.2013.874378
Horner, R.H., & Carr, E.G. (1997). Behavioral support for students with severe disabilities: Functional assessment and comprehensive intervention. *Journal of Special Education, 31*(1), 84–104.
Horner, R., Carr, E., Halle, J., McGee, G., Odom, S., & Wolery, M. (2005). The use of single subject research to identify evidence-based practice in special education. *Exceptional Children, 71,* 165–180.
Horner, R.H., & Day, H.M. (1991). The effects of response efficiency on functionally equivalent competing behaviors. *Journal of Applied Behavior Analysis, 24,* 719–732.
Horner, R.H., Diemer, S.M., & Brazeau, K.C. (1992). Educational support for students with severe problem behaviors in Oregon: A descriptive analysis from the 1987–1988 school year. *Journal of The Association of Persons with Severe Handicaps, 17*(3), 154–169.
Horner, R.H., O'Neill, R.E., & Flannery, K.B. (1993). Building effective behavior support plans from functional assessment information. In M. Snell (Ed.), *Systematic instruction of persons with severe handicaps* (4th ed., pp. 184–214). Columbus, OH: Charles E. Merrill Publishing.
Horner, R.H., & Sugai, G. (2000). School-wide behavior support: An emerging initiative (special issue). *Journal of Positive Behavioral Interventions, 2,* 231–233.
Horner, R.H., & Sugai, G. (2001). "Data" need not be a four-letter word: Using data to improve schoolwide discipline. *Beyond Behavior, 11*(1), 20–22.
Horner, R.H., & Sugai, G., (2005). School-wide positive behavior support: An alternative approach to discipline in schools. In L. Bambara & L. Kern (Eds.), *Individualized supports for students with problem behavior: Designing positive behavior plans.* (pp. 359–390). New York, NY: Guilford Press.
Horner, R.H., Sugai, G., Smolkowski, K., Eber, L., Nakasato, J., Todd, A.W., & Esperanza, J. (2009). A randomized, wait-list controlled effectiveness trial assessing school-wide positive behavior support in elementary schools. *Journal of Positive Behavior Interventions, 11*(3), 133–144.
Hyppa-Martin, J., Reichle, J., Dimian, A., & Chen, M. (2013). Communication modality sampling for a toddler with Angelman syndrome. *Language, Speech, and Hearing Services in Schools, 44*(4), 327–336.
Irvin, L.K., Tobin, T.J., Sprague, J.R., Sugai, G., & Vincent, C.G. (2004). Validity of office discipline referral measures as indices of school-wide behavioral status and effects of school-wide behavioral interventions. *Journal of Positive Behavior Interventions, 6*(3), 131–147.
Iwata, B.A., Dorsey, M.F., Slifer, K.J., Bauman, K.E., & Richman, G.S. (1994). Toward a functional analysis of self-injury. *Journal of Applied Behavior Analysis, 27,* 197–209. (Reprinted from *Analysis and Intervention in Developmental Disabilities, 2,* 3–20, 1982)
Janney, D.M., Umbreit, J., Ferro, J.B., Liaupsin, C.J., & Lane, K.L. (2013). The effect of the extinction procedure in function-based intervention. *Journal of Positive Behavior Interventions, 15*(2), 113–123.

Jenson, W.R., Clark, E., Kircher, J.C., & Kristjansson, S.D. (2007). Statistical reform: Evidence based practice, meta-analyses, and single subject designs. *Psychology in the Schools, 44,* 483–494.

Johnson, L., Reichle, J., & Monn, E. (2009). Longitudinal mentoring with school-based positive behavioral support teams: Influences on staff and learner behavior. *Evidence-Based Communication Assessment and Intervention, 3,* 113–130.

Johnston, S.S., Reichle, J., Feeley, K.M., & Jones, E.A. (2012). *AAC strategies for individuals with moderate to severe disabilities.* Baltimore, MD: Paul H. Brookes Publishing Co.

Kahng, S., Iwata, B.A., DeLeon, I.G., & Worsdell, A.S. (1997). Evaluation of the "control over reinforcement" component in functional communication training. *Journal of Applied Behavior Analysis, 28,* 261–268.

Kazdin, A.E. (1971). The effect of response cost in suppressing behavior in a prepsychotic retardate. *Journal of Behavior Therapy and Experimental Psychiatry, 2,* 137–140.

Kelm, J.L., & McIntosh, K. (2012). Effects of school-wide positive behavior support on teacher self-efficacy. *Psychology in the Schools, 49*(2), 137–147.

Kemp, D.C., & Carr, E.G. (1995). Reduction of severe problem behavior in community employment using a hypothesis-driven multicomponent intervention approach. *Journal of The Association for Persons with Severe Handicaps, 20*(4), 229–247.

Kern, L., Choutka, C.M., & Sokol, N.G. (2002). Assessment-based antecedent interventions used in natural settings to reduce challenging behavior: An analysis of the literature. *Education and Treatment of Children, 25*(1), 113–130.

Kern, L., Gallagher, P., Starosta, K., Hickman, W., & George, M.L. (2006). Longitudinal outcomes of functional behavioral assessment-based intervention. *Journal of Positive Behavior Interventions, 8,* 67–78.

Klingner, J.K., & Edwards, P.A. (2006). Cultural considerations with response to intervention models. *Reading Research Quarterly, 41*(1), 108–117.

Lalli, J.S., Casey, S., & Kates, K. (1995). Reducing escape behavior and increasing task completion with functional communication training, extinction, and response chaining. *Journal of Applied Behavior Analysis, 28,* 261–268.

Lauderdale-Littin, S., Howell, E., & Blacher, J. (2013). Educational placement for children with autism spectrum disorders in public and nonpublic school settings: The impact of social skills and behavior problems. *Education and Training in Autism and Developmental Disabilities, 48*(4), 469–478.

Lehr, C.A., Sinclair, M.F., & Christenson, S.L. (2004). Addressing student engagement and truancy prevention during the elementary school years: A replication study of the Check and Connect model. *Journal of Education for Students Placed at Risk, 9,* 279–301.

Lewis, T.J., Colvin, G., & Sugai, G. (2000). The effects of pre-correction and active supervision on the recess behavior of elementary students. *Education and Treatment of Children, 23,* 109–21.

Lipsey, M.W., & Wilson, D.B. (2001). *Practical meta-analysis.* Thousand Oaks, CA: Sage Publications.

Loeber, R., Farrington, D.P., & Petechuk, D. (2003). *Child delinquency: Early intervention and prevention.* Washington, DC: U.S. Department of Justice, Office of Juvenile Justice and Delinquency Prevention.

Loman, S.L., & Horner, R.H. (2014). Examining the efficacy of a basic functional behavioral assessment training package for school personnel. *Journal of Positive Behavior Interventions, 16*(1), 18–30.

Lovaas, O.I., Freitag, G., Gold, V.J., & Kassorla, I.C. (1965). Experimental studies in childhood schizophrenia: Analysis of self-destructive behavior. *Journal of Experimental Child Psychology, 2,* 67–84.

Lovaas, O.I., & Simmons, J.Q. (1969). Manipulation of self-destruction in three retarded children. *Journal of Applied Behavior Analysis, 2,* 143–157.

Lowe, K., Allen, D., Jones, E., Brophy, S., Moore, K., & James, K. (2007). Challenging behaviors: Prevalence and topographies. *Journal of Intellectual Disability Research, 51*(8), 625–636.

Lucyshyn, J. M., Horner, R. H., Dunlap, G., Albin, R. W., & Ben, K. R. (2002). Positive behavior support with families. *Families and positive behavior support: Addressing problem behavior in family contexts,* 3-43.

Luczynski, K.C., & Hanley, G.P. (2013). Prevention of problem behavior by teaching functional communication and self-control skills to preschoolers. *Journal of Applied Behavior Analysis, 46*(2), 355–368.

Luiselli, J.K., Dunn, E.K., & Pace, G.M. (2005). Antecedent assessment and intervention to reduce physical restraint (proactive holding) of children and adolescents with acquired brain injury. *Behavioral Interventions, 20,* 51–65.

Ma, H. (2006). An alternative method for quantitative synthesis of single subject researches: Percentage of data points exceeding the median. *Behavior Modification, 30,* 598–617.

Maag, J.W. (2001). Rewarded by punishment: Reflections on the disuse of positive reinforcement in schools. *Exceptional Children, 67*(2), 173–186.

Mace, F.C., & Lalli, J.S., & Lalli, E.P. (1991). Functional analysis and treatment of aberrant behavior. *Research in Developmental Disabilities, 12,* 155–180.

Machalicek, W., O'Reilly, M.F., Beretvas, N., Sigafoos, J., & Lancioni, G. (2007). A review of intervention strategies to decrease challenging behavior in school settings for students with autism spectrum disorders. *Research in Autism Spectrum Disorders, 1,* 229–246.

Manolov, R., & Solanas, A. (2008). Randomization tests for ABAB designs: Comparing data-division-specific and common distributions. *Psicothema, 20,* 291–297.

March, R.E., & Horner, R.H. (2002). Feasibility and contributions of functional behavioral assessment in schools. *Journal of Emotional and Behavioral Disorders, 10,* 158–170.

McClannahan, L.E., & Krantz, P.J. (1999). *Activity schedules for children with autism: Teaching independent behavior.* Bethesda, MD: Woodbine House.

McIntosh, K., Campbell, A., Carter, D.R., & Dickey, C.R. (2009). Differential effects of a tier 2 behavioral intervention based on function of problem behavior. *Journal of Positive Behavior Interventions, 11,* 82–93.

McIntosh, K., Filter, K.J., Bennett, J.L., Ryan, C., & Sugai, G. (2010). Principles of sustainable prevention: Designing scale-up of school-wide positive behavior support to promote durable systems. *Psychology in the Schools, 47*(1), 5–21.

McLaren, E.M., & Nelson, C.M. (2009). Using functional behavior assessment to develop behavior interventions for students in Head Start. *Journal of Positive Behavior Interventions, 11*(1), 3–21.

Millar, D. (2009). Effects of AAC on the natural speech develop of individuals with autism spectrum disorders. In P. Mirenda & T. Iacono (Eds.), *Autism spectrum disorders and AAC* (pp.171–194). Baltimore, MD: Paul H. Brookes Publishing Co.

Millard, T., Wacker, D.P., Cooper, L.J., Harding, J., Drew, J., Plagmann, L.A., Jensen-Kovalan, P. (1993). A brief component analysis of potential treatment packages in an outpatient clinic setting with young children. *Journal of Applied Behavior Analysis, 26*(4), 475–476.

Miller, G.E., & Prinz, R.J. (1990). The enhancement of social learning family interventions for childhood conduct behavior. *Psychological Bulletin, 108,* 291–307.

Mirenda, P. (1997). Functional communication training and augmentative communication: A research review. *Augmentative and Alternative Communication, 13,* 207–225.

Murphy, G.H. (1978). Overcorrection: A critique. *Journal of Intellectual Disability Research, 22*(3), 161–173.

Murphy, G.H., Beadle-Brown, J., Wing, L., Gould, J., Shah, A., & Holmes, N. (2005). Chronicity of challenging behavior in people with severe intellectual disabilities and/or autism: A total population sample. *Journal of Autism and Developmental Disorders, 35,* 267–280.

Myers, C.L., & Holland, K.L. (2000). Classroom behavioral interventions: Do teachers consider the function of the behavior? *Psychology in the Schools, 37*(3), 271–280.

Najdowski, A.C., Wallace, M.D., Ellsworth, C.L., MacAleese, A.N., & Cleveland, J.M. (2008). Functional analyses and treatment of precursor behavior. *Journal of Applied Behavior Analysis, 41,* 97–105.

Nathan, P., & Gorman, J.M. (2002). *A guide to treatments that work.* New York, NY: Oxford University Press.

National Professional Development Center on Autism Spectrum Disorders. (2014). *What are evidence-based practices (EBP)?* unpublished manuscript. Frank Porter Graham Center. University of North Carolina-Chapel Hill, Chapel Hill, N.C.

Noltemeyer, A., & Sansosti, F.J. (2012). Tiered models of integrated academic and behavioral support: Effect of implementation level on academic outcomes. *Contemporary School Psychology, 16*(1), 117–127.

Odom, S.L. (2009). The tie that binds: Evidence-based practice, implementation science, and outcomes for children. *Topics in Early Childhood Special Education, 29*(1), 53–61.

Odom, S.L., Brantlinger, E., Gersten, R., Horner, R.D., Thompson, B., & Harris, K.

(2004). *Quality indicators for research in special education and guidelines for evidence-based practices: Executive summary*. Arlington, VA: Council for Exceptional Children, Division for Research.

O'Neill, R., & Reichle, J. (1993). Addressing socially motivated challenging behaviors by establishing communicative alternatives: Basics of a general-case approach. In J. Reichle & D.P. Wacker (Eds.), *Communicative alternatives to challenging behavior: Integrating functional assessment and intervention strategies* (pp. 205–235). Baltimore, MD: Paul H. Brookes Publishing Co.205-235.

O'Neill, R.E., & Sweetland-Baker, M. (2001). Brief report: An assessment of stimulus generalization and contingency effects in functional communication training with two students with autism. *Journal of Autism and Developmental Disorders, 31*(2), 235–240.

O'Neill, R. E., Vaughn, B. J., & Dunlap, G. (1997). Comprehensive behavioral support: Assessment issues and strategies. In Wetherby, A. M., Warren, S. F., & Reichle, J. (Eds.). *(1998). Transitions in prelinguistic communication (Vol. 7).* Paul H Brookes Publishing Company., 313-341.

O'Reilly, M., Sigafoos, J., Lancioni, G., Edrisinha, C., & Andrews, A. (2005). An examination of the effects of a classroom activity schedule on levels of self-injury and engagement for a child with severe autism. *Journal of Autism and Developmental Disabilities, 35,* 305–311.

Pace, G.M., Dunn, E.K., Luiselli, J.K., Cochran, C.R. & Skowron, J. (2005). Antecedent interventions in the management of maladaptive behaviors in a child with brain injury. *Brain Injury, 19*(5), 365–369.

Parker, R.I., & Hagan-Burke, S. (2007). Median-based overlap analysis for single case data. *Behavior Modification, 31*(6), 919–936.

Parker, R.I., Hagan-Burke, S., & Vannest, K. (2007). Percentage of all non-overlapping data (PAND): An alternative to PND. *Journal of Special Education, 40,* 194–204.

Parker, R.I., & Vannest, K.J. (2009). An improved effect size for single-case research: Nonoverlap of all pairs. *Behavior Therapy, 40,* 357–367.

Parker, R.I., Vannest, K.J., Davis, J.L., & Sauber, S.B. (2011). Combining nonoverlap and trend for single-case research: Tau-U. *Behavior Therapy, 42,* 284–299.

Parker-McGowan, Q., Chen, M., Reichle, J., Pandit, S., Johnson, L., & Kreibich, S. (2014). Describing treatment intensity in milieu teaching interventions for children with developmental disabilities: A review. *Language, Speech, and Hearing Services in Schools, 45,* 351-364.

Patterson, G.R. (1986). Performance models for antisocial boys. *American Psychologist, 41,* 432–444.

Pinkston, E.M., Reese, N.M., LeBlanc, J.M., & Baer, D.M. (1973). Independent control of a preschool child's aggression and peer interaction by contingent teacher attention. *Journal of Applied Behavior Analysis, 6,* 115–124.

Reeve, C.E., & Carr, E.G. (2000). Prevention of severe behavior problems in children with developmental disorders. *Journal of Positive Behavior Interventions, 2*(3), 144–160.

Reichle, J. (1990). *National working conference on positive approaches to the management of excess behavior: Final report and recommendations.* Minneapolis, MN: Institute on Community Integration, University of Minnesota.

Reichle, J., Drager, K., & Davis, C.A. (2002). Using requests for assistance to obtain desired items and to gain release from non-preferred activities: Implications for assessment and intervention. *Education and Treatment of Children, 25,* 47–66.

Reichle, J., Johnson, L., Monn, E., & Harris, M. (2010). Task engagement and escape maintained challenging behavior: Differential effects of general and explicit cues when implementing a signaled delay in the delivery of reinforcement. *Journal of Autism and Developmental Disorders, 40,* 709–720.

Reichle, J., & McComas, J. (2004). Conditional use of a request for assistance. *Disability and Rehabilitation, 26,* 1255–1262.

Reichle, J., McEvoy, M., Davis, C., Rogers, E., Feeley, K., Johnston, S., & Wolff, K. (1996). Coordinating preservice and in-service training of early interventionists to serve preschoolers who engage in challenging behavior. In L.K.K. Koegel, R.L. Koegel, & G. Dunlap (Eds.), *Positive behavioral support: Including people with difficult behavior in the community* (pp. 227–259). Baltimore, MD: Paul H. Brookes Publishing Co.

Reichle, J., & Wacker, D.P. (1993). *Communicative alternatives to challenging behavior: Integrating functional assessment and intervention strategies.* Baltimore, MD: Paul H. Brookes Publishing Co.

Reichle, J., & Wacker, D. (2014). *Functional communication training.* Unpublished manuscript, Department of Educational Psychology, University of Minnesota, Minneapolis.

Reichle, J., York, J., & Sigafoos, J. (1991). *Implementing augmentative and alternative communication.* Baltimore, MD: Paul H. Brookes Publishing Co.

Reinke, W.M., Herman, K.C., & Stormont, M. (2013). Classroom-level positive behavior supports in schools implementing SW-PBIS: Identifying areas for enhancement. *Journal of Positive Behavior Interventions, 15*(1), 39–50.

Richman, D.M., Wacker, D.P., Asmus, J.M., & Casey, S.D. (1998). Functional analysis and extinction of different behavior problems exhibited by the same individual. *Journal of Applied Behavior Analysis, 31*(3), 475–478.

Rimm-Kaufman, S., Pianta, R., & Cox, M. (2000). Teachers' judgments of problems in the transition to kindergarten. *Early Childhood Research Quarterly, 15,* 147–166.

Rishel, C.W., Morris, T.L., Colyer, C., & Gurley-Calvez, T. (2014). Preventing the residential placement of young children: A multidisciplinary investigation of challenges and opportunities in a rural state. *Children and Youth Services Review, 37,* 9–14.

Rogers, S.J., & Vismara, L.A. (2008). Evidence based comprehensive treatments for early autism. *Journal of Child and Adolescent Clinical Psychology, 37*(1), 8–38.

Rosenthal, R. (1991). *Meta-analysis procedures for social science research.* Thousand Oaks, CA: Sage Publications.

Sadler, C., & Sugai, G. (2009). Effective behavior and instructional support: A district model for early identification and prevention of reading and behavior problems. *Journal of Positive Behavior Interventions, 11,* 35–46.

Sailor, W., Dunlap, G., Sugai, G., & Horner, R. (2009). *Handbook of positive behavior support.* New York, NY: Springer.

Sailor, W., Guess, D., Rutherford, G., & Baer, D.M. (1968). Control of tantrum behavior by operant techniques during experimental verbal training. *Journal of Applied Behavior Analysis, 1,* 237–243.

Sampers, J., Anderson, K.G., Hartung, C.M., & Scambler, D.J. (2001). Parent training programs for young children with behavior problems. *Infant Toddler Intervention, 11,* 91–110.

Schindler, H., & Horner, R. (2005). Generalized reduction of problem behavior of young children with autism: Building trans-situational interventions. *American Journal on Mental Retardation, 110*(1), 36–47.

Schwartz, I.S., & Baer, D.M. (1991). Social validity assessments: Is current practice state of the art? *Journal of Applied Behavior Analysis, 24,* 189–204.

Scott, T.M., Nelson, C.M., & Liaupsin, C.J. (2001). Effective instruction: The forgotten component in preventing school violence. *Education and Treatment of Children, 24,* 309–322.

Scotti, J.R., Evans, I.M., Meyer, L.H., & Wacker, P. (1991). A meta-analysis of intervention research with problem behavior: Treatment validity and standards of practice. *American Journal on Mental Retardation, 96,* 233–256.

Scruggs, T.E., Mastropieri, M.A., & Casto, G. (1987). The quantitative synthesis of single subject research: Methodology and validation. *Remedial and Special Education, 8,* 24–33.

Sedlak, A.J., & McPherson, K. (2010). *Survey of youth in residential placement: Youth's needs and services.* Rockville, MD: Westat.

Sellers, T.P., Bloom, S.E., Samaha, A.L., Dayton, E., Lambert, J.M., & Keyl-Austin, A.A. (2013). Evaluation of some components of choice making. *Journal of Applied Behavior Analysis, 46*(2), 455–464.

Shadish, W.R., Hedges, L.V., & Pustejovsky, J.E. (2014). Analysis and meta-analysis of single-case designs with a standardized mean difference statistic: A primer and applications. *Journal of School Psychology, 52,* 123–147.

Shirley, M.J., Iwata, B.A., Kahng, S., Mazaleski, J.L., & Lerman, D.C. (1997). Does functional communication training compete with ongoing contingencies of reinforcement? An analysis during response acquisition and maintenance. *Journal of Applied Behavior Analysis, 30,* 93–104.

Simonsen, B., Britton, L., & Young, D. (2010). School-wide positive behavior support in an alternative school setting: A case study. *Journal of Positive Behavior Interventions, 12*(3), 180–191.

Sinclair, M.F., Christenson, S.L., Evelo, D.L., & Hurley, C.M. (1998). Drop-out prevention for youth with disabilities: Efficacy of a sustained school engagement procedure. *Exceptional Children, 65,* 7–21.

Sinclair, M.F., Christenson, S.L., & Thurlow, M.L. (2005). Promoting school completion of urban secondary youth with emotional or behavioral disabilities. *Exceptional Children, 71*(4), 465–482.

Solomon, B.G., Klein, S.A., Hintze, J.M., Cressey, J.M., & Peller, S.L. (2012). A meta-analysis of school-wide positive behavior support: An exploratory study using single-case synthesis. *Psychology in the Schools, 49*(2), 105–121.

Sparks, S.C., & Cote, D.L. (2012). Teaching choice making to elementary students with mild to moderate disabilities. *Intervention in School and Clinic, 47*(5), 290–296.

Spaulding, S.A., Irvin, L.K., Horner, R.H., May, S.L., Emeldi, M., Tobin, T.J., & Sugai, G. (2010). Schoolwide social-behavioral climate, student problem behavior, and related administrative decisions: Empirical patterns from 1,510 schools nationwide. *Journal of Positive Behavior Interventions, 12*(2), 69–85.

Stokes, T.F., & Baer, D.M. (1977). An implicit technology of generalization. *Journal of Applied Behavior Analysis, 10,* 349–367.

Sugai, G., & Horner, R.H. (2006). A promising approach for expanding and sustaining school-wide positive behavior support. *School Psychology Review,* 35(2), 245–259.

Sugai, G., O'Keeffe, B.V., & Fallon, L.M. (2012). A contextual consideration of culture and school-wide positive behavior support. *Journal of Positive Behavior Interventions, 14*(4), 197–208.

Sulzer-Azaroff, B., & Mayer, G.R. (1977). *Applying behavior analysis procedures with children and youth.* Austin, TX: Holt, Rinehart & Winston.

Thomas, D.R., Becker, W.C., & Armstrong, M. (1968). Production and elimination of disruptive classroom behavior by systematically varying teacher's behavior. *Journal of Applied Behavior Analysis, 1,* 35–45.

Tincani, M. (2004). Comparing the Picture Exchange Communication System and sign language training for children with autism. *Focus on Autism and Other Developmental Disabilities, 19,* 152–164.

Todd, A.W., Campbell, A.L., Meyer, G.G., & Horner, R.H. (2008). The effects of a targeted intervention to reduce problem behaviors. *Journal of Positive Behavior Interventions, 10,* 46–55.

Turtura, J.E., Anderson, C.M., & Boyd, R.J. (2014). Addressing task avoidance in middle school students: Academic behavior check-in/check-out. *Journal of Positive Behavior Interventions, 16*(3), 159–167.

Vincent, C.G., & Tobin, T.J. (2011). The relationship between implementation of school-wide positive behavior support (SWPBS) and disciplinary exclusion of students from various ethnic backgrounds with and without disabilities. *Journal of Emotional and Behavioral Disorders, 19*(4), 217–232.

Volkert, V.M., Lerman, D.C., Call, N.A., & Trosclair-Lasserre, N. (2009). An evaluation of resurgence during treatment with functional communication training. *Journal of Applied Behavior Analysis, 42,* 145–160.

Wacker, D.P., Steege, M.W., Northup, J., Sasso, G., Berg, W., Reimers, T., Donn, L. (1990). A component analysis of functional communication training across three topographies of severe behavior problems. *Journal of Applied Behavior Analysis, 23*(4), 417–429.

Wacker, D.P., Wiggins, B., Fowler, M., & Berg, W.K. (1988). Training students with profound or multiple handicaps to make requests via microswitches. *Journal of Applied Behavior Analysis, 21*(4), 331–343.

Warren, S.F., Fey, M.E., & Yoder, P.J. (2007). Differential treatment intensity research: A missing link to creating optimally effective communication interventions. *Mental Retardation and Developmental Disabilities Research Reviews, 13*(1), 70–77.

Watson, J. (2003, May 14). *Report to the 4J school board.* Eugene, OR: 4J School District.

West, S.G., & Hepworth, J.T. (1991). Statistical issues in the study of temporal data: Daily experiences. *Journal of Personality, 59*(3), 609–662.

Winborn, L., Wacker, D.P., Richman, D.M., Asmus, J., & Geier, D. (2002). Assessment of mand selection for functional communication training packages. *Journal of Applied Behavior Analysis, 35,* 295–298.

Wolf, M.M. (1978). Social validity: The case for subjective measurement, or how behavior analysis is finding its heart. *Journal of Applied Behavior Analysis, 11,* 203–214.

Yoder, P.J., & Layton, T.L. (1988). Speech following sign language training in autistic children with minimal verbal language. *Journal of Autism and Developmental Disorders, 18,* 217–229.

4

Research on Communication Intervention for Children Who Are Deafblind

Charity Mary Rowland and Amy T. Parker

Maria

Maria was born at 29 weeks gestation and was diagnosed with periventricular leukomalacia (PVL), a type of brain injury. Maria was also diagnosed with spastic quadriplegia and seizure disorder while she was in the neonatal intensive care unit. In addition, Maria was diagnosed with cortical visual impairment (CVI) and hearing impairment associated with PVL after she left the hospital. Maria was the firstborn child of a 19-year-old mother and 20-year-old father from Mexico who lived in an apartment with seven other adult relatives and friends in an urban setting.

Maria was seen by several therapists through her in-home early intervention program, including one with advanced training in sensory impairments. Fortunately, Maria's early intervention program had begun implementing a family-centered, play-based curriculum that focused on therapy teams working closely with families, including Spanish-speaking families, during typical routines. Maria's extended family partnered with her early intervention therapists over the course of 3 years to recognize how her basic bathing, feeding, playing, and sleeping routines could be used to help her anticipate what should happen next and participate in her environment. Maria received a functional vision evaluation that revealed the sorts of objects, lights, and colors she could see. Maria's family gradually began to recognize that Maria could orient toward familiar objects, although it took significant processing time for her to respond to them. Maria responded to and reached for objects that were red, and her team incorporated the color red into most of her daily routines. She was interested in familiar objects, often looking away from them while she reached to find them. Acoustically, Maria responded to sounds such as her mother's voice repeatedly singing her name when she came in the door. Maria also would orient to the sound of the physical therapist slapping a large red therapy ball, even when she could not see the ball. Maria's hearing was tied to routines, just like her vision. She was more responsive when there was little background noise and sounds were repeated patterns. She laughed when her mother sang to her, and she enjoyed the sound of cellophane crinkling. With the help of her early intervention team, Maria's mother had begun playing a game of waiting for Maria to "ask" for more crinkle paper by kicking her legs.

Before making the transition to the preschool setting, Maria's mother began working with the team to list Maria's preferences in order to help her future teachers get to know her. One of the early intervention team members suggested that Maria might use a red Big Mac™ microswitch with a recording of her mother saying, "crinkle paper" to request this preferred activity. The team hoped that Maria's new preschool teachers would recognize her subtle communication signals and incorporate the strategies that helped her participate more fully in her routines.

Thaddeus

Thaddeus was born with total blindness and moderate to severe bilateral sensorineural hearing loss. He was ambulatory at 18 months of age but had little in the way of intentional communication. He became tactually defensive, resisting manipulation of his hands, after intensive early intervention sessions that focused on hand-in-hand signing. The focus at home and preschool shifted to providing systematic input through touch cues and environmental input and responding to spontaneous movements and vocalizations that were clearly intentional and might be shaped into intentionally communicative signals. Because he loved movement-based activities, regular routines were established around the equipment in the school playroom with the indoor slide, the therapy ball, a rocking boat, and a trampoline, all of which Thaddeus required assistance to use. These 20-minute routines were conducted daily at school. Thaddeus became less dependent as he became more confident; he began to reach out to other people and touch them, guide their hands or touch desired objects to indicate his desires, and request help. He developed very specific body movements to show exactly how he wanted to be placed on the therapy ball and trampoline and whether he wanted to go down the slide forward or backward.

After Thaddeus became confident at indicating exactly what he wanted presymbolically (e.g., tapping objects or hand guiding to make choices, mimicking part of a movement to request an action, touching someone to gain attention), it became clear that it was time to introduce some sort of symbol system to him. Because he had no useful vision, three-dimensional symbols were created for his favorite playroom items and fashioned out of similar materials. At first, the symbols were attached to the corresponding items with Velcro. Each time Thaddeus used a plaything, he was assisted to run his hand over the attached symbol so that he began to gain an understanding of the association between each symbol and its referent. The next step was to teach him to pick up the symbol and give it to his partner as a request to use the play equipment. He was always required to gain his partner's attention in conjunction with learning how to use the symbols to communicate. After he became adept at gaining attention, taking the symbol from the equipment, and handing it to his partner to request access, the symbols were removed from the equipment and presented in progressively larger arrays. Thaddeus learned to scan an array of symbols attached by Velcro to a clipboard and select the one associated with the piece of equipment he had already indicated he wanted. This was a long, but rewarding process that lasted 3 years in total; baby steps were taken so Thaddeus was never confronted by demands that would frustrate him and he was quickly successful at each new step.

WHAT IS DEAFBLINDNESS?

Gaining an understanding of the deafblind population is central to any discussion of the challenges of studying individuals who are deafblind. Under the definition of a child with a disability, Code of Federal Regulations for Title 34-Education specifies that

> Deaf-blindness means concomitant hearing and visual impairments, the combination of which creates such severe communication and other developmental and educational needs that they cannot be accommodated in special education programs solely for children with deafness or children with blindness. (34 CFR 300.7[c][2])

Deafblindness is more explicitly defined in the Helen Keller National Center Act (as amended by the Rehabilitation Act Amendments of 1992 [PL 102-569]), which specifies that someone who is deafblind means any individual

> (A) (i) who has a central visual acuity of 20/200 or less in the better eye with corrective lenses, or a field defect such that the peripheral diameter of visual field subtends an angular distance no greater than 20 degrees, or a progressive visual loss having a prognosis leading to one or both these conditions;
>
> (ii) who has a chronic hearing impairment so severe that most speech cannot be understood with optimum amplification, or a progressive hearing loss having a prognosis leading to this condition; and
>
> (iii) for whom the combination of impairments described in clauses (i) and (ii) cause extreme difficulty in attaining independence in daily life activities, achieving psychosocial adjustment, or obtaining a vocation;
>
> (B) who despite the inability to be measured accurately for hearing and vision loss due to cognitive or behavioral constraints, or both, can be determined through functional and performance assessment to have severe hearing and visual disabilities that cause extreme difficulty in attaining independence in daily life activities, achieving psychosocial adjustment, or obtaining vocational objectives. (U.S. Code Title 29, Chapter 21)

National Child Count Data

The reality is that the deafblind label is a functional descriptor that is associated with a vast array of etiologies, disorders, and health conditions. The National Child Count of Children and Youth Who Are Deaf-Blind (Killoran, 2007; Schalock & Bull, 2012) tracks individuals from birth to 21 years through the efforts of each state's federally funded technical assistance project. The total census since the mid-2000s has hovered between 9,000–10,000 nationally. The census lists 11 hereditary syndromes, prenatal/congenital complications, and postnatal/noncongenital conditions most commonly associated with deafblindness, in addition to complications of prematurity (12%) and a large number for whom no etiology has been determined (18%). Most children who are diagnosed as deafblind have additional disabilities, including orthopedic, cognitive, speech-language impairments, behavior disorders, and complex health care needs. In fact, the census data show that 40% have four or more additional disabilities, the most common of which is intellectual (69%). Important, most children who are deafblind actually have some vision and hearing. Vision impairment ranges from low vision to total blindness, and 28% are known to have CVI. Hearing impairment ranges from mild to total deafness. Only 29% of 3- to 5-year-old children on the census are educated to any degree in general education settings, whereas 60% of those in the 6- to 21-year-old range are educated to any degree in general settings. All of these data illustrate the extreme heterogeneity of this population in terms of underlying condition, functional capacities, and educational experience.

Functional Ramifications of Deafblindness

The impact of entering the world with compromised auditory and visual input is highly individual and difficult to calculate. Many children born deafblind will be sociable and cuddly, whereas others for whom every touch is a complete surprise may become tactually defensive, withdrawn, and difficult to bond with or engage. Children who cannot predict what will happen to them next may develop learned helplessness (Seligman, 1975). Many children who are deafblind will appear to have severe intellectual impairment, although it may be impossible to assess cognitive status in any meaningful way. Even the most basic understanding that the self is distinct from the rest of the world or that people are fundamentally different from objects may take a long time to develop, compromising the understanding of contingent relationships between the self and other people or objects. Joint attention, a hallmark of communication development, may be difficult to achieve when awareness of the environment is severely limited. Even once some communicative behaviors appear, it may be difficult to discover common ground about which to communicate. Intentional communication involves the relaying of one's own experience and knowledge to other people, as well as gaining knowledge from others, based on shared experience (Rowland & Schweigert, 2003). General world experience provides a common platform of behavioral expectations that govern interactions as well as a common knowledge base that facilitates meaningful conversations, even between strangers. This common knowledge base cannot be taken for granted in individuals with sensory, physical, and cognitive limitations. Why would we expect a child who does not share our life experience to share our means of communicating that experience?

Impact of Age at Onset

The disease or condition associated with dual sensory impairment is of huge import. Those whose sensory losses occur later in life may learn a language system prior to the sensory loss. Even if expressive speech is not an option, these individuals may be able to map an alternative language system directly onto an existing receptive language system that functioned prior to the sensory loss. Helen Keller was one of these children—although it was no easy task, she eventually learned to connect tactually presented manual signs to the remnants of speech perception and production that she had achieved prior to her illness. Intervention for these individuals has little in common with intervention for children who are born with severe sensory losses and may not spontaneously develop either receptive or expressive language. This chapter addresses the needs of this latter group, which has more complex and diverse needs.

Communication and Deafblindness

Children born with deafblindness are likely to have unusual communication patterns. Because most of these children have some sight and some hearing, it may be possible to harness one or both senses for receptive and/or expressive communication. It is common for an individual who is deafblind to use one mode (or modes) for expressive communication and a different mode (or modes) for receptive communication. For instance, a child might have enough sight to be able to perceive manual signs executed in very close proximity, but might have orthopedic limitations that prevent him or her from using manual signs expressively. He or she might instead use large line drawings to communicate to others. Receptive communication strategies that may be used for children without useful vision include touch cues, hand-in-hand manual signs, three-dimensional symbols, and brailled words. Children with some functional vision may be able to gain information from gestures, facial expressions, two-dimensional symbols, and visually presented manual signs. Children who also have some functional hearing may benefit from spoken input; even if they are not able to discriminate between or understand specific words, they may gain information from the paralinguistic features of voice, such as volume and tone. Children born with deafblindness may use any of the following means for expressive communication: vocalizations, speech, manual signs, two-dimensional symbols, three-dimensional symbols, gestures, facial expressions, or speech-generating devices (SGDs) into which a symbolic system is embedded. These children are likely to use multiple modes of expressive communication, just as their partners are likely to provide multiple forms of input to maximize understanding.

Data on Children with Deafblindness from the Communication Matrix Database

The online Communication Matrix (www.communicationmatrix.org) is a communication assessment targeting the earliest stages of communication (Rowland, 2009). It is used to document the communicative intents and modes (both typical and alternative) that an individual uses for expressive purposes. The data collected are retained in a database that has currently accumulated information on 1,490 U.S. residents between birth and 21 years old who are deafblind and have been assessed by teachers, speech-language pathologists (SLPs), and other professionals (additional parent assessments are also captured in the database). This is not a representative sample, but rather a sample of children who are operating at the earliest stages of communication development. Nevertheless, the sample constitutes a number equal to 16% of the population based on the latest (2011) deafblind census. These data provide information about the level of communication, the communicative intents, and the specific behaviors that these children are actually using to communicate. Figures 4.1–4.2 show data on various aspects of communication scored as either mastered or merging in this sample, grouped into 5-year age brackets for ages 1.0–20.11 years. Note that these are cross-sectional data, rather than longitudinal data.

Figure 4.1 shows that at least 75% of the matrix sample is communicating at an intentional presymbolic level using nonconventional gestures (Level 3) across age groups; and at least 50% of children ages 6 and older have some conventional presymbolic communication (Level 4). Twenty-five percent to 49% of the youngest age group and 50%–75% of the three older age groups use some sort of concrete symbols that bear a perceptual relationship to their referents; fewer than

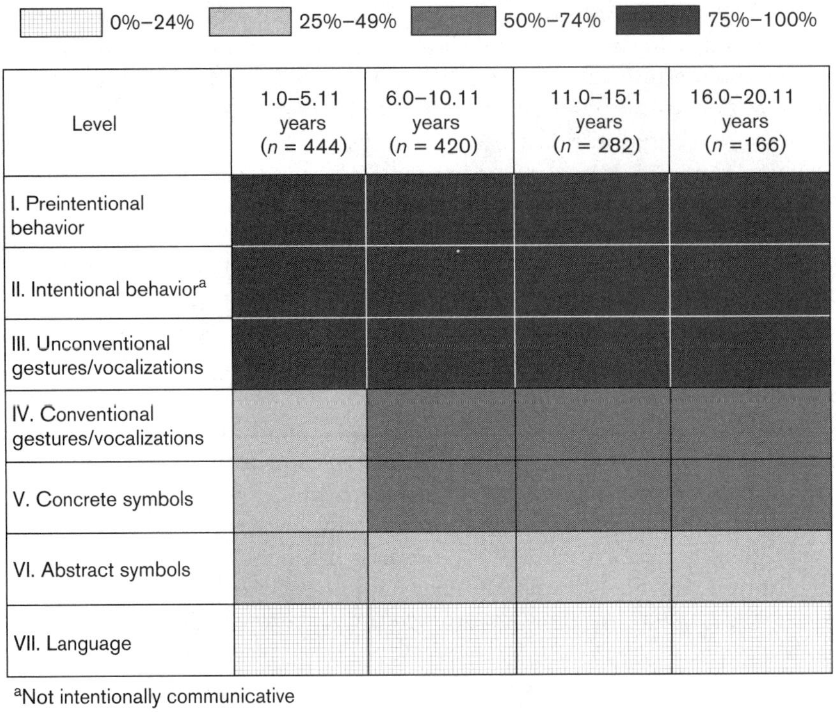

0%–24% | 25%–49% | 50%–74% | 75%–100%

Level	1.0–5.11 years (n = 444)	6.0–10.11 years (n = 420)	11.0–15.1 years (n = 282)	16.0–20.11 years (n =166)
I. Preintentional behavior	75%–100%	75%–100%	75%–100%	75%–100%
II. Intentional behavior[a]	75%–100%	75%–100%	75%–100%	75%–100%
III. Unconventional gestures/vocalizations	75%–100%	75%–100%	75%–100%	75%–100%
IV. Conventional gestures/vocalizations	25%–49%	50%–74%	50%–74%	50%–74%
V. Concrete symbols	25%–49%	50%–74%	50%–74%	50%–74%
VI. Abstract symbols	25%–49%	25%–49%	25%–49%	25%–49%
VII. Language	0%–24%	0%–24%	0%–24%	0%–24%

[a]Not intentionally communicative

Figure 4.1. Percent of children demonstrating each level of communicative behavior (Communication Matrix database).

50% of any age group use any sort of abstract symbol; and fewer than 25% of any age group use language (combinations of two or more symbols). Figure 4.2 shows the specific communicative intents used by the four age groups. Refusing is well within the abilities of all age groups, but no other intent is expressed by at least 75% of all age groups. The intents most commonly used are related to obtaining desired items, with requesting more of an action being the most frequently noted intent under this category. Only 50%–74% of individuals across all age groups are able to gain attention or show affection in the Social Interaction category. Twenty-five percent to 49%of the two middle age groups express greetings, and a similar percentage of the oldest group directs attention. All remaining intents related to social interaction and all of those related to information exchange are expressed by fewer than 25% of all age groups. What is most discouraging about these data is the lack of improvement from one age group to another. One would expect that older children would tend to show higher levels of communication and larger repertoires of communicative intent, even among these early communicators.

Information about specific behaviors of particular interest that these children use to communicate can be gleaned by collapsing data across all ages and assessments. The use of a simple switch device to communicate (e.g., a calling device) was scored as mastered in only 5% of assessments. The ability to direct another person's attention to something is a crucial marker of communication

0%–24% | 25%–49% | 50%–74% | 75%–100%

Reason to communicate	Specific intent	1.0–5.11 years (*n* = 444)	6.0–10.11 years (*n* = 420)	11.0–15.11 years (*n* = 282)	16.0–20.11 years (*n* = 166)
Refuse	Refuses, rejects	75%–100%	75%–100%	75%–100%	75%–100%
Obtain	Requests more action	50%–74%	75%–100%	50%–74%	50%–74%
	Requests new action	25%–49%	25%–49%	25%–49%	25%–49%
	Requests more object	50%–74%	50%–74%	50%–74%	50%–74%
	Makes choices	50%–74%	50%–74%	50%–74%	50%–74%
	Requests new object	25%–49%	25%–49%	25%–49%	25%–49%
	Requests absent object	0%–24%	0%–24%	25%–49%	25%–49%
Social interaction	Requests attention	50%–74%	50%–74%	50%–74%	50%–74%
	Shows affection	50%–74%	50%–74%	50%–74%	50%–74%
	Greets people	0%–24%	25%–49%	25%–49%	0%–24%
	Offers/shares	0%–24%	0%–24%	0%–24%	0%–24%
	Directs attention	0%–24%	0%–24%	0%–24%	25%–49%
	Polite social forms	0%–24%	0%–24%	0%–24%	0%–24%
Information exchange	Answers yes/no questions	0%–24%	0%–24%	0%–24%	0%–24%
	Asks questions	0%–24%	0%–24%	0%–24%	0%–24%
	Names things/people	0%–24%	0%–24%	0%–24%	0%–24%
	Makes comments	0%–24%	0%–24%	0%–24%	0%–24%

Figure 4.2. Percent of children demonstrating each communicative intent (Communication Matrix database).

development, but it is typically accomplished through vision-based means. It is not surprising that pointing was scored as mastered in only 14% of assessments and alternating gaze in only 15% in this sample of children with compromised vision. Eight types of symbolic behavior were scored as mastered across assessments: three-dimensional symbols (18%); two-dimensional symbols (17%); mimicking sounds, such as making a kissing sound to request a kiss (4%); pantomiming actions, such as moving hands as if turning a steering wheel to request a ride in the car (7%); spoken words (10%); brailled words (1%); written words (2%); and manual signs (17%).

RESEARCH ON COMMUNICATION INTERVENTION FOR THIS POPULATION

Perhaps it is not surprising that little intervention research has been conducted with individuals who are deafblind (Parker, Davidson, & Banda, 2007; Parker & Ivy, 2014; Ronnberg & Borg, 2001; Sigafoos et al., 2008). As has been noted by leaders in the broader field of special education, although there is a greater emphasis on the need for evidence-based approaches to intervention, a simultaneous downward trend in intervention research funding has occurred, particularly research that concerns the needs of low-incidence disability groups (Gersten, Baker, Flojo, & Hagan-Burke, 2004). This lack of research funding naturally contributes to the lack of recent research studies. Multiple search terms that are necessary to identify the few studies that do exist compound the problem because researchers may use a variety of descriptors to describe participants with dual sensory impairments (Parker et al., 2007; Parker & Ivy, 2014; Ronnberg & Borg, 2001). The heterogeneity of the population and the impact of various conditions on both senses may mean that a research participant may be described as having limited vision in one part of a report and then later described as having severe to profound sensorineural hearing loss, requiring a very intentional reader to identify the participant as deafblind. Reviewers of the literature also have found that study participants are often identified by their etiologies and not necessarily by the terms *deafblindness* or *dual sensory impairments.* The true number of individuals with deafblindness who have been included in intervention research may be impossible to determine. Warburg (2008) conducted an epidemiological study and found that visual impairment was more than 200 times more likely to be found in populations of people with multiple disabilities than in populations with no identified disabilities. Recognizing the impact of sensory impairments on research participants is vital in order to evaluate whether the approaches were effective despite the participants' dual sensory impairments or whether they might be more effective if adaptations or alterations were made to the intervention.

A review of the recent literature (Parker and Ivy, 2014) related to communication intervention for children who are deafblind suggests that several major strategies have been investigated, either through clinical applications or research studies. Broadly speaking, the intervention approaches that have been successfully implemented for beginning communicators who are deafblind may be organized into three categories—multicomponent partner-based interventions, the use of tangible/object symbols, and the use of microswitches/SGDs. A small number of studies have been conducted on the use of abstract symbol systems.

Multicomponent Partner-based Interventions

The most salient component of multicomponent partner-based approaches is intense training and support of partners to recognize and respond to the communication behaviors of participants within natural routines. Communication partners include parents or other caregivers, paraprofessionals, teachers, early intervention providers, and the researchers themselves. All of these approaches involve assessment of the child's preferences, a review of sensory information systems, and a focus on typical routines. Many of these interventions rely on video analysis as a way for communication partners to note what behaviors the child demonstrates so that they will not miss communication opportunities. Although partner coaching and support are the hallmarks of these interventions, many also involve providing access to various types of alternative media for communication, such as calendar systems, anticipation shelves, or object symbols (Parker, Grimmett, & Summers, 2008).

Child-guided Assessment and Intervention Many of the intervention approaches described in the literature have been influenced by the work of Jan van Dijk, a researcher from the Netherlands whose child-guided strategies for assessment and intervention start by recognizing and responding to the child's unique repertoire of behaviors as communication. van Dijk's work throughout the 1960s and 1970s had a profound influence on the educational programs that were created for individuals who are deafblind in Europe, the United States, and Canada.

Van Dijk's early work focused on movement: the communication partner learned to move co-actively with the child to increase engagement, initiation, and turn-taking. The goal of this intervention was to decrease the child's isolation by responding to the child using a shared movement-based system. van Dijk and colleagues outlined the patterns of missed communication opportunities between teachers and students, using video analysis within single-subject design studies (Vervloed van Dijk, Knoors, & van Dijk, 2006). Findings from van Dijk's ongoing work with other prominent colleagues, such as Catherine Nelson, have offered parents and teachers practical ways to increase the level of engagement that the child may have with communication partners and emphasize increasing the child's quality of life as well as communication exchanges. A practitioner book was published in 2010 that described the van Dijk method of assessment and intervention for students with multiple and sensory disabilities, including students who are deafblind (Nelson, van Dijk, McDonnell, & Thompson, 2002; Nelson, van Dijk, Oster, & McDonnell, 2010).

Diagnostic Intervention As an outgrowth of van Dijk's work, Janssen and colleagues codified both student and communication partner behaviors using intensive and regular video analysis to graph how the partner's behavior systematically influences the interaction of students who are deafblind (Janssen, Riksen-Walraven, & van Dijk, 2002, 2003, 2004, 2006). Janssen and colleagues measured six areas of partner behavior that can be influenced to improve the communication, self-regulation, and participation of students who are deafblind. Teaching the child's communication partners, including support staff and family members, to systematically respond to the child's unique communication behaviors is the intervention's main emphasis. Their analysis of the videotaped interactions indicated that the adult communication partner's supportive responses are linked to increases in the child's communication initiations and to the number of exchanges.

Path to Symbolism Bruce and colleagues have contributed several qualitative research studies to the literature that richly describe the topography, rate, and function of communication behaviors of students who are deafblind, as well as those with severe and sensory disabilities (Bruce, Godbold, & Naponelli-Gold, 2004; Bruce, Mann, Jones, & Gavin, 2007; Bruce & Vargas, 2007). These authors described the idiosyncratic communication behaviors, initiations, communication functions, and gestures of these participants and connected empirically based descriptions of student behavior to interventions in order to influence teacher practices. Bruce expanded on the communication assessment framework outlined by Rowland (1990, 2004) and infused the observation and documentation of student communication into teacher in-services, coaching, and action planning sessions (Bruce, 2002, 2003, 2008). Within this action research approach to intervention, Bruce documented changes in the fidelity of implementation of teacher action plans for students who are deafblind, noting increases in the implementation of strategies for supporting students' communication forms, functions, and topics within school contexts. Bruce also reported case studies in the areas of communication and literacy of a student who was congenitally deafblind (Bruce & Conlon, 2005; Bruce, Randall, & Birge, 2008).

Adaptations to Prelinguistic Milieu Training Brady and Bashinski (2008) conducted research over the course of 3 years on the efficacy of prelinguistic milieu teaching (PMT) for teaching gestures to students with deafblindness during typical routines. Their adaptations to the PMT protocol (Yoder & Stone, 2006) involved interactions that emphasized touch and movement to accommodate the participants' limited vision and hearing. Other adaptations to the protocol included hand-under-hand teaching, the use of touch and object cues, and an emphasis on the direction of communication exchanges between partners. Specific gestures were taught to students in communication interactions and games. Although the students increased their use of approximately 15 natural gestures, the behaviors did not generalize outside of the teaching environment or to other communication partners. Subsequent replications have confirmed a lack of generalization to nonintervention contexts (Brady & Bashinski, 2008).

Promoting Learning Through Active Interaction Chen, Klein, and Haney (2007) used a family-centered approach and conducted a 3-year field test of the Promoting Learning Through Active Interaction (PLAI) curriculum to promote interactions with infants who had complex disabilities, including deafblindness. The first phase of the field test involved 27 infants in two states. Family members and early intervention teams implemented the five modules—understanding the child's cues (documenting arousal as well as behaviors); noting the child's high and low preferences across people, activities, and objects; establishing predictable routines with the child; establishing turn-taking games; and encouraging/responding to communication initiations within routines. Videos of the family-based assessment and intervention were used as a structured part of field testing for both English- and Spanish-speaking families. The field test findings, which were replicated in additional states, indicated that families could implement these naturalistic approaches to increase their infant's communication behaviors.

Project Supporting Adaptations for Learning to Use Touch Effectively, SALUTE In a 5-year model demonstration grant, Downing and Chen (2003) used a panel of experts, focus groups, a literature review, student observation, and curriculum field testing to develop a manual of socially valued methods for supporting tactile learning strategies for children who are deafblind. The investigators collaborated with English- and Spanish-speaking families to create a resource that would be culturally relevant as well as practically oriented to families with young children. The model demonstration project developed a list of recommendations for families and service providers that included using hand-under-hand strategies, employing object cues paired with adapted signs consistently in the child's routines, increasing wait time before prompting, increasing communication partner responsiveness, and employing consistent touch cues in routines.

Response Prompting in Embedded Instruction Grisham-Brown and colleagues (Grisham-Brown, Schuster, Hemmeter, & Collins, 2000) conducted a single-subject design study and used video training of paraprofessionals to help teach a response-prompting protocol for four preschoolers with deafblindness in an inclusive setting. Although the approach was not restricted to communication intervention, some of the activities involved communication requests or social interactions with peers within preschool routines. These authors found that using specific most-to-least prompts was effective in teaching the deafblind student to request "more" during a preschool routine. Other strategies included constant time delay to allow participants to choose peers to engage in play activities.

Tangible Symbols, Object Symbols, Objects as Referents

Rowland and Schweigert (1989, 2000b) first used the term *tangible symbols* to describe symbols that can be manipulated and that bear a clear physical and conceptual relationship to their referents. They include both two-dimensional drawings or photographs and three-dimensional symbols under this rubric. Three-dimensional object symbols share tactual features such as scale, weight, texture, and size, as well as visual features, which may be useful for users with some functional vision. They may be used for environmental access and receptive and expressive communication purposes. The rationale for categorizing these approaches based on the symbol system is the strategic use of an iconic referent to teach individuals with deafblindness symbolic behaviors when abstract symbols are not accessible.

Tangible Symbol Systems Rowland and Schweigert (2000b) led a second study on the use of tangible symbols for expressive communication and conducted a quasi-experimental study of 41 children with severe/multiple disabilities, including deafbindness in self-contained public school classrooms. The success of the instructional approach, manualized in Rowland and Schweigert (2000a), was measured using pre-post tests of communication development, symbol acquisition rate, and observational data on the frequency of symbol use. All but eight students acquired the use of tangible symbols for communication, and a few progressed to the use of abstract symbols, such as speech or sign language.

Other Object Symbol Systems Trief (2007) conducted a quasi-experimental study and examined the use of object symbols for 25 participants with multiple disabilities attending a school for the blind. Trief reported that 15 of the 25 participants were able to acquire the use of object symbols for communication purposes. Group data on skill acquisition demonstrated that the object symbols were used more for environmental awareness, developing student activity schedules, and receptive communication than for expressive communication by individual students. A greater degree of iconicity of the object symbol was associated with greater adoption and use by participants. In the practitioner literature, object symbols have been incorporated within the practice of using tactile calendars, activity schedules, experience books, interactive games, or environmental labeling for people with deafblindness as well as those with vision loss and multiple disabilities (Blaha, 2001; Hagood, 2008; Lewis & Tolla, 2003).

Adaptations of the Picture Exchange Communication System The use of object symbols has been successfully embedded in the Picture Exchange Communication System (PECS; Bondy & Frost, 2001), which is another type of augmentative and alternative communication (AAC) intervention for individuals with visual impairments and multiple disabilities. One of the main adaptations to the PECS protocol in each of these studies involved the use of individualized, three-dimensional object symbols to allow participants to request preferred items (Ali, McFarland, & Umbreit, 2011; Ivy, Hatton & Hooper, 2014; Lund & Troha, 2008; Parker, Banda, Davidson, & Liu-Gitz, 2010). Each of these single-subject studies found that participants acquired the use of the adapted PECS system at a similar rate to participants with typical visual acuities in previous PECS studies.

Microswitches and Speech-Generating Devices

The use of microswitches and SGDs has been around since the mid-1980s. *Microswitch interventions* are defined as supportive speech output systems or devices that serve the purpose of building communication interactions, contingency awareness, or choice-making associations (Lancioni et al., 2002). Many studies in this category have examined microswitch interventions as a means to build choice making and other purposeful communication capacities of participants who experience severe orthopedic impairment as well as sensory impairment. Most studies that have included individuals who are deafblind have included young adults with deafblindness and severe disabilities in single-subject designs.

Saunders and collaborators (2001) taught three young adults with severe disabilities and deafblindness who used wheelchairs and lived in a skilled care facility to request preferred leisure activities by using head movements to activate microswitch devices with voice output. Lancioni and collaborators (2002, 2004) taught young adults to use a microswitch to request preferred objects from support staff. In one instance, Lancioni and collaborators (2002) used the scent of coffee beans to help the participant orient to the switch to make a request. It is important to note that numerous studies that include individuals with visual impairments and severe disabilities (with no hearing impairments noted) also have been conducted by Lancioni and colleagues. A variety of movements have been used successfully to help individuals with severe disabilities and visual impairments make meaningful requests using microswitches (Parker et al., 2008).

Abstract Symbolic Systems

If there are few recent studies that involve children who are beginning communicators, then there have been fewer still that describe interventions for children who are able to use abstract symbols to communicate. One such study described the communication supports needed by children who were deafblind and were attending a segregated recreation and leisure camp (Arndt, Lieberman, & Pucci, 2004). All participants were fluent communicators in using manual sign language and some were fluent in braille. These researchers reported that methods for supporting communication emphasized allowing plenty of time for object and environmental exploration, consulting with the individual or someone who knows the child well to avoid misunderstandings during activities, and planning frequent breaks during instruction to allow for feedback.

In order to address the dearth of instructional materials to support the development of manual sign language systems, Blaha and Carlson (2007) created an assessment and intervention book that outlines strategies for appropriate assessment and teaching of sign language by adapting a framework based on the child's available vision. This product is disseminated by the National Consortium on Deafblindness and is widely respected by practitioners, but it is not research based.

RESEARCH CHALLENGES FOR THIS POPULATION

The intervention studies previously summarized do not include any traditional experimental designs, and for good reason. The challenges to conducting high-quality research on children who are deafblind are myriad, including issues related to sampling, the study design, implementation factors, and measurement factors. These issues are not unique to this particular low-incidence category, but they are exacerbated by the extreme heterogeneity of the population.

Defining the Sample

Any research involving intervention with this population will necessarily have a small *n* in any one site. Couple the low incidence with the extreme heterogeneity of the population in terms of etiology and functional capacities, and it is impossible to obtain a local study sample that is homogenous in any meaningful way or to constitute a well-matched control group. Informed consent must be obtained first from a school district, then from educational professionals and parents. It is unlikely that the final sample will be representative of any particular sector of the population once all of the parties involved have consented. Appropriate participants are likely to be scattered throughout a school district with teachers who have different experience levels and skill sets. A very small school district may have only one child who is deafblind, if any. The psychosocial history and socioeconomic status of participants will vary markedly. Their educational histories, which are crucial to the development of communication skills, will also differ markedly.

Designing the Study

The willingness of parents, teachers, and administrators to get involved with a study that involves random assignment to a no-treatment group is minimal. A wait-list control group, although more appealing to families, is likely to have dwindled to a much reduced number after sufficient time has elapsed to generate meaningful improvement in the treatment group (typically at least a school term, if not a school year). Furthermore, it is impossible to control the nature of interventions that wait-list participants will experience over the course of a lengthy wait period. Even if two different treatments are compared with random assignment to groups, it is unlikely that expectations of success are really the same for both treatments, posing serious ethical concerns. Finally, "business as usual" as a control treatment is difficult to define and highly variable, especially across multiple sites.

Single-subject baseline/withdrawal designs are traditionally used to examine withdrawable treatments and/or involve behaviors that are subject to control through the manipulation of contingencies. Communication behavior is different from other behavior. Once learned, natural forms of communication should occur spontaneously. And, once a child has learned to communicate anything specific, the last thing a teacher would want to do is risk suppressing communication by ceasing to respond to it for the sake of a withdrawal phase. It is true that if treatment involves the provision of an aided communication system, then that system is easily withdrawn; but it is hardly informative to demonstrate that a child denied a communication system will be unable to communicate.

Alternating treatments that systematically introduce new independent variables or target new behaviors across multiple participants are much more appropriate for this population, although more difficult to analyze. A design that has been widely employed in AAC intervention research involves the use of multiple baseline designs that allow the researcher to repeatedly compare the impact of a specific intervention on individuals who have begun the intervention phase against participants who are having baseline measures drawn at intervals before their intervention begins (Kennedy, 2005). The multiple baseline design eliminates the need for withdrawal of the intervention, which is problematic for intervention that teaches a new skill such as communication or literacy (Kennedy, 2005). The visual analysis of trend lines across participants allows the researcher to look for patterns of impact of the intervention. The analysis of percent of nonoverlapping data points (Mastropieri & Scruggs, 1985–1986) and variations of this measure provides a useful quantitative estimate of the effect of treatment. Kratochwill et al. (2012) described challenges and other approaches to the estimate of treatment effects in single-subject designs. Horner, Carr, Halle, Odom, and Wolery (2005) described the challenge in establishing the effect of an intervention across several well-conducted single-subject studies involving at least nine replications across research teams and settings. The low numbers and geographic spread of the population also presents a challenge that requires skillful coordination.

Defining the Independent Variables (Treatment Conditions)

High-quality research involves a well-defined, replicable treatment. Unfortunately, the more diverse the sample, the more flexible and individualized the treatment needs to be to meet the needs of each participant. Motivation is the be-all and end-all of success for children who are at the earliest stages of intentional communication or who have not even reached that stage. When communication has not developed spontaneously (and when it has failed to develop despite intense intervention attempts), new communication methods will be embraced only to the extent that they free a child from the prison of being unable to express needs and desires. Attempts to teach a beginning vocabulary that is standard across participants is unlikely to harness the intrinsically motivating elements of every child's life and will meet with varying degrees of success. The treatment dose will also vary from participant to participant, depending on prior history, teacher skill levels, the appropriateness of treatment, and the stamina and interest of each child. Many children with deafblindness experience health conditions that keep them out of school for significant periods, adding another factor that makes it difficult to implement a standard treatment dose. Finally, fidelity of implementation across different teachers or SLPs may be difficult to assess.

Defining the Dependent Variable (Measurement)

Communication is complex and subjective, making the measurement of communicative behavior difficult. Communicative behavior is not just motor behavior; so merely observing behavior that takes the form of a spoken word, a manual sign, or a point toward a tangible symbol does not necessarily constitute meaningful communication. Such behaviors produced without the intent of affecting the behavior of another person are not communicative. Similarly, the use of symbols without evidence of a clear understanding of the one-to-one correspondence between each symbol and its referent is not meaningful.

Collecting meaningful performance data that is uniform across participants is challenging in large part due to the fact that what is a meaningful outcome measure for one participant may not be meaningful for another. Any group of children who are deafblind are likely to use a variety of presymbolic and symbolic communicative behaviors to express a wide variety of intents under a range of instructional conditions. Even if the same communicative behavior were targeted for several different children, the criteria for success might differ between them. The following are some of the parameters of a targeted communicative behavior that might be measured:

- Rate (greets at least four peers as they enter the classroom each day)
- Duration (maintains touch for at least 2 seconds to gain attention)
- Latency (answers questions within 5 seconds)
- Independence (spontaneously points to object array to make choices)
- Correctness/accuracy (chooses correct symbols when asked to name items needed for vocational task)
- Generalization (uses SGD in classroom, cafeteria, and on school bus)
- Rate of learning (acquires six new symbols by end of Fall term and an additional 12 new symbols by end of Spring term)

Rate of learning reflects one of the signal properties of good instruction—a learning-to-learn effect demonstrated by an increase in the acquisition rate over the course of instruction. Rowland and Schweigert (1989) demonstrated a 50% reduction in the number of sessions required to meet acquisition criteria for new tangible symbols in a group of seven children with deafblindness (from a mean of 13 sessions per symbol to a mean of 7 sessions). A larger study showed a similar increase in acquisition rate (from a mean of 7 sessions per new symbol to a mean of 3) in a group of 35 children that included five who were deafblind (Rowland & Schweigert, 2000b). Twenty-one of these children essentially became one-trial learners. In essence, the accomplishment of these learners was not only the acquisition of a specific vocabulary, but also in the generic ability to use tangible symbols to communicate and in the ability to learn the meaning of new symbols. This accomplishment suggests the phenomenon of fast mapping (Crais, 1992), or the ability to learn new symbols with very little exposure to them. Romski, Sevcik, Robinson, Mervis and Bertrand (1995) demonstrated fast mapping in students with intellectual disability who learned to use graphic symbols in a short-term (15-day) follow-up study. Fast mapping is a feature of teaching strategies promoted by Beukelman and Mirenda (2013) and a dependent variable that deserves further study.

Coding Issues Taking performance data often requires snap judgments by the data taker, which may be quite subjective. For instance, the intentionality of a presymbolic behavior may be questionable, as when two observers disagree on whether a child intentionally activates a switch. As another example, two educational assistants may disagree on whether a child who says/signs CRACKER has any understanding of what that sign means. It may be possible to videotape interactions and code behavior at leisure in a funded research project, but this does not resolve the problems of the ambiguity of behavior and differences in its interpretation between observers.

Social Validity of Dependent Measures The dependent variables reported in intervention studies of communication learning occasionally are ones that have little social validity or for which validity has not been evaluated (Parker et al., 2007). Different stakeholders will have different opinions of the social validity of any particular behavior that is the target of intervention. Family members, the learner, communication partners, teachers, paraprofessionals, interveners, and peers may view the behavior through different lenses. The culprit in an unsuccessful intervention is sometimes the fact that a key stakeholder does not value the targeted response. This is an area of study that deserves attention.

Pre–Post Measures Performance measures are often combined with more global measures of communication development to provide a broader view of the effect of intervention. Learning ideally involves the successive acquisition of more communicative behaviors, and the totality of the impact of intervention needs to be captured. Standardized instruments are generally not useful for three reasons—first, they are likely to take a speech-centric approach to communication development, which is inappropriate for a child who uses alternative means to communicate; second, they generally do not break down early communication into small enough steps to track progress in a child with complex needs; and, finally, there is no standard child with deafblindness, so the very notion of norms for this population is unrealistic. Chen, Rowland, Stillman, and Mar (2009), Rowland, Stillman, and Mar (2010), Rowland (2011), and Rowland and Fried-Oken (2010) described the challenges of assessing this population and outlined authentic assessment practices.

SOME SUGGESTIONS

Despite the bleak picture previously painted, we have some suggestions for improving research efforts that involve children who are deafblind. These suggestions involve design, independent, and dependent measures.

Defining Meaningful Control Conditions

A common sense approach to evaluating the success of intervention is in order. Demonstrating changes in trivial outcomes without social validity is not helpful; and ignoring the face value of changes that could not possibly occur without intervention is foolish. If interventionists assume no or little change in communication skills based on previous history, and they see more than that, then they may assume that the change is caused by the intervention. For instance, an 8-year-old child who has never shown any clearly intentional communication now reliably kicks his or her leg to gain attention after laborious efforts to provide a contingently responsive environment, which is an achievement of incalculable import that no doubt is the result of the new contingencies. Similarly, the 15-year-old child who grasps for the first time the one-to-one correspondence between a few tangible symbols and their referents and understands that they convey meaning to someone else has made the astounding leap to symbolic communication. No child is going to spontaneously start using AAC forms such as sign language or tangible symbols—when those behaviors appear, they must be the result of intervention. In essence, the participant's prior history serves as the control condition. The more important question to answer is whether the new behaviors are used intentionally and with understanding.

A Taxonomy of Treatment Variables

Although intervention needs to be flexible to accommodate the needs of diverse children, it should be possible to describe the principles and components of intervention with precision. Rowland and Schweigert (1997) conducted a longitudinal study of tangible symbols acquisition by 52 children with complex communication needs (CCN) (including some children with deafblindness) and tracked every change made in the instructional programs for each participant for the first half of the project. Those changes were then grouped into logical categories and prospectively tracked for the second half of the project. These variables were used to guide intervention and monitor progress, documenting every change made along the way to generate a precise record of customized intervention for each participant. Figure 4.3 presents the variables used to describe presymbolic and symbolic interventions as detailed in Rowland and Schweigert (2000a, 2004). A taxonomy of treatment parameters along these lines might be useful for standardizing the description of intervention strategies to aid in the meta-analysis of research.

Using Appropriate Pre–Post Measures

Some assessment instruments are available that are appropriate for children who are deafblind and who are at the earliest stages of communication development. The Communication Matrix (www.communicationmatrix.org; Rowland, 1990, 2004) covers communication development from birth up to the use of two- to three-symbol utterances and has been the subject of reliability and validity studies. It is already widely used to assess children who are deafblind. The Communication Complexity Scale (Brady et al., 2012) measures early communication behaviors from reactions to environmental changes to the production of symbols. It provides a quantitative measure of functioning at the prelinguistic level that is sensitive to change over time. Children who are deafblind were included in the test development sample.

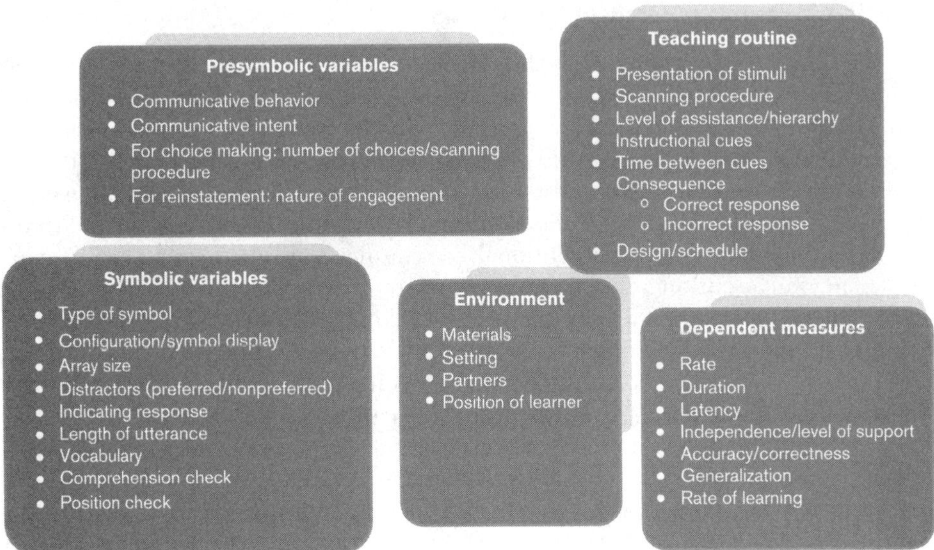

Figure 4.3. Generic variables related to communication intervention. (*Source:* Rowland & Schweigert, 2000b and Rowland & Schweigert, 2004.)

The Infant Social and Communication Behavior Scales (ISCBS; Cress, Olson, & Wetherby, in preparation) is a prototype communication assessment that is being nationally normed at time of this article, in preparation for publication. The ISCBS is a dynamic assessment of pre-intentional communication for children of all ages (that will be normed for infants 2-12 months) that accommodates sensory and motor impairments into the assessment tasks as well as scoring. Items are scored by modality-independent communicative intent (e.g. Shows wanting for an object) rather than by specific typical expected behavior (e.g. Reaches for an object). It is based on the Communication and Symbolic Behavior Scales (Wetherby & Prizant, 2003) and uses similar procedures and scoring. Any of these instruments would make good pre-post measures for this population.

Generic Dependent Variables

The most logical way to define targeted communicative behavior in a precise but flexible way is to describe its function. For instance, three examples of identical communicative intents expressed in completely different ways by two different students follow:

- Johnny may be learning to tap a desired object to make a choice, whereas Sherry may be activating a symbol on an SGD to express the same intent.
- Sydney may be learning to gain attention by turning her head to activate a single switch with voice output, whereas Jonas may be learning to vocalize and tap someone for the same purpose.
- Manolo may be learning to request a book by picking up and giving a line drawing of the book out of an array of 10 symbols, whereas Lucinda may ask for a book after being assisted to scan an array of two three-dimensional symbols and touching the one for BOOK.

Each pair of learners could be viewed as having similar outcome measures, even though each member of the pair is learning a completely different behavior. Generic definitions of communicative behavior could provide another way to combine data from multiple studies.

WHAT DOES THE FUTURE HOLD?

Future developments in the areas of technology, advances in public policy, and a shift toward a more functional approach toward disability hold promise in terms of improving research on communication intervention for individuals who are deafblind.

Promise of Technology

It is impossible to predict the advances in technology that will profoundly affect the lives of children with dual sensory impairments. Advances are already underway that will radically improve hearing and vision, leveling the playing field for many children born with deafblindness. Cochlear implants are already playing an important role in diminishing effects of congenital hearing impairment, and the number of children receiving implants at an early age will only increase. Promising research in regenerating retinas through the use of embryonic stem cells or by chemically triggering the transformation of nonneuronal cells into progenitor cells are examples of new approaches that may ultimately bring a measure of vision to children born without it. There is no question that many of the hearing and vision impairments common to deafblindness will be subject to improvement, if not compete reversal, in the future; the only question is how long it will take for new breakthroughs to occur and to reach the level of common practice.

Shifts in Public Policy

Access to assistive technology (AT) is often facilitated or hindered by government and educational policies. For instance, new Federal Communications Commission rules on the provision of Relay Services for Deafblind Individuals (adopted in 2011) mandate the distribution of specialized equipment to individuals who are deafblind to allow access to telecommunication services, the Internet, and advanced communications. Similarly, educational entities may mandate higher levels or types of services through school programs. As new technologies become ubiquitous, public health policies and related medical insurance coverage may change to bring additional types of AT within the reach of children who need them. The U.S. Department of Education used to fund grants specifically to investigate needs and solutions for children who are deafblind. Perhaps such funding will once again become available with an improved economic climate.

Functional Approaches to Assessment, Intervention, and Research

The uniting factor experienced by this population of children is the profound affect that diminished sensory input has on their development and on their access to opportunities for learning, as opposed to a specific etiology or set of etiologies. There is a tendency to allow diagnosis to drive intervention, as opposed to the functional characteristics of the child. For instance, a child with autism may automatically be given a set of picture symbols; or a child with deafblindness may be expected to learn tactile signs. It is more appropriate to prescribe intervention based on the current functional capacities of the child (Rowland, 2005). The international community is increasingly embracing a functional approach to disability by adopting the International Classification of Functioning, Disability, and Health (ICF) (WHO) to describe the functional status of individuals independent of disease condition. The ICF emphasizes the ability of the individual to fully participate in society through functional capacities that transcend any particular etiology. A number of efforts are underway in this and other countries to derive core sets or code sets of items from the ICF that speak to various aspects of function. One such effort has developed a tool that incorporates ICF items relevant to communication and specifically to the use AAC to help educators and therapists develop appropriate educational goals (available at www.csi-cy.org) (Rowland et al., 2012). This is just one example of a functional approach to intervention that may be helpful for heterogeneous populations such as children with deafblindness.

CONCLUSION

Communication intervention for children who are deafblind has been studied for a surprisingly long time, both in this country (with the support of the U.S. Department of Education) and in Europe. Despite and perhaps because of the heterogeneity and geographic dispersion of the population of students, creative approaches have been applied to bridge the profound gaps that individuals face in communicating with partners. Although relatively little research has been conducted, and none of it could be described as satisfying the gold standard, a close-knit community of practitioners, researchers, and family members continues to search for practical solutions to the communication challenges faced by this population. Perhaps it is within such a close-knit, low-incidence community that new opportunities may be forged through more coordinated approaches to intervention research. In the end, both highly descriptive and empirical intervention approaches are called for in order to support more children in engaging effectively with people in the world around them. In achieving this end, new opportunities for practitioners and researchers alike to listen and learn from individuals who are deafblind will be provided.

REFERENCES

Ali, E., McFarland, S.Z., & Umbreit, J. (2011). Effectiveness of combining tangible symbols with the Picture Exchange Communication System to teach requesting skills to children with multiple disabilities, including visual impairment. *Education and Training in Autism and Developmental Disabilities, 46*(3), 425–435.

Arndt, K., Lieberman, L.J., & Pucci, G. (2004). Communication during physical activity for children who are deafblind: research to practice. *Teaching Exceptional Children Plus, 1*(2), Article 1.

Beukelman, D.R., & Mirenda, P. (2013). *Augmentative and alternative communication: Supporting children and adults with complex communication needs* (4th ed.). Baltimore, MD: Paul H. Brookes Publishing Co.

Blaha, R. (2001). *Calendars for students with multiple impairments including deafblindness.*

Austin, TX: Texas School for the Blind and Visually Impaired.

Blaha, R., & Carlson, B. (2007). Assessment of deafblind access to manual language systems (ADAMLS). Retrieved from http://www.dblink.org/pdf/adamls.pdf

Bondy, A., & Frost, L.A. (2001). The Picture Exchange Communication System. *Behavior Modification, 25*, 725–744.

Brady, N.M., & Bashinski, S.M. (2008). Increasing communication in children with concurrent vision and hearing loss. *Research and Practice for Persons with Severe Disabilities, 33*(1-2), 59–70.

Brady, N., & Bashinski, S. M. (2008, August). *Teaching communicative gestures to children with deaf-blindness through adapted prelinguistic milieu teaching: Results of a research study*. Poster presented at the International Society for Augmentative and Alternative Communication (ISAAC) Bi-Annual Conference, Montreal, Quebec, Canada.

Brady, N., Fleming, K., Thiemann-Bourque, K., Olswang, L., Dowden, P., Saunders, M.D. (2012). Development of the Communication Complexity Scale. *American Journal of Speech-Language Pathology, 21*, 16–28.

Bruce, S.M. (2002). Impact of a communication intervention model on teachers' practice with children who are congenitally deaf-blind. *Journal of Visual Impairment and Blindness, 96*(3), 154–168.

Bruce, S.M. (2003). Importance of shared communication forms. *Journal of Visual Impairment and Blindness, 97*(2), 106–109.

Bruce, S. (2008). The use of action plans to support communicative programming for children who are deafblind. *RE:view, 39*(2), 71–83.

Bruce, S., & Conlon, K. (2005). Colby's daily journal: A school–home effort to promote communication development. *Teaching Exceptional Children Plus, 2*(1). Article 3. http://escholarship.bc.edu/education/tecplus/vol2/iss1/3

Bruce, S., Godbold, E., & Naponelli-Gold, S. (2004). An analysis of communicative functions of teachers and their students who are congenitally deafblind. *RE:view: Rehabilitation Education for Blindness and Visual Impairment, 36*(2), 81–92.

Bruce, S.M., Mann, A., Jones, C., & Gavin, M. (2007). Gestures expressed by children who are congenitally deaf-blind: topography, rate, and function. *Journal of Visual Impairment and Blindness, 101*(10), 637–652.

Bruce, S.M., Randall, A., & Birge, B. (2008). Colby's growth to language and literacy: The achievements of a child who is congenitally deafblind. Retrieved from http://www.pathstoliteracy.org/sites/default/files/uploaded-files/Colby_growth.pdf

Bruce, S.M., & Vargas, C. (2007). Intentional communication acts expressed by children with severe disabilities in high-rate contexts. *Augmentative and Alternative Communication, 23*(4), 300–311.

Chen, D., Klein, D., & Haney, M. (2007). Promoting interactions with infants who have complex multiple disabilities: Development and field-testing of the PLAI curriculum. *Infants and Young Children: An Interdisciplinary Journal of Early Childhood Intervention, 20*(2), 149–162.

Chen, D., Rowland, C., Stillman, R., & Mar, H. (2009). Authentic practices for assessing communication skills of young children with sensory impairments and multiple disabilities. *Early Childhood Services, 3*(4), 328–339.

Crais, E. (1992). Fast mapping: A new look at word learning. In R. Chapman (Ed.), *Processes in language acquisition and disorders* (pp. 159–185). St. Louis, MO: Mosby.

Cress, C.J., Olson, A., & Wetherby, A.M. (in preparation). *Infant Social and Communication Behavior Scales*. Baltimore, MD: Paul H. Brookes Publishing Co.

Downing, J.E., & Chen, D. (2003). Using tactile strategies with students who are blind and have severe disabilities. *Teaching Exceptional Children, 36*(2), 56–60.

Gersten, R., Baker, S.K., Flojo, J.R., & Hagan-Burke, S. (2004). A tale of two decades: Trends in support for federally funded experimental research in special education. *Exceptional Children, 70*(3), 323–332.

Grisham-Brown, J., Schuster, J.W., Hemmeter, M.L., & Collins, B.C. (2000). Using an embedding strategy to teach preschoolers with significant disabilities. *Journal of Behavioral Education, 10*(2/3), 139–162.

Hagood, L. (2008). *Better together: Building relationships with people who have visual impairments and autism spectrum disorder (or atypical social development)*. Austin, TX: Texas School for the Blind and Visually Impaired.

Helen Keller Act, 29 U.S.C. §§ 1903. PL102-569, 1992.

Horner, R.H., Carr, E.G., Halle, J., Odom, S., & Wolery, M. (2005). The use of single-subject research to identify evidence-based practice in special education. *Exceptional Children, 71,* 165–179.

Ivy, S.E., Hatton, D.D., & Hooper, J.D. (2014). Using the Picture Exchange Communication System with students with visual impairment. *Exceptional Children, 46,* 101–143.

Janssen, M.J., Riksen-Walraven, M., & van Dijk, J. (2002). Enhancing the quality of interaction between deaf-blind children and their educators. *Journal of Developmental and Physical Disabilities, 14,* 87–109.

Janssen, M.J., Riksen-Walraven, M., & van Dijk, J. (2003). Contacts: Effects of an intervention program to foster harmonious interactions between deaf-blind children and their educators. *Journal of Visual Impairment and Blindness, 97,* 215–229.

Janssen, M.J., Riksen-Walraven, M., & van Dijk, J. (2004). Enhancing the interactive competence of deaf-blind children: Do intervention effects endure? *Journal of Developmental and Physical Disabilities, 16,* 73–94.

Janssen, M.J., Riksen-Walraven, M., & van Dijk, J. (2006). Applying the diagnostic intervention model for fostering harmonious interactions between deaf-blind children and their educators: a case study. *Journal of Visual Impairment and Blindness, 100,* 91–105.

Kennedy, C.H. (2005). *Single-case designs for education research.* New York, NY: Pearson Education.

Killoran, J. (2007). The national deafblind child count: 1998–2005 in review. Monmouth, OR: National Technical Assistance Consortium.

Kratochwill, T.R., Hitchcock, J., Horner, R., Levin, J.R., Odom, S.L. Rindskopf, D.M. & Shadish, W.R. (2012). *Single case designs technical documentation.* Retrieved from http://ies.ed.gov/ncee/wwc/pdf/reference_resources/wwc_scd.pdf

Lancioni, G.E., O'Reilly, M.F., Singh, N.N., Campodonico, F., Marziani, M., & Oliva, D. (2004). A microswitch program to foster simple foot and leg movements in adult wheelchair users with multiple disabilities. *Cognitive Behavior Therapy, 33*(3), 137–142.

Lancioni, G.E., Singh, N.N., O'Reilly, M.F., Oliva, D., Baccani, S., & Canevaro, A. (2002). Using simple hand-movement responses with optic microswitches with two persons with multiple disabilities. *Research and Practice for Persons with Severe Disabilities, 27,* 276–279.

Lewis, S., & Tolla, J. (2003). Creating and using tactile experience books for young children with visual impairments. *Teaching Exceptional Children, 35*(3), 22–28.

Lund, S.K., & Troha, J.M. (2008). Teaching young people who are blind and have autism to make requests using a variation on the Picture Exchange Communication System with tactile symbols: A preliminary investigation. *Journal of Autism and Other Developmental Disorders, 38,* 719–730.

Mastropieri, M.A., & Scruggs, T.E. (1985–1986). Early intervention for socially withdrawn children. *Journal of Special Education, 19,* 429–441.

Nelson, C., van Dijk, J., McDonnell, A.P., & Thompson, K. (2002). A framework for understanding young children with severe multiple disabilities: The van Dijk approach to assessment. *Research and Practice for Persons with Severe Disabilities, 27*(2), 97–111.

Nelson, C., van Dijk, J., Oster, T. & McDonnell, A.P. (2010). *Child-guided strategies: The van Dijk approach to assessment.* Lexington, KY: American Printing House for the Blind.

Parker, A.T., Banda, D.R., Davidson, R., & Liu-Gitz, L. (2010). Adapting the Picture Exchange Communication System (PECS) for a student with visual impairment and autism: A case study. *AER Journal: Research and Practice in Visual Impairment and Blindness, 3*(1), 2–11.

Parker, A.T., Davidson, T.C., & Banda, D.R. (2007). Emerging evidence from single-subject research in the field of deafblindness. *Journal of Visual Impairment and Blindness, 101*(11), 690–700.

Parker, A.T., Grimmett, E., & Summers, S. (2008). Evidence-based communication practices for children with vision loss and additional disabilities: an examination of single-subject design studies. *Journal of Visual Impairment and Blindness, 102*(9), 540–52.

Parker, A.T., & Ivy, S. (2014). Communication development of children with visual impairment and deafblindness: A synthesis of intervention research. In D.D. Hatton (Ed.), *Current issues in the education of students with visual impairments* (pp. 101–143). United Kingdom: London Academic Press.

Project SALUTE (n.d.). *Successful adaptations for learning to use touch effectively.* Retrieved from http://www.projectsalute.

net/Description/Descriptionhtml/Descriptionmain.html

Rehabilitation Act Amendments of 1992, PL 102-569, 29 U.S.C., §§ 701 *et seq.*

Romski, M.A., Sevcik, R., Robinson, B., Mervis, C., & Bertrand, J. (1995). Mapping the meanings of novel visual symbols by youth with moderate or severe mental retardation. *American Journal on Mental Retardation, 100,* 391–402.

Ronnberg, J., & Borg, E. (2001). A review and evaluation of research on the deafblind from perceptual, communicative, social and rehabilitative perspectives. *Scandinavian Audiology, 30,* 67–77.

Rowland, C. (1990, 2004). *Communication Matrix.* Portland, OR: Design to Learn Projects.

Rowland, C. (2005). But what can they do? Assessment of communication skills in children with severe and multiple disabilities. *Perspectives on Alternative Communication, 14,* 7–12.

Rowland, C. (2009). *Communication Matrix* [Web site]. Portland, OR: Oregon Health and Science University, Design to Learn Projects.

Rowland, C. (2011). Using the Communication Matrix to assess expressive skills in early communicators. *Communication Disorders Quarterly, 32,* 190–201.

Rowland, C., & Fried-Oken, M. (2010). Communication Matrix: A clinical and research assessment tool targeting children with severe communication disorders. *Journal of Pediatric Rehabilitation Medicine, 3,* 319–329.

Rowland, C., Fried-Oken, M., Steiner, S.A.M., Lollar, D., Phelps, R., Simeonsson, R.J. & Granlund, M. (2012). Developing the ICF-CY for AAC Profile and code set for children who rely on AAC. *Augmentative and Alternative Communication, 28*(1), 21–32.

Rowland, C., & Schweigert, P. (1989). Tangible symbols systems: Symbolic communication for individuals with multisensory impairments. *Augmentative and Alternative Communication, 5,* 225–234.

Rowland, C., & Schweigert, P. (1997). *Demonstrating the benefits of "tangible symbol systems:" An innovative use of "low-tech" materials for students with severe and multiple disabilities.* Retrieved from http://www.ohsu.edu/xd/research/centers-institutes/institute-on-development-and-disability/design-to-learn/completed-projects/upload/Demonstrating-the-Benefits-of-Tangible-Symbol-Systems.pdf

Rowland, C., & Schweigert, P. (2000a). *Tangible symbol systems.* Portland, OR: Design to Learn Products.

Rowland, C., & Schweigert, P. (2000b). Tangible symbols, tangible outcomes. *Augmentative and Alternative Communication, 16,* 61–78.

Rowland, C., & Schweigert, P. (2003) Cognitive skills and AAC: Where we've been, what we know and the questions we should ask. In J. Light, D. Beukelman, & J. Reichle (Eds.), *Communicative competence for individuals who use AAC* (pp. 241–275). Baltimore, MD: Paul H. Brookes Publishing Co.

Rowland, C., & Schweigert, P. (2004). *First things first: Early communication for the presymbolic child with severe disabilities.* Portland, OR: Design to Learn Products.

Rowland, C., Stillman, R., & Mar, H. (2010). Current assessment practices for young children who are deafblind. *AER Journal: Research and Practice in Visual Impairment and Blindness, 3*(3), 63–70.

Saunders, M.D., Questad, K.A., Kedziorski, T.L., Boase, B.C., Patterson, E.A., & Cullinan, T.B. (2001). Unprompted mechanical switch use in individuals with severe multiple disabilities: An evaluation of the effects of body position. *Journal of Developmental and Physical Disabilities, 13*(1), 27–39.

Schalock, M.D., & Bull, R. (2012). *The 2011 national child count of children and youth who are deaf-blind.* Monmouth, OR: National Consortium on Deaf-blindness, Teaching Research Institute, Western Oregon University.

Seligman, M. (1975). *Helplessness: On depression, development and death.* New York, NY: W.H. Freeman.

Sigafoos, J., Didden, R., Schlosser, R., Green, V., O'Reilly, M., & Lancioni, G. (2008). A review of intervention studies on teaching AAC to individuals who are deaf and blind. *Journal of Developmental and Physical Disabilities, 20,* 71–99.

Trief, E. (2007). The use of tangible cues for children with multiple disabilities and visual impairment. *Journal of Visual Impairment and Blindness, 101,* 613–619.

Vervloed, M., van Dijk, R., Knoors, H., & van Dijk, J. (2006). Interaction between the teacher and the congenitally deafblind child. *American Annals of the Deaf, 151,* 336–344.

Warburg, M. (2008). Visual impairment in adult people with intellectual disability:

Literature review. *Journal of Intellectual Disability Research, 45,* 424–438.

Wetherby, A.M., & Prizant, B.M. (2003). *Communication and Symbolic Behavior Scales (CSBS), Normed Edition.* Baltimore, MD: Paul H. Brookes Publishing Co.

Yoder, P., & Stone, W.L. (2006). A randomized comparison of the effect of two prelinguistic communication interventions on the acquisition of spoken communication in preschoolers with ASD. *Journal of Speech, Language, and Hearing Research, 49,* 698–711.

5

Are We There Yet?

Targeted and Phenotypic Communication Interventions for Children with Down Syndrome or Autism Spectrum Disorder

Stephanie Yoshiko Shire and Connie Kasari

Young children with disabilities often have specific impairments in their understanding and expression of spoken language. As a result, early interventions rely heavily on strategies to improve communication and language skills. Despite the increasing knowledge of the etiology of various disorders associated with delays in communication and language development, few interventions have been designed to address the specific impairments associated with these different etiologies (Fidler & Nadel, 2007; Kasari & Hodapp, 1996; Kasari & Sigman, 1996). Two disorders that are similar in language delays and impairments but differ significantly in other areas of development are of particular interest. The inherently social nature of children with Down syndrome (DS) is a natural contrast to children with autism spectrum disorder (ASD) who experience core challenges in social interaction. Although this and many other differences in the behavioral phenotype of these two groups exist, both require intervention for their communication and language impairment (Abbeduto, Warren, & Conners, 2007). Let's examine two cases: Brian, a 6-year-old boy with a diagnosis of ASD, and Sarah, a 3-year-old girl who has a diagnosis of DS. Looking at both children in the context of play with toys, challenges are apparent in communication, play, and joint engagement that would be key targets in early intervention programming for both children.

This chapter was based on a presentation by Connie Kasari at a conference hosted by Georgia State University in June 2011. We thank our funders for support in writing this chapter: the Autism Intervention Research Network in Behavioral Health from the Maternal and Child Health Research Program, Maternal and Child Health Bureau (Combating Autism Act Initiative), Health Resources and Services Administration (HRSA), Department of Health and Human Services (Grant # UA3MC11055), Autism Speaks (# 7495), NIMH RO1MH084864 and NICHD/NIDCD RO1HD073975 awarded to second author.

Brian

Brian's parents report that he did not speak until he was 4 years old. He now has five words—*more, go, mama, cookie,* and *want*—that he uses to ask for his favorite foods, people, and toys. Brian's parents also report that he loves LEGO blocks and animals, but he often plays with those toys alone at home by lining up the blocks by color and then lining up his animals. Brian's parents and his older sister Emily frequently try to play with Brian, but he tends to push them away as he always wants to play with the LEGO blocks and animals in the same way. Brian's parents would like to learn how to play with Brian and how to get Brian to share his ideas by talking about his LEGO blocks, animals, and other items in his environment.

Sarah

Sarah's parents feel like she understands when they talk with her or give her directions, but Sarah is very hard to understand when she speaks. Sarah shows interest in toys for short periods of time. She has difficulty turning and fitting small pieces into toys (e.g., puzzles, building blocks). Sarah loves to sing songs and play tickle games with her mother. Sarah's mother is concerned because her daughter likes to approach other children but does not seem to know how to play with them, and other children have difficulty understanding Sarah's words.

How could we help Brian and Sarah's families engage their children in activities that can help them learn the communication and play skills they need to interact with others more successfully?

Children with other disabilities also present with communication and language delays, but this chapter focuses on DS and ASD, two of the most common disorders with a biological basis, because there are few studies even describing the differences in any one developmental area, let alone communication. Thus, this chapter's purpose is to review the extant literature, examining targeted and comprehensive intervention programs focused on social communication and spoken language for children with ASD and children with DS who have limited expressive language skills.

SOCIAL-COMMUNICATION DEVELOPMENT: CHILDREN WITH AUTISM SPECTRUM DISORDER AND CHILDREN WITH DOWN SYNDROME

Flexible and functional spoken language skills are delayed for many children with ASD or DS compared with typically developing milestones (Abbeduto et al., 2007). Although children with ASD have also been found to demonstrate greater delays in receptive language than expressive language (Hudry et al., 2010; Weismer, Lord, & Esler, 2010), both groups demonstrate delays in the acquisition of spoken vocabulary. Children with DS also have greater difficulty with articulation and intelligibility (Fidler, 2005) due to differences in vocal tract anatomy and frequent recurring otitis media that hinder their communicative clarity (Rice, Warren, & Betz, 2005). Several groups have described an expressive language impairment for children with DS, a profile also described for children with ASD. This profile includes delays in the development of expressive spoken language that are incongruent with the children's nonverbal cognitive abilities (see Chapman, 1997; Rice et al., 2005; Tager-Flusberg, Paul, & Lord, 2005). This mismatch is such that delays in expressive language for groups of children with either DS or ASD are often greater than would be expected for their nonverbal cognitive level. Therefore, this disconnect between nonverbal cognitive abilities and expressive communication skills may be a relevant characteristic of both groups.

There is great heterogeneity among children with DS and children with ASD. Children are often delayed in their spoken language skills during the preschool years, but the expectation is that they will learn to speak, albeit later than typically developing children. These children are considered preverbal, whereas school-age children who continue to have limited vocabularies (e.g., fewer than 20 spontaneous, functional words) may be considered minimally verbal (Tager-Flusberg & Kasari, 2013). Focusing on the development of early nonverbal and intentional social-communication skills for children who are preverbal or minimally verbal may be especially important for further communicative development.

Children use gestures to request and to share for the purpose of joint attention. These gestures emerge within the first and second years of life, allowing children to communicate with those around them prior to the emergence of spoken language (Mundy, Sigman, Kasari, & Yirmiya, 1988). Gestures used to request (e.g., pointing to or reaching for something in order to obtain it; also called *proto-imperative gestures*) and gestures used to share attention or topic (e.g., pointing to something of interest; also called *proto-declarative gestures*) are often addressed in early intervention programs. Proto-declarative, joint attention gestures, however, are more difficult to teach given the abstract nature of the target (sharing attention to an event rather than obtaining an object). In addition, the difficulties children with DS and ASD have with gestures vary and, thus, affect how one might address interventions for these behaviors.

Joint Attention and Requesting Gestures in Down Syndrome

Studies are mixed on whether joint attention gestures are impaired in children with DS, with some studies suggesting delays (Walden, Blackford, & Carpenter, 1997) and others not when different groups of children are matched on mental age (Mundy et al., 1988). Children with DS may engage in frequent coordinated joint looks—a lower level joint attention behavior in which the child looks between an event and another person to share with somewhat more difficulty than using higher level pointing and giving and showing joint attention gestures—because of the social nature of joint attention (Mundy et al., 1988). In contrast, gestures used to request are specifically delayed in children with DS (Fidler et al., 2006; Mundy et al., 1988; Smith et al., 1987). When children with DS are compared with children with mixed disabilities and typically developing peers, children with DS demonstrated fewer gestures to request, yet an equal number of initiations to begin social routines with partners (Fidler, 2005). As such, social initiations may be viewed as a strength while requesting skills requires further development, a profile opposite to many children with ASD.

Joint Attention and Requesting Gestures in Autism Spectrum Disorder

There is consensus among studies that the majority of children with ASD show delays and differences in their use of joint attention gestures. Mundy, Sigman, and Kasari

(1990) found that joint attention skills were specifically impaired compared with children with intellectual disabilities when matched for mental age or language age. Joint attention skills were more impaired than requesting skills, and the impairment in joint attention skills remained stable over 13 months. Furthermore, joint attention skills were found to be predictive of children's later language skills, whereas requesting, initial language level, and IQ were not. Joint attention has been considered one of the earliest behavioral core impairments of autism because of the convergence of evidence using well-matched comparison samples and, as such, is included as an early diagnostic marker (e.g., Lord et al., 2000; Robins, Fein, Barton, & Green, 2001).

Social-Communication Interventions

Despite these phenotypic differences of DS and ASD children, an intervention will generally address both requesting and joint attention functions depending on the child's presentation (Fidler, 2005; Mundy et al., 1988; Smith et al., 1987). There is more evidence supporting early social-communication interventions for children with ASD than DS. Despite the greater impairment in joint attention for children with ASD, the majority of studies address requesting gestures and are overrepresented by single-case designs with mixed results (Kasari, Shire, Factor, & McCracken, 2014). Within these studies, change is often obtained on lower level behaviors, such as responding to joint attention, rather than higher level initiations of joint attention, which are more difficult to improve. Maintenance and generalization of taught skills are weak when change is documented. Another issue with studies on children with ASD is that researchers often report an outcome measure that combines requesting and joint attention gestures. Combined reporting of both functions does not clearly demonstrate if joint attention skills improved for children with ASD or if the outcomes were primarily driven by change in requesting. Although children with DS have shown specific difficulty in requesting gestures, interventions specifically reporting on this function have not been reported.

Some interventions have used play routines as a means to jointly engage children, rather than teaching discrete skills in adult–child teaching contexts, so they can learn the forms of different gestures within a naturalistic context (e.g., Kasari, Freeman, & Paparella, 2006). One might expect children with DS to enter into periods of joint engagement with another person relatively easily because they are highly social at a young age. Joint engagement, however, requires that the child be actively engaged in the activity with the person; he or she cannot be passive, either by watching or contributing little in terms of the interaction (Adamson, Bakeman, Deckner, & Romski, 2009). This context of a shared interaction around an activity sets up opportunities for learning about communication and language. The difficulty in joint engagement for children with DS, however, may be the preference for engaging with the person and showing limited interest in the activity. Thus, several studies have found that children with DS engage in an increased number of social bids with an experimenter during a difficult task (e.g., Kasari & Freeman, 2001; Pitcairn & Wishart, 1994), or they fail to make connections between the person and the activity (Kasari & Freeman, 2001). Combining social and cognitive aspects of an interaction is difficult for children with DS, leading them to spend less time jointly engaged (Adamson et al., 2009).

Children with ASD also experience little time jointly engaged compared with typically developing peers as well as children with DS (Adamson et al., 2009). Unlike children with DS who may focus exclusively on people, children with ASD spend more time focused exclusively on objects (Adamson et al., 2009). The demands of social interactions with symbol use may also be particularly challenging for children with ASD. Children with DS and children with ASD demonstrate difficulties managing the social and cognitive load required during periods of joint engagement, although differences are present in their profile of preference for exclusive person or object engagement. Therefore, both children with ASD and children with DS may benefit from communication interventions that focus on supporting children's joint engagement with people and objects.

DEVELOPMENT OF PLAY SKILLS: CHILDREN WITH AUTISM SPECTRUM DISORDER AND CHILDREN WITH DOWN SYNDROME

The context for learning social-communication for young children typically revolves around play with others. Indeed, children spend a great deal of time playing. Historically, it has been hypothesized that play at the symbolic level is a context that facilitates the development of other symbolic skills such as language (Piaget and Inhelder, 1969; Vygotsky, 1980). Correlational research indicates that the attainment of higher level play skills in the preschool years is associated with greater language vocabulary at age 8 and 9 years for children with ASD (Kasari et al., 2012). Play interactions provide the context in which children can learn language, but if children have impairments in learning to play, then play skills may need to be specifically taught.

The nature of play interactions has been studied with children with DS and children with ASD. Children with DS demonstrate more stereotyped and repetitive functional play as well as more frequent nonfunctional acts such as mouthing and throwing of objects compared with typically developing peers (e.g., Krakow & Kopp, 1983). The play behavior of children with ASD has also been found to be repetitive in nature, lacking the flexibility and diversity of play skills demonstrated by typically developing children (e.g., Lifter, Sulzer-Azaroff, Anderson, & Cowdery, 1993). The social nature of play, however, leads to seemingly greater impairments for children with ASD than children with DS. Given that play skills are often demonstrated in the context of engaging with others, children with ASD have difficulty with peers and with caregivers (Chang, Shih, & Kasari, 2015; Kasari, Sigman, Mundy, & Yirmiya, 1990; Sigman, Mundy, Sherman, & Ungerer, 1986). Thus, in addition to delays in play skills, children with ASD may also resist playing with others, as seen in the case of Brian. Altogether, the targets of increasing play diversity and play level are crucial for intervention because of the limited play repertoire of both children with ASD and DS, as well as the increase in repetitive nonfunctional play.

CURRENT REVIEW

Although children with ASD and children with DS have different strengths and challenges, they also have many similarities. Joint attention appears more impaired in children with ASD, and requesting seems more impaired in children with DS (Mundy et al., 1988). Yet, both groups show difficulties in joint engagement and spoken language. The mechanisms for these difficulties may differ, but interventions that can build engaging social interactions with many opportunities to learn social-communication skills will likely be needed. Intervention packages may need to be tailored to the unique needs and strengths of these populations. The following sections examine the extant literature on communication and play interventions.

METHODS

Search Strategy

A search of six electronic databases was conducted in October 2014, including ERIC, Google Scholar, Linguistics and Language Behavior Abstracts, PsycINFO, PsychArticles, and Web of Science. The search was primarily designed to capture communication interventions for children with DS and children with ASD. Search terms were related to the participant population (e.g., *children with Down syndrome, autism*), communication (e.g., *language, joint attention, joint engagement, gestures*), and intervention (e.g., *treatment, parent mediated, preschool*). A detailed description of the search string and the full set of searches can be obtained from the first author. In addition to the electronic search, snowball sampling (Greenhalgh & Peacock, 2005) was used to further broaden the search by scanning reference lists to identify research groups who examine communication interventions for children with developmental disorders, examination of references of related articles, and contact with researchers relevant to the field.

Study Selection

No restrictions were placed on the date published or the language in which the manuscript was written. Grey literature was not included due to the increased risk of bias through the inclusion of non–peer-reviewed articles. The inclusion criteria were designed to select experimental quantitative studies that provided empirical data examining communication interventions for children with ASD and children with DS. Studies included in this chapter met the following inclusion criteria: 1) included children with a diagnosis of ASD or DS, 2) included an intervention targeting communication or play as the primary study outcome or a secondary target outcome, and 3) utilized a randomized controlled trial (RCT) design when examining interventions for children with ASD or included quasi-experimental designs when examining interventions for children with DS. We originally intended to include only randomized experimental group designs—those with the highest levels of scientific rigor (Logan, Hickman, Harris, & Heriza, 2008). It was necessary to broaden the inclusion criteria to include quasi-experimental designs, however, due to the limited body of intervention research utilizing RCT designs that focused on children with DS. Studies using quasi-experimental designs were not included due to the greater number of RCTs examining interventions for children with ASD. Studies using quasi-experimental designs are identified in Table 5.1.

RESULTS

Search Results

The electronic search returned 2,082 results on which snowball sampling was also applied. A total of 34 studies met inclusion criteria, including 33 RCTs and one quasi-experimental design. Participant characteristics, intervention, outcomes, and findings are detailed in Table 5.1.

Table 5.1. Communication interventions and outcomes for children with autism spectrum disorder and children with Down syndrome: Randomized controlled trials

Study	Population and *n*	Developmental level (*mean*)	Intervention and dosage	Communication outcomes and findings
Primary study outcome: Communication				
Adamson, Romski, Bakeman, and Sevcik (2010) (secondary analysis of Romski et al., 2010)	Down syndrome (DS) and Developmental Delays (DD), *n* = 57 Toddlers	MSEL composite 59 (spoken communication; SC)/ 60 (augmented communication input; ACI)/ 59 (augmented communication output; ACO)	24 sessions of SC, ACI, ACO	Parent training; significant gains in symbol-infused supported joint engagement for children in all three groups
Burgoyne, Duff, Clarke, Buckley, Snowling, & Hulme (2012)	DS, *n* = 57 Early elementary	NVIQ block design 13.4 treatment (tx)/ 11.7	Daily 40-minute language and literacy sessions for 20 weeks versus wait list	Teaching assistant training; increase in taught vocabulary over wait list; no change in nontaught receptive or expressive vocabulary
Carter et al. (2011)	Autism spectrum disorder (ASD), *n* = 62 Toddlers	MSEL composite 63.8/64.9	Hanen's More than Words over 3.5 mo versus no treatment (tx) control	Parent training; no main effects of parent education intervention on children's communication, initiations of joint attention (IJA), or initiations of behavior regulation (IBR)
Drew et al. (2002)	ASD, *n* = 24 Preschoolers	NVIQ 88.1 (tx)/ 66.0	Parent training versus community tx	Parent training; significant increase in parent-reported (MB-CDI) vocabulary over community control
Fey et al. (2006)	DS (*n* = 26), DD (*n* = 25) Toddlers and preschoolers	Bayley Raw score 96.2 (tx)/ 97.0	6-month responsivity education prelinguistic milieu teaching versus no tx control	DS diagnosis did not predict differential outcome; significant increase in intentional communication for treatment over no treatment control
Goods, Ishijima, Chang, and Kasari (2013)	ASD, *n* = 15 Preschoolers	MSEL MA in mo 17.2 (tx)/ 13.9	Applied behavior analysis (ABA) plus JASPER versus ABA-only control	Pilot study showing significant increase in number of types of play acts and IBR in class and decrease in time unengaged over control; no difference in IJA

(continued)

Table 5.1. (*continued*)

Study	Population and *n*	Developmental level (*mean*)	Intervention and dosage	Communication outcomes and findings
Primary study outcome: Communication				
Green et al. (2010)	ASD, *n* = 152 Toddlers and preschoolers	MSEL range in mo across sites 21.2–31.4	6 mo of 2-hour biweekly PACT versus community tx	Small effect on language scores on PLS raw scores over community tx; significant gains on CSBS-DP social-communication and parent-reported vocabulary (MB-CDI) over community tx
Howlin, Gordon, Pasco, Wade, and Charman (2007)	ASD, *n* = 84 Elementary school children	MSEL developmental quotient 25.9 (tx)/ 22.7	PECS immediate tx versus delayed tx versus control	Significant increase in initiations of communication and PECS usage; no change in frequency of speech through class observation or scores on expressive and receptive language tests
Jocelyn, Casiro, Beattie, Bow, and Kneisz (1998)	ASD, *n* = 35 Preschoolers	Leiter-R NVIQ 58.4 (tx)/ 67.1	12-week child care intervention program versus control	Teacher training; increase in language on autism behavior checklist for treatment over control
Kaale , Smith, & Sponheim (2012)	ASD, *n* = 61 Preschoolers	MSEL MA in mo 25.6 (tx)/ 30.3	8 weeks JASPER and preschool versus preschool control	Teacher training; increase in IJA and time jointly engaged with parent over preschool-only control
Kaiser and Roberts (2013)	ASD (*n* = 16), DS (*n* = 18), DD (*n* = 43)	Leiter-R NVIQ 70.7 (parent tx)/ 69.8	36 × 30-minute EMT sessions parent and therapist versus therapist only	Parent training; no main effect of either tx on standardized tests of communication or parent report measures; observed outcomes including mean length of utterance (MLU) and number of different words were not significantly different by group at exit, but differed in favor of parent and therapist training at 6-month follow-up with MLU also significant at 12-month follow-up
Kasari, Freeman, and Paparella (2006)	ASD, *n* = 58 Preschoolers	MSEL DQ 58.3 (joint attention; JA)/ 58.9 (symbolic play; SP)/ 52.0 (control)	30 minutes x 6 weeks JA and ABA versus SP and ABA versus ABA-only control	Significant increase in IJA show and responding to JA for JA tx over SP and control; increase in coordinated looks, gives, and shows over SP and control; children in SP made greatest gains in mastered play levels

Kasari, Paparella, Freeman, and Jahromi (2008)	ASD, *n* = 58 Preschoolers	MSEL DQ 58.3 (JA)/ 58.9 (SP)/ 52.0 (control)	30 minutes × 6 weeks JA and ABA versus SP and ABA versus ABA-only control	Significant growth in IJA (Early Social Communication Scales) and time jointly engaged with parent in both tx over control; greatest growth in language (Reynell) in JA tx over SP and control at 1-year follow-up.
Kasari, Gulsrud, Wong, Kwon, and Locke (2010)	ASD, *n* = 42 Toddlers	MSEL DQ 64.8 (tx)/ 59.8	24 × 30 minutes JASPER parent mediated sessions versus wait list	Parent training; children in tx increased in time jointly engaged with caregiver, responses to JA, and types of functional play over wait list; no significant increase in IJA.
Kasari, Lawton, et al. (2014)	ASD, *n* = 112 Preschoolers	MSEL MA in mo 23.6 (tx)/ 26.3	3 mo JASPER parent mediated versus group parent education	Parent training; children in JASPER individual tx increased in time jointly engaged, IJA (ESCS), and types of symbolic play over group parent education
Kasari, Kaiser, et al. (2014)	ASD, *n* = 61 Early elementary	Leiter-R Brief IQ—three sites: 68.2/ 68.8/ 67.7	SMART design—initial randomization JASPER + EMT + speech-generating device (SGD) versus JASPER + EMT	Clinician implemented plus parent training; increase in spontaneous communicative utterances, different words, and comments favoring JASPER + EMT + SGD
Kasari, Siller, et al. (2014)	At-risk ASD, *n* = 66 Toddlers	MSEL DQ 65.78 (tx), 66.66 (control)	12 sessions parent education intervention versus control—4 sessions behavior support	Parent training; significant gains in parental responsivity; no main effect of treatment on children's communication outcomes
Lawton and Kasari (2012)	ASD, *n* = 16 Preschoolers	MSEL MA in mo 30.3 (tx)/ 33.8	6 weeks preschool plus JASPER versus preschool-only control	Teacher training pilot; significant increase in IJA and time jointly engaged over preschool-only control
McConachie, Randle, Hammal, and Le Couteur (2005)	ASD (*n* = 29), at risk (*n* = 22) Toddlers and preschoolers	Not reported	3 mo Hanen's More Than Words versus wait list control	Parent training; significant increase postintervention on parent-reported MB-CDI vocabulary for tx over wait list; no significant difference for Autism Diagnostic Observation Schedule (ADOS) social-communication scores

(continued)

Table 5.1. *(continued)*

Study	Population and *n*	Developmental level (*mean*)	Intervention and dosage	Communication outcomes and findings
Primary study outcome: Communication				
Oosterling et al. (2010)	ASD, *n* = 75 Preschoolers	PEP-R DQ 58.4 (tx)/ 58.0	12 mo focus parent training versus community tx	Parent training; no significant effect of treatment on parent-reported MB-CDI vocabulary (Dutch version: MCDI-Netherlands) or Dutch speech test
Paul, Campbell, Gilbert, and Tsiouri (2014)	ASD, *n* = 17 Toddlers and preschoolers	MSEL visual reception age equivalent 22.6 (rapid motor imitation antecedent; RIMA)/ 22.2 (milieu communication training; MCT)	12 weeks of RIMA versus MCT	Significant increase in words observed on CSBS and through parent report noted in each tx condition using separate analyses
Romski et al. (2010)	DS and DD, *n* = 68 Toddlers	MSEL composite 59 (SC)/ 60 (ACI)/ 59 (ACO)	24 sessions of SC, ACI, ACO	Parent training; ACO significant increase in number of augmented words over ACI; ACO maintained more spoken words than those in ACI or SC at exit; gains from baseline across groups in utterances, MLU, and turn rate with parent
Siller, Hutman, and Sigman (2012)	ASD, *n* = 70 Preschoolers	MSEL expressive language 16.5 (tx), 15.1	Focused playtime intervention 12 × 90-minute sessions	Parent training; tests of residual gain scores indicate main effect of treatment on maternal synchrony; no significant main effect of treatment on children's language scores
Wetherby et al. (2014)	ASD, *n* = 82 Toddlers	MSEL composite 75.56 (individual tx), 74.05 (group tx)	6 mo early social interaction (ESI) individual home sessions (3 times a week) plus 3 mo (2 times a week) versus ESI group (1 time a week)	Parent training; significantly greater gains for children in individual tx on CSBS composite, MSEL receptive language, and parent-reported Vineland adaptive behavior composite score.

Wong and Kwan (2010)	ASD, *n* = 17 Toddlers and preschoolers	MA in mo 17.9 (tx)/ 17.9	Autism 1-2-3, 10 × 30-minute sessions over 2 weeks versus control	Brief intervention with frequent testing intervals (every 2 weeks); no clear main effect of treatment on ADOS items; no differential effect of tx over control on parent stress or parent report of child behavior
Wong (2013)	ASD, *n* = 33 Preschoolers	MSEL MA in mo 36.3/ 27.4/ 30.4	SP then JA, JA then SP, versus wait list	Teacher training; significant gains in joint engagement, IJA, and responding to JA over wait list; change in play in class observation but not semistructured measure (Structured Play Assessment SPA).
Yoder and Stone (2006)	ASD, *n* = 36 Preschoolers	NVMA 18.7 mo	RPMT versus PECS; both 60 minutes a week for 6 mo	No differential effects of treatment allocation on initiations of JA
Yoder and Warren (2002)	DS (*n* = 17) and DD (*n* = 22) Toddlers	Bayley MA 14 mo	6 mo (three to four times a week) RPMT versus no treatment control	Parent training; no main effect of RPMT on children's initiations of requests or comments or their lexical density; children with DS greater growth in control
Yoder, Woynaroski, Fey, and Warren (2014) *Quasi Group*	DS (*n* = 35), ID (*n* = 29) Toddlers	Bayley MA in mo 12.3 (DS)/ 12.8 (ID)	MCT for 5 hours a week for 9 mo versus MCT for 1 hour a week	Participants in ID group experienced greater gains in parent-reported spoken vocabulary (MB-CDI) than DS group; participants in high-dose MCT showed greater parent-reported gains in spoken vocabulary over low-dose MCT
Secondary study outcome: Communication				
Aldred, Green, and Adams (2004)	ASD, *n* = 28 Toddlers and preschoolers	Not reported	Social-communication intervention: 12 sessions over 1 year versus community tx	Significant gains in MB-CDI reported expressive vocabulary over community tx; no difference between groups in receptive vocabulary
Dawson et al. (2010)	ASD, *n* = 48 Toddlers	MSEL composite 59.4/61.0	ESDM: 20 hour per week for 2 years versus community tx	MSEL receptive and expressive language—no significant difference after 1 year, significant differences post-2 years, favoring ESDM over community tx

(continued)

Table 5.1. (*continued*)

Study	Population and *n*	Developmental level (*mean*)	Intervention and dosage	Communication outcomes and findings
Secondary study outcome: Communication				
Landa, Holman, O'Neil, and Stuart (2011)	ASD, *n* = 50 Toddlers	MSEL VR T score 27.5 (tx)/ 31.1	6 mo classroom and interpersonal synchrony versus classroom only	No difference between groups on IJA or MSEL language scales
Smith, Groen, and Wynn (2000)	ASD, *n* = 28 Preschoolers	Bayley IQ 50.7 (parent) 50.5 (intensive)	3–9 mo of parent training versus intensive therapy (average 24.52 hours per week)	Parent training; no significant difference in Reynell or parent reported (Vineland) language scores over intensive intervention
Strain and Bovey (2011)	ASD, *n* = 294 across 56 classroom randomized Preschoolers	MSEL composite 59.6 (tx)/ 63.2	2-year LEAP-coached teacher training versus manual-only LEAP	Significant gains for coaching LEAP tx over manual only on standardized language tests (PLS, MSEL language scales)

Abbreviations in table: mo = months; tx = treatment; DQ = developmental quotient; MA = mental age; NVIQ = nonverbal intelligence quotient; MB-CDI = MacArthur-Bates Communicative Development Inventory; MSEL = Mullen Scales of Early Learning; ESDM = Early Start Denver Model; PACT = Preschool Autism Communication Trial; LEAP = Learning Experiences and Alternate Program for Preschools and their Parents; PLS = Preschool Language Scales; CSBS-DP = Communication and Symbolic Behavior Scales Developmental Profile; RPMT = Responsive Education and Prelinguistic Milieu Training; JASPER = joint attention, symbolic play, engagement, and regulation; PECS = Picture Exchange Communication System; PEP-R = Psychoeducational Profiles–Revised

Participant Characteristics

Twenty-eight studies included children with ASD, whereas only seven studies included either children with DS in mixed-diagnosis samples or children with DS alone (Adamson et al., 2011; Burgoyne et al., 2012; Fey et al., 2006; Kaiser & Roberts, 2013; Romski et al., 2010; Yoder & Warren, 2002; Yoder, Woynaroski, Fey, & Warren, 2014). Overall, participants included young children, most frequently toddlers and/or preschool-age children, with an additional two studies including elementary school-age children (Burgoyne et al., 2012; Kasari, Kaiser, et al., 2014). Studies assessed developmental level using a variety of tools providing group mean scores for characteristics such as mental age and developmental quotient. Measures and average scores by group can be found in Table 5.1.

Interventions and Primary Target Outcomes

Studies included in this review were divided into those examining communication, language, and play as a primary study outcome and those examining communication, language, or play as secondary outcomes. Table 5.1 provides measures, outcomes, and findings by study.

The majority of the interventions targeting communication as a primary outcome combined behavioral and developmental perspectives. Strategies were often based in the principles of applied behavior analysis (ABA) and delivered in natural contexts, including caregiver and child play (e.g., joint attention, symbolic play, engagement, and regulation [JASPER]: Kasari, Gulsrud, Wong, Kwon, & Locke, 2010; Kasari, Lawton, et al., 2014), caregiver and child daily routines (e.g., Hanen's More than Words [MTW]: Carter et al., 2011; McConachie, Randle, Hammal, & Le Couteur, 2005; Early Social Interaction [ESI]: Wetherby et al., 2014), preschool classroom interactions with teachers (e.g., JASPER: Kaale et al., 2012; Lawton & Kasari, 2012), and child care settings (e.g., Jocelyn, Casiro, Beattie, Bow, & Kneisz, 1998). Furthermore, 17 of these studies included parent or teacher education or training.

Studies that included communication/language as a secondary outcome often applied comprehensive treatments targeting goals broader than communication, including discrete trial teaching (DTT; Smith, Groen, & Wynn, 2000), Early Start Denver Model (ESDM; Dawson et al., 2010), and Learning Experiences and Alternative Program for Preschoolers and Their Parents (LEAP; Strain & Bovey, 2011). The majority of these comprehensive treatments provided a large dose or number of hours of treatment (e.g., 6–24 months and multiple hours per week), whereas the modular interventions focused on communication as a primary outcome provided relatively brief doses of targeted treatments most often delivered within a 3-month time frame (e.g., Kasari et al., 2010; Wong & Kwan, 2010). Only one of the studies providing comprehensive intervention (Smith et al., 2000) included substantive parent training beyond psychoeducation/information in which the parent implemented the treatment provided to the child.

Summary of Outcomes Overall, the comprehensive interventions that were not specific to communication reported mixed findings using standardized measures of language development, parent-reported vocabulary, and observed communicative behavior. In contrast, the shorter targeted communication interventions largely led to gains in communication outcomes. These studies targeted a variety of specific communication skills. For example, early nonverbal social-communication skills including initiations of joint attention (IJA) and initiations of behavior regulation (IBR) were targeted in 10 studies examining targeted communication interventions. Eight of these 10 studies examined JASPER intervention in which six demonstrated gains in children's IJA through either semistructured assessments or observations of parent– or teacher–child interactions. In contrast, no main effect of treatment on IJA was found through MTW parent education (Carter et al., 2011), responsive milieu prelinguistic teaching, Picture Exchange Communication System (PECS) (Yoder & Stone, 2006), or the comprehensive preschool interpersonal synchrony intervention (Landa, Holman, O'Neil, & Stuart, 2011). Furthermore, gains specific to IJA could not be determined for the SCERTS® (Social Communication, Emotional Regulation and Transactional Support)-based ESI project by Wetherby et al. (2014) because only composite scores combining requesting and joint attention were reported.

Examination of requesting behavior occurred less frequently. IBR (gestures to request) was examined in only two studies. Gains in IBR observed in classrooms were reported post–JASPER intervention (Goods, Ishijima, Chang, & Kasari, 2013); however, no main effect of treatment on IBR was found post MTW (Carter et al., 2011). Requesting behavior was also examined via picture exchange behavior. Howlin, Gordon, Pasco, Wade, and Charman (2007) reported an increase in PECS usage post–PECS training, whereas Yoder and Stone (2006) found no main effects of PECS treatment on children's communication. Requesting behavior was not examined for children with DS.

Finally, spoken language outcomes varied and were largely examined through parent-reported vocabulary, most commonly using the MacArthur Communication Development Inventory (Fenson et al., 2007). Mixed effects were found via parent report with six of seven studies reporting increases over control treatment or a lower dosage of the same treatment. Using standardized tests of language (e.g., Preschool Language Scale: Zimmerman, Steiner, & Pond, 2002; Reynell Developmental Language Scales: Reynell & Gruber, 1990), gains were documented for the group who received JASPER intervention in addition to their ABA classroom intervention compared with the group who received ABA alone (Kasari, Paparella, Freeman, & Jahromi, 2008), whereas no effects were found post–PECS training (Howlin et al., 2007) or EMT (Kaiser & Roberts, 2013). Comprehensive interventions demonstrated mixed effects. Gains were demonstrated in an evaluation of LEAP delivered with teaching coaching versus LEAP delivered by giving teachers a LEAP manual to read on their own (Strain & Bovey, 2011). Furthermore, an evaluation of ESDM over community control demonstrated few gains that were demonstrated only after 2 years of intensive treatment (Dawson et al., 2010). Finally, no additive effects of treatment were found for parent-mediated DTT compared with DTT delivered only by a clinician (Smith et al., 2000) or interpersonal synchrony intervention delivered in a classroom early intervention setting compared with preschool-only control (Landa et al., 2011).

Finally, eight studies documented gains in spoken language observed in interaction with others. Kasari and colleagues (2014) demonstrated gains for elementary school-age children with ASD who were minimally verbal at study entry. In addition to the social-communication intervention protocol, children with access to speech-generating devices (SGDs) showed greater gains in spontaneous communicative utterances, comments, and word variety in the 6 months of treatment compared with the same treatment without SGDs. Romski and colleagues (2010) also compared a spoken communication arm with augmented communication interventions using SGDs. In this trial, two augmented communication arms that varied by whether the interventionist demanded expressive output from the child (Augmented Communication-AC input versus AC output). Overall, toddlers with developmental delays, including DS, demonstrated the greatest and quickest increases in the AC output arm, including the odds of spoken language. Additional examination of gains in intentional communication and communication initiations for children with ASD and children with DS were also observed in comparison with no treatment control groups (Fey et al., 2006; Howlin et al., 2007).

DISCUSSION

A total of 34 RCTs included children with ASD and examined interventions targeting communication skill. A handful of these studies also examined play as a study outcome. Furthermore, 16 of the studies included training/education or mediation in which a community stakeholder (e.g., parents, teachers) delivered the intervention to the child. Altogether, these studies report positive findings for children's communication; however, the body of literature is limited by small sample sizes and frequent inclusion of parent report as the primary measure of language outcomes. RCTs that include small samples with unbalanced allocation to treatment conditions risk bias in highly heterogeneous samples in which randomization with only a few participants may not fully alleviate the influence of confounding participant factors (Piantadosi, 1990). Small RCTs also have limited power to detect effects. As such, small or more varied effects that may still hold clinical relevance may not be detected in such trials, thereby leading to an incorrect conclusion regarding the efficacy or effectiveness of the intervention.

The appropriate application of statistical analyses is another methodological consideration particularly relevant in light of the small sample sizes of many of the included studies. The application of many statistics tests on a small sample can lead to spurious findings due to increases in type 1 error (Abdi, 2007). The likelihood of finding a rare chance effect increases as the number of tests on a small sample increases (Abdi, 2007). Although corrections for multiple comparisons can reduce type 1 error, studies should be designed to test primary a priori hypotheses to ensure adequate power and reduce spurious findings (Benjamini & Yekutieli, 2001). Furthermore, statistical analyses need to address the effects of time in treatment, treatment allocation, and the interaction between time and treatment group when a trial is designed to compare outcomes for children randomized to two intervention conditions in order to examine differential effects of treatments. The comparison and control for threats to internal validity, including children's natural maturation and development, is lost when comparative studies are deconstructed to examine change only within one treatment group. The tests in such cases become an analysis of a one group pre-post design in which a statement cannot be made about the effect of treatment on the children's behavior versus natural maturation (Campbell & Stanley, 1963). Overall, it is important that the reader keep these and other important methodological limitations in mind when considering the findings produced from trials, even those using designs that are considered to be the highest level of rigor available.

Although a growing number of RCTs are examining the efficacy and effectiveness of communication interventions for children with ASD, there is a clear paucity of literature providing a rigorous examination of communication interventions for children with DS. Considering the lack of group trials providing evidence for interventions targeting communication and play skills for children with DS, researchers and clinicians may start by examining interventions explored with children with ASD. In doing so, however, one must consider the similarities and differences between the social-communication and play needs of young children with ASD or DS who are preverbal or minimally verbal.

Functions of Communication: Requesting and Social Initiations

Early social-communication skills are of particular relevance for children who are preverbal or minimally verbal. Mixed results were found across the various interventions for children with ASD who demonstrate significant delays in the development of IJA gestures. Studies examining JASPER intervention provided the bulk of the evidence with six of eight studies finding significant increases over control treatment arms. The emergence of gestures to request is more relevant to communicative development for children with DS. The limited examination specific to requesting behavior restricts interventionists' understanding of the needs of children with DS. IBR, otherwise known as requesting through gesture, were examined in only two studies with children with ASD and showed mixed findings. Implementation of PECS (Bondy & Frost, 2001) in two studies, however, provided evidence for increase in the rate of picture exchanges to request (Howlin et al., 2007; Yoder & Stone, 2006). No main effect of treatment was found for other areas of communication, however, beyond exchanges to request. Inclusion of PECS programming to foster requesting skills may be particularly beneficial to children with DS, considering the challenges experienced with requesting gestures; however, further examination of the influence of PECS teaching on other communicative functions is required.

An additional two studies included other forms of augmentative and alternative communication (AAC) systems to enhance children's expressive communication (Kasari, Kaiser et al., 2014; Romski et al., 2010). These two studies included SGDs to provide access to communication within early social-communication interventions delivered by a combination of clinicians and caregivers. Kasari, Kaiser, and colleagues (2014) found faster gains in spoken socially communicative utterances, variety of words, and comments favoring children ages 5–8 who received the social-communication intervention as well as access to an SGD than children who received the same intervention but with no access to an SGD. Romski et al. (2010) similarly found that children who were allocated to treatment arms that included SGDs, but varied by emphasizing either language input or demanding language output, made greater gains in both augmented and spoken words. Together, these two studies provide support for the potential of AAC to bolster spoken communication in early communicators across diagnostic groups. Considering the substantial challenges experienced by children with ASD and children with DS in the domain of expressive language, AAC systems may be a tangible option to provide access to communication for many children with either diagnosis. Both low-tech PECS and high-tech SGDs may have benefits for children with

DS. Boosting spoken communication through the inclusion of AAC, specifically SGDs, may have application for preverbal and early communicators who have DS as well. An SGD may provide additional access to visual communication models as well as a second mode of expressive communication. This combination may lead to increases in symbol infusion during joint engagement. Adamson, Romski, Bakeman, and Sevcik (2010) conducted an examination of this relationship. Adamson et al. explored joint engagement with the participants enrolled in the Romski et al. trial and found that gains in symbol-infused joint engagement were correlated to increases in the number of augmented words produced by the children, providing further evidence for the role of joint engagement and symbolic development. Further examination is required of the role of AAC in communication interventions for both populations.

Spoken language outcomes were targeted in additional studies; however, the findings were largely limited by a lack of direct observation or structured evaluation of the child's communication. Rather, studies included parent report as the primary measure to evaluate change in children's vocabulary or overall communicative skills with mixed findings. Therefore, interventionists' cumulative understanding of the efficacy and effectiveness of early intervention programs to facilitate children's initiations of spoken language is limited and should be a target for further evaluation.

Intervention Targeting Developmental Domains Other than Communication

A small body of literature utilizing RCTs designs, including children with DS, targeted outcomes other than communication, including parents' behavior and children's broader development. These small studies have mixed findings. For example, Roux, Sofronoff, and Sanders (2013) demonstrated changes in parents' interaction style as well as parent report of children's overall developmental level after participation in Stepping Stones/Triple P, a broad positive parenting intervention. Piper and Pless (1980) also included parents in a largely clinician-delivered intervention designed to increase developmental scores; however, no differences between treatment and control groups were found.

Notably, there were studies found through the electronic search that included children with DS and used a group design to examine an intervention targeting play. Children with DS have been found to have difficulty sustaining attention and functional play with toys (e.g., Krakow & Kopp, 1983) and tend to spend more time passive in the session than typically developing peers (Linn, Goodman, & Lender, 2000). Furthermore, children with DS have been reported to demonstrate more indiscriminant or nonfunctional actions on objects such as mouthing and throwing (e.g., Krakow & Kopp, 1983), although findings for the complexity of play of children with DS is mixed (Beeghly, Perry, & Cicchetti, 1989; Lender, Goodwin, & Linn, 1998). Therefore, this population warrants the development and examination of intervention protocols to increase engagement as well as the range and level of play skills. Children with ASD also demonstrate impairments in the development of flexible, diverse, and higher level play skills (e.g., Rutherford, Young, Hepburn, & Rogers, 2007). The way that play skills are taught affects the maintenance and generalizability of play. Direct teaching approaches (e.g., DTT) that use repetition of adult-directed commands, often out of the natural context of play, have limited success in generalization as evidenced by interventionists who must specifically program for generalization. Play that is taught outside the natural context and is not linked to the child's current developmental level often does not maintain or generalize (Lifter et al., 1993). In other words, teaching symbolic play when children have not yet mastered earlier levels of play likely takes longer, and the symbolic skill, once mastered in a discrete, adult-directed way, likely will not be generalized.

JASPER intervention uses an initial play assessment in order to identify developmentally appropriate play targets. These play targets are engineered within play routines that are contextually and developmentally appropriate (e.g., Kasari, Freeman, & Paparella, 2006). This approach differs from others that are adult directed and driven by the child's response. For example, several models use child choice (as initially determined by the adult with two choices presented to the child). Once the child chooses the toy, the adult teaches the child what to do with the toy. The teaching activity may be embedded within a play routine, but it is often adult driven. Several studies within this review examined play skills through implementation of the JASPER intervention (e.g., Kasari et al., 2010). Children demonstrated an increase in play types (flexible and diverse play acts) post–JASPER intervention (e.g., Goods et al., 2013; Kasari et al., 2006; Kasari, Lawton, et al., 2014). These same studies also provided evidence toward increases in time spent jointly engaged in the context of play and in increases in level of play. Therefore, JASPER intervention strategies may represent an appropriate starting point for play and engagement intervention for children with DS due to the similarities in challenges experienced in play and joint engagement for children with ASD as well as children with DS.

Clinical Implications

Joint Engagement The bulk of the intervention studies focused on JASPER intervention. JASPER focuses on supporting periods of joint engagement in which a child attends to both the intervention partner and the shared activity. Although Brian and Sarah who were introduced earlier in this chapter have different developmental diagnoses, they both struggle to jointly engage with their caregivers. Focusing on joint engagement as the context for developing communication skills may lead to gains for many children because this is a clear impairment for children with ASD and is limited in the context of play for other populations of children with developmental disabilities.

Furthermore, these studies demonstrate that brief, targeted, and developmentally appropriate intervention can lead to gains in social-communication skills for young children with ASD and provide the most consistent findings for increasing children's initiations of joint attention, a difficult core challenge to influence. The included studies highlight the need to focus on the type of communication that is targeted during the treatment. It is important that clinicians include target goals for requesting as well as social commenting. Although early communicators may have few words in their vocabulary, several included studies demonstrated that children who are minimally verbal or preverbal can make gains not only in requesting to have their needs met but also in commenting to socially participate in the interaction.

Including Augmentative and Alternative Communication Two RCTs that included SGDs in their protocols provide further evidence to demonstrate that not only young children but also school-age early communicators can benefit from this mode of AAC. Furthermore, these participants demonstrated not only gains in augmented communication but also spoken words. The SGDs were incorporated in the context of two different interventions that included naturalistic settings focused on increasing children's communication skills. Notably, spoken language outcomes for children in Romski et al. (2010) were greater for children who received intervention with the SGD compared with those who had access only to spoken language. Children who received access to the SGD using a teaching method that demanded output from the child as well as those children who were enrolled in the treatment arm that did not demand output (focused on modeling use of the device) obtained similar spoken language outcomes. Similarly, Kaiser, et al. (2014) focused on modeling communication via the SGD in session with limited demand for child output. Children receiving the SGD condition produced more spoken language than children receiving only the spoken language intervention similar to Romski's et al.) findings with younger children. Further examination of the differences in these teaching methods will better inform clinical practice.

CONCLUSION AND FUTURE DIRECTIONS

An increasing evidence base has been accrued on the social-communication impairments of children with ASD and children with DS, but not on other disorders associated with intellectual and developmental disabilities (IDD). Few phenotypically targeted interventions for children with IDD are available, despite this knowledge. Although there are more interventions targeted on core social-communication impairments in children with ASD, many of these interventions do not measure change in these core areas of impairment. Others measure social-communication as an outcome but do not obtain change. Such is the evidence that these types of impairments are very difficult to improve, and likely require targeted, intensive interventions.

Some evidence shows that improving these areas of social-communication can improve language outcomes in children with ASD (Kasari et al., 2008; Kasari, Kaiser, et al., 2014); however, some interventions using the same methods over a brief period have not obtained improvement in language outcomes (Kaale et al., 2014; Kasari et al., 2010). Thus, future research needs to examine the dose, both length of time and density of intervention, and the agent of change (parent, therapist, or parent plus therapist) that is needed to obtain change on broader outcomes of development. Other characteristics also need further study, including the severity of ASD, developmental age of child, types of interventions received, and so forth.

Given the success of interventions at improving core social-communication impairments in children with ASD, future studies need to test whether similar interventions can affect change in children with DS and other neurodevelopmental disorders. For example, focusing on social-communication gestures (particularly requesting gestures), task-related social behaviors, and the management of attention and persistence may benefit the language development of children with DS. Social-communication interventions for children with the genetic disorder

Dup15q who have a high comorbidity with ASD need to also consider motor impairment common to these children and the application of augmented communication support. Linking treatment components to particular areas of impairment that uniquely define the disorder call for a modular approach to interventions rather than an uninformed or whole-hog application of comprehensive models.

Finally, studies are needed that examine the mechanisms of change for children with ASD and children with DS. Interventionists need to be able to tease apart dose from content from approach used to obtain developmental improvements in children. A goal for future interventions is to deliver intervention when needed and to better personalize these interventions to obtain maximal benefit.

REFERENCES

Abbeduto, L., Warren, S., & Conners, F.A. (2007). Language development in Down syndrome: From the prelinguistic period to the acquisition of literacy. *Mental Retardation and Developmental Disabilities Research Reviews, 13,* 247–261.

Adamson, L.B., Bakeman, R., Deckner, D.F., & Romski, M. (2009). Joint engagement and the emergence of language in children with autism and down syndrome. *Journal of Autism and Developmental Disorders, 39,* 84–96.

Adamson, L.B., Romski, M., Bakeman, R., & Sevcik, R.A. (2011). Augmented language intervention and the emergence of symbol-infused joint engagement. *Journal of Speech, Language, and Hearing Research, 53,* 1769-1773

Adbi, H. (2007). The Bonferonni and Sidak Corrections for Multiple Comparisons. In N. Salkind (Ed.) *Encyclopedia of Measurement and Statistics.* Thousand Oaks: Sage.

Aldred, C., Green, J., & Adams, C. (2004). A new social communication intervention for children with autism: Pilot randomized controlled treatment study suggesting effectiveness. *Journal of Child Psychology and Psychiatry, 45,* 1420–1430.

Beeghly, M., Perry, B.W., & Cicchetti, D. (1989). Structural and affective dimensions of play development in young children with Down syndrome. *International Journal of Behavioral Development, 12,* 257–277.

Benjamini, Y., & Yekutieli, D. (2001). The control of the false discovery rate in multiple testing under dependency. *The Annals of Statistics, 29,* 1165-1188.

Bondy, A., Frost, L. (2001). The picture exchange communication system. *Behavior Modification, 25,* 725–744.

Burgoyne, K., Duff, F.J., Clarke, P.J., Buckley, S., Snowling, M.J., & Hulme, C. (2012). Efficacy of a reading and language intervention for children with Down syndrome: A randomized controlled trial. *The Journal of Child Psychology and Psychiatry, 53,* 1044–1053.

Campbell, D.T., & Stanley, J.C. (1963). Experimental and Quasi-Experimental Designs for Research. Boston: Houghton Mifflin Company.

Carter, A.S., Messinger, D.S., Stone, W.L., Celimli, S., Nahmias, A.S., & Yoder, P. (2011). A randomized controlled trial of Hanen's "More Than Words" in toddlers with early autism symptoms. *Journal of Child Psychology and Psychiatry, 52,* 741–752.

Chang, C., Shih, W., & Kasari, C. (2015). Friendship in preschool children with autism spectrum disorder: What holds them back, child characteristics or teacher behavior?. *Autism.* Doi: 10.1177/1362361314567761

Chapman, R.S. (1997). Language development in children with Down syndrome. *Mental Retardation and Developmental Disabilities, 3,* 307–312.

Chapman, R.S., Seung, H., Schwartz, S.E., & Kay-Raining Bird, E. (1998). Language skills of children and adolescents with Down syndrome. *Journal of Speech, Language, and Hearing Research, 41,* 861–873.

Dawson, G., Rogers, S., Munson, J., Smith, M., Winter, J., Greenson, J., Varley, J. (2010). Randomized, controlled trial of an intervention for toddlers with autism: The Early Start Denver Model. *Pediatrics, 125,* e17–e23.

Drew, A., Baird, G., Baron-Cohen, S., Cox, A., Slonims, V., Wheelwright, S., Charman, T. (2002). A pilot randomized control trial of a parent training intervention for preschool children with autism: Preliminary findings and methodological challenges. *European Child and Adolescent Psychiatry, 11,* 266–272.

Fenson, L., Marchman, V.A., Thal, D.J., Dale, P.S., Reznick, J.S., & Bates, E. (2007). *MacArthur-Bates Communicative Development Inventories User's Guide and Technical Manual, Second Edition.* Baltimore, MD: Paul H. Brookes Publishing Co.

Fey, M.E., Warren, S.F., Brady, N., Finestock, L.H., Brendin-Oja, S.L., Fairchild, M., Yoder, P. (2006). Early effects of responsivity education/prelinguistic milieu teaching for children with developmental delays and their parents. *Journal of Speech, Language, and Hearing Research, 49,* 526–547.

Fidler, D.J. (2005). The emerging Down syndrome behavioral phenotype in early childhood: Implications for practice. *Infants and Young Children, 18,* 86–103.

Fidler, D.J., Hepburn, S., & Rogers, S. (2006). Early learning and adaptive behaviour in toddlers with Down syndrome: Evidence for an emerging behavioural phenotype. *Down Syndrome Research and Practice, 9,* 37–44.

Fidler, D.J., & Nadel, L. (2007). Education and children with Down syndrome: Neuroscience, development, and intervention. *Mental Retardation and Developmental Disabilities Research Reviews, 13,* 262–271.

Goods, K.S., Ishijima, E., Chang, Y., & Kasari, C. (2013). Preschool based JASPER intervention in minimally verbal children with autism: Pilot RCT. *Journal of Autism and Developmental Disorders, 43,* 1050–1056.

Green, J., Charman, T., McConachie, H., Aldred, C., Slonims, V., Howlin, P., the PACT Consortium. (2010). Parent-mediated communication-focused treatment in children with autism (PACT): A randomized controlled trial. *Lancet, 375,* 2152–2160.

Greenhalgh, T., & Peacock, R. (2005). Effectiveness and efficiency of search methods in systematic reviews of complex evidence: Audit of primary sources. *British Medical Journal, 331,* 1064–1065.

Howlin, P., Gordon, R.K., Pasco, G., Wade, A., & Charman, T. (2007). The effectiveness of Picture Exchange Communication System (PECS) training for teachers of children with autism: A pragmatic group randomized controlled trial. *Journal of Child Psychology and Psychiatry, 48,* 473–481.

Hudry, K., Leadbitter, K., Temple, K., Slonims, V., McConachie, H., Aldred, C., the PACT Consortium (2010). Preschoolers with autism show greater impairment in receptive compared with expressive language abilities. *International Journal of Language & Communication Disorders, 45,* 681–690. doi: 10.3109/13682820903461493

Jocelyn, L.J., Casiro, O.G., Beattie, D., Bow, J., & Kneisz, J. (1998). Treatment of children with autism: Randomized controlled trial to evaluate a caregiver-based intervention program in community day-care centers. *Developmental and Behavioral Pediatrics, 19,* 326–334.

Kaale, A., Fagerland, M.W., Martinsen, E.W., & Smith, L. (2014). Preschool-based social communication treatment for children with autism: 12 month follow-up of a randomized trial. *Journal of the American Academy of Child and Adolescent Psychiatry, 53,* 188–198.

Kaale, A., Smith, L., Sponheim, E. (2012). A randomized controlled trial of preschool-based joint attention intervention for children with autism. *The Journal of Child Psychology and Psychiatry, 53,* 97–105.

Kaiser, A.P., & Roberts, M.Y. (2013). Parent-implemented enhanced milieu teaching with preschool children who have intellectual disabilities. *Journal of Speech, Language, and Hearing Research, 56,* 295–309.

Kasari, C., & Freeman, S.F.N. (2001). Task-related social behavior in children with Down syndrome. *American Journal on Mental Retardation, 106,* 253–264.

Kasari, C., Freeman, S., & Paparella, T. (2006). Joint attention and symbolic play in young children with autism: A randomized controlled intervention study. *Journal of Child Psychology and Psychiatry, 47*(6), 611–620.

Kasari, C., Gulsrud, A., Freeman, S., Paparella, T., & Helleman, G. (2012). Longitudinal follow-up of children with autism receiving targeted interventions on joint attention and play. *Journal of the American Academy of Child and Adolescent Psychiatry, 51,* 487–495.

Kasari, C., Gulsrud, A.C., Wong, C., Kwon, S., & Locke, J. (2010). A randomized controlled caregiver mediated joint engagement intervention for toddlers with autism. *Journal of Autism and Developmental Disorders, 40,* 1045–1056.

Kasari, C., & Hodapp, R.M. (1996). Is Down syndrome different? Evidence from social and family studies. *Down Syndrome Quarterly, 1,* 1–8.

Kasari, C., Kaiser, A., Goods, K., Nietfeld, J., Mathy, P., Landa, R., Almirall, D. (2014).

Communication interventions for minimally verbal children with autism: A sequential multiple assignment randomized trial. *Journal of the American Academy of Child and Adolescent Psychiatry, 53,* 635–646.

Kasari, C., Paparella, T., Freeman, S., & Jahromi, L.B. (2008). Language outcome in autism: Randomized comparison of joint attention and play interventions. *Journal of Consulting and Clinical Psychology, 76,* 125–137.

Kasari, C., Lawton, K., Shih, W., Barker, T.V., Landa, R., Lord, C., Senturk, D. (2014). Caregiver-mediated intervention for low-resourced preschoolers with autism: An RCT. *Pediatrics, 134,* e72–e79.

Kasari, C., Shire, S.Y., Factor, R., & McCracken, C. (2014). Psychosocial treatments for individuals with autism spectrum disorder across the lifespan: New developments and underlying mechanisms. *Current Psychiatry Reports, 16,* 512–524.

Kasari, C., & Sigman, M. (1996). Expression and understanding of emotion in atypical development: Autism and Down syndrome. In M. Lewis & M. Sullivan (Eds.), *Emotional development in atypical populations* (pp. 109–130). Mahwah, NJ: Lawrence Erlbaum Associates.

Kasari, C., Sigman, M., Mundy, P., & Yirmiya, N. (1990). Affective sharing in the context of joint attention interactions of normal, autistic, and mentally retarded children. *Journal of Autism and Developmental Disabilities, 20,* 87–100.

Kasari, C., Siller, M., Huynh, L.N., Shih, W., Swanson, M., Hellemann, G.S., & Sugar, C.A. (2014). Randomized controlled trial of parental responsiveness intervention for toddlers at high risk for autism. *Infant Behavior and Development, 37,* 711–721.

Krakow, J.B., & Kopp, C.B. (1983). The effects of developmental delay on sustained attention in young children. *Child Development, 54,* 1143–1155.

Landa, R.J., Holman, K.C., O'Neil, A.H., & Stuart, E.A. (2011). Intervention targeting development of social synchronous engagement in toddlers with autism spectrum disorder: A randomized controlled trial. *Journal of Child Psychology and Psychiatry, 52,* 13–21.

Lawton, K., & Kasari, C. (2012). Teacher-implemented joint attention intervention: Pilot randomized controlled study for preschoolers with autism. *Journal of Consulting and Clinical Psychology, 80,* 687–693.

Lender, J.L., Goodman, J.F., & Linn, G.I. (1998). Repetitive activity in the play of children with mental retardation. *Journal of Early Intervention, 21,* 308–322.

Lifter, K., Sulzer-Azaroff, B., Anderson, S.R., & Cowdery, G.E. (1993). Teaching play activities to preschool children with disabilities: The importance of developmental considerations. *Journal of Early Intervention, 17,* 139–159.

Linn, M.I., Goodman, J.F., & Lender, W.L. (2000). Played out? Passive behavior by children with Down syndrome during unstructured play. *Journal of early Intervention, 23,* 264–278.

Logan, L.R., Hickman, R.R., Harris, S.R., & Heriza, C.B. (2008). Single-subject research design: Recommendations for levels of evidence and quality rating. *Developmental Medicine and Child Neurology, 50,* 99–103.

Lord, C., Risi, S., Lambrecht, L., Cook, E.H., Leventhal, B.L., DiLavore, P.C., Rutter, M. (2000). The autism diagnostic observation schedule-generic: A standard measure of social communication deficits associated with the spectrum of autism. *Journal of Autism and Developmental Disorders, 30,* 205–223.

McConachie, H., Randle, V., Hammal, D., & Le Couteur, A. (2005). A controlled trial of a training course for parents of children with suspected autism spectrum disorder. *Journal of Pediatrics, 147,* 335–340.

Mundy, P., Sigman, M., & Kasari, C. (1990). A longitudinal study of joint attention and language development in autistic children. *Journal of Autism and Developmental Disabilities, 20,* 115–128.

Mundy, P., Sigman, M., Kasari, C., & Yirmiya, N. (1988). Nonverbal communication skills in Down syndrome children. *Child Development, 59,* 235–249.

Oosterling, I., Visser, J., Swinkels, S., Rommelse, N., Donders, R., Woudenberg, T., Buitelaar, J. (2010). Randomized controlled trial of the focus parent training for toddlers with autism: One-year outcome. *Journal of Autism and Developmental Disorders, 40,* 1447–1458.

Paul, R., Campbell, D., Gilbert, K., & Tsiouri, I. (2014). Comparing spoken language treatments for preschoolers with autism spectrum disorder. *Journal of Autism and*

Developmental Disorders. doi: 10.1007/s10803-012-1583-z.

Piaget, J., & Inhelder, B. (1969). *The psychology of the child*. New York, NY: Basic Books.

Piantadosi, S. (1990). Hazards of small clinical trials. *Journal of Clinical Oncology, 8,* 1–3.

Piper, M.C., & Pless, I.B. (1980). Intervention for infants with Down syndrome: A controlled trial. *Pediatrics, 65,* 463–468.

Pitcairn, T.K., & Wishart, J.G. (1994). Reactions of young children with Down syndrome to an impossible task. *British Journal of Developmental Psychology, 12,* 485–489.

Reynell, J., & Gruber, C.P. (1990). *Reynell Developmental Language Scales: Manual.* Los Angeles, CA: Western Psychological Services.

Rice, M.L., Warren, S.F., & Betz, S.K. (2005). Language symptoms of developmental language disorders: An overview of autism, Down syndrome, fragile X, specific language impairment, and Williams syndrome. *Applied Psycholinguistics, 26,* 7–27.

Robins, D.L., Fein, D., Barton, M.L., & Green, J.A. (2001). The modified checklist for autism in toddlers: An initial study investigating the early detection of autism and pervasive developmental disorders. *Journal of Autism and Developmental Disorders, 31,* 131–144.

Romski, M., Sevcik, R.A., Adamson, L.B., Cheslock, M., Smith, A., Barker, R.M., & Bakeman, R. (2010). Randomized comparison of augmented and non-augmented language interventions for toddler with developmental delays and their parents. *Journal of Speech, Language, and Hearing Research, 53,* 350–364.

Roux, G., Sofronoff, K., & Sanders, M. (2013). A randomized controlled trial of group stepping stones triple P: A mixed-disability trial. *Family Process, 52,* 411–424.

Rutherford, M.D., Young, G.S., Hepburn, S., & Rogers, S.J. (2007). A longitudinal study of pretend play in autism. *Journal of Autism and Developmental Disorders, 37,* 1024–1039.

Sigman, M., Mundy, P., Sherman, T., & Ungerer, J. (1986). Social interactions of autistic, mentally retarded and normal children and their caregivers. *Journal of Child Psychology and Psychiatry, 27,* 647–656.

Smith, T., Groen, A.D., & Wynn, J.W. (2000). Randomized trial of intensive early intervention for children with pervasive developmental disorder. *American Journal on Mental Retardation, 105,* 269–285.

Strain, P.S., & Bovey, E.H. (2011). Randomized, controlled trial of the LEAP model of early intervention for young children with autism spectrum disorders. *Topics in Early Childhood Special Education, 31,* 133–154.

Tager-Flusberg, H., & Kasari, C. (2013). Minimally verbal school-age children with autism: The neglected end of the spectrum. *Autism Research, 6,* 468–478.

Tager-Flusberg, H., Paul, R., & Lord, C. (2005). Language and communication in autism. *Handbook of Autism and Pervasive Developmental Disorders, 1,* 335–364.

Vygotsky, L.S. (1980). *Mind in society: The development of higher psychological processes.* Cambridge, MA: Harvard University Press.

Walden, T., Blackford, J., & Carpenter, K.L. (1997). Differences in social signals produced by children with developmental disabilities. *American Journal on Mental Retardation, 102,* 292–305.

Wetherby, A., Guthrie, W., Woods, J., Schatschneider, C., Holland, R.D., Morgan, L., & Lord, C. (2014). Parent-implemented social intervention for toddlers with autism: An RCT. *Pediatrics, 134,* 1–10.

Weismer, S.E., Lord, C., & Esler, A. (2010). Early language patterns of toddlers on the autism spectrum compared to toddlers with developmental delay. *Journal of Autism and Developmental Disorders, 40,* 1259–1273.

Wong, V.C., & Kwan, Q.K. (2010). Randomized controlled trial for early intervention for autism: A pilot study of the autism 1-2-3 project. *Journal of Autism and Developmental Disorders, 40,* 677–688.

Wong, C.S. (2013). A play and joint attention intervention for teachers of young children with autism: A randomized controlled pilot study. *Autism, 17,* 340–357.

Yoder, P., & Stone, W.L. (2006). Randomized comparison of two communication interventions for preschoolers with autism spectrum disorders. *Journal of Consulting and Clinical Psychology, 74,* 426–435.

Yoder, P., & Warren, S. (2002). Effects of prelinguistic milieu teaching and parent responsivity education on dyads involving children with intellectual disabilities. *Journal of Speech, Language, and Hearing Research, 45,* 1158–1174.

Yoder, P., Woynaroski, T., Fey, M., & Warren, S. (2014). Effects of dose frequency of early communication intervention in young children with and without Down syndrome. *American Journal on Intellectual and Developmental Disabilities, 119,* 17–32.

Zimmerman, I.L., Steiner, V.G., & Pond, R.E. (2002). *Preschool language scale* (Vol. 3). San Antonio, TX: Psychological Corporation.

6

Augmented Language Interventions for Children with Severe Disabilities

Ashlyn L. Smith, R. Michael Barker, Andrea Barton-Hulsey, MaryAnn Romski, and Rose A. Sevcik

Children with severe disabilities who use augmentative and alternative communication (AAC) are a very heterogeneous group that comprise a range of medical etiologies, can exhibit mild to significant intellectual and developmental disability (IDD), and have a range of physical abilities. Despite the heterogeneity of this group of children, a hallmark feature for many children with a severe disability is great difficulty acquiring language and communication skills. Children are often identified by their communication profile rather than their medical etiology because of this range in etiologies. Although many children with severe disabilities learn to speak, there are some children who either do not develop speech even after extensive language intervention efforts or who have difficulty using speech to meet all of their communication needs. Significant delays in communication can affect all aspects of a child's development. Therefore, interventions that incorporate the use of AAC strategies can address the communication needs of children who cannot consistently rely on speech for communication. This chapter begins with a case example of a young girl's experience with an AAC intervention.

Emily

Emily was a 27-month-old girl with a diagnosis of Down syndrome (DS). Emily and her mother were participants in a longitudinal study in which children and a participating parent were randomly assigned to one of three parent-coached language interventions; two that involved an augmented component with the incorporation of a speech-generating device (SGD) and one that incorporated spoken language intervention components. At the

A preliminary version of the material in this chapter was presented at the National Joint Committee for the Communication Needs of Persons with Severe Disabilities Research Conference, Atlanta, GA (2011, June), by MaryAnn Romski.

beginning of the intervention, Emily exhibited expressive and receptive language skills of 16 and 20 months, respectively, on a standardized language assessment. Emily's mother reported on a parent-report vocabulary checklist that Emily had nine intelligible spoken words, understood 46 words, and used 16 signs. She had hearing and vision within normal limits. She was receiving speech-language therapy through the early intervention program provided by her state of residence. Emily and her mother participated in the augmented communication input (AC-I) intervention in which the interventionist (and later the parent) provided communication input to the child using the SGD and the verbal modality. The input was vocabulary models to the child using the SGD with visual-graphics symbols positioned in the environment to mark referents. The vocabulary models were an individualized set of vocabulary with visual graphic symbols and spoken words (chosen by her parent and speech-language pathologist [SLP]) that Emily did not say or understand. Emily had 19 total vocabulary words that were available to her on the SGD during the course of the intervention. The intervention consisted of 24 sessions. Eighteen sessions took place in the laboratory setting, and six sessions took place in the child's home so that the parent could generalize the strategies to routines at home. Sessions were 30 minutes in length and consisted of three 10-minute blocks of play, book reading, and snack, in that specific order.

Emily had made significant gains in her speech and language skills at the conclusion of the 24-session intervention. Analysis and coding of the session transcripts indicated that she independently used 7 of the 19 symbols (37%) on her device during session 24. Although her mean length of utterance remained below 1, her proportion of intelligible utterances increased from 0.05 at baseline to 0.14 at session 24, her utterance rate increased from 2.67 utterances per minute to 7.57 utterances per minute, and her total communicative turns increased from 76 to 193. Emily also made gains on the standardized measures of vocabulary and language. She made gains of 8 months and 4 months on receptive and expressive language, respectively, on the Sequenced Inventory of Communication Development (SICD; Hedrick, Prather, & Tobin, 2000). Emily's mother reported on the MacArthur-Bates Communication Development Inventory (MB-CDI; Fenson et al., 2006), a parent-report vocabulary checklist, that Emily had 46 intelligible spoken words and understood 254 words. Of these 254 words that Emily understood, 13 were words that were part of her target vocabulary set that included 19 words that she did not understand or say prior to the intervention. In addition, Emily's mother was able to successfully learn the intervention strategies, apply them with fidelity in interactions with Emily, and maintain the use of the strategies when the intervention was transitioned to the home environment. This intervention was successful for not only teaching Emily how to use her SGD for communication, but it also facilitated communication interaction between Emily and her mother.

AAC strategies can provide both input and output modes for the child as well as intervention techniques that are tailored to the child's developmental level. Augmented language interventions can incorporate a wide range of strategies including unaided modes of communication, such as gestures and manual signs, and aided modes of communication, such as communication boards and SGDs. This chapter explores the historical summary and provides a contemporary review of the empirical research base for augmented language interventions for children with severe disabilities with a focus on research from the year 2000 to the present.

It also discusses research design challenges and measurement issues when conducting AAC intervention studies. Finally, the chapter explores future areas of research that will be important to address in order to maximize intervention outcomes for children with severe disabilities.

REVIEWS OF THE LITERATURE

Three literature reviews were published that addressed studies conducted from 1992 to 2009. Recent reviews of the literature have provided evidence for where the field now stands in terms of findings from AAC interventions.

Snell, Chen, and Hoover (2006) examined 40 studies using single-subject experimental design between 1997 and 2003 on AAC communication interventions for individuals with severe disabilities from birth to 21 years of age. *Severe disability* was defined in this review as severe to profound intellectual disability (ID) alone or in combination with additional disabilities such as autism, or young children who demonstrated extensive developmental delays but lacked a specific diagnosis. They found that the greatest improvements in AAC communication occurred when a variety of child-directed antecedents (prompting, proximity, enhancing motivation, creating opportunities) were used in combination with consequences (specific and contingent reinforcement).

Lancioni et al. (2007) examined 37 studies conducted between 1992 and 2006 for effectiveness of the Picture Exchange Communication System (PECS) and voice output communication aid (VOCA) approaches for requesting with students who had developmental disabilities (ID, autism, pervasive intellectual and behavior disorder). Seventeen of the studies used PECS and found that out of 173 participants, all but three were able to succeed in learning the PECS strategies. Sixteen studies used VOCAs and found that out of 39 participants, all but three showed various levels of success. Participants specifically showed increases in learning to use a single message to request a single item or use a variety of messages to request preferred items. Four studies compared the use of PECS versus VOCAs and found that all 11 students experienced some level of success, regardless of the mode. More specifically, all students were able to acquire requesting skills in both modes, with acquisition rates favoring PECS in only one study. Students varied in the degree to which they preferred the VOCA or PECS.

Rispoli, Franco, van der Meer, Lang, and Camargo (2010) reviewed 35 studies from 1992 to 2009 that specifically examined the use of SGDs in communication interventions for children and adults with IDD. For the purposes of this chapter, we only examined the findings from the studies that specifically focused on children ($n = 75$). The results were generally positive for these 75 children. Children learned to use the SGDs to request preferred items, help, and attention; label actions and objects; and participate in social interactions.

As a whole, these reviews of AAC intervention research did not differentiate between children with autism and those with other IDD and used samples of children that were heterogeneous in terms of the severity of disability. In addition, they were all single-subject design studies and primarily used school-age children (age range from 2 to 21 years). Regardless, findings from these studies indicate that there is evidence for the effectiveness of AAC interventions in teaching requesting and, to a lesser extent, labeling and social-communication.

This chapter aims to add to the previous intervention reviews by examining studies employing AAC interventions targeted for children with severe disabilities from 2000 to 2014. A search of the literature revealed a total of 18 studies using a variety of research designs during this time period that were specifically communication intervention studies using AAC for children with severe disabilities. Table 6.1 summarizes participants, procedures, and results for all studies included in this chapter. The studies chosen for this chapter were identified using the Google Scholar search engine (scholar.google.com). Google scholar searches the Internet for journal articles, theses, dissertations, abstracts, and books contained in multiple databases from a single web page. This included the full catalog of holdings of two universities, numerous databases (e.g., Education Resources Information Center, EBSCO host, PsycINFO, and MEDLINE), and journal publishers' web sites (e.g., *Augmentative and Alternative Communication, Journal of Speech, Language, and Hearing Research*). We searched for the following terms: *augmentative and alternative communication, AAC, speech-generating device, SGD, voice output communication aid, VOCA, intervention, or intellectual or developmental disabilities.* In addition, we investigated the reference lists of articles that fit our search criteria for articles that may not have been found in the online search. The studies had to meet the following criteria in order to be included in this review: 1) include children with a diagnosed IDD, 2) include participants who had a severe speech impairment requiring the use of AAC, and 3) include a systematic intervention with measurable outcomes prior to and at the conclusion of the intervention.

A review of the studies revealed that the interventions in these studies focused on teaching the communicative function of requesting (n = 11), using aided language stimulation (n = 4) as a general strategy to learn to use AAC systems, or teaching specific target vocabulary (n = 3). By focusing our discussion on children with severe disabilities and these types of interventions, we will take a more specific look at methodological issues that surround conducting interventions with this population and provide directions for future intervention research.

TEACHING THE COMMUNICATIVE FUNCTION OF REQUESTING

The ability to request a preferred item is an important task for any child to learn. It is the earliest communication function to emerge in children who are typically developing (Bruner, 1983). Children who have difficulties with communication may use prelinguistic forms of communication such as pointing, reaching, eye gaze, or facial expressions to request a preferred item. These types of behaviors, however, are often difficult to interpret or may be unclear. This, in turn, may lead the child to exhibit difficult or challenging behaviors when his or her requests are not understood. Having access to an AAC mode of communication can help the child not only have his or her requests understood but also progress beyond prelinguistic forms of communication.

Participants and Procedures

Children who participated in the 11 studies reviewed and focused on requesting ranged from 2 to 18 years of age. Sixty-six children with severe disabilities were included in the studies that examined requesting; although 41 were in the same study (Rowland & Schweigert, 2000). The children in these studies had a variety

Table 6.1. Summary of augmentative and alternative communication included intervention studies

Citation	Participant characteristics	Intervention target	Intervention procedures	Results
Barton, Sevcik, and Romski (2006)	4 males, ranging from 2 years, 4 months to 3 years 8 months; significant speech-language delays (1 year behind CA on SICD)	Teaching vocabulary (e.g., six words that children did not comprehend)	Acquire meanings of iconic Blissymbols and arbitrary Lexigrams via observational experiential language intervention; 8 sessions over 4 weeks for a total of 96 experiences per symbol; comprehension and production assessed after 2, 4, 6, and 8 sessions	In production, all 4 participants demonstrated symbol–referent relationships. In comprehension, 3 of the 4 demonstrated emerging symbol–referent relationships. No differences according to iconicity of symbol.
Brady (2000)	1 female (5 years), 1 male (5 years, 11 months) with severe cognitive disabilities and limited expressive language (assessed at 20 months)	Requesting preferred items using VOCA and improving comprehension for object names	Case study design completed in a small room at participants' public school classroom; graphic symbols of vocabulary items placed on a VOCA (switches); teaching occurred in a joint activity routine with requesting opportunities provided throughout; comprehension probes administered periodically; criterion for acquisition was 90% unprompted responses over three consecutive sessions	The female participant met criterion after 11 sessions for the glitter activity and after 13 sessions for snack activity. Her comprehension also improved. The male participant met criterion after 30 sessions in the tape player routine and after 5 sessions in the glitter activity. His comprehension also improved.
Bruno and Trembath (2007)	9 children, ranging from 4 years, 8 months to 14 years, 5 months; all had complex communication needs	Aided language stimulation to compare SGD versus communication board on complexity of aided messages independently composed	Two 45-minutes sessions per day for 5 consecutive days; interventionists modeled messages that were one step more advanced than his or her mean modeled message length in each condition	Younger participants made greater gains in complexity of aided messages. Participants with less augmentative and alternative communication (AAC) experience performed better when using communication board over SGD.
Cosbey and Johnston (2006)	3 females, ranging from 3 years, 6 months to 6 years, 6 months, severe, multiple disabilities (no functional verbal communication)	Requesting access to preferred items or peers using VOCA	Multiple-baseline design implemented each day participant was in school during free-choice activities in the classroom; Step 1: opportunities for social interaction created by identifying high-interest objects; Step 2: activation of VOCA to request access to preferred item or peer with assistance from interventionist; Step 3: interventionist inserted time delay to allow participant to independently request	All three participants exhibited increase in correct, unprompted VOCA use. Peers responded to participants with either positive or neutral responses.

(continued)

Table 6.1. *(continued)*

Citation	Participant characteristics	Intervention target	Intervention procedures	Results
Dada and Alant (2009)	1 male, 3 females; ranging from 8 years, 1 month to 12 years, 1 month; significant speech-language impairment (fewer than 15 intelligible words)	Aided language stimulation for acquisition of target vocabulary items	Single-subject multiple-probe design across three activities with eight vocabulary items taught within each activity: arts and crafts, food preparation, and storytime; sessions took place at school every day for a total of 3 weeks.	All four participants acquired the target vocabulary items but differed in the rate of acquisition.
DiCarlo and Banajee (2000)	2 males; 24 and 28 months of age; significant speech-language impairment (expressive language scores 6–8 months for P1 and 3–5 months for P2)	Requesting; use of VOCA to initiate communicative behaviors to gain attention or objects	Single-subject multiple-baseline design during snack time; data was collected over a 4-month period that consisted of 24 20-minute sessions; each communicative behavior recorded one time during each 30-second interval	Both participants increased their initiations. Unclear initiations and adult-prompted communication behaviors decreased when VOCAs were used.
Drager et al. (2006)	1 male (4 years), 1 female (4 years, 5 months); significant speech-language impairment (fewer than 30 functional words)	Aided language modeling on symbol comprehension and expression of target vocabulary items	Single-subject multiple-baseline design across three activities individually chosen for each participant with four vocabulary words in each activity; sessions occurred at the child care center attended by both children; sessions conducted twice a week over 5 months for a total of 37 sessions	Both participants demonstrated increased symbol comprehension and elicited symbol production. Symbol production lagged behind symbol comprehension for both children.
Dyches, Davis, Lucido, and Young (2002)	1 female (17 years); one or two functional words	Requesting preferred items (i.e., "have," "want," "French fries," "chicken nuggets")	Single-subject alternating treatments design using a communication board in one treatment and a VOCA in second treatment, with 11 symbols on each; sessions conducted in self-contained school and during community outings; 7 trials for each mode over course of 7 days (14 total sessions); 8 trials for each mode over course of a 3-week period in 16 different community facilities	Participant learned to use both communication systems when prompting was faded across 14 training sessions. The participant was able to generalize these skills to community settings, but not all interactions were effective.

Harding, Lindsay, O'Brien, Dipper, and Wright (2011)	2 males (6 years, 2 months and 6 years 4 months) with profound and multiple disabilities; nonverbal with gestures and a range of vocalizations to communicate	Requesting to make choices for preferred items (e.g., bubbles, balloons)	Intervention took place for 5 weeks within the classroom during music, free play, and lunchtime (30-minutes per day each) with teacher and speech-language pathologist. In addition, researchers worked with each child twice a week for 30 minutes within the classroom context.	Both participants learned to make independent choices for preferred items with less reliance on physical and verbal prompting.
Harris and Reichle (2004)	2 females, 1 male (ranging from 3 years, 10 months to 5 years, 4 months) with moderate cognitive disabilities who were functionally nonspeaking (fewer than 30 words)	Aided language stimulation to increase symbol comprehension and production (object labeling)	Single-subject multiple-probe design across three symbol sets and activities; sessions took place over the course of an academic year and summer session; at school during the year and at home or child care during vacation and summer session	All three participants demonstrated increases in symbol comprehension and production, but the rates differed for each participant.
Lancioni, O'Reilly, Oliva, and Coppa (2001)	2 males (9 years, 7 months and 13 years, 3 months) with severe and multiple disabilities and no speech	Requesting for preferred items using microswitches (e.g., music and songs, animal sounds, foods, kisses)	Single-subject modified multiple-probe design; sessions took place in rehabilitation center four to six times per day for 10 minutes each; items and events were chosen based on individual responses prior to intervention	Both participants were successfully able to use microswitches (either individually or in combinations of two or three) to obtain a variety of positive environmental events.
Lancioni et al., (2006)	1 male (9 years, 2 months) and one female (12 years, 3 months) with severe to profound intellectual disability (ID) and no speech	Requesting preferred (e.g., potato chips, music) and nonpreferred (e.g., clip on hair, cola drink) stimuli using yes/no responses via a microswitch	Single-subject multiple-probe design across stimuli; intervention continued until child exceeded 85% correct responding over set of 80 trials	The male participant showed fewer correct responses during baseline and a greater number of intervention trials to reach criterion compared with the female participant.
Lancioni et al. (2008)	One male (16 years) and one female (18 years) with profound ID and no speech	Requesting preferred stimuli (e.g., songs, familiar objects, familiar voices) using microswitches and requesting social contact using a VOCA	Single-subject modified multiple-probe design across responses; intervention consisted of four to eight 10-minute sessions per day until participant acquired the skill	Both participants learned to use the microswitches to request preferred items and the VOCA to request social contact consistently when all three were simultaneously available.

(continued)

Table 6.1. *(continued)*

Citation	Participant characteristics	Intervention target	Intervention procedures	Results
Romski et al. (2010)	62 children (*M* = 29.60 months) with developmental delay and fewer than 10 spoken words	Teaching target vocabulary that children did not comprehend or speak; vocabulary individualized for each child	Each child and his or her parent randomly assigned to one of three parent-coached language interventions (augmented input, augmented output, spoken communication); 24 intervention sessions (18 in the lab, 6 at home) that were 30 minutes in length with three 10-minute blocks of play, book reading, and snack	Children in the two augmented intervention groups used augmented and spoken words for target vocabulary, with children in the augmented output condition making the greatest gains. Children in the spoken intervention produced fewer spoken words. Children in the augmented conditions had a larger overall vocabulary size.
Rowland and Schweigert (2000)	41 children (*M* = 6 years) with a range of intellectual and developmental disabilities (IDD) and 10 or fewer abstract symbols for expressive communication and little, if any, conventional communication skills	Requesting for preferred items individualized for each child using tangible symbols	Pre-post descriptive design with intervention provided for 6.5 months on average, with one-to-one instruction from project staff for one activity that lasted 15–20 minutes out of every day that participant attended school; intervention approaches were prescribed and individualized but provided in a naturalistic and spontaneous manner during motivating activities	35 of 41 participants learned to use tangible symbols to request items, and 10 participants progressed beyond tangible symbols and learned how to use abstract symbol systems including speech.
Rudd, Grove, and Pring (2007)	8 children, ranging from 6 years, 11 months to 10 years, 11 months with moderate to severe ID with poor speech intelligibility	Requesting for preferred items using modified signs (e.g., house, ball, circle, walk)	Pre-post descriptive design in which participants were seen in pairs in 12 30-minute intervention sessions twice a week for 6 weeks; modified signs were taught in pairs, with a new sign paired with one that had just been taught; children were taught to modify signs through modeling, imitation with or without physical guidance, questions, and elicitation of signs	All children were able to learn modified signs to request. Productive use of these signs in a generative and consistent way occurred at postintervention for seven of eight children.

Sevcik, Romksi, and Adamson (2004)	1 male child (4 years) with severe developmental delays who had little functional speech	Teaching 34 vocabulary items based on parent's perception of child and his communication needs using the System for Augmenting Language (SAL)	Case study design; 30-minute videotaped samples of communicative interaction obtained before and after introduction of the SAL; videotapes were coded for child engagement state, child communicative events, and adult spoken/augmented communicative input; parents also kept diary of vocabulary and communicative use at home after introduction of SAL	Child engagement state was stable in the therapy setting and increased at home. Child communicative attempts increased following introduction of AAC system.
Sigafoos and Drasgow (2001)	1 male (14 years) with moderate to severe ID and communication impairment (expressive speech limited to a few single words used infrequently)	Teaching the child to request for more of reinforcing item using the aided device when it was present and signs when it was not	Single-subject ABCD design; baseline phase (A) followed by acquisition training for both manual sign (B) and VOCA (C), VOCA present versus VOCA absent (D); two clinical sessions lasting about 90 minutes each; each session involved three activities; intervention conducted in a therapy room; sessions coded for four target behaviors: reaching for preferred item, aided requesting with VOCA, manual signing, or speech	Participant learned to request using both manual signs and the VOCA. During the final phase of the intervention, the participant learned to conditionally discriminate and always used manual sign when VOCA was absent and used the VOCA when it was present.

Note: CA = chronological age; VOCA = Voice Output Communication Aid; SGD = Speech Generating Device; SICD = Sequenced Inventory of Communication Development of disability diagnoses, including cerebral palsy, Angelman syndrome, severe ID, motor impairments, vision/hearing impairment, chromosomal abnormality, DS, Smith-Magenis syndrome, or disorder of unknown origin. There was considerable variability across studies in how the cognitive skills of the participants were reported. DiCarlo and Banajee (2000) reported that a 2-year, 4-months-old participant had cognitive skills in the 16–19 months range and a 2-year-old participant had cognitive skills in the 6–8 month range. Brady (2000) reported that one 5-year-old participant had an age equivalent of 18 months on the Bayley Scales of Infant Development (Bayley, 1993), according to school records. All other studies did not report formal cognitive skill scores other than to describe their participants as having cognitive delays (Cosbey & Johnston, 2006; Rowland & Schweigert, 2000) or moderate to profound ID (Dyches, Davis, Lucido, & Young, 2002; Lancioni et al., 2006, 2008; Lancioni, O'Reilly, Oliva, & Coppa, 2001; Rudd, Grove, & Pring, 2007; Sigafoos & Drasgow, 2001). Although they did not report formal cognitive scores, Rowland and Schweigert (2000) reported Communication Matrix levels on all their participants. This measure provided a sense of how children were doing developmentally (see Chapter 4), and they reported that the majority of children exhibited intentional behavior and intentional presymbolic communicative behavior (unconventional). A minority of the children exhibited intentional presymbolic communicative behavior (conventional) and used concrete or tangible symbols.

Similar variability existed in how studies reported the receptive and expressive language skills of their participants. The work of Lancioni and colleagues (2001, 2006, 2008) did not report any formal language assessments but indicated that all of their participants were nonverbal. DiCarlo and Banajee (2000) reported results of language assessments and indicated that children were exhibiting delays on average of 12 months for receptive language and 20 months for expressive language. Rudd et al. (2007) did not report expressive language scores but indicated that children in their study were exhibiting receptive language delays of 5 years, on average. Dyches et al. (2002) did not report expressive language skills but indicated that the 17-year-old participant exhibited receptive vocabulary at the 8-year, 3-month level. Brady (2000) reported receptive language scores of 9 months and 16 months for both participants respectively, and expressive language scores of 20 months for both participants.

Other studies did not report results of language assessments but instead descriptively indicated how their participants used and understood language. Receptively, children in these studies understood some spoken words (Sigafoos & Drasgow, 2001), gestures, facial expressions, and tactile signals (Rowland & Schweigert, 2000). Expressively, children in these studies used a few single words infrequently (Sigafoos & Drasgow, 2001), used gestures and a few speech approximations (Harding, Lindsay, O'Brien, Dipper, & Wright, 2011; Rowland & Schweigert, 2000), and exhibited communicative behaviors such as crying, smiling, vocalizations used with meaning, and occasional use of simple one-word utterances (Cosbey & Johnston, 2006; Harding et al., 2011).

The majority of studies used single-subject research designs to investigate the effects of AAC interventions on teaching requesting. Descriptive pre-post designs were the exception to these research designs (Brady, 2000; Harding et al., 2011; Rowland & Schweigert, 2000; Rudd et al., 2007). Targeted requesting skills included using microswitches to activate favorite songs, familiar voices, and animal sounds and making single-word requests using an SGD, tangible symbol, or modified sign to gain access to a preferred snack, activity, or to request MORE. Intervention settings included therapy rooms at rehabilitation centers, clinics, and schools, as well as the child's home or an inclusive classroom; interventionists included trained research assistants, teachers, and trainers. There was quite a bit of variation in the length of the intervention as well as the length of sessions. Several studies included multiple (10 minutes on average) sessions per day until the child reached the set criterion, which lasted anywhere from 14 days to 6 months. Other studies carried out sessions twice a week for 4 months, 6 weeks, or until the child reached the set criterion.

Results

Results from these studies showed strong and relatively consistent results for teaching requesting using augmented means for children with severe disabilities and are in line with the findings of Snell et al. (2006) (see Brady, Snell, & McLean). Results from pre- to post-intervention indicated that the majority of participants demonstrated increases in comprehension and learned to increase their microswitch activations, increased their initiations/requests using the AAC device while simultaneously decreasing their unclear initiations/requests, learned to use tangible symbols as an effective means of communication, and learned to modify their signs to express different meanings. In addition, the use of SGDs did not inhibit vocalizations when measured, and some children exhibited significant increases in their spoken communication as evidenced by becoming more verbal in communications with both familiar and unfamiliar people (Dyches et al., 2002) or demonstrating an increase in single words that corresponded to their target words (Sigafoos & Drasgow, 2001). Rowland and Schweigert (2000) found that spoken words increased from 3 to 53 for students who began the intervention with some speech or speech approximations, and four children began to use speech as their primary mode of communication during the course of the intervention. None of the studies that examined requesting used standardized assessments to measure child outcome.

Only one of the 11 studies specifically measured generalization of outcomes (Rudd et al., 2007), whereas two studies measured maintenance of outcomes (Lancioni et al., 2008; Sigafoos & Drasgow, 2001). Rudd et al. found that all participants demonstrated generalization of a modified sign for both items that were taught and items that were not taught. Sigafoos and Drasgow included a postacquisition phase of the intervention to determine if the child was able to conditionally discriminate between the SGD and manual sign when each were available. They found that the child was able to conditionally discriminate between the two and always used a manual sign when the SGD was absent and used the SGD when it was present. Lancioni et al. (2008) assessed maintenance of the use of microswitches using a postintervention check in which participants received 12 sessions that were the same as those received during intervention, 1.5 months after the intervention. They found that maintenance of acquired skills occurred as children's performance during these sessions were comparable with those during the intervention.

IMPLEMENTING AIDED LANGUAGE STIMULATION

Aided language stimulation is an AAC strategy that can be implemented by anyone in the child's environment, including teachers, therapists, parents, or aides. It involves pointing to picture symbols on a communication board in conjunction with providing ongoing language stimulation (Beukelman & Mirenda, 2013; Goossens, 1989). The premise behind aided language stimulation is that it is not only giving the child a mode for expression of language but it can also serve as an input strategy aimed at increasing a child's language comprehension (Goossens, Jennings, & Kinahan, 2000), which is an important predictor of intervention success (Romski & Sevcik, 2003). Individuals who implement this type of AAC intervention strategy should follow certain criteria for optimal effects. First, they should provide input that has more comments than questions, which permits the child to receive more input without emphasizing output or expression from the child. Second, aided language stimulation should be provided 70% of the time, such that when the interventionist speaks a word that is represented on the communication board (or SGD), the child points to the appropriate symbol 70% of the time.

Participants and Procedures

Research on the effects of aided language stimulation has studied children between 3 and 14 years of age. Twenty children with severe disabilities have been included in four studies on the effects of aided language stimulation on both symbol comprehension and production. As with the other topics, there was considerable variability in the range of disabilities for the children included in this research. They included but were not limited to DS, cerebral palsy, autism, schizencephaly, severe developmental delay, and ID of unknown origin. Participants in these studies had fewer than 30 functional or intelligible words, and their receptive language skills ranged from being unable to achieve a basal score on tests of receptive language to scores within normal limits. There was considerable variability in how these studies reported the cognitive skills of the participants. Drager et al. (2006) reported cognitive scores and indicated that participants were exhibiting cognitive delays of 30.5 months on average. Although Harris and Reichle (2004) did not report cognitive scores, they did indicate that their participants had moderate cognitive disabilities, and Dada and Alant (2009) indicated that their participants attended a school specifically for children with cognitive impairments. Cognitive information was not reported for Bruno and Trembath (2006).

Three of these studies used a single-subject research design and one used a group design. Intervention settings included therapy rooms at school, home, child care, and on the grounds of a camp for children who used AAC. Three of these studies examined the effects of aided language stimulation using communication boards only, whereas one study examined the effects for communication boards versus SGDs (Bruno & Trembath, 2006). Interventionists for these studies included SLPs, trained experimenters, and researchers. Intervention sessions were variable, with some studies conducting sessions every day from 1 week up to 3 weeks, whereas others were conducted twice a week for 5 months (Bruno & Trembath, 2006; Dada & Alant, 2009; Drager et al., 2006). One study did not indicate an intervention length but indicated that sessions took place during the academic year as well as during the summer (Harris & Reichle, 2004).

Results

As a whole, results from these studies suggest that providing varying forms of augmented models and input increased symbol comprehension and/or production and highlighted the role of the communication partner for young children. When examining the results more closely, it is evident that there was considerable variability in individual performance. Dada and Alant (2009) found that aided language stimulation facilitated acquisition of most of the 24 target words for all three children, and the performance was maintained during weeks when aided language stimulation was stopped for a particular activity. Harris and Reichle (2004) studied three preschool children and found that two of the children had a faster rate of comprehension than production for the first two symbol sets and had an equal rate and a faster rate of acquisition for production, respectively, on the last symbol set. The third child had equal rates of comprehension and production for the first two symbol sets but had a faster rate of acquisition for comprehension on the last symbol set. Bruno and Trembath (2006) conducted a study examining improvement in syntactic performance following aided language stimulation and found that the youngest participants made the greatest gains in syntactic complexity. They also found that participants who had less overall AAC experience performed better when using the manual communication board as opposed to the SGD, due to the demands associated with constructing a sentence. Drager et al. (2006) found that when aided language stimulation was used with three activities, one child showed a lag in symbol production as compared with comprehension for all three activities, whereas the other child had less success with symbol production on the first activity but quickly exhibited success for both comprehension and production for the remaining two activities.

Two of the four studies examining aided language stimulation examined maintenance of intervention strategies. Drager et al. (2006) conducted maintenance probes after criterion was reached for each activity. They conducted three probes for comprehension of graphic/visual symbols and symbol production at the end of the children's school year. They found that one child maintained criterion-level performance for both comprehension and production, whereas the other child maintained criteria for comprehension for all but the third probe and the final two probes for production. Harris and Reichle (2004) conducted maintenance probes of both graphic and spoken symbols and found that all three children maintained performance criterion for comprehension with the exception of one child who did not maintain criterion for the first two maintenance probes for comprehension.

TEACHING VOCABULARY

Children who are at the beginning stages of communication rely primarily on nonsymbolic modes of communication, do not demonstrate communicative intentionality, and are just learning to use aided or unaided symbols (Beukelman & Mirenda, 2013). Romski, Sevcik, and Fonseca (2003) also described beginning communicators as children with a spoken and/or symbol vocabulary of fewer than 50 words. The task of learning vocabulary can be an important step in the language acquisition process for these children. Children with severe speech-language difficulties may have a hard time understanding the relationship between a symbol and its referent. AAC can be used to help children understand the symbol–referent relationship by focusing on teaching specific vocabulary that children do not yet know in order to encourage both language and vocabulary growth (Beukelman & Mirenda, 2013).

Participants and Procedures

Children who participated in the three studies focused on teaching vocabulary ranged from 2 years to 6 years of age. Sixty-seven children (62 in one study by Romski et al., 2010) participated in these three studies aimed at teaching vocabulary. Similar to other AAC intervention studies, there was considerable variability in the range of disabilities for the children included in this research. They included but were not limited to DS, cerebral palsy, autism, schizencephaly, severe physical disability, and ID of unknown origin. Participants in these studies had fewer than 10 functional or intelligible words, and their receptive language skills ranged from being unable to achieve a basal score on tests of receptive language to a standard score of 28. Cognitive skills were not available for any children, but Romski et al. (2010) reported that children received on average a composite score of 60 on the Mullen Scales of Early Learning (Mullen, 1995), which indicates the presence of a severe developmental delay.

One study employed a case study design (Sevcik, Romski, & Adamson, 2004), one used a repeated measures experimental design (Barton, Sevcik, & Romski, 2006), and one used an experimental design with children randomly assigned to one of three interventions (Romski et al., 2010). Intervention settings included therapy rooms at school, in the classroom, at the home, and in the laboratory. Interventionists for these studies included trained research assistants, learning support assistants, investigators, and SLPs. Intervention sessions were variable and ranged from eight sessions over a period of 4 weeks (Barton et al., 2006), two sessions per week for 12 weeks (Romski et al., 2010), and weekly speech therapy sessions over 9 months (Sevcik et al., 2004). Two of these studies incorporated SGDs (Romski et al., 2010; Sevcik et al., 2004) and one compared iconic Blissymbols with arbitrary lexigrams (Barton et al., 2006).

Results

Results from these studies suggest that children can successfully acquire vocabulary that was previously unknown to them. Sevcik et al. (2004) used the intervention approach known as the System for Augmenting Language (SAL; Romski & Sevcik, 1996; Romski, Sevcik, Cheslock, & Barton, 2006) and found that the child increased both the quantity and frequency of utterance attempts using the SGD over a 9-month period. In addition, parents incorporated the use of the SAL into their spoken communication, which allowed for increased engagement for both the parent and child. Barton et al. (2006) found that all four children demonstrated learning of at least one symbol that they did not previously understand, whereas three of the four children were able to both comprehend and produce at least one symbol. Children with better receptive language skills before intervention demonstrated the greatest gains in comprehension and production of learned vocabulary. This learning was demonstrated on both iconic Blissymbols and arbitrary lexigrams, indicating that symbol learning was not contingent on the iconicity of the symbols. Romski et al. (2010) found that children randomly assigned to the augmented interventions used more vocabulary words on the SGD and produced more target spoken vocabulary words for communication than children assigned to the spoken communication intervention. In addition, parents were able to successfully implement the augmented interventions, which, in turn, facilitated better parent–child interaction.

Of the three studies, one reported maintenance of intervention outcomes (Romski et al., 2010) and examined maintenance of intervention procedures and generalization to the home after 9 weeks of intervention in the lab. They found that children maintained their use of augmented words and parents maintained their implementation of intervention strategies after the intervention was generalized to the home. This finding lends further support to the idea that parent coaching can be a useful way to include parents in interventions with their children.

RESEARCH DESIGN CHALLENGES AND MEASUREMENT ISSUES

Conducting AAC intervention research is complex, and there are several challenges that make developing the evidence base difficult. First, there are issues with research design that can affect the generalizability of the findings. Individuals with severe disabilities represent a low-incidence population. The number of children in each study we reviewed was 10 or less, with a few exceptions (Romski et al., 2010; Rowland & Schweigert, 2000). It will be important to replicate and expand these studies by using larger numbers of participants, examine intervention approaches across time, and target more advanced language skills. Investigators typically use single-subject designs and pre-post designs due to the small sample sizes used in many of these studies. One approach is to scale up to randomized control studies, which are generally considered the gold standard for intervention research (Kratochwill et al., 2010), although Barker and Francis raise some questions about doing this (see Chapter 10). This can be done by employing multisite studies and carrying out work over time. It will also be useful to create a clearinghouse for data similar to the Child Language Data Exchange System (CHILDES; MacWhinney, 2000) in which researchers can pool their resources from these small studies. For example, Grela (2002) utilized data sets drawn from CHILDES to examine verb use in children with DS compared with typically developing children. Finally, very few of the studies included in this chapter reported treatment integrity/fidelity or generalization and maintenance of outcomes. It will be important to consider guidelines for reporting these aspects of AAC intervention studies as all are integral to determining if these interventions contribute to the standards for evidence-based practice.

Second, there are measurement issues that researchers must consider when conducting AAC intervention research. First, there is a need for greater consistency in reporting about an individual's language skills. The expressive language skills of the children in the studies that were included in this chapter ranged from no speech to talking. There was not a consistent description of what it meant for a child to be nonspeaking at any point in development. Some researchers described nonspeaking as fewer than 10 intelligible words, whereas others described nonspeaking as fewer than 30 intelligible words. In addition to the variability in what it means to be nonspeaking, there is also variability in the terminology used to describe this population. There is increased use of the term *minimally verbal* in the autism literature to describe children with autism who have a small repertoire of spoken words and fixed phrases used communicatively; usually fewer than 20 functional words (Kasari, Brady, Lord, & Tager-Flusberg, 2013). The term *complex communication needs* has been used in the AAC literature to describe individuals who cannot meet all of their communication needs using speech (Light & McNaughton, 2012). Although these are likely similar individuals in terms of their need for AAC, the inconsistent description of their language skills and different terms used to describe them may lead to some confusion. For example, children with some speech may be very different in terms of their language skills from those with no speech. Rowland and Schweigert (2000) found that children that began their intervention with some speech showed the greatest gains in their use of tangible symbols. Evidence in the general language intervention literature suggests that children who begin intervention with higher expressive and receptive language skills (albeit significantly delayed) and/or more sophisticated prelinguistic skills demonstrate greater language gains during intervention (Fey, Yoder, Warren, & Bredin-Oja, 2013; Kasari, Paparella, Freeman, & Jahromi, 2008; Yoder & Stone, 2006; Yoder & Warren, 2002; Yoder, Woynaroski, Fey, & Warren, 2014). In that sense, it is important to examine to whom results of these interventions apply. Having a more consistent definition of what these terms mean will permit greater generalizability across studies.

Considering the measurement tools that are chosen to describe participants prior to and following intervention also is important. Very few of the AAC intervention studies included in this chapter and in other reviews of the literature have used standardized measures to assess outcomes. Most used measures specific to the study, such as the comprehension and production of target words (either spoken or symbol), as well as frequency of initiations and requests. In a similar vein, very few studies included a description of the individual's receptive language skills. Because receptive language skills can be an important predictor of intervention success, not knowing the receptive language skills of those children who receive AAC interventions can raise questions about potential response to intervention. The relationship between comprehension and production of spoken words and symbols is a complex one that is not yet fully understood (Romski et al., 2010; Sevcik & Romski, 2002). AAC strategies can serve as a language teaching tool that can target receptive language skills and give children a foundation on which expressive communication skills can develop. These strategies illustrate the real-world meaning of symbols and the many functions they can serve (Romski & Sevcik, 2003).

Finally, ancillary outcomes of these interventions and what else should be measured in addition to child outcomes should be considered. The role of the individual's communication partners, such as parents or others in the child's environment who work with them on communication, is one such outcome. A long history of research demonstrates that parents can successfully learn to use spoken language intervention strategies with their children and positive effects can result for both parent and child (see Chapter 7; Kaiser, Hancock, & Hester, 1998; Kaiser & Hancock, 2003; Kaiser & Roberts, 2013; Yoder & Warren, 2002. There recently has been a larger focus on training parents and other communication partners to use AAC strategies with their children. The work of Binger and colleagues has demonstrated that an eight-step cognitive communication partner instruction approach can be used to successfully teach both parents (Binger, Kent-Walsh, Berens, Del Campo, & Rivera, 2008; Kent-Walsh, Binger, & Hasham, 2010) and educational assistants (Binger, Kent-Walsh, Ewing, & Taylor, 2010) to implement an AAC modeling approach using either communication boards or SGDs. In addition, children in these studies demonstrated positive outcomes such as increases in producing multisymbol messages, communicative turns, and semantic concepts.

The work of Romski and colleagues has also demonstrated that not only can parents be taught to implement intervention strategies with their children using a naturalistic parent-coaching model but that there can also be positive effects on parent stress and how parents perceive their children's language development. Romski, Sevcik, Adamson, Cheslock, and Smith (2007) demonstrated that parents can successfully learn to use augmented language intervention strategies with their children and that these strategies could be implemented with fidelity to the intervention protocol. In addition, children who participated in the AAC interventions demonstrated increases in both augmented and spoken words during the course of the intervention, and this was maintained after the intervention was transitioned to the home and implemented solely by parents (Romski et al., 2010). There are also important outcomes parents need to consider. There are decreases in parent perceptions of the severity of their children's communication difficulty (Romski et al., 2011) without accompanying increases in parent stress (Smith, Romski, Sevcik, Adamson, & Bakeman, 2011) when parents successfully learn these augmented strategies. Parents of children who had better expressive language prior to intervention perceived their children's communication difficulties as less severe and reported less parent stress following language intervention (Smith et al., 2011). There are also differences in parent outcomes based on the etiology of the children (Smith, Romski, Sevcik, Adamson, & Barker, 2014). Parents of children with DS reported lower levels of total stress, child-related stress, and stress surrounding the parent–child interaction. Parents of all children reported that they felt successful in their ability to affect their children's communication development. Parents of children with DS, however, perceived their children's communication difficulties as less severe despite similar language skills across groups. The role of the communication partner in AAC interventions cannot be understated and should be included in any AAC intervention approach. The role of social validity in assessing the effects of AAC interventions is also important (see Chapter 15). Finally, results highlight the importance of considering etiology when assisting families raising a child with a disability.

FUTURE DIRECTIONS FOR AAC INTERVENTION RESEARCH

There are many exciting new areas to develop to further increase knowledge as AAC research moves forward. Considering the contribution of different components of the intervention, such as length and intensity, is one such area. To date, AAC interventions are widely variable with respect to their length and intensity, and it is unclear as to the importance of each (see Chapter 2). Recent research has shown that intensity of intervention does not have a strong effect on child outcomes for speech-language interventions that do not include the use of AAC intervention strategies (Fey et al., 2013). It will be important to determine if the same finding applies to AAC interventions.

More direct comparisons need to be made among different AAC modes and intervention techniques, such as aided versus unaided techniques and SGD versus non–SGD interventions. Although there was considerable variation in performance, Bruno and Trembath (2006) found that gains were more pronounced when participants used a manual communication board as opposed to a dynamic display SGD. They suggested that this was related to both the demands associated with constructing the message on the SGD and the fewer opportunities to practice targeted message forms in the SGD condition. Kasari et al. (2014) found that children with autism who were minimally verbal who began intervention with an SGD integrated into a blended developmental/behavioral intervention produced more spontaneous communicative utterances, novel words, and comments than children who began the intervention without an SGD. They suggested that including an SGD at the start of intervention may provide the most benefit to children who are minimally verbal. More studies of this kind would shed greater light on the conditions under which one communication mode might be more optimal or preferred to ensure the greatest communicative success.

An enormous increase in the use of tablets and smartphones for communication has resulted in AAC being incorporated into the mainstream in a way that has never been seen before. Because they are relatively inexpensive, families can obtain these new technologies quickly without having to wait for clinical recommendations or insurance waivers (Couper et al., 2014). These devices also provide social value in that individuals can use them without appearing different from their typically developing peers (Light & McNaughton, 2012). In fact, parents and teachers report more positive perceptions about this technology as compared with other forms of AAC. They report that their children/students learn to use this technology faster and that they were superior in terms of preference and effectiveness compared with other forms of AAC (Alzrayer, Banda, & Koul, 2014). Research is only beginning to systematically examine the efficacy of using these devices as a viable mode for communication. As part of a larger review of the use of iPods and iPads, Kagohara et al. (2013) examined eight studies using these technologies that focused on teaching communication skills. They found that not only could children be successfully taught to use this technology as an SGD but that it was also a viable communication aid for individuals with disabilities because they were successfully able to use them to name pictures and gain access to preferred stimuli. In addition, these studies showed that although children did not make more requests using these technologies as compared with low-technology communication aids, they generally preferred the SGDs and demonstrated better maintenance with the SGD. They suggested that future research target purposes such as greeting, conversation, and commenting, as well as social validation. Although requesting is an important skill, it is also important that children receive intervention on these other skills in order to be successful communicators.

Further exploration into the complex relationship between language comprehension and production is another area for future research. A closer examination of the intervention studies included in this chapter indicate that children's comprehension skills may have played a role in the intervention outcomes. One of the two participants in the DiCarlo and Banjee (2000) study had higher receptive language and clearly had better initiations using AAC than the other participant with lower receptive language. They did not discuss this information in their results or discussion, however, as a possible factor in the different outcomes of the participants. Although both Dada and Alant (2009) and Bruno and Trembath (2006) stated that comprehension may have been a factor contributing to the children's performance, they did not indicate whether there were any actual differences in performance based on participants' receptive language skills. Harding et al. (2011) stated that focusing intervention around children's receptive language ability was key, but they did not discuss differences in performance. Romski et al. (2010) found that although children randomly assigned to both augmented interventions developed more augmented and spoken words than children in the spoken intervention, children who were asked to produce augmented words spoke more. This finding was counter to their hypothesis that children who received a model via augmented input would exhibit better outcomes than children who were not given that added model for comprehension. They suggested that it will be important to integrate comprehension and production into one intervention focus so that children can observe and actively engage in the communicative process. Romski et al. (in preparation) did just that in a follow-up randomized control trial. They compared the effects of the intervention that asked children to produce augmented words with a hybrid intervention that provided an augmented model and asked children to produce augmented words. They found that the hybrid intervention, which combined augmented input and output, provided the strongest use of augmented and spoken words. The second study supported and clarified the findings of Romski et al. (2010). The role of receptive language skills at the onset of intervention still requires more attention.

Bruno and Trembath (2006) did make a clear statement regarding differences in performance based on comprehension scores. They reported that the children in their study with the lowest sentence comprehension scores made fewer gains using the SGD but did better when they used the manual board for sentence production. They posited that children with lower comprehension skills may have had more trouble sequencing through levels of a dynamic display SGD versus using a manual board in which they had equal/simultaneous access to all the vocabulary. These results suggest that the relationship between comprehension and production may not be as clear cut as once thought and should be explored further so that the best way to target interventions for children with severe disabilities is better understood.

CONCLUSION

Follow-up on Emily

As discussed at the beginning of this chapter, Emily showed significant gains in her language and communication skills following her participation in a 3-month augmented language intervention. Emily had the opportunity to participate in a second study several years later to follow up on the sample of toddlers to examine their speech-language skills as they entered into school. These data reveal that at 10 years of age, Emily primarily communicated using sentences and was largely independent in her communication. She exhibited age equivalents of 7 years, 10 months and 4 years, 11 months on tests of receptive and expressive language, respectively. She was able to identify all of her letters and identify enough words on a test of reading mastery to place her at an age equivalent of 7 years, 7 months. Cognitively, Emily exhibited age equivalents of 4 years, 6 months on verbal cognition and 5 years, 6 months on nonverbal cognition. In a 10-minute interaction with her older sister, Emily's proportion of intelligible utterances was .80; she exhibited a mean length of utterance of 2.26, used 56 different words, used 5.69 utterances per minute, and exhibited 40 turns in the interaction. Although it was not possible to disentangle the effects of the intervention from later interventions Emily received or maturation during the approximately 3 months of intervention, the fact that Emily significantly improved her comprehension and production of language outside of the target vocabulary indicates that language interventions involving AAC can facilitate language skills.

The results of the studies presented in this chapter demonstrate that AAC interventions for children with severe disabilities can foster positive language and communication outcomes for children at any age and can aid development of a variety of important communicative functions that allow children with severe disabilities to more fully participate in the world around them.

REFERENCES

Alzrayer, N., Banda, D.R., & Koul, R.K. (2014). Use of iPad/iPods with individuals with autism and other developmental disabilities: A meta-analysis of communication interventions. *Review Journal of Autism and Developmental Disorders, 1,* 179–191. doi:10.1007/s40489-014-0018-5

Barton, A., Sevcik, R.A., & Romski, M.A. (2006). Exploring visual-graphic symbol acquisition by pre-school age children with developmental and language delays. *Augmentative and Alternative Communication, 22,* 10–20. doi:10.1080/07434610500238206

Bayley, N. (1993). *Bayley Scales of Infant Development* (2nd ed.). San Antonio, TX: The Psychological Corporation.

Beukelman, D.R., & Mirenda, P. (2013). *Augmentative and alternative communication: Supporting children and adults with complex communication needs* (4th ed.). Baltimore, MD: Paul H. Brookes Publishing Co.

Binger, C., Kent-Walsh, J., Berens, J., Del Campo, S., & Rivera, D. (2008). Teaching Latino parents to support the multi-symbol message productions of their children who require AAC. *Augmentative and Alternative Communication, 24,* 323–338. doi:10.1080/07434610802130978

Binger, C., Kent-Walsh, J., Ewing, C., & Taylor, S. (2010). Teaching educational assistants to facilitate the multi-symbol message productions of young students who require augmentative and alternative communication. *American Journal of Speech-Language Pathology, 19,* 108–120.

Brady, N. (2000). Improved comprehension of object names following voice output communication aid use: Two case studies. *Augmentative and Alternative Communication, 16,* 197–204.

Bruner, J. (1983). *Child's talk: Learning to use language.* London, England: Fontana.

Bruno, J., & Trembath, D. (2006). Use of aided language stimulation to improve syntactic performance during a weeklong intervention program. *Augmentative and Alternative Communication, 22,* 300–313. doi:10.1080/07434610600768318

Cosbey, J.E., & Johnston, S.S. (2006). Using a single-switch voice output communication aid to increase social access for children with severe disabilities in inclusive classrooms. *Research and Practice for Persons with Severe Disabilities, 31,* 144–156.

Couper, L., van der Meer, L., Schafer, M.C.M., McKenzie, E., McLay, L., O'Reilly, M.F., Sutherland, D. (2014). Comparing acquisition of and preference for manual signs, picture exchange, and speech-generating devices in nine children with autism spectrum disorder. *Developmental Neurorehabilitation, 17,* 99–109. doi:10.3109/17518423.2013.870244

Dada, S., & Alant, E. (2009). The effect of aided language stimulation on vocabulary acquisition in children with little or no functional speech. *American Journal of Speech-Language Pathology, 18,* 50–64.

DiCarlo, C.F., & Banajee, M. (2000). Using voice output devices to increase initiations of young children with disabilities. *Journal of Early Intervention, 23,* 191–199.

Drager, K.D., Postal, V.J., Carrolus, L., Castellano, M., Gagliano, C., & Glynn, J. (2006). The effect of aided language modeling on symbol comprehension and production in 2 preschoolers with autism. *American Journal of Speech-Language Pathology, 15,* 112–125.

Dyches, T.T., Davis, A., Lucido, B., & Young, J. (2002). Generalization of skills using pictographic and voice output communication devices. *Augmentative and Alternative Communication, 18,* 124–131.

Fenson, L., Marchman, V.A., Thal, D.J., Dale, P.S., Reznick, S.J., & Bates, E. (2006). *MacArthur-Bates Communicative Development Inventories: User's guide and technical manual, Second Edition.* Baltimore, MD: Paul H. Brookes Publishing Co.

Fey, M.E., Yoder, P.J., Warren, S.F., & Bredin-Oja, S.L. (2013). Is more better? Milieu communication teaching in toddlers with intellectual disabilities. *Journal of Speech, Language, and Hearing Research, 56,* 679. doi:10.1044/1092-4388(2012/12-0061)

Goossens, C. (1989). Aided communication intervention before assessment: A case study of a child with cerebral palsy. *Augmentative and Alternative Communication, 5*(1), 14–26. doi:10.1080/07434618912331274926

Goossens, C., Jennings, D., & Kinahan, D. (2000). *Facilitating strategies for group activities in engineered AAC classrooms.* Presented at the Preconference workshop presented at the Ninth Biennial Conference of ISAAC, Washington, DC.

Grela, B. (2002). Lexical verb diversity in children with Down syndrome. *Clinical, Linguistics, and Phonetics, 16,* 251–263. doi:10.1080/02699200210131987

Harding, C., Lindsay, G., O'Brien, A., Dipper, L., & Wright, J. (2011). Implementing AAC with children with profound and multiple learning disabilities: A study in rationale underpinning intervention. *Journal of Research in SpecialEducationalNeeds, 11,* 120–129. doi:10.1111/j.1471-3802.2010.01184.x

Harris, M.D., & Reichle, J. (2004). The impact of aided language stimulation on symbol comprehension and production in children with moderate cognitive disabilities. *American Journal of Speech-Language Pathology, 13,* 155–167.

Hedrick, D.L., Prather, E.M., & Tobin, A.R. (2000). *Sequenced Inventory of Communication Development Manual—Revised Edition.* Los Angeles, CA: Western Psychological Services.

Kagohara, D.M., van der Meer, L., Ramdoss, S., O'Reilly, M.F., Lancioni, G.E., Davis, T.N., Sigafoos, J. (2013). Using iPods and iPads in teaching programs for individuals with developmental disabilities: A systematic review. *Research in Developmental Disabilities, 34,* 147–156. doi:10.1016/j.ridd.2012.07.027

Kaiser, A.P. & Hancock, T.B. (2003). Teaching parents new skills to support their young children's development. *Infants and Young Children, 16,* 9–21.

Kaiser, A.P., Hancock, T.B., & Hester, P.P. (1998). Parents as cointerventionists: Research on applications of naturalistic language teaching procedures. *Infants and Young Children, 10*(4), 46–55.

Kaiser, A.P. & Roberts, M.Y. (2013). Parent-implemented enhanced milieu teaching with preschool children who have intellectual disabilities. *Journal of Speech Language Hearing Research, 56,* 295-309. doi: 10.1044/1092-4388(2012/11-0231

Kasari, C., Brady, N., Lord, C., & Tager-Flusberg, H. (2013). Assessing the minimally verbal school-aged child with autism spectrum disorder. *Autism Research, 6,* 479–493. doi:10.1002/aur.1334

Kasari, C., Kaiser, A., Goods, K., Nietfeld, J., Mathy, P., Landa, R., Almirall, D. (2014). Communication interventions for minimally verbal children with autism: A sequential multiple assignment randomized trial. *Journal of the American Academy of Child and Adolescent Psychiatry, 53,* 635-646. doi:10.1016/j.jaac.2014.01.019

Kasari, C., Paparella, T., Freeman, S., & Jahromi, L.B. (2008). Language outcome in autism: Randomized comparison of joint attention and play interventions. *Journal of Consulting and Clinical Psychology, 76,* 125–137. doi:10.1037/0022-006X.76.1.125

Kent-Walsh, J., Binger, C., & Hasham, Z. (2010). Effects of parent instruction on the symbolic communication of children using augmentative and alternative communication during storybook reading. *American Journal of Speech-Language Pathology, 19,* 97–107.

Kratochwill, T.R., Hitchcock, J., Horner, R.H., Levin, J.R., Odom, S.L., Rindskopf, D.M., & Shadish, W.R. (2010). *Single-case designs technical documentation.* Retrieved from http://ies.ed.gov/ncee/wwc/aboutus/

Lancioni, G.E., O'Reilly, M.F., Cuvo, A.J., Singh, N.N., Sigafoos, J., & Didden, R. (2007). PECS and VOCAs to enable students with developmental disabilities to make requests: An overview of the literature. *Research in Developmental Disabilities, 28,* 468–488. doi:10.1016/j.ridd.2006.06.003

Lancioni, G.E., O'Reilly, M.F., Oliva, D., & Coppa, M.M. (2001). Using multiple microswitches to promote different responses in children with multiple disabilities. *Research in Developmental Disabilities, 22,* 309–318. doi:10.1016/S0891-4222(01)00074-9

Lancioni, G.E., O'Reilly, M.F., Singh, N.N., Sigafoos, J., Oliva, D., & Severini, L. (2008). Enabling two persons with multiple disabilities to access environmental stimuli and ask for social contact through microswitches and a VOCA. *Research in Developmental Disabilities, 29,* 21–28. doi:10.1016/j.ridd.2006.10.001

Lancioni, G.E., Singh, N.N., O'Reilly, M.F., Sigafoos, J., Oliva, D., & Baccani, S. (2006). Teaching "yes" and "no" responses to children with multiple disabilities through a program including microswitches linked to a vocal output device. *Perceptual and Motor Skills, 102,* 51–61.

Light, J., & McNaughton, D. (2012). Supporting the communication, language, and literacy development of children with complex communication needs: State of the science and future research priorities. *Assistive Technology, 24*(1), 34–44. doi:10.1080/10400435.2011.648717

MacWhinney, B. (2000). *The CHILDES project: Tools for analyzing talk* (3rd ed.). Mahwah, NJ: Lawrence Erlbaum Associates.

Mullen, E. M. (1995). *Mullen Scales of Early Learning.* Circle Pines, MN: American Guidance Service.

Rispoli, M.J., Franco, J.H., van der Meer, L., Lang, R., & Camargo, S.P.H. (2010). The use of speech generating devices in communication interventions for individuals with developmental disabilities: A review of the literature. *Developmental Neurorehabilitation, 13,* 276–293. doi:10.3109/17518421003636794

Romski, M.A., & Sevcik, R.A. (1996). *Breaking the speech barrier.* Baltimore, MD: Paul H. Brookes Publishing Co.

Romski, M.A., & Sevcik, R.A. (2003). Augmented input: Enhancing communication development. In J.C. Light, D.R. Beukelman, & J. Reichle (Eds.), *Communicative competence for individuals who use AAC: From research to effective practice* (pp. 147-162). Baltimore, MD: Paul H. Brookes Publishing Co.

Romski, M.A., Sevcik, R.A., Adamson, L.B., Cheslock, M., & Smith, A. (2007). Parents can implement AAC interventions: Ratings of treatment implementation across early language interventions. *Early Childhood Services, 1,* 100–115.

Romski, M.A., Sevcik, R.A., Adamson, L.B., Cheslock, M., Smith, A., Barker, R.M., & Bakeman, R. (2010). Randomized comparison of augmented and nonaugmented language interventions for toddlers with developmental delays and their parents. *Journal of Speech, Language, and Hearing Research, 53,* 350–364. doi:10.1044/1092-4388(2009/08-0156)

Romski, M.A., Sevcik, R.A., Adamson, L.B., Smith, A., Cheslock, M., & Bakeman, R. (2011). Parent perceptions of the language development of toddlers with developmental delays before and after participation in parent-coached language interventions. *American Journal of Speech-Language Pathology, 20*(2), 111–118. doi:10.1044/1058-0360(2011/09-0087)

Romski, M.A., Sevcik, R.A., Cheslock, M., & Barton, A. (2006). The system for augmenting language: AAC and emerging language intervention. In R.J. McCauley & M.E. Fey (Eds.) *Treatment of language disorders in children* (pp. 123–148). Baltimore, MD: Paul H. Brookes Publishing Co.

Romski, M.A., Sevcik, R.A., & Fonseca, A.H. (2003). Augmentative and alternative communication for persons with mental retardation. In L. Abbeduto (Ed.) *International review of research in mental retardation: Language and communication* (pp. 255–280). New York: Academic Press

Rowland, C., & Schweigert, P. (2000). Tangible symbols, tangible outcomes. *Augmentative and Alternative Communication, 16,* 61–78.

Rudd, H., Grove, N., & Pring, T. (2007). Teaching productive sign modifications to children with intellectual disabilities. *Augmentative and Alternative Communication, 23,* 154–163. doi:10.1080/07434610601124867

Sevcik, R.A., & Romski, M.A. (2002). The role of language comprehension in establishing early augmented conversations. In J. Reichle, D.R. Beukelman, & J.C. Light (Eds.), *Exemplary practices for beginning communicators* (pp. 453-474). Baltimore, MD: Paul H. Brookes Publishing Co.

Sevcik, R.A., Romski, M.A., & Adamson, L.B. (2004). Research directions in augmentative and alternative communication for preschool children. *Disability and Rehabilitation, 26,* 1323–1329. doi:10.1080/09638280412331280352

Sigafoos, J., & Drasgow, E. (2001). Conditional use of aided and unaided AAC: A review and clinical case demonstration. *Focus on Autism and Other Developmental Disabilities, 14,* 152–161. doi:10.1177/108835760101600303

Smith, A., Romski, M.A., Sevcik, R.A., Adamson, L.B., & Bakeman, R. (2011). Parent stress and its relation to parent perceptions of communication following parent-coached language intervention. *Journal of Early Intervention, 33,* 135–150.

Smith, A., Romski, M., Sevcik, R.A., Adamson, L.B., & Barker, R.M. (2014). Parent stress and perceptions of language development: Comparing Down syndrome and other developmental disabilities. *Family Relations, 63,* 71–84. doi:10.1111/fare.12048

Snell, M.E., Chen, L.-Y., & Hoover, K. (2006). Teaching augmentative and alternative communication to students with severe disabilities: A review of intervention research. *Research and Practice for Persons with Severe Disabilities, 31,* 203–214.

Yoder, P.J., & Stone, W.L. (2006). A randomized comparison of the effect of two prelinguistic communication interventions on the acquisition of spoken communication in preschoolers with ASD. *Journal of Speech, Language, and Hearing Research, 49,* 698–711.

Yoder, P.J., & Warren, S.F. (2002). Effects of prelinguistic milieu teaching and parent responsivity education on dyads involving children with intellectual disabilities. *Journal of Speech, Language, and Hearing Research, 45,* 1158–1174.

Yoder, P.J., Woynaroski, T., Fey, M., & Warren, S. (2014). Effects of dose frequency of early communication intervention in young children with and without Down syndrome. *American Journal on Intellectual and Developmental Disabilities, 119,* 17–32. doi:10.1352/1944-7558-119.1.17

7

Parents as Partners in Effective Communication Intervention

Ann P. Kaiser, Lauren H. Hampton, and Megan Y. Roberts

Including parents in their children's communication intervention is not a new idea. Beginning in the 1980s, researchers and clinicians argued that parents should be included as powerful and important partners in interventions to improve language and communication outcomes for children with developmental disabilities (MacDonald, 1989). An environmental systems perspective strongly supports the inclusion of partners in children's everyday lives as part of a comprehensive approach to early communication intervention (Kaiser, 1993). Research, both randomized controlled trial (RCTs) and single-case design studies, demonstrating the effectiveness of parent-implemented intervention in improving child outcomes has expanded since the mid-2000s (Barton & Fettig, 2013; Roberts & Kaiser, 2011).

In this context, the key question about including parents as partners in their children's communication intervention has shifted from "Can including parents in communication intervention improve child outcomes?" to "How can we maximize the impact of including parents in intervention?" This shift in perspective has been supported by research that indicates parental responsiveness improves child outcomes from therapist-provided naturalistic intervention (Yoder & Warren, 1998) as well as research reporting improved generalized and maintained child outcomes of intervention when parents are trained (Roberts & Kaiser, 2012). In addition, there is increasing evidence that systematic adult teaching can ensure that parents deliver intervention with a high degree of fidelity and that fidelity of intervention is related to child outcomes (Roberts & Kaiser, 2015; Walker, Carta, Greenwood, & Buzhardt, 2008). As a result, new approaches to parent training focus on documenting the methods for training, measuring fidelity of parent implementation, and increasing the efficiency of parent training. These include hybrid treatments, such as parent plus therapist and parent training as part of a comprehensive intervention to provide optimal support

Preparation of this manuscript was supported in part by grants from HRSA 117453 (2014–2017), NIH HD073975 (2012–2017), John Merck Foundation (2014–2018), IES R324A090181 (2009–2013), IES H325D100034A (2011–2014).

for children's communication (Kaiser & Roberts, 2013b), and technology-based strategies to increase the efficiency as well as effectiveness of teaching parents to support their children's communication (Marturana & Woods, 2012).

This chapter provides a contemporary perspective on including parents in interventions to promote their children's communication development framed primarily around research on naturalistic language intervention, particularly enhanced milieu teaching (EMT; Kaiser, 1993). The chapter has five sections. First, it considers developmental and behavioral perspectives on parents as partners in language learning. Then, it discusses findings from a meta-analysis of parent-implemented language intervention and recent research on EMT. Next, the chapter discusses the triadic model of parent training and the assumptions that frame the triadic model in general and when applied with EMT as the primary language intervention. After considering emergent directions for EMT parent-implemented research, it discusses issues related to fidelity of implementation and suggests directions for research and practice in the field to advance the inclusion of parents as partners in early communication intervention.

ROLE OF PARENTS IN CHILDREN'S LANGUAGE DEVELOPMENT

Most young children learn to communicate in the context of interactions with their parents and caregivers without intervention for either the parents or the children. The dependable transactional process that supports language learning is complex and multilayered and relies on adult behaviors that reinforce social-communication through providing input for language learning, opportunities for social interactions, and social linguistic input. Three key parent components contributing to child language learning are 1) frequent input (Hart & Risley, 1995), 2) meaningful responsiveness (Kaiser et al., 1996; Kaiser & Delaney, 2001; Mahoney & McDonald, 2003), and 3) the social-communicative interaction itself (Adamson, Bakeman, & Deckner, 2004; Brady, Marquis, Fleming, & McLean, 2004). Parents vary widely in the extent to which they provide these three components, and these variations in parent behavior are associated with differences in child language outcomes in children who are at risk and children who are typically developing (Bottema-Beutel, Yoder, Hochman, & Watson, 2014; Yoder & Warren, 1998). Children also vary in the skills they bring to the task of language learning and their interests and ability to participate in social-communication. Thus, the outcomes of this generally dependable but dynamic and transactional process are not perfectly predictable in terms of the timing or extent of child language learning and use.

Developmental Perspectives

From a developmental perspective, the provision of social-communication opportunities and linguistic input specific to the child's heritage language is an essential factor in developing language for all children (Hoff, 2006), including children at risk for language delays due to primary language impairment or a secondary impairment associated with a specific disability or condition (Abbeduto, Warren, & Conners, 2007; Mundy, Sigman, & Kasari, 1990). The underlying joint attention processes that emerge in dyadic interactions in the first year of life lay the foundation for children to become intentional communicators (Mundy et al., 2007). Shared attention to objects and people, as well as the introduction of symbolic representation (usually spoken language) into joint attention, provides the ideal environment for children to learn the function and meaning of words. Attention to social cues and language input in context may vary based on children's cognitive skills, development of visual and auditory memory, and ability to integrate symbols while socially engaged with a partner (Adamson et al., 2004).

Parents' skills in noticing; responding; scaffolding coordinated attention to person, object, and symbol; and modeling language at their child's cognitive and linguistic level support children's learning to communicate. Parents match their language teaching to their children's emerging skills (Hart & Risley, 1999). For example, they use a relatively small set of words to reference objects and events that are in close proximity to children's focus of attention during the first 12–18 months (Tomasello & Farrar, 1986). Parents become less explicit in their modeling of vocabulary over time, except when teaching new words that have unique meaning or are of special interest to the child. Parents implicitly assess their children's comprehension as well as production and adjust their language input accordingly. Parents focus less on providing their children with words or more elaborated or correct phrases to express their intentions and become more interested in the content of conversations as their children master early sentence forms and pragmatic functions (Moerk, 1974).

In typical development, the fine tuning of parent teaching and support for language learning to match the child's emerging communication skills occurs relatively easily. The child's development appears to lead the parent in providing models of language that are slightly more advanced than the child's productive skills and are tuned to the child's interests and understanding (Moerk, 1974). The finely tuned process may be disrupted by difficulties in language production or comprehension for children with primary or second language impairment. Motivation for social interaction and the ability to engage in sustained interactions with partners and objects may limit the opportunities for parents to model language and respond to children's communication (Adamson, Bakeman, Deckner, & Romski, 2009). The process of language learning may be slowed or changed by children's early emerging abilities as a social-communication partner, even when parents are responsive, consistent, and engaging partners who model developmentally appropriate language (Mundy, Kasari, Sigman, & Ruskin, 1995). In addition, parents who have difficulty providing linguistic input and social support for learning because of acute stress, depression, or their own limited language skills may reduce the language learning efficiency of children with typical social and cognitive skills and significantly affect children with language impairment.

From a developmental perspective, language teaching and learning in parent–child dyads is a dance in which both partners are sensitive to the steps executed by the other. The goal is a smooth, flowing tour around the dance floor, even as the music changes from slow and mellow to fast and exciting. Children develop strategies for extracting meaning and morpho-syntactic regularities as needed for the development of complex language skills. Parents provide the intensive input needed to acquire early language forms and functions and then move the focus of their interactions to other aspects of interaction (Tomasello, 1995).

Parent training in a developmental perspective emphasizes the quality of the parent–child interactions, responsiveness, and provision of linguistic input that the child needs to develop language. Balancing interactions to maintain synchrony and flow may be important for long-term communication outcomes (Siller & Sigman,

2002). Parent training supports parents in noticing and responding to their children's communicative cues. Parent training will help parents match their input to their children's cognitive, social, and linguistic abilities. Parent training in a social synchronous engagement intervention resulted in greater socially engaged imitation for young children with autism (Landa, Holman, O'Neill, & Stuart, 2011), which has been suggested as an important predictor of language outcomes for these children (Ingersoll & Schreibman, 2006). Parents in both groups received training in this study, but it was the specific training in social synchrony that resulted in the significantly improved social imitation, further emphasizing the importance of improving parent–child social engagement.

Behavioral Perspectives

A behavioral perspective emphasizes the processes that have been demonstrated to result in language learning and social use of language in experimental instructional settings—imitation, reinforcement, discrimination, and generalization (Skinner, 2014). Children learn from the models of language provided by parents and through observation, but it is the imitation of observed behavior that is a primary process in language learning (Speidel & Nelson, 1989). Children practice communicating by imitating the language forms used by their parents and other salient partners. Parents provide models as well as contingent responses, which reinforce child attempts to communicate (Sundberg & Sundberg, 2011). Parents support children in learning correct linguistic forms through modeling, shaping, and differential feedback (Rheingold, Gewirtz, & Ross, 1959). Learning the forms of language (words, phrases, sentences) is specifically linked to the functions those forms serve in the natural environment. Children learn early forms for making requests because those forms are functional for getting their needs and wants addressed. Commenting emerges because of the positive, functional social consequences resulting from expressing shared interest with a partner. Specific functions such as greetings or seeking information are learned by observing and imitating the forms used for those functions and then experiencing functional consequences for producing the form.

A behavioral perspective emphasizes how children learn the forms and functions of language from the environment and the contingencies for language use. Relatively less emphasis is placed on the complexity of transactional processes compared with a developmental perspective. Parents are still presumed to be critical partners for their child's language learning, however. Parents frequently model functional language and provide powerful and naturally reinforcing consequences for attempting to communicate through their continued attention and ensuring access to preferred objects and activities (Hart & Risley, 1975).

Parent training in a behavioral framework focuses on teaching specific language targets using modeling and reinforcement in direct instruction or in naturalistic, incidental teaching (Delprato, 2001). Parents might be taught to model language targets, respond contingently, and provide specific positive or corrective feedback contingent on child communication attempts. Parents may also learn systematic strategies for prompting communication. Parents involved in naturalistic behavioral interventions are taught to prompt when children are interested and requesting and, thus, when there are reinforcing natural consequences. Parent training from a behavioral perspective provides more learning trials for children and may promote generalization and maintenance by ensuring that the dosage of the intervention is greater and that the training occurs across settings, contexts, and people (Kaiser, Hancock, & Hester, 1998; Kaiser & Roberts, 2013a; Roberts & Kaiser, 2011; Woods, Kashinath, & Goldstein, 2004).

Although behavioral and developmental perspectives differ in their views of the underlying process and the emphasis on transactional versus instructional approaches to parents as language teachers, they share a common view that parents are important in language learning. Both perspectives believe that preparing parents to be efficient and effective in their role as social-communicative partners for their children with language impairment is an important component of effective early intervention to promote language development.

Constraints and Challenges for Parents as Language Teachers

It is important to consider why parents may be limited in their role as language teachers for children who have primary or secondary language impairment. First, parents are primarily parents. Their role in caregiving, nurturing, and providing a stable emotional and physical environment for their children supersede their role as systematic teachers of new language skills. Although language teaching naturally occurs in the context of many parent–child interactions, it is not the primary focus of most interactions. Second, children who evidence early indications of language impairment are often difficult partners in social interaction. Parents may not only need specific skills to teach children with language impairment effectively, but they may also need support to sustain their teaching with sufficient intensity over long periods of time. Parents must be able to respond to infrequent and iconic social initiations when their children have autism or disabilities that directly affect their social motivation for communication. Although the period of intensive language teaching primary spans the infant and toddler years for parents of typically developing children, the period when high levels of responsiveness, language modeling, prompting, and functional reinforcement is needed for children with language impairment may extend throughout childhood and adolescence. Finally, nearly all typically developing children learn the heritage language of their family in spoken form. Augmentative and alternative communication (AAC) may be essential for children with significant communication impairment. Teaching and modeling language using dual modes (spoken and secondary augmented mode), responding to children's use of these modes, and providing opportunities to learn new forms may be especially challenging for parents whose children use AAC (Romski, Sevcik, & Adamson, 1997).

Parents need systematic training and professional partnerships to be effective language teachers for children with language impairment. Although they play an important role in their children's language learning, it is not their only role. Teaching parents to provide extraordinary language support to their children requires strategies that are efficient, effective, practical, and compatible with parents' multiple roles. Teaching parents requires the development and use of evidence-based practices as the basis for what is taught and how it is taught.

IS PARENT-IMPLEMENTED LANGUAGE INTERVENTION EFFECTIVE?

Systematic models of supporting and teaching parents to implement language intervention practices must be effective at two levels; the parent must learn the strategies and the child must make progress as a result of the parent's implementation. Recent research has focused on measuring effectiveness at both of these levels within a systematic framework that specifies what the parent is supposed to learn and how the interventionist should train them.

Effects of Parent-Implemented Language Interventions: Evidence from Meta-analysis

Systematic evidence across child populations and measures shows that parent-implemented interventions positively affect child language outcomes (Roberts & Kaiser, 2011). Roberts and Kaiser reported outcomes from a meta-analysis of 18 group experimental design studies. The review included 14 studies that compared parent-implemented interventions with a control condition and four studies that compared parent-implemented with therapist-implemented treatments. Interventions varied in focus from general language support to targeted behavioral instruction; generally, the content of interventions was not well described in the individual studies. Responsiveness, language modeling using expansions, and increasing rate of linguistic input were the three strategies for supporting child language most often described. Eight studies used variations of the Hanen model (Girolametto, Pearce, & Weitzman, 1996). Positive and statistically significant effects for expressive language, receptive language, expressive vocabulary, receptive vocabulary, and expressive morpho–syntax were found in studies that compared parent-implemented intervention with a community or business-as-usual control condition. Effect sizes (ES) ranged from $g = 0.35$, 95% CI (0.05, 0.65} for receptive language to $g = 0.82$, 95% CI (0.37, 1.38) for expressive syntax. The ES for overall language was moderate ($g = 0.42$, 95% CI [-0.02, 0.92]) but not statistically significant ($p = 0.06$). Parents reported that children receiving parent-implemented interventions had an average of 52 more words than parents reported for children in the control group. Significant positive ES were indicated for only two of seven language constructs when parent-implemented interventions were compared with therapist-implemented interventions: receptive language $g = 0.41$, 95% CI [0.08, 0.76] and expressive syntax $g = 0.41$, 95% CI [0.06, 0.79]. Parents reported that children in the parent-implemented interventions had on average 22 more words than parents reported for children in the therapist group, but this difference was not significant ($p = 0.42$). The positive effects on children's language across studies were not statistically different for children with and without intellectual disabilities (ID).

Although the evidence indicating that parent-implemented language intervention is positive, the findings from the meta-analysis suggest there is still a need for evidence linking specific strategies for teaching parents to parent implementation and, subsequently, to children's developmental outcomes. Roberts and Kaiser (2011) reported that half of the studies did not adequately describe how parents were trained, and fewer than 30% measured parent training fidelity. Slightly more than half (55%) of the 18 studies measured parent implementation before and after training.

Barton and Fettig (2013) reported a similar finding in a review of selected parent-implemented interventions for children with disabilities that included language interventions. Only 29% (7) of a sample of 24 single-case and group design studies reported implementation of fidelity for parent training. Describing how parents are trained and reporting fidelity of parent training in addition to measuring and reporting parent implementation of the language support strategies are essential in establishing a strong evidence base for parent-implemented language intervention.

Evidence from Research on Enhanced Milieu Teaching

EMT is a naturalistic communication intervention that builds on both developmental and behavioral principles for language learning and teaching (Kaiser, 1993). EMT is a systematic extension of principles of incidental teaching (Hart & Risley, 1980) adapted for children with significant language impairment (Hart & Rogers-Warren, 1978). EMT was developed as an intervention approach to be used by children's significant communication partners to teach functional language in everyday interactions (Kaiser, Hemmeter, & Alpert, 1992). EMT has five core components—environmental arrangement to support child communication, noticing and responding to child communication, modeling and expanding, time delay, and milieu prompting episodes. EMT is typically used to teach child-specific targets that may include specific words and phrases, classes of words, generative phrases that represent early semantic relationships, simple syntax, complex syntax, and speech sounds. Targets are selected that are functional for the child in the natural setting and that are teachable in the context of ongoing interactions. EMT has been used with both sign language and speech-generating devices as AAC modes (Kaiser & Wright, 2013).

More than 50 studies have investigated the effects naturalistic teaching similar to EMT across populations, interventionists, and settings. This chapter highlights findings for four studies that are representative of research on parent-implemented EMT (see Table 7.1) (Kaiser & Roberts, 2013a; Roberts, Kaiser, Wolfe, Bryant, & Spidalieri, 2014; Roberts & Kaiser, 2015; Wright & Kaiser, in press). These studies were designed to addresses two questions: 1) "Can parents be taught EMT to high levels of fidelity?" and 2) "What are the effects of parent-implemented EMT on their children's language?"

Parents were sequentially taught the components of EMT in each of the four studies. A total of 90 parents received parent training across the four studies. Two studies were randomized group designs (Kaiser & Roberts, 2013a; Roberts & Kaiser, 2015). Two were single-case research designs with four parent participants in each study (Roberts et al., 2014; Wright & Kaiser, in press). Three studies included workshop training and extended modeling by the therapist (Roberts et al., 2014; Roberts and Kaiser, 2015; Wright & Kaiser, in press), and all studies included practice sessions with coaching and review. The number of individual practice sessions varied from 24- to sessions. All parents learned the EMT strategies, and parents met predetermine criterion levels for most behaviors. Parents in the Kaiser and Roberts (2013) study met criterion on responsiveness, modeling, and expansions but were lower than criterion levels for milieu prompting episodes. Parents generalized across untrained contexts in the three studies in which home generalization was assessed (Kaiser & Roberts, 2013a; Roberts et al., 2014; Wright & Kaiser, in press).

The effects of parent-implemented EMT on their children's language outcomes have varied. There were significant ES for receptive language and number

Table 7.1. Recent studies of parent-implemented enhanced milieu teaching

Study	Population	Design	How parents were trained	Parent outcomes	Child outcomes
Kaiser and Roberts (2013)	77 preschoolers (ages 30–60 months; MN 41 months) with intellectual disabilities (ID) (MN NV IQ 70) and their parents ASD =16 (21%) DS = 18 (23%) DD = 43 (56%)	Randomized treatment parent-implemented enhanced milieu teaching (EMT) versus therapist-implemented EMT	Individually, in 36 individual sessions across clinic (24) and home (12) Preteaching, coaching, feedback in each session	Trained parents met criterion on responsiveness, modeling, and expansions. ES 0.92–1.63 across trained and untrained activities.	No differences between standardized assessments. Children whose parents were trained used more targets over time (ES 0.40–0.76) had longer MLUw (ES 0.39–0.60) and greater NDW (ES .10-.62) in trained activities. Differences were greater at 3- and 6-month follow-up than immediately after intervention.
Roberts et al. (2014)	4 toddlers (ages 25–38 months; MN 30.8 months) with receptive and expressive language delays and their parents	Single-subject multiple baseline across 4 EMT strategies, replicated across parents	Individually, in 4 workshops, minimum of 24 individual sessions across clinic and home TMCR model	Caregivers learned all EMT strategies to criterion fidelity. All caregivers used more strategies at home at 3- and 6-month follow-up but varied in terms of individual strategies and maintenance of fidelity.	3 of 4 children demonstrated a functional relationship between caregiver use of EMT and spontaneous language use. Children generalized and maintained language use across most activities over 6-month follow-up.
Roberts and Kaiser (2015)	97 toddlers (ages 24–42 months; MN 30.4 months) with receptive and expressive language delays and their parents	Randomized treatment and control: parent-implemented EMT versus community business-as-usual	Individually, in 4 workshops, 24 individual sessions across clinic and home TMCR model	Trained parents met criterion on all EMT strategies to criterion fidelity. ES ranged from 0.43 to 3.19. Parents generalized to untrained activities at home. Parents maintained some EMT strategies at follow-up.	Children in parent training group had significantly better receptive language skills (ES 0.27–0.35), greater number of different words (ES 0.38).
Wright and Kaiser (in press)	4 toddlers (ages 28–33 months; MN 29.5 months) with DS and their parents; children used signs and words	Single-subject multiple baseline across 5 EMT strategies, replicated across parents	Individually in 4 workshops, 27–36 (MN 31) individual sessions across clinic (50%) and home (50%) TMCR model	Parents learned all strategies to criterion fidelity. Parents generalized to uncoached probes at fidelity. Parents maintained most EMT strategies at fidelity at 4- to 5-week follow-up	Child outcomes varied; 2 of 4 children demonstrated a relationship between parent EMT and rate of words and signs.

Key: DS = Down syndrome; ASD = Autism Spectrum Disorder; DD = Developmental Delay; EMT = Enhance Milieu Teaching; MN = Mean; ES = Effect size(s); MLUw = Mean Length of Utterance in words; TCMR = Teach-Model-Coach-Review (*Source:* Kaiser & Roberts, 2013b).

of different words in the RCT of toddlers with receptive and expressive delays (Roberts & Kaiser, 2015), Three of four children in the single-case design with toddlers with receptive and expressive delays demonstrated increases in spontaneous language use during training and generalized and maintained effects over 6 months of follow-up. Kaiser and Roberts (2103) compared a multisetting EMT therapist intervention with parent-implemented EMT for preschoolers with ID in a randomized treatment comparison. They found significant effects for child use of targets and weighted Mean Length Utterance in activities at home (in both trained and untrained activities) that favored the parent-implemented group, but there were no main effects between groups on standardized assessments in the clinic. The effects of parent-implemented intervention were largest for children with autism spectrum disorder in home observations and in standardized assessments within the sample that varied in diagnosis. Wright and Kaiser (in press) observed a functional relationship between parent-implemented EMT including spoken words and signs as the mode of communication for only one of four toddlers with Down syndrome (DS). All children did show increases in communication over time, but these changes were not clearly linked to the sequential training across EMT conditions provided to their training. Overall, there appear to be differences in the impact of parent-implemented EMT, depending on child diagnosis, with children with DS responding less to the treatment than children with receptive and expressive language delays. No EMT studies have found that child outcomes were related to parent fidelity; however, fidelity has been measured only through direct observation in clinic and selected home activities. Important variations in implementation may not have been observed because much of the impact of parent-implemented interventions is presumed to occur over time outside of the training and observed generalization sessions.

A TRIADIC MODEL OF COMMUNICATION INTERVENTION

The process for intervention becomes triadic when parents become partners in communication intervention. Therapists become teachers and coaches for parents who, in turn, teach their children. In triadic communication intervention, parents assume the roles of adult learners who are acquiring new skills for supporting their children's language, and they simultaneously assume the role of language teachers for their children. The role shifts required in triadic intervention pose a range of challenges. Therapists will need skills for teaching adults that they have not acquired during their professional training to assess and teach children. Parents will continue in their primary role as parents but must also function as adult learners and as language teachers implementing systematic strategies to support language with their children. Effective triadic communication intervention requires well-defined language intervention strategies that can be implemented in naturalistic settings and systematic procedures for teaching parents to implement these strategies

Three critical questions must be asked and answered in formulating an effective triadic teaching model. 1) What is the role of parents in supporting their children's communication? This question asks if parents are primarily communication partners, incidental or naturalistic teachers, or direct instructors with their children. 2) What are parents being taught to do? This question asks about the conceptual framework for intervention and the specific skills and strategies that parents will be taught. Ideally, benchmarks or criteria for parents' performance of the use of strategies will be provided, and these benchmarks will be linked empirically to child outcomes. 3) How will parents be taught? This question is about the method for training parents and includes questions about the approach to training, the setting, the duration, and the specific instructional strategies used to teach parents as well as the specific language intervention content taught to parents. Thus, a triadic model of parent training in language intervention must systematically encompass each critical component around the parent's role, what they are being taught, and how they are being taught.

Teach-Model-Coach-Review Process: Teaching Parents to Implement Enhanced Milieu Teaching in a Triadic Model

A systematic model has been developed for therapists to teach parents to implement EMT with their children who have language impairment. Teach-Model-Coach-Review (TMCR) builds on instructional strategies that demonstrated effectiveness in teaching specific skills to adult learners (Dunst, Trivette, & Hamby, 2010; Trivette, Dunst, Hamby, & O'Herin, 2009). A comprehensive description of this model may be found in Roberts et al. (2014). The therapist using TMCR teaches the core principles of EMT to parents using multiple modes (verbal instruction, handouts, videos, role playing, and discussion) at the beginning of each segment of training within an individualized workshop introducing the five EMT strategies (environmental arrangement, notice and respond, model and expand, time delay, and milieu teaching prompts). Teaching also briefly occurs at the beginning of each session with the parent and child. The therapist models EMT during every session by working directly with children while their parents observe. The therapist points out what he or she is doing and provides brief rationales for his or her teaching during these observations. Training occurs in the clinic (workshops and initial practice sessions) and at home. The therapist provides examples and models in the specific contexts in which parents interact with their children (e.g., home routines, family chores and activities, play at home). Parents practice with their children for 15–30 minutes and receive coaching during practice. The parent reviews the session and asks questions and provides feedback to the therapist about the training. The parent and therapist together discuss the parent's use of strategies and how parent use of the EMT strategies is affecting child language and communication. The therapist uses the TMCR model throughout the training to help parents notice the effects of their behavior on their children's use of language and communication skills. The TMCR model has been used in four studies (Kaiser & Roberts, 2013a; Roberts & Kaiser, 2015; Roberts et al., 2014; Wright & Kaiser, in press)

What Is the Role of Parents in Enhanced Milieu Teaching? EMT assumes that the first and most important role for parents is that of a communication partner. Interpersonal connection and availability as a communication partner lays the foundation for specific teaching. It is assumed that all children are communicating in some way right now, and therapists begin by teaching parents to notice and appreciate the many ways in which their children already communicate. It is expected that parents will be responsive teachers. That is, they will teach in response to their children's interests and attempts to communicate, and they will teach in response to the context in which their children are attempting to communicate. Supporting parents to assume the role of responsive communication partners is the primary objective of EMT training. If parents are comfortable and dependable in this role, then it is possible to teach them to become more systematic by teaching them to model and prompt language- and communication-specific forms at their children's target level. Close collaboration with their children's therapist may allow some parents to provide targeted specific instruction or opportunities to generalize specific forms that are being taught in another instructional context. The exact role parents assume depends on their interest and on their skill in continuing to be a responsive communication partner while focusing on modeling and teaching target language.

What Are Parents Taught in Enhanced Milieu Teaching? Parents are taught the core philosophy and specific language teaching components of EMT. What is taught is tailored to children's behavior and communication skills as well as their parents' abilities as teachers. EMT begins with three core principles: 1) every child is communicating now, 2) communication happens in contexts that specify function of communication, and 3) responsive partners are essential for learning to communicate. The five components of EMT are nested within these three principles—environmental arrangement, notice and respond, model and expand, time delay, and milieu teaching prompts.

Parents are taught to select home routines and arrange activities and materials that offer opportunities for children to communicate about objects and events of interest to them. Activities in which language is needed are ideal settings for teaching, but therapists often begin with activities that are preferred and fun before teaching in difficult routines in which children are reluctant communicators or unengaged participants. Environmental arrangement with time delays and milieu teaching prompts are used later to help children make choices and ask for assistance.

The majority of the initial instructional time with parents is spent building on the principle that every child is a communicator and teaching parents strategies for becoming responsive partners. Parents are taught to notice and respond to their children's current and emergent communication and to engage nonverbally with their children through turn-taking and supporting children's engagement. Parents whose children are early communicators are taught strategies for increasing joint attention using selected strategies from Kasari, Freeman, and Paparella (2006) to infuse language during episodes of joint attention. Parents create space and opportunities for children to initiate and respond by balancing turns, pacing to match the child, responding to every communication attempt, and limiting questions and instructions.

Because linguistic input tailored to children's abilities is essential, parents are taught to model language at their children's target level and sometimes to model specific target forms or word combinations as a foundation for beginning language. The precision of modeling depends on the parents' mastery of responsive interaction principles, which is an indication that they are solid as responsive partners and can focus on the content of their responses. Expansions are child-contingent models that respond to child communicate attempts (the form and function used by the child) and add additional linguistic information while reflecting the child's intention. Expansions are powerful because they occur contingent on child attempts to communicate or act, when attention is focused, and when the child has a cognitive representation of the event. The principle of expansion can be applied to extend play and engagement as well as language (Frey & Kaiser, 2010).

Time delays are a specific strategy that uses the environment, the child's interests and requests, and the established pattern of contingent responding. The parent pauses, focuses on the child, and waits for the child's communicative initiation when using a time delay. Parents span the gap between prompted responding and truly independent initiated communication by setting up the environment to provide an opportunity to make a choice or ask for assistance. Time delays may signal the beginning of a milieu prompting episode (as described next) or may focus the child when the adult models specific language form. For example, when parents offer choices early on and children reach to indicate their choice, parents are taught to respond with the name of the object (e.g., "truck") and give the chosen object to the child. Prompting can be easily introduced for both parents and children when time delay routines are well established. How time delays are used depends on parents' skills and fluency in responding to their children and their children's tolerance for prompting.

EMT includes prompting that supports children's practice of new language forms in contexts in which they are motivated to communicate. Prompting provided by skilled interventionists is effective in teaching new communication forms. Over many years of teaching parents to use EMT, the emphasis on prompting has been systematically reduced when teaching parents. Again, responsive communication is the foundation of parent-implemented EMT. Prompting can be difficult for parents to embed in interactions while maintaining a conversational focus. Prompting disrupts the flow of turn-taking for some children. Other children are resistant to prompting and may not respond or may respond only when their parents persist. The decision to teach parents to prompt is individualized and based on their skills and their children's abilities.

How Are Parents Taught Enhanced Milieu Teaching? The TMCR model is used to teach parents EMT, with individualization to fit the parent, the child, the context for teaching, and the amount of time available for teaching. Parents were taught using a combination of workshops and individual training sessions in the clinic and at home (Roberts & Kaiser, 2015; Roberts et al., 2014). Core EMT content was introduced in four interactive workshops that included PowerPoint, video examples with the target child, handouts and worksheets, and discussion lead by the therapist. Each workshop lasted about 45 minutes, and the content was individually tailored to the parent and the child. After each workshop, parents practiced the skills set in the clinic and at home across routines during four to six sessions. The therapist assisted with setting up interactions and the environment. She observed, coached, and supported parents while they interacted with their child; she offered formative feedback during coaching throughout the session and at the end of the session. After the parent practiced, the therapist evaluated the session and together they discussed the child's communication, focusing on how the parent's use of EMT was affecting the child and overall progress.

Fidelity in Teaching Parents Enhanced Milieu Teaching Fidelity of implementation in a triadic training model is important in both therapists' training of parents and parents' implementation of EMT with their children. Fidelity of the therapist's training of the parent in workshops, clinic practices, and at home was monitored and reported for about 20% of sessions, and parent fidelity of implementing EMT in the clinic and at home was monitored in 20% of sessions (Roberts & Kaiser, 2015; Roberts et al., 2014). Fidelity on training parents was more than 90% across settings and types of instruction. Fidelity of parent implementation in the clinic and at home across routines was also more than 90% on all EMT components. The child outcomes in these two studies were strong and relatively consistent across children. Variability in child outcome was not associated with the level of parent fidelity in the Roberts and Kaiser (2015) study, possibly because parents were trained to criterion and fidelity was uniformly high across families.

Much is unknown about parent fidelity in using EMT across the day and over time and, thus, much is unknown about the impact of parent fidelity on child outcomes. First, interventionists assume that the effects of parent-implemented EMT on children's language outcomes are the result of using the strategies across the day, not only within the sessions observed for fidelity. Fewer than 2 hours of parent–child interaction was directly observed each week in most EMT studied, and data was reported for only a small time sample. Thus, it is unknown if variability in parent-generalized use of the strategies, either in terms of dosage or quality of implementation, may have contributed to variability in child outcomes. Second, although levels of fidelity for parent implementation have been established based on previous studies, the relationship between criterion fidelity levels and child outcomes has not been established empirically. Finally, intervention as received by the child, which is one of the most important measures of fidelity (Schulte, Easton, & Parker, 2009), has never been measured in EMT or other language intervention studies. Children vary in the extent to which they receive the EMT intervention because some intervention components are delivered in response to child behavior (e.g., expansions) and children may respond differently to other components (e.g., modeling, time delay, milieu prompting episodes).

Advancing Research and Practice in Parent-Implemented Language Interventions

This section briefly discusses the next steps in research and practice in parent-implemented language interventions (see Table 7.2). Issues related to internal validity in parent training studies are not directly addressed because standards for internal validity in intervention studies using group designs and single-case research designs have been clearly articulated (c.f., Council for Exceptional Children, 2014; What Works Clearinghouse [http://ies.ed.gov/ncee/wwc/]). Fidelity in a triadic intervention model and the need for professional training in evidence-based language interventions and strategies for training parents are the focus.

Assessing Fidelity Consistent with a Triadic Intervention Model Assessing fidelity of parent training procedures and demonstrating parents' fidelity in using the trained procedures are critical to establishing an evidence base for parent-implemented interventions (Barton & Fettig, 2013). Studies of parent-implemented interventions should measure and report data on each of the three levels of the intervention reflected in a triadic model of intervention: 1) procedural fidelity on training techniques used to teach parents to use intervention strategies, 2) fidelity measures or observational data demonstrating parents' use of the intervention

Table 7.2. Components of the Teach-Model-Coach-Review and criteria for implementation fidelity

Component	Indicators	Criterion
Teach	4 1-hour workshops • Defined language facilitation strategy • Provided rationale • Described how to do the strategy • Showed video examples • Answered questions First 15 minutes of each intervention session • Restated the strategy, gave example • Role played • Discussed ways to use strategy	80% of items completed correctly
Model	10–15 minutes of each intervention session • Modeled language facilitation strategy • Highlighted strategy use	Modeled and highlighted target strategy at least two times
Coach	15 minutes of each intervention session • Coached with caregiver while she practiced the strategy with the child	Coached caregiver at least once every minute
Review	Last 15 minutes of each intervention session • Discussed the session • Linked caregiver and child behaviors • Made a plan for home use of strategies	80% of times completed correctly

Note: Times are based on Roberts and Kaiser (2015); times for each component have slightly varied across studies. (*Source:* Roberts & Kaiser, 2015.)

strategies as a result of training during the intervention (single-case designs) or before and after the intervention (group design), and 3) the child outcomes as a result of the parents' use of the strategies, either during the intervention phase (single-case designs using time series data) or before and after the intervention (group design studies) (Roberts & Kaiser, 2011). Positive child outcomes, when parent-implementation has been verified, can be considered further indication of the fidelity of intervention by indicating the extent to which the intervention was received by the child (Schulte et al., 2009).

The assessment of implementation of fidelity is complex in a triadic intervention. Schoenwald et al. (2011) summarized treatment fidelity as consisting of therapist adherence, therapist competence, treatment differentiation, and highlighted the overlap among these indicators of fidelity. *Adherence* refers to the extent to which the therapist uses prescribed intervention procedure. Procedural adherence in triadic interventions includes use of prescribed procedures for teaching parents and accurately teaching the content of the language intervention that will be implemented by parents. For example, adherence in training parents to implement EMT includes teaching parents specific strategies using the procedures described in the TMCR model and accurately teaching the specific content of the EMT intervention through modeling, teaching, and coaching parents. A manualized treatment protocol and checklists that operationalize both types of information is used to evaluate the method for teaching parents and the extent to which the content of the language intervention was correctly taught. An example checklist that evaluates both TMCR teaching procedures and EMT language intervention content is in Table 7.3. The strategies for teaching parents are listed, and the specific EMT content to be taught using those methods during a single session is specified. Meeting

Table 7.3. Example fidelity criterion for Teach-Model-Coach-Review on play and language expansions

	Criterion
Teach	Therapist reviews the three strategies: 1. Model and expand play 2. Model all of the child's language targets (list child's targets) 3. Expand all of the child's communication by adding one to two words Therapist and caregiver discuss how to play with the toys: 1. At least two ways to expand play 2. At least two routines with the play Therapist reviews the child's targets and gives examples of each target. Therapist reviews types of expansion: We are going to add one to two words every time your child communicates. 1. Vocalization: respond with a target (e.g., what you would want him or her to say). 2. Gestures: imitate the gesture and then add a target (e.g., what you would want him or her to say). 3. Words: imitate the word and add a word. Words can come before or after the child's word (e.g., *eat:* cow eats or eat apple). Therapist practices one gesture and one word expansion with caregiver. Therapist reviews coaching plan with caregiver. Therapist checks for understanding and invites caregiver questions.
Model	Therapist highlights modeling and expanding play at least two times. Therapist highlights targets at least two times. Therapist highlights expansions at least two times. Session lasts for 15 minutes. Therapist implementation of enhanced milieu teaching: 1. Therapist responds to at least 90% of all child communication. 2. Therapist uses child target language during 50%–70% of adult utterances. 3. Therapist uses proximal language targets during 30%–50% of adult utterances. 4. Therapist expands at least 40% of all child utterances. 5. Therapist completes time delays with an average rating of 3.5/4.0. 6. Therapist completes milieu prompting episodes with an average rating of 8.0/10.
Coach	Therapist gives caregiver positive or training feedback at least once per minute. Session lasts for 15 minutes.
Review	At the end, the therapist asks the caregiver how he or she felt about the session. Therapist summarizes how the caregiver modeled and/or expanded communication and/or play. Therapist relates the caregiver's behavior and child's behavior during the practice session at least once.

criterion for implementation in this example requires teaching the specific content (expansions) using the components of TMCR at criterion levels.

Therapist competence is the level of skill and judgment used in executing the treatment (Schoenwald et al., 2011). Assessing the competence of the therapist separately from adherence has not been done frequently in parent-implemented language intervention. Two general approaches have been used in studies of EMT. First, for the modeling component of TMCR, the therapist is observed implementing EMT and fidelity is scored from observational data, exactly as is done for parents (see Roberts & Kaiser, 2013). The second aspect of therapist competence is assessed by rating indicators of a specific construct assumed to index therapist competence. For example, building positive relationships with parents is an important aspect of competent parent training. Behaviors that contribute to building a relationship might be observed during training sessions; however, rating individual behaviors may not be sufficient for judging overall therapist competence. For example, the relationship-building related items in the example checklist (see Table 7.3) include greeting the parent, asking the parent about his or her impressions of the session, responding to the parent's questions, and providing a positive assessment of the parent's and child's progress. Rating specific indicators may discriminate trainers' abilities to perform specific behaviors but may not fully index competence. An earlier study found that new trainers had difficulty clearly explaining intervention strategies and responding with direct, accurate answers to parents' questions (Kaiser, Hester, Alpert, & Whiteman, 1995). New trainers improved their skills with practice and feedback. Few instruments are available at this time for assessing the competence of therapists as parent trainers. Development and validation of such instruments, as well as specific professional training to ensure such competence, are needed.

Treatment differentiation, or the extent to which the treatment being evaluated is different from other treatments on critical dimensions, is the third aspect of fidelity (Schoenwald et al., 2011). Specification of both the parent training procedures and the language intervention procedures is required to judge the adequacy of treatment differentiation in a triadic model. Although it is possible to differentiate the components of one language intervention from another (e.g., milieu teaching from responsive interaction) (Yoder et al., 1995) and milieu teaching from focused stimulation (Scherer, D'Antonio, & McGahey, 2008), no studies of parent-implemented language intervention have differentiated one model of parent training from another. This is due, in part, to the lack of specification of parent training models and empirical data indicating which components of parent training are critical to parent outcomes. specification, differentiation, and comparison of models of teaching parents and linking the models of parent training to child outcomes are important next steps in parent training research.

In addition to the fidelity of the parent training, the fidelity of the parent implementation of the language intervention with the child must be measured. The same constructs of adherence, competence, and differentiation should be evaluated. Measures of adherence and differentiation can be obtained through observation in training sessions, home practice sessions across activities, and in pre- and post-assessments of parent–child interaction in a clinic or natural setting. Parent performance can be evaluated against established criterion levels for critical language intervention behaviors (see Roberts & Kaiser, 2015) to indicate the degree of adherence to the intervention protocol. Measure the critical behaviors associated with the targeted intervention method and with other intervention strategies that are not part of the targeted intervention to determine differentiation. This has been done in treatment comparison studies implemented by researchers and teachers (e.g., Yoder et al., 1995). EMT treatment implementation has been differentiated from nontreatment in studies in which parent training was not provided in one of the experimental conditions (e.g., Kaiser & Roberts, 2013a; Roberts & Kaiser, 2015).

Determining the competence of the parent as the implementer of a language intervention is complex, just as evaluating the competence of parent trainers is complex. The central issue for competent parent implementation of a language intervention has to do with whether the parent provides the intervention with sufficient dosage, precision, and generality to affect the child's language development. In addition, competence might include implementing the intervention in a manner consistent with core principles that guide the intervention. For example, competence in EMT would include not only adhering to the specific treatment protocol but also being an available and responsive communicative partner over time, supporting the child in his or her mode of communication, and adapting linguistic input and prompting strategies as the child's language changes and the contexts for conversation vary. Competence might be indexed by generalization, maintenance, and generative adaptations consistent with the child's development. If so, it is important to have methods for assessing these aspects of competence and benchmarks to indicate when parents have met the indicators for competence in the natural setting. Most studies of parent training report measures of generalization and maintenance under specific conditions—assessments in the clinic with novel materials, probes across untrained activities at home over time, and parent report of the frequency of use of the intervention strategies. Observational data from generalization and maintenance are evaluated using the same standards as primary data—frequency and percentage of accurate implementation and, sometimes, overall fidelity summaries or ratings. It may become easier to estimate parent competence in natural settings without the reactive influence of observers with the advent of new video and telecommunication technology. Current technologies that record audio and summarize rates of parent turns and child-directed speech are useful for a limited set of behaviors, but transcription of the recordings is still required to assess the precise implementation of an intervention such as EMT (Ford, Baer, Xu, Yapanel, & Gray, 2008).

Child outcomes are an index of the effectiveness of the parent-implemented language intervention. Child outcomes are the highest standard for impact of fidelity of parent implementation when the research design provides the internal validity conditions for assessing the causal linkage between parent implementation and child outcome. When child outcomes are variable, however, interventionists must return to the transactional model of parent–child interactions and consider how child characteristics directly and indirectly affect parent efforts to teach language. Children with significant language impairment vary in the skills they bring to the task of learning language in natural environments and the extent to which they are responsive to their parents' language intervention efforts. Child outcomes may vary even when parents appear to have implemented an intervention with acceptable fidelity. Kaiser and Roberts (2013) found children with autism had better language outcomes across measures when their parents were trained, but outcomes for children with DS did not differ when the intervention was delivered by only the therapist, by their parents alone, or combined with therapist intervention. Parents in both groups had similar levels of fidelity of implementation of the EMT intervention.

Conceptualizing, measuring, and reporting fidelity of implementation in triadic, parent-implement intervention research will advance both scientific understanding of how change in child language outcomes are best achieved and provide guidance for standards in clinical practice.

Preparing Therapists to Teach Parents Effective parent trainers have skills in both the primary language intervention and procedures for teaching parents that correspond to the aspects of fidelity just discussed (see Table 7.4). Training therapists in preparation for teaching parents requires providing instruction and practice in

Table 7.4. Recommendations for advancing effective parent-implemented language intervention

	Adherence	Differentiation	Competence
Assess treatment fidelity consistent with a triadic intervention model:			
For therapists	Does the therapist implement the parent-training model at criterion levels?	Does the therapist implement the specific components of the parent training model and not implement training procedures associate with other models?	Is the therapist competent in use of training procedures and principles of parent training (e.g., effective communication, relationship building, family-centered practice)?
For parents	Does the parent implement the language intervention at criterion levels?	Does the parent implement only the components associated with the trained language intervention and not implement intervention procedures associated with other models?	Is the parent competent in use of the intervention procedures and principles of the intervention (e.g., available communication partner, changing input and teaching targets as child advances, supporting child's mode)?
Establish criterion levels (benchmarks for implementation)			
For therapists	Criteria for essential parent training behaviors consistent with the selected model of parent training	Indicators of parent training behavior that are not consistent with the selected model of parent training	Indicators of competence in parent training in addition to criterion for adherence
For parents and therapists	Criteria for therapist and parent implementation of the targeted language intervention	Indicators of therapist and parent implementation that are not consistent with the targeted language intervention	Indicators of competence in implementing the intervention that include indicators of implementation across settings and over time (especially for parents)
Train professionals to criterion levels of implementation in: ▪ Evidence-based language intervention ▪ Evidence-based parent training interventions	Primary instruction, analysis of evidence, and practical experience in language intervention and parent training Introduction to methods of assessing adherence to protocols for language intervention and parent training	Primary instruction in a range of language intervention and parent training models Practice in implementing components of different language intervention and parent training models Use of observation and rating instruments for determining differentiation of models of language intervention and parent training	Demonstration of competence in language intervention using specific intervention models, including planning, assessment, implementation, outcome evaluation for target population; mastery of specific components of the intervention and demonstrated use of core principles Demonstration of competence in parent training using specific parent training model, including all specific procedures, core principles, and management and evaluation of the parent training and parent implementation process

evidence-based child language intervention. Instruction about evidence-based language intervention procedures, practicing those procedures in clinical settings, and demonstrating fluency in the language intervention across children with varying needs is already part of many training programs. An important addition to expected clinical training is teaching new therapists about evidence-based practices in parent training, providing them with opportunities to use one or more practices to teach an evidence-based language intervention to parents, and evaluating their overall competence in parent training after they have had several opportunities to master the procedural aspects of parent training. Fostering competence in parent training requires opportunities to work with experienced parent trainers in apprenticeship or internship arrangements and may require additional training in skills that are common across intervention models and approaches to parent training (e.g., effectively communicating with parents, supporting parents in managing behavior when it interferes with communication intervention, collecting and using data on parent implementation and child progress to make treatment decisions). Given the intensive curriculum for preservice training for speech-language pathologists and early interventionists who are the most likely professional to provide parent training for language intervention, continuing educational opportunities and advanced professional training should be made available through professional organizations and universities. As research on effective parent-implemented intervention continues and advances in implementation science provide guidelines for how to best implement evidence-based practices, it is critical that training for professionals is accessible and driven by the advances in research and implementation science.

CONCLUSION

Although there is systematic evidence that parent-implemented language interventions can result in positive child language outcomes, a considerable gap still exists between research and practice in this important area of early communication intervention. This chapter discussed the theoretical foundations for parents as partners in communication intervention, provided examples of parent-implemented intervention from research on EMT, described the triadic model of parent-implemented interventions, and discussed issues related to ensuring treatment fidelity in a triadic model of intervention. Closing the research-to-practice gap depends on evidence from effective communication intervention and the application of models for teaching parents these communication interventions. Developing standards for implementation fidelity is an important step advancing both research and clinical training.

REFERENCES

Abbeduto, L., Warren, S.F., & Conners, F.A. (2007). Language development in Down syndrome: From the prelinguistic period to the acquisition of literacy. *Mental Retardation and Developmental Disabilities Research Reviews, 13*(3), 247–261.

Adamson, L.B., Bakeman, R., & Deckner, D.F. (2004). The development of symbol-infused joint engagement. *Child Development, 75*(4), 1171–1187.

Adamson, L.B., Bakeman, R., Deckner, D.F., & Romski, M. (2009). Joint engagement and the emergence of language in children with autism and Down syndrome. *Journal of Autism and Developmental Disorders, 39*(1), 84–96.

Barton, E.E., & Fettig, A. (2013). Parent-implemented interventions for young children with disabilities: A review of fidelity features. *Journal of Early Intervention, 35,* 194–219. doi:1053815113504625

Bottema-Beutel, K., Yoder, P.J., Hochman, J.M., & Watson, L.R. (2014). The role of supported joint engagement and parent utterances in language and social communication development in children with autism spectrum disorder. *Journal of Autism and Developmental Disorders, 44*(9), 2162–2174. doi:10.1007/s10803-014-2092-z

Brady, N.C., Marquis, J., Fleming, K., & McLean, L. (2004). Prelinguistic predictors of language growth in children with developmental disabilities. *Journal of Speech, Language, and Hearing Research, 47*(3), 663–677.

Council for Exceptional Children. (2014). Council for Exceptional Children standards for evidence-based practices in special education. *Exceptional Children, 80*(4), 504–511.

Delprato, D.J. (2001). Comparisons of discrete-trial and normalized behavioral language intervention for young children with autism. *Journal of Autism and Developmental Disorders, 31*(3), 315–325. doi:10.1023/A:1010747303957

Dunst, C.J., Trivette, C.M., & Hamby, D.W. (2010). Meta-analysis of the effectiveness of four adult learning methods and strategies: Supplemental tables and references. *Learning, 3*(1), 91–112.

Ford, M., Baer, C.T., Xu, D., Yapanel, U., & Gray, S. (2008). *The LENA™ language environment analysis system: Audio specifications of the DLP-0121.* Boulder, CO: LENA Foundation.

Frey, J.R., & Kaiser, A.P. (2010). The use of play expansions to increase the diversity and complexity of object play in young children with disabilities. *Topics in Early Childhood Special Education, 31*(2), 99–111. doi:10.1177/0271121410378758

Girolametto, L., Pearce, P.S., & Weitzman, E. (1996). Interactive focused stimulation for toddlers with expressive vocabulary delays. *Journal of Speech, Language, and Hearing Research, 39*(6), 1274–1283.

Hart, B., & Risley, T.R. (1975). Incidental teaching of language in the preschool. *Journal of Applied Behavior Analysis, 8*(4), 411–420.

Hart, B., & Risley, T.R. (1980). In vivo language intervention: Unanticipated general effects. *Journal of Applied Behavior Analysis, 13*(3), 407–432.

Hart, B., & Risley, T.R. (1995). *Meaningful differences in the everyday experience of young American children.* Baltimore, MD: Paul H. Brookes Publishing Co.

Hart, B., & Risley, T.R. (1999). *The social world of children: Learning to talk.* Baltimore, MD: Paul H. Brookes Publishing Co.

Hart, B., & Rogers-Warren, A. (1978). Milieu teaching approaches. In R.L. Schiefelbusch (Ed.), *Language intervention strategies* (Vol 2, pp. 192–235). Baltimore, MD: University Park Press.

Hoff, E. (2006). How social contexts support and shape language development. *Developmental Review, 26*(1), 55–88.

Ingersoll, B., & Schreibman, L. (2006). Teaching reciprocal imitation skills to young children with autism using a naturalistic behavioral approach: Effects on language, pretend play, and joint attention. *Journal of Autism and Developmental Disorders, 36*(4), 487–505. doi:http://dx.doi.org.proxy.library.vanderbilt.edu/10.1007/s10803-006-0089-y

Kaiser, A.P. (1993). Parent-implemented language intervention: An environmental system perspective. *Enhancing children's communication: Research foundations for intervention* 63–84.

Kaiser, A.P., & Delaney, E.M. (2001). Responsive conversations: Creating opportunities for naturalistic language teaching. *Young Exceptional Children Monograph Series, 3,* 13–23.

Kaiser, A.P., Hancock, T.B., & Hester, P.P. (1998). Parents as cointerventionists: Research on applications of naturalistic language teaching procedures. *Infants and Young Children, 10*(4), 46–55.

Kaiser, A. P., Hemmeter, M. L., & Alpert, C. L. (1992). Alternative intervention strategies for the treatment of communication disorders in young children with developmental disabilities. *Advances in school psychology,* 8, 7-43.

Kaiser, A.P., Hemmeter, M.L., Ostrosky, M.M., Fischer, R., Yoder, P., & Keefer, M. (1996). The effects of teaching parents to use responsive interaction strategies. *Topics in Early Childhood Special Education, 16*(3), 375–406.

Kaiser, A.P., Hester, P.P., Alpert, C.L., & Whiteman, B.C. (1995). Preparing parent trainers: An experimental analysis of effects on trainers, parents, and xhildren. *Topics in Early Childhood Special Education, 15*(4), 385–414.

Kaiser, A.P., & Roberts, M.Y. (2013a). Parent-implemented enhanced milieu teaching with preschool children who have intellectual disabilities. *Journal of Speech, Language, and Hearing Research, 56*(1), 295–309.

Kaiser, A.P., & Roberts, M.Y. (2013b). Parents as communication partners: An evidence-based strategy for improving parent support for language and communication in everyday settings. *Perspectives on Language Learning and Education, 20*(3), 96–111.

Kaiser, A.P., & Wright, C. (2013). Enhanced milieu teaching: Incorporating AAC into naturalistic teaching with young children and their partners. *Perspectives on Augmentative and Alternative Communication, 22*(1), 37–50.

Kasari, C., Freeman, S., & Paparella, T. (2006). Joint attention and symbolic play in young children with autism: A randomized controlled intervention study. *Journal of Child Psychology and Psychiatry, 47*(6), 611–620. doi:http://dx.doi.org.proxy.library.vanderbilt.edu/10.1111/j.1469-7610.2005.01567.x

Landa, R.J., Holman, K.C., O'Neill, A.H., & Stuart, E.A. (2011). Intervention targeting development of socially synchronous engagement in toddlers with autism spectrum disorder: A randomized controlled trial. *Journal of Child Psychology and Psychiatry, 52*(1), 13–21. doi:http://dx.doi.org.proxy.library.vanderbilt.edu/10.1111/j.1469-7610.2010.02288.x

MacDonald, J.D. (1989). *Becoming partners with children: From play to conversation. A developmental guide for professionals and parents.* Retrieved from http://eric.ed.gov/?id=ED386267

Mahoney, G., & McDonald, J. (2003). *Responsive teaching: Parent-mediated developmental intervention.* Baltimore, MD: Paul H. Brookes Publishing Co.

Marturana, E.R., & Woods, J.J. (2012). Technology-supported performance-based feedback for early intervention home visiting. *Topics in Early Childhood Special Education, 32*(1), 14–23.

Moerk, E. (1974). Changes in verbal child–mother interactions with increasing language skills of the child. *Journal of Psycholinguistic Research, 3*(2), 101–116.

Mundy, P., Block, J., Delgado, C., Pomares, Y., Van Hecke, A.V., & Parlade, M.V. (2007). Individual differences and the development of joint attention in infancy. *Child Development, 78*(3), 938–954. doi:10.1111/j.1467-8624.2007.01042.x

Mundy, P., Kasari, C., Sigman, M., & Ruskin, E. (1995). Nonverbal communication and early language acquisition in children with Down syndrome and in normally developing children. *Journal of Speech and Hearing Research, 38*(1), 157–167.

Mundy, P., Sigman, M., & Kasari, C. (1990). A longitudinal study of joint attention and language development in autistic children. *Journal of Autism and Developmental Disorders, 20*(1), 115–128.

Rheingold, H.L., Gewirtz, J.L., & Ross, H.W. (1959). Social conditioning of vocalizations in the infant. *Journal of Comparative and Physiological Psychology, 52*(1), 68–73.

Roberts, M.Y., & Kaiser, A.P. (2011). The effectiveness of parent-implemented language interventions: A meta-analysis. *American Journal of Speech-Language Pathology, 20*(3), 180–199. doi:10.1044/1058-0360(2011/10-0055)

Roberts, M.Y., & Kaiser, A.P. (2015). Early intervention for toddlers with language delays: A randomized controlled trial. *Pediatrics, 135(4),* 686-693.

Roberts, M.Y., Kaiser, A.P., Wolfe, C.E., Bryant, J.D., & Spidalieri, A.M. (2014). Effects of the Teach-Model-Coach-Review instructional approach on caregiver use of language support strategies and children's expressive language skills. *Journal of Speech, Language, and Hearing Research, 57*(5), 1851–1869.

Romski, M.A., Sevcik, R., & Adamson, L. (1997). Framework for studying how children with developmental disabilities develop language through augmented means. *Augmentative and Alternative Communication, 13*(3), 172–178.

Scherer, N.J., D'Antonio, L.L., & McGahey, H. (2008). Early intervention for speech impairment in children with cleft palate. *Cleft Palate-Craniofacial Journal, 45*(1), 18–31.

Schoenwald, S.K., Garland, A.F., Chapman, J.E., Frazier, S.L., Sheidow, A.J., & Southam-Gerow, M.A. (2011). Toward the effective and efficient measurement of implementation fidelity. *Administration and Policy in Mental Health and Mental Health Services Research, 38*(1), 32–43.

Schulte, A.C., Easton, J.E., & Parker, J. (2009). Advances in treatment integrity research: Multidisciplinary perspectives on the conceptualization, measurement, and enhancement of treatment integrity. *School Psychology Review, 38*(4), 460-475.

Siller, M., & Sigman, M. (2002). The behaviors of parents of children with autism predict the subsequent development of their children's communication. *Journal of Autism and Developmental Disorders, 32*(2), 77–89.

Skinner, B.F. (2014). *Verbal behavior.* Retrieved from https://books.google.ca/books?hl=en&lr=&id=v4CeAwAAQBAJ&oi=fnd&pg=PT1&dq=verbal+behavior&ots=9eVXMx_6Cp&sig=32fCOqRC9D3YLywAR7SW1REoXMU

Speidel, G.E., & Nelson, K.E. (1989). A fresh look at imitation in language learning. Speidel, G. E., & Nelson, K. E. (Eds.). In *The many faces of imitation in language learning* (pp. 1–21). New York, NY: Springer.

Sundberg, M.L., & Sundberg, C.A. (2011). Intraverbal behavior and verbal conditional discriminations in typically developing children and children with autism. *Analysis of Verbal Behavior, 27,* 23–43.

Tomasello, M. (1995). Joint attention as social cognition. Moore, C., & Dunham, P. (Eds.). In *Joint Attention: Its Origins and Role in Development,* (pp. 103–130) New York, NY:Psychology Press.

Tomasello, M., & Farrar, M.J. (1986). Joint attention and early language. *Child Development, 57*(6), 1454–1463. doi:10.2307/1130423

Trivette, C.M., Dunst, C.J., Hamby, D.W., & O'Herin, C.E. (2009). Characteristics and consequences of adult learning methods and strategies. *Winterberry Research, 2*(2), 1–33.

Walker, D., Carta, J.J., Greenwood, C.R., & Buzhardt, J.F. (2008). The use of individual growth and developmental indicators for progress monitoring and intervention decision making in early education. *Exceptionality, 16*(1), 33–47.

Woods, J., Kashinath, S., & Goldstein, H. (2004). Effects of embedding caregiver-implemented teaching strategies in daily routines on children's communication outcomes. *Journal of Early Intervention, 26*(3), 175–193.

Wright, C.A., & Kaiser, A.P. (in press). Teaching parents enhanced milieu teaching with words and signs using the Teach-Model-Coach-Review model. *Topics in Early Childhood Special Education.*

Yoder, P.J., Kaiser, A.P., Goldstein, H., Alpert, C., Mousetis, L., Kaczmarek, L., & Fischer, R. (1995). An exploratory comparison of milieu teaching and responsive interaction in classroom applications. *Journal of Early Intervention, 19*(3), 218–242.

Yoder, P.J., & Warren, S.F. (1998). Maternal responsivity predicts the prelinguistic communication intervention that facilitates generalized intentional communication. *Journal of Speech, Language, and Hearing Research, 41,* 1207–1219.

8

Putting It Together

Discussion Synthesis of Communication Interventions for Individuals with Severe Disabilities

Ellin B. Siegel, Diane Paul, and Lorraine Sylvester

This chapter provides an overview of the discussions surrounding the section of the conference on communication interventions for individuals with severe disabilities. The presentations provided summaries of research, research design challenges, measurement issues, research challenges, and recommendations for future clinical/educational research. The topics included an overview of research evidence (Brady and Snell), prelinguistic communication interventions (Warren), challenging behavior and replacement communication (Reichle), communication interventions for children who are deafblind (Rowland), communication interventions for children with specific etiologies (Kasari), augmentative and alternative communication (AAC) interventions (Romski and Sevcik), and parent training and communication interventions (Kaiser). This chapter provides a synthesis of these primary topics and the themes identified during the discussion.

WHAT IS THE STATE OF EVIDENCE?

Drs. Nancy Brady and Martha Snell presented the outcomes of a research review conducted by the National Joint Committee (NJC) for the Communication Needs of Persons with Severe Disabilities that appraised and synthesized communication research spanning 20 years with individuals who have severe disabilities (Snell et al., 2010; see Chapter 1). The review included 116 of 269 articles that met these criteria: 1) the research described an intervention study, 2) one or more participants had severe disabilities, and 3) the intervention was applied addressing one or more areas of communication. The 116 research articles that met the inclusionary criteria displayed the following primary characteristics: 1) sample included few participants (mean = 4), 2) participants were children (mean age of 13 years, 7 months), and 3) participants presented with intellectual disabilities (ID), autism spectrum disorder (ASD), or multiple disabilities. In addition, the participants communicated at emergent or prelinguistic levels, and the majority of the interventions focused on expression of behavior or emotional regulation with few focusing on receptive communication or language. More than 95% of the 116 studies reported positive, immediate results in target communication following intervention.

Common research challenges discussed included lack of specificity regarding treatment dosage (frequency or duration of instruction), limited reports of generalization outcomes (51%), as well as infrequently reported fidelity of treatment (32%), long-term effects (25%), social validity (16%), or intrarater reliability (3%). Brady and Snell discussed a number of recommendations for enhancing future research outcomes: 1) distinct participant descriptions, 2) assessment and reporting of generalization and maintenance data, and 3) stronger description of the distinct intervention practices. In addition, Brady and Snell shared ways to enhance future research by comparing naturalistic approaches (e.g., functional goals, multiple settings, distributed trials) and using a variety of AAC technology.

Discussion Synthesis

The discussion of the state of the evidence covered both broad and specific topics that can provide professionals with guidance to develop and implement more effective communication research outcomes and translate these outcomes into effective interventions and teaching methods. Expert panel members acknowledged that the NJC evidence-based practice research summary was valuable and also that the state of the science was modest, based on this review. The topic themes of discussion included specificity of information to allow replication, detailed description of participants, assessment of capabilities of individuals with severe disabilities, systematic and large-scale studies, and evaluation of published materials.

Specificity and Replicable Description The essential nature of relaying research methods that allow replicability and comparison of findings was the focus of the theme of specificity and replicable description. Small *n*, single-subject design research is valuable in demonstrating success and informing practice. It is essential that research methods of these studies are clearly delineated (see Chapters 9 and 11). Many of the studies reported salient measurement methods. Yet, the need to report specific dosage parameters was a primary concern that was discussed. Participants deliberated and agreed that future research reports could better inform practice by including these essential features—measurement of generalization, fidelity of treatment, long-term effects, social validity, and intrarater reliability.

Participant Description and Assessment Clear participant descriptions that include operationally defined pretreatment skills in terms of both receptive and expressive communication surfaced as a major recommendation to positively affect future research outcomes. It is critical for researchers to present a comprehensive and holistic view of participants' skills. Expert panel members shared the common scientific tradition of using assessment information to help predict an individual's learning outcomes. The panel and discussion participants, however, emphasized use of caution to ensure that these measures are not used to marginalize individuals if outcomes are not achieved. It is essential that the researchers describe the language and communication assessment outcomes of individual participants. Dr. Snell connected research to practice by recommending that assessments focus on describing who the person is and how he or she communicates and learns. This information can then be used in the context of describing the value of the intervention and specific, measured pre-post intervention outcomes.

Systematic, Large-Scale Studies Discussants acknowledged that there has been a growth in research in the area of severe disabilities. One expert panel member reflected on the Snell et al. (2010) systematic review and acknowledged that inclusion criteria were used to identify research articles. This panel member shared that it was rather sobering to realize the small number of included articles that were published with a relatively small number of participants. Although there is a paucity of research with large participant numbers, this same panel member pointed out that focusing on individuals with severe communication challenges makes a large contribution to what is known about language intervention and, in fact, may be overrepresented in spite of being a low-incidence population. If practitioners hope to use evidence-based interventions, then researchers must implement a broader scientific agenda, including systematic, large-scale studies that reflect and expand the knowledge of how individuals with the most severe challenges learn.

Published Materials with Evidence Basis A short discussion transpired about the practical needs in the field for practitioners to have materials available that address the question, "What intervention should I use?" The need to develop and test interventions that can be implemented by professionals in clinical and educational settings is essential. To that end, it is imperative to publish practical and evidence-based sources that are focused on interventions for individuals with severe disabilities.

Themes

The most critical theme discussed was the need for research that meets more stringent criteria. Outcomes must result in interventions that can be used in schools, homes, and communities across the communication partners who live and work with these individuals. It is essential that these partners (e.g., teachers, speech-language pathologists [SLPs], family members, other providers) have practical resources that are evidence based and have been demonstrated to promote relevant communication of individuals with severe disabilities in their daily lives.

PRELINGUISTIC INTERVENTIONS

Dr. Warren's presentation (see Chapter 2) focused on the topics of prelinguistic intervention and briefly reviewed basic intervention approaches, including prelinguistic milieu teaching, parent responsivity training, AAC approaches, and combinations of these three approaches. Dr. Warren explained that basic research findings document that parents and others can be taught to respond in ways that should enhance and support communication development. Responsivity alone demonstrates weak evidence to support its use for enhancing communication outcomes for young children with intellectual and developmental disabilities.

An overview of published preliminary results from a randomized, clinical trial involving prelinguistic milieu teaching and parent responsivity training was presented (Warren, Fey, & Yoder). Children were randomly assigned to 1 hour per week or 5 hours per week of intervention across 9 months with follow-up 6 months after treatment. All assessment and coding was performed by study personnel who were blind to the treatment assignment of the children they tested. There were no clinically significant effects or interactions involving either the low-intensity or high-intensity treatment groups. Tentative conclusions were that those most likely to benefit from as much as 5 hours of direct training per week among children with developmental delays who do not have ASD are children who start with a broad range of interests in toys/objects and numerous schemes for relating to them meaningfully. Dr. Warren acknowledged that 5 hours per week is low intensity in the context of the child's day and experiences.

Romski et al. (2010) shared evidence regarding using AAC to enhance speech production in young children with prelinguistic ability when compared with speech-only approaches. Dr. Warren recommended that future research focus on larger scale studies with children with developmental delays using AAC intervention combined with language-based intervention, such as milieu and parent responsivity approaches.

Research design challenges also surfaced in Warren's presentation. Prelinguistic intervention research has only recently moved beyond Phase 1 investigations that focus on developing interventions and conducting small *n* studies, which are useful tools for early research. Phase 2 research emphasizes studies that compare distinct interventions as well as comparing similar treatment at different intensities. The growing number of randomly controlled trials in the literature is promising. Further progress in these types of studies will be demonstrated with well-controlled differential treatment intensity, better proximal and distal measures, and better treatment fidelity. Innovative use of technology, such as the LENA System (Language ENvironment Analysis; www.lenafoundation.org), can enhance treatment fidelity and outcome measures. The lack of a standard definition of treatment intensity in behavioral research must be addressed with a focus on duration of treatment. It is imperative that the interventions that occur be explicitly described.

Discussion Synthesis

Prelinguistic intervention research focused on specific exchange of information regarding the Warren, Fey, and Yoder (2007) randomized, clinical trial research as well as general implications to communication intervention research. Themes identified throughout this discussion included intensity of treatment, technology tools used to collect data, critical participant factors, and methodological issues required in large-scale behavioral research.

Technology Tools: Automatic Language Data Collection LENA is an automatic language collection and analysis tool created by the nonprofit organization, LENA Research Foundation. This tool was used in the randomized, clinical trial study presented by Dr. Warren. The expert panel and conference participants asked for more information during this conference discussion period. Many studies have used this technology for a variety of purposes and it has potential as a valuable clinical tool. As reported by the Lena Research Foundation, LENA analyzes every millisecond of the audio file and produces core reports as well as segmented data for researchers to conduct additional analysis. The reports generated by this technology can provide numbers for many variables, including adult words, conversational turns, and child vocalizations, as well as comparative information across participants. This technology holds promise for the communication intervention research area and other areas of behavioral and educational research. A limitation of this technology is that it relies on auditory data collection and, thus, is not applicable to those individuals who do not use speech.

Treatment Intensity for Optimal Outcomes Discussion focused on the need to investigate the impact of quantifying intensities of treatment on outcomes. Discussion of variability in definitions of the term *treatment intensity* within research and clinical practice include 1) quality and quantity of service, 2) number of hours of intervention, 3) level of participation in a service, 4) ratio of children in a service context, and 5) quantification of specific intervention episodes. Dr. Warren proposed that defining intensity in the context of duration of treatment may prove advantageous in behavioral research as it is easily understood by a range of audiences (e.g., parents, teachers, policy makers). He cautioned that the specific prelinguistic interventions also must be quantified to predict factors that influence optimal outcomes. This can help answer the essential questions, "What are the primary variables of the intervention that resulted in positive outcomes for children?" and "How much of the intervention produced positive effects?"

Critical Child Variables Analogous to Brady and Snell's opening discussion of research challenges, attendees again explored the issue of including distinct descriptions of participant variables. Discussion focused on the fundamental need to define and report child-specific information regarding pre- and postintervention, including receptive and expressive skills and imitation and spontaneous communication, as well as cognition and learning.

Methodological Issues Dr. Warren and the expert panelists discussed the basic requirements of true clinical trials being infused into behavioral research focused on interventions for those with severe communication challenges. The fundamental methods of providing controls such as testers and coders being masked to conditions and child-specific information, thorough treatment fidelity measurement, and proximal and distal measures (immediate and generalization impacts) are critical as part of expanding the scientific approach to large-scale, systematic studies in communication intervention research.

Themes

It is critical that more prelinguistic research be focused on Phase 2 randomized, clinical trials. An expansion of responsivity intervention with milieu teaching that incorporates AAC warrants exploration and expansion. The communication intervention for individuals with severe communication challenges must be informed through more high-quality, large-scale research efforts.

CHALLENGING BEHAVIOR AND REPLACEMENT COMMUNICATION

Dr. Joe Reichle discussed the extent and persistence of challenging behaviors in children and the use of alternatives or communicative replacement behavior. He indicated that problem behaviors beyond the first few years will likely persist. He provided a summary of studies that show the correlation of challenging behavior with other serious problems, such as lower educational achievement, antisocial behavior, juvenile gang membership, and stress for families. Challenging behavior ranks as one of the top concerns by educators.

Problem behaviors were addressed for many years by trying to overpower the behavior with punishment procedures (e.g., time-out, overcorrection, response cost). These procedures, however, model undesirable behavior, are labor-intensive, and are ineffective. Differential reinforcement of communication behavior achieves better maintenance and generalization of lower levels of challenging behavior. This procedure uses differential reinforcement to promote desired communication behavior that serves the same function as existing challenging behavior. Reinforcement focuses on the more socially appropriate communicative alternative rather than the challenging behavior. The plan encourages the learner to choose the socially appropriate alternative more frequently. Contemporary approaches also recognize the need for functional equivalence in which a new alternative behavior is functionally equivalent to the problem behavior (e.g., escape, gain, or maintain access to objects, task, or activity). Reichle stressed that response efficiency also needs to be considered when identifying a communicative alternative to challenging behavior.

Reichle reported on a systematic review of studies that focus on functional communication training (FCT) for challenging behavior with people with severe disabilities. *FCT* uses alternative, more socially acceptable, communication behavior to replace challenging behavior (Kuhn, Chirighin, & Zelenka, 2010). Findings indicated that recipients of FCT are often nonverbal (42%), and approximately one third use primarily single words. Most of the FCT is implemented outside of the classroom (52%). Other settings include general education classrooms (22%) and special education classrooms (20%). About 53% of the FCT is implemented by trained experimenters. Prompting procedures used in implementing FCT follows a most-to-least prompt hierarchy (50%) or, less frequently, a least-to-most prompt hierarchy (28.6%).

Future research efforts surrounding challenging behavior can address crucial areas by incorporating examination of collateral behavioral gains (e.g., vocal production, speech comprehension), exploring social functions of communication, incorporating cultural influences in selecting and implementing interventions, and considering physiological influences as setting events for challenging behavior. Topics of intervention delivery strategies, methodological areas for scientific inquiry, and the need for better procedural fidelity were shared.

Discussion

Research design issues surfaced during the discussion of investigations about challenging behavior. Most of these studies focus on attempts to make the behavior of children and adults less challenging. Few studies, however, address ways to train those who implement interventions (e.g., staff, professionals) or how to achieve intervention fidelity of those providing the interventions. Improvements in preservice education and follow-up at the in-service level are critical to optimize services and supports for children and adults with severe disabilities. A major goal is to train staff and professionals on ways to respond to challenging behavior and use procedures to limit its resurgence.

Themes

One primary theme focused on educating preprofessional personnel about challenging behavior (preservice). A second theme focused on providing more systematic education for professionals (inservice).

Preservice and In-service Training Issues Personnel preparation for those who will work with children who have challenging behaviors can be improved. Ideas shared included 1) creating courses that include high-technology simulation education for preservice students and practitioners, 2) providing opportunities for practice with students who have challenging behaviors, 3) offering mentoring in classrooms as a part of in-service training, and 4) providing on-the-job training. Fidelity and maintenance are key variables to address in personnel training. Systematic, hands-on training is needed for preservice students and practitioners to learn and apply intervention techniques with fidelity.

Intervention Strategies A combination of intervention approaches should be considered for children and adults with challenging behaviors. For example, FCT often is mentioned in isolation. An isolated approach, however, only solves problems in the short term. Antecedent-focused training was one strategy suggested to be paired with FCT.

COMMUNICATION INTERVENTIONS FOR CHILDREN WHO ARE DEAFBLIND

Dr. Charity Rowland defined deafblindness and provided a count of children and youth who are deafblind. Defining features of individuals who are deafblind are central visual acuity of 20/200 or less, chronic severe hearing loss, and extreme difficulty attaining independence in daily life activities, achieving psychosocial adjustment, or obtaining a vocation (U.S. Code Title 29, Chapter 21). Approximately 10,000 individuals from birth to 21 years in the United States are deafblind. Forty percent have four or more additional disabilities, with the most common being a cognitive impairment (78%). Known causes are hereditary syndromes/disorders (e.g., CHARGE (Coloboma of the eye; Heart defects; Atresia of the choanae; Retardation of growth and development; Genital and/or urinary abnormalities; Ear abnormalities and deafness), Usher syndrome, Down syndrome [DS]), prenatal congenital complications (e.g., cytomegalovirus, micro or hydrocephaly, rubella), postnatal/noncongenital complications (e.g., asphyxia, meningitis, traumatic brain injury, encephalitis), and complications of preterm births.

Deafblindness has a strong impact on many facets of life. Rowland discussed the effects on social-emotional functioning and cognitive skills. Social-emotional consequences include attachment difficulty and learned helplessness. Cognitive skills are affected in the areas of awareness, communicative intent, world knowledge, memory, symbolic representation, and metacognition. Rowland described the communication-related issues, such as receptive strategies (e.g., gestures, touch cues, tangible cues, hand-in-hand manual signs) and expressive strategies (e.g., movement-based approaches, presymbolic gestures/facial expressions, tangible two- and three-dimensional symbols). Rowland discussed the need to document outcomes and the need for communication intervention and instructional strategies to be partner focused and individualized.

Research studies pertaining to communication intervention for children who are deafblind are scarce and primarily use case studies, single-subject, and pre-post designs. Research challenges are numerous and include 1) small sample (e.g., small numbers of individuals and difficulty finding matched controls due to the heterogeneity of the population), 2) independent variable (treatment) issues (e.g., highly individualized interventions, difficulty withdrawing or waiting for treatment), 3) the dependent variable (e.g., dependent on context and partner; finding meaningful measurement parameters, such as rate, initiation, clarity), 4) implementation (e.g., fidelity, experience of practitioners, length of treatment time), 5) analysis (e.g., meeting statistical assumptions, limitations of single-subject/multiple baseline data, clinical versus educational significance), and 6) measurement (e.g., collecting meaningful performance data, demonstrating generalization and social validity, lacking appropriate standardized instruments).

Rowland suggested that technological advances and new education and health care policies may help in the future by correcting sensory impairments, improving access to world experience, and identifying ways for children with deafblindness to communicate more effectively.

Themes

Primary themes discussed were implementing dynamic adjustments within instructional programs and the importance of monitoring progress.

Dynamic Instruction Rowland discussed the need for constant adjustments in instructional programs for children who are deafblind so that interventions can be beneficial. Every change in presymbolic and symbolic intervention variables is designed to promote success.

Ongoing Monitoring The discussion also focused on the theme of ongoing monitoring to track progress. Individual student outcomes should be monitored and regularly tracked on intervention record forms by families and practitioners. Adjustments in presymbolic and symbolic intervention variables and consistent tracking may improve outcomes for others with severe disabilities.

COMMUNICATION INTERVENTION FOR CHILDREN WITH SPECIFIC ETIOLOGIES (DOWN SYNDROME AND AUTISM SPECTRUM DISORDER)

Dr. Connie Kasari reviewed evidence surrounding communication interventions for children with specific etiologies, which include DS and ASD. Communication interventions for this group of children are not consistent, and treatment effectiveness is often difficult to discern. The specific behavior patterns demonstrated by children with varied diagnoses such as DS and ASD suggest that targeted interventions are effective; however, evidence supporting effectiveness is mixed. Communication is part of a greater whole of intervention with goals and outcomes that are different, especially for children with ASD. Research revealed that interventions for children with ASD were comprehensive and sometimes targeted. The treatments, however, often were focused on core deficits in ASD, not specifically communication and language, even though communication is one of the core deficits associated with this population. Comprehensive interventions usually have broader goals with outcomes reflecting standardized measures (e.g., IQ, adaptive behavior, language age). Targeted interventions have goals that are more specific to core deficits, and the outcomes were observational and based on experimental tests. For example, a number of group-design studies investigated changes in IQ as the outcome (not specifically elements of communication). Intervention outcomes were dependent and related to the intervention approach used. It is essential to consider the intervention provider (clinician versus parent-mediated treatment) as well as the treatment strategies implemented. Studies may have demonstrated individual child improvement; few, if any, showed significant treatment differences (Landa, Holman, O'Neill, & Stuart, 2011; Sallows & Graupner, 2005; Yoder & Stone, 2006). One factor contributing to this finding is that significant treatment differences may not be discernable if children receive multiple and/or simultaneous interventions while researchers focus on just one. Finally, many intervention studies reported limited follow-up after the interventions were provided; that is, it was not always clear that the results generalized across settings and were maintained over time.

Comprehensive versus Targeted Interventions for Children with Autism Spectrum Disorder

Studies showed large dosing differences between comprehensive and targeted interventions for children with ASD but rarely reported results that specifically compare one intervention to another. Comparative efficacy studies are rare and do not rule out dose issues for the business-as-usual control. Business as usual, notwithstanding the intervention, can mean different things to different clinicians and researchers. These studies may demonstrate individual child improvement, but few, if any, showed significant treatment differences (Landa et al., 2011; Sallows & Graupner, 2005; Yoder & Stone, 2006). Although active influences involved in treatment effectiveness need to be considered, evidence suggests that these are not clearly delineated in most intervention studies. A study may focus on one aspect of intervention; however, researchers may neglect to consider the myriad of other interventions that a child with ASD may be getting simultaneously.

In the effort to tease out the impact of various treatment mediators, Kasari used a randomized control group design to investigate communication changes for children with ASD in early intervention who were in a 5- to 6-week program. Results indicated that outcomes are not only related to skills taught, but that supported engagement also is critical to improving a child's communication, regardless of whether sessions are parent or clinician mediated.

Research Challenges Kasari highlighted many research challenges as part of the conference discussion. What is taught and how it is taught matters. Evidence that indicates treatment effectiveness is important, but researchers and clinicians also need to know if communication changes are meaningful. In other words, how do they determine the correct level of responsiveness, especially in a heterogeneous population? What is the best sequence of interventions, and how are they selected given the current evidence base? Clinicians and researchers need to be concerned with developmental abilities of children and focus treatment at their level. Using a model that considers only the child's developmental level is not the same as targeting the child's development. Research designs need to be rigorous and outcomes need to be meaningful.

Dr. Kasari echoed the findings and discussions from the first presentation (Brady and Snell) in terms of challenges to research surrounding targeted communication interventions for children with ASD. Kasari identified a number of themes surrounding intervention strategies and research design that focus on implementing developmental, social, and communicatively matched skills; strategies to develop and maintain caregiver buy-in to the interventions; and ways to develop sequential, multiple assignment, randomized trial (SMART) research designs.

Themes

Themes that emerged during the discussion were 1) selecting interventions that match development and social communication, 2) selecting specific treatment outcomes, and 3) ensuring parental acceptance and implementation of the interventions.

Matching Current Development and Social-Communication Play Skills Kasari discussed the importance of knowing the child's development and current social-communication play skills before choosing an intervention model and before moving to a higher communication level. It is critical to discern the core communication deficits that a child exhibits and match interventions to these core areas. Once interventionists know which areas to address, then a determination is made regarding the primary ingredients within the treatment program and the outcomes are investigated based on factors such as dose, provider, setting, and the most important components of the intervention.

Intervention Acceptance It is critical to implement strategies that promote caregiver buy-in to the interventions and document how well parents accept and implement the programs. Research can consider buy-in related to how intervention is viewed by family members (e.g., using rating scales to see how well families implement treatment) and also can address challenges of completing interventions within a reasonable amount of time. Some of the discussion focused on equating timely completion of treatment (e.g., considering cancellations) to the buy-in and to the relative density of the treatment because this may relate to outcomes ultimately achieved.

Research Design Concerns arose regarding how researchers and interventionists determine responsiveness that is related to meaningful changes in communication. Considerations must include the heterogeneity of the population and sequencing interventions. Some discussion was about conducting studies with greater power (at the second randomization) using a SMART design (Murphy, 2010). More information and references on SMART designs are available at http://home.isr.umich.edu/releases/susan-murphy-wins-2013-macarthur-genius-grant.

AUGMENTATIVE AND ALTERNATIVE COMMUNICATION INTERVENTIONS

Drs. Mary Ann Romski and Rose Sevcik reported findings from studies surrounding AAC interventions, discussed challenges with research design in these studies related to measurement, and proposed future research areas. Individuals with severe disabilities who use AAC form a heterogeneous group that spans chronological age from infancy to adulthood and a wide range of medical etiologies. This group exhibits mild to significant levels of ID and is identified by communication profile rather than etiology. These individuals often have a wide range of physical disabilities and an array of access modes and communication responses, similar to findings from Roberts and Kasari (2011).

AAC interventions include both aided (e.g., communication boards, Picture Exchange Communication System [PECS], speech generating devices [SGDs]) as well as unaided communication (e.g., gestures, manual signs). SGDs are now more affordable and available to a broader range of users, and these may include smartphone and tablet applications, an important change in access over the last generation, although these are not yet research based in the applications. This typical technology is available to all children, thus increasing access for students with disabilities as new integrated technology emerges.

AAC interventions address communication needs of children and adults who cannot consistently rely on speech for communication for a variety of reasons. AAC was historically used for individuals with output problems, specifically older individuals and those who had not acquired verbal communication. AAC was perceived to be a last resort treatment after other communication interventions failed in its early days of implementation. Children who had ID often were not afforded AAC interventions because clinicians believed the children needed a prerequisite set of cognitive and prelinguistic skills in order for AAC to be effective. These skills had to be fully intentional and include a predefined cognitive level. These prerequisite skills often set up barriers and, in fact, denied opportunities for successful communication using AAC devices with many children.

Although it is apparent that children respond robustly to AAC in combination with other intervention strategies, Romski indicated that adults' responses would depend on the experiences the adults bring to the communication task. For example, adults with good comprehension skills demonstrate greater frequency of expression.

Discussion

Romski and Sevcik reiterated Kasari's findings that children demonstrated more communication behaviors when they were within their own developmental comfort zone. Augmented input can be helpful if children are not processing auditory-linguistic symbols alone. The additional modality (AAC) provides support for comprehension and learning. Romski and Sevcik focused on several themes: 1) working within the child's developmental comfort zone, 2) the importance of using AAC in combination with other approaches, 3) designing intervention approaches that affect overall communication rather than limited word use, 4) recognizing that there are no prerequisites for children or adults to gain access to AAC interventions, and 5) the impact of AAC intervention on communication of adults with severe disabilities.

Themes

Primary themes included 1) implementing AAC in a way that matches developmental level, 2) using a hybrid of input and output interventions, and 3) targeting interventions that focus on language use beyond single words.

Developmental Comfort Zone Children and parents are generally responsive to AAC, especially if the program is tailored to what parents identify as communication needs. Romski suggested that the nature of the intervention tends to ground the children in familiar and developmentally comfortable routines.

Combinatorial Approaches Romski suggested that a hybrid model of input/output gives the best effect on vocabulary learning. AAC interventions are viable approaches for children with severe disabilities and are a tool for language development. Use of AAC does not hinder development of speech. AAC can be used as a strategy to move children into speaking as well as improve language and communication for individuals who will never speak.

AAC to Move Beyond Limited Word Use to More Complete Language It is sometimes difficult for practitioners to know how to provide augmented input when the child only uses single words. Therefore, it is critical to use modeling and traditional language intervention strategies that focus on word combinations and early syntactic structures for a child with minimal language experience. Clinicians must move beyond single words into combinations and more complete language. Admittedly, it is difficult to develop strategies, protocols, and routines to extend language; clinicians can use less focused input as the child develops more sophisticated language.

Teach Individuals to Use Augmentative and Alternative Communication AAC interventions enable many children and adults with significant disabilities to communicate more effectively. There has been a shift in recent years away from thinking that children need prerequisite cognitive and/or prelinguistic skills before they can benefit from AAC interventions. The NJC has worked hard to eliminate the misconception that an individual must demonstrate particular prerequisite skills in order to gain access to AAC interventions. Although no child or adult with severe disabilities should be denied the opportunity to use AAC communication strategies based on lack of prerequisite skills, interventionists still need to expect to teach children how to communicate using AAC (NJC, 2002, 2003).

Adults with Disabilities Using Augmentative and Alternative Communication Similarities and differences exist between AAC use in children and adults. When interventionists consider using augmented input and output for adults, they see similarities and differences comparable to children. Clinicians must look at what an adult brings to the communication task, especially an adult that has acquired communication impairments. They need to consider the adult's prior experiences that promote or negate positive communication interaction.

PARENT-IMPLEMENTED INTERVENTIONS

It is common for parents to be involved in training their children and enhancing their communication. Parent training makes sense and is effective from developmental and behavioral perspectives. Parents support language learning using multiple communication patterns and are tuned into both input and responsivity during the interactions with their children (Kushnir & Wellman, 2010; Perry, 2015). Input, social interaction, joint attention, and scaffolding are all strategies that parents and all communication partners can and should use to promote effective communication across the lifespan. Outcome measures for individuals with severe disabilities may need to be more sensitive, however, and include 1) a number of spontaneous, socially communicative utterances, 2) independent communication attempts, rather than number of words uttered, and 3) a range of contexts in which communication is used. Communication behavior may vary depending on the level and type of partner support. This multilayered process is not easily replicated in intervention studies, however, especially when there are varying support levels between individuals in different diagnostic groups (e.g., differences between children with varying developmental disabilities) or differences with regard to socioeconomic or cultural diversity.

Impact of Diversity on Interventions and Outcomes

The conference discussion focused on the impact of cultural and socioeconomic diversity on communication behaviors and outcomes. If parent training can increase the impact of early language interventions, then it is essential to examine the criteria that can determine effectiveness. Researchers and practitioners need to consider the influence of variables such as socioeconomic status, culture, and how parents respond within these demographic parameters. These influences raise concern about participation disparities within communication research. That is, those families that become involved in studies are a small subset of children and families who are likely more motivated to participate in the studies. Therefore, research lacks diversity. The discussion concluded that it is important that researchers address how to gain family members participation across demographic parameters.

Impact of Parent-Implemented Interventions Kaiser and her colleagues conducted a meta-analysis of parent-implemented language interventions to determine the extent to which parent-implemented language interventions were effective for enhancing the language skills of children between 18 and 60 months of age (Roberts & Kaiser, 2011). They examined whether parent-implemented intervention positively affected language outcomes of young children with language impairments and which aspects of outcomes were affected by the interventions. In addition, the meta-analysis focused on how the effects of parent-implemented interventions differed for children with and without ID.

Kaiser and colleagues (Roberts & Kaiser, 2011) found that parent training changes parent behavior, with the largest effects found for responsiveness, expressive language, and expressive syntax. Parent-implemented interventions hold the advantage when compared with clinician-implemented interventions. There are similar effects, though smaller and less significant, for receptive language and expressive syntax during parent-implemented sessions. Parent-implemented interventions are found to be effective for children with and without disabilities. Larger effect sizes, however, are noted for the children who had only language (without cognitive) limitations.

Research limitations relative to fidelity of parent training and generalizability over time and settings were of concern during the conference discussion. The meta-analyses were unclear about the parent training methods used, specifically when distinguishing between parent education and parent training. Parent education tends to be more general and supportive, whereas parent training takes a more systematic approach. The effectiveness of specific language teaching strategies also were not reported. Generalization to other settings was not measured after interventions were accomplished in clinics, nor were there follow-up studies regarding language development over time. Finally, none of the included studies investigated parent-implemented interventions in combination with clinician-implemented interventions. Nevertheless, outcomes provide modest evidence that parent-implemented interventions can result in positive language outcomes.

Impact of Combined Clinician–Parent Intervention Kaiser and Roberts' study (2013) investigated the impact of a combined parent–clinician-implemented intervention to discern the added effect to typical clinician-implemented models; that is, would language outcomes be more robust with this combined approach? Kaiser and Roberts used a randomized control design, counter-balanced study to determine what parent and child characteristics predicted children's growth in language. Results showed big differences in parent behavior but no statistically significant differences in standardized outcome measures. They found statistically significant outcomes in children's use of functional language at home and across time, however. Differences between trained and untrained parents were apparent in every case. Parents that were trained saw generalized results across routines at home and retained core strategies over time after the intervention ceased. Children's results generalized in both groups but were stronger for the children whose parents were trained relative to those in the untrained routines, particularly with children who had ASD. Although study results were not generalizable due to the small sample size, children with parent training still demonstrated more positive outcomes compared with clinician-only interventions.

Discussion

Kaiser and conference participants identified a number of issues and themes surrounding parent-implemented interventions. First and foremost, parents are powerful partners in communication intervention from developmental and behavioral perspectives. Although clinicians have demonstrable evidence of the effectiveness of parent- implemented interventions, Kaiser discussed how these findings may differ from previous discussions during this conference. The key to the success of her team's parent-implemented interventions surrounded the use of systematic strategies for training parents/partners while maintaining a high level of training fidelity, which should enable parents to achieve the maintenance and generalization of skills over time. Fidelity of the parent training is the primary factor in determining the effectiveness of parent-implemented treatment for children with severe disabilities. Training parents to implement communication interventions improves child outcomes in a variety of venues: parents as primary interventionists, parents partnering with SLPs or other practitioners, and parents as part of a team of practitioners that support communication.

Themes

Parents as Partners Parent-implemented intervention is effective in realizing child communication outcomes. Research now needs to focus on ways to maximize the impact of parent training while considering models of change for the parent/partner that lead to the effects of increased communication support for the child. Clinicians need to 1) further investigate the impact of training fidelity on parents, parent implementation, and response to treatment models over time as children get older; 2) identify the component differences and similarities relative to the adaptations or protocol deviations needed to accomplish the parent training and interventions; and 3) identify the proximal and distal measures using varying supports in different contexts relative to outcomes that include independent communication and social utterances.

Parent Training Styles Kaiser discussed the fact that some parents prefer to observe and model before getting into direct training; it is important to recognize that parents may exhibit varying preferences relative to the amount and type of interaction they have with their children during intervention. Interventionists need to consider the diverse cultural, linguistic, and socioeconomic status relative to the disproportionate representation of middle-class and upper middle-class participants in the majority of research that has been conducted. Parent training and parent implementation of intervention sessions may be disrupted by a number of issues, most notably, the health of the child or family.

Diversity Kaiser discussed that sample diversity will remain a challenge, especially when considering children with ASD who do not speak. Supporting the social process and parental responsiveness is the critical piece for children with ASD. Parents need to become skilled at supporting their child's communication. Parents of children with DS may be more supportive and systematic when children are younger, but the changes are less dramatic compared with other children (with ASD).

Protocol deviations are needed when families are non–English speaking, have low incomes, or have other family interruptions. Delivering effective interventions for struggling families needs to be learned. Research outcome results are often quite different for children with ASD compared with other developmental disabilities, likely due to incomparable child and parent groups.

Interventionists need to take care and not mistake poverty issues for cultural diversity. Yet, they recognize that many minority groups are disproportionately impoverished. Although interventionists work with low-income families, they generally do not get the opportunity to work with parents who do not sign the consent forms or do not have their children in school. Kaiser reported that neither socioeconomic status, race, ethnicity, education level, nor willingness to be trained predicted any difference in the way parent training or intervention was provided. Getting parents to intervention sessions on a regular basis so that the treatment did not become diluted was challenging. Parents involved in the studies previously described were generally educated mothers and some fathers and grandparents, with minimal racial diversity. Kaiser expressed concern about the fact that research has allowed interventionists to learn a lot about a small number of children, but the most challenging children are the ones they know the least about.

Overall Themes About Communication Interventions from Day One Discussions

- Research conducted with individuals with severe communication needs must clearly delineate the interventions used.
- Research should focus on interventions that are meaningful and usable to educators, clinicians, and family members within the practical life context of individuals and families.
- Families exhibit greater buy-in to communication interventions when they understand outcomes and can see the value for themselves and their children.
- AAC intervention continues to provide viable communication options for children and adults with severe disabilities, alone or in combination with other strategies to enhance communication skills.
- New technology to collect data should be investigated across intervention settings for children with severe communication challenges who may or may not have speech.
- Research on effective parent-implemented and clinician-implemented practices needs continued exploration.
- Parents and children with cultural and socioeconomic diversity should be included as participants in communication intervention research.
- The use of large-scale research (randomized, clinical trial) for individuals with severe communication challenges needs to increase.

REFERENCES

Kaiser, A.P., & Roberts, M.Y. (2013). Parent-implemented enhanced milieu teaching with preschool children who have intellectual disabilities. *Journal of Speech, Language, and Hearing Research, 56,* 295–309.

Kuhn, D.D., Chirighin, A.E., & Zelenka, K. (2010). Discriminated functional communication: A procedural extension of functional communication training. *Journal of Applied Behavior Analysis, 43*(2), 249–264.

Kushnir, T., Xu, F., & Wellman, H.M. (2010). Young children use statistical sampling to infer the preferences of other people. *Psychological Science, 21,* 1134–1140.

Landa, R.J., Holman, K.C., O'Neill, A.H., & Stuart, E.A. (2011). Intervention targeting development of socially synchronous engagement in toddlers with autism spectrum disorder: A randomized controlled trial. *Journal of Child Psychology and Psychiatry and Allied Disciplines, 52*(1), 13–21.

Murphy, S. (2010). *Computer science, adaptive treatment strategies, and SMART. Behavioral intervention optimization: Capitalizing on engineering, computer science, and technology.* Bethesda, MD: National Institute on Drug Abuse.

National Joint Committee for the Communication Needs of Persons with Severe Disabilities. (2002). *Access to communication services and supports: Concerns regarding the application of restrictive "eligibility" policies* [Technical report]. Retrieved online from http://www.asha.org/policy/TR2002-00233.htm

National Joint Committee for the Communication Needs of Persons with Severe Disabilities. (2003). *Position statement on access to communication services and supports: Concerns regarding the application of restrictive "eligibility" policies.* Retrieved online from http://www.asha.org/policy/PS2003-00227.htm

Perry, B.D. (2015). *How young children learn language.* Retrieved from www.scholastic.com/teachers/article/how-young-children-learn-language

Picture Exchange Communication System (PECS). Developed by Andrew S. Bondy, Ph.D. & Lori Frost, M.S., CCC/SLP as retrieved online at http://www.pecsusa.com/pecs.php

Roberts, M.Y., & Kaiser, A.P. (2011). The effectiveness of parent-implemented language interventions: A meta-analysis. *American Journal of Speech-Language Pathology, 20,* 180–199.

Romski, M.A., Sevcik, R.A, Adamson, L.A., Cheslock, M., Smith, A., Barker, R.M., & Bakeman, R. (2010). Randomized comparison of augmented and nonaugmented language interventions for toddlers with developmental delays and their parents. *Journal of Speech, Language, and Hearing Research, 53,* 350–364.

Sallows G.O., & Graupner, T.D. (2005). Intensive behavioral treatment for children with autism: Four-year outcome and predictors. *American Journal on Mental Retardation, 110*(6), 417–438.

Snell, M.E., Brady, N., McLean, L., Ogletree, W., Siegel, E., Sylvester, L., Sevcik, R. (2010). Twenty years of intervention research on the communication intervention research on the communication interaction of individuals who have severe disabilities. *American Journal on Intellectual and Developmental Disabilities, 115,* 363–380.

Warren, S.F., Fey, M.E., & Yoder, P.J. (2007). Differential treatment intensity research: A missing link to creating optimally effective communication interventions. *Mental Retardation and Developmental Disabilities Research Reviews, 13*(1), 70–77.

Warren, S., Gilkerson, J., Richards, J., Oller, K., Xu, D., Yapanel, U., & Gray, S. (2010, April). *Using LENA to map the language learning environments and vocal behavior of young children with ASD.* Conference proceedings by the first LENA User's Conference, Denver, CO.

Yoder, P., & Stone, W. (2006). A randomized comparison of the effect of two prelinguistic communication interventions on the acquisition of spoken communication in preschoolers with ASD. *Journal of Speech, Language, and Hearing Research, 49,* 698–711.

II

Challenges for Communication Intervention Research

Design Methods Issues

9

Behavioral Heterogeneity in People with Severe Intellectual Disabilities

Integrating Single-Case and Group Designs to Develop Effective Interventions

William J. McIlvane, Anne-Therese Hunt, Joanne B. Kledaras, and Curtis K. Deutsch

Most people with intellectual and developmental disabilities (IDD) were consigned to institutions until a sustained national effort was initiated in the United States more than 50 years ago. Although often called schools, institutions provided little education. There was little to no effective methodology for teaching people with IDD—some questioned whether they could learn at all. Negative opinions left many people with IDD relegated to care that often isolated them socially and sometimes led to neglect and abuse. The history and evolution of thinking concerning IDD in the United States has been summarized in an extensive scholarly treatment by Trent (1994).

The negative prospects for people with IDD began to change in the middle of the last century, due in no small measure to the efforts of Eunice Kennedy Shriver and her family. For example, the National Institute of Child Health and Human Development was established in part to develop a national biomedical and behavioral science research initiative through its Mental Retardation branch (since renamed the Intellectual and Developmental Disabilities branch). Other institutes (e.g., National Institute on Deafness and Other Communication Disorders, National Institute of Mental Health) also committed a portion of their resources to meet the challenges of people with IDD and their families. In parallel, other agencies (e.g.,

The research program described here has received long-term support from the National Institutes of Health, particularly the National Institute of Child Health and Human Development (NICHD). Preparation of this chapter was supported by an Intellectual and Developmental Disabilities Research Center grant from NICHD (HD04147), by individual grants to Dr. McIlvane from NIDCD and NIMH (DC10365, MH90272), and by funding from the Commonwealth Medicine Division of the University of Massachusetts Medical School.

Administration on Developmental Disabilities, Maternal and Child Heath Bureau) launched training and service initiatives that sought to create the infrastructure needed to support people with IDD and their families, initially within the institutions and subsequently in increasing numbers of community programs.

Fast forward to the present day. Many people with IDD are reasonably well integrated within society. Individuals with IDD remain with their families to the extent possible during their lifetimes. Children often attend public schools, may be included in classrooms with typically developing children, and have individualized education programs. Individuals with IDD of all ages are now visible in society, engage in sports via typical routes or in the Special Olympics, may have gainful employment, and generally experience a fuller range of life's benefits and challenges than people with IDD who lived out their lives in institutions earlier in the 20th century.

SEVERE INTELLECTUAL DISABILITIES

Gratifying as the successes have been, individuals remain who need help overcoming de facto (if not physical) isolation from the social environment—people whose development of effective communication skills is such that they have great difficulty expressing needs, preferences, and other aspects of social discourse. Although augmentative and alternative communication (AAC) systems have helped many people engage socially to some degree (cf. Beukelman & Miranda, 2013; Romski & Sevcik, 1996), others may make little-to-no progress with AAC or other forms of communication intervention.

Although a low-incidence group, service provision can prove very costly. Children who fail to develop adequate communication skills are at high risk for expensive residential treatment in progressive areas of the United States (tuitions in Massachusetts may exceed $200,000 annually). Opportunities for developing communication skills and adequate social adjustment may be negligible in areas where these supports are not available; individuals may be susceptible to unmet needs or even abuse. Communication impairments that are left uncorrected are often associated with chronic aberrant behavior (CAB) that can be dangerous to the individual and others (e.g., Durand, 1990). In turn, amelioration of communication impairments may prevent or replace CAB (Frea, Arnold, & Vittimberga, 2001; Mirenda, 1997; see Chapter 3). Thus, effective intervention for communication impairments has a high potential impact. In that light, one might be surprised that the National Institutes of Health (NIH) RePORTER indicates the needs of people with severe disabilities have attracted only very modest support from the NIH. This chapter 1) suggests reasons why the challenges of severe IDD have not attracted more attention and support, 2) describes efforts to resolve these challenges, which may be more tractable than they might appear, and 3) discusses approaches and methodologies for conducting research to inform evidence-based intervention.

RESEARCH ISSUE: DEVELOPING EVIDENCE-BASED INTERVENTION FOR SEVERE INTELLECTUAL AND DEVELOPMENTAL DISABILITIES

A critical research issue is how to structure research and procedure development to produce the evidence needed to support evidence-based communication intervention for people with severe IDD. This population presents a number of conceptual and logistical challenges that must be overcome, including difficulties in effectively communicating with these individuals, complexities of managing the behavioral heterogeneity that one regularly encounters, and obstacles relating to recruiting samples of the size needed to establish the reliability and generality of findings that undergird evidence-based intervention.

The authors of this chapter represent members of a research group at the Shriver Center that has been engaged in relevant research for more than 50 years. Experimental designs used in the research have included a miscellany of single-case designs (Barlow, Nock, & Hersen, 2009) and designs that involve comparing groups of individuals to assess, for example, the relative effectiveness of different teaching procedures or the impact of different diagnoses on behavior (e.g., Dickson, Deutsch, Wang, & Dube, 2006). The perspective present here has been developed over decades of struggling with research issues previously outlined.

Among the group's best-known early contributions was translation of procedures from basic research with nonhumans to develop effective instructional technology for people with severe IDD. Shriver researchers learned early on that teaching challenges could often (perhaps virtually always) be formulated in terms of increasing the effectiveness of communication. Sidman and Stoddard conveyed this perspective when they wrote

> At the very outset of our work we were struck by an observation that has formed the basis for all of our subsequent investigations. The most pressing initial question is 'How do I communicate with this patient?' In our work we have assumed the responsibility for finding methods of communication when we are able to communicate with the [child with ID] s/he is capable of responding [to teaching], often at levels far higher than anyone would have expected. (1966, p. 152)

Sidman and Stoddard's 1966 chapter in the *International Review of Research in Mental Retardation* describes processes in developing a procedure for evaluating aspects of visual perception—via a circle-ellipse discrimination task—that does not rely on verbal instruction (and thus can be effective even with people who do not understand verbal instructions). Beyond the details of the specific techniques employed, the project illustrates a methodological approach by which even people with severe IDD can be taught new skills efficiently.

The goal of the research conducted by the Shriver group has been nothing less than development of methodologies that are routinely effective across a broad range of individuals and populations with communication challenges (e.g., individuals with severe IDD, neurological patients, nonhumans), thus rendering them useful for application by neurologists and other professionals conducting clinical assessments.

In developing their circle-ellipse program, Sidman and Stoddard (1966) evaluated many program enhancements as their numbers of participants grew over time. These enhancements were mainly studied with individuals or small groups and were incorporated into the program based on apparent effectiveness. With much diligent effort, they arrived at a program that approaches the goal of broad effectiveness with the populations that they studied.

CHALLENGES IN INTERVENTION RESEARCH FOR PEOPLE WITH SEVERE INTELLECTUAL AND DEVELOPMENTAL DISABILITIES

Behavioral Heterogeneity in Severe Intellectual and Developmental Disabilities

In retrospect, Sidman and Stoddard (1966) addressed a key issue early on that continues to be important today—how to manage the substantial behavioral heterogeneity associated with the many etiologies (known and unknown) that are associated with severe IDD. Notably, they made most of their progress in program development with single-subject or small-*n* research designs.[1]

Sidman and Stoddard (1966) took on broad range of people, largely without regard for etiology, when developing their circle-ellipse program. Whenever some step of their teaching program proved deficient with one or more individual(s), they revised it with the goal of remediating the program deficiencies and preventing future failures. Program revisions were evaluated during these formative stages through apparent effectiveness with an expanding number of participants and decreasing failures overall as program development proceeded—not with a group design of the type traditionally used in intervention research. Thus, Sidman and Stoddard were using single-subject and small-*N* methods to develop evidence-based intervention that addressed the critical issues of generality of effectiveness (i.e., whether their program was appropriate to use on a wide scale with the expectation that its application would have the intended outcome with virtually everyone who received it).

The program eventually developed to the point that it appeared broadly effective across individuals and ready for formal efficacy evaluation of the type expected at that time. Sidman and Stoddard (1967) conducted a group study comparing their program with trial-and-error training, which was the prevalent primary alternative at the time. Each of seven children with severe IDD who had learned to discriminate a form (i.e., the circle on a lit background) versus no form (only a lit background) went on to master the circle-ellipse discrimination via the program. Only three of six children in the trial-and-error group did so, and they made many more errors than any of the seven program children.[2]

From contemporary perspectives on behavioral phenotypes in neurodevelopmental disorders (cf. Deutsch & McIlvane, 2012; McIlvane & Deutsch, 2004), one might view the Sidman and Stoddard (1967) program goal as a naïve product of its times. The program and test groups in the 1967 study were comprised of mixed diagnoses, including Down syndrome (DS), IDD relating to known neurological insult, and IDD resulting from unknown etiologies. Today it is recognized that people with IDD characteristically exhibit both etiologic and behavioral heterogeneity. Heterogeneity is seen even within well-established diagnoses (e.g., DS, autism spectrum disorder [ASD], Prader-Willi syndrome, fragile X syndrome, comorbid attention-deficit/hyperactivity disorder). One intervention typically does not fit all.

---

[1]Many disciplines in the helping professions that formerly relied on group designs are being drawn to single-subject or small-*N* designs. Examples include personalized medicine, medical genetics, and the pharmaceutical industry (cf. Zhao & Zeng, 2013). Genetic profiles and comorbid conditions are now used to tailor diagnosis and therapeutic interventions. sample sizes dwindle, however, as patients' rare or unique characteristics are taken into account. Single-subject and small-*N* designs have been embraced out of necessity. Now there is a call for the development of yet additional analytic techniques for complex disorders (Alemi, Erdman, Griva, & Evans, 2009), and new academic programs have been designed to cater to these needs.

[2]Although their circle-ellipse program proved more effective than its trial-and-error comparison procedure, Sidman and Stoddard must have been disappointed by another aspect of their results. The initial form versus no form discrimination component unsuccessful with some children, despite protracted training. These children apparently required more involved programming to direct attending to the relevant features of the discrimination task (e.g., McIlvane, Kledaras, Callahan, & Dube, 2002) and to forestall the development of error patterns that were shown to become pervasive, highly resistant to reduction by the programmed contingencies, and major impediments to subsequent learning.

If students who trained with Sidman and Stoddard applied for grant funds in today's environment and proposed to evaluate methodologies using two small, mixed etiology groups like those in the 1967 study, then the review outcome would likely be disastrous. After all, how could anything possibly be learned from comparing two small groups comprised of members whose diagnoses implied a great deal of heterogeneity in behavior—even if between-group variables such as CA and IQ were controlled reasonably well?

Viewed from another perspective, Sidman and Stoddard contributed a great deal indeed. For example, their 1967 paper has been cited in hundreds of scholarly publications about behavioral assessment and intervention for people with neurodevelopmental and neurological disorders. Modest as that 1967 scientific contribution might seem in retrospect, its effect has been substantial, perhaps because its findings were consistent with other science using single-subject and small-*N* designs with both humans and animal models (e.g., McIlvane, 1992; Sidman & Stoddard, 1966; Terrace, 1963a, b).

Perhaps another reason that this program has had continuing influence pertains to the logistical limitations of working with populations comprised of people with severe IDD. Many disorders associated with severe IDD are rare and/or not yet diagnosed. Sidman and Stoddard structured their program to implicitly recognize the reality that such people do not typically come to clinicians and educators in large numbers or in tidy groups that make for clean, easily implemented group research designs. Assembling and characterizing groups to be compared may prove financially impractical or even logistically impossible.

Do the characteristics of the population of people with severe IDD make it impractical or impossible to address their manifest needs? We think "No" and have been guided in our research by 1) lessons that derive from the early work of Sidman, Stoddard, and their colleagues and students; 2) increased consideration of the behavioral phenotypes for disorders associated with severe IDD; 3) long-standing appreciation for the potency of and need for single-subject and small-*N* experimental designs in collecting evidence of intervention effectiveness; and 4) a growing need to incorporate such designs within a larger effort to inform evidence-based intervention for people with severe IDD. The remainder of this chapter discusses such designs and their relationship to the larger issue of establishing generality of findings of intervention research. It reviews analytic procedures geared to both single-subject and small-*N* studies and provides some practical suggestions for the investigator and clinician.

QUANTITATIVE ANALYSIS OF SINGLE-SUBJECT AND SMALL-*N* STUDIES: AN OVERVIEW

Single-Subject Research Designs

Single-subject research designs are used profitably in speech-language research to examine the efficacy of intervention (e.g. Byiers, Reichle, & Symons, 2012; Connell & Thompson, 1986; Kearns, 1986; Robey, Schultz, Crawford, & Sinner, 1999) and are suitable to many types of interventions in which individualized treatment is the goal. This level of analysis is of inherent interest and may fit the bill when heterogeneity is at issue. They also may be used in exploratory research leading to subsequent large-scale traditional group-comparisons or clinical trials.

A typical single-subject study compares outcomes measures from one or more interventions over time. An intervention not applied during a baseline phase serves as a basis for comparison. It must be stable as a benchmark (Kazdin, 2010). Thus, several baseline measurements are usually taken to minimize error. Given steady-state performance or an observable trend, the intervention follows a duration that should be as long or longer than the baseline phase (Barlow et al., 2009). Clinically significant positive shifts in outcome level, trend, or variability following intervention indicate an efficacious intervention.

Common Single-Subject Designs

Despite their name, single-subject designs may involve the study of more than one participant, but data are analyzed for each individual separately (de Vries & Morey, 2013).

Preexperimental AB Design A baseline (A) is established and an intervention (B) follows, thus providing an immediate initial assay. Although it does not control for other factors that may influence changes (e.g., the passage of time, other experience outside the intervention setting), it may efficiently set the stage for controlled follow-up work.

ABA/ABAB (withdrawal) designs assess whether the outcome compared with baseline (A) changes with introduction (B), withdrawal (second A), and reintroduction of intervention (in the ABAB model). This design improves experimental control but assumes that intervention effects are reversible and withholding an effective intervention, once applied, is ethical.

Multiple baseline designs examine intervention effects across multiple conditions or participants. It can be seen as a series of AB studies successively conducted across a number of conditions and/or participants. Interventions are introduced one by one while baseline data collection continues for the remainder, thus resulting in some level of experimental control. The primary advantage is that this design does not require intervention withdrawal. The primary disadvantage is that some participants must wait for a potentially effective intervention. Multiple probe variants of this design use probe techniques (i.e., brief tests embedded within conditions) to establish the baseline level(s) of target behavior(s) for comparison to the level(s) seen after intervention is applied (see Horner & Baer, 1978).

Multiple treatment designs examine effects of multiple interventions on an outcome measure and make comparisons among them as well as to baseline measures. Typical designs for two interventions would be the ABCABC or ABCBCA structures (with the C component being the second intervention). The latter assesses order effects. Although such designs allow the researcher to simultaneously consider two or more hypotheses, a concern may be influence/interference (carryover) from prior interventions.

Visual Analysis of Single-Subject Data Sets

Visual analysis provides a simple, albeit subjective, approach to assessing change over time and intervention effects (Parsonson & Baer, 1986; see Fisher, Piazza, & Roane, 2011). Visual analysis is also used to detect cyclic patterns, nonlinear trends, lagged responsiveness, and variability within phases. Moreover, it can be used in conjunction with common descriptive and regression-based statistics, such as mean levels per phase and trends in slope across time.

Although specific guidelines for visual analysis of single-subject designs have been suggested (Jones, Vaught, & Weinrott, 1977), the lack of formalized interpretation rules is a limitation. Several reliability studies have found poor interrater agreement (Deprospero & Cohen, 1979; Gibson & Ottenbacher, 1988; Gottman & Glass, 1978; Jones et al., 1977; Ottenbacher & Cusick, 1991). Thus, visual analysis should be supplemented with more objective, precise, and reliable methodologies when visual results support the effectiveness of the intervention.

Inferential statistics methods have been proposed for analysis of single-subject data (e.g., inclusion of time series analysis) (Borckhardt et al., 2008) and bootstrapping methodologies (Wilcox, 2001). Conventional parametric and nonparametric analytic approaches, however, are seldom suitable due to the lack of independence among data points *(autocorrelation)*. Thus, one may want to focus on effect size (ES) as a means of quantification of improvement.

Power and Effect Size

Understanding the definitions of and relationships among ES, *p*-values, and statistical power is crucial in quantitative management of single-subject and small-*N* samples. What do we mean by *power?* It is the probability that a study will detect an effect that is actually there to be detected. In statistical terms, it is the probability that the test will reject a false null hypothesis. For example, if one is analyzing the difference in scores between two groups, then the effect is the difference found. The ES is a measure of the strength of the result based on the magnitude of the effect (i.e., it does not depend on sample size, thus making it especially useful when samples are small as they are in many studies of people with severe IDD). But is that result generalizable to a population? This is where *p*-values take on importance. A *p*-value indicates the likelihood that the result found is not due to chance or sampling error, and it very much depends on the number of observations.

Suppose a researcher conducting a pilot study wants to know if there is a difference in mean scores between a group that has received an intervention (*int*) and a no-intervention group (*ctl*) (e.g., $N = 4$ in each group). The sample (*N*) for each group, the group means, and the group standard deviation (*SD*) are presented below, along with the calculation for a simple ES measure of the mean difference, often referred to as *d* (Cohen, 1988)

$$N_{int} = 4, \text{Mean}_{int} = 90, SD_{int} = 5$$
$$N_{ctl} = 4, \text{Mean}_{ctl} = 85, SD_{ctl} = 5$$
$$ES = (\text{Mean}_{int} - \text{Mean}_{ctl})/\text{pooled } SD = (90 - 85)/5 = 1.0$$

The ES of 1.0 is considered a large effect when assessing the difference between two means (Cohen, 1988). If an inferential test to determine whether these results are generalizable (e.g., a nonparametric Mann-Whitney U test) is used, then there is a nonsignificant *p*-value—despite the large effect—likely because the number of observations is small. To determine the *N* needed to test for generality, ES is used to compute the requisite *N* needed to conduct statistical analysis with conventional setting of power (power analysis). In the example, 14 participants would be needed in each group to demonstrate adequacy of the effect with inferential statistics (i.e., using *p*-values set at 0.05 level).

A dilemma exists that clearly applies to an interest in assessing communication interventions for people with severe IDD. Small-*N* studies may show large effects but may not yield statistically significant *p*-values. Large-*N* studies may have small, perhaps inconsequential effects but yield statistical significance. If one is interested in testing broad applicability of a new or enhanced intervention, then one should report ES, *p*-value, and results of a power analysis. Notably, there is handy, easy-to-use software for performing the latter (e.g., Faul, Erdfelder, Lang, & Buchner, 2007).

Effect Size Measures for Single-Subject Designs

As the clinical significance of individual change following intervention is often more important than generalizability in single-subject designs with limited numbers data points, ES measures that do not depend on *N* can provide an appropriate index for quantifying change (Busk & Serlin, 1992; Jensen, Clark, Kircher, & Kristjansson, 2007; Mitchell & Hartmann, 1981).

Many ES measures have been proposed for use in single-subject designs to quantify changes seen through visual inspection. Perhaps the simplest is percent of nonoverlapping data (PND; Scruggs, Mastropieri, & Casto, 1987). For example, the data on program errors in Sidman and Stoddard's 1967 study comprised two distributions (program, trial and error), and there was no overlap in those distributions (PND = 0%). With respect to this characteristic of the findings, statistical evaluation would have added nothing more than visual inspection made obvious.

Most other methods focus on some measure of overlap and include percent of data points exceeding the median value (PEM) (Ma, 2006), percent of all nonoverlapping data (PAND) (Parker, Hagan-Burke, & Vannest, 2007), percent of zero data points (PZD) (Johnson, Reichle, & Monn, 2009; Scotti, Evans, Meyer, & Walker, 1991), and mean baseline reduction (MBR) (Campbell, 2003, 2004; Lundervold & Bourland, 1988; O'Brien & Repp, 1990). A brief review follows.

In calculating PND, a straight line is drawn from a representative baseline data point across the intervention phase (see Figure 9.1), the number of data points above or below the line are then added, and this sum is divided by the total number of data points in the intervention. A PND of 70%–90% is often considered a fairly effective intervention, and a PND > 90% is considered a highly effective intervention (Scruggs, Mastropieri, Cook, & Escobar, 1986). Despite simplicity and intuitive appeal, this approach may be sensitive to baseline outliers as it depends on a single baseline data point (Riley-Tillman & Burns, 2009).

PEM calculation begins with locating the median value of the baseline data (see Figure 9.1). A horizontal line is then drawn through this baseline median value across the intervention phase, and the percentage of intervention points above this line is calculated if intervention was expected to increase the outcome

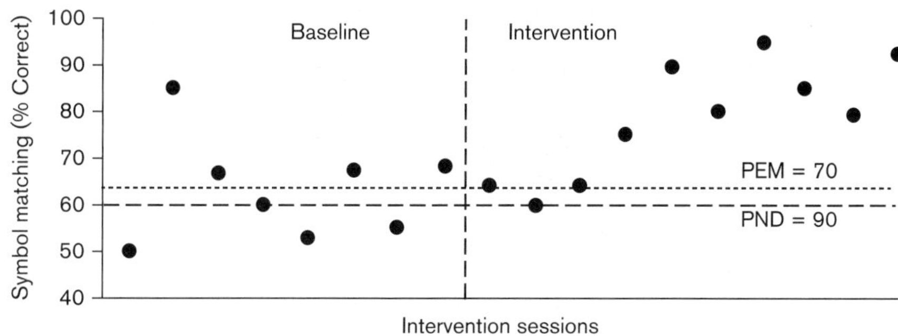

Figure 9.1. Hypothetical data plot for a symbol-matching task that shows a difference in results when comparing PND and PEM visual inspection data analysis techniques.

or below the line if intervention was expected to decrease the outcome. PEM is usually expressed as a decimal value, with the range being 0–1. Scores of > 0.7 and > 0.9 indicate reasonable and high intervention success, respectively. Also, PEM is a simple and intuitively appealing measure so it is not sensitive to the magnitude of the data points above the median, nor does it consider trend across the intervention phase.

PAND totals the data values that do not overlap between the baseline and intervention phases. The resulting total is then divided by the total number of data points. This percent of overlapping data is subtracted from 100 to yield the PAND. Such results may then be translated to *Phi* and Phi^2 which can then be converted to Cohen's *d* for a common ES interpretation (Parker & Hagan-Burke, 2007). This method has the advantage of using the data points in both the baselines and intervention phases. It is limited in that it measures only mean shifts in the data.

PZD is useful for interventions aimed at bringing the level of targeted variable(s) to zero (e.g., failure to respond to a communication bid). The first zero point is noted, and the percent of data points afterward that remain at zero is calculated. Levels of PZD > 55% indicate a reasonably effective intervention, with > 80% often deemed very effective.

MBR is also suitable when the goal is reduction in behavior. One calculates the difference in the means of the last three points of the baseline phase and of the intervention phase, and then multiplies by 100. Limitations of MBR include disregarding early data in both phases and sensitivity to outliers as it is based on only three values from each phase.[3]

[3]Notably, calculating effect size measures reviewed here requires little more than paper and pencil and simple graphs. Excel can create graphics and handle basic calculations (Carr & Burkholder, 1998). The open-source product R also provides software (SSD for R) for analyzing single-subject designs using a variety of methods (Auerbach & Schudrich, 2013). Bayesian methods are also available in the R product (BayesSimpleSub R package). There have also been several regression-based techniques developed for summarizing single-subject designs (Allison & Gorman, 1993; Beretvas & Chung, 2008; Faith, Allison, & Gorman, 1996; Huitema & McKean, 2000; van der Noortgate & Onghena, 2003) and Bayesian approaches to analysis (de Vries & Morey, 2013). These are more complex and beyond the scope of this chapter, but, in practice, these approaches are increasing in popularity among statisticians.

Inferential Analysis of Small-*N* Designs

Although small-*N* studies seldom allow inferences beyond the sample at hand, they can suggest generalizability when effects seen are sufficiently large or when there are multiple observations per subject (i.e., repeated measures). The ability to generalize results through inferential testing is highly affected by the combination of the power, the number of observations, and the ES as previously discussed. Thus, small samples can yield statistically significant inferential findings when the ES is large or there are repeated measures.

Visually inspecting the data and calculating descriptive statistics and ES, as with single-subject designs, is the most common analytic approach to small-*N* studies. Small-*N* studies may be viewed and analyzed as a series of single-subject studies in some cases. If, however, ES are sufficiently large and clinically meaningful, then it is reasonable to proceed with inferential testing using nonparametric methods to examine hypotheses of interest. Small samples do not usually meet the distributional assumptions needed for more powerful parametric methods readers may be familiar with (e.g., *t-test,* ANOVA), but nonparametric methods tend to be more robust and do not have such distributional limitations and, thus, are particularly well suited to small sample analysis.[4]

There is analogous nonparametric technique for most parametric methods that can use be used with small samples not meeting distributional assumptions, even though it is less powerful. For example, the popular *t-test* used to test the difference in means between two independent samples can be analyzed with a Wilcoxon Rank Sum or Mann-Whitney U test nonparametrically, examining differences in the ranks of the data values between samples rather than their actual values. This can be extended to the three or more independent sample case (analogous to ANOVA) using the nonparametric Kruskal-Wallis test. The nonparametric Sign Test may be used for the single-sample case when the sample size is small, rather than the parametric one-sample *t-test.*

Similarly, the comparisons of two related samples would be analyzed parametrically with the paired *t-test,* but nonparametrically with the Wilcoxon Signed Rank test; the repeated measures ANOVA parametric test analogy would be the nonparametric Friedman test in the three-sample case. For correlation analysis, the comparable nonparametric method to the Pearson correlation coefficient would be the Spearman rank correlation coefficient.

Although the nonparametric methods previously discussed are appropriate only to outcome data that is ordinal, interval, or ratio in nature, nonparametric techniques are also available for the analysis of nominal data. For example, exact permutation tests such as the 2 × 2 table Fisher's exact test is used in small sample studies to compare independent samples of nominal data and is comparable to the Chi-square statistic (also a nonparametric method) for the larger sample case (Deutsch, Lauer, Patel, & Mehta, 2001). Similarly, the nonparametric McNemar

[4]Decades ago all nonparametric analysis was done by hand. Now, with readily accessible computers, nonparametric methods are available in popular statistical packages, among them SPSS, SAS, and Stata, R, Epi-Info, MATLAB Statistics Toolbox, BMDP, Minitab, JMP, SPlus, Statistica, Mathematica, GraphPad, and Prism. There are also specialized products that focus on nonparametric methods, such as the StatXact software package. Some products, such as R (open source) and Epi-Info (public domain), are available at no cost.

test may be used for related samples of nominal data. Refer to the classical text by Siegel (1956) for a more comprehensive review of nonparametric statistical methods with examples.

RESOLVING CHALLENGES IN EVIDENCE-BASED INTERVENTION FOR PEOPLE WITH SEVERE INTELLECTUAL AND DEVELOPMENTAL DISABILITIES

As the preceding material suggests, there is a diverse, maturing, and increasingly well-accepted quantitative methodology for testing the evidence collected through single-subject and small-*N* research designs. Also suggested, however, is that single-subject and small-*N* designs are inherently limited in their ability to provide evidence in support of intervention approaches that are generalizable to the broad, heterogeneous population of people with severe IDD and associated communication limitations—or even a major subset thereof. Finally, this population presents certain logistical challenges that further complicate efforts (e.g., difficulties in recruiting adequate samples for large-scale clinical/educational research, variability in response to extant intervention methods).

For discussion purposes, let's assume that broadly generalizable intervention approaches are both programmatically desirable and realistically achievable from a practical standpoint. The former seems self-evident but the latter does not. Returning to the history of our research group, did the research program initiated by Sidman and his colleagues in the 1960s inspire development of whole classes of comparably effective nonverbal teaching and assessment programs? Regrettably, it did not.

The main outcome of that research program was to illustrate what could be accomplished given sufficient time, focus, and resources. That said, the careful, evidence-based approach of the Sidman group was apparently deemed impractical for routine applications by clinicians and educators who had 1) limited time for and expertise in materials development, 2) a variety of different student needs to serve, and 3) few resources beyond the minimum necessary for their jobs. Under the parsimony principle of Etzel and LeBlanc (1979), professionals were encouraged to use simple methods first (e.g., trial and error, extra stimulus [or noncriterion related] prompting procedures [Schreibman, 1975]) and resort to advanced methods only after the methodologically simpler ones had failed. That principle, however, seemed to de-emphasize the demonstrated fact that error histories from failed methods may severely interfere with subsequent learning (e.g., Sidman & Stoddard, 1967; Stoddard & Sidman, 1967).

There will likely be a reconsideration of the parsimony principle based on evolving computer technologies that will provide better support for clinicians and educators. The primary objection to using advanced programming techniques was their complexity and labor-intensive nature. Today, one can envision development and dissemination of computer methodologies that reduce or eliminate virtually all of the former challenges. One sees already widespread availability of computer-generated graphics in apps aimed at AAC applications. One also sees development of utility programs that bypass aspects of the time-consuming process of generating trial-based training and assessment procedures (e.g., Gerard,

Mackay, Thompson, & McIlvane, 2014). These contributions are only the beginning, however. Our own research group and others that we communicate with have much more powerful tools under development that we think have great potential for optimizing learning opportunities for learners with severe IDD.

MOVING TOWARD INTEGRATION OF SINGLE-SUBJECT AND GROUP METHODOLOGIES

The chapter concludes by suggesting approaches in which single-subject and small-*N* designs can be used in concert with other methodologies to establish intervention procedures that have greater generality. Single-subject and small-*N* designs are useful for developing hypotheses that might be pursued in follow-up studies using group designs, as Sidman and Stoddard (1966, 1967) demonstrated. The logic of the single-subject and small-*N* work reported in their 1966 chapter, however, need not point inevitably to ultimate validation via a group design.

Approach 1: Integrating Single-Subject and Small-*N* Designs

Another approach to establishing generality is to adopt certain practices of the early Shriver group to design interventions that require no validation beyond efficiency assessments because the failure rate is so low that questions about whether intervention had a strong evidence base would seem inappropriate. The current Shriver group has demonstrated this approach in researching relational learning processes that are essential for the success of AAC and other forms of symbolic communication. For example, recognizing when symbols are members of the same or different stimulus classes is a pivotal skill in learning to communicate with visual symbols in an AAC format. If the basis for classification is physical similarity, then such classes are termed as *feature classes* (i.e., classification is based on common physical features rather than common functions) (cf. McIlvane, Dube, Green, & Serna, 1993). If the basis for classification is another common property (i.e., functional use in the same manner and context), then such classes are termed as *symbolic or equivalence classes* (cf. Wilkinson & McIlvane, 2001a, b).

Much research by current members of our group has proceeded with a goal similar to that of Sidman and Stoddard (1966)—developing instructional technology for establishing stimulus classes that will be effective across a broad range of people with severe IDD. Because population heterogêneity is inevitable given this objective, our target is not merely a single linear program but rather a minicurriculum comprised of different components and program branching options. The components are validated through single-subject and small-*N* research designs. The overall goal, however, is to develop instructional technology that has near-universal success provided that the learner meets certain basic entry requirements (e.g., sensory functions are intact, effective reinforcing consequences have been identified, evidence of at least minimally necessary attending to relevant stimuli).

The most advanced efforts concern development of feature classes. We usually test this skill using some form of identity matching-to-sample (IDMTS) and/or sorting procedure. The goal is generalized sameness-difference judgments. Such judgments were once thought beyond the capabilities of children with IDD and mental ages less than 4 years (cf. Soraci & Carlin, 1992). That picture began to change circa 1990 due to research by our group and others. For example, it was found that people with low mental ages could acquire generalized IDMTS and oddity very rapidly merely by increasing the number of non-odd distractors (e.g., Mackay, Soraci, Carlin, Dennis, & Strawbridge, 2002; Serna & Carlin, 2001).

As new instructional methods were developed, refined, and validated, the goal became organizing them into a minicurriculum that could be effective with virtually any learner—verbal or nonverbal—who met minimal entry requirements—mastery of a simple form discrimination. The approach was to 1) carefully task-analyze the learning requirements, 2) match those requirements to the best available procedures, 3) rapidly screen out any candidates who could be taught with conventional procedures, and 4) further research any apparent limitations in the instructional technology, including procedural inefficiency. Like Sidman and Stoddard, we included people with a broad range of diagnoses, anticipating that branching options available within the minicurriculum could effectively manage heterogeneity of response to components.

This research was highly productive. More than 20 publications documented various component behavior analyses. Prior to 1990, successes in teaching generalized IDMTS were about 30% with children with severe IDD. The minicurriculum largely achieved the original objective—near universal effectiveness with children who had little or no functional language and/or other symbolic communication skills—when the development formally concluded (Dube & Serna, 1998; Serna, Dube, McIlvane, 1997).

We are not advocating that this approach become the standard of clinical research and practice because we are mindful that this type of program development is costly in terms of time, energy, and money. This effort was conducted in part to ascertain whether an extension of the Sidman and Stoddard approach could 1) be effected in the domain of relational learning and 2) reveal behavioral potential beyond what might be predictable from typical clinical or educational research and practice. Pertinent to the theme of this chapter, it also demonstrated that single-subject and small-*N* methodologies can be used artfully to provide the basis of evidence that can support a case for intervention effectiveness across a broad range.

Regarding how this type of work might be integrated with traditional group designs, the relational learning program was quite time- and labor-intensive for some of the participants, especially those whose level of behavioral functioning was very low. Given that one has a program with near-universal effectiveness such as this (e.g., demonstrating sufficiency), the logical question is whether the same learning outcomes might be achieved via extended exposure to procedurally simpler alternatives (e.g., trial and error, time-delay prompting). If procedural necessity need be established, then one can consider a group design, perhaps supplemented with a multiple baseline across participants design to assess necessity for any individuals who fail to learn via the simpler alternative.

Approach 2: Meta-analyses of Single-Subject and Small-*N* Designs

As previously noted, a critical issue when using such designs is evaluating the degree of generalizability from a study sample to an entire population (cf. Polit & Hungler, 1991). Here the distinction is made between statistical generalization (as the term *generalization* is typically described in the statistics literature) and an empirical form of generalization (not statistical in nature but verifiable by observation or experience). Stake (1995) referred to the latter as a more naturalistic form of generalization, extending results from a single study to others that are similar in scope, rather than to a population. In contrast, Gomm, Hammersley, and Foster (2009) defined empirical generalization as the drawing of conclusions about the features of a finite population (all members of a theoretical category) based analysis of a sample drawn from it. Both the type of generalization and the nature of the population to which it is applied should be taken into consideration when generalizing the results of single-subject research.

How can single-subject research be extended to evidence-based practice? Meta-analysis is one widely used method in which several comparable single-subject studies are taken into account. The component studies must be valid and relevant to the design at hand in order to perform a meta-analysis (Moher et al., 1999), and their ES must be calculated—and interpreted if not comparable in type —to yield an average ES. Here, the average is weighted by the number of observations across the studies, which may vary in numbers of participants or time points under investigation.

Several meta-analytic techniques for aggregating study results have been proposed for single-study research, many of them computationally complex (e.g., Busk & Serlin, 1992; Robey et al., 1999; Van den Noortgate & Onghena, 2003). A potential advance has been put forward by Kuppens, Heyvaert, Van den Noortgate, and Onghena (2011). The authors focus on the concept of *sufficiency*—whether a sequential collection of studies yields convincing statistical evidence, or in the authors' words, "whether there are enough pieces to unravel the puzzle" (p. 720). Their method combines cumulative meta-analysis of single-case experimental data with formal sequential testing of the type that have been used in earlier large-*N* studies. The approach guides the investigator in deciding whether the added value of a new study materially adds to the existing base of knowledge. This strategy can conceivably provide an early, efficient determination of the benefit or failure of an intervention.

We previously outlined how forms of generalization from single-subject testing to the population are attainable. Some critics, however, take the position that single-subject studies may not lend themselves to generalization if there has been heterogeneity across their single-subject evaluations (e.g., if participants in the component studies were not randomly sampled by the investigator or if they were not representative of a population) (Lieberson, 1991; Simons, 1980, 2009; Yin, 1984). Others have countered that these single-subject evaluations are indeed useful, not only in attaining generalization but also in formulating hypotheses that can be subsequently tested within more powerful, large-*N* studies (Bennett & Elman, 2006; Gomm et al., 2009; Stake, 1995). Although both positions have merit, we tend to agree more with the latter. Whatever their limitations, accumulated single-subject studies may constitute the best evidence available to guide a clinician. The starting point that they suggest seems likely to be at least a good—and arguably better than—uniformed guesses or practices rooted more in ideology than in the best available evidence.

CONCLUSION

We hope the reader has come to appreciate two main points:

1. Collecting and evaluating the evidence necessary to inform communication intervention practice for people with severe IDD presents many challenges that are difficult to overcome.

2. Although difficult, there are approaches that can be used successfully to make progress toward the resolution of those challenges. Let us grant for the moment that the gold standard in evaluating intervention research is the randomized controlled/clinical trial (RCT). Let us grant also that it is logistically difficult and sometimes impractically expensive to staff and conduct quality RCTs with low-prevalence, etiologically, and behaviorally heterogeneous populations.

If one is to improve on the standard of care/intervention, then he or she seems to have two paths before him or her. First, one can pursue the dream of ultimately securing the human, financial, and infrastructure resources needed for conducting RCTs that can evaluate intervention procedures based on current evidence and that which will emerge in the future. There are models that could inform development of the networks of intervention programs that would be needed for large-scale RCTs (e.g., the Research Units for Pediatric Psychopharmacology [Arnold et al., 2012]). Development of such RCT networks, however, would appear to require a long-term effort and investment by many individuals and agencies.

A second path that can be followed in the interim would be attending to the challenge of assembling and reducing evidence from single-subject and small-*N* studies that can be accomplished without an extensive, expensive, regional, or national infrastructure. We are particularly interested in approaches of the type suggested by Kuppens et al. (2011) regarding judging the sufficiency of an accumulating body of single-subject and small-*N* studies. If one is not logistically capable of conducting a group RCT within extant infrastructure, one may have no better alternative than using a formal method to assess results of well-controlled single-subject and small-*N* studies. The concept of sufficiency seems particularly attractive in this context. If one has evidence that is arguably sufficient to inform communication intervention, then one is likely to be less concerned about the inability to offer evidence that meets the RCT standard.

REFERENCES

Alemi, F., Erdman, H., Griva, I., & Evans, C.H. (2009). Improved statistical methods are needed to advance personalized medicine. *Open Translational Medicine Journal, 1,* 16–20.

Allison, D.B., & Gorman, B.S. (1993). Calculating effect sizes for meta-analysis: The case of the single case. *Behaviour Research and Therapy, 31,* 621–631.

Arnold, L.E., Aman, M.G., Li, X., Butter, E., Humphries, K., Scahill, L., Stigler, K.A. (2012). Research Units of Pediatric Psychopharmacology (RUPP) Autism Network randomized clinical trial of parent training and medication: One-year follow-up. *Journal of the American Academy of Child and Adolescent Psychiatry, 51,* 1173–1184.

Auerbach, C., & Schudrich, W. (2013). SSD for R: A comprehensive statistical package to analyze single-system. *Research on Social Work Practice, 23,* 346–353.

Barlow, D.H., Nock, M.K., & Hersen, M. (2009). *Single case experimental designs: Strategies for studying behavior change* (3rd ed.). Boston, MA: Allyn & Bacon.

Bennett, A., & Elman, C. (2006). Qualitative research: Recent developments in case study methods. *Annual Review of Political Science, 9,* 455–476.

Beretvas, S.N., & Chung, H. (2008). *Computation of regression-based effect size measures.* Paper presented at the annual meeting of the International Campbell Collaboration Colloquium, Vancouver, British Columbia, Canada.

Beukelman, D., & Mirenda, P. (2013). *Augmentative and alternative communication: Supporting children and adults with complex communication needs, Fourth edition.* Baltimore, MD: Paul H. Brookes Publishing Co.

Borckardt, J.J., Nash, M.R., Murphy, M.D., Moore, M., Shaw, D., & O'Neil, P. (2008). Clinical practice as natural laboratory for psychotherapy research: A guide to case-based time-series analysis. *American Psychologist, 63,* 77–95.

Busk, P.L., & Serlin, R.C. (1992). Meta-analysis for single-case research. In *Single case research design and analysis: New directions for psychology and education* (pp. 187–212). Mahwah, NJ: Lawrence Erlbaum Associates.

Byiers, B., Reichle, J., & Symons, F. (2012). Single-subject experimental design for evidence-based practice. *American Journal of Speech and Language Pathology, 21,* 397–414.

Campbell, J.M. (2003). Efficacy of behavioral intervention for reducing problematic behaviors in persons with autism: A quantitative synthesis of single-subject research. *Research in Developmental Disabilities, 24,* 120–138.

Campbell, J.M. (2004). Statistical comparisons of four effect sizes for single-subject designs. *Behavior Modification, 28,* 234–246.

Carr, J.E., & Burkholder, E.O. (1998). Creating single-subject design graphs with Microsoft Excel. *Journal of Applied Behavior Analysis, 31,* 245–251.

Cohen, J. (1988). *Statistical power analysis for the behavioral sciences* (2nd ed.). Mahwah, NJ: Lawrence Erlbaum Associates.

Connell, P.K. & Thompson, C.K. (1986). Flexibility of single subject design. Part III: Using flexibility to design or modify experiments. *Journal of Speech and Hearing Disorders, 51,* 214–225.

de Vries, R.M., & Morey, R.D. (2013). Bayesian hypothesis testing for single-subject designs. *Psychological Methods, 18,* 165–185.

DeProspero, A., & Cohen, S. (1979). Inconsistent visual analyses of intrasubject data. *Journal of Applied Behavior Analysis, 12,* 573–579.

Deutsch, C.K., Lauer, E., Patel, N., & Mehta, C. (2001). Exact nonparametric statistical methods in behavior analysis. *Experimental Analysis of Human Behavior Bulletin, 19,* 19–21.

Deutsch, C.K., & McIlvane, W.J. (2012). Non-mendelian etiologic factors in neuropsychiatric illness: Pleiotropy, epigenetics, and convergence. *Behavioral and Brain Science, 35,* 363–364.

Dickson, C.A., Deutsch, C.K., Wang, S.S., & Dube, W.V. (2006). Matching-to-sample assessment of stimulus overselectivity in students with intellectual disabilities. *American Journal on Mental Retardation, 111,* 447–453.

Dube, W.V., & Serna, R.W. (1998). Reevaluation of a programmed method to teach generalized identity matching to sample. *Research in Developmental Disabilities, 19,* 347–379.

Durand, V.M. (1990). *Functional communication training: An intervention program for severe behavior problems.* New York, NY: Guilford Press.

Etzel, B.C., & LeBlanc, J.M. (1979). The simplest treatment alternative: The law of parsimony applied to choosing appropriate instructional control and errorless-learning procedures for the difficult-to-teach child. *Journal of Autism and Developmental Disorders, 9,* 361–382.

Faith, M.S., Allison, D.B., & Gorman, B.S. (1996). Meta-analysis of single-case research. In *Design and analysis of single-case research* (pp. 245–277). Mahwah, NJ: Lawrence Erlbaum Associates.

Faul, F., Erdfelder, E., Lang, A.G., & Buchner, A. (2007). G*Power 3: A flexible statistical power analysis program for the social, behavioral, and biomedical sciences. *Behavior Research Methods, 39,* 175–191.

Fisher, W.W., Piazza, C.C., & Roane, H.S. (Eds.). (2011). *Handbook of behavior analysis.* New York, NY: Guilford Press.

Frea, W.D., Arnold, C., & Vittimberga, G.L. (2001). A demonstration of the effects of augmentative communication on extreme aggressive behavior on a child with autism within an integrated preschool setting. *Journal of Positive Behavioral Interventions, 3,* 194–198.

Gerard, C.J., Mackay, H.A., Thompson, B., & McIlvane, W.J. (2014). Rapid generation of balanced trial distributions for discrimination learning procedures: A technical note. *Journal of the Experimental Analysis of Behavior, 101,* 171–178. doi: 10.1002/jeab.58

Gibson, G., & Ottenbacher, K.J. (1988). Inconsistent visual analysis of intrasubject data: An empirical analysis. *Journal of Applied Behavioral Science, 24,* 298–314.

Gomm, R., Hammersley, M., & Foster, P. (Eds.). (2009). *Case study method: Key issues, key texts.* London, England: Sage.

Gottman, J.M., & Glass, G.V. (1978). Analysis of interrupted time-series experiments.

In T.R. Kratochwill (Ed.), *Single-subject research: Strategies for evaluating change* (pp. 197–235). San Diego, CA: Academic Press.

Horner, R.D., & Baer, D.M. (1978). Multiple-probe technique: A variation of the multiple baseline. *Journal of Applied Behavior Analysis, 11,* 189–196.

Huitema, B.E., & McKean, J.W. (2000). Design specification issues in time-series intervention models. *Educational and Psychological Measurement, 60,* 38–58.

Jenson, W., Clark, E., Kircher, J., & Kristjansson, S. (2007). Statistical reform: Evidence-based practice, meta-analyses, and single-subject designs. *Psychology in the Schools, 44,* 483–493.

Johnson, L., Reichle, J., & Monn, E. (2009). Longitudinal mentoring with school-based positive behavioral support teams: Influences on staff and learner behavior. *Evidence-Based Communication Assessment and Intervention, 3,* 113–130.

Jones, R.R., Vaught, R.S., & Weinrott, M. (1977). Time-series analysis in operant research. *Journal of Applied Behavior Analysis, 10,* 151–166.

Kazdin, A.E. (2010). *Single-case research designs: Methods for clinical and applied settings* (2nd ed.). New York, NY: Oxford University Press.

Kearns, K.P. (1986). Flexibility of single-subject experimental designs: Part II: Design selection and arrangement of experimental phases. *Journal of Speech and Hearing Disorders, 51,* 204–214.

Kuppens, S., Heyvaert, M., Van den Noortgate, W., & Onghena, P. (2011). Sequential meta-analysis of single-case experimental data. *Behavior Research Methods, 43,* 720–729.

Lieberson, S. (1991). Small N's and big conclusions: An examination of the reasoning in comparative studies based on a small number of cases. *Social Forces, 70,* 307–320.

Lundervold, D., & Bourland, G. (1988). Quantitative analysis of treatment of aggression, self-injury and property destruction. *Behavior Modification, 12,* 590–617.

Ma, H. (2006). An alternative method for quantitative synthesis of single-subject researchers: Percentage of data points exceeding the median. *Behavior Modification, 30,* 598–617.

Mackay, H.A., Soraci, S.A., Carlin, M.T., Dennis, N.A., & Strawbridge, C.P. (2002). Guiding visual attention during acquisition of matching to sample. *American Journal on Mental Retardation, 107,* 445–454.

McIlvane, W.J. (1992). Stimulus control analysis and nonverbal instructional technology for people with intellectual handicaps. In N.R. Bray (Ed.), *International review of research in mental retardation* (Vol. 18, pp. 55–109). San Diego, CA: Academic Press.

McIlvane, W.J., & Deutsch, C.K. (2004). Behavioral phenotypes in neurodevelopmental disabilities: Some possible interactions with behavioral contingencies. In L. Williams (Ed.), *Handbook of behavioral intervention in developmental disabilities* (pp. 63–80). Oakland, CA: Context Press.

McIlvane, W.J., Dube, W.V., Green, G., & Serna, R.W. (1993). Programming conceptual and communication skill development: A methodological stimulus-class analysis. In A.P. Kaiser & D.B. Gray (Eds.), *Enhancing children's communication* (pp. 243–285). Baltimore, MD: Paul H. Brookes Publishing Co.

McIlvane, W.J., Kledaras, J.B., Callahan, T.C., & Dube, W.V. (2002). High probability stimulus control topographies with delayed S+ onset in a simultaneous discrimination procedure. *Journal of the Experimental Analysis of Behavior, 77,* 189–198.

Mirenda, P. (1997). Functional communication training and augmentative and alternative communication for students with autism: Manual signs, graphic symbols, and voice output communication aids. *Language, Speech, and Hearing Services in Schools, 34,* 202–215.

Mitchell, C., & Hartmann, D.P. (1981). A cautionary note on the use of omega squared to evaluate the effectiveness of behavioral treatments. *Behavioral Assessment, 3,* 93–100.

Moher, D., Cook, D., Eastwood, S., Okin, I., Rennie, D., & Stroup, D. (1999). The QUOROM group: Improving the quality of reports of meta-analyses of randomized controlled trials. *The Lancet, 354,* 1896–1900.

O'Brien, S., & Repp, A.C. (1990). Reinforcement-based reductive procedures: A review of 20 years of their use with persons with severe of profound mental retardation. *Journal of The Association for Persons with Severe Handicaps, 15,* 148–159.

Ottenbacher, K.J., & Cusick, A. (1991). An empirical investigation of inter-rater agreement for single-subject data using graphs with and without trend lines. *Journal of The Association for Persons with Severe Handicaps, 16,* 48–55.

Parker, R.I., & Hagan-Burke, S. (2007). Median-based overlap analysis for single case data: A second study. *Behavior Modification, 31,* 919–936.

Parker, R.I., Hagan-Burke, S., & Vannest, K. (2007). Percentage of all non-overlapping data (PAND): An alternative to PND. *Journal of Special Education, 40,* 194–204.

Parsonson, B.S., & Baer, D.M. (1986). The graphic analysis of data. In A. Poling & R. W. Fuqua (Eds), *Research methods in applied behavior analysis: Issues and advances* (pp. 157–186). New York, NY: Plenum Press.

Polit, D., & Hungler, B. (1991). *Nursing research: Principles and methods.* New York, NY: JB Lippincott.

Riley-Tillman, T.C., & Burns, M.K. (2009). *Single case design for measuring response to education intervention.* New York, NY: Guilford Press.

Robey, R.R., Schultz, M.C., Crawford, A.B., & Sinner, C.A. (1999). Single-subject clinical-outcome research: Designs, data, effect sizes, and analyses. *Aphasiology, 13,* 445–473.

Romski, M.A., & Sevcik, R.A. (1996). *Breaking the speech barrier: Language development through augmented means.* Baltimore, MD: Paul H. Brooks Publishing Co.

Schreibman, L. (1975). Effects of within-stimulus and extra-stimulus prompting on discrimination learning in autistic children. *Journal of Applied Behavior Analysis, 8,* 91–112.

Scotti, J.R., Evans, I.M., Meyer, L.H., & Walker, P. (1991). A meta-analysis of intervention research with problem behavior: Treatment validity and standards of practice. *American Journal on Mental Retardation, 96,* 233–256.

Scruggs, T.E., Mastropieri, M.A., & Casto, G. (1987). The quantitative synthesis of single-subject research: Methodology and validation. *Remedial and Special Education, 8,* 24–33.

Scruggs, T.E., Mastropieri, M.A., Cook, S.B., & Escobar, C. (1986). Early intervention for children with conduct disorders: A quantitative synthesis of single-subject research. *Behavioral Disorders, 1,* 260–271.

Serna, R.W., & Carlin, M.T. (2001). Guided visual attention in individuals with mental retardation. In L.M. Glidden (Ed.), *International review of research in mental retardation* (Vol. 24, pp. 321–357). San Diego, CA: Academic Press.

Serna, R.W., Dube, W.V., & McIlvane, W.J. (1997). Assessing same/different judgments in individuals with severe intellectual disabilities: A status report. *Research in Developmental Disabilities, 18,* 343–368.

Sidman, M., & Stoddard, L.T. (1966). Programming perception and learning for retarded children. In N.R. Ellis (Ed.), *International review of research in mental retardation* (Vol. 2, pp. 151–208). San Diego, CA: Academic Press.

Sidman, M., & Stoddard, L.T. (1967). The effectiveness of fading in programming a simultaneous form discrimination for retarded children. *Journal of the Experimental Analysis of Behavior, 10,* 3–15.

Siegel, S. (1956). *Nonparametric statistics.* New York, NY: McGraw-Hill.

Simons, H. (Ed.). (1980). *Towards a science of the singular: Essays about case study in educational research and evaluation.* Norwich, England: Centre for Applied Research in Education, University of East Anglia.

Simons, H. (2009). *Case study research in practice.* London, England: Sage.

Soraci, S.A., & Carlin, M.T. (1992). Stimulus organization and relational learning. In N.W. Bray (Ed.), *International review of research in mental retardation* (Vol. 18, pp. 29–53). San Diego, CA: Academic Press.

Stake, R. (1995). *The art of case research.* Thousand Oaks, CA: Sage Publications.

Stoddard, L.T., & Sidman, M. (1967). The effects of errors on children's performance on a circle-ellipse discrimination. *Journal of the Experimental Analysis of Behavior, 10,* 261–270.

Terrace, H.S. (1963a). Discrimination learning with and without "errors." *Journal of the Experimental Analysis of Behavior, 6,* 1–27.

Terrace, H.S. (1963b). Errorless transfer of a discrimination across two continua. *Journal of the Experimental Analysis of Behavior, 6,* 223–232.

Trent, J.W. (1994) *Inventing the feeble mind: A history of mental retardation in the United States.* Berkeley, CA: University of California Press.

Van den Noortgate, W., & Onghena, P. (2003). Hierarchical linear models for the quantitative integration of effect sizes in single-case research. *Behavior Research Methods, Instruments, and Computers, 35,* 1–10.

Wilcox, R.R. (2001). *Fundamentals of modern statistical methods: Substantially improving power and accuracy.* New York, NY: SpringerVerlag.

Wilkinson, K.M., & McIlvane, W.J. (2001a). Considerations in teaching graphic symbols. In J. Reichle, D. Beukelman, & J. Light (Eds.), *Exemplary strategies for beginning communicators: Implications for AAC* (pp. 273–21). Baltimore, MD: Paul H. Brookes Publishing Co.

Wilkinson, K.M., & McIlvane, W.J. (2001b). Methods for studying symbolic behavior and category formation: Contributions of stimulus equivalence research. *Developmental Review, 21,* 355–374.

Yin, R. (1984). *Case study research: Design and methods.* Thousand Oaks, CA: Sage Publications.

Zhao, Y., & Zeng, D. (2013). Recent development on statistical methods for personalized medicine discovery. *Frontiers of Medicine, 7,* 102–110.

10

Randomized Controlled Trials

Do They Tell Us What We Want to Know About Interventions for People with Severe Disabilities?

R. Michael Barker and David J. Francis

Randomized controlled trials (RCTs) are considered the gold standard methodology to demonstrate whether and to what extent a treatment has an impact on outcomes (Jadad & Enkin, 2008). RCTs were once the purview of medicine but are increasingly being used in the behavioral and health sciences as a way to demonstrate the influence that behavioral and language interventions have on behavioral outcomes. There is good reason for this; RCTs are both simple in design (although they can become quite complex) and extremely powerful in the causal inferences that can be drawn from them. This chapter briefly introduces RCTs and their potential application to research for individuals with severe disabilities. It also discusses some of the problems associated with RCTs, many of which are exacerbated when considering the complexities of working with individuals who have severe disabilities. Finally, the chapter discusses some alternative research design approaches that may better address some of the shortcomings of RCTs when used with individuals with severe disabilities.

A BRIEF INTRODUCTION TO RANDOMIZED CONTROLLED TRIALS

The RCT is an experimental approach used to evaluate the impact of some treatment on a specific study population. An RCT in its simplest form compares the relative effects of a treatment in one sample of individuals (i.e., the treatment group) on a specific outcome with the same outcome in another sample of

---

A preliminary version of the material in this chapter was presented as part of the panel discussion, "Options for Research Design: Integrating Group and Single-Subject Designs: How Do We Advance the Evidence Base?" at the National Joint Committee for the Communication Needs of Persons with Severe Disabilities Research Conference, Atlanta, GA (2011, June).

individuals from the same population who did not receive the treatment (i.e., the control group). The power of RCTs (power in the sense of the validity of the causal inferences, not in the statistical sense of sensitivity to treatment impacts) comes from the fact that participants are randomly assigned in a predetermined fashion to either the treatment group or the control group. In other words, any given participant has a known probability of receiving the treatment, or not. This random assignment ensures that both groups, in the absence of treatment effects, have the same probability distribution for posttreatment outcomes. As such, following treatment, differences between the treatment and control groups are inferred to result from causal impacts of the treatment. A popular framework for thinking about causal impacts of treatments comes from Rubin (2005) and is based on the notion of potential outcomes. Although the potential outcomes framework can be applied in both RCTs and nonexperimental studies, this chapter focuses on the experimental context. Let t represent the time of observation posttreatment. Each person in the simplest RCT scenario has two potential outcomes at time t. One potential outcome is the score the person would have earned if he or she had been assigned to treatment, and the other potential outcome is the score the person would have earned had he or she been assigned to the control. The difference between these two potential outcomes at time t is the causal impact of the treatment at time t. Of course, only one of the two potential outcomes can be observed for any given person. Thus, researchers can only estimate the difference in expected outcomes (i.e., the average effect of the treatment). Researchers estimate this average treatment effect in a true experiment using the average difference between individuals assigned to treatment and individuals assigned to control. Randomization assures researchers that, in the absence of treatment impacts, these two sample averages have the same probability distribution and are, thus, probabilistically equivalent.

Many different types of group-based RCTs are available, and the details of each are outside the scope of this chapter (see Jadad & Enkin, 2008). RCTs have one thing in common, namely, they estimate average impacts of a treatment or intervention in the accessible population of interest. The expected potential outcomes for the groups are equivalent, in the absence of treatment impacts, because of random allocation of participants to treatment conditions. Observed differences between group means reflect the impact that the treatment has, on average, in the accessible population along with sampling variability.

It is widely acknowledged that the population of individuals with severe disabilities is varied and heterogeneous (Snell et al., 2010). Individuals with severe disabilities come from all walks of life, any socioeconomic background, and have varied education histories. Their disabilities may be acquired or congenital, and of known or unknown origins. Consider for a moment a sample of children taking part in an RCT to determine the impact of an augmentative and alternative communication intervention on communication. The sample of children selected to participate will certainly have one thing in common—they will have great difficulty communicating using speech. Consider further that the researchers placed the inclusion criteria that participants have fewer than 10 intelligible words to an unfamiliar communication partner. Multiple precipitating factors could result in children being able to participate in this study. They may have one of any number of genetic syndromes such as Angelman syndrome, Down syndrome, or Fragile X syndrome—all of which have unique characteristics. In addition, they may have relatively intact language but with severe speech problems, or, they may have severe language delay and little, intact speech. Furthermore, some children with an acquired disability, such as a traumatic brain injury, will likely meet the selection criteria for this study and will have many of the same concerns just described, but for very different reasons. The presence of an intellectual disability and the degree of intellectual impairment may also be a factor in some cases.

The heterogeneity and resulting variability on many characteristics of interest in the accessible population presents methodological challenges for researchers who work with individuals with severe disabilities and are attempting to determine the impact of a specific treatment or intervention. As previously described, group-based RCTs lend themselves naturally to estimating the average causal impacts of a treatment on a defined outcome. But practitioners and researchers interested in low-incidence and/or severe disabilities tend to favor more idiographic rather than nomothetic formulations of treatments and their impacts. This distinction reflects their more individualized focus on the members of society who suffer from the disorders and conditions to be treated, in lieu of a more nomothetic or generalized focus on the disorders and conditions. This distinction is also present in modern day medicine as physicians attempt to focus treatment on specific patients through personalized medicine (Hamburg & Collins, 2010), a movement signaled through the promise of research on the human genome, which signifies the uniqueness of individuals and their potential response to disease and treatment.

Preoccupation with the estimation of average treatment impacts can be problematic for a science in which the accessible population may be small and/or extremely heterogeneous. There are no magic bullet treatments for many of the issues affecting individuals with severe disabilities, and many of the best interventions demonstrate small-to-moderate average impacts (see Fey, Yoder, Warren, & Bredin-Oja, 2013; Roberts & Kaiser, 2011; Romski et al., 2010; Yoder & Warren, 2001). High variability among participants within and across treatment groups make it particularly difficult to detect these small-to-moderate average impacts. In other words, high variability can hide the small-to-moderate influences that an intervention may have on potential outcomes. Moreover, when the accessible population is small, conducting well-controlled group-based RCTs with a sufficiently large sample to detect small-to-moderate treatment impacts can prove difficult without the creation of national or international consortia to increase the size of the accessible population.

ISSUES THAT MAY MAKE THE USE OF RANDOMIZED CONTROLLED TRIALS CHALLENGING WITH THIS POPULATION

The influence of population heterogeneity on the results of group-based RCTs creates several challenges and considerations that researchers must take into account. A primary concern is how to manage or otherwise address the high variability in treatment groups. One method involves placing more restrictive inclusion and exclusion criteria when selecting participants. Researchers could set cutoff scores for language and intelligence measures. They could limit selection of participants to a single syndrome, etiology, or disability (e.g., only focusing on children with Down syndrome or cerebral palsy). Utilizing this approach, however, creates other problems. First, individuals with the same diagnoses can vary widely in terms of language and cognitive abilities as well as many other characteristics of interest. Consequently, focusing on a single diagnosis or syndrome likely will not adequately reduce heterogeneity in the accessible population to facilitate the study of treatment impacts. Second, restrictive inclusion and exclusion criteria, particularly those that focus on cutoff scores, may pose problems not only for participant recruitment, but also for using statistical methods to control for the influence of measurable characteristics on patient outcomes, which can often be used to increase power in studies of treatments with small-to-moderate impacts. Whether statistical control will be more effective than controlling heterogeneity through inclusion criteria is not always known at the time of study design.

Severe disabilities, by definition, are low-incidence disabilities. It is likely that placing recruitment restrictions that would successfully address heterogeneity could result in sample sizes that were too small for many data analysis approaches. This is particularly true considering the small-to-moderate impacts anticipated for intervention outcomes, which necessarily require large samples in order to be detected. In sum, instituting restrictive sampling to help control the high heterogeneity that threatens statistical power in studies of individuals with severe disabilities may force researchers to settle for smaller sample sizes, which also reduce statistical power. Consequently, attempts to control population heterogeneity through restrictive sampling may result in a zero-sum game.

A broader consideration is whether the results of group-based RCTs really address the important questions surrounding communication interventions for individuals who have severe disabilities. Is the average impact of an intervention or treatment approach the most important thing to know in a relatively low-incidence population? The treatment or treatments in a group-based RCT are typically given in the exact same manner across all individuals in a treatment group, so called standardized treatment protocols. Treatments of severe and low-incidence disabilities, however, must frequently be tailored to meet the specific needs of individuals in ways that go beyond milligrams per kilogram in drug trials. Although it is possible to study individualized treatment plans in a group-based RCT (see Vaughn et al., 2011 for an example in the area of middle school reading disabilities), such studies are rare and require that the individualization of treatment can be manualized and sufficient numbers of treatments units are available for randomization across the collection of study sites. Researchers working in the area of severe and low-incidence disabilities are more often interested in what treatment(s) will result in the most improved outcomes, for whom, and how the treatment can be adapted for individual cases without negatively affecting its efficacy.

In addition, group-based RCTs often fall short of characterizing how, and to what extent, treatment impacts may vary with time, or with respect to other dimensions of interest, because they measure the average treatment for a specific period. For example, the treatment may have a strong effect for any given individual at some points during the study, whereas the effect may be small or nonexistent at other times. These fluctuations in treatment efficacy may vary differently for different children and may be the result of intrinsic or extrinsic factors. This temporal variation may be studied explicitly or treated as measurement error in RCTs that use multiple measurement occasions. It is common, however, that temporal factors and other treatment effect moderators are ignored and focus is placed on estimating treatment impacts at the end of treatment or at a narrowly defined follow-up interval without an explicit focus on heterogeneity of treatment impacts in a manner that would support causal inference (Angrist, 2004).

RCTs also have limited utility in determining the optimal intensity or dosage of a treatment in a heterogeneous sample. Participants would have to be randomly assigned to one of many different dosage groups, each of which differs in the dose of the treatment, ranging from a high-dosage group to a low-dosage group, or to assign dosages to treatment groups as a random impacts factor. Having many treatment groups creates problems with sample size and power because there is a finite number of available participants. Small sample size further compound problems that result from high, within-group variability. Again, many populations with severe disabilities may be too small to support large RCTs.

Although group-based RCTs are an important tool for determining treatment impacts in the broader general population of children with disabilities, it may be the case that such designs provide answers to questions that are of less importance for treating severe disabilities and for understanding and caring for the individuals affected by them. The answer to the question, "What is the average impact of a treatment on an average participant?" may not be as important as, "What is the best treatment approach for an individual with certain characteristics in certain circumstances?" The potential outcomes framework for generalized causal inference fortunately is not limited to causal inference in group-based RCTs. Indeed, there may be alternative approaches to investigating treatment efficacy that are better suited to the challenges of low-incidence, high-severity disabilities and to the questions posed by researchers in this area.

DESIGN ALTERNATIVES TO GROUP-BASED RANDOMIZED CONTROLLED TRIALS

The development of a taxonomy of individuals and the treatments that best correspond to their unique situations should be the overarching goal of research programs that focus on treatments for individuals with severe disabilities. As such, there are several research methods and statistical approaches that researchers can leverage to work toward establishing such taxonomy.

Single-subject experimental research designs, which are often maligned and misunderstood by some researchers, are a powerful method that can be deployed when attempting to determine the impacts of treatments on specific individuals with severe disabilities. Single-subject research designs involve obtaining repeated measures or observations on an individual under different treatment assignments so that the individual serves as his or her own control (Haynes & Johnson, 2009; Kratochwill et al., 2010) across repeated exposures to two or more treatment conditions. This is in contrast to between-subjects, group-based RCT designs in which control groups are comprised of different people (i.e., different individuals are observed in different treatment conditions), each assigned to a single treatment condition, and also different from within-subjects group-based RCT designs in which the same people are assigned to multiple treatments at different occasions. Although each person serves as his or her own control in the latter design, data are nevertheless aggregated across individuals to assess treatment impacts, and it is rare that the same treatments are readministered after having been withdrawn.

Single-subject experimental designs involve establishing a baseline on a characteristic or behavior of interest over many observations and then documenting change in that baseline as a function of some experimental manipulation, most likely an intervention or treatment. However, treatments and time are confounded for an individual person when there is only one change of conditions (i.e., from baseline to active treatment). This confounding of time and treatment renders causal inferences about treatment impacts ambiguous. A strong, unambiguous causal inference about treatment impacts in single-subject designs requires additional demonstrations of the impact of the treatment on the behavior(s) of interest. The inability to aggregate data across individuals for analysis in single-subject designs typically requires that the same treatments be administered during multiple treatment/nontreatment periods in order to remove the confounding of treatment and time. Alternatively, treatments are administered to different behaviors at different periods of time in an effort to show that behavior change is tied to the onset of treatment and not simply the passage of time.

Several types of single-subject experimental designs can be helpful in determining treatment efficacy. These generally fall under two classes of design: A-B-A-B (or multiple treatment sequence) and multiple baseline. In multiple baseline designs, baselines are established for multiple behaviors and treatment is applied to different behaviors at different points in time, or baselines are established in multiple individuals and treatments are begun with different individuals at different points in time. Unlike treatment sequence designs, multiple baseline designs do not require treatment to be withdrawn or reversed, which is rarely ethically appropriate and sometimes logistically impossible with behavioral interventions. For example, removing a new instructional method that is used to teach a student a new behavior might prevent new learning from occurring but would not necessarily result in the loss of the behavior already acquired. Multiple baselines can be evaluated across behaviors, participants, and/or settings.

A multiple baseline across behaviors design allows researchers to measure two or more functionally distinct behaviors (i.e., dependent variables), obtain a stable baseline on both, and introduce an intervention that should only affect the two dependent variables differently. This approach allows researchers to evaluate the impact of the treatment on the two dependent variables independently and helps establish the specificity of the treatment.

A multiple baseline across participants design allows researchers to estimate the impact of an intervention across a (typically, small) group of individuals. All participants in the group are measured at the same time to establish a baseline on a specified dependent variable, and an intervention is then introduced to one individual at a time while measurement of the dependent variable continues for all participants. An effective intervention would result in change in the dependent variable for the individual(s) who received the intervention, and those who have not yet received the intervention should demonstrate unchanged baselines. This type of design allows researchers to estimate the impact of the intervention while accounting for the influence of time on the dependent variables of interest.

A multiple baseline across settings design allows researchers to determine the impact of an intervention within the same individual across different treatment settings. Stable baselines are established across the settings of interest (e.g., classroom, home), and intervention is started in one setting. Measuring dependent variables across different settings allows researchers to establish the extent to which the impacts of interventions generalize to settings other than the ones in which the intervention is conducted.

Not only is it possible to conduct studies that combine elements of each of these multiple baseline designs, but it is also possible to apply sophisticated multilevel modeling (MLM) to the data (Moeyaert, Ferron, Beretvas, & Van den Noortgate, 2014; Ugille, Moeyaert, Beretvas, Ferron, & Van den Noortgate, 2012). MLM generally requires a minimum of 15–30 experimental units for estimation of variance components (i.e., the random impacts in the model). The random impacts in a single-subject design might be the single-subject averages under each of the treatment conditions and/or the difference in the single-subject averages between the treatment periods. Both the within-person focus of the single-subject design and the repeated measurements that are characteristic of single-subject designs help to assuage this requirement. In actuality, the sample size requirements for estimating the variance in the random impacts in a MLM depend on how precisely the individual random impacts have been estimated. With greater precision in the estimates of the individual random impacts, fewer experimental units are required to estimate the variance in those random impacts. All other things being equal, having more observations per person per condition translates into more precise estimation of the individual random impacts. The repeated measures from single-subject studies, however, serve as multiple observations that are nested within behavior, treatment, or setting and, ultimately, the individual. The typically large number of individual observations per treatment period in a single-subject experiment generally translates into precise estimates of individual random impacts. Consequently, researchers can apply sophisticated modeling to carefully designed, single-subject studies in order to answer questions typically answered by RCTs using group-based designs. In addition, concerns about heterogeneity are greatly reduced, although not eliminated, because participants serve as their own control.

Advances in the development of adaptive designs and their application with students with autism (Kasari et al., 2014) and students with attention-deficit/hyperactivity disorder (Pelham & Fabiano, 2008) have spurred interest in their potential application to students with severe disabilities. These designs represent creative ways to employ randomization and, thus, strong causal inferences in the development of adaptive treatments or treatment sequences, as well as to develop and understand the effective components of multicomponent treatments. At first glance these strengths seem to make sequential, multiple assignment, randomized trials (SMART) designs well suited to the study of treatments used with individuals with severe disabilities, in which treatments might need to be adapted based on responses to earlier treatment stages. Researchers and practitioners, however, must recognize that a traditional group randomized trial represents the final step in a SMART design, following the development of an adaptive treatment. Thus, although we would not rule out the possible continued development of SMART designs that might be well suited to addressing the problems associated with randomized trials in the study of treatments for individuals with severe disabilities, we do not see that current SMART designs address the challenges to group randomized trials in the treatment of severe disabilities previously discussed.

LUMPING VERSUS SPLITTING: THE SEARCH FOR LATENT CONSISTENCY AMIDST MANIFEST HETEROGENEITY

Group-based treatment designs have at their heart a notion that like units can be combined to study treatment efficacy because these units share something in common that renders them sensitive to the impacts of a particular treatment. This communality is often directly observable in the etiology or symptomatology associated with disorders or disabilities. This manifest communality is often not present in the case of severe disabilities. Indeed, the manifest heterogeneity is often so stark that there is a tendency to view all individuals ideographically, as unique unto themselves, and to presume that aggregation of like units is futile. However, as more and more information becomes publicly available on larger and larger numbers of individuals with severe disabilities, and these data follow common designs and collect information on similar behaviors, it becomes possible to employ statistical methods that attempt to identify homogeneous classes of individuals, in which class membership may not be directly observable, but only latent in the individuals' patterns of behavior over time, or in response to competing treatments. Two such classes of models are mixture models, in particular latent growth mixture models, and latent class models (Francis, Fletcher, & Morris, 2009). Research using these types of models is possible on individuals with severe disabilities with public or privately accessible archives of treatment-outcome data, but it is unlikely that sufficiently large study samples could ever be collected to allow questions of this type to be answered without such archives.

For example, mixture models can be applied to data from many single-subject experiments that were collected using similar designs and interventions across individuals that might differ substantially in their manifest characteristics but are being exposed to similar or comparable treatments. Mixture models attempt to identify subgroups of individuals within the sample who show similar developmental trajectories, responses to treatment, or patterns of behavior (see Boscardin, Muthén, Francis, & Baker, 2008; Jones, Nagin, & Roeder, 2001). The method essentially seeks to lump together individuals whose behavior profiles are similar and to separate into different classes those individuals whose behavior profiles are similar to one another and distinct from the profiles of individuals in the other classes. The objective of the analysis is to determine the number of latent classes and the probability of membership for each individual in each of the latent classes. Mixture models are quite flexible in that they allow different relationships to exist between and among the independent and dependent variables for each subpopulation. This method could be applied to treatment-outcome data and used to seek out subgroups of individuals and examine treatment impacts within similar subgroups that are defined based on their pattern of baseline behavior. This approach would control for baseline variability that would otherwise be treated as error if all individuals were lumped together, thereby increasing the likelihood of finding a significant impact of the intervention on outcomes within subpopulations. More important, this approach to addressing heterogeneity of samples eliminates the necessity to sample using restrictive inclusion and exclusion criteria. Furthermore, the results provide information about the impact of interventions on individuals who may be from different manifest subpopulations, which begins to address the all-important question of which interventions work for whom.

Finally, latent class analysis is another statistical approach that can be used to identify subgroups of individuals based on responses to test or survey items. Latent class models are similar to mixture models in that they seek to identify latent subgroups of individuals who are similar in their response patterns to one another and different in their response patters to other latent subgroups. Latent class, factor mixture models, growth mixture models, and generalized growth mixture models are simply types of covariance structure models that attempt to cluster people (i.e., respondents) in the way that factor analysis attempts to cluster variables (McCutcheon, 1987; Magidson & Vermunt, 2004). Latent class models historically referred to the search for latent subgroups of individuals in responses to test or survey items (i.e., dichotomous or polytomous items), whereas latent profile analysis referred to the search for latent subgroups using continuously measured variables. The subgroups in both cases were posited to account for all of the covariation among the items/measures. That is, items/measures within a class were independent and items/measures between classes were correlated. This restriction is no longer applied, and these models (latent class and latent profile models) are just special cases of latent mixture models.

More important, all of these models seek to identify meaningful homogeneity and heterogeneity within a population. The quality of the solution will depend on the quality of the information that goes into the analysis. Finding meaningful ways to study this heterogeneity must be a priority in a field that is marked by concern over heterogeneity. Assembling the appropriate datasets appears to be the challenge in applying these methods to the study of severe disabilities. Although retrospective analysis of the literature using meta-analysis, which is characterized by studies with relatively small numbers of participants, would be a step in addressing the question of which interventions work for whom, this enterprise is fundamentally different from the search for latent classes of individuals and the manifest features of individuals that can predict membership in those classes. Coupled with prospective treatment studies that exploit information about latent subgroups in matching individuals to treatments, these models could be useful in the evolution of the scientific study of severe and low-incidence disabilities and the discovery of what treatments work for whom and under what conditions.

CONCLUSION

Group-based RCTs are an important scientific tool for determining the impact of treatment. They do so by determining the average impact of treatment on an outcome measure for a group of individuals relative to the average of the same outcome measure for another group of individuals in a contrast or control condition. Unfortunately, when considering treatments or interventions for people with severe or low-incidence disabilities, the question of the average impact may be less important than the question of what intervention works best for whom when individuals within a disability group appear at the manifest level to be quite distinct from one another. Consequently, alternative methods that address the high heterogeneity of the population and focus more on the individual should be considered when conducting intervention research with individuals with severe and/or low-incidence disabilities. Single-subject experimental designs, coupled with MLM that capitalizes on repeated measures and mixture and latent class models that identify subpopulations and how interventions affect them, begin to address the question of what interventions work best and for whom.

REFERENCES

Angrist, J.D. (2004). Heterogeneity of treatment effects in theory and practice. *Economic Journal, 114,* C52–C83.

Boscardin, C.K., Muthén, B., Francis, D.J., & Baker, E.L. (2008). Early identification of reading difficulties using heterogeneous developmental trajectories. *Journal of Educational Psychology, 100,* 192–208. doi: 10.1037/0022-0663.100.1.192

Fey, M.E., Yoder, P.J., Warren, S.F., & Bredin-Oja, S.L. (2013). Is more better? Milieu communication teaching in toddlers with intellectual disabilities. *Journal of Speech, Language, and Hearing Research, 56,* 679–693. doi: 10.1044/1092-4388(2012/12-0061)

Francis, D.J., Fletcher, J.M., & Morris, R.D. (2009). Recent methodological advances in the analysis of developmental data: An introduction to growth mixture models. In K. Pugh and P. McCardle (Eds.), *How children learn to read: Current issues and new directions in the integration of cognition, neurobiology and genetics of reading and dyslexia research and practice* (pp. 65–85). New York, NY: Psychology Press.

Hamburg, M.A., & Collins, F.S. (2010). The path to personalized medicine. *New England Journal of Medicine, 363,* 301–304.

Haynes, W.O., & Johnson, C.E. (2009). *Understanding research and evidence-based practice in communication disorders: A primer for students and practitioners.* Boston, MA: Pearson Education.

Jadad, A.R., & Enkin, M.W. (2008). *Randomized controlled trials: Questions, answers and musings.* Malden, MA: Blackwell Publishing.

Jones, B.L., Nagin, D.S., & Roeder, K. (2001). A SAS procedure based on mixture models for estimating developmental trajectories. *Sociological Methods and Research, 29,* 374–393. doi: 10.1177/0049124101029003005

Kasari, C., Kaiser, A., Goods, K., Nietfeld, J., Mathy, P., Landa, R., Almirall, D. (2014). Communication interventions for minimally verbal children with autism: A sequential multiple assignment randomized trial. *Journal of the American Academy of Child and Adolescent Psychiatry, 53,* 635–646. doi: 10.1016/j.jaac.2014.01.019

Kratochwill, T.R., Hitchcock, J., Horner, R.H., Levin, J.R., Odom, S.L., Rindskopf, D.M., & Shadish, W.R. (2010). *Single-case design technical documentation.* Retrieved from http://ies.ed.gov/ncee/wwc/pdf/wwc_scd.pdf

Magidson, J., & Vermunt, J.K. (2004). Latent class models. In D. Kaplan (Ed.), *The sage handbook of quantitative methodology for the social sciences* (pp. 549-553). Thousand Oaks, CA: Sage Publications.

McCutcheon, A.L. (1987). *Latent class analysis.* Thousand Oaks, CA: Sage Publications.

Moeyaert, M., Ferron, J.M., Beretvas, S.N., & Van den Noortgate, W. (2014). From a single-level analysis to a multilevel analysis of single-case experimental designs. *Journal of School Psychology, 52,* 191–211. doi: 10.1016/j.jsp.2013.11.003

Pelham, W.E., & Fabiano, G.A. (2008). Evidence-based psychosocial treatments for attention-deficit/hyperactivity disorder. *Journal of Clinical Child and Adolescent Psychology, 37,* 184–214. doi: 10.1080/15374410701818681

Roberts, M.Y., & Kaiser, A.P. (2011). The effectiveness of parent-implemented language interventions: A meta-analysis. *American Journal of Speech-Language Pathology, 20,* 180–199. doi: 10.1044/1058-0360 (2011/10-0055)

Romski, M.A., Sevcik, R.A., Adamson, L.B., Cheslock, M., Smith, A., Barker, R.M., & Bakeman, R. (2010). Randomized comparison of augmented and non-augmented language interventions for toddlers with developmental delays and their parents. *Journal of Speech, Language, and Hearing Research, 53,* 350–364. doi: 10.1044/1092-4388(2009/08-0156)

Rubin, D.B. (2005). Causal inference using potential outcomes. *Journal of the American Statistical Association, 100,* 322–331.

Snell, M.E., Brady, N.C., McLean, L., Ogletree, B.T., Siegel, E., Sylvester, L., Sevcik, R. (2010). Twenty years of communication intervention research with individuals who have severe intellectual and developmental disabilities. *American Journal on Intellectual and Developmental Disabilities, 115,* 364–380. doi: 10.1352/1944-7558-115-5.364

Ugille, M., Moeyaert, M., Beretvas, S.N., Ferron, J., & Van den Noortgate, W. (2012).

Multilevel meta-analysis of single-subject experimental designs: A simulation study. *Behavior Research Methods, 44,* 1244–1254. doi: 10.3758/s13428-012-0213-1

Vaughn, S., Wexler, J., Roberts, G., Barth, A.A., Cirino, P.T., Romain, M.A., Denton, C.A. (2011). Effects of individualized and standardized interventions for middle school students with reading disabilities. *Exceptional Children, 77,* 391–407.

Yoder, P.J., & Warren, S.F. (2001). Relative treatment effects of two prelinguistic communication interventions on language development in toddlers with developmental delays vary by maternal characteristics. *Journal of Speech, Language, and Hearing Research, 44,* 224–237.

11

Boxed in by Small Sample Size?

Some Ways Out of the Box

Roger Bakeman

For researchers seeking to demonstrate and evaluate more effective ways of intervening with individuals with severe disabilities, statistical and research design consultants too often seem like people who delight in saying no. They may say that sample sizes are too small for conventional statistical tests, which would be so underpowered as to be pointless. But many researchers are stuck in a practical world in which the cases of interest to them are few and access is often difficult and time consuming. What should you as a researcher do when a respectable number of cases might take decades to accumulate?

Possible approaches, especially appealing in clinical contexts, include *N* of one studies and qualitative reports. Such possibilities have been addressed at length by others and are not discussed here. Instead, I would like to focus on some quantitative approaches that need not be out of reach for researchers with few cases to consider. These approaches emphasize simplicity. They build on core quantitative knowledge that, although now forgotten or only dimly remembered, typically lies in most researchers' academic past. The ideas presented here are not especially new, although some of them may require you to put together what you already know in new ways, ways that I hope will prove to be simple and productive.

I will make five suggestions. Specifically, I recommend greater use of the sign test, which may be one of the simpler statistical tests; suggest that the pursuit of statistical significance may be overrated; urge that effect sizes (ES) such as the odds ratio and Cohen's *d* or Hedges' *g* be emphasized; suggest that individual results may become important later when used for meta-analyses; and recommend that data visualizations be used at all stages of data analysis. Almost all of these

A preliminary version of the material in this chapter was presented as part of the panel discussion, "Options for Research Design: Integrating Group and Single-Subject Designs: How Do We Advance the Evidence Base?" at the National Joint Committee for the Communication Needs of Persons with Severe Disabilities Research Conference, Atlanta, GA (2011, June).

suggestions have been made before, repeatedly, yet their influence on the published literature remains difficult to discern. For an especially useful explication of these and related suggestions, see Wilkinson and the American Psychological Association's Task Force on Statistical Inference (1999) guidelines.

SELECT SIMPLE OUTCOMES AND TESTS

Complexity often rules the research roost, perhaps in the hope that if enough different bits of data are collected and fed into the computer, then something must result—an enterprise that is often rightly called *fishing*, although chickens scratching might be a more apt metaphor. An alternative is simplicity—and no assessment is simpler than a binary, yes/no, or true/false one. In many investigations, it is relatively easy to define outcome in binary terms—the child improved or not. Doing so has two advantages: the descriptive statistic (e.g., 78% improved) is easily understood and its statistical significance is easily tested. All that is needed is a sign test (also called a *binomial test*).

If you can categorize an outcome for individual cases as "yes" or "no" and believe that "yes" should be more frequent (a one-tailed test), then you would be disappointed if only half the cases were "yes" (p["yes"] = .5); such a result would not let you claim an effect. But how many "yes" cases would let you claim an effect? The exact number, which varies with the number of cases, is given by the binomial expansion (see Bakeman & Robinson, 2005). Critical values for various numbers of cases (e.g., participants, dyads) are shown graphically in Figure 11.1. For example, if 15 of 20 cases improved—following usual null-hypothesis testing conventions—then you would say that such a result would occur by chance alone less than 5% of

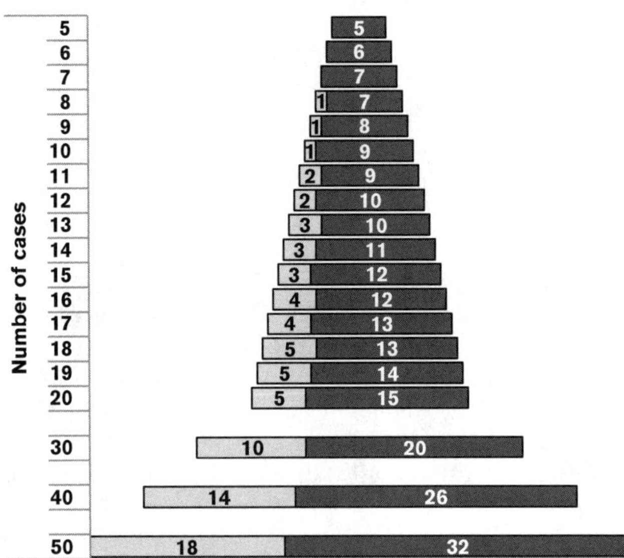

Figure 11.1. Critical values for a one-tailed sign test. The numbers to the right (white on a dark background) are the number of cases that need to be coded "yes" (or other binary value), given the specified total number of cases, in order to infer an effect. If the probability of a "yes" is 50%, then the probability of this many cases being coded "yes" is fewer than 5%. Critical values for a two-tailed test differ by at most 1.

the time if the true probability of "yes" were .5, and so you would declare the result statistically significant, $p < .05$. Other probabilities than .5 can be used, although a suitable rationale is required; and tests can be two tailed if you do not specifically hypothesize that one response will be more frequent.

But here's the puzzle. Why is the simple, straightforward, and easy-to-understand sign test so seldom used? And why do so many of my colleagues return a blank stare when I mention it? Part of the reason may be the dismaying sameness and limited scope of almost all undergraduate textbooks designed to teach statistics to budding behavioral scientists. Their focus is almost exclusively on parametric statistics—means, standard deviations, correlation, simple regression, and analysis of variance—that assume measurement on an equal-interval scale (often called *continuous*). Nonparametric statistics—statistics that deal with count variables—are usually represented only by chi square, with the sign test rarely mentioned, and are relegated to a final chapter that, in practice, is often skipped in the interest of time. Even figuring out how to do a sign test with a standard statistical package can be complex. For example, in SPSS (Release 18) you first need to select Analyze > Nonparametric Tests > One Sample, then select variable (Test Fields) under the Fields tab, next select Customize Tests under the Settings tab, and finally check Compare observed binary probability to hypothesized (Binomial test). The test is two tailed (there is not a one-tailed option), but you can specify a hypothesized probability other than the default .5.

In the context of multiple regression, Cohen and Cohen (1983) recommended segregating explanatory variables into three levels: those the research was designed to appraise, those of secondary interest, and those of the "I wonder if" variety (p. 171). Similarly, I recommend, whenever feasible and no matter how many secondary analyses follow, first addressing your central research questions and asking whether they are amenable to a sign test. Is there a binary outcome of central interest and a binary explanatory variable whose influence on outcome that needs to be tested? If so, analyses should begin with a sign test. The test statistic—percentage coded "yes"—is easily and instantly understood; even with as few as five cases, if all five were "yes," then you can claim a result that is statistically significant, $p < .05$ (exact probability per the binomial expansion = .03125; see Bakeman & Robinson, 2005). The sign test is not only exact and simple—too simple, apparently, to receive much attention from introductory statistical textbooks—but it also works well when samples are small. If you start looking for places to apply it, you may be surprised how many there are.

PUT STATISTICAL SIGNIFICANCE IN PERSPECTIVE

Statistical consultants are not the only ones who like to say no; sometimes journal reviewers do too, but for the opposite reason—too little, as opposed to too much, reading of current statistical literature. When queried, most of my colleagues report that a reviewer has chastised them at least once for mentioning a result whose p-value fails to fall below the conventional .05 threshold for statistical significance. This can be especially problematic when N is small. As is widely appreciated, results that are not statistically significant when N is small become so when N is larger. For example, when $N = 5$, 100% must be "yes" to claim a significant sign test effect, but only 90% when $N = 10$ and 75% when $N = 20$.

Rigidity at the .05 barricade is understandable; the impulse is to avoid error and, when null-hypothesis testing logic and statistical theory are less understood, rigid interpretation seems the safer course. The rigidity is not supported by most statistical experts. For example, Jacob Cohen (1990) wrote, ".05 is not a cliff but a convenient reference point along the possibility–probability continuum" (p. 1311; see also Cohen, 1994). Aware of how often "* $p < .05$, ** $p < .01$, *** $p < .001$" appear at the bottom of journal article tables, and a bit tongue-in-cheek but with a nod to the moral fervor with which the .05 cliff is sometimes enforced, Cohen commented further,

> The atmosphere that characterizes statistics as applied in the social and biomedical sciences is that of a secular region (Salsburg, 1985), apparently of Judeo-Christian derivation, as it employs as its most powerful icon a six-pointed cross, often presented multiply for enhanced authority. (pp. 1306–1307)

Rosnow and Rosenthal (1989) commented, "Surely, God loves the .06 nearly as much as the .05" (p. 1277).

The knowledgeable rule follower understands when rules can be bent. One of the stronger arguments for not breaking .05 discipline occurs when many tests are in play (e.g., examining all of the 45 pair-wise correlations 10 variables produce). Such fishing courts Type I error (the risk of making false claims)—the thing that null-hypothesis testing is designed to guard against. In contrast, a good argument for loosening .05 discipline occurs when, in the spirit of Cohen's suggestion to order variables from most to least important, you have identified a few tests of primary importance. Like the gambler who can win only by naming the horse before the race, identifying your most important tests beforehand gives you latitude. In such cases it makes sense to talk about effects significant at, for example, "only" .063. As Cohen (1990) noted, .05 is a continuum, not a cliff.

EMPHASIZE EFFECT SIZE

The antidote to an exclusive emphasis on statistical significance is an equal, if not greater, emphasis on the magnitude of effects (Wilkinson and the Task Force on Statistical Inference, 1999). Simply put, size matters. As noted in the *Publication Manual of the American Psychological Association* (APA), *Sixth Edition* (2010), "For the reader to appreciate the magnitude or importance of a study's findings, it is almost always necessary to include some measure of effect size in the Results section" (p. 34). Effect measures are many, but they share a common defining characteristic—unlike statistical significance, their magnitude does not change with *N*. For a comprehensive list, the APA Publication Manual recommends Grissom and Kim (2005); another excellent source is Cooper, Hedges, and Valentine (2009); and a brief introduction is provided by Bakeman (2006). ES measures include members of the *r* family (bivariate association including the familiar Pearson correlation coefficient), the *d* family (comparison of two means; see McCartney & Rosenthal, 2000), and various squared indexes such as the change in R^2 of hierarchic multiple regression and the conceptually similar partial eta squared (η_p^2) of analyses of variance. By way of introduction, here I describe two of the simplest (simple, in part, because they compare two groups)—the odds ratio (for count data) and Cohen's *d* and Hedges' *g* (for interval-scaled data).

The Odds Ratio

The odds ratio (OR) is unique among statistics in that its name states what it is and how to compute it. It is appropriate whenever count data can be arranged in a 2 × 2 table. For purposes of exposition, here I will assume two groups, labeled Alpha and Beta (thus, group is the independent variable); these groups might be formed experimentally (e.g., treatment group, control group) or they might result from measurement (e.g., boys, girls). I will also assume a simple outcome, labeled "yes" and "no" (e.g., "yes" might indicate improvement, however defined). Cases can then be tallied in a 2 × 2 table with rows labeled Alpha and Beta and columns labeled "Yes" and "No."

The number of summary statistics that can be computed for a 2 × 2 table is legion. The Pearson chi-square (which is also appropriate for larger tables) is the one behavioral scientists are most likely to know—thanks to that last, often overlooked chapter in introductory statistical textbooks. The odds ratio (which is limited to 2 × 2 tables) is less well known. Although not part of the behavioral science canon, it deserves to be. Its magnitude has concrete meaning, which makes its interpretation intuitive—this is perhaps its major merit. Consider a 2 × 2 table with cells labeled *a, b, c,* and *d,* as shown in Figure 11.2. The odds of "yes" (Column 1) are a/b for the Alpha group (Row 1) and c/d for the Beta group (Row 2). The odds ratio is simply the ratio of the Row 1 to the Row 2 odds.

If there is no effect (i.e., the groups do not differ), then the odds are the same for each row and their ratio is 1. If the odds of "yes" are higher for the Alpha group, then the odds ratio is greater than 1 (and becomes larger as the effect becomes stronger, approaching infinity). This lends itself to clear descriptive statements such as, "The odds of improving are three times greater for the Alpha group than the Beta group." If the odds of "yes" are higher for the Beta group, then the odds ratio

Odds ratio (OR)	$\text{OR} = \frac{a/b}{c/d} = \frac{ad}{bc}$ (cells: a b / c d)
Natural log of OR	lnOR = LN(OR)
Standard error of log odds ratio	$\text{SElnOR} = \sqrt{\frac{1}{a} + \frac{1}{b} + \frac{1}{c} + \frac{1}{d}}$
95% confidence low and high limits for log odds ratio and odds ratio	ln95%lo = lnOR − 1.96 * SElnOR ln95%hi = lnOR + 1.96 * SElnOR 95%lo = EXP(ln95%lo) 95%hi = EXP(ln95%hi)

Figure 11.2. Definitional and computational formulas for the odds ratio, a useful descriptive statistic and measure of effect size for 2 × 2 tables. An odds ratio is said to be significant, $p < .05$, if its 95% confidence interval excludes 1. Its 95% confidence interval is easily computed from the natural logarithm of the odds ratio and its standard error, as shown. LN indicates taking the natural logarithm (i.e., determining the exponent for the mathematical constant e that gives the specified value). EXP is the reverse; it indicates exponentiation (i.e., raising the mathematical constant *e* to the power indicated).

is less than 1 (and approaches zero as the effect becomes stronger). If statements such as "the odds of improving for the Alpha group are one third of those for the Beta group" seem awkward, then simply swap rows and columns (or compute the reciprocal, 1/OR) and report that the odds of improving are three times greater for the Beta group than the Alpha group.

The magnitude of the odds ratio has meaning that the magnitude of the chi-square does not. For example, imagine that 10 children received an intervention and another 10 did not, and that 80% of the Alpha group improved, whereas only 50% of the Beta group did. In this case, the odds ratio is 4.00 and the Pearson chi-square is 1.98. The odds of improving were four times greater for the intervention compared with the control group. The chi-square of 1.98 affords no comparable, concrete interpretation. Moreover, if the counts were doubled—20 in each group—but the 80% and 50% remained the same, then the odds ratio would remain the same as well (this is what magnitude of effect statistics do), but the Pearson chi-square would become 3.96, no more interpretable than the 1.98.

Statistical significance can be computed for both the odds ratio and the Pearson chi-square—and would be essentially the same—but is actually easier to compute for the odds ratio (see Figure 11.2). Using a spreadsheet program (probably easier than the alternatives), compute the odds ratio (*ad/bc,* the computational formula, is less vulnerable to zero cell problems than the definitional formula), the natural logarithm of the odds ratio, its standard error, the 95% confidence interval (CI) in log units (low and high), and finally the 95% CI (low and high) converted back into odds-ratio units. If 1, which indicates no effect, lies outside the 95% CI, then the odds ratio is said to be statistically significant, $p < .05$.

Understanding how statistical significance is computed for an odds ratio illuminates the problem researchers with small N face. As N becomes smaller, cell sizes become smaller as well, but the reciprocals of the cell sizes become larger, as does the standard error (SElnOR in Figure 11.2), which is computed from the sum of these reciprocals. And, with a larger standard error, an OR of 1 becomes more likely to fall within the embrace of the 95% CI, leading to the conclusion that the effect is not statistically significant. To return to the example given a couple of paragraphs earlier, when $N = 20$ the OR is not statistically significant (95% CI = 0.55 – 29.1), but when $N = 40$ the OR is almost significant at the .05 level (95% CI = 0.98 – 16.27). Yet, the odds ratio for both was 4.00—the same ES but different significance due to the sample size.

Working with and truly assimilating the computations shown in Figure 11.2 is important because it promotes understanding, thereby making errors of interpretation less likely. I worry that too many graduate students (and too many of my colleagues) have joined another chorus of those who say no—those who will not use a statistic unless they can point and click and have the desired statistic pop out of the appropriate computer program. The question, "How do I compute that?" should be a question about actual computations, but too often the desired answer is simply the name of a computer program—a magic black box replacing competence, a fish replacing learning to fish. If you understand and implement computations like those shown in Figure 11. 2 using a spreadsheet or other computing device, then you are less likely to make conceptual errors later. Only then should you use a statistical package; and, even then, figuring out how to produce an odds ratio may not be immediately obvious. For example, in SPSS (Release 18), you need to select

Analyze > Descriptive Statistics > Crosstabs, then your Row and Column variables, then Statistics, and check Risk. This gives you the odds ratio and its 95% CI; to get an exact probability you need to select Analyze > Regression > Binary Logistic, then your Dependent (here, outcome or column) and Covariate (here, independent or row) variables, then Options, and check 95% CI (other percentages can be specified). The odds ratio is labeled "Exp(B)" in the output, something you might understand only if you had worked through the equations in Figure 11.2.

Odds ratios, such as *p*-values, constitute a continuum, not a cliff. Nonetheless, qualitative terms for ranges of values can be useful. For example, Cohen's (1988) widely used categories for correlation coefficients—values of .1 suggest a small, .3 a medium, and .5 a large effect—provide a consistent way to describe such results. Similarly, and based in part on a suggestion by Haddock, Rindskopf, and Shadish (1998), Bakeman and Quera (2011) suggested that odds ratios more than 3.00 (or less than 0.3) be regarded as large, between 2.00–3.00 (or 0.33–0.50) as medium, and between 1.25–2.00 (or 0.50–0.80) as small, with odds ratios between 0.80–1.25 regarded as negligible. All such guidelines are arbitrary but have the merit of bringing some consistency to discussions of effect size.

Consider this example from Romski et al. (2010) describing the effect of a randomized trial with three interventions. The odds that children in the AC-I and AC-O interventions would use spoken words at the end of intervention was 2.9 and 4.8 greater than the odds that children in the SC intervention would. The first was a medium effect and not statistically significant (95% CI = 0.78–10.9, p = .11), whereas the second was a large effect and statistically significant (95% CI = 1.25–18.4, p=.02).

Cohen's *d* and Hedges' *g*

When characteristics of interest, such as the number of words a child understands or expressive language ability measured on a standardized test, are assessed for children from two groups (again, these could be intervention and control groups or groups of boys and girls), one direct measure of ES is simply the difference between the (arithmetic) means of the two groups. But scales vary; number of words might vary from 0 to 400, whereas a standardized scale might produce scores that can vary from 4 to 36. The solution is to standardize the difference between the two means, which is what Cohen's *d* and Hedges' *g* do.

Standardization is achieved for both statistics by dividing the difference between the means of the two groups by the standard deviation of the (pooled) scores (see Figure 11.3). The only difference is in how the standard deviation is computed: Cohen assumes, in effect, that the sample is the population and so divides the pooled sum of squares (SS) by the sample size, whereas Hedges assumes that the sample is used to estimate the population and so divides the pooled SS by the degrees of freedom (two less than the sample size), providing a less biased estimate. On this basis, Hedges' *g* would seem preferable, but Cohen's *d* appeared first in the literature, which may account for its continued frequent use. Values of Hedges' *g* will always be somewhat smaller than Cohen's *d,* as the computational formulas based on the *t* statistic show (Figure 11.3). As a practical matter, the differences between *d* and *g* are small when *N* is large but become greater as *N* decreases. For this reason, it may make sense for investigators with small *N*

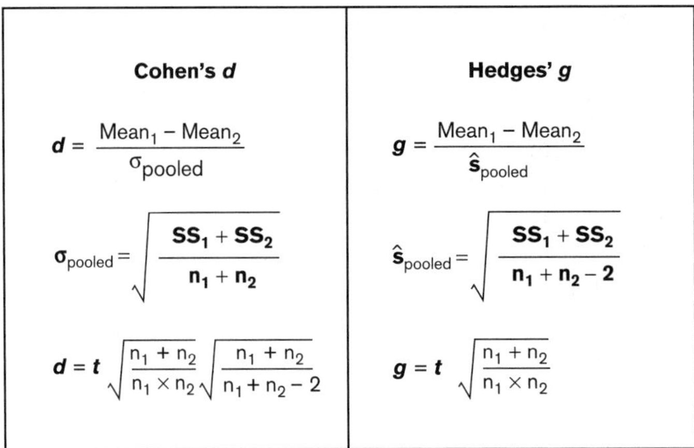

Figure 11.3. Definitional and computational formulas for Cohen's *d* and Hedges' *g*, useful effect size measures for assessing the difference between the means of two groups. SS is the sum of squares (i.e., deviations of each score from its mean, squared, and summed). Cohen's *d* and Hedges' *g* are easily computed from the *t*-test statistic, as shown. Cohen regards *d*s of 0.2, 0.5, and 0.8 as indicating small, medium, and large effects, respectively.

to favor Hedges' *g*. One caveat: both of these statistics work best when variability of scores within the two groups is roughly comparable. When variability differs, other solutions may be warranted (see Cooper et al., 2009); and when the distributions of scores are badly skewed (i.e., when means may be misleading), it may be better to abandon standardized mean differences in favor of data visualization, as discussed shortly.

FEED THE SYNTHESIZERS

There is more than one way to view our toils in the research trenches. Understandably, when in the midst of a particular project, we seldom focus much beyond the trench; we are too involved with finding and keeping participants, ensuring the faithful execution of procedures, and monitoring the careful performance of assessments. Our attention focuses on understanding the results of our single study. But others can take a longer view. Since the beginning of our literature, review articles have sought pattern across published reports. But what were once primarily qualitative narratives and box scores (percentage of studies finding an effect) have now taken a quantum leap in sophistication. Now review articles, which are called meta-analyses or research syntheses, employ a variety of sophisticated—and evolving—statistical procedures (e.g., Cooper et al., 2009), which provide a considerably more accurate overview than articles in the past.

Thus, any single result produced—this is a second way to view behavioral scientists' toils—can become grist for subsequent meta-analysts. Small *N* matters less from this point of view. A reasonable ES may not be statistically significant when *N* is small, but if the preponderance of studies shows effects, then a research synthesis can reveal—and quantify—the pattern. Several attitudes need to shift for this to work well. First, individual researchers need to become less intimidated by the bludgeon of statistical significance and emphasize ES more; they should not relegate insignificant results to the file drawer in which later meta-analysts may not be able to find them. Second, reviewers and journal editors need to become less dismissive of insignificant findings, thereby reducing the publication bias meta-analysts rightly find problematic. But mainly, everyone needs to recognize science as the communal, accumulative process it can be—and the role research syntheses can play in helping behavioral scientists move toward that goal.

Let me present a simple example to illustrate how this can work. Imagine 10 studies, with *N*s varying from 10 to 40, each with two groups and a simple binary outcome. Based on data I made up to illustrate meta-analysis, I computed odds ratios and 95% CIs for these 10 studies (see Figure 11.4). Because the *N*s are small, the 95% CIs are quite large, as the figure shows. In fact, only one of these studies achieved a conventional level of statistical significance. Yet, although one study showed no effect and another a negative effect, the remaining eight all showed positive effects: following the conventions presented earlier, 1 was negligible, 2 were small, 2 were medium, and 3 were large; but a box-score style review would note that only 1 of 9 studies showed a significant effect.

Meta-analysis provides methods for quantitatively combining individual results, a bit like computing a mean for a set of scores. The summary odds ratio produced by meta-analysis is shown at the bottom of Figure 11.4 along with its CI. This summary odds ratio is 1.79, a small but nonetheless statistically significant effect, $p < .05$. (Technically, I assumed that each study estimates a common population effect size—a fixed effects model—and used the Mantel-Haenszel summary estimate—a method appropriate for combining several small studies; see Shadish & Haddock, 2009.) The moral is that the whole can be greater than the sum of its parts, and—especially with small *N* studies—individual contributions may matter most when combined with other, similar studies in a subsequent research synthesis.

EMBRACE DATA VISUALIZATION

Research can be a time-consuming but glacially moving process, a trial for the impatient. Perhaps that is why, once the last participant is processed and the last bit of data entered, researchers too often rush to analysis. But this elides a key step. Before anything else, data should be looked at using graphical methods that show all data points (Wilkinson and the Task Force on Statistical Inference, 1999). A

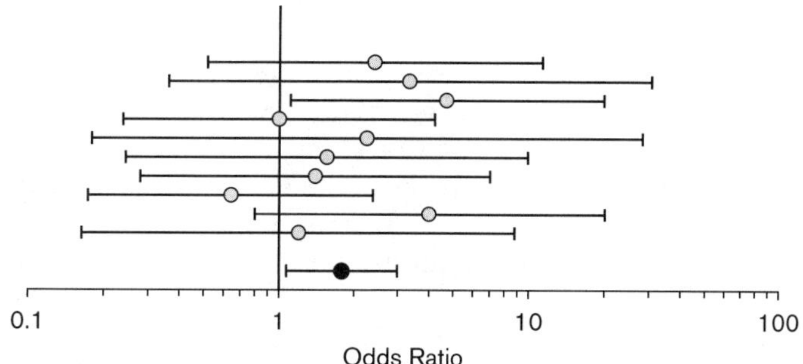

Figure 11.4. An example of a meta-analysis. When synthesized, the 10 studies represented with their odds ratios (lighter circles) and 95% confidence intervals result in the statistically significant, $p < .05$, odds ratio (darker circle) shown at the bottom.

graduate student I advised once excitedly showed me how a theoretically interesting—and predicted—two-way interaction was almost significant ($p = .063$). I asked her to prepare a figure that showed individual data points illustrating how the predicted interaction had played out. In fact, the near-significant result was due to just one extreme outlier who—given the score—probably should not have been included in the sample in the first place. Visual examination of the data before analysis would have created less excitement, but less disappointment as well, and is especially important when N is small because of the greater vulnerability of small samples to extreme scores.

Data visualization is equally, if not more, important when presenting results. Wilkinson and the Task Force on Statistical Inference (1999) wrote, "Figures attract the reader's eye and help convey global results. It is time for authors to take advantage of them and for editors and reviewers to urge authors to do so" (p. 601). Many instructive examples are presented by Edward Tufte in his stimulating *The Visual Display of Quantitative Information* (1983). Most of his illustrations go well beyond what behavioral researchers are likely to employ, but he presents a few easily applied and helpful guidelines. Tufte wrote of the data–ink ratio and recommended that it be large. Use only as much ink—in a figure, in a table, in prose—as needed to clearly convey the data; more is unnecessary and unnecessarily distracting. For example, the three-dimensional bars that are produced too easily by Excel and seen in too many journal articles and PowerPoint presentations diminish the data–ink ratio, clutter the screen or page, and provide no useful information. Tufte rightly called them *chart-junk*—something to avoid.

As an example of data visualization, consider Figure 11.5, which shows three ways of displaying data (see Oller, Buder, Ramsdell, Warlaumont, & Bakeman, 2013). The figure shows two groups, labeled Alpha and Beta, each with 20 scores that are measured on an interval scale (e.g., scores on a language test). A bar graph is on the left. This is perhaps the most commonly used type of figure seen in journal articles and is one of the least informative. The height of the bar represents the (arithmetic) mean for its group. The bar is sometimes presented unadorned without error bars, which conveys even less information than the example shown here. At least error bars (the usual assumption is that they represent the standard error of the mean, unless stated otherwise) convey some information about how much scores vary, but they provide little information about how scores are distributed.

A plot showing each data point is in the center of Figure 11.5. This type of plot is most useful when initially examining data and is almost never seen in published reports. Here, the longer and shorter horizontal lines indicate each group's median and mean, respectively. This is the most informative display because each data point is shown separately; from the smallest to the largest score, we can see exactly how the scores are distributed. In particular, we can see that scores in the Alpha group tend to be smaller than those in the Beta group, the range of scores is similar in both groups only because one Alpha score is quite a bit higher than the others, and scores in both groups are positively skewed (the means are bigger than the medians).

A box-and-whisker plot (Tukey, 1977) is on the right of Figure 11.5 and is useful when initially examining data and when presenting results. It is seldom seen in journal articles, which is unfortunate; the information it presents is considerably more informative than the usual bar graph, and for this reason box-and-whisker

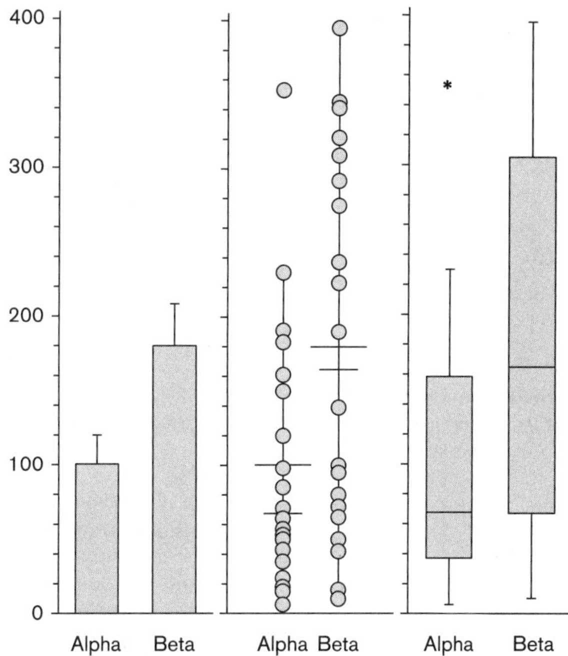

Figure 11.5. Three ways of visually portraying data for two groups, here with 20 cases in each group. Bars (at left) represent means and error bars their standard errors. Circles (in the middle) represent individual data points, and longer and shorter horizontal lines represent means and medians, respectively. See the text for details concerning the box-and-whisker plots (at right).

plots deserve to become the standard. Their construction is straightforward (although no current, commonly used computer program quite produces a publication-quality figure). The top of the box indicates the 75th percentile, the horizontal line in the middle indicates the median, and the bottom of the box indicates the 25th percentile. Thus, the box embraces 50% of the scores. The potential upper and lower limits for the whiskers are defined as the 75th percentile plus 1.5 times the interquartile range (IQR, the 75th percentile minus the 25th percentile) and the 25th percentile minus the IQR, respectively. The upper whisker indicates the highest score that falls at or below the potential upper limit, and the lower whisker indicates the lowest score that falls at or above the lower limit. Any scores outside the whiskers are regarded as extreme and are indicated with some symbol (e.g., an asterisk or a circle).

The Alpha group in Figure 11.5 has one extreme high score. The second highest score is considerably below it, as indicated by a whisker that is clearly less than 1.5 times the IQR. No other scores were extreme, so in those cases the whiskers indicate the lowest and highest scores. The box-and-whisker plot shows that both distributions are positively skewed, the Alpha somewhat more than the Beta group, and that Beta scores tend to be higher than Alpha ones, a difference that is confirmed with a Mann-Whitney U test ($p = .001$). Box-and-whisker plots occasionally have no whiskers, which simply means that more than 25% of the scores at either the top or the bottom were the same; but box-and-whisker plots always give a more nuanced view of how scores are distributed than bar graphs, which are impoverished by comparison.

CONCLUSION

Researchers with few cases need not despair or feel bludgeoned by statisticians who say no. Rely mainly on simple statistics, do not feel intimidated by statistical significance or its lack, emphasize ES above all, understand that synthesizers may see patterns that are elusive, and seek ways to visualize data. With apologies to the poet e e cummings, a pretty graph that clarifies is worth a million *t*-tests.

REFERENCES

American Psychological Association. (2010). *Publication manual of the American Psychological Association* (6th ed.). Washington, DC: Author.

Bakeman, R. (2006). The practical importance of findings. In K. McCartney, M.R. Burchinal, & K.L. Bub (Eds.), *Best practices in quantitative methods for developmentalists* (pp. 127–145). *Monographs of the Society for Research in Child Development, 71*(3, Serial No. 285).

Bakeman, R., & Quera, V. (2011). *Sequential analysis and observational methods for the behavioral sciences.* Cambridge, UK: Cambridge University Press.

Bakeman, R., & Robinson, B.F. (2005). *Understanding statistics in the behavioral sciences.* Mahwah, NJ: Lawrence Erlbaum Associates.

Cohen, J. (1988). *Statistical power analysis for the behavioral sciences* (2nd ed.). Hillsdale, NJ: Lawrence Erlbaum Associates.

Cohen, J. (1990). Things I have learned (so far). *American Psychologist, 45,* 1304–1312.

Cohen, J. (1994). The earth is round (p < .05). *American Psychologist, 49,* 997–1003.

Cohen, J., & Cohen, P. (1983). *Applied multiple regression/correlation analysis for the behavioral sciences* (2nd ed.). Hillsdale, NJ: Lawrence Erlbaum Associates.

Cooper, H., Hedges, L.V., & Valentine, J.C. (Eds.). (2009). *The handbook of research synthesis and meta-analysis* (2nd ed.). New York, NY: Russell Sage Foundation.

Grissom, R.J., & Kim, J.J. (2005). *Effect sizes for research: A broad practical approach.* Mahwah, NJ: Lawrence Erlbaum Associates.

Haddock, C., Rindskopf, D., & Shadish, W. (1998). Using odds ratios as effect sizes for meta-analysis of dichotomous data: A primer on methods and issues. *Psychological Methods, 3,* 339–353.

McCartney, K., & Rosenthal, R. (2000). Effect size, practical importance, and social policy for children. *Child Development, 71,* 173–180.

Oller, D.K., Buder, E.H., Ramsdell, H.L., Warlaumont, A.S., & Bakeman, R. (2013). Functional flexibility of infant vocalization and the emergence of language. *Proceedings of the National Academy of Sciences, 110,* 6318–6323.

Romski, M.A., Sevcik, R., Adamson, L.B., Cheslock, M., Smith, A., Barker, R.M., & Bakeman, R. (2010). Randomized comparison of augmented and non-augmented language interventions for toddlers with developmental delays and their parents. *Journal of Speech, Language, and Hearing Research, 53,* 350–364.

Rosnow, R.L., & Rosenthal, R. (1989). Statistical procedures and the justification of knowledge in the psychological sciences. *American Psychologist, 44,* 1276–1284.

Salsburg, D. S. (1985). The religion of statistics as practiced in medical journals. *The American Statistican, 39,* 220–223

Shadish, W.R., & Haddock, C.K. (2009). Combining estimates of effect size. In H. Cooper, L.V. Hedges, & J.C. Valentine (Eds.), *The handbook of research synthesis and meta-analysis* (2nd ed., pp. 257–278). New York, NY: Russell Sage Foundation.

Tufte, E.R. (1983). *The visual display of quantitative information.* Cheshire, CT: Graphics Press.

Tukey, J.W. (1977). *Exploratory data analysis.* Reading, MA: Addison-Wesley.

Wilkinson, L., and the Task Force on Statistical Inference. (1999). Statistical methods in psychology journals: Guidelines and explanations. *American Psychologist, 54,* 594–604.

Challenges for Communication Intervention Research

Measuring Outcomes

12

Recent Innovations in the Assessment of Auditory Discrimination Abilities in Individuals with Intellectual Disabilities Who Are Nonspeaking

Richard W. Serna

This chapter describes efforts to develop auditory discrimination assessment methods for use with individuals whose language capabilities make it difficult to assess their skills using conventional means. The methods described here represent one experimental approach to assessment development from a behavior analytic perspective. Although much remains to be done, the ultimate goal of these efforts is to set the stage for universal, widely available, and relatively easy-to-administer auditory discrimination assessment methods for individuals who are not speaking.

To put the experimental approach to assessment development into a broader perspective, it is important to recognize the research path that some evidence-based methods take to become relatively accessible to clinicians. For example, methods based on applied behavior analysis (ABA) have been an integral part of treatment for establishing fundamental communication, preacademic, self-help, and other skills for severe intellectual disabilities (ID). Moreover, such methods are evidence based, and are the most widely used treatment option for those with autism spectrum disorder (ASD; Eikeseth, 2009; Odom, Boyd, Hall, & Hume, 2010). The full development of many evidence-based ABA treatment methods may have progressed through three distinct research traditions within the field of behavior analysis—basic, translational, and applied research. Basic research within the field examines the fundamental principles and processes of learning; applied research involves the application of basic principles to individual, community, and world problems that have social significance (Baer, Wolf, & Risley, 1968). McIlvane et al. (2011)

Preparation of this chapter was supported, in part, by grants from the Eunice Kennedy Shriver National Institutes of Health, P01HD25995 and P30HD004147, to the University of Massachusetts Medical School.

distinguished translational research from basic and applied: One utilizes principles from basic research in translational research to investigate engineered procedures that may benefit application in the longer term. Whereas applied research is conducted in treatment settings with individuals that may directly benefit from the methods under investigation, translational research often is conducted under more tightly controlled laboratory conditions. The experimental approach described in this chapter is translational can play an important role in the development of applied treatment and assessment methods, as illustrated next.

To illustrate translational research, consider the issue of same-different judgments by individuals with severe ID. The ability to judge and report whether pairs of objects, letters, numbers, or other visual stimuli are the same or different from one another is critical to learning more complex skills involving those stimuli. Same-different judgments historically have been difficult to teach to individuals with severe ID (Greenfield, 1985; House, Brown, & Scott, 1974). Thus, clinicians and researchers were faced with a problem. In the early 1990s, researchers at the Eunice Kennedy Shriver Center undertook efforts to solve this issue through several translational research studies (see Serna, Dube, & McIlvane, 1997). The research ultimately showed that virtually any individual with the necessary motor and visual prerequisites could make same-different judgments with the methods developed via translational research. Furthermore, applied research that adopted these methods to teach generalized same-different judgments also showed their effectiveness (Mahon et al., 2004). Notably, it was the translational research effort that set the stage for application of same-different judgment teaching methods.

Similarly, the translational research efforts described in this chapter arose from another problem faced by those concerned with individuals with severe ID: Auditory assessment methods often require verbal instructions to orient the participant to the task requirements, or they require a spoken response from the participant (e.g., Bonnel et al., 2003; Jones et al., 2009). For example, Jones et al. assessed auditory discrimination of frequency (pitch), intensity (loudness), and duration dimensions of pure tones. One of the groups of participants was described as an ASD population,with a mean full-scale IQ of 87.79. Pairs of auditory stimuli were presented as coming from separate cartoon dinosaurs, one standing on a yellow box (the left side of the computer screen) and the other on a red box (right). Participants were to indicate their selections by either pointing to one or the other dinosaur or by calling out the color name of the box on which one or the other dinosaur stood. A selection-based procedure such as this one has value in that it does not require the participant to understand the concepts of first and second or left and right in the absence of something visual. Verbal preparation using other concepts was required, however, in the Jones et al. study. Participants were instructed to make their selections based on which sound was "higher" or "longer" or "louder." These instructions and the conceptual understanding needed to carry them out were sufficient for individuals functioning at a relatively high intellectual level. The Jones et al. task would be virtually impossible to complete for individuals with severe ID who lack fundamental listening or speaking skills or who cannot readily grasp the higher/longer/louder concepts. Such procedures and requirements necessarily preclude the use of such tasks with a significant proportion of those with severe ID (Serna, Preston, & Thompson, 2009).

This chapter's purpose is to describe translational research efforts to develop auditory discrimination assessment methods for use with individuals with severe ID. This chapter first explicates the need and rationale for such assessments in the ID population, including the perspective of the historical literature on language deficits in children with ID. This chapter then conceptualizes the requirements of accurate auditory discrimination from a behavior analytic perspective, as a starting point for better understanding why some individuals show difficulty with auditory discrimination. Finally, the chapter presents a detailed description of new methodology developed to date to assess auditory discrimination capabilities in individuals with ID who are not speaking. The chapter concludes with a view of future possibilities for further development and use of related methodology.

AUDITORY DISCRIMINATION AND INTERVENTION

Auditory discrimination necessarily plays an important role in receptive language/ listening skills. Whether listening to single words or a full sentence, Individuals who are capable of hearing must be able to differentiate or discriminate the different elements of speech that are being presented to them. Accurate auditory discrimination skills allow the listener to then act on or vocally respond to the sounds. The ubiquity of auditory discrimination in instructional tasks in special education teaching is obvious; auditory stimuli appear as part of virtually all instruction, from task instructions to verbal labels for words, letters, and other symbols.

It is well known from the field of speech perception that even seemingly simple words involve potentially complex auditory features that must be discriminated from one another. Consider the spoken word "bat." At the phonetic level, "bat" can be discriminated from "pat" on the basis of the voiced versus voiceless plosives at the beginning of the words. These words have other dimensions that are important for auditory discrimination, however, such as the pitch, the rise and fall, and the amplitude, or loudness, of the sounds. All these dimensions of speech sounds combine to distinguish words from one another. Moreover, the prosody of speech can be altered within the same word based on these dimensions: "bat?" versus "bat!" is a discrimination that must be made for a listener to extract the proper meaning.

Children who are typically developing tend to acquire auditory discrimination of speech sounds relatively easily and quickly. Auditory learning is reported to be difficult, however, in some children with ID (Abbeduto, Furman, & Davies, 1989; Chapman, Schwartz, & Kay-Raining Bird, 1991; Miller, 1987). The lack of effective auditory discrimination skills may unfortunately limit the success of communication interventions. This may be particularly evident in individuals whose ID is more severe; such individuals may lack sufficient entry skills to fully benefit from intervention programs based on augmentative and alternative communication (AAC) training and treatments.

Historically, there have been intermittent attempts to develop effective auditory discrimination teaching procedures to address the issue (e.g., Green, 1990; McIlvane & Stoddard, 1981, 1985; Serna, Stoddard, & McIlvane, 1992; Stoddard, 1982; Stoddard & McIlvane, 1989). Although often successful, these procedures are not universally so. This may be accounted for, in part, by converging evidence from speech-language perception and psychophysiological research suggesting that individuals with ID, particularly those with ASD, may be prone to deficits in verbal performance (compared with visual), speech perception (compared with nonspeech sound), and auditory sensory processing, respectively (Bomba & Pang, 2004; Joseph, Tager-Flusberg & Lord, 2002; Kuhl, Coffey-Corina, Padden, & Dawson, 2005). This research suggests that improving the ability to effectively ameliorate deficits in auditory discrimination requires a better characterization of the auditory discrimination problems among individuals with ID. Thus, from an intervention perspective, it is argued here that it is critical to first assess the extant fundamental auditory discrimination abilities of the individual for whom an intervention is designed.

LANGUAGE DEFICITS IN CHILDREN WITH INTELLECTUAL DISABILITIES

It has been known for some time that children with ID experience language deficits among the impairments of various domains of cognitive functioning (Schiefelbusch & Lloyd, 1974). The type and degree of the deficit has been shown to vary widely, however, given the heterogeneity of the population (Cromer, 1981; Miller & Chapman, 1984). A number of studies have documented the existence of a language comprehension and nonverbal cognitive performance discrepancy in children with ID. For example, Miller, Chapman, and Bedrosian (1978) reported that 25% of their sample showed deficits in comprehension over and above nonverbal cognitive delays. Abbeduto et al. (1989) reported this same discrepancy in 55% and 60%, respectively. Similar findings and characterizations have been reported by Bartel, Bryen, and Keehn (1973), Dewart (1979), Hartley (1982, 1986), Miller (1987), and Chapman et al. (1991).

Difficulties assessing verbal performance have been found in some studies in which the intellectual functioning of the participants varied. For example, the participants in the Dewart (1979) study had mental ages ranging from 1.83 to 7.08. The task studied (acting out simple active- and passive-voice sentences), however, yielded interpretable results only with the participants whose mental ages were at the high end of the range. Difficulties in assessing nonverbal performance using standardized measures with this population have also been reported by Chapman et al. (1991). Barker-Collo, Jamieson, and Boo (1995) and Vause, Martin, and Yu (2000), however, have shown that auditory discrimination performance correlates highly with communication ability in individuals with moderate to profound ID.

ASD is notoriously associated with language and communication deficits. For example, approximately 25% of individuals with ASD never develop functional language (Klinger, Dawson, & Renner, 2002). Language and communication deficits vary widely within this population, however (Kjelgaard & Tager-Flusberg, 2001; Lord & Paul, 1997; Munson et al., 2008). Nevertheless, on the whole, evidence suggests that individuals with ASD generally show poorer verbal than nonverbal performance skills (Rapin, 1991; Rutter, 1984). Lincoln, Courchesne, Allen, Hanson and Ene (1998) published a 23-paper meta-analytic review of the cognitive profiles of individuals with ASD and reported that performance IQ generally exceeded verbal IQ scores. Joseph et al. (2002) found that the verbal–nonverbal discrepancy was most pronounced in younger children, suggesting some amelioration of the language deficit with age. It should be noted, however, that these studies tended to focus on relatively high-functioning participants, likely because of their ability to perform on standardized tests. Very little is known, however, about how widespread verbal–nonverbal performance discrepancies might be in individuals for whom interpretable IQ scores cannot be obtained.

HISTORICAL BEHAVIORAL EVIDENCE OF AUDITORY DISCRIMINATION DEFICITS IN INDIVIDUALS WITH INTELLECTUAL DISABILITIES

There exists an historical literature demonstrating the difficulty of individuals with ID acquiring even basic auditory discrimination skills. Many such studies have been conducted with individuals with severe and profound ID, and significant numbers of participants never achieved any level of successful auditory discrimination, despite reasonable efforts. These findings mirror those from clinical observations—some will learn, and some will not.

Clinical Studies of Auditory Discrimination

Evidence of difficulty in acquiring auditory discriminations is often found in clinical reports. Although negative results are rarely published, evidence of difficulty with auditory discrimination can be found in studies that produce positive outcomes in other ways. Studies of simultaneous (total) communication (SC) training and stimulus overselectivity are two examples.

Simultaneous Communication SC training involves the use of both spoken words and signs in teaching language skills to children with ID and ASD (cf. Carr, 1979; Clarke, Remington, & Light, 1988; Yoder & Layton, 1988). The goals are to 1) teach comprehension and production of signs as an alternative to spoken language and 2) foster such acquisition with respect to spoken words. The prevalent outcome is that virtually all children learn the desired performances involving the signs, but many show no control by spoken words. In his early review of SC work, Carr (1979) noted that less than one fourth of children with ASD who are mute and who received SC training acquired some vocal speech; moreover, speech that was acquired was extremely limited.

Studies by Carr and his colleagues have related these negative outcomes to a limited or nonexistent vocal imitation repertoire ("verbal imitation hypothesis"; Carr, Binkoff, Kologinsky, & Eddy, 1978; Carr & Dores, 1981; Carr, Pridal, & Dores, 1984). This relationship received support in a study by Yoder and Layton (1988) conducted with 60 children with ASD. Yoder and Layton interpreted their results as showing "general visual overselectivity: That is, autistic low verbal imitators selectively failed to process speech in favor of sign and nonsign visual stimuli" (p. 227). Verbal imitation proved to be the critical variable when IQ and initial expressive language levels were controlled. Carr and Dores (1981) made a similar observation with respect to mental age.

Stimulus Overselectivity Studies on stimulus overselectivity supply examples of the ineffectiveness of pairing visual and auditory stimuli to achieve auditory stimulus control. *Stimulus overselectivity* refers to a tendency by some individuals to focus on one stimulus dimension to the exclusion of others. Stimulus control is achieved when there is clear evidence that the participant will respond appropriately in the presence of one or more stimuli under investigation. Participants in such studies are trained to discriminate the presence versus absence of a stimulus complex, which might include both visual and auditory stimuli. When control by each component of the complex is tested, lack of control by one or more of the components (i.e., stimulus overselectivity) is typical. When an auditory stimulus is one component, a number of participants fail to display control by that component (Lovaas & Schreibman, 1971; Lovaas, Schreibman, Koegel, & Rehm, 1971; Rincover & Koegel, 1975). Overselectivity has also been seen when all components of the complex are auditory (Reynolds, Newsom, & Lovaas, 1974; Schreibman, 1975; Schreibman, Kohlenberg, & Britten, 1986). The study by Schreibman and colleagues (1986) is particularly relevant because the stimulus complexes did not include arbitrary sounds such as tones or buzzers but were two-syllable nonsense words that differed both in phonetic content and intonation. The results, along with those of Rincover and Koegel who sought to establish control by spoken instructions, highlight common problems in establishing control by multisyllabic words and word sequences. A final example comes from work conducted by Stoddard and McIlvane (1989). Pairing of auditory and visual stimuli in a study with several participants with profound ID did not suffice to establish control by the auditory component, even though it was a spoken reinforcer name. Pairing did suffice with most high-functioning participants (Stoddard, 1982).

Behavior Analytic Studies of Auditory Discrimination Learning

Additional historical evidence suggesting the difficulty of establishing auditory discriminations in individuals with ID comes from the behavior-analytic, stimulus-control literature. These studies are grouped according to the type of auditory discrimination task. The tasks range from seemingly simple ones (e.g., detecting the whether an auditory stimulus is either present or absent) to quality discriminations (e.g., discriminating two auditory stimuli that differ from one another) to relatively complex tasks, such as conditional auditory-visual matching (e.g., spoken word-symbol relations).

Presence versus Absence Discriminations Attempts to teach individuals with severe ID and other difficult-to-test participants to discriminate the presence versus absence of pure tones was the focus of many early studies. The focus of this work was on audiometric assessment (e.g., Fulton, Gorzycki, & Hull, 1975; Spradlin, Lloyd, Hom, & Reid, 1968). The effectiveness of standard conditioning procedures (e.g., prompting, differential reinforcement) varied widely across studies, apparently due to participant variables. Of the 41 children with severe ID studied, 26 learned a presence versus absence discrimination after 7–50 training sessions (a success rate of only 64%). Success has also been reported with other stimuli, such as white noise (Koegel & Schreibman, 1976; Lovaas et al., 1971; Lovaas & Schreibman, 1971) and a buzzer (Schreibman, 1975), when these stimuli were presented alone in training. Reports of these studies unfortunately do not supply details of acquisition. Some attempts have been made to errorlessly teach presence versus absence control by pairing auditory and visual stimuli and gradually removing the visual component. One study directed at audiometric assessment (Woolcock & Alferink, 1982) taught control by a panel light, paired the light with a pure tone, and removed the light by intensity fading. This study is flawed, however, by lack of detail on participant characteristics, by the omission of acquisition data, and by puzzling features of the procedures and audiometric data that make the actual stimulus control of performances difficult to interpret.

Discriminations of Different Auditory Stimuli (a Quality Discrimination) Few studies have addressed the issue of training quality discriminations between different auditory stimuli. The studies by Schreibman (1975) and Schreibman and colleagues (1986) illustrate the use of a Go/No-Go method (described next) to obtain such discriminations. The training procedures were straightforward, involving prompting and differential reinforcement. Difficulties were noted with a number of children, particularly in the 1975 study when the procedures involved pairing a training stimulus with an already effective stimulus (termed *extrastimulus prompting*). Success was achieved only by use of within-stimulus prompts that served to emphasize critical stimulus differences.

Conditional Auditory Stimulus Control Discrimination between stimuli can also be studied through conditional discrimination methods. A conditional discrimination task is one in which the response to a particular stimulus is conditional on the presence of another stimulus. Perhaps the simplest level of conditional control is seen in two-choice discriminations of words that control responses to different objects, such as food names (Stoddard, 1982) or positions (e.g., right versus left; Rincover & Koegel, 1975). As yet, however, there is virtually no truly solid information on how to teach the first instances of conditional auditory control to individuals with severe ID. It may be that such problems stem from more fundamental auditory discrimination difficulties.

When conditional auditory stimulus control is established (by whatever means), the next goal is to extend and refine the control. Some success in refining fairly gross auditory conditional discriminations was reported by Meyerson and Kerr (1977). Four participants with severe and profound ID (no other participant information was provided) were initially taught to discriminate auditory stimuli via a visual fading procedure. That is, a visual stimulus that already controlled performance was used as a prompt. Many participants unfortunately could not perform the subsequent criterion auditory conditional discrimination.

AUDITORY DISCRIMINATION STIMULUS-CONTROL REQUIREMENTS

Breaking down auditory discrimination requirements in stimulus control terms provides a useful pathway for assessing auditory discrimination skills. Moreover, knowledge of the behavioral manifestation of certain cortical auditory processing problems, particularly at the individual level, may prove quite valuable to the development of behavioral intervention procedures for addressing auditory discrimination difficulties. Thus, efforts to assess extant auditory discrimination skills represent initial steps toward better understanding of why auditory matching-to-sample (MTS) performance goes awry. This, in turn, would likely directly contribute to the training goals of various clinical applications, particularly those routinely used in the education of children with ID (e.g., communication, preacademic skills, instruction following).

Teaching Tasks

It is important to delineate the requirements for auditory discriminations to begin to answer why its success is not higher in some individuals with ID. Typical teaching tasks used in a variety of interventions for rudimentary communication training help illustrate those requirements.

ABA-based teaching methods often make use of discrete trial training (DTT) procedures (Smith, 2001). These procedures present a series of displays, each of which occasions a response of some type and, as appropriate, feedback. One example is the flashcard procedure, which is used to teach number facts, sight word vocabulary, and so forth. Another DTT procedure involves certain psychophysical procedures presenting a series of comparison stimuli; the participant indicates whether the comparison stimuli are the same as or different from a standard stimulus. The MTS and related tasks are often used in both experimental research and in applied settings in the context of DTT to teach fundamental visual or auditory discriminations. For example, MTS is often used to teach symbol–referent relations (Wilkinson, Rosenquist, & McIlvane, 2009). The learner in a typical MTS procedure is required to look at a visual sample stimulus (e.g., the printed word *cat*) or listen to an auditory sample stimulus (e.g., the spoken word "cat") and then select an appropriate comparison stimulus. The correct comparison stimulus may 1) be physically identical to the sample (identity matching), 2) be the only different stimulus in the display (nonmatching or oddity), or 3) bear some other relation with the sample, such as a spoken word and its corresponding printed word (arbitrary matching). The learner's response and the teacher's feedback constitutes a discrete trial in each sequence of the presentation of a sample and an array of comparisons; sessions consist of multiple trials. Evidence exists that when a learner reliably selects a given comparison in the presence of a given sample, then the learner's responses are under the stimulus control of the samples and comparisons. Put another way, a symbol–referent relation has been learned.

The MTS procedure, particularly if conducted in a simple trial-and-error fashion, has not been universally effective in establishing relations between different stimuli with individuals with ID. In response, much translational behavioral research has been conducted in an effort to better understand why MTS does not result in better performance. This has been done by more closely examining the stimulus-control requirements of a teaching task and then engineering various solutions (e.g., Dube, Iennaco, & McIlvane, 1993; Dube & Serna, 1998; Saunders & Spradlin, 1989, 1990). Most of this research has been conducted with visual stimuli, and it has proven very successful, especially in the case of identity matching (Serna et al., 1997). Much less engineering/translational research has been conducted with tasks that involve auditory stimuli (cf. Serna et al., 1992). This may be due in part to the fact that successive discrimination is inherently more difficult than simultaneous discrimination (Carter & Eckerman, 1975), as described next. Whatever the reason, discrimination-training research historically has favored visual rather than auditory stimuli in terms of concerted, long-term research efforts.

Conceptualizing the Auditory Discrimination Process

It is useful to expand the view beyond behavioral variables and include biological variables in order to conceptualize the auditory discrimination process. For example, consider the auditory discrimination aspects of the MTS task previously described for teaching a relation between the spoken word "cat" and the printed word *cat* and between "dog" and *dog*. As previously described, ample evidence suggests that many individuals with severe ID have difficulties with tasks that involve auditory stimuli, which sometimes stands in stark contrast to their ability to discriminate visual stimuli. Why might such difficulties occur?

The obvious first question asked in the context of typical clinical screening is whether there is hearing loss that interferes with the discrimination needed between the spoken words "cat" and "dog." If so, then can it be corrected with amplification via hearing aid? Also, might the problem stem from abnormalities in auditory brain stem responses? If these problems are insurmountable, so too will be problems in auditory learning.

A less obvious question is whether auditory discrimination learning problems can be directly attributed to problems in cortical auditory processing. Indeed, evidence is mounting that many children with ASD, for example, show abnormalities at the cortical level of auditory processing (e.g., Bruneau, Bonnet-Brilhault, Gomot, Adrien, & Barthélémy, 2003; Gervais et al., 2004). These abnormalities may contribute to poor behavioral discrimination in auditory tasks. Moreover, abnormalities may be either enhancements or deficits, depending on certain individual sound features of an auditory stimulus, such as pitch, duration, or phonetic processing (Bonnel et al., 2010; Lepisto et al., 2005). Finally, implicit in questions about auditory processing abilities is whether the structural characteristics of the stimuli are important (e.g., speech versus nonspeech sounds), as some research with children with typical development suggests (Kuhl et al., 2005).

At least three types of auditory stimulus control must be present at the behavioral level. First, stimulus control must exist between different auditory stimuli, such as spoken words. That is, an individual must be able to distinguish one auditory stimulus from another. Second, stimulus control must exist between the different sound features within an auditory stimulus, such as a spoken word. For example, words are comprised of many different features, such as pitch, duration, and rise and fall. Third, stimulus control must exist when the presentation of stimuli is separated in time. Unlike many visual discrimination tasks in which two or more visual stimuli might be simultaneously available for visual inspection and comparison, auditory stimuli are necessarily presented successively. Although a child may be able to discriminate between two auditory stimuli presented in relatively rapid succession, auditory discrimination in the context of a typical learning task such as MTS requires that the child be able to make this discrimination when the auditory stimuli are separated in time, as might occur across discrete trials. For example, in a typical teaching context one does not simultaneously present "cat" and "dog" to a learner, as one does simultaneously present the printed words *cat* and *dog*. Instead, "cat" and "dog" are presented separately across trials, and they may be separated by several seconds or even minutes.

A NEW APPROACH TO EVALUATING BEHAVIORAL AUDITORY DISCRIMINATION

Previous attempts to establish auditory stimulus control in some individuals with ID have not always been successful. The research described next illustrates how a new approach, one that manipulates the auditory stimuli more directly, set the stage for the current assessment methods described in this chapter.

Presence/Absence Discriminations

Serna et al. (1992) was the seminal paper on this new approach to auditory discrimination. Participants TML, a 20-year-old woman (Peabody Picture Vocabulary

Test—Revised [PPVT-R] age equivalent score: 2.2 years), and LAM, a 64-year-old woman (PPVT-R age equivalent score: 4.4 years), both with severe ID, were exposed to procedures designed to teach the presence versus absence of a spoken word. Participants were seated before a computer screen illuminated only with a light gray rectangle. The digitally recorded positive stimulus (the S+), "Touch," was repeated by the computer at 1-second intervals for 5 seconds during each trial. A touch to the screen during that period was followed by reinforcement. TML responded to the presence of the auditory S+ on most trials; responses in the absence of the auditory S+ gradually declined, occurring in fewer than 10% of the intervals. LAM responded with perfect accuracy to the S+ and refrained from making any responses in its absence after only a single session. Additional research conducted at the University of Massachusetts Medical School's Shriver Center lab showed that 11 individuals (individuals with severe ID and typically developing preschoolers) all acquired a presence/absence auditory discrimination.

Quality Discriminations of Different Auditory Stimuli

An additional research question was whether TML and LAM would discriminate "Touch" from an S- word, "Wait." TML and LAM were presented with 10 trials of "Wait," interspersed among 40 S+ (i.e., "Touch") trials. These contingencies constituted a Go/No-Go task (e.g., D'Amato & Colombo, 1985). If the participants touched in the presence of "Wait," then the auditory S- continued to repeat for the full 5 seconds and no reinforcers were delivered. The results for LAM showed perfect performance during her first session and near perfect performance during subsequent maintenance sessions. TML, however, responded to 40% of the S- presentations and to only 52% of the S+ presentations, thus demonstrating a lack of stimulus control between the two words. TML was then taught to discriminate "Touch" versus "Wait" using a partial-word duration fading procedure. "Wait" was gradually introduced in 10 fading steps. Fading was performed in the following manner: only the middle 10% of the acoustical wave form that corresponded to "Wait" was presented in Step 1; increasing percentages were presented in succeeding steps. Errors in the presence of either "ouch" (a failure to touch) or "Wait" (touching) resulted in a backup to the previous fading level. This procedure was effective.

Type of Task Matters

Although the procedures described in Serna et al. (1992) were successful, subsequent tests of the Go/No-Go task yielded less successful results with several additional participants with ID. Briefly, the primary pattern of responding for these additional participants was a tendency to respond regardless of whether the S+ or S- was present. Subsequent training and testing capitalized on this propensity to respond through a change in the task: Instead of requiring participants to refrain from responding to one of the two auditory stimuli presented, a Go-Left/Go-Right (GL/GR) procedure was instituted. As the name implies, participants were required to touch a white circle positioned on the left side of the computer screen given auditory stimulus 1 and touch the white circle positioned on the right side of the computer screen given auditory stimulus 2. Both white circles were identical and remained on the screen at all times, except during reinforcement. This procedure has a successful history with nonhuman participants (e.g., D'Amato & Worsham, 1974). This procedure improved the ability of participants to differentiate two auditory stimuli (Serna, Jeffery, & Stoddard, 1996) and served as the basis for the work described in this chapter.

CURRENT METHODS FOR ASSESSING AUDITORY DISCRIMINATION IN INDIVIDUALS WHO ARE NONSPEAKING

Several studies have been conducted in which auditory discrimination in clinical populations has been assessed (e.g., Bonnel et al., 2003; Jones et al., 2009). The tasks used in these studies, however, may not be possible with individuals who are either nonspeaking or who may not meet the language requirements of the assessment tasks. A task was developed for these individuals that requires no spoken language instructions and is based on the GL/GR procedure previously described. Such assessment requires three stages: 1) baseline acquisition, 2) threshold training and 3) threshold testing. Each will be described next.

Baseline Acquisition

Figure 12.1 illustrates the same-different, GL/GR task as applied to a baseline pitch discrimination task. For example, a participant might be asked (nonverbally) whether two successively presented tones are the same or different. That is,

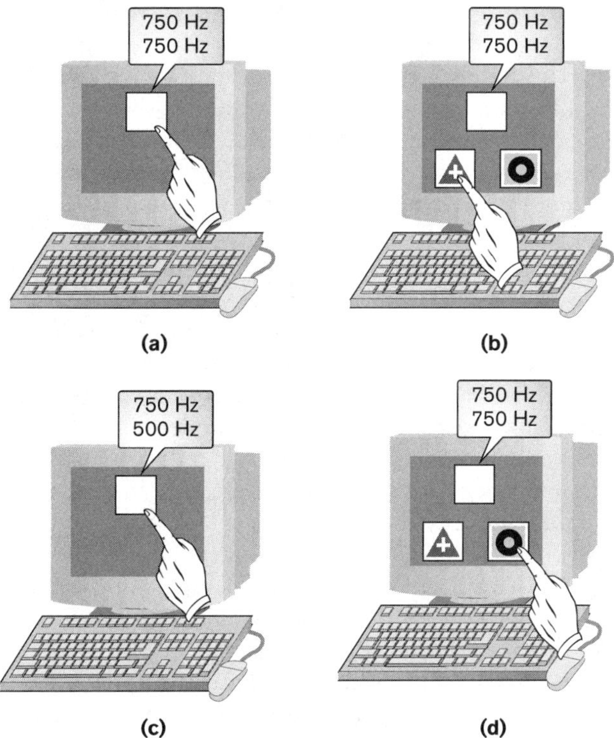

Figure 12.1. Illustration of the basic same-different, Go-Left/Go-Right task. Panels a and b illustrate a "same" trial; panels c and d illustrate a "different" trial. Note that the disparity between the different tones was 250 Hz.

participants are required to make a same-different judgment about two successively presented auditory stimuli. Participants are seated before a computer equipped with a touch-sensitive screen. Each trial begins with the simultaneous presentation of a white square in the upper center portion of the screen and two sine-wave tones, each 150 milliseconds (ms.) in duration and each separated by 500 ms. The set of two auditory stimuli are repeated every 1,200 ms. throughout the trial. The upper portion of Figure 12.1 (Panels a and b) illustrate a "same" trial in which the two auditory stimuli are identical. A response to the white square (either by clicking an appropriately positioned mouse cursor or touching the stimulus, if a touch-sensitive screen in use) produces two form stimuli in the bottom corners of the screen. If the two auditory stimuli are the same, then a response to the left form results in a reinforcer. If the two auditory stimuli are different, then a touch to the right form results in a reinforcer (lower portion of Figure 12.1, Panels c and d). Only minimal prompting has been required for some participants to establish reliable performance on the baseline task. For example, for the first several trials, only the correct choice appeared in the lower portion of the screen, a prompt that is easily removed. More elaborate prompting measures have been required, such as superimposition and fading and stereo-field prompting, for other participants.

Superimposition and Fading Superimposing the difficult stimuli onto the easy stimuli and then physically fading out the easy stimuli is a common prompting method in the visual stimulus domain for transferring control from an easy set of stimuli to a more difficult set of stimuli (Etzel & LeBlanc, 1979; Serna, 2004; Serna & Carlin, 2001; Terrace, 1963). An example from visual discrimination superimposition and fading will help illustrate the procedure: Suppose a child with ID has difficulty discriminating between two black-and-white line drawings. Further suppose that child had no difficulty discriminating between two squares of different colors. To prompt the discrimination between the line drawings, one could superimpose the color stimuli onto them so that each stimulus consisted of a square of color and a different line drawing. The color stimuli would be gradually faded out over a number of trials once reliable performance has been established. This fundamental prompting procedure has been adapted for use with auditory stimuli to promote accurate baseline performance on the same-different, GL/GR procedure.

Serna et al. (2009) found that some participants who cannot readily acquire baseline pitch discrimination with sine-wave tone stimuli nevertheless can do so if the stimuli are digitally recorded spoken words, such as "dog" and "cat." For example, one participant consistently selected the left comparison stimulus when the auditory sample was either "dog"–"dog" or "cat"–"cat" and selected the right comparison stimulus when the auditory sample was "dog"–"cat" or "cat"–"dog." Another participant could perform the baseline task with the words *house* and *tree*. Neither could perform the baseline task, however, when the stimuli were sine-wave tones. Table 12.1 illustrates the basic modified superimposition and fading procedure used to transfer control from spoken words to the tones. First, accurate performance on the same-different, GL/GR task with only the spoken words is verified. Next, the tones are superimposed onto the spoken words by gradually increasing the intensity (dB level) of the tones in eight steps. The tones were constructed such that they were the same duration as their spoken-word counterparts. Four trial blocks (two same trials and two different trials, randomly distributed)

Table 12.1. Superimposition and fading procedure

Stage	Stimulus intensity percent of approximately 65 dB	Same stimuli	Different stimuli
Words only	100%	"dog"–"dog"	"dog"–"cat"
Fade-in tones (eight steps)	100% 0–100%	"dog"–"dog" 3,500 Hz–3,500 Hz	"dog"–"cat" 3,500 Hz – 2,500 Hz
Words and tones (superimposed)	100% 100%	"dog"–"dog" 3,500 Hz–3,500 Hz	"dog"–"cat" 3,500 Hz–2,500 Hz
Fade-out words	100–0% 100%	"dog"–"dog" 3,500 Hz–3,500 Hz	"dog"–"cat" 3,500 Hz–2,500 Hz
Tones only	100%	3,500 Hz–3,500 Hz	3,500 Hz–2,500 Hz
Tones only (standardized duration)	100%	3,500 Hz–3,500 Hz	3,500 Hz–2,500 Hz

were available at each fading step to accomplish fading in of the tones. A titration protocol dictated progression through the fading steps. Accurate performance on blocks of trials at one step advanced the participant to the next step; errors resulted in a backup to the previous step. After verifying accurate performance when both the tones and words are simultaneously presented at their full intensity, the spoken words were gradually faded out in the same fashion that the tones were faded in. A tones-only stage verified that the participant could accurately respond in the absence of spoken-word prompts. Finally, the duration was standardized across the tones to ensure that accurate baseline performance was under the control of the tone pitch and not the tone duration. Serna et al. (2009) showed that this procedure was effective for two participants with ID.

Stereo-field Prompting Using the stereo field of the auditory stimuli to guide responses to either the left or right keys is another prompting method that has proven successful. The procedure has its roots in auditory discrimination research with nonhumans. Several studies have demonstrated that the acquisition of auditory discrimination can be enhanced by locating the response manipulandum close to the source of the sound (D'Amato & Colombo, 1985; Harrison, 1992; Neill & Harrison, 1987; Wright, Shyan, & Jitsumori, 1990). Soraci, Stoddard, Serna, McIlvane, and Carlin (1994) exploited these findings to develop an auditory spatial-location prompt. Three young children with ID first were given a two-choice auditory-visual MTS task in which selection of a correct visual comparison depended on which of two auditory samples was presented. Each dictated sample initially sounded with equal loudness from speakers adjacent to each visual comparison. A trial-and-error method proved ineffective in teaching correct responding. A prompting procedure was introduced such that the sound of each auditory sample was localized on its corresponding speaker adjacent to the correct visual comparison. It was found that the responses of all three children were controlled by the localization prompt. This is an important finding; sound location was shown to be an effective starting point for gaining initial auditory stimulus control without the use of visual prompts. A third condition of the Soraci et al. study suggested the effectiveness of subsequent fading out of the prompts: The prompts were removed by slightly decreasing and slightly increasing the volume from the speakers adjacent to the correct and incorrect comparisons, respectively.

Figure 12.2 illustrates how Soraci et al.'s (1994) procedure was modified for use in the same-different, GL/GR task. If the correct choice is the left visual comparison on the screen (e.g., a trial in which the two auditory stimuli are the same), then the tone pairs are localized to the left speaker of the headphones (see upper Panel a). If the correct choice is the right visual comparison on the screen, then the tone pairs are localized to the right speaker of the headphones (see Panel b). Once participants demonstrate reliable same-different performance with the stimulus pairs appropriate localized in the stereo field, this prompt is gradually removed by altering the stereo field over trials until the stimulus pairs are presented in the center of the stereo field (see Panels c and d). Like the superimposition-and-fading method, progression through the steps occurs in a titration fashion. Stereo-field prompting and fading has been used successfully with several participants to establish the same-different, GL/GR baseline.

Threshold Training

More refined auditory discrimination assessments can be made from the baseline performance of the type previously described. For example, not unlike traditional

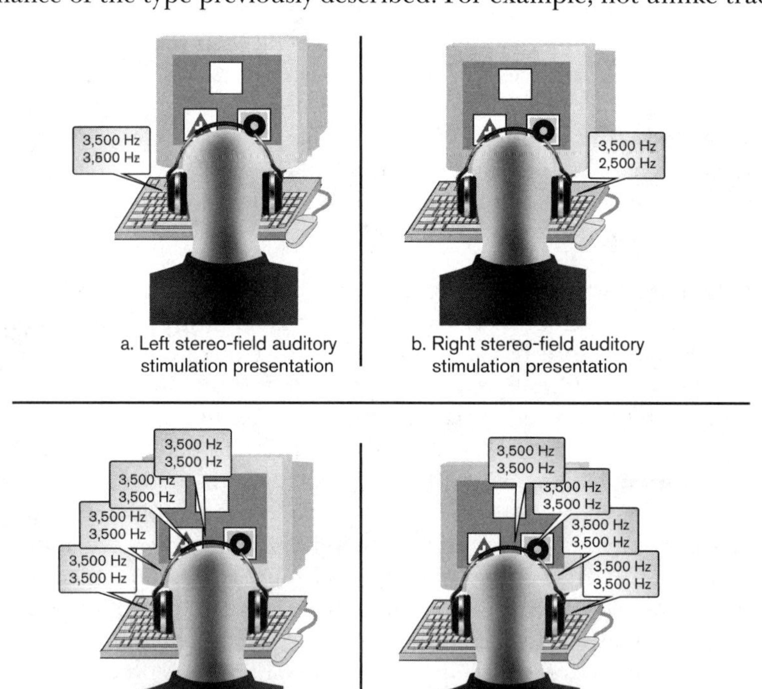

Figure 12.2. Illustration of the initial stereo-field prompts for "same" (left) and "different" (right) trials in the upper two panels (a and b) and stereo-field prompt fading in the lower two panels (c and d).

psychometric assessments in which a participant is asked to verbally report whether pairs are the same or different, one could use the same-different, GL/GR task to determine a discrimination threshold between pairs of stimuli. This will be illustrated with pitch discrimination as an example, although this method could be used with other characteristics of sound, such as duration or intensity.

A participant who successfully performs a baseline same-different, GL/GR task with auditory stimuli of 3,500 Hz and 2,500 Hz is demonstrating discrimination of a 1,000 Hz disparity. The term *disparity value* describes the difference in Hz between some standard and the absolute value of the other stimulus-pair member. The question for pitch assessment is as follows. At what point of Hz disparity between two tones will the participant no longer be able to reliably discriminate the difference? To answer this question, participants first are prepared by the training of pitch discriminations until they reach a stable threshold. This is followed by a more formal test, described in the next section.

To train pitch discrimination, participants are exposed within the same-different, GL/GR task to progressively more difficult-to-discriminate auditory stimulus pairs using the psychophysical staircase method (Levitt, 1971). Each staircase step consists of four trials: two "different" and two "same" trials (see the upper portion of Table 12.2). Assessment and control trials often appear equally, although they are presented randomly without replacement within each block. The "same" trials serve as control trials to ensure that the participant is not indiscriminately choosing one visual form or one side of the computer screen over the other. The values of the tones depend on where in the staircase the participant has progressed. A typical set of disparity values (the disparity down from 3,000 Hz) is shown in the lower portion of Table 12.2. Assess values are the absolute Hz value of a given stimulus that differs from 3,000 Hz. Thus, the value for all four assess values in the block of four trials in the first step of the staircase is 2,000 Hz (3,000 Hz minus 1,000 Hz equals 2,000 Hz). The assess value for the second step is 2,500 Hz and so forth. All correct responses are reinforced during threshold

Table 12.2. Auditory stimulus pairs and disparity values

Assessment stimulus pairs (different)		Control stimulus pairs (same)	
3000 Hz—Assess value*		3000 Hz—3000 Hz	
Assess value—3000 Hz		Assess value—Assess value	
Disparity values			
1000 Hz	90 Hz	35 Hz	8 Hz
750 Hz	80 Hz	30 Hz	7 Hz
500 Hz	70 Hz	25 Hz	6 Hz
250 Hz	60 Hz	20 Hz	5 Hz
200 Hz	50 Hz	15 Hz	4 Hz
150 Hz	45 Hz	10 Hz	3 Hz
100 Hz	40 Hz	9 Hz	2 Hz

*Assess values are the absolute Hz value of a given stimulus that differs from 3,000 Hz.

training. If the participant is correct on all four trials within a step, then he or she progresses to the next step. Any errors result in a backup to the previous step. It has been found that participants with ID can tolerate approximately 75–100 trials per session. Thus, later iterations of the threshold-training protocol reduced the number of trials within the blocks to just two: one "same" trial and one "different" trial. Subsequent sessions (e.g., the next day) do not begin with the 1,000 Hz disparity value. Instead, those sessions begin well within the range of accuracy shown during the previous session. Training proceeds until the participant's threshold value is stable. That is, the threshold values do not vary more than 20% across three sessions.

The peak and valley method (Levitt, 1971) is used to calculate the threshold. To illustrate this method, Figure 12.3 shows the fifth threshold-training session for Participant 1869 (Serna & Preston, 2010). The peaks and valleys refer to upward and downward runs of consecutive-correct step performance. For example, the data in Figure 12.3 show 20 peaks and valleys across the session. A 50% threshold would be calculated by averaging the disparity values of the peaks and valleys. The first three peaks and valleys are excluded from the calculation to account for the fact that sessions commenced a disparity value that was easy for the participant and for warm-up effects. Thus, the estimated threshold achieved by Participant 1869 for Session 5 was a disparity of 12.21 Hz.

Threshold Testing

The final threshold test makes use of the method of constant stimuli (Fechner, 1860/1912). This method is considered more accurate because the pairs of stimuli from different disparity values are randomly presented across trials, unlike the staircase method (Goldstein, 2010).

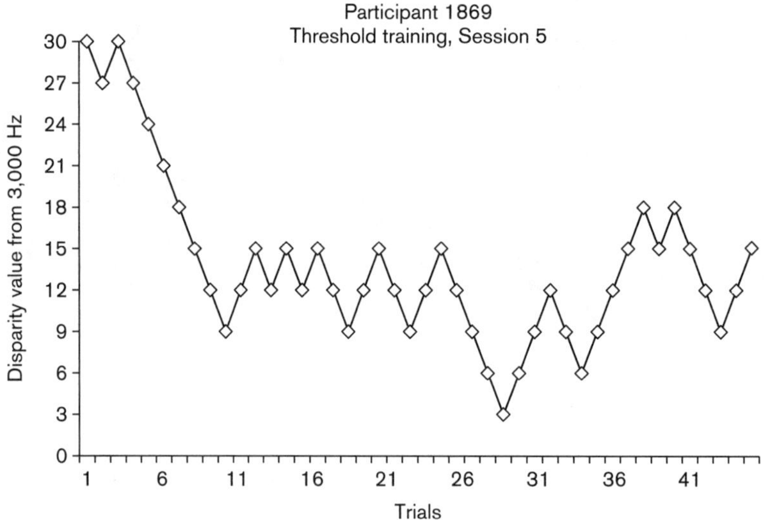

Figure 12.3. Representative data from the fifth session of threshold training for Participant 1869. Serna, R.W. & Preston, M.A. (2010). [Nonverbal methods for determining pitch-discrimination thresholds in individuals with intellectual disabilities]. Unpublished raw data.

Threshold testing proceeds as follows. First, participants are given warm-up trials. The warm up consists of "same" and "different" trials in which the values 3,000 Hz and 2,872 Hz (disparity value of 128 Hz) are used. The warm-up trials continue until the participant makes 10 consecutive correct responses. All correct trials are reinforced. If the criterion is met, then the task in repeated, but none of the trials are reinforced. Providing unreinforced trials prepares the participant for the unreinforced test. (The final threshold test is provided with reinforcement for some participants who do not maintain accurate performance in the absence of reinforcement.)

The final threshold test made use of six disparity values—128, 64, 32, 16, 8, and 4 Hz. (These values easily bracket the thresholds found during threshold training, and, thus, they are therefore appropriate for testing in an ID population.) One hundred and forty-four trials—72 assessment trials ("different") and 72 control trials ("same"), all distributed randomly—are needed to complete the threshold test. The test is administered across three, 48-trial sessions. Each disparity value determines the assess value used for four different trial types of stimulus pairs: 1) 3,000 Hz—assess value (× 4 presentations), 2) 3,000 Hz—3,000 Hz (× 4), 3) assess value—3,000 Hz (× 4) and 4) assess value—assess value (× 4).

Figure 12.4 shows the threshold test results from Participant 1869 (Serna & Preston, 2010). The less the disparity (i.e., the more difficult the discrimination), the less accurate was the performance for this participant. These results showed an estimated 50% auditory discrimination threshold of 21.44 Hz disparity.

Effectiveness

To date, the auditory discrimination procedure previously described—or variations of it—has been tested with a variety of individuals, including those with ASD

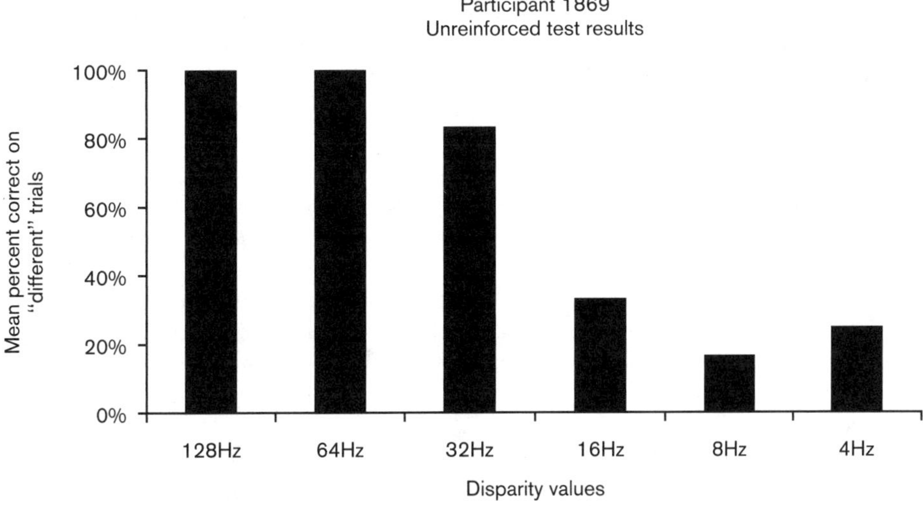

Figure 12.4. Percent correct performance on "different" trials across six disparity values. Each bar represents the mean of 12 trials. This test resulted in an estimated 50% auditory discrimination threshold of 21.44 Hz disparity. Serna, R.W. & Preston, M.A. (2010). [Nonverbal methods for determining pitch-discrimination thresholds in individuals with intellectual disabilities]. Unpublished raw data.

and comorbid ID, ID alone, high-functioning ASD, and typically developing individuals. As expected, the most success was obtained with individuals from the latter two populations. About half of the participants with ID complete all the stages of auditory discrimination assessment. The performance of participants who were unsuccessful in completing the protocol broke down in several different ways. For example, accurate same-different, GL/GR baseline performance could not be established for several participants with ID, despite the use of elaborate prompting procedures. Superimposition and fading was successful for another participant, but he was unable to generalize baseline performance to threshold training. This participant apparently learned the absolute requirements of the task but not a generalized same-different judgment of pairs of auditory stimuli, a performance necessary to succeed during threshold training. As yet, it is unknown why the procedures were not universally successful. Nevertheless, the positive results to date suggest that the reach of auditory discrimination assessment can be extended beyond what is currently available.

CONCLUSION

Although many studies have been conducted to assess auditory discrimination in clinical populations, most have focused on populations whose functioning is high enough to accommodate conventional, spoken-oriented measures. Those measures require either receptive language capabilities sufficient to understand the instructions of the assessment task or a spoken language response from the participant. Such measures unfortunately cannot gain access to the skills of individuals who are nonspeaking or who lack the spoken language capabilities to understand relatively complex task directions. As reviewed in this chapter, there is ample evidence that many individuals with ID struggle with auditory discrimination, which, in turn, may account for deficits in listening skills required in a variety of learning contexts, including those involving AAC instruction. This chapter described efforts to date to develop measures that can be used with individuals with ID whose auditory discrimination capabilities cannot be assessed by conventional means. The initial results have been very promising. Although the methods to date have not yet been universally successful, their effectiveness strongly suggest that further development could ultimately extend the reach of those whose auditory discrimination capabilities can be assessed.

Several related goals define the ways in which this area of research and development should proceed in the future, each of which is elaborated upon next. First, additional research needs to be conducted that will determine additional training steps for those who do not succeed with the methods reported here. Second, research and development efforts need to be extended to stimulus dimensions of auditory discrimination beyond pitch. Finally, the methods need to be consolidated and distributed in such a way that they are readily available not only to researchers but also to clinicians.

Additional exploration is needed of the conditions necessary to succeed for an individual who can acquire the baseline same-different, GL/GR task but whose performance deteriorates during threshold testing. As noted earlier, these circumstances likely represent a lack of generalization beyond the stimuli used in the baseline task. It would seem that additional baseline training explicitly geared toward promoting and verifying generalization would be required prior to introducing the threshold training. Methods adapted from the promotion of generalization in similar tasks with visual stimuli may prove useful, such as fading-out-the-fading procedures used to teach some forms of MTS (Dube et al., 1993; Dube & Serna, 1998). Perhaps the biggest challenge for future research and development in this area involves individuals who have difficulty acquiring same-different, GL/GR baseline performance in the first place. Although elaborate prompting methods such as superimposition and fading and stereo-field prompting and fading have been successful with many participants with ID, they were not universally so. Additional subskills would help some participants ultimately perform the same-different, GL/GR task. For example, in addition to the same-different judgments required between pairs of auditory stimuli, accurate responding requires the participant to shift responses from left to right, conditional on the sample, across trials. Generalized conditional discrimination capability is by no means a given with many individuals who have ID, even if all stimuli are visual (Saunders, Johnston, Tompkins, Dutcher, & Williams, 1997; Serna, 2004). This issue could be addressed in two separate ways in the future: 1) provide generalized conditional discrimination training to participants who do not acquire the baseline same-different, GL/GR task, or 2) explore methods that do not require a conditional discrimination.

Although the methods described in this chapter were applied to pitch discrimination, there does not appear to be any reason why the methods cannot be applied to other rudimentary dimensions of sound or speech. For example, tone duration assessment was piloted with four individuals with high-functioning ASD. All stimuli were 3,000 Hz in pitch during baseline. "Same" pairs were each 640 ms in duration; "different" pairs were 640 ms versus 420 ms in duration. Participants were exposed to threshold training and threshold testing in which a range of duration values were used, and orderly thresholds for all four participants were obtained. Other dimensions that could be tested include detection of gaps between sounds, rise and fall of pitch, speech versus nonspeech sounds, and so forth. The method described in this chapter could also be useful for detecting stimulus overselectivity (Dube, 2009) within speech or other sounds. For example, to what aspects of sound do individuals with ID attend? Could overselective responding to pitch, for example, account for some difficulties in auditory discrimination? These methods could prove very useful in this regard.

Finally, as noted earlier, the ultimate goal of the present research and development efforts is to deliver a reliable auditory discrimination assessment technology that can be used by researchers and clinicians alike. Consider the development of the same-different judgment technology that was described in the beginning of this chapter in order to provide a context for how an auditory discrimination technology might be completed. That effort resulted in an ability to teach same-different judgments to virtually any individual who met the basic motor and visual prerequisites, regardless of functioning level. Reaching that point required years of translational research to achieve a complete understanding of all the stimulus control requirements of the teaching methods prior to the development of a comprehensive curriculum. Analogously, an auditory discrimination assessment technology that reaches virtually all those that meet fundamental entry requirements also will require a complete understanding of the stimulus-control issues involved in the technology, and procedural gaps need to be eliminated. Meeting such requirements will lead to a well-specified path to assessment success, with appropriate and individual training deviations along the way. Ultimately, such a technology should be readily accessible to researchers and clinicians, otherwise it is of little use. Thus, given the necessary complexity of the envisioned technology, the system will need to be integrated into easy-to-use software. Once that is achieved, research and clinical work can proceed to better characterize the extant auditory discrimination skills in those individuals whose cannot be assessed by conventional means.

REFERENCES

Abbeduto, L., Furman, L., & Davies, B. (1989). Relation between the receptive language and mental age of persons with mental retardation. *American Journal on Mental Retardation, 93,* 535–543.

Baer, D.M., Wolf, M.M., & Risley, T.R. (1968). Some current dimensions of applied behavior analysis. *Journal of Applied Behavior Analysis, 1,* 91–97.

Barker-Collo, S., Jamieson, J., & Boo, F. (1995) Assessment of Basic Learning Abilities test: Prediction of communication ability in persons with developmental disabilities. *International Journal of Practical Approaches to Disability, 19,* 23–28.

Bartel, N.R., Bryen, D., & Keehn, S. (1973). Language comprehension in the mentally retarded child. *Exceptional Children, 39,* 375–382.

Bomba, M. D., & Pang, E. W. (2004). Cortical auditory evoked potentials in autism: a review. *International Journal of Psychophysiology 53,* 161–169.

Bonnel, A., Mottron, L., Peretz, I., Trudel, M., Gallun, E., & Bonnel, A. (2003). Enhanced pitch sensitivity in individuals with autism: A signal detection analysis. *Journal of Cognitive Neuroscience, 15*(2), 226–235.

Bonnel, A., McAdams, S., Smith, B., Berthiaume, C., Bertone, A., Ciocca, V., Mottron, L. (2010). Enhanced pure-tone pitch discrimination among persons with autism but not Asperger syndrome. *Neuropsychologia, 48*(9), 2465–2475. doi:10.1016/j.neuropsychologia.2010.04.02

Bruneau, N., Bonnet-Brilhault, F., Gomot, M., Adrien, J., & Barthélémy, C. (2003). Cortical auditory processing and communication in children with autism: Electrophysiological/behavioral relations. *International Journal of Psychophysiology, 51*(1), 17–25.

Carr, E.G. (1979). Teaching autistic children to use sign language: Some research issues. *Journal of Autism and Developmental Disorders, 9,* 345–359.

Carr, E.G., & Dores, P.A. (1981). Patterns of language acquisition following simultaneous communication training with autistic children. *Analysis and Intervention in Developmental Disabilities, 1,* 347–361.

Carr, E.G., Binkoff, J.A., Kologinski, E., & Eddy, M. (1978). Acquisition of sign language by autistic children. I: Expressive labeling. *Journal of Applied Behavior Analysis, 11,* 489–501.

Carr, E.G., Pridal, C., & Dores, P.A. (1984). Speech versus sign comprehension in autistic children: Analysis and prediction. *Journal of Experimental Child Psychology, 37,* 587–597.

Carter, D.E., & Eckerman, D.A. (1975). Symbolic matching by pigeons: Rate of learning complex discriminations predicted from simple discriminations. *Science, 187,* 662–664.

Chapman, R.S., Schwartz, S.E., & Kay-Raining Bird, E. (1991). Language skills of children and adolescents with Down syndrome: I. Comprehension. *Journal of Speech and Hearing Research, 34,* 1106–1120.

Clarke, S., Remington, B., & Light, P. (1986). An evaluation of the relationship between receptive speech skills and expressive signing. *Journal of Applied Behavior Analysis, 19*(3), 231–239.

Cromer, R. (1981). Reconceptualizing language acquisition and cognitive development. In R.L. Schiefelbusch & D.D. Bricker (Eds.), *Early language: Acquisition and intervention* (pp. 51–138). Baltimore, MD: University Park Press.

D'Amato, M.R., & Colombo, M. (1985). Auditory matching-to-sample in monkeys (Cebus apella). *Animal Learning and Behavior, 13,* 375–382.

D'Amato, M.R., & Worsham, R.W. (1974). Retrieval cues and short-term memory in capuchin monkeys. *Journal of Comparative and Physiological Psychology, 86,* 274–282.

Dewart, M.H. (1979). Language comprehension processes of mentally retarded children. *American Journal of Mental Deficiency, 84,* 177–183.

Dube, W.V. (2009). Stimulus overselectivity in discrimination learning. In P. Reed (Ed.), *Behavioral theories and interventions for autism* (pp. 23–46). New York, NY: Nova Science Publishers.

Dube, W.V., & Serna, R.W. (1998). Reevaluation of a programmed method to teach generalized identity matching. *Research in Developmental Disabilities, 19,* 347–379.

Dube, W.V., Iennaco, F.M., & McIlvane, W.J. (1993). Generalized identity matching to sample of two-dimensional forms in individuals with intellectual disabilities. *Research in Developmental Disabilities, 14,* 457–477.

Eikeseth, S. (2009). Outcomes of comprehensive psycho-educational interventions for young children with autism. *Research in Developmental Disabilities, 30,* 158–178.

Etzel, B.C., & LeBlanc, J.M. (1979). The simplest treatment alternative: The law of parsimony applied to choosing appropriate instructional control and errorless-learning procedures for the difficult-to-teach child. *Journal of Autism and Developmental Disorders, 9,* 361–382.

Fechner, G.T. (1860/1912). Elements of psychophysics: Sections VII and XVI (H.S. Langfeld, Trans.). In B. Rand (Ed.), *The classical psychologists* (pp. 562–572). Boston, MA: Houghton Mifflin.

Fulton, R.T., Gorzycki, P.A., & Hull. W.L. (1975). Hearing assessment with young children. *Journal of Speech and Hearing Disorders, 40,* 397–404.

Gervais, H., Belin, P., Boddaert, N., Leboyer, M., Coez, A., Sfaello, I., Zilbovicius, M. (2004). Abnormal cortical voice processing in autism. *Nature Neuroscience, 7,* 801–802. doi:10.1038/nn1291

Goldstein, E.B. (2010). *Sensation and perception* (8th ed.). Belmont, CA: Wadsworth/Cengage Learning.

Green, G. (1990). Differences in development of visual and auditory-visual equivalence relations. *American Journal on Mental Retardation, 95,* 260–270.

Greenfield, D.B. (1985). Facilitating mentally retarded children's relational learning through novelty-familiarity training. *American Journal of Mental Deficiency, 90,* 342–348.

Harrison, J.M. (1992). Avoiding conflicts between the natural behavior of the animal and the demands of discrimination experiments. *Journal of the Acoustical Society of America, 92,* 1331–1345.

Hartley, X.Y. (1982). Receptive language processing of Down's syndrome children. *Journal of Mental Deficiency Research, 29,* 197–205.

Hartley, X.Y. (1986). A summary of recent research into the development of children with Down syndrome. *Journal of Mental Deficiency Research, 30,* 1–14.

House, B.J., Brown, A.L., & Scott, M.S. (1974). Children's discrimination learning based on identity or difference. In H.W. Reese (Ed.), *Advances in child development and behavior* (Vol. 9, pp. 1–45). San Diego, CA: Academic Press.

Jones, C.R.G., Happé, F., Baird, G., Simonoff, E., Marsden, A.J.S., Tregay, J., Harman, T. (2009). Auditory discrimination and auditory sensory behaviours in autism spectrum disorders. *Neuropsychologia, 47,* 2850–2858.

Joseph, R.M, Tager-Flusberg, H., & Lord, C. (2002). Cognitive profiles and social-communicative functioning in children with autism spectrum disorder. *Journal of Child Psychology and Psychiatry, 43,* 807–821.

Kjelgaard, M.M., & Tager-Flusberg, H. (2001). An investigation of language impairment in autism: Implication for genetic subgroups. *Language and Cognitive Processes, 16,* 287–308.

Klinger, L., Dawson, G., & Renner, P. (2002). Autistic disorder. In E. Mash & R. Barkley (Eds.), *Child psychopathology* (2nd ed., pp. 409–454). New York, NY: Guilford Press.

Koegel, R.L., & Schreibman, L. (1976). Identification of consistent responding to auditory stimuli by a functionally "deaf" autistic child. *Journal of Autism and Childhood Schizophrenia, 6,* 147–156.

Kuhl, P.K., Coffey-Corina, S., Padden, D., & Dawson, G. (2005). Links between social and linguistic processing of speech in preschool children with autism: Behavioral and electrophysiological measures. *Developmental Science, 8,* F1–F12.

Levitt, H. (1971). Transformed up-down methods in psychoacoustics. *Journal of the Acoustical Society of America, 49,* 467–477.

Lincoln, A.J., Courchesne, E., Allen, M., Hanson, E., & Ene, M. (1998). Neurobiology of Asperger syndrome: Seven case studies and quantitative magnetic resonance imaging findings. In E. Schopler, G. Mesibov, & L.J. Kunce (Eds.), *Asperger syndrome or high-functioning autism?* (pp. 145–166). New York, NY: Plenum.

Lepisto, T., Kujala, T., Vanhala, R., Alku, P., Huotilainen, M., & Naatanen, R. (2005). The discrimination of and orienting to speech and non-speech sounds in children with autism. *Brain Research, 1066,* 147–157.

Lord, C., & Paul, R. (1997). Language and communication in autism. In D.J. Cohen & F.R. Volkmar (Eds.), *Handbook of autism and pervasive developmental disorders* (2nd ed., pp. 195–255). New York, NY: Wiley.

Lovaas, O.I., & Schreibman, L. (1971). Stimulus overselectivity of autistic children in two-stimulus situation. *Behavior Research and Therapy, 9,* 305–310.

Lovaas, O.I., Schreibman, L., Koegel, R.L., & Rehm, R. (1971). Selective responding by autistic children to multiple sensory input. *Journal of Abnormal Psychology, 77,* 211–222.

Mahon, K.L., Serna, R.W., Porter, A.F., Smith, E.R., Warecki, E.A., Lockerbie, A.M., & Saunders, E. (2004). Teaching visual stimulus same/different judgments to children with severe intellectual disabilities: Investigating the efficacy of the StartMatching! Curriculum. *Proceedings of the 37th Annual Gatlinburg Conference on Research and Theory in Mental Retardation and Developmental Disabilities, 130.*

McIlvane, W.J., Dube, W.V., Serna, R.W., Lionello-DeNolf, K.M., Barros, R.S., & Galvão, O.F. (2011). Some current dimensions of translational behavior analysis: From laboratory research to intervention for persons with autism spectrum disorders. In J.A. Mulick & E.A. Mayville (Eds.), *Behavioral foundations of effective autism treatment* (pp. 155–181). Cornwall-on-Hudson, NY: Sloan Publishing.

McIlvane, W. J., & Stoddard, L. T. (1981). Acquisition of matching-to-sample performances in severe mental retardation: Learning by exclusion. *Journal of Mental Deficiency Research, 25,* 33–48.

McIlvane, W. J., & Stoddard, L. T. (1985). Complex stimulus relations and exclusion in mental retardation. *Analysis and Intervention in Developmental Disabilities, 5,* 307–321.

Meyerson, L., & Kerr, N. (1977). Teaching auditory discriminations to severely retarded children. *Rehabilitation Psychology, 24* (Monograph Issue), 123–128.

Miller, J.F. (1987). Language and communication characteristics of children with Down syndrome. In S. Pueschel, C. Tinghey, J. Rynders, A. Crocker, & C. Crutcher (Eds.), New Perspectives on *Down Syndrome* (pp. 233–262). Baltimore, MD: Paul H. Brookes Publishing Co.

Miller, J.F., & Chapman, R.S. (1984). Disorders of communication: Investigating the development of language of mentally retarded children. *American Journal of Mental Deficiency, 88,* 536–545.

Miller, J.F., Chapman, R.S., & Bedrosian, J. (1978). The relationship between etiology, cognitive development, and communicative performance. *New Zealand Speech Therapist's Journal, 13,* 2–17.

Munson, J., Dawson, G., Sterling, L., Beauchaine, T., Zhou, A., Koehler, E., Abbott, R. (2008, November). Evidence for latent classes of IQ in young children with autism spectrum disorder. *American Journal of Mental Retardation, 113*(6), 439–452. doi: 10.1352/2008.113:439-452

Neill, J.C. & Harrison, J.M. (1987). Auditory discrimination: Konarski's quality-location effect. *Journal of the Experimental Analysis of Behavior, 48,* 81–95.

Odom, S.L., Boyd, B.A., Hall, L.J. & Hume, K.A. (2010). Evaluation of comprehensive treatment models for individuals with autism spectrum disorders. *Journal of Autism and Developmental Disabilities, 40,* 425–437.

Rapin, I. (1991). Autistic children: diagnosis and clinical features. *Pediatrics, 87,* 751–760.

Reynolds, B.S., Newsom, C.D., & Lovaas, O.I. (1974). Auditory overselectivity in autistic children. *Journal of Abnormal Child Psychology, 2,* 253–263.

Rincover, A., & Koegel, R.L. (1975). Setting generality and stimulus control in autistic children. *Journal of Applied Behavior Analysis, 8,* 235–246.

Rutter, M. (1984). Cognitive deficits in the pathogenesis of autism. *Journal of Child Psychology and Psychiatry, 24(4),* 513–521.

Saunders, K.J., Johnston, M.D., Tompkins, B.F., Dutcher, D.L., & Williams, D.C. (1997). Generalized identity matching of two-dimensional forms by individuals with moderate to profound mental retardation. *American Journal on Mental Retardation, 102,* 285–291.

Saunders, K.J., & Spradlin, J.E. (1989). Conditional discrimination in mentally retarded adults: The effect of training the component simple discriminations. *Journal of the Experimental Analysis of Behavior, 52,* 1–12.

Saunders, K.J., & Spradlin, J.E. (1990). Conditional discrimination in mentally retarded adults: The development of generalized skills. *Journal of the Experimental Analysis of Behavior, 54,* 239–250.

Schiefelbusch, R.L., & Lloyd, L.L. (1974). *Language perspectives: Acquisition, retardation and intervention.* Baltimore, MD: University Park Press.

Schreibman, L. (1975). Effects of within-stimulus and extra-stimulus prompting on discrimination learning in autistic children. *Journal of Applied Behavior Analysis, 8,* 91–112.

Schreibman, L., Kohlenberg, B.S., & Britten, K.R. (1986). Differential responding to content and intonation components of a complex auditory stimulus by nonverbal and verbal autistic children. *Analysis and Intervention in Developmental Disabilities, 6,* 109–125.

Serna, R.W. (2004). Recent advances in discrimination learning with individuals with developmental disabilities. In L. Williams (Ed.), *Developmental disabilities: Etiology, assessment, intervention, and integration.* (pp. 81–104). Reno, NV: Context Press.

Serna, R.W., & Carlin, M.T. (2001). Guiding visual attention in individuals with mental retardation. In L.M. Glidden (Ed.) *International review of research in mental retardation.* (Vol. 24, pp. 321–357). San Diego, CA: Academic Press.

Serna, R.W. & Preston, M.A. (2010). [Nonverbal methods for determining pitch-discrimination thresholds in individuals with intellectual disabilities]. Unpublished raw data.

Serna, R.W., Dube, W.V., & McIlvane, W.J. (1997). Assessing same/different judgments in individuals with severe intellectual disabilities: A status report. *Research in Developmental Disabilities, 18,* 343–368.

Serna, R.W., Jeffery, J.A., & Stoddard, L.T. (1996). Establishing go-left/go-right auditory discrimination baselines in an individual with severe mental retardation. *Experimental Analysis of Human Behavior Bulletin, 14,* 18–23.

Serna, R.W., Preston, M.A., & Thompson, G.B. (2009). Assessing nonverbal same/different judgments of auditory stimuli in individuals with intellectual disabilities: A methodological investigation. *Brazilian Journal of Behavior Analysis, 5,* 69–87.

Serna, R.W., Stoddard, L.T., & McIlvane, W.J. (1992). Developing auditory stimulus control: A note on methodology. *Journal of Behavioral Education, 2,* 391–403.

Smith, T. (2001). Discrete trial training in the treatment of autism. *Focus on Autism and Other Developmental Disabilities, 16*(2), 86–92.

Soraci, S.A., Stoddard, L.T., Serna, R.W., McIlvane, W.J., & Carlin, M.T. (1994). Auditory spatial location in auditory-visual matching to sample: A preliminary investigation. *Experimental Analysis of Human Behavior Bulletin, 12,* 14–16.

Spradlin, J.E., Lloyd, L.L., Hom, G.L., & Reid, M. (1968). Establishing tone control and evaluating the hearing of severely retarded children. In G.A. Jervis (Ed.), *Expanding concepts in mental retardation* (pp. 170–180). Springfield, IL: Charles C. Thomas.

Stoddard, L.T. (1982). An investigation of automated methods for teaching severely retarded individuals. In N.R. Ellis (Ed.), *International review of research in mental retardation* (Vol. 8, 163–207). San Diego, CA: Academic Press.

Stoddard, L.T., & McIlvane, W.J. (1989). Generalization after intradimensional discrimination training in 2-year old children. *Journal of Experimental Child Psychology, 47,* 324–334.

Terrace, H.S. (1963). Errorless transfer of a discrimination across two continua. *Journal of the Experimental Analysis of Behavior, 6,* 223–232.

Vause, T., Martin, G.L., & Yu, D.C.T. (2000) ABLA test performance, auditory matching, and communication ability. *Journal on Developmental Disabilities, 7,* 123–141.

Wilkinson, K.M., Rosenquist, C., & McIlvane, W.J. (2009). Exclusion learning and emergent symbolic category formation in individuals with severe language impairments and intellectual disabilities. *Psychological Record,* 59, 187–206.

Woolcock, J.E., & Alferink, L.A. (1982). An operant tracking procedure in the auditory assessment of profoundly retarded individuals. *Animal Learning and Behavior, 18,* 287–294.

Wright, A.A., Shyan, M.R., & Jitsumori, M. (1990). Auditory same/different concept learning by monkeys. *Animal Learning and Behavior, 18,* 287–294.

Yoder, P.J., & Layton, T.L. (1988). Speech following sign language training in autistic children with minimal verbal language. *Journal of Autism and Developmental Disorders, 18,* 217–229.

13

The Role of Cultural, Ethnic, and Linguistic Differences

Katherine T. Rhodes and Julie A. Washington

The population of individuals with severe disabilities is a diverse group, varying along a number of dimensions, including biology, cognition, behavior, age, race, gender, ethnicity, and social and economic resources. Issues of identification, measurement, and treatment of disabilities can be complicated by the presence of any mix of these important group and individual variables, regardless of the severity level of the disability. This chapter focuses on children with severe disabilities who have cultural, ethnic, and linguistic differences from the White, middle-class, Standard American English dialect-speaking norm in the United States.

First, the chapter explores definitions and theoretical models of disability that govern practitioners' and researchers' work, including the diagnosis and prevalence estimates of children with severe disabilities. Next, it examines cultural, ethnic, and linguistic differences (CELD) as important but largely unexplored variables for consideration when diagnosing and treating individuals with severe disabilities, including discussion of potential sources of misunderstanding when serving CELD children and their families. Finally, the chapter considers remedies for existing disparities in the experiences of disability from a social-ecological framework, emphasizing community-based participatory action intervention.

WHAT IS DISABILITY?

Before discussing the unique challenges faced by CELD children with severe disabilities, the conceptualization of disability in general needs to be outlined. As a construct, disability may be simply defined as a natural part of the human experience that is subject to the social climate of a particular era (Iezzoni & Freedman, 2008; Smart & Smart, 2006). The language used to describe disability is a strong indicator of the social concept of disability at the time, so disability is also in part a social construction. A society's understanding of disability is a function of both an era and a culture. For scientists and practitioners disability is usually defined formally, using a model, which is simply a conceptual framework for identifying, explaining, and predicting phenomena.

The model chosen to define disability affects prevalence estimates, inclusionary and exclusionary research decisions, treatment decisions, and treatment outcome expectations. For some time, scientists, policy makers, researchers, and clinicians have recognized the utility of a standardized classification system within their models of disability. In addition to a standardized classification system, a good model of disability should allow its users to make inferences about populations, measure multiple dimensions of health, distinguish between different types of health experiences, predict service needs, predict functional outcomes, and create policies for social inclusion and access to resources (World Health Organization [WHO], 2002).

Disabilities have historically been conceptualized using 1) a medical model, 2) a functional-environmental model, 3) a sociopolitical model, or 4) some combination of these. Importantly, the definition of disability embraced by CELD clients or participants may diverge from the model employed by the practitioners and researchers who serve them. Ignoring these points of divergence can significantly affect the success of assessments and interventions, so it is crucial that practitioners and researchers are aware of the models they use to conceptualize disability.

Traditional Models for Defining Disability

The experience of disability often has been defined using a medical model because many disability categories include a concomitant medical diagnosis (Gilson & Depoy, 2000; Gleeson, 1997). Several other models of disability have been proposed more recently. The leading models of disability are briefly discussed in the following sections.

Medical Model The medical model describes disability as some form of biological, physical, behavioral, cognitive, or sensory impediment located within individuals, rendering individuals with disabilities deficient in some way when compared to a segment of a population without disabilities (Gilson & Depoy, 2000; Gleeson, 1997; Quinn, 1997; Shakespeare & Waston, 1997). According to a medical model of disability, the problem resides within an individual, and treatment and rehabilitation are defined in terms of returning the individual to full functioning or a developmentally normative state. For individuals experiencing acute or temporary disabilities, rehabilitation and recovery are possible using a medical model (Smart & Smart, 2006). However, within this model individuals with developmental disabilities or chronic disabling conditions have little chance of recovery or rehabilitation and have traditionally been isolated and institutionalized (Smart & Smart, 2006).

Functional-Environmental Model Functional-environmental models of disability are defined in terms of the interaction between individuals and environments (Smart & Smart, 2006). According to this model of disability, an individual's biological, physical, cognitive, behavioral, or sensory status interacts with environmental demands and access to create functional limitations (Gilson & Depoy, 2000). Treatment is defined in terms of both rehabilitation and recovery for individuals and environmental changes and adjustments to allow for individual inclusion (Gilson & Depoy, 2000). Acute and chronic cases of disability are considered in terms of maximizing each individual's potential level of function (Gilson & Depoy, 2000).

Sociopolitical Model The sociopolitical model of disability defines disability in terms of the social prejudice, discrimination, and marginalization experienced by individuals with disabilities (Smart & Smart, 2006). This model of disability allows individuals to define themselves, rejecting medical diagnoses and discriminatory language, while focusing on achieving equitable social and political inclusion as a minority group (Smart & Smart, 2006). The disability community (including individuals with disabilities, their families, and their advocates) utilizes the sociopolitical model to form a culture all its own (Gilson & Depoy, 2000). Treatment is defined in terms of political and social actions that enable a minority group to achieve equity and social justice.

Sociopolitical models of disability often appear in policy and legislation aimed at decreasing the discrimination experienced by individuals with disabilities as a minority group. The Americans with Disabilities Act (ADA) of 1990 (PL 101-336) and the Individuals with Disabilities Education Improvement Act (IDEA) of 2004 (PL 108-446) arguably have been the most influential pieces of legislation for advancing equitable treatment in employment, community, and educational contexts. The ADA was designed to increase community access and participation and to reduce the experiences of discrimination experienced by individuals with disabilities. IDEA was designed to increase access to and participation in education and stresses the importance of family participation in service delivery for all children and young adults with disabilities (see U.S. Department of Education, 2010). These two pieces of legislation combined have done the most to influence the lives of individuals with disabilities at home, in the community, in the workplace, and at school.

Toward a Multidimensional Model of Disability

Overall, the medical model of disability continues to prevail among most members of the general public, policy makers, researchers, and practitioners. Some argue that its continuing use is due to its strengths in terms of explaining, classifying, and measuring disability (Smart & Smart, 2006). Medical models of disability also have important practical applications in health care settings because reimbursement for diagnostic or intervention services is frequently tied to the ability to establish that an individual's symptoms are consistent with established disability categories (e.g., *Diagnostic and Statistical Manual of Mental Disorders, Fifth Edition [DSM-V;* American Psychiatric Association, 2013]. Medical models of disability have been criticized for failing to consider contexts outside of the individual and locating problems within individuals who are experiencing disabilities (Lollar & Crews, 2003). Although functional-environmental and sociopolitical models of disability may be willing to consider contexts outside of the individual as important predictors of disabling experiences, many of them still rely on some aspect of individual impairment or less-than-ideal health conditions to define and measure disability (Lollar & Crews, 2003). Thus, many scientists and practitioners have argued the need for a model of disability that can reliably identify, explain, and recommend treatment without stigmatizing individuals who have disabilities.

In an effort to address criticisms of the medical model that arose from within the disability community, the World Health Organization (WHO, 2002) established the International Classification of Functioning, Disability and Health (ICF; Pfeiffer, 1998; Pfeiffer, 2000). The ICF is a classification system for functioning and disability designed to focus on inclusiveness as well as equity and quality of life (WHO, 2002). Thus, the ICF incorporates some of the broad concerns of the sociopolitical and functional-environmental models of disability. The resulting bio-psycho-social model of disability defines disability as an interaction between health conditions, environmental factors, and internal factors. Treatment under this model of disability can be designed and implemented for individuals' bodies, individuals' functional capacities in various contexts, and/or social environments' restrictions in participation.

Including Cultural, Ethnic, and Linguistic Differences in Models of Disability

Culture is often a major predictor of the ways in which families and communities interpret disability status. Specifically, culture predicts the ways in which families act to treat severe disability, the emphasis they may place on early intervention, and the hopes they may have for long-term outcomes. Cultural beliefs may also influence the community support that families will receive for engaging in certain treatment services.

In some cases, a family's model and understanding of disability may collide with scientists' and practitioners' models of disability to produce cross-cultural miscommunications. For example, many families may interpret their child's disability within a larger spiritual framework (e.g., the disability is a punishment for past transgressions or, conversely, represents a divine gift; Groce & Zola, 1993). Practitioners using a traditional medical model, which does not incorporate the family's spiritual beliefs, may encounter cross-cultural miscommunications when they attribute the child's disability to a medical condition or physical impairment. The medical model may simply be incompatible with the values of the family in this case, resulting in noncompliance with treatment recommendations.

Other cultural belief systems may lead families to view disability as a shameful or embarrassing condition and, therefore, to isolate their children from social inclusion opportunities in order to protect the children and the family from ridicule (Groce & Zola, 1993). Practitioners approaching the family within a functional-environmental framework may recommend environmental changes and accommodations that conflict with families' cultural values regarding disability as a private concern and children with disabilities as needing protection. Treatment recommendations for accommodations inside the family's home may be acceptable, but making exterior modifications or publicly advocating for social inclusion may be uncomfortable or even humiliating. Functional-environmental treatment recommendations may be met with less resistance if the attempts to modify the child's level of functioning or make environmental changes and accommodations take the family's cultural values around privacy into account.

Thus, it is essential that scientists and practitioners discuss the perceived causes, outcome expectations, needs, and goals of families and caregivers in order to help families and children with severe disabilities achieve the levels of community participation that suit the specific needs of the family and the child. When cultural miscommunications are encountered, resolutions must begin with a willingness to consider families' perspectives.

EXPLAINING DISPARITIES IN DISABILITY PREVALENCE AMONG CULTURALLY, ETHNICALLY, AND LINGUISTICALLY DIFFERENT POPULATIONS

Beyond influencing intervention outcome expectations and collaborations between family members and researchers/practioners, the models used to define and discuss disability also influence the estimation of disability prevalence (see Table 13.1). This is a particularly relevant issue for individuals from CELD populations for whom disability prevalence estimates are often entangled with cultural differences.

Disparities in Diagnosis

Racial and ethnic minorities within the United States tend to be identified with disabilities at a disproportionately high rate compared with White, non-Hispanic Americans (Smart & Smart, 1997), and this is especially true for African Americans. The 2010 U.S. Census Survey of Income and Program Participation (SIPP; Brault, 2010) estimated that approximately 22.3% of African Americans ages 6 and older experienced disabilities under the WHO's ICF multidimensional model of disability (in impairments, activity limitations, and participation restrictions). Comparatively, Hispanics had reported disabilities at a rate of 17.8%, and White, non-Hispanic Americans had reported disabilities at a rate of 17.4%. These disparities in disability diagnosis have been consistently noted by both researchers and policy makers (Bowe, 1984; Hayes-Bautista, 1992; Klingner et al., 2005; Smart & Smart, 1997; Thornhill & HoSang, 1988).

Why Do Children with Cultural, Ethnic, and Linguistic Differences Experience Disparities in Disability?

This apparent racial/ethnic disparity in disability prevalence has been linked to 1) lower socioeconomic status and access to resources, 2) lower levels of education, 3) lack of access to quality care, and 4) biased testing and diagnostic services, especially

Table 13.1. Estimating disability prevalence globally and within the United States

Source	Population	Disability model	Estimate
World Health Survey	Adults 18 years and older globally	Bio-psycho-social	15.6%
Global Burden of Disease	Children and adults 14 years and older globally	Medical	12%
American Community Survey	Americans 0–75 years	Medical/functional environmental	12%
Current Population Survey	American adults 18–64 years	Functional environmental	8.1%
U.S. Census (2000)	American adults and children 5–64 years	Medical/functional environmental	15.5%

*See source for the data at the end of the chapter.

for cognitive disabilities (Smart & Smart, 1997). For example, minorities (especially African Americans and Latinos) in public schools are more likely to be diagnosed with learning or behavior problems and less likely to be placed in mainstream classrooms (Lester & Kelman, 1997). In particular, CELD students are disproportionately represented in high-incidence special education categories such as learning disabilities, intellectual disability (ID), and emotional impairments (Klingner et al., 2005). Furthermore, minority children are more likely to be diagnosed with more severe forms of intellectual and developmental disabilities (IDD; Emerson, 2012) and less likely to be differentially diagnosed with autism spectrum disorder (ASD) as opposed to ID (Mandell et al., 2009). These diagnostic disparities most often have been attributed to issues of cultural and linguistic bias in assessment instruments used to diagnose impairments (Figueroa, 1989; Smart & Smart, 1997).

Cultural, Ethnic, and Linguistic Differences in Language and Communication

Differences in cultural and linguistic practices and the general lack of understanding of these practices by practitioners may be an invisible source of disparity for both disability status and treatment outcomes for minority children. Different cultures also vary in their language usage and preferred cultural communication styles. These two sources of cultural variation must be considered when assessing disability prevalence, planning community interactions, delivering services, and evaluating outcomes. These sources of cultural variance are discussed in the following sections.

CULTURAL VARIANCE IN LANGUAGE USAGE

Cultural differences in language use have been widely reported for children who are nonnative speakers of English and those who use cultural or regional dialects of American English. Although the United States has no official national language, Mainstream American English (MAE) is largely the language of commerce, diplomacy, and education (Huntington, 2004). Ample evidence shows that mastery of MAE improves academic, social, and economic outcomes (Cargile, 2000; Charity, Scarborough, & Griffin, 2004; Connor, 2008). For those CELD families who do not speak English as a first language or MAE dialect as the primary language of their community, experiences of being a linguistic minority may collide with the challenges of caring for a child with a severe disability in ways that require thoughtfulness and sensitivity from practitioners and researchers.

Immigrants with Cultural, Ethnic, and Linguistic Differences

Estimates of the number of children with disabilities who immigrated to the United States are difficult to find, and they vary across measurement instruments and models of disability. For example, using a functional-environmental model of disability, results from the 2002 National Survey of America's Families (NSAF; Urban Institute & Child Trends, 2007) indicate that approximately 8.6% of foreign-born naturalized U.S. citizen children and approximately 6.5% of foreign-born noncitizen children have physical, learning, or mental health conditions that limit participation in daily life activities.

Disability may not have been diagnosed or recognized prior to entry in the United States for many immigrants, and access to treatment and/or social inclusion may have been limited, regardless of their diagnostic status. For example, of the estimated 5% of children (ages 14 years or younger) who have a moderate to severe disability worldwide (UNICEF, 2013), approximately 98% of those living in developing countries are not given access to education (Blankenship & Madson, 2007). Of the 1%–2% of these children who are given access to education, boys are more likely to be chosen for educational inclusion than girls (Blankenship & Madson, 2007). Experiences of violence, war, and trauma also may have affected family structure, disability status, mental health, and access to services for those CELD immigrants who are in the United States as refugees and asylum seekers (Blankenship & Madson, 2007). These and other experiences prior to arrival in the United Sates may complicate the experience of disability identification, measurement, and treatment for CELD immigrant children and their families.

Successful identification, measurement, and treatment/intervention for CELD immigrant children with severe disabilities will likely involve some collaboration with families (Blankenship & Madson, 2007). These collaborations must begin with an understanding of the social barriers these families face as well as sensitivity to their specific needs and perspectives.

Identifying families who are eligible for services is one major issue complicating service delivery. CELD immigrants with severe disabilities and their families often have difficulty navigating social systems within the United States. In general, children in immigrant families are more likely to experience fair or poor health (as opposed to good health), more likely to be uninsured, more likely to have limited access to a regular source of health care, and less likely to take advantage of public benefits and social services such as Temporary Assistance for Needy Families (TANF) or food vouchers (Capps, Fix, Ost, Reardon-Anderson, & Passel, 2004). Immigration resettlement plans may attempt to help families navigate available services, but these are only offered for a limited time after resettlement (Blankenship & Madson, 2007).

Even if parents are aware that their child has a disability and that certain services are available, the parents of CELD immigrant children with severe disabilities may be hesitant to seek out services for several reasons. The availability of economic resources is a major concern for many immigrant families. Young children of immigrants experience much higher poverty rates than children of families who are native to the United States, and this is especially true for young children of immigrants below the age of 6 years (56% are below the poverty level) (Capps et al., 2004). Researchers and practitioners should note which recommended treatment services can be paid for using existing social service programs and which will require additional funds from the family. For families experiencing economic hardships, hesitation to adhere to treatment or intervention suggestions may reflect concerns about costs rather than willingness to trust professional expertise.

Fear of visibility may also be a barrier to participation for many families. An estimated 29% of young children of immigrants live in families with at least one undocumented parent, but most (93%) of these children are United States citizens (Capps et al., 2004). Fear of immigration enforcement actions may constitute an additional barrier to service delivery and full social participation for these families. Practitioners and researchers should be aware that several pieces of federal legislation ensure that CELD immigrant children with severe disabilities are legally allowed participation in the public education system and other federally funded programs. For example, the U.S. Supreme Court ruling in *Plyler v. Doe* (1982) established that denying children access to school enrollment and educational funding on the basis of their legal immigration status is in violation of the 14th Amendment to the U.S. Constitution, which guarantees equal protection under the law to people within the jurisdiction of the United States. Title I (providing additional resources to disadvantaged and minority children) and Title III (providing educational services to English language learners [ELLs]) of the Elementary and Secondary Education Act Amendments of 1968 (PL 90-247) (reauthorized as No Child Left Behind Act [NCLB] of 2001, PL 107-110) also apply to CELD immigrant children.

Regardless of immigration status, limited English proficiency is another major social barrier for an estimated 60% of parents of young immigrant children (Capps et al., 2004). Thus, understanding the communication needs of CELD immigrant children with severe disabilities and their families must begin with assessments of home language profiles. More than 150 home languages are spoken by ELLs nationally, but the vast majority of ELLs ages 5–18 years enrolled in schools speak Spanish at home (73.1%; Batalova & McHugh, 2010). The most frequent home languages for ELLs after Spanish are Chinese (3.8%), Vietnamese (2.7%), French/Haitian Creole (2.1%), Hindi and related dialects (1.8%), Korean (1.5%), German (1.5%), Arabic (1.2%), Russian (1.1%), and Miao/Hmong (1.1%; Batalova & McHugh, 2010). An estimated one third of immigrant families are linguistically isolated, meaning that all people age 14 years and older in the household have limited English language proficiency (Capps et al., 2004). Successful collaboration with these families will require sensitivity to families' educational backgrounds, levels of English language proficiency, and literacy levels in native languages and in English.

Children with Disabilities Who Have Cultural, Ethnic, and Linguistics Differences and Are Bilingual

Issues in bilingual education affect children with severe disabilities whether they are ELLs who are relatively new to English or have been exposed to another language concurrently with English (bilinguals or multilinguals). Bilingual education continues to be a controversy in the United States (see Bialystok, 2001, 2007, 2011).

Professionals often recommend that children with severe disabilities who may have general difficulty in language acquisition (Carlo et al., 2004) be raised in monolingual English environments (Kay-Raining Bird, Cleave, Trudeau, Thordardottir, Sutton, & Thorpe, 2005); however, there is little empirical evidence to suggest that bilingual education is detrimental to children with language impairments. Studies of typically developing children indicate that bilingualism may, in fact, be beneficial for children and may increase their metalinguistic awareness (see Bialystok, 2001, 2007, 2011). More research is needed to determine whether CELD children with disabilities demonstrate a metalinguistic advantage similar to their typically developing peers; however, the few research studies on CELD children with disabilities and bilingualism indicate that children with severe disabilities can and do learn more than one language without adverse effects to their English language learning.

Bilingual children with Down syndrome (DS) have English language skills that are comparable with their monolingual peers with DS, and they evidence similar patterns of receptive language strength and difficulties with expressive language (especially with morphosyntax) in both languages (Kay-Raining Bird et al., 2005). Although their second language skills vary widely, children with DS can learn languages in addition to English (Kay-Raining Bird et al., 2005). In general, those children with DS who are more developmentally advanced and have better vocabulary comprehension skills tend to be more successful in their second language learning (Kay-Raining Bird et al., 2005).

Research also indicates that bilingual children with ASD can and do learn more than one language (Kay-Raining Bird, Lamond, & Holden, 2011). Families of children with ASD also reported that these children were able to extend their bilingualism across a variety of communication modalities, including oral language, sign language, Picture Exchange Communication System, and augmentative and alternative communication (AAC) devices (Kay-Raining Bird et al., 2011). Although these children varied widely in their language skills, the rates of language comprehension and production abilities among bilingual children with ASD were similar to those of monolingual children with ASD (Kay-Raining Bird et al., 2011). Variability in language acquisition success for bilingual children with ASD appears to be related to a number of contextual and individual factors, including home language input and child cognitive linguistic profile.

Recommending English-only language usage within the homes of CELD children with disabilities may not be feasible, regardless of one's theoretical and professional orientation toward bilingual education. Practitioners and researchers working with these children and their families should address families' values around bilingualism and biculturalism as well as families' language proficiencies in all of the languages spoken at home. Bilingualism is a necessity for many families due to issues of language proficiency, and families may also place a high value on bilingualism because their children may need to learn more than one language in order to fully participate in their communities and communicate with their loved ones (Kay-Raining Bird et al., 2011). Families who have chosen to raise their CELD children in bilingual or multilingual home environments, whether out of necessity or due to personal beliefs, may need assistance in navigating available services and social supports for their children. If bilingualism is a family goal, then successful collaboration between the family, practitioners, and researchers will foster open discussion about desired communication outcomes.

African American English Dialect Users

African American English dialect (AAE) is spoken by most but not all African Americans who, until recently, were the largest minority group in the United States (Stockman, 2010). AAE is the most studied dialect of American English (Wolfram & Thomas, 2002) and affects the morphology, phonology, and syntax of English in very predictable ways. The pragmatics of language are also known to be affected in AAE speakers, but are less well documented than structural differences. This is an unfortunate omission because it is these differences that often lead to communicative misunderstanding and differential responses to treatment, as discussed in the following section. AAE has been identified as a factor in educational attainment, assessment, and service delivery for African American children and adults (e.g., Figueroa, 1989; Grogger, 2011; Smart & Smart, 1997). For example, Washington and colleagues (Craig & Washington, 1995; Craig, Washington, & Thompson-Porter, 1998) determined that although African American children who are from low-income families and who speak AAE are linguistically sophisticated at the time of school entry, continued use of AAE in school settings often has a negative impact on educational attainment. In a similar vein, Terry and Connor (2012) found that the use of dialect in kindergarten predicted development of reading skills in kindergarten and beyond, such that students who were low users of dialect developed reading skills at a similar rate to their MAE peers, whereas those using higher levels developed the same skills at a slower rate. In addition, the presence of AAE complicates attempts to identify and diagnose disabilities because the most common features of AAE are also common in MAE speakers who have language impairments.

Impact of Language Difference

For children who are linguistic minorities within the United States, research has demonstrated that linguistic differences can be an important variable influencing the disparities in disability identification experienced in the special education system, including both under- and overidentification in various disability categories (Figueroa, 1989; Oswald, Coutinho, & Best, 2002; Smart & Smart, 1997). In particular, standardized assessment instruments have been implicated for their insensitivity to variations in language usage that constitute cultural linguistic differences as opposed to those variants that are indicative of language disorders. Investigations of test bias concerns have focused on instruments across language domains, including vocabulary (Qi, Kaiser, Milan, & Hancock, 2006; Restrepo et al., 2006; Stockman, 2000; Thomas-Tate, Washington, Craig, & Packard, 2006; Washington & Craig, 1999), articulation (Cole & Taylor, 1990; Laing & Kamhi, 2003), and syntax (Adler & Birdsong, 1983; Campbell, Dollaghan, Needleman, & Janosky, 1997; Charity, 2010).

The influence of these linguistic differences is neither well documented nor well understood in those CELD children who have severe disabilities. Many of these children have limited verbal skills, including significant difficulty producing intelligible speech. Accordingly, cultural concerns related to standardized assessment of communication output are often regarded as low priority or ignored entirely in the design of language acquisition interventions for this population. The influence of culture on expectations for performance and for designing and delivering interventions must still be considered, however.

Cultural variance in the use of language in the home and community will influence the nature of the input that CELD children with disabilities receive and expect to hear. Children develop linguistic expectations of their communication partners and environments based on the language inputs (e.g., phonology, semantics, syntax, pragmatics) to which they are exposed in their homes and communities (Saffran, 2003). For example, Pickl (2011) noted that children who use AAC devices and who come from multilingual families must figure out the language of school, home, and the pictorial communication system of the AAC device. These differences in the input received at home and school should influence the AAC interventions that are selected for use as well as the manner in which these interventions are delivered and introduced to the family. Making these differentiated decisions requires that practitioners be well informed about the cultural and linguistic expectations of children and their families.

CULTURAL VARIANCE IN COMMUNICATION STYLE

There is more to communication than the words people choose and the syntax and grammar used to arrange them. A large portion of the content of communication lies in metalinguistic communication, or communication style (Hall, 1976, 1983; Hecht, Ribeau, & Alberts, 1989; Tannen, 2006), often referred to as the pragmatic domain of language. Communication styles are largely culturally determined, and the cultural appropriateness of a given individual's communication style will vary with region, age, gender, and socioeconomic status. What people are allowed to say, how they are expected to say it, how they convey their messages, and how individuals ensure that their messages have been received are all products of both individual styles and larger sociocultural contexts. Figure 13.1 outlines these metalinguistic features of communication. The following sections consider a few selected features of communication style with attention to differences between mainstream American (White, middle class) styles and the communication styles of various CELD minority groups within the United States.

Taboo Topics

Every culture has taboo topics. Many people in the United States would consider topics such as religion, politics, income level, and sexuality to be off limits for polite conversation with relatively new communication partners; however, it would be

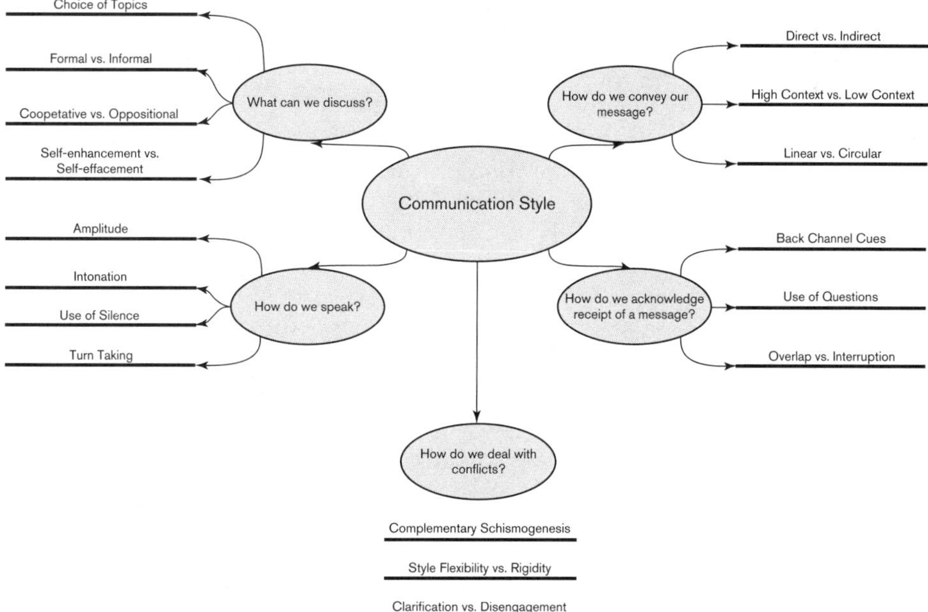

Figure 13.1. Selected features of metalinguistic communication, or communication style. (*Source:* Hall, 1976, 1983; Hecht, Ribeau, & Alberts, 1989; Tannen, 2006.)

perfectly acceptable to discuss these topics with new communication partners in other cultures (e.g., Western European nations such as Germany; Tannen, 2006). In collectivistic cultures, such as China and Japan, communication partners tend to have more taboo topics, even within the context of close friendships (Goodwin & Lee, 1994). When working with CELD children and their families, it is important for researchers and practitioners to identify these taboo topics and to consider the fact that they are taboo while communicating.

Although discussion of taboo topics is not generally considered culturally appropriate in the United States, it is perfectly acceptable within the context of American communication intervention research and practice for professionals to ask families questions about taboo topics such as personal demographics, medical histories, family structures, and educational achievements without first establishing a bond of familiarity as communication partners. This expert–patient interaction is arguably a holdover from the medical model; however, it is important for researchers and practitioners to acknowledge that despite the formality of the context and the power dynamic inherent in the expert–patient interaction, discussion of such taboo, personal topics with a relatively new communication partner is difficult if not impossible for some CELD families from collectivistic cultures because it is culturally unacceptable for a relative stranger to ask such personal questions.

Parents, and young parents in particular, may also feel uncomfortable discussing the topic of parenting a child with a severe disability without members of the extended family present. Family structure in many collectivistic cultures is viewed as encompassing extended family, especially older relatives with many years of experience in child rearing (Groce & Zola, 1993). Although young professionals may feel qualified to approach these families using an expert–patient model of interaction, families may not be willing to accept young professionals as experts on child rearing.

Turn-taking and Back Channel Cues: Overlap Versus Interruption

Different cultures have different expectations for how long communication turns should last, when turns should be taken, and how listeners should show support and engagement while a communication partner is speaking. Listeners show support and engagement with the use of back channel cues (e.g., head nods, subvocalizations such as "mhm" or "uhuh," repetitions of words or sentences) (Tannen, 2006). These back channel cues are standard demonstrations of engagement or even agreement with a speaker; in some cultures, the use of certain back channel cues constitutes an interruption and may be seen by the speaker as an impolite bid for the floor (Tannen, 2006).

Turn-taking in White American culture is highly regulated by formality and power; the communication partner with the most power or status will subtly determine when turns switch hands (Kochman, 1981). Contrary to the White American turn-taking style, African Americans tend to allow the content of a conversation to dictate the turn-taking (i.e., anyone with something to add to the content under discussion may comfortably make a bid for the conversational space; Kochman, 1981). Miscues about when a speaker is signaling the availability of a turn can lead White Americans to see African Americans as rude and disrespectful of formal power structures, whereas African Americans may see Whites as uptight or disengaged.

For example, the call-and-response verbalizations (i.e., shout outs) used across many settings in African American culture to show contextually mandated participation and engagement (e.g., religious services, greetings, audience participation in public speaking events) are seen as rude, loud, and disorderly by many Whites; however, remaining completely silent in these contexts would be viewed as snobbish or cold by African Americans (Hughes & Baldwin, 2002; Kochman, 1981; Smitherman, 1977).

The use of back channel cues also differs between Whites and African Americans. For example, whereas Whites often use perpendicular head-nodding to indicate agreement or understanding of a speaker's message, African Americans often use perpendicular head-nodding to convey an invitation for a communication partner to take the floor or a signal that a turn-taking opportunity has arrived (Asante & Davis, 1985; Hughes & Baldwin, 2002). What may be interpreted by an African American listener as an invitation to speak, could lead a White speaker to feel interrupted.

These differences in turn-taking styles and back channel cues can lead to cross-cultural miscommunications between Whites and African Americans. For example, Whites often misinterpret African American listeners' back channel cue usage to mean that African American listeners are not interested or not paying attention to what is being said, leading Whites to use more repetitions and slowed clarifications when speaking to African Americans (Hughes & Baldwin, 2002), which, in turn, may lead African American listeners to interpret their White communication partners as being condescending (Hughes & Baldwin, 2002).

Cultural turn-taking rules also vary for children. In White American culture, children are encouraged to converse with adults as full communication partners (Stewig & Jett-Simpson, 1995). However, in African American and Latino cultures, children are not considered equal communication partners with adults. Children are expected to be silent while adults are conversing, interruptions are not tolerated, and children are expected to wait until all adult turn-taking has concluded before they attempt to enter adult conversations (Fantini, 1978; Heath, 1983). The child-directed communication focus of many popular intervention and therapy contexts may be culturally incompatible with many CELD children and their families. Families for whom child-directed communication is not a natural communication style may need to be convinced of the value of this approach and may need to be coached on the use of this style in a community that does not typically endorse child-directed communication.

High-Context versus Low-Context Communication Styles

In low-context cultures the communication partner who is sending the message is responsible for explicitly delivering it to the person receiving the message (Bennett, 1999; Hall, 1976, 1983). Context is not relied on for interpretation of the message, rather the message itself is relied on for the interpretation of meaning. The low-context style of communication is generally linked with more individualistic cultures (Hall, 1976, 1983; Sanchez-Burks et al., 2003).

In high-context cultures the person who is receiving the message is responsible for interpreting implicit cues from the communication context in order to correctly derive the message (Hall, 1976, 1983; Sanchez-Burks et al., 2003). Context is essential in interpretation of the message, and the message itself is relied on less than context for the interpretation of meaning. This style of communication is generally linked with more collectivistic cultures (Hall, 1983; Sanchez-Burks et al., 2003).

Many White American communicators tend to use a low-context communication style and may miss communicative intent when conversing with a partner from a high-context culture simply because they do not rely on contextual cues to determine meaning. Low-context listeners may be perceived as being crude and unsubtle in this regard. Conversely, high-context listeners may miss communicative intent when conversing with a partner from a low-context culture simply because they rely on context to read messages in which perhaps no contextual cues were intended. As speakers, individuals from high-context cultures may be viewed as indirect and unclear by individuals from low-context cultures who are not reading contextual cues to derive meaning.

High- and low-context cultures also tend to differ in the formality of their communications and their turn-taking expectations. Most low-context cultures tend to rely on formality in order to determine when turns should be taken and when new speakers may enter a conversation (Bennett, 1999). Interruptions are expected to be timed so that they align with the end of a conversational topic because the messages being relayed are essential to communication partners' understandings of the communication interaction (Bennett, 1999). The messages being relayed in high-context cultures, however, depend more on the context for communication, and turn-taking rules or introductions of new speakers are less formal (Bennett, 1999). A new communication partner can be welcomed into a conversation without it being perceived as an interruption (Bennett, 1999).

For CELD children and families who are from a high-context cultures, adhering to a treatment or intervention routine that does not fit into the family's existing communication styles and routines may mean relegating treatment and intervention to a very specific context (e.g., a laboratory, a clinic, the kitchen table, the child's bedroom). It may be difficult for high-context families to extend the intervention or treatment demands to multiple contexts (e.g., school communication, family communication, community gatherings), and relying on a specific and limited context may be the natural means by which these families are able to incorporate culturally different communication routines into their lives. Researchers and practitioners should be aware that the extent to which an intervention or treatment deviates from the natural cultural practices of CELD children and families will undoubtedly affect treatment fidelity.

Coping with Cross-Cultural Miscommunications

Even when these various components of communication style are considered separately, the potential for miscommunications between communication partners from different cultural, ethnic, and linguistic backgrounds is obvious. However, as each of the dimensions of communication style is combined within individuals to create an individual's global communication style, the potential for cross-cultural miscommunications is enormous. Many of the practitioners delivering language interventions for CELD children with severe disabilities are White and middle class, due in large part to stark differences in social and cultural capital and, by implication, educational attainment in the United States (Sullivan, 2001). As such, their communication styles will not necessarily reflect the styles of CELD children and families receiving services and interventions.

Researchers and practitioners who wish to engage in effective cross-cultural communication with families from diverse cultural and linguistic backgrounds can work to prevent cross-cultural miscommunications by acknowledging 1) that they have a particular communication style that is influenced by individual personality as well as the larger sociocultural conventions of what is an acceptable communication style for a person in their region, of their gender, age, and socioeconomic status; 2) that as a member of their culture, they have been bombarded with certain culturally sanctioned stereotypes about individuals from other cultures, and the first step in questioning those stereotypes is a willingness to acknowledge that they exist; and 3) that resolving miscommunications will require some communication style flexibility, and much of the responsibility for that flexibility falls to them because service providers and researchers are in the role of expert.

CONCLUSION

The National Joint Committee for the Communicative Needs of Persons with Severe Disabilities (1992) emphasized the importance of modifications to the environment as well as collaboration between family members and professionals in order to facilitate communication. These two tenets should guide work with all children with disabilities and are particularly critical for CELD children and their families.

Modifications to Accommodate Communication Must Begin with Valid Measurement

Practitioners cannot begin to identify the environmental features that should be modified for communication if they have not assessed the child and his or her environment using culturally valid instruments. Evaluation of CELD children with severe disabilities can be negatively affected by culturally biased assessment instruments; however, finding assessment instruments that are sensitive and appropriate for children with severe disabilities can be challenging or impossible. It is critical that only instruments with proven track records for use with CELD populations be selected, when possible, and that they be developed for use with CELD populations in instances where they do not yet exist. Failure to utilize culturally valid instruments can result in biased results and inappropriate treatment decisions, particularly when the child comes from a home in which a different dialect or language constitutes the primary language environment.

Successful intervention with children and families from CELD backgrounds may require special consideration of language usage not only during the measurement phase of intervention but also during the planning, implementation, and evaluation stages. Beyond the use of culturally valid measurement instruments, explicit questions regarding language status (as opposed to only race and ethnicity) should be included in the measurement of demographic variables because linguistic minority status is arguably more predictive of community membership and involvement than the categories of race or ethnicity that are traditionally measured.

After the initial measurement phase of intervention, the planning and implementation phases should incorporate an explicitly identified model of disability, family language usage, and communication style into intervention design and delivery. The evaluation phase of intervention must reflect the measurements taken during initial assessment and the goals established during intervention design; however, the ultimate success of the intervention will depend on the extent to which families' and researchers'/practitioners' were able to collaborate, identify, and resolve divergent models of disability, expectations for disability outcomes, and cultural and linguistic communication values.

Collaboration Between Family Members and Professionals

Children with severe disabilities are often defined by their disabilities rather than their cultures, but culture has a tremendous impact on many aspects of intervention, including participation and compliance. Recognizing and acknowledging differences in communication styles and perceptions of disability is key to designing and implementing culturally appropriate interventions, establishing collaborative relationships with families, and considering families' beliefs and expectations in intervention designs.

Future research should focus on developing community-based participatory action models of research and intervention that emphasize active and equal partnerships between researchers, practitioners, children, families, and communities (O'Fallon & Dearry, 2002). In these models, researchers and practitioners begin by evaluating their own language status, preferred communication styles, and models of disability and work closely to identify those points of departure from the families that they serve. Furthermore, the family's inputs and goals are explicitly identified and incorporated into communication interventions. Intervention implementation constitutes an ongoing partnership between professionals, families, and community stakeholders. Finally, results from intervention evaluation are actively disseminated and discussed.

Overall, it is important for practitioners and researchers to be aware of the cultural, ethnic, and linguistic background of the children and families that they serve and study and to adapt their expectations and service delivery models to accommodate the differences that they encounter. Successful evaluation and intervention with CELD children and families demands maximal flexibility and understanding on the part of both researchers and practitioners.

REFERENCES

Adler, S., & Birdsong, S. (1983). Reliability and validity of standardized testing tools used with poor children. *Topics in Language Disorders, 3*(3), 76–88.

American Psychiatric Association. (2013). *Diagnostic and Statistical Manual of Mental Disorders, Fifth Edition (DSM-V)*. Arlington, VA: Author.

Americans with Disabilities Act (ADA) of 1990, PL 101-336, 42 U.S.C. §§ 12101 *et seq.*

Asante, M., & Davis, A. (1985). Black and white communication: Analyzing work place encounters. *Journal of Black Studies, 16,* 77–93.

Batalova, J., & McHugh, M. (2010). *Top languages spoken by English language learners nationally and by state.* Washington, DC: Migration Policy Institute.

Bennett, C. (1999). *A comprehensive multicultural education* (4th ed.). Boston, MA: Allyn & Bacon.

Bialystok, E. (2001). *Bilingualism in development: Language, literacy, and cognition.* Cambridge, United Kingdom: Cambridge University Press.

Bialystok, E. (2007). Acquisition of literacy in bilingual children: A framework for research. *Language Learning, 57,* 45–77.

Bialystok, E. (2011). Reshaping the mind: The benefits of bilingualism. *Canadian Journal of Experimental Psychology, 65*(4), 229–235.

Blankenship, D., & Madson, N. (2007). *Resource guide for serving refugees with disabilities.* Washington, DC: United States Committee for Refugees and Immigrants.

Bowe, F. (1984). *U.S. Census and disabled adults.* Hot Springs, AR: University of Arkansas, Arkansas Rehabilitation Services, Arkansas Rehabilitation Research and Training Center.

Brault, M. (2010). Americans with disabilities: 2010. In U.S. Census Bureau (Ed.), *Current population reports* (pp. 70–131). Washington, DC: U.S. Census Bureau.

Campbell, T., Dollaghan, C., Needleman, H., & Janosky, J. (1997). Reducing bias in language assessment: Processing-dependent measures. *Journal of Speech, Language, and Hearing Research, 40*(3), 519-525.

Capps, R., Fix, M., Ost, J., Reardon-Anderson, J., & Passel, J.S. (2004). *The health and well-being of young children of immigrants.* Washington, DC: The Urban Institute.

Cargile, A.C. (2000). Evaluations of employment suitability: Does accent always matter? *Journal of Employment Counseling, 37*(3), 165–177.

Carlo, M.S., August, D., McLaughlin, B., Snow, C.E., Dressler, C., Lippman, D.N., White, C.E. (2004). Closing the gap: Addressing the vocabulary needs of English language learners in bilingual and mainstream classrooms. *Reading Research Quarterly, 39*(2), 188–215.

Charity, A.H., Scarborough, H.S., & Griffin, D.M. (2004). Familiarity with school English in African American children and its relation to early reading achievement. *Child Development, 75*(5), 1340–1356.

Charity Hudley, A.H. (2010). Standardized assessment of African American children: A sociolinguistic perspective. In M. Farr, L. Seloni, & J. Song (Eds.), *Ethnolinguistic diversity and education: Language, literacy, and culture* (pp. 167–192). New York, NY: Routledge.

Cole, P.A., & Taylor, O.L. (1990). Performance of working class African-American children on three tests of articulation. *Language, Speech, and Hearing Services in Schools, 21*(3), 171-176.

Connor, C.M. (2008). Language and literacy connections for children who are African American. *Perspectives on Communication Disorders and Sciences in Culturally and Linguistically Diverse Populations, 15*(2), 43–53.

Craig, H.K. & Washington, J.A. (1995). African American English and linguistic complexity in preschool discourse: A second look. *Language, Speech, and Hearing Services in Schools, 26*(1), 87–93.

Craig, H.K., Washington, J.A., & Thompson-Porter, C. (1998). Average c-unit lengths in the discourse of African American children from low income, urban homes. *Journal of Speech and Hearing Research, 41*(2), 433–444.

Elementary and Secondary Education Act Amendments of 1968, PL 90-247, 20 U.S.C. §§ 877b *et seq.*

Emerson, E. (2012). Deprivation, ethnicity, and the prevalence of intellectual and developmental disabilities. *Journal of Epidemiology and Community Health, 66,* 218–224.

Fantini, A.E. (1978). *Language acquisition of a bilingual child: A sociolinguistic perspective.* Putney, VT: Experimental Press.

Figueroa, R. (1989). Psychological testing of linguistic minority students: Knowledge gaps and regulations. *Exceptional Children, 56,* 145–152.

Gilson, S.F., & Depoy, E. (2000). Multiculturalism and disability: A critical perspective. *Disability and Society, 15*(2), 207–218.

Gleeson, B. (1997). Disability studies: A historical materialist view. *Disability and Society, 12*(2), 179–202.

Goodwin, R., & Lee, I. (1994). Taboo topics among Chinese and English friends: A cross-cultural comparison. *Journal of Cross-Cultural Psychology, 25,* 325–338.

Groce, N.E., & Zola, I.K. (1993). Multiculturalism, chronic illness, and disability. *Pediatrics, 91,* 1048–1055.

Grogger, J. (2011). Speech patterns and racial wage inequality. *Journal of Human Resources, 46,* 1–25.

Hall, E.T. (1976). *Beyond culture.* New York, NY: Anchor Press/Doubleday.

Hall, E.T. (1983). *The dance of life: The other dimension of time.* New York, NY: Doubleday.

Hayes-Bautista, D. (1992). Latino health indicators and the underclass model: From paradox to new policy models. In A. Furino (Ed.), *Health policy and the Hispanic* (pp. 32–47). Boulder, CO: Westview.

Heath, S. (1983). *Ways with words: Language, life and work in communities and classrooms.* Cambridge, United Kingdom: Cambridge University Press.

Hecht, M.L., Ribeau, S., & Alberts, J.K. (1989). An Afro-American perspective on interethnic communication. *Communication Monographs, 56,* 385–410.

Hughes, P.C., & Baldwin, J.R. (2002). Black, white, and shades of gray: Communication predictors of stereotypic impressions. *Southern Communication Journal, 68,* 40–56.

Huntington, S. (2004). Mexican immigration and Hispanization. In *Who are we? The challenges to America's national identity* (pp. 221–256). New York, NY: Simon & Schuster.

Iezzoni, L.I., & Freedman, V.A. (2008). Turning the disability tide: The importance of definitions. *JAMA, 299*(3), 332–334.

Individuals with Disabilities Education Improvement Act (IDEA) of 2004, PL 108-446, 20 U.S.C. §§ 1400 *et seq.*.

Kay-Raining Bird, E., Cleave, P., Trudeau, N., Thordardottir, E., Sutton, A., & Thorpe, A. (2005). The language abilities of bilingual children with Down syndrome. *American Journal of Speech-Language Pathology, 14,* 187–199.

Kay-Raining Bird, E., Lamond, E., & Holden, J. (2011). Research report: Survey of bilingualism in autism spectrum disorders. *International Journal of Language and Communication Disorders, 47,* 52–64.

Klingner, J.K., Artiles, A.J., Kozleski, E., Harry, B., Zion, S., Tate, W., & Riley, D. (2005). Addressing the disproportionate representation of culturally and linguistically diverse students in special education through culturally responsive educational systems. *Education Policy Analysis Archives, 13,* n38.

Kochman, T. (1981). *Black and white styles in conflict.* Chicago, IL: University of Chicago Press.

Laing, S.P., & Kamhi, A. (2003). Alternative assessment of language and literacy in culturally and linguistically diverse populations. *Language, Speech, and Hearing Services in Schools, 34*(1), 44–55.

Lester, G., & Kelman, M. (1997). State disparities in the diagnosis and placement of pupils with learning disabilities. *Journal of Learning Disabilities, 30,* 599–607.

Lollar, D., & Crews, J. (2003). Redefining the role of public health in disability. *Annual Review of Public Health, 24,* 195–208.

Mandell, D., Wiggins, L., Carpenter, L., Daniels, J., DiGuiseppi, C., Durkin, M., Kirby, R. (2009). Racial/ethnic disparities in the identification of children with autism spectrum disorders. *American Journal of Public Health, 99,* 493–498.

National Joint Committee for the Communication Needs of Persons with Severe Disabilities. (1992). *Guidelines for meeting the communication needs of persons with severe disabilities* [Guidelines]. Retrieved from http://www.asha.org/njc

No Child Left Behind Act of 2001, PL 107-110, 115 Stat. 1425, 20 U.S.C. §§ 6301 *et seq.*

O'Fallon, L., & Dearry, A. (2002). Community-based participatory research as a tool to advance environmental health sciences. *Environmental Health Perspectives, 110,* 155–159.

Oswald, D.P., Coutinho, M.J., & Best, A.M. (2002). Community and school predictors of overrepresentation of minority children in special education. In D.J. Losen, G. Orfield, & J.M. Jeffords (Eds.), *Racial inequity in special education* (pp. 1–13). Cambridge, MA: Harvard Educational Publishing Group.

Pfeiffer, D. (1998). The ICIDH and the need for its revision. *Disability and Society, 13,* 503–523.

Pfeiffer, D. (2000). The devils are in the details: The ICIDH2 and the disability movement. *Disability and Society, 15,* 1079–1082.

Pickl, G. (2011). Communication intervention in children with severe disabilities and multilingual backgrounds: Perceptions of pedagogues and parents. *Augmentative and Alternative Communication, 27,* 229–244.

Plyler v. Doe, 457 U.S. 202 (1982).

Qi, C.H., Kaiser, A.P., Milan, S., & Hancock, T. (2006). Language performance of low-income African American and European American preschool children on the PPVT-III. *Language, Speech, and Hearing Services in Schools, 37*(1), 5–16.

Quinn, P. (1997). *Understanding disability: A lifespan approach.* Thousand Oaks, CA: Sage Publications.

Restrepo, M.A., Schwanenflugel, P.J., Blake, J., Neuharth-Pritchett, S., Cramer, S.E., & Ruston, H.P. (2006). Performance on the PPVT-III and the EVT: Applicability of the measures with African American and European American preschool children. *Language, Speech, and Hearing Services in Schools, 37*(1), 17–27.

Saffran, J.R. (2003). Statistical language learning mechanisms and constraints.

Current directions in psychological science, 12(4), 110–114.

Sanchez-Burks, J., Lee, F., Choi, I., Nisbett, R., Zhao, S., & Koo, J. (2003). Conversing across cultures: East-West communication styles in work and non-work contexts. *Journal of Personality and Social Psychology, 85*(2), 363–372.

Shakespeare, T., & Waston, N. (1997). Defending the social model. *Disability and Society, 12*(2), 293–300.

Smart, J., & Smart D. (1997). The racial/ethnic demography of disability. *Journal of Rehabilitation, 63,* 9–15.

Smart, J.F., & Smart, D.W. (2006). Models of disability: Implications for the counseling profession. *Journal of Counseling and Development, 84*(1), 29–40.

Smitherman, G. (1977). *Talkin' and testifyin': The language of black Americans.* Boston, MA: Houghton Mifflin.

Stewig, J.W., & Jett-Simpson, M. (1995). *Language arts in the early childhood classroom.* Belmont, CA: Wadsworth.

Stockman, I.J. (2000). The new Peabody Picture Vocabulary Test–III: An illusion of unbiased assessment? *Language, Speech, and Hearing Services in Schools, 31*(4), 340–353.

Stockman, I. (2010). A review of developmental and applied language research on African American children: From a deficit to difference perspective on dialect differences. *Language, Speech, and Hearing Services in Schools, 41,* 23–38.

Sullivan, A. (2001). Cultural capital and educational attainment. *Sociology, 35*(4), 893–912.

Tannen, D. (2006). Language and culture. In R. Fasold & J. Connor-Linton (Eds.), *An introduction to language and linguistics* (pp. 343–372). New York, NY: Cambridge University Press.

Terry, N.P., & Connor, C.M. (2012). Changing nonmainstream American English use and early reading achievement from kindergarten to first grade. *American Journal of Speech-Language Pathology, 21,* 78–86.

Thomas-Tate, S., Washington, J.A., Craig, H.K., & Packard, M.E.W. (2006). Performances of African American preschool and kindergarten students on the Expressive Vocabulary Test. *Language, Speech, and Hearing Services in Schools, 37,* 143–149.

Thornhill, H., & HoSang, D. (1988). Poverty, race, and capability. In S. Walker, J. Fowler, R. Nicholls, & K. Turner (Eds.), *Building bridges to independent employment successes, problems, and needs of African Americans with disabilities* (pp. 148–157). Washington, DC: Howard University School of Education, Center for the Study of Handicapped Children and Youth.

UNICEF. (2013). *The state of the world's children 2013: Children with disabilities.* Retrievedfromhttp://www.uis.unesco.org/Library/Documents/state-world-children-2013-children-with-disabilities-en

Urban Institute & Child Trends. (2007). *National Survey of America's Families (NSAF): 2002.* Ann Arbor, MI: Inter-university Consortium for Political and Social Research.

U.S. Department of Education. (2010). *Thirty-five years of progress in educating children with disabilities through IDEA.* Retrieved from http://www2.ed.gov/about/offices/list/osers/idea35/history/idea-35-history.pdf

Washington, J.A., & Craig, H.K. (1999). Performances of at-risk, African American preschoolers on the Peabody Picture Vocabulary Test–III. *Language, Speech, and Hearing Services in Schools, 30*(1), 75–82.

Wolfram, W., & Thomas, E. (2002). *The development of African American English.* Oxford, UK: Blackwell Publishers.

World Health Organization. (2002). *Towards a common language for functioning, disability, and health: ICF.* Retrieved from http://www.who.int/classifications/icf/training/icfbeginnersguide.pdf

SOURCE FOR THE DATA IN TABLE 1

Global Disability Prevalence Estimates

One of the most informative estimates of world-wide disability prevalence is the WHO's World Health Survey (WHS), collected across 70 countries during 2002 – 2004. The WHS used face-to-face surveys with questions generated from the ICF's bio-psycho-social model of disability. Results from this survey indicated that globally, approximately 15.6% (approximately 650 million) of adults 18+ years of age experience significant difficulties in functioning in their everyday lives. This estimate tended to be higher in lower income countries (18.0%; WHO, 2011, Chapter 2). Approximately 2.2% of adults 18+ years of age experienced very significant difficulties (WHO, 2011). Although this survey did not include disability prevalence estimates for children and adolescents, the WHO noted that across the countries surveyed, other vulnerable groups (e.g., women, those experiencing poverty, elderly adults) had higher prevalence of disability. The WHO also noted that despite using the ICF as a model of measuring disability across persons, activities, and environments, the cultural differences in the perception and expectations of disability and environmental factors contributing to functioning were not necessarily captured across the many cultural contexts included in the WHS (WHO, 2011).

The WHO's, World Bank's, and Harvard School of Public Health's Global Burden of Disease (GBD) study is another leading source for global estimates of disability prevalence; however, the GBD defines disability in terms of loss of health due to limitations in function (including limitations in mobility, cognition, hearing, and vision) without explicit consideration of environmental factors that may interact with individuals to produce these limitations in functioning (WHO 2008 Chap 2; GBD). This model of disability, while it may appear to be functional-environmental on the surface, is arguably a medical model of disability because it does not account for sources of disability that might be located outside of individuals experiencing disability. The GBD estimated the prevalence of severe disability at around 19 million people worldwide (approximately 3%) and the prevalence of moderate to severe disability at around 80 million people worldwide (approximately 12%; WHO, 2008). Unlike the World Health Survey, the Global Burden of Disease study did account for children in its global estimates of disability prevalence. Of those persons experiencing moderate and severe disabilities, approximately 5% were children under the age of 14 years (WHO, 2008). The WHO noted that consistently, the prevalence of moderate to severe disability was related to national income and age, with higher rates of disability experienced in low to middle-income countries and among older individuals (WHO, 2008).

United States National Disability Prevalence Estimates

Within the U.S. estimates of disability prevalence also vary across studies, and these differences can be largely attributed to differences in the definitions of disability. For example, the American Community Survey (ACS; Erickson, Lee, & von Schrader, 2013) uses six questions to assess disability prevalence among respondents. ACS questions address auditory, visual, ambulatory, cognitive, and self-care disabilities within persons, arguably from a medical model perspective of disability. However, the ACS also includes one question regarding disability in the domain of independent living (i.e., doing errands alone), which is arguably approaching disability from a functional-environmental perspective. The most recent ACS survey estimated that approximately 12% of Americans ages 0 to 75+ years experienced disabilities (Erickson, Lee, & von Schrader, 2013).

The Current Population Survey defines disability in terms of an inability to work or an impediment to the amount and type of work respondents can undertake (CPS; Nazarov & Lee, 2012). In this sense, the CPS defines disability as a functional limitation under a functional-environmental model of disability. The most recent CPS estimated the prevalence of disability within the U.S. at approximately 8.1% of adults aged 18 to 64 years (Nazarov & Lee, 2012).

Perhaps the most popular measure of disability prevalence in the U.S. is the U.S. Census, which includes questions about disability in the sensory, physical, mental, and self-care domains. Respondents who indicate the presence of physical impairments (e.g., deafness, blindness), or functional limitations (e.g., difficulty walking, learning, concentrating, dressing, or bathing) are considered to have a disability using the Census long form (Erickson & Lee, 2005). In this sense, the U.S. Census blends the traditional medical model with the newer functional-environmental model of disability. The 2000 U.S. Census estimated disability prevalence at approximately 9.7% for adults age 16 to 64 years and 5.8% for children age 5 to 15 years, placing the total American prevalence of disability at approximately 15.5% (Erickson & Lee, 2005).

Table 1 presents a summary of the disability prevalence estimates reviewed. In general, estimates of disability vary across surveys due to survey methodologies, models of disability employed, ages included, and cultural contexts. Across surveys, estimating disability prevalence among children is difficult, which may be especially worrisome given the importance of early intervention in facilitating positive long-term outcomes for individuals with developmental disabilities. It is also important to note that across surveys, the disability prevalence in vulnerable populations (including women, children, elderly adults, individuals experiencing poverty, and minorities) is higher than disability prevalence in the general population.

REFERENCES

Erickson, W., Lee, C., von Schrader, S. (2013). Disability Statistics from the 2011 American Community Survey (ACS). Ithaca, NY: Cornell University Employment and Disability Institute (EDI). Retrieved from www.disabilitystatistics.org.

Erickson, W., Lee, C. (2005). Disability Statistics from the Decennial Census 2000. Ithaca, NY: Cornell University Rehabilitation Research and Training Center on Disability Demographics and Statistics (StatsRRTC). Retrieved from www.disabilitystatistics.org

Nazarov, Z., & Lee, C. (2012). Disability Statistics from the Current Population Survey (CPS). Ithaca, NY: Cornell University Rehabilitiation Research and Training Center on Disability Demographics and Statistics (StatsRRTC). Retrieved from www.disabilitystatistics.org.

WHO. (2008). *The global burden of disease: 2004 update*. Geneva, Switzerland: World Health Organization.

WHO (2011). World report on disability. Geneva, Switzerland: World Health Organization. Retrieved from www.who.int.

14

Measuring Communication and Language Skills in Individuals with Severe Intellectual Disabilities

Billy T. Ogletree

Society's attitudes about individuals with severe disabilities have become more inclusive, resulting in this group's increased participation in most activities of everyday life. The population's greater presence in educational, community, and work settings has placed new pressures on researchers and allied health providers to generate and implement effective therapeutic practices. This chapter explores one area of this effort—the measurement of communication and language skills.

Efforts to measure communication and language have traditionally occurred for the following purposes: 1) to determine the presence of a disability, 2) to consider the magnitude of that disability relative to preset standards to provide rationale for therapeutic services, and 3) to assess the effects of intervention services received. The last of these purposes is of primary importance in the case of individuals with severe disabilities. That is, although the presence of a disability is obvious and eligibility for services via normative or other comparisons is less than relevant, the ability to measure treatment gains is critical to setting a meaningful intervention course. This chapter shows how treatment success has been and can be measured.

The chapter attempts to provide context by defining individuals with severe disabilities and reviewing seminal literature specific to communication and language measurement with this population. It concludes by describing the challenges associated with measuring communication and language and proposes new directions for researchers and practitioners.

DEFINING SEVERE DISABILITIES

The American Association on Intellectual and Developmental Disabilities (AAIDD) stated that intellectual disability (ID) originates before the age of 18 and "is characterized by significant limitations in both intellectual functioning and adaptive behavior as expressed in conceptual, social, and practical adaptive skills" (2010, p. 1). Westling and Fox (2014) reported that the AAIDD definition emanates from a theoretical model that considers specific ID, adaptive behavior, health, participation, and life contexts. These model dimensions interact reciprocally with the support received by an individual to contribute to overall functioning. For example, a child with significantly impaired intellectual and adaptive abilities and relatively good health may function well in his or her daily environment when provided ongoing support.

Although AAIDD eliminated categories of ID based in intelligence quotient in 1992, the classification of people by level of ID has been reported to be useful (Shapiro & Batshaw, 2013). Individuals categorized with severe ID have measured IQs from 20 to 40, whereas those with profound ID present IQs less than 20 (Westling & Fox, 2014). This said, categorization by IQ alone has limited utility. In contrast, an appreciation of typical ranges of developmental or adaptive functioning can assist with understanding these groups, both independently and collectively. Developmental functioning has been reported to range from 1 year to 30 months for people with severe ID and less than 1 year for those who are profoundly impaired (Sternberg, 1988; Westling & Fox, 2014). Both groups present significantly limited adaptive abilities. Individuals with severe impairments likely need assistance or reminders to be independent with daily activities (e.g., feeding, dressing, self-care) and present limited academic abilities (e.g., reading, writing, manipulating money). People with profound ID present a range of functioning that includes relative independence to total dependence with self-care and other tasks (Westling & Fox, 2014). These groups are exceptionally heterogeneous when collectively considered. This is nowhere more apparent than in the area of communication in which functioning can range from the absence of intentional communication to the use and understanding of symbols, including some speech and short sentences.

Although AAIDD uses the notion of support to explain functioning, another specific definition of severe ID is much more explicit in this regard. TASH, an organization formerly known as The Association for Persons with Severe Handicaps and presently advocating for opportunities for all individuals with disabilities, defines people with severe ID as people

> of all ages who require extensive ongoing support in more than one major life activity to participate in integrated community settings and to enjoy a quality of life that is available to citizens with fewer or no disabilities. Support may be required for life activities such as mobility, self-care, and learning as necessary for independent living, employment, and self-sufficiency. (Meyer, Peck, & Brown, 1991, p. 19)

The TASH definition strongly suggests that successful community access and integration for people with severe disabilities depends on support across all life areas. Interestingly, effective communication plays a critical role in each of the areas mentioned in the definition. Focusing on support rather than IQ or developmental/adaptive functioning results in the inclusion of more people under the severe classification. For example, individuals traditionally classified as presenting moderate ID could have high support needs, making them severely disabled, according to TASH. Both TASH and AAIDD suggest that individuals with disabilities must be viewed with regard to support needs rather than developmental/adaptive deficits or measured IQ. IQ is a unitary concept and, thus, counterintuitive to the notion of individual complexity.

People with severe disabilities can be best defined by their heterogeneous, yet relatively limited, functioning compared with those with less or no disability. This range of abilities and subsequent needs requires significant and ongoing support for the achievement of objectives in the areas of education, community integration, employment, and self-determination. Traditional groups frequently integrate under a broad definition of severe disabilities, including individuals with moderate, severe, or profound ID; concomitant physical, sensory, and ID; and some on the autism spectrum (Westling & Fox, 2014).

For the purpose of this chapter, individuals with severe disabilities are considered according to their communication characteristics. A thorough knowledge of communication abilities and needs obviously helps those involved in this groups' care understand their functioning and plan for their supports and accommodations.

McLean and Snyder-McLean (1988) applied a pragmatics model to the description of expressive abilities in people with severe disabilities, noting that communicative behaviors can be locutionary, illocutionary, and perlocutionary. They described locutionary communication as being expressed through specialized communicative forms (e.g., speech, other symbols). Locutionary communication has been referred to as symbolic and, for some, linguistic. McLean and Snyder-McLean described illocutionary communication as dual focused and expressing communicative intent. These behaviors were noted to be persistent and purposeful, yet nonsymbolic. In contrast, perlocutionary communication has also been referred to as pre- or nonintentional and was described by McLean and Snyder-McLean as single focused and dependent on partners for interpretation. Each individual also presents receptive abilities that are either nonsymbolic or symbolic, regardless of the complexity of one's expressive abilities. Those individuals who understand symbols may or may not understand spoken language. The review that follows considers the measurement of nonsymbolic and symbolic expressive and receptive communication and language abilities in individuals with severe disabilities.

MEASURING COMMUNICATION AND LANGUAGE: AN HISTORICAL REVIEW

Joseph Spradlin stated the following in his early chapter on assessment and ID, "When one engages in speech and language research, he is immediately faced with measurement problems" (1963, p. 8). The challenges faced by Spradlin and others measuring the communication and language of people with ID have not abated since the early 1960s. That said, theorists and practitioners have worked tirelessly to describe and account for behavior changes in this population. Measurement has evolved in ways largely consistent with changing theoretical views of language development. The review that follows considers the question of what measurement is and presents a historical context for the measurement of communication and language in people with severe disabilities.

For the purpose of this chapter, measurement is considered the collection of data on specific targets relevant to communication and language. It involves the targets of investigation (dependent variables) and the processes used to collect data. Clearly, measurement can include expressive or receptive targets specific to the communicator. It has also grown to include much more, such as characteristics of communicative partners and environments (Siegel-Causey & Bashinski, 1997).

McCarthy (1946) identified four evaluation targets most often used in the measurement of children's speech and language.

1. Age of first words
2. Vocabulary size
3. Grammatical constructions
4. Articulatory competence

Unfortunately, during the early 20th century, children with ID were likely excluded from assessments according to these or other metrics due to their limited access to educational and therapeutic services. Their exclusion primarily related to a prevailing belief that this population could not benefit from language training (Schroeder & Reese, 2007). This opinion was particularly true for those individuals presenting severe disabilities.

In the 1960s, a behavioral view of language acquisition provided an initial impetus for the measurement of speech-language structures in individuals with ID. Much of the early work came from the University of Kansas' Communication and Language Program, which functioned under the assumption that the speech and language of people with ID could be improved through the application of systematic behavioral principles (Romski & Sevcik, 2000; Saunders, Spradlin, & Sherman, 2006; Schiefelbusch & Lloyd, 1974).

Spradlin (1963) reported selecting a Skinnerian model (Skinner, 1953, 1957) in his development of measurement targets and procedures due to the model's focus on environmental conditions and their role in language behaviors. He described the importance of recording mand behaviors (e.g., verbal or gestural demanding, commanding, requesting, asking), tact behaviors (e.g., verbal naming, gesturally descriptive responses in the presence of discriminative stimuli), and verbal behavior under the control of verbal stimuli (e.g., echoic, intraverbal, comprehension responses). Spradlin's inclusion of comprehension with behavior under the control of verbal stimuli is interesting. He described comprehension as a construct evident when a person offers a differential response to a verbal behavior bearing some relationship to that behavior (e.g., a nod after hearing, "Are you Okay?"). The measurement of comprehension in people with severe disabilities has long been a difficult, if not avoided, task, which will become apparent throughout this chapter (Sevcik & Romski, 2002).

Spradlin (1963) described the Parsons Language Sample (PLS) (not to be confused with the Preschool Language Scales [Steiner & Pond, 2011]) as a systematic attempt to sample language behavior. He created seven subtests and 123 test items consistent with the Skinnerian model previously described. Spradlin's Tact subtest consisted of objects or pictures that are named by the child after being asked, "What is it?" or "What do you call it?" The examiner spoke words or sentences of varying complexity during the Echoic subtest that the child was expected to repeat. The Gesture subtest presented motor acts to mimic. The acts were accompanied by pointing or the verbal request to "Do this." In a similar fashion, the Comprehension subtest presented the child with a series of motor requests paired with gestural or vocal directions. The Intraverbal subtest presented the child with simple questions or incomplete sentences requiring verbal responses, whereas the Intraverbal Gesture subtest presented questions designed to elicit gestural responses (e.g., "Where is your ear?"). Finally, the PLS Mand subtest consisted of items interspersed throughout other subtests. Items could elicit either gestural or vocal responses and included actions such as holding a desirable wind-up toy in sight of the child, winding it and letting it deactivate, and putting it away. These activities were clearly designed to evoke imperative responses from the child.

Spradlin (1963) provided guidelines for administering and scoring all of the subtests. He also provided test–retest reliability and predictive utility data from the administration of the PLS with 275 children with ID who were institutionalized but ambulatory between 7 and 16 years old. Spradlin's early efforts with PLS can be summarized by saying that he measured symbolic and nonsymbolic receptive and expressive communication forms through various elicitation tasks that included verbal questioning and verbal and nonverbal modeling. He also used expectant delay and some verbal directives. Although Spradlin's recommendations were consistent with research standards of his day, he emphasized measurement targets exclusively specific to the child and most relevant for locutionary communicators. In addition, his elicitation procedures, with the exception of the Mand subtest, did not reflect naturally occurring tasks and were largely contextual.

By the 1960s and early 1970s, Chomsky's (1959) criticisms of Skinner had shifted thoughts about the very nature of language. Psycholinguists developed more intense interests in proposed innate aspects of grammar. As a result, theorists studying people with ID began to measure the acquisition of grammatical forms taught through behavioral principles (Baer & Guess, 1973; Guess, Sailor, Rutherford, & Baer, 1968). Others considered language complexity (as measured by mean length of utterance) in comparison with children without ID (Dooley, 1976). Coinciding with these efforts, researchers also measured growth in generative receptive language abilities after the application of behavioral instruction (Baer & Guess, 1971; Striefel & Wetherby, 1973).

Although several training efforts previously mentioned were successful, many individuals with ID did not benefit from instruction targeting speech, which caused researchers to explore the use of alternative symbol systems such as manual signs or geometric shapes created from three-dimensional materials and computers (Carrier, 1974; Moores, 1974; Schiefelbusch, 1980). Training efforts with nonspeech targets (e.g., sign language, communication boards) eventually grew into the present-day field of augmentative and alternative communication (AAC). The work of Premack and Premack (1974), Rumbaugh (1977), and Schiefelbusch and Hollis (1979) was central to this effort. These investigators began their work with primates after initial observations that children with ID presented language comprehension deficits and, along with others (Romski & Sevcik, 1996; Romski, White, Millen, & Rumbaugh, 1984), reported intervention outcomes for individuals who were institutionalized in the areas of symbol use, symbol combinations, word recognition, morphological and grammatical distinctions, and sentence comprehension.

The investigative focus on syntax was eventually supplanted by interest in semantics (language meaning) in the ID literature during the 1970s. Research in ID expanded to measuring receptive and expressive lexical size and diversity as well as referential capacity (Dooley, 1976). As with prior measures of expressive complexity, abilities were compared with those of children without disabilities. Pragmatics, or the use of language in context, emerged as a defining construct of language by the early 1980s. Correspondingly, researchers broadened measurement efforts to prelinguistic events, such as the emergence and expression of communicative intent as a forerunner to first words and word combinations. Studies measured the form, function, and rate of prelinguistic intentional communicative behaviors in individuals with severe disabilities (Cirrin & Rowland, 1985; Labato, Berrera, & Feldman, 1981; McLean, McLean, Brady, & Etter, 1991; McLean, Snyder-McLean, & Cirrin, 1981; Ogletree, Wetherby, & Westling, 1992).

The movement toward a pragmatic focus on communication coincided in large part with a general push for the instruction of functional skills in inclusive settings (Baine & Sobsey, 1983). By the 1980s and 1990s, successful outcomes for individuals with severe ID were measured not only in growth in this population's expressive and receptive communicative behaviors but also in changes in their environments and partners that promoted greater communicative success (Calculator & Jorgenson, 1994; Siegel-Causey, & Bashinski, 1997; Siegel & Cress, 2002; Siegel & Wetherby, 2006). Targets of child-directed intervention efforts included nonsymbolic forms and functions, emergent graphic symbol use with and without voice output, and speech (Ogletree, Fischer, & Turowski, 1996; Romski, Sevcik, & Pate, 1988). Targets for partners and environments included interactive patterns and settings that facilitated communication (Ogletree et al., 1996). Most important, social validity also emerged as a valued construct that encouraged the measurement of outcomes, which illustrated social worth in a broad context (see Chapter 15).

Parameters defining the measurement of communication and language of individuals with severe disabilities were largely set by the turn of the 21st century. Theorists and practitioners were evaluating existing speech for the locutionary communicator, in addition to a host of nonspoken symbolic forms. These efforts primarily focused on expressive abilities, and therapeutic gains were increasingly reported in the pursuit of functional and socially valid outcomes. Measurement for the illocutionary communicator focused on nonsymbolic forms and functions, whereas only limited efforts to measure movement and behavioral state as interpretable behaviors were being initiated on behalf of perlocutionary communicators (Sternberg, Pegnatore, & Hill, 1983; Sternberg & Richards, 1989; Stillman, Williams, & Linam, 1997).

As targets of measurement grew, so did the tools used in their assessment. Although research efforts continued to employ the elicitation techniques pioneered by Spradlin (1963) for PLS, they often applied test products developed for children who were typically developing (Rowland, Stillman, & Mar, 2010). Broen (1988) described the use of norm-referenced tests that yield either developmental scores (e.g., age-equivalent scores) or relative standing scores (scores comparing performance with a normative sample). Developmental scores must be interpreted with caution due to the variance of typical functioning evident throughout childhood. Limitations with scores based on a normal sample include problems with the application of normative data to individuals who are chronologically older and lower functioning (Bruce, 2011). Broen mentioned the use of criterion-referenced tests, which compare performance with content or subject matter mastery, as an alternative to norm-referenced instruments. These types of tests are limited by the degree to which they elicit a reliable response and are valid measures of the content presented. Both norm- and criterion-referenced instruments also have limitations with many individuals with ID due to physical requirements of task completion. A list of every infant–toddler test used with individuals with severe disabilities is not possible. That said, a nonexhaustive list of products reported to be frequently used with this population is provided in the following list (Rowland et al., 2010).

Battelle Developmental Inventory–Second Edition (Newborg, 2005)

Bayley Scales of Infant Development–Third Edition (Bayley, 2005)

Brigance Diagnostic Inventory of Early Development–Second Edition (Brigance, 2004)

Carolina Curriculum (Johnson-Martin, Attermeir, & Hacker, 2007)

*Communication and Symbolic Behavior Scales (Wetherby & Prizant, 1992)

*Communication and Symbolic Behavior Scales–Developmental Profile (Wetherby & Prizant, 2001)

Hawaii Early Learning Profile (Parks & Furuno, 2004)

Peabody Picture Vocabulary Test–Fourth Edition (Dunn & Dunn, 2007)

Receptive Expressive Emergent Language Test–Third Edition (Bzoch, League, & Brown, 2003)

*Rossetti Infant–Toddler Language Scale (Rossetti, 2006)

Vineland Adaptive Behavior Scales–Second Edition (Sparrow, Balla, & Cicchetti, 2006)

*Not included in citation

Aside from the previous infant–toddler assessment tools, a few products have been generated for people with severe disabilities. These instruments typically measure discrete behaviors unique to the communicator and provide a description of communication performance. The Communication Matrix is a commonly used example (Rowland, 2011), is a direct observation tool developed through several revisions (1990, 1996, 2004), and is useful with the description of emergent communication behavior from a sociopragmatic framework. The Communication Matrix describes presymbolic to symbolic expressive behaviors, including all forms of AAC. Interrater reliability with the Communication Matrix has been reported (Parker, 2009), and the instrument has proven to be sensitive to communicative change over time (Rowland & Schweigert, 2002). Rowland et al. (2010) reported that the Communication Matrix compared quite positively with infant–toddler tests when assessing the communication skills and describing the strengths and needs of children with severe disabilities. The Communication Matrix is now easily accessible online (http://www.communicationmatrix.org/whatis.aspx) and is available in Spanish (Rowland & Fried-Oken, 2010; see Chapter 4).

The Dimensions of Communication is also an instrument useful in the description of expressive communication in individuals with severe disabilities (Mar & Sall, 1999). The authors claim that it can be most useful in the absence of appropriate standard language assessment tools and note its attention to nonsymbolic and emergent symbolic forms, including AAC (Mar & Sall, 1999). The Dimensions of Communication is also unique for its attempt to link assessment and intervention planning. There has been no effort to document psychometric properties of the Dimensions of Communication, and it has primarily been used as a descriptive tool to inform treatment direction and is available online at http://documents.nationaldb.org/products/dimensions-of-communication.pdf.

The tools mentioned thus far provide a framework for clinical observation(i.e., they guide the examiner by highlighting critical skills as targets to observe, describe, and record). For example, the Communication Matrix provides illustrative descriptions of seven levels of communicative competence, including preintentional, intentional, unconventional, conventional, concrete, abstract, and language-related signal/symbol use. These frames of reference assist examiners by grounding observations and promoting consistency across assessment periods. Rowland and Schweigert (2000) used components of the matrix to provide an assessment in the changes in communication following a tangible symbol intervention for 41 children with a variety of developmental disorders.

Aside from guided observation, more casual observation of interactive episodes is also a critical component of most assessment protocols considering the expressive and receptive abilities of people with severe disabilities. Casual observations can include regarding a child and his or her mother as they interact in their home prior to formal assessment, watching an adult with a disability as he or she meets a new interactive partner in his or her work setting, or simply observing a group in a leisure activity. The use of casual observation in assessment allows examiners to appreciate the sequential and complex nature of communication (Bakeman & Gottman, 1997) and is a socially valid aspect of assessment. Romski, Sevcik, Adamson, and Bakeman (2005) adapted a standard partner observational protocol to assess the communication skills of school-age adolescents with severe disabilities after 5 years of experience with a speech-generating device. This protocol provided a way to obtain consistent information about communication across children.

Most researchers and clinicians have used structured elicitation tasks and sampling over time to supplement scores or descriptions of behavior derived from instruments like those mentioned in the previous sections. Spradlin's (1963) early PLS assessment tool relied heavily on the elicitation of behaviors. For example, his Mand subtest employed activities that placed recipients in near obligatory response contexts, such as winding and deactivating a toy and awaiting a response. The notion of sampling through enticing contexts gained credibility in the 1980s as researchers used elicitation protocols to encourage symbolic and nonsymbolic communication from children and adults with severe disabilities (Brady, McLean, McLean, & Johnston, 1995; Cirrin & Rowland, 1985; Labato et al., 1981; McLean et al., 1981; McLean et al., 1991; Ogletree et al., 1992). The Communication and Symbolic Behavior Scales (CSBS; Wetherby & Prizant, 1992, 1993) is one popular protocol. The CSBS is an infant–toddler assessment tool that provides guidelines for enticing examiner–child engagement across several assessment domains, including communication and play. Furthermore, the CSBS utilizes a popular structured sampling sequence to elicit expressive abilities. Ogletree et al. (1992) used tasks similar to those in the CSBS to assess emergent communication in people with severe disabilities (see Table 14.1). A review of the tasks in Table 14.1 makes one problem with elicitive sampling procedures painfully apparent—they require physical responses that are frequently absent in individuals with severe disabilities. Brady and Bashinski (2008) addressed this issue by adapting tasks so that they are applicable to all individuals, regardless of their motor and sensory competence (see Table 14.2).

The sampling procedures described in this chapter are most appropriate for illocutionary and emergent locutionary communicators. It can be appropriate to conduct language sampling for children who are symbolic communicators. Rosenberg

Table 14.1. Example of a structured communication sampling protocol

Tasks

- Eating a desired food item in front of the child without offering food.
- Activating a wind-up toy, letting it deactivate, and handing it to the child.
- Giving the child four blocks to drop in a box, then giving the child something different, such as a small toy, to drop in the box.
- Looking through a few books with the child.
- Opening a jar of bubbles, blowing bubbles over several turns, then closing the jar and handing it to the child.
- Initiating a social game such as Peekaboo with the child until he or she expresses pleasure, then stopping the game and waiting.
- Blowing up a balloon, letting it deflate, then holding the balloon to your mouth and waiting.
- Offing a food item the child dislikes.
- Placing the child's hands in a cold or sticky substance.
- Waving bye-bye to toys as you put them away.

(Republished with permission of American Association on Intellectual and Developmental Disabilities, Profile of the prelinguistic intentional communicative behaviors of children with profound mental retarda, Ogletree, Wetherby, & Westling, 97, 2, 1992; permission conveyed through Copyright Clearance Center, Inc.)

and Abbeduto (1993) cited several examinations of morphosyntactic development in children with ID that utilized mean length of utterance in morphemes as their metric. Other comprehensive language sampling procedures such as the Systematic Analysis of Language Transcripts (SALT; Miller & Chapman, 1985) can also be useful. SALT software manages the process of eliciting, transcribing, and analyzing language samples and, although appropriate for a smaller segment of individuals with severe disabilities who demonstrate at least a minimal degree of language/symbol complexity, can provide information about interactions specific to turn-taking, the input received by conversational partners, word usage, and intelligibility (see Romski et al., 2010 for an example of use with codes for AAC).

A discussion of measurement tools and procedures would not be complete without noting the absence of instruments available to assess variables external to the child. This review has already reported the expansion of measurement targets beyond the communicator to variables relevant to his or her partners and environments. Researchers and practitioners measuring such variables have largely been dependent on observational methodologies. There is, however, at least guidance

Table 14.2. Sample adaptations of a structured sampling protocol for people who are impaired

Imitating the child's motor acts. For example, if the child stomps on the floor, then the examiner would also stomp while touching the child's leg.

Taking turns with a preferred object. For example, the examiner would introduce a vibrating ball to the child, then take turns handling the ball.

Providing choice-making opportunities. For example, the examiner could place one object in each of the child's hands, then pull the objects just out of reach without losing contact with the child.

Bouncing a child on a small trampoline, then stopping and waiting.*

Introducing aversive smells to a child.*

*Not included in the citation

(From Brady, N. C., & Bashinski, S. M. (2008). Increasing communication in children with concurrent vision and hearing loss. *Research and Practice for Persons with Severe Disabilities*, 33, 59–70. Adapted with permission.)

in this area. The National Joint Committee (NJC) on the Communicative Needs of Persons with Severe Disabilities published the *Communication Supports Checklist,* which includes observable behaviors across three areas: assessment practices, goal setting, and program implementation (McCarthy et al., 1998). Each section includes directives specific to partners and environments. For example, under assessment, the checklist recommends the measurement of partners' responsiveness to communication. Likewise, in the program implementation section, the document recommends the measurement of adaptations and modifications to the learner's environment that optimize communicative success.

CURRENT PRACTICES IN MEASUREMENT

Interest in the communicative abilities of people with severe ID has grown over the years. Researchers have begun to conduct large-scale literature reviews in an attempt to describe data trends. One review considered communication treatment efficacy with people with severe ID (Snell et al., 2010). One hundred and sixteen studies published in refereed journals between 1987 and 2007 were reviewed. All studies described a communication intervention, included at least one person with severe ID, and addressed one or more areas of communication performance. Although the primary finding of the study was its strong support for intervention, secondary findings revealed specific insights regarding the measurement of communication and language during the past two decades. This study was not designed to identify targets of measurement independent of the individual with disability (i.e., it did not address partners and environments). Table 14.3 provides an overview of dependent variables reported by Snell et al. (2010), whereas a more complete review of this study occurs in Chapter 1. Percentages in Table 14.3 were calculated based on the entire sample of 116 studies.

Table 14.3. Dependent variables measured in studies included in Snell et al. (2010)

Dependent variable	Percent of studies including variable
Expressive communication	81%
Speech	41.4%
Unaided augmentative and alternative communication (AAC)	21.6%
Aided AAC	61.2%
Aided AAC without voice output	36%
Comprehension of receptive language	17.2%
AAC with or without voice output	10.4%
Speech	9.5%
Unaided AAC/gesture or contextual understanding	6%
Interaction or conversation	30%
Turn-taking	11.2%
Joint attention	9.5%
Imitation	6.9%

Communicative forms were primarily taught to regulate the behavior of others (i.e., request or protest). (*Source:* Snell, M., Brady, McLean, Ogletree, Siegel, Sylverster, L. and Sevcik, 2010.)

The absence of measurement efforts related to comprehension is the most striking conclusion to be drawn from a review of Table 14.3. This likely relates to both the inherent complexity and subjectivity often associated with this task (Miller & Paul, 1995). Significant emphasis on the expressive measurement of speech and other symbolic forms is a second notable finding. These two categories clearly account for the vast majority of dependent variables in this group of intervention studies, which is somewhat surprising given the burgeoning interest in nonsymbolic communication since the late 1990s. Once again, a lack of measurement in this area may be the result of difficulty with defining and measuring nonsymbolic communication. A final obvious comment is the lack of dependent variables specific to both form and function in Snell et al.'s (2010) sample.

The Snell et al. (2010) study was not intended to measure communication variables independent of the communicator (i.e., partner, environmental targets). Some of the investigations included did, however, measure social validity defined by Snell et al. as "any measure of acceptability or benefit of the intervention from the perspectives of experts or individuals who interact with the participant" (p. 373).

There is less clarity when one attempts to use Snell et al. (2010) to discern how variables of interest were measured. Examination of experimental designs of included studies provides some insight. Of the 116 investigations reviewed, experimental single-subject research designs predominated (67.2%), followed by quasi-experimental designs (19%), qualitative designs (9.5%), and experimental group designs (3.4%).

Researchers clearly used observational techniques to measure behavior, given the designs previously mentioned. Interestingly, interrater agreement was reported in almost all studies (89.5%), yet intrarater agreement (i.e., consistency of measurement over time) was only reported 2.6% of the time. Finally, a little more than half of the studies made observations of skill generalization (51.3%), yet only 25% measured skill maintenance after 3 months.

The preceding review provides an overview of the state of communication and language measurement for people with severe disabilities. What follows is a presentation of measurement challenges and ideas for consideration as this field of inquiry moves forward.

CHALLENGES AND FUTURE DIRECTIONS IN MEASUREMENT

Myriad variables complicate the measurement of communication and language in individuals with severe disabilities. These can be viewed within the broad context of a tri-focus framework initially described by Siegel-Causey and Bashinski (1997) and later developed by Siegel and Wetherby (2006) and Siegel and Cress (2002). Siegel and colleagues presented a dynamic relationship between learners, environments, and partners and suggested that each of these areas must be 1) analyzed for a complete understanding of communication and 2) actively incorporated into treatment if meaningful outcomes are to be achieved. Using a tri-focus approach, what measurement challenges do researchers and practitioners face?

Learner challenges include the idiosyncratic nature of communication by this population. As part of the panel discussion at the NJC conference, the less than conventional use of communicative forms and functions places increased pressure on the observer to recognize and record behaviors reliably. This clearly affects an examiner's ability to interpret communication attempts with certainty, and measurement of expressive competence is potentially flawed without such certainty. The use of unconventional communicative or response behaviors also complicates the measurement of comprehension. For example, observing compliance, movement, expression, and emotion as evidence of comprehension of the symbolic or nonsymbolic communication attempts of partners is questionable at best. Capturing one's understanding of these types of behaviors is difficult, regardless of the presence of disability. Performance variability is an additional learner challenge complicating the response issues previously described. Individuals with severe ID experience significant fluctuations in performance as a result of behavior state variance, fatigue, or health conditions. Measurement must account for performance variability if it is to accurately portray the communicative abilities of this population.

Rhodes and Washington (see Chapter 13) also presented measurement challenges specific to partners and environments. They suggested that changing national demographics with respect to cultural and linguistic diversity mandate that measurement be pursued by culturally competent partners. Failing to conduct measurement in this way may compromise the representative nature of reported research and therapeutic findings. They also noted challenges specific to measuring behaviors too narrowly. Behaviors occur within broader life and family contexts that need to be recognized and acknowledged. Discrete reports of learner performance that fail to consider the multiple spheres of life (e.g., immediate and extended family, health, resource access) provide narrow and often incomplete descriptions of abilities.

The field of applied behavior analysis has much to contribute to measurement challenges facing researchers and practitioners (see Chapter 12). For example, discrimination and relational learning tasks, thought to be foundational to comprehension, can be added to measurement paradigms in cases in which individuals struggle to respond to conventional testing. Serna specifically recommended measuring visual and auditory discrimination in addition to "same" and "different" categorization. These researchers also called for the need to develop nonverbal tasks to measure discrimination in general and strongly suggested the need for increased measurement fidelity.

Measurement challenges similar to those previously mentioned could be addressed several ways. The application of rising technologies in assessment process and systematic/rigorous research procedures could bring clarity to the otherwise murky waters of communication measurement.

The application of new technologies, such as the Language Environment Analysis System (LENA) and eye-tracking technology, could make the measurement of communication from and to individuals with severe disabilities less subjective than it is now. LENA applies a digital language processor and speech reception software to provide an ongoing recording of auditory interaction. Communicative partners wear unobtrusive recording devices that provide easily downloadable audio files for analysis (language analysis software is provided). One can imagine that the use of LENA and other noninvasive audio and video recording devices could assist with interpretation of communication subtleties frequently evident in individuals with severe disabilities. Brady, Anderson, Hahn, Obermeier, and Kapa (2014) explored the use of eye-tracking technology to examine the comprehension skills of children with autism. This technology could provide assessment strategies that do not rely on a direct response from the child.

Serna et al. (2011) made several suggestions that could affect validity and reliability of efforts to measure communication and language. First, they called for critical descriptions of subjects in research. Little can be made of the claims of researchers without such descriptions. Snell et al. (2010) also saw a critical need for clear subject descriptions and noted that the lack of such descriptions is a considerable source of ambiguity in current research findings. Second, Serna et al. also questioned the pursuit of ill-defined dependent variables, such as functional communication. Once again, clarity in all aspects of research yields stronger findings. Third, these researchers supported the creation and application of innovative sampling procedures that engage communicators in socially valid ways. The work of Brady and Bashinski (2008) provided a nice example of useful and socially valid sampling procedures. Fourth, Serna et al. questioned how differences associated with cultural, linguistic, or other forms of diversity affect measurement. They specifically pointed to the inadequacy of current methodologies when attempting to capture the essence of performance within a broad cultural context and questioned cultural influences on all aspects of the research process. Possible solutions in this regard include the active presence of researchers and practitioners in diverse communities and the continued pursuit of assessment instruments sensitive to diversity.

A call for social validity as a target of measurement is a final overarching challenge for researchers and practitioners. Goldstein notes the importance of three validity dimensions, including consumer satisfaction (including desirability and feasibility), valued and perceptual behavior change, and change relative to a normative group (see Chapter 15). With respect to the first two dimensions, Goldstein suggests that perceptions may differ depending on consumer groups. For example, parents may view satisfaction differently than peers.

Goldstein raises an interesting point about researchers' reports of effect sizes (ES) regarding findings. ES assists in the quantification of a difference between two groups, drawing attention to the size of the difference (Coe, 2002). Goldstein suggests that large ES, which are pleasing to researchers, are unimpressive unless they are reported with correspondingly positive social validity data. Unfortunately, Goldstein reports that too few studies measure social validity, especially when reporting results pertinent to individuals with severe disabilities. The addition of social validity measures to intervention outcome studies would provide a strong complement to ES data.

CONCLUSION

The purpose of this chapter has been to overview issues specific to the measurement of communication and language in people with severe disabilities. Interest in this area has expanded since the work of Spradlin (1963) to include a broader consideration of targets of measurement and at least some new developments specific to measurement tools. The most important new ideas being offered are specific to how researchers and practitioners apply tools of measurement. These include calls to 1) include and clearly describe all communicators, regardless of the uniqueness of their communication; 2) consider broad contexts of communication, including partners and environments; 3) apply emerging technologies to understand better the nuances of communicative behavior; 4) apply and interpret culturally and linguistically sensitive measurement procedures; and 5) consider the impact of what is measured through the lenses of socially validity. Extending measurement efforts in these directions will help document meaningful change in the communicative abilities of people with severe disabilities.

REFERENCES

American Association on Intellectual and Developmental Disabilities. (2010). *Intellectual disability: Definition, classification, and systems of support.* Washington, DC: Author.

Baer, D., & Guess, D. (1971). Receptive training of adjectival inflections in mental retardates. *Journal of Applied Behavior Analysis, 4,* 129–139.

Baer, D., & Guess, D. (1973). Teaching productive noun suffixes to severely retarded children. *American Journal on Mental Deficiency, 77,* 498–505.

Baine, D., & Sobsey, R. (1983). Implementing transdisciplinary services for severely handicapped persons. *Special Education in Canada, 58*(11), 12–14.

Bakeman, R., & Gottman, J. (1997). *Observing interaction: An introduction to sequential analysis.* New York, NY: Cambridge University Press. Bayley, N. (2005). *Bayley Scales of Infant Development (3rd ed.).* San Antonio, TX: Pearson.

Bayley, N. (2005). *Bayley Scales of Infant and Toddler development,* Third Edition (Bayley III). San Antonio, TX: Psychological Corporation

Brady, N., Anderson, C., Hahn, L., Obermeier, S., & Kapa, L. (2014). Eye tracking as a measure of receptive vocabulary with autism spectrum disorders. *Augmentative and Alternative Communication.* 30 (2), 147–159.

Brady, N.C., & Bashinski, S.M. (2008). Increasing communication in children with concurrent vision and hearing loss. *Research and Practice for Persons with Severe Disabilities, 33,* 59–70.

Brady, N.C., McLean, J.E., McLean, L.K., & Johnston, S. (1995). Initiation and repair of intentional communication acts by adults with severe to profound cognitive disabilities. *Journal of Speech and Hearing Research, 38,* 1334–1348.

Brigance, A.H. (2004). *Brigance Diagnostic Inventory of Early Development II.* North Billerica, MA: Curriculum Associates.

Broen, P.A. (1988). The ongoing assessment of language. In R.L. Schiefelbusch & L.L. Lloyd (Eds.), *Language perspectives: Acquisition retardation and intervention* (2nd ed., pp. 299–320). Austin, TX: PRO-ED.

Bruce, S. (2011). Severe and multiple disabilities. In J.M. Kauffman & D.P. Hallahan (Eds.), *Handbook of special education* (pp. 291–303). New York, NY: Routledge Press.

Bzoch, K.R., League, R., & Brown, V.L. (2003). *Receptive Expressive Emergent Language Test (3rd ed.).* Austin, TX: PRO-ED.

Calculator, S., & Jorgensen, C. (1994). *Including students with severe disabilities in schools.* San Diego, CA: Singular.

Carrier, J. (1974). None speech noun usage training with severely and profoundly retarded children. *Journal of Speech and Hearing Research, 17,* 510–517.

Chomsky, N. (1959). A review of B.F. Skinner's verbal behavior. *Language, 35,* 26–58.

Cirrin, F.M., & Rowland, C.M. (1985). Communicative assessment of nonverbal youths with severe and profound mental retardation. *Mental Retardation, 23,* 52–62.

Coe, R. (2002). *It's the effect size, dummy: What is effect size and why is it important.* Unpublished paper presented at the annual conference of the British Educational Research Association, University of Exeter, England.

Dooley, J. (1976). Language acquisition and Down's syndrome: A study of early semantics and syntax. Unpublished doctoral dissertation, Harvard University, Cambridge, MA.

Dunn, L.M., & Dunn, D.M. (2007). *Peabody Picture Vocabulary Test (4th ed.).* San Antonio, TX: Pearson.

Guess, D.A., Sailor, W., Rutherford, G., & Baer, D.M. (1968). An experimental analysis of linguistic development: The productive use of the plural morpheme. *Journal of Applied Behavior Analysis, 2,* 55–64.

Johnson-Martin, S., Attermier, S., & Hacker, B. (2007). *Carolina Curriculum.* Baltimore, MD: Paul H. Brookes Publishing Co.

Johnson-Martin, N.M., Attermeier, S.M. & Hacker, B.J. (2004). *The Carolina curriculum for infants and toddlers with special needs.* Baltimore, MD: Paul H. Brookes.

Labato, D., Berrera, R.D., & Feldman, R.S. (1981). Sensorimotor functioning and prelinguistic functioning in profoundly retarded individuals. *American Journal of Mental Deficiency, 85,* 489–496.

Mar, H.H., & Sall, N. (1999). *Dimensions of communication. Part I: Developing a communication profile [and] Part II: Designing an intervention plan. An instrument to assess the communication skills and behaviors of individuals with disabilities.* Patterson, NJ: St Joseph's Children's Hospital.

McCarthy, C.F., McLean, L.K., Miller, J., Paul-Brown, D., Romski, M.A., Rourk, J.D., & Yoder, D. (1998). *Communication supports checklist for serving individuals with severe disabilities.* Baltimore, MD: Paul H. Brookes Publishing Co.

McCarthy, D. (1946). Language development in children. In L. Carmichael (Ed.), *Manual of child psychology* (pp. 476–581). New York, NY: Wiley.

McLean, J.E., McLean, L.K.S., Brady, N.C. & Etter, R. (1991). Communication profiles of two types of gesture using nonverbal persons with severe to profound mental retardation. *Journal of Speech and Hearing Research, 34,* 294–308.

McLean, J.E., & Snyder-McLean, L. (1988). Application of pragmatics to severely mentally retarded children and youth. In R.L. Schiefelbusch & L.L. Lloyd (Eds.), *Language perspectives: Acquisition retardation and intervention* (2nd ed., pp. 255–290). Austin, TX: PRO-ED.

McLean, J., Snyder-McLean, L., & Cirrin, F. (1981*). Communication performatives and representative behaviors in severely mentally retarded adolescents.* Unpublished paper presented at the annual meeting of the American Speech-Language-Hearing Association, Los Angeles, California.

Meyer, L.H., Peck, C.A., & Brown, L. (Eds.). (1991). *Critical issues in the lives of people with severe disabilities.* Baltimore, MD: Paul H. Brookes Publishing Co.

Miller, J., & Chapman, R. (1985). *Systematic analysis of language transcripts (SALT).* Madison, WI: Waisman Center on Mental Retardation and Human Development.

Miller, J., & Paul, R. (1995). *Clinical assessment of language comprehension.* Baltimore, MD: Paul H. Brookes Publishing Co.

Moores, D.F. (1974). Nonvocal systems of verbal behavior. In R.L. Schiefelbusch & L.L. Lloyd (Eds.), *Language perspectives: Acquisition retardation and intervention* (pp. 347–376). New York, NY: Macmillan.

Newborg, J. (2005). *Battelle Developmental Inventory (2nd ed.).* Itasca, Il: Riverside.

Ogletree, B.T., Fischer, M.A., & Turowski, M. (1996). Assessment targets and protocols for nonsymbolic communicators with profound disabilities. *Focus on Autism and Other Developmental Disabilities, 11*(*1*), 53 58

Ogletree, B.T., Wetherby, A.M., & Westling, D. (1992). Profile of the prelinguistic intentional communicative behaviors of children with profound mental retardation. *American Journal on Mental Retardation, 97*(2), 186–196.

Parker, A. (2009). *Measuring an adapted form of Picture Exchange Communication System (PECS) for young children with visual impairments and developmental disabilities.* Unpublished doctoral dissertation, Texas Tech University, Lubbock, Texas.

Parks, S., & Furuno, S. (2004). *Hawaii Early Learning Profile.* Palo Alto, CA: VORT Corp.

Premack, D., & Premack, A.J. (1974). Teaching visual language to apes and language-deficient persons. In R.L. Schiefelbusch & L.L. Lloyd (Eds.), *Language perspectives: Acquisition retardation and intervention* (pp. 377–418). New York, NY: Macmillan.

Romski, M.A., & Sevcik, R.A. (1996). *Breaking the speech barrier: Language development through augmented means.* Baltimore, MD: Paul H. Brookes Publishing Co.

Romski, M.A., & Sevcik, R.A. (2000). Communication, technology, and disability. In M. Wehmeyer & J.R. Patton (Eds.), *Mental retardation in the 21st century* (pp. 299–313). Austin, TX: PRO-ED.

Romski, M.A., Sevcik, R.A., Adamson, L.B., & Bakeman, R. (2005). Communication patterns of individuals with moderate or severe cognitive disabilities: Interactions with unfamiliar partners. *American Journal on Mental Retardation, 110,* 226–239.

Romski, M.A., Sevcik, R.A., Adamson, L.B., Cheslock, M., Smith, A., Barker, R.M., & Bakeman, R. (2010). Randomized comparison of augmented and nonaugmented language interventions for toddlers with developmental delays and their parents. *Journal of Speech, Language, and Hearing Research, 53,* 350–365.

Romski, M.A., Sevcik, R.A., & Pate, J.L. (1988). The establishment of symbolic communication in persons with severe retardation. *Journal of Speech and Hearing Disorders, 53,* 94–107.

Romski, M.A., White, R., Millen, C.E., & Rumbaugh, D.M. (1984). Effects of computer keyboard teaching on the symbolic communication of severely retarded persons: Five case studies. *Psychological Record, 34,* 39–54.

Rosenberg, S. & Abbeduto, L. (1993). *Language and cognition in mental retardation: Development, processes, and intervention.* Mahwah, NJ: Lawrence Erlbaum Associates.

Rossetti, L. (2006). The Rossetti Infant Toddler Language Scale. East Moline, IL: LinguaSystems.

Rowland, C. (2011). Using the Communication Matrix to assess expressive skills in early communicators. Communication Disorders Quarterly, 32, 190–201.

Rowland, C., & Fried-Oken, M. (2010). Communication Matrix: A clinical and research assessment tool targeting children with severe communication disorders. Journal of Pediatric Rehabilitation Medicine. 3, 319–321.

Rowland, C., & Schweigert, P. (2000). Tangible symbols, tangible outcomes. *Augmentative and Alternative Communication, 16,* 61–78.

Rowland, C., & Schweigert, P. (2002). Functional problem solving skills for children with pervasive developmental disorders. Retrieved from http://www.ohsu.edu/oidd/d21/doc/PDD%20final%20report11-25-08x.pdf

Rowland, C., Stillman, R., & Mar, H. (2010). Current assessment practices for young children who are deafblind. AER Journal: Research and Practice in Visual Impairment and Blindness, 3(3), 63–70.

Rumbaugh, D. (1977). *Language learning by a chimpanzee: The LANA project.* San Diego, CA: Academic Press.

Saunders, R.R., Spradlin, J.E., & Sherman J.A. (2006). Communication of people with mental retardation program project. In R.L. Schiefelbusch & S.R., Schroeder (Eds.) *Doing science and doing good: A history of the bureau of child research and the Schiefelbusch institute for life span studies 1921-2006* (Book II, Ch. 7). Baltimore, MD: Paul Brooks Publishing.

Schiefelbusch, R.L. (1980). *Nonspeech language and communication: Analysis and intervention.* Baltimore, MD: University Park Press.

Schiefelbusch, R.L., & Hollis, J. (1979). *Language intervention from ape to child.* Baltimore, MD: University Park Press.

Schiefelbusch, R.L., & Lloyd, L. (1974). *Language perspectives: Acquisition, retardation, intervention.* Baltimore, MD: University Park Press.

Schroeder, S., & Reese, M. (2007). Historical overview of assessment in intellectual disability. In J. Matson (Ed.), *International review of research in mental retardation: Handbook of assessment in persons with intellectual disabilities* (Vol. 34, pp. 1–18). San Diego, CA: Academic Press.

Serna, R., Washington, J., Goldstein, H., & Ogletree, B.T. (2011). *Measurement issues: What type of measurement tools do we have? What types to we need to develop or adapt?* Panel session at the NJC Research Conference, Georgia State University, Atlanta, Georgia.

Sevcik, R.A., & Romski, M.A. (2002). The role of language comprehension in establishing early augmented conversations. In J. Reichle, D. Beukelman, & J. Light (Eds.), *Implementing an augmentative communication system: Exemplary strategies for beginning communicators* (pp. 453–474) Baltimore, MD: Paul H. Brookes Publishing Co.

Shapiro, B.K., & Batshaw, M.L. (2013). Developmental delay and intellectual disability. In M.L. Batshaw, N.J. Roizen, & G.R. Lotrecchiano (Eds.), *Children with disabilities* (7th ed., pp. 291–306). Baltimore, MD: Paul H. Brookes Publishing Co.

Siegel, E., & Cress, C. (2002). Overview of the emergence of early AAC behaviors. In J. Reichle, D.R. Beukelman & J.C. Light (Eds.), *Implementing an augmentative communication system: Exemplary practices for beginning communicators* (pp. 25–57). Baltimore, MD: Paul H. Brookes Publishing Co.

Siegel, E., & Wetherby, A. (2006). Nonsymbolic communication. In M.E. Snell & F. Brown (Eds.), *Instruction of students with severe disabilities* (6th ed., pp. 405–446). Upper Saddle River, NJ: Merrill/Prentice Hall.

Siegel-Causey, E., & Bashinski, S.M. (1997). Enhancing initial communication and responsiveness of learners with multiple disabilities: A tri-focus framework for partners. *Focus on Autism and Other Developmental Disabilities, 12,* 105–120.

Skinner, B.F. (1953). *Science and human behavior.* New York, NY: Macmillian.

Skinner, B.F. (1957). *Verbal behavior.* New York, NY: Appleton-Century-Crofts.

Snell, M., Brady, N.C., McLean, L.K., Ogletree, B.T., Siegel, E., Sylverster, L., Sevcik, R. (2010). Twenty years of communication intervention research with individuals who have severe intellectual disabilities. *American Journal on Intellectual and Developmental Disabilities, 115*(5), 324–380.

Sparrow, S., Balla, D.A., & Cicchetti, D.V. (2006). *Vineland Adaptive Behavior Scales (2nd ed.).* Upper Saddle River, NJ: Pearson.

Spradlin, J.E. (1963). Assessment of speech and language of retarded children: The Parsons language sample. *Journal of Speech and Hearing Disorders Monograph, 10*, 8–31.

Sternberg, L. (Ed.). (1988). *Educating students with severe or profound handicaps.* Austin, TX: PRO-ED.

Sternberg, L., Pegnatore, L., & Hill, C. (1983). Establishing interactive communication behaviors with profoundly handicapped students. *Journal of The Association for the Severely Handicapped, 8*(2), 39–46.

Sternberg, L., & Richards, S. (1989). Assessing levels of state and arousal in individuals with profound handicaps: A research integration. *Journal of Mental Deficiency Research, 33,* 381–387.

Stillman, R., Williams, C., & Linam, A. (1997). Communications directed to students with severe and profound disabilities. *Focus on Autism and Other Developmental Disabilities, 12,* 130–141.

Striefel, S., & Wetherby, B. (1973). Instruction-following behavior of a retarded child and its controlling stimuli. *Journal of Applied Behavior Analysis, 6,* 663–670.

Steiner, V.G., & Pond, R.E. (2011). *Preschool Language Scales (5th ed.).* Upper Saddle River, NJ: Pearson.

Westling, D., & Fox L. (2014). Teaching students with severe disabilities. Upper Saddle River, NJ: Pearson.

Wetherby, A.M., & Prizant, B.M. (1992). *Communication and Symbolic Behavior Scales.* Chicago, IL: Applied Symbolix.

Wetherby, A.M., & Prizant, B.M. (2003). *Communication and Symbolic Behavior Scales Developmental Profile (CSBS DP) Infant-Toddler Checklist and Easy-Score.* Baltimore, MD: Paul H. Brookes Publishing Co.

15

Where does Social Validity Measurement Fit into Identifying and Developing Evidence-Based Practices?

Howard Goldstein

This chapter discusses criteria for judging the evidence for clinical and educational practices that are often overlooked. One such dimension is social validity. Wolf (1978) introduced the concept of social validity to the field more than 35 years ago. He argued that investigators should attend to how others value treatments and treatment effects, rather than merely whether effects are demonstrated experimentally. Yet, the recommendation to include social validity assessments in treatment studies has yet to gain widespread acceptance (Armstrong, Ehrhardt, Cool, & Poling, 1997; Carr, Austin, Britton, Kellum, & Bailey, 1999; Kennedy, 1992; Lindo & Elleman, 2010; Schwartz & Baer, 1991).

Social validity is a component of external validity. The continued focus on stressing the internal validity of intervention research is one reason for the limited use of social validity assessment. In the larger context of developing and evaluating interventions, practitioners must recognize the tension in planning studies that strike a balance between internal versus external validity. Krathwohl (2009) offered a useful framework that juxtaposes what he calls linking power (internal validity) and generalizing power (external validity). Krathwohl outlined the myriad decisions made in designing studies that can yield a tightly controlled, laboratory study that may have little generality to real-world conditions or a study conducted under real-world conditions with less control over potentially confounding variables. The balance between such considerations might be expected to shift as science progresses in studying a phenomenon of interest. If generalizing power is not adequately considered, then the ability to identify evidence-based practices may be

Preparation of this chapter was supported in part by Cooperative Agreement R324C080011 from the U.S. Department of Education, Institute of Education Sciences.

hindered. Social validity has the potential to offer measurement strategies that will contribute to generalizing power and also serve to advance research on interventions for individuals with severe disabilities.

WAYS OF IDENTIFYING EVIDENCE-BASED PRACTICES

There has been a great deal of interest among numerous clinical and educational professions in identifying evidence-based practices. One might characterize the evidence-based practice movement as an evolution, if not a revolution, in clinical decision making. It recognizes that clinical decisions should not be based on unsystematic, clinical observation and claims of clinical expertise. Even pronouncements and theories of authorities in the field need to be questioned. Instead, clinical decisions should be based on the best evidence available from systematic clinical research. Professionals are being asked to rely on systematic, unbiased, and reproducible observations. The evidence-based practice movement seeks to increase accountability among service providers and improve services within these professions. It also highlights the need for high-quality research that develops, evaluates, and refines clinical and educational practices. Like clinicians, researchers face a host of decisions as they seek to inform practitioners' scientific knowledge of interventions for individuals with severe disabilities. For example, some of the questions with which researchers must grapple include, "What behaviors are likely to have the greatest impact?" "What intervention strategies are likely to produce significant changes in behavior?" "How are changes in behavior assessed?"

Numerous organizations have recognized the need to help professionals identify evidence-based practices and keep up with the evidence being generated. For example, the field of special education and related fields have sought syntheses of such information from a variety of sources, including government agencies (e.g., U.S. Department of Education's What Works Clearinghouse), professional organizations (e.g., Research Division of the Council for Exceptional Children, School Psychology Division of the American Psychological Association, the National Center for Evidence-Based Practice in Communication Disorders), and information clearinghouses (e.g., Cochrane Group, The National Academies, and Scottish Intercollegiate Guidelines Network).

The criteria for making quality judgments that can be applied to individual studies and bodies of literature vary widely. Judgments may be based on types of experimental design. Many limit their reviews to evidence derived only from randomized controlled trials (RCTs). Others have developed question sets for different types of studies. A great deal of stock is placed on summarizing literature via meta-analyses. Judgments are thought to be most objective if based on effect sizes and confidence intervals. Most of these evaluation criteria stress the internal validity of studies.

A number of limitations exist in applying the current systems of evaluating evidence. In particular, numerous problems are found in simply adopting RCTs as the gold standard for intervention research. First, they are rare in research on severe disabilities and other low-incidence populations. Second, too few RCTs have identified interventions that have been developed to the point of producing robust effects, especially in real-world implementation conditions. Third, the bulk of experimental research is often omitted from systematic reviews because single-subject experiments are hardly acknowledged. Single-subject experimental designs typically are inaccurately thought of as case studies or quasi-experimental studies. Yet, they constitute the vast majority of the evidence in many areas in the behavioral sciences and especially research on severe disabilities.

Although it may take considerable time for the field to adopt systems that remedy these limitations, efforts are underway to expand perspectives on identifying evidence-based practices. Integrative frameworks with broadly applicable and interpretable criteria are needed because so many systems are being applied. For example, Cook, Tankersley, and Landrum (2009) proposed an evaluation system based on the quality indicators for group and single-subject experimental designs published in *Exceptional Children* (Gersten et al., 2005; Horner et al., 2005). Review teams applied this system to the special education literature for five frequently used interventions—cognitive strategy instruction, repeated reading, self-regulated strategy development, time delay, and function-based interventions (Baker, Chard, Ketterlin-Geller, Apichatabutra, & Doabler, 2009; Browder, Ahlgrim-Delzell, Spooner, Mims, & Baker, 2009; Chard, Ketterlin-Geller, Baker, Doabler, & Apichatabutra, 2009; Lane, Kalberg, & Shepcaro, 2009; Montague & Dietz, 2009). Cook et al. (2009) summarized review teams' recommendations identified to remedy shortcomings in the evaluation system. Reviewers suggested refinements in the definitions of quality indicators. Reviewers were concerned about the lack of transparency and interpretability when dichotomous ratings for multiple criteria are simply added to obtain an overall quality score and recommended weighting their importance. Although they acknowledged the potential difficulty in establishing interrater agreement, they suggested a multilevel rating system for the quality indicators. Finally, they noted a need for flexibility in aggregating studies based on participant characteristics, intervention types, dependent variables, and other features.

The School Psychology Division of the American Psychological Association also developed a rating system for both group and single-subject experimental designs that sought to evaluate individual studies using a broad set of criteria (Kratochwill & Stoiber, 2002). Goldstein, Lackey, and Schneider (2014) extended these evaluation systems in a way that sought to maximize the consistency in applying criteria across group and single-subject experimental designs. Four common dimensions are proposed to judge the quality of group and single-subject experimental designs: 1) measurement and reliability features, 2) design characteristics, 3) evaluation of treatment effects, and 4) dimensions of external validity. Figure 15.1 presents the criteria applied and illustrates the parallels in the quality indicators used for evaluating group and single-subject experimental designs. This framework for evaluating individual studies allows a graphic representation of the quality of studies across multiple dimensions, much like a *Consumer Reports* approach to reviewing consumer products. This method is proposed as a means of extending researchers' ability to review literature in a more comprehensive, transparent, and critical manner. This chapter focuses on the criteria considered to rate dimensions of external validity.

Application of Evaluation Criteria for Group Design Studies

Citations	Average Rating	Design characteristics & internal validity				Measurement & reliability features			Evaluation of treatment effects				Dimensions of external validity			
		Design	Group Equivalence	Comparison Group	Attrition	Measurement	Reliability	Implementation Fidelity	Rationale	Robust tx effects	Statistics	Maintenance & generalization	Implementation site	Participant selection	**Consumer satisfaction**	**Social validity**
Subheading																
Study 1		●	◕	◔	○											
Study 2																
Study 3																
Average rating by criterion																

Application of Evaluation Criteria for Single-Subject Experimental Design Studies

Citations	Average Rating	Design characteristics	Measurement & reliability features			Evaluation of treatment effects						Dimensions of external validity			
		Design	Measurement	Reliability	Implementation Fidelity	Rationale	Robust tx effects	Quality of Baseline	Visual Analysis	Statistics	Maintenance & generalization	Implementation site	Participant selection	**Consumer satisfaction**	**Social validity**
Subheading															
Study 1															
Study 2															
Study 3															
Average rating by criterion															

Exemplary--4 ●
Acceptable--3 ◕
Minimal--2 ◔
Unacceptable--1 ○

Figure 15.1. Evaluation criteria for group and single-subject experimental designs. (*Source:* Goldstein and Schneider, 2014.)

DIMENSIONS OF EXTERNAL VALIDITY

Few systems for evaluating evidence-based practices consider dimensions of external validity, especially social validity. Four dimensions of external validity need to be evaluated: implementation site, participant selection, consumer satisfaction, and social validity. The chapter discusses each dimension in turn and focuses on the last two, which comprise major dimensions of social validity.

If an investigator chooses to maximize external validity (i.e., generalizing power), then one would expect intervention to be implemented in natural environments with peers or family members. In contrast, a laboratory setting would indicate low generalizing power (Krathwohl, 2009). A clinical setting that attempts to simulate a natural environment might be considered contributing moderate generalizing power. Thus, the criterion for rating a quality indicator for the implementation site might distinguish among an

- Exemplary rating for a high level of external validity with respect to everyday contexts and environments
- Acceptable rating for a simulated or somewhat contrived environment (e.g., resource room), which diminishes external validity

- Minimal rating for a laboratory, clinical, or segregated setting but sufficient description to judge degree of generalizability to natural contexts and environments
- Unacceptable rating for no attempt to relate findings to the real world

Participant selection also contributes to judgments of the external validity of a study. Thus, it is important to provide enough information to judge who the participants represent, which is a major decision point as investigators determine who to recruit and enroll in their studies. Participant selection may vary from applying highly constrained selection criteria (more linking power) to minimally restrictive selection criteria (more generalizing power). The characteristics described may vary based on the clinical problem and the type of disabilities under study. For example, the inclusion criteria should at least involve assessment practices consistent with current clinical practice. For example, exemplary ratings for participant selection would involve an excellent description of participants (including gender, race/ethnicity, and socioeconomic status) with a high degree of generalizability to a broad population of interest and with inclusion and exclusion selection criteria specified. The description may have less to do with generalizability in the case of severe disabilities, but it must be detailed enough to facilitate replicability. In contrast, an unacceptable rating would be a study for which one is unable to determine which and why participants were selected and the sample has seemingly poor generalizability or replicability. Although the number of participants influences dimensions of the design, (e.g., the power for detecting intervention effects), it is the information provided about how the sample is selected and characterized that influences one's ability to generalize to similar individuals or to the population represented.

The diagnosis itself is insufficient in the case of small *n* studies and especially single-case experimental designs. Children with the same disability label may have very different strengths and weaknesses. Reporting detailed descriptions about the assessments used to evaluate a number of domains or skills not only facilitates replication but also aids clinicians in choosing appropriate interventions for specific students.

Operationalizing Social Validity

Wolf (1978) defined *social validity* as the extent to which potential consumers of research results and products judge them as useful and practical. Social validity involves judgments of the significance of targeted treatment goals, the acceptability of procedures, and the importance of treatment effects by consumers expected to use or benefit from treatments under study. Wolf argued that when behavioral researchers attend to the social validity of their research, the probability that their research would be endorsed and implemented increases.

Wolf's (1978) original conception of social validity has been expanded as investigators have sought to develop methods for conducting social validity assessments. For example, Goldstein (1990) proposed three dimensions of clinical significance:

1. Consumer satisfaction—desirability and feasibility of the treatment
2. Changes in behavior are readily perceptible and valued

3. Resulting changes in behavior are comparable with an appropriate normative group

This conceptualization separates the acceptability of the treatment procedures (consumer satisfaction) from the two dimensions that relate to behavior change (goals and outcomes). The latter is referred to as *social validity* in the following scheme.

In the Goldstein et al. (2014) framework for evaluating the quality of studies that contribute to judgments of evidence-based practices these three types of social validity assessment served as a basis for two criteria that should be considered in making judgments about evidence-based practices (see Figure 15.1). The first criterion is consumer satisfaction and is most consistent with Wolf's (1978) original conceptualization of social validity. Ratings should consider whether and how consumer satisfaction is assessed and reported in high-quality treatment studies. Ratings might include an

- Exemplary rating for studies with comprehensive and objective assessments of consumers' satisfaction with the treatment and its outcomes
- Acceptable rating for studies with some systematic assessment of consumers' satisfaction with the treatment or its outcomes
- Minimal rating for studies with some mention of consumers' satisfaction or willingness to continue the treatment
- Unacceptable rating for studies with no mention of consumers' satisfaction with the treatment or outcomes

The social validity criterion takes into account two aspects that could inform the clinical significance of the study. First, one might ask raters to judge whether intervention outcomes are perceptible and valued, which is usually accomplished by having naïve raters view participants before and after intervention and provide ratings about whether changes are clinically significant. For example, the perceptions of naïve, albeit interested judges (e.g., peer, parent, teacher group) would augment the use of objective measures of the primary and secondary dependent variables.

Comparing outcomes to a normative comparison condition is a second way to determine the clinical significance of the intervention effects. Investigators may have well-established norms for clinical diagnoses or they may have to collect normative information for outcomes that represents norms for the phenomenon under study. Some individuals with severe disabilities may not demonstrate skills commensurate with typically developing peers following intervention. Normative information, however, could provide benchmarks to help evaluate clinical significance of behavior changes associated with intervention. For example, the frequency of social interaction among typically developing children could be gathered in the same contexts (e.g., group size, materials, time) as the experimental context. Based on these considerations, study ratings for social validity might include an

- Exemplary rating for studies with 1) objective, blind assessment by multiple judges of perceived outcomes and 2) normative data presented
- Acceptable rating for studies with either 1 or 2 above
- Minimal rating for studies with some subjective assessment presented that bears on clinical significance or educational relevance

- Unacceptable rating for studies that do not mention clinical significance or educational relevance of outcomes or if data indicate that social validity was poor

PREVALENCE OF SOCIAL VALIDITY ASSESSMENTS IN RESEARCH ON SEVERE DISABILITIES

The sad truth is that social validity and consumer satisfaction assessment are not commonplace in intervention research in severe disabilities. A number of investigators have reviewed bodies of literature to determine the extent to which social validation measures are reported and whether their inclusion is increasing. Storey and Horner (1991) found 189 articles that included social validity assessments in 15 journals that published articles on developmental disabilities between 1972–1988. Kennedy (1992) found that about 20% of behavior analytic studies reported social validity data in the *Journal of Applied Behavior Analysis* (1968–1990) and *Behavior Modification* (1977–1990). Carr et al. (1999) found that fewer than 13% of studies reported social validity data in 31 years of *Journal of Applied Behavior Analysis.* Armstrong et al. (1997) examined 5 years of *Journal of Developmental and Physical Disabilities* (1991–1995) and found that 13% of 39 intervention articles included some form of social validation assessment. Lindo and Elleman (2010) reviewed 82 experimental evaluations of reading interventions (2000–2006). Although 90% of these studies were conducted in authentic field settings and 59% used teaching staff as implementers, only 28% of the studies reported any teacher feedback, and 11% of the studies sought feedback from students.

Goldstein et al. (2014) conducted a systematic review of social skills interventions for preschoolers with autism (66 studies conducted over 30 years). This review applied the coding scheme previously described for judging the quality of consumer satisfaction and social validity dimensions of each study. Out of a total of 58 single-subject experimental design studies, the consumer satisfaction criterion was rated exemplary 11 times, acceptable 1 time, minimal 6 times, and unacceptable 40 times. Similarly, the social validity criterion was rated exemplary 4 times, acceptable 5 times, minimal 13 times, and unacceptable 36 times. For the 9 group design studies, the consumer satisfaction criterion was rated acceptable 1 time and unacceptable 8 times. The social validity criterion was rated minimal 1 time and unacceptable 8 times. Overall, out of 67 studies analyzed, 30% achieved a rating of exemplary or acceptable for at least one dimension of social validity or consumer satisfaction. These dimensions stand in contrast to the ratings for the other dimensions of external validity coded. Implementation site was coded as exemplary or acceptable for 79% of the studies, and participant selection was coded as exemplary or acceptable for 81% of the studies.

Although one could question how best to characterize social validity, consumer satisfaction, or related constructs such as acceptability or feasibility, it is clear that investigators fail to attend to the social validity of their treatments, goals, and outcomes routinely. Researchers are left with incomplete knowledge of how treatments developed for people with severe disabilities stack up in real-world contexts as judged by families, individuals with disabilities, peer groups, and interventionists. Perhaps in the context of scientific progress practitioners assume that they can work out the logistics of implementation after they have developed robust treatments. Unfortunately, at this point practitioners have relatively little information to inform that process.

SOCIAL VALIDITY AND IMPLEMENTATION SCIENCE

Implementation research has taken up the challenge of identifying how to transmit innovative programs and practices to service delivery. The so-called science of implementation brings greater attention to feasibility and sustainability of interventions. The importance of this perspective is clear when practitioners are reminded that they should expect positive intervention outcomes only when effective practices and programs are fully implemented. Consequently, implementation scientists have outlined strategies that are designed to promote full implementation. Consider the hierarchy of stakeholders that are involved in implementation when one attends to the following factors:

- What policies, regulations, and funding are in place (locally and federally) to create a hospitable environment for implementation?
- How are local stakeholders interested in implementing effective interventions involved in selecting and evaluating programs and procedures?
- How are organizations selected with necessary infrastructure in place to facilitate implementation?
- How are practitioners selected, and how are they trained, coached, and evaluated to ensure full implementation?

Implementation scientists have noted that there are so many named interventions that practitioners need to identify core components or kernel elements that seem to be a part of many successful interventions (Embry & Biglan, 2008; Fixsen, Naoom, Blase, Friedman, & Wallace, 2005). Furthermore, Fixsen et al. suggested that these components need to be researched in applied settings and include measures of social validity to increase external validity.

A thoughtful analysis of social validity focusing mainly on consumer satisfaction and treatment acceptability has outlined potential threats to social validity (Seekins & White, 2013). These include threats posed by 1) selecting irrelevant issues for research, 2) a lack of clarity about important consumer goals, 3) misunderstanding the acceptability of research and evaluation strategies, 4) misunderstanding the range of acceptability of intervention approaches and procedures, 5) ignoring criteria that potential adopters would use to judge a successful outcomes, 6) misinterpreting results, and 7) lacking generality of findings to real-life contexts. Seekins and White (2013) proposed ways in which consumers might be involved in participatory action research of various sorts to help protect against these threats to social validity. A key proposition in their approach is that social validity needs to be ongoing and not relegated to a posthoc assessment at the end of a study, as is so often the case.

Schwartz and Baer (1991) defined *social invalidity* as the behavior of consumers who disapprove of some component(s) of an intervention. Moreover, that disapproval is reflected by a variety of behaviors, such as rejection of or withdrawal from an intervention, a lack of adoption or sustainability of an intervention, and potentially conveying their disapproval to others. These are not simply outcomes to be avoided; these are outcomes that need to be understood and remedied, when possible. A proper analysis of social invalidity depends on the ability to 1) ask the right consumers or stakeholders, 2) ask the right questions, and 3) use the information appropriately. Their argument highlights a need to develop a technology for accurately and validly assessing social validity.

First, Schwartz and Baer (1991) argued that interventionists need to think more broadly about who constitutes the consumers of interventions. They offered a distinction among direct recipients and users; indirect patients, patients' families or peers; and interventionists. Implementation could be undermined if any of these consumer groups have reservations about the treatment goals, the treatment, or the treatment effects. Direct recipients need to be convinced that a change in behavior is warranted, the proposed change is worth the effort, and participation in the treatment protocol is acceptable and feasible. Indirect recipients need to be convinced that participation is worth the money and the effort expended to gain access to the treatment. Family members and peers also need to be willing to encourage participation in the treatment and reinforce the desired behavior changes. Likewise, the interventionists need to be willing to commit the time and resources needed to learn how to implement the treatment and expend the effort necessary to carry out the treatment competently and with good fidelity. Deciding among possible augmentative and alternative communication systems to implement with an individual with severe disabilities is a good example of the need to consider a number of consumers.

Second, Schwartz and Baer (1991) recognized that asking the right questions is far from easy. A true concern with social validity means that practitioners need to gather accurate and useful information about possible trouble and not design their assessments to garner false praise for their efforts. The common practice of assessing social validity at the end of an investigation is not sufficient if practitioners take seriously their desire to address and correct problems. They typically ask consumers to rate their satisfaction at the end of a treatment to which they have devoted considerable resources and after they have worked with an investigator with whom they have developed a positive relationship (hopefully); one might reasonably expect a halo effect when conducting social validity assessments at that point. Deeper analyses and perhaps an ongoing assessment process are needed. The information gathered should be sufficient to elucidate what aspects of the intervention are viewed most positively and what are the sources of negative reactions. Practitioners conduct brief assessments, mindful that they should not overburden consumers and to help ensure a high response rate. Perhaps with a truly participatory approach, the consumers will welcome the opportunity to voice their opinions and welcome deep and probing questions that will help improve the value and acceptability of treatment efforts.

This goal of asking the right questions should make practitioners rethink how they conduct social validity assessments. Implementation research can be advanced if practitioners can develop a toolkit of measures that have been shown to be reliable, valid, and useful. Measurement development provides the analytic procedures for determining reliability and validity. The utility dimension, however, may depend on how generalizable developed measures turn out to be. Will good questions (assessment items) in one treatment context be relevant in other contexts? Can sets of questions be formulated that will still have utility with wording changes specific to the treatment? How can social validity assessments be devised so that bias will be minimized on the part of consumers?

These questions highlight the opportunity to apply test and measurement development procedures to social validity measures. To this end, research efforts have sought to evaluate the psychometric properties of survey instruments that have been used to assess social validity (Finn & Sladeczek, 2001). A number of survey instruments focusing on treatment acceptability have been developed—the Treatment Evaluation Inventory (Kazdin, 1980), the Intervention Rating Profile-15 (Martens, Witt, Elliott, & Darveaux, 1985), the Abbreviated Acceptability Rating Profile (Tarnowski & Simonian, 1991), and the Behavior Intervention Rating Scale (Von Brock & Elliott. 1987). Efforts have sought to expand on the singular dimension of acceptability. For example, Chafouleas, Briesch, Riley-Tillman, and McCoach (2009) developed the Usage Rating Profile-Intervention. They used a factor analytic approach to evaluate an instrument developed to measure four factors of consumer satisfaction. They argued that moving beyond treatment acceptability as the sole dimension of consumer satisfaction would increase the likelihood of implementation of interventions. They included four dimensions: acceptability (e.g., "I am motivated to try this intervention"), understanding (e.g., "The directions for using this intervention are clear to me"), feasibility (e.g., "The amount of time required for record-keeping with this intervention is reasonable"), and systems support (e.g., "Implementation of this intervention would require support from my coworkers"). Further research is needed to determine how robust this tool might be in different contexts and to determine when and how it may be useful and whether these items are adequately providing information that would guide refinements to intervention packages.

Third, Schwartz and Baer (1991) urged interventionists to use social validity information. Only then can they justify the time and effort on the part of those who are asked to complete assessments. If the information is ignored, then the process of refining the intervention is hindered. Plus, the credibility of investigators is undermined, which may affect one's ability to gather such information in the future and/or affect the acceptability or adoption of an intervention. Interventionists need to think carefully about how to best incorporate participatory action research features into scientifically rigorous experiments. They will need to think about how to sequence studies designed to develop and refine interventions, which would seem to argue for conducting a series of smaller studies, often single-subject experimental designs, rather than large-scale studies. This tactic would better enable interventionists to use social validity results along with primary outcomes measures to help guide the development of better goals, better assessments, better intervention procedures, and better outcomes that ultimately will be successfully endorsed, selected, and implemented.

RECOMMENDATIONS

1. Recognize the balance between internal validity (linking power) and external validity (generalizing power) (Krathwohl, 2009). Krathwohl provided a useful analysis of the numerous decisions made in designing studies that reflect the degree to which internal validity versus external validity is emphasized. Traditionally, the scientific progression often emphasized the former

in the initial stages of intervention development and more emphasis on external validity later in the development of an intervention. Wolf (1978), Kazdin (1977), and others questioned the wisdom of this progression. Those advocating for the importance of implementation science also have suggested that external validity dimensions should be considered from the outset of intervention development (Fixsen et al., 2005). Indeed, the implementation science perspective seems to be most consistent with Wolf's (1978) original conceptualization of social validity that was focused on the viability and sustainability from those expected to adopt and implement the intervention.

2. Discussions of clinical significance and evidence-based practice have expanded the conceptualization of social validity. There seems to be value in attending to at least three aspects of social validity measurement and to do so regardless of experimental design. First, high-quality studies should assess consumers' satisfaction with the goals and procedures undergoing investigation. Second, social validity should be informed by data that provide a normative basis of comparison for evaluating outcomes. Third, investigators should assess the degree to which relevant stakeholders perceive and value changes in behavior that are functionally related to the intervention under investigation. Although social validity has received more attention among applied behavior analysts who often are using single-subject experimental designs, it is equally relevant to group experiments.

3. It would be useful for investigators to develop generally accepted social validity measurement methods and tools. For example, if judges are asked to rate pre- versus postintervention effects, then conventions might be developed for selecting representative samples of participants' behavior before and after intervention. Storey and Horner (1991) suggested that multiple stakeholders should be involved in making judgments about the social importance of effects, the social significance of goals, the appropriateness of procedures, and the optimal levels of performance. Incorporating multiple dimensions of social validity into measurement plans requires investigators to infuse considerable effort and methodological rigor into measurement development.

   The development of efficient and reliable survey tools has received some attention. Few investigations, however, have begun to explore what dimensions will help inform implementation. Moreover, interview protocols with branching steps that permit deeper analysis as needed would be helpful. The interest in implementation science has the potential to help guide the development of a broader array of social validity measures.

4. The evidence-based practice movement would benefit from an acknowledgment of the need to develop interventions before investing in large-scale studies that are designed to provide the actuarial data that would greatly benefit policy makers. Scientists, however, need to acknowledge and advocate for an iterative and disciplined refinement process that is characteristic of scientific progress. If that scientific progress is predicated on following the data, then those data also should include social validity assessments. It is imperative that interventionists are guided by social validity assessments as well as their

objective assessments of primary and secondary outcomes as experiments are moved into real-world conditions.

5. Expectations for social validity results need to be calibrated. Social validity measures are not always going to yield, nor should they yield, positive results. Care should be taken to avoid halo effects expressed by friendly consumers. Honest, thoughtful feedback is needed to improve the utility and practicality of interventions for people with severe disabilities and their families. Philosophical and pedagogical perspectives may limit acceptability when it comes to behavior change. Indeed, universal acceptance of an intervention may not be achievable. Nevertheless, social validity assessments should help market efficacious interventions more accurately and to relevant stakeholders.

6. The incorporation of social validity assessments into intervention research should not be relegated to an afterthought. Investigators should strive to inform intervention development before, during, and after implementation through social validity assessment. Investigators need to develop a suite of sound and useful social validity measures that have the potential to guide intervention development. This will provide tools that will improve the science around implementation research and boost efforts to accelerate adoption of efficacious, useful, and practical interventions for people with severe disabilities.

CONCLUSION

Social validity measurement has an important role to play in efforts to identify and develop evidence-based practices. There is a growing awareness that investigators need to pay attention to dimensions of external validity (generalizing power) to make judgments about evidence-based practices. In particular, those criteria will help stakeholders discern whether interventions are ready for large-scale evaluation, widespread implementation, and broad dissemination.

The infrequent use of social validity assessments during intervention development can only be rectified if there is an expectation that they be included. A transparent scheme for applying a set of criteria to evaluations of evidence in extant research as previously outlined (see Figure 15.1) would help to set that expectation. Moreover, clinical scientists would become better at formulating useful social validity measures and at using the data that results if it became a common expectation.

Finally, one might foresee far-ranging effects on services for people with severe disabilities and their families. The inclusion of social validity measures would help ensure that researchers focus on what really matters to individuals with disabilities, their families, and their peer groups. The expectation is that greater consideration of dimensions of external validity would clarify the goals of intervention efforts. For example, the inclusion of normative comparisons may help determine what skills and environmental changes are needed for people with severe disabilities to successfully participate successfully in natural environments. The recognition of the importance of environmental changes is critical to the development of sustainable interventions. Social validity assessments can help determine what aspects of intervention protocols are perceived as more and less acceptable and sustainable.

REFERENCES

Armstrong, K.J., Ehrhardt, K.E., Cool, R.T., & Poling, A. (1997). Social validity and treatment integrity data: Reporting in articles published in the *Journal of Developmental and Physical Disabilities*, 1991-1995. *Journal of Developmental and Physical Disabilities, 9,* 359–367.

Baker, S.K., Chard, D.J., Ketterlin-Geller, L.R., Apichatabutra, C., & Doabler, C. (2009). Teaching writing to at-risk students: The quality of evidence for self-regulated strategy development. *Exceptional Children, 75,* 303–318.

Browder, D., Ahlgrim-Delzell, L., Spooner, F., Mims, P.J., & Baker J.N. (2009). Using time delay to teach literacy to students with severe developmental disabilities. *Exceptional Children, 75,* 343–364.

Carr, J.E., Austin, J.L., Britton, L.N., Kellum, K.K., & Bailey, J.S. (1999). An assessment of social validity trends in applied behavior analysis. *Behavioral Interventions, 14,* 223–231.

Chard, D.J., Ketterlin-Geller, L.R., Baker, S.K., Doabler C., & Apichatabutra, C. (2009). Repeated reading interventions for students with learning disabilities: Status of the evidence. *Exceptional Children, 75,* 263–281.

Chafouleas, S.M., Briesch, A.M., Riley-Tillman, T.C., & McCoach, D.B. (2009). Moving beyond assessment of treatment acceptability: An examination of the factor structure of the Usage Rating Profile–Intervention (URP-I). *School Psychology Quarterly, 24,* 36–47.

Cook, B.G., Tankersley, M., & Landrum, T.J. (2009). Determining evidence-based practices in special education. *Exceptional Children, 75,* 365–383.

Embry, D.D., & Biglan, A. (2008). Evidence-based kernels: Fundamental units of behavioral influence. *Clinical Child and Family Psychology Review, 11,* 75–113. doi 10.1007/s10567-008-0036-x

Finn, C.A., & Sladeczek, I.E. (2001). Assessing the social validity of behavior interventions: A review of treatment acceptability measures. *School Psychology Quarterly, 16,* 76–206. doi: 10.1521/scpq.16.2.176.18703.

Fixsen, D.L., Naoom, S.F., Blase, K.A., Friedman, R.M. & Wallace, F. (2005). *Implementation research: A synthesis of the literature.* Tampa, FL: University of South Florida, Louis de la Parte Florida Mental Health Institute, The National Implementation Research Network (FMHI Publication #231).

Gersten, R., Fuchs, L.S., Compton, D., Coyne, M., Greenwood, C., & Innocenti, M.S. (2005). Quality indicators for group experimental and quasi-experimental research in special education. *Exceptional Children, 71,* 149–164.

Goldstein, H. (1990). Assessing clinical significance. In L.B. Olswang, C.K. Thompson, S.F. Warren, & N.J. Minghetti (Eds.), *Treatment efficacy research in communication disorders* (pp. 91–98). Rockville, MD: American Speech-Language-Hearing Foundation.

Goldstein, H., Lackey, K.C., & Schneider, N.J. (2014). A new framework for systematic reviews: Application to social skills interventions for preschoolers with autism. *Exceptional Children, 80,* 262–280. doi: 10.1177/0014402914522423

Horner, R.H., Carr, E.G., & Halle, J. (2005). The use of single-subject research to identify evidence-based practice in special education. *Exceptional Children, 71,* 165–179.

Kazdin, A.E. (1977). Assessing the clinical and applied importance of behavior change through social validation. *Behavior Modification, 1,* 427–451. doi: 10.1177/014544557714001

Kazdin, A.E. (1980). Acceptability of alternative treatments for deviant child behavior. *Journal of Applied Behavior Analysis, 13,* 259–273.

Kennedy, C.H. (1992). Trends in the measurement of social validity. *Behavior Analyst, 15,* 147–156.

Krathwohl, D.R. (2009). *Methods of educational and social science research: An integrated approach.* Long Grove, IL: Waveland Press.

Kratochwill, T.R., & Stoiber K.C. (2002). Evidence-based interventions in school psychology: Conceptual foundations of the procedural and coding manual of division 16 and the society for the study of school psychology task force. *School Psychology Quarterly, 17,* 341–389. doi:10.1521/scpq.17.4.341.20872

Lane, K.L., Kalberg, J.R., & Shepcaro, J.C. (2009). An examination of the evidence base for function-based interventions for students with emotional and/or behavioral disorders attending middle and high schools. *Exceptional Children, 75,* 321–340.

Lindo, E.J., & Elleman, A.M. (2010). Social validity's presence in field-based reading intervention research. *Remedial and Special Education, 31,* 489–499. doi: 10.1177/0741932510361249

Martens, B.K., Witt, J.C., Elliott, S.N., & Darveaux, D.X. (1985). Teacher judgments concerning the acceptability of school-based interventions. *Professional Psychology: Research and Practice, 16,* 191–198.

Montague, M., & Dietz, S. (2009). Evaluating the evidence base for cognitive strategy instruction and mathematical problem solving. *Exceptional Children, 75,* 285–302.

Schwartz, I.S., & Baer, D.M. (1991). Social validity assessment: Is current practice state of the art? *Journal of Applied Behavior Analysis, 24,* 186–212. doi: 10.1901/jaba.1991.24-189

Seekins, T., & White, G.W. (2013). Participatory action research designs in applied disability and rehabilitation science: Protecting against threats to social validity. *Archives of Physical Medicine and Rehabilitation, 94*(1 Suppl 1), S20–29.

Storey, K., & Horner, R.H. (1991). An evaluative review of social validation research involving persons with handicaps. *Journal of Special Education, 25,* 352–401.

Tarnowski, K.J. & Simonian, S.J. (1992). Assessing treatment acceptance: The Abbreviated Acceptability Rating Profile. *Journal of Behavioral Therapy and Experimental Psychiatry, 23,* 101–106.

Von Brock, M., & Elliott, S. (1987). Influence of treatment effectiveness information on the acceptability of classroom interventions. *Journal of School Psychology, 25,* 131–144.

Wolf, M.M. (1978). Social validity: The case for subjective measurement or how applied behavior analysis is finding its heart. *Journal of Applied Behavior Analysis, 11,* 203–214. doi: 10.1901/jaba.1978.11-203

16

Section Discussion Summary

State of the Evidence: Research Design and Measurement Issues

Krista M. Wilkinson, Beth A. Mineo, Diane Paul, & Christine Regiec

Finding interventions that work is the overwhelming driver of research in the area of significant communication disabilities. The challenges in doing so are many—the heterogeneity of the population; the low-incidence nature of the disabilities leading to limited numbers of research participants in any given location; assumptions about the incompatibility of small *n* studies and the use of statistical methods; the lack of validated assessment measures; and the lack of precision in descriptions of research participants and intervention methods. The NJC research conference, *Research Challenges and Future Directions in Evidence-Based Communication Interventions for Individuals With Severe Disabilites,* featured two panels charged with examining these issues more closely and speculating about what might—and should—be done to refine and strengthen the evidence base. The first panel discussion explored how the field might advance the evidence base via a continuum of group and single subject designs, and the second discussion focused on measurement issues. Each panel featured four panelists; their prepared remarks served as the foundation for additional discussion. This chapter summarizes information shared by each panelist as well as the themes that emerged during the presentations and ensuing discussion.

RESEARCH DESIGN AND METHODS PANEL

William McIlvane, Peg Burchinal, Roger Bakeman, and David Francis

William McIlvane began by emphasizing the value of single-case research in identifying how characteristics of both the participant and the intervention influence outcomes. He reflected on his experiences learning from his mentor, Murray Sidman, and how those experiences continue to inform his approach to the development of effective assessment and intervention techniques. Sidman's perspective was that quantitative methods were useful once the experimental methodology had been refined to the point of controlling all controllable variables; at that point, remaining core variability can be statistically managed. The identification of controllable variables emerges during an iterative refinement of methods that seeks to explain outlier behaviors. Once adequate control of the variables that influence behavior is achieved, the resulting assessment/intervention technology can be used to generate data that provide a common point of reference for other behaviors. To illustrate, McIlvane noted that he has been engaged in work spanning two decades to devise a methodology for same-different discrimination that works with almost all children, an achievement that signifies the maturation of the technique. This example reinforces the value of single-case research in pinpointing the mechanism of operation of an intervention.

Peg Burchinal also addressed the role of different research designs, although her focus was on group design, specifically growth curve modeling. She echoed McIlvane's observations on the merits of single-subject design, yet noted that there is not much true statistical evaluation done in the context of those designs. She contrasted the purpose of single-subject design—describing the behavior of a single individual—with the purpose of group designs, which is to determine how well an intervention works for a given population, yet noted that practice-oriented researchers have difficulty abandoning the focus on the individual because they are interested in the real-world impact of an intervention at that level. Burchinal suggested that growth curve modeling might be the compromise that allows one to marry the benefits of single-subject examinations with group designs because it can be used to examine interindividual (across-individual) differences in intraindividual (within-individual) patterns of change. Although growth curve modeling assumes that research participants get the same treatment, it can allow for differences such as time-in-treatment, fidelity, and intentional variations in treatment. It also can be used to probe what is and is not working within a treatment. Before concluding, Burchinal offered a few additional observations about research with those who have significant communication challenges. She warned against defaulting to single-subject designs merely because the population is heterogeneous; rather, she urged the adoption of new strategies for managing heterogeneity within research designs. She reiterated the problems that arise from the lack of standardized measures for this population, yet noted that standardized measures often are not adequate for describing the behaviors of interest among typically developing research participants as well. Finally, she observed that researchers too often consider only proximal outcomes; if they fail to also include distal outcomes in their designs, then they lose the opportunity to measure how new behaviors generalize beyond what was directly taught. She concluded with an admonition that research in this domain needs to more often describe impact in statistical terms in order to determine what works—and for whom—in practice.

Roger Bakeman posited that those conducting research with individuals having significant communication challenges rely on single-subject designs because of mistaken assumptions about the applicability of statistical tests to small sample sizes. Contrary to the belief of many researchers—and some statisticians—a number of relatively simple statistical tests can be applied quite appropriately in the context of small n studies. For example, the sign test provides a clear descriptive statistic as well as a significance level in designs featuring a binomial distribution. Regarding statistical significance, Bakeman urged reason with regard to the sacred p value set at .05, citing Cohen, who characterized it as merely "a convenient reference point along the possibility-probability continuum" (1990, p. 1311). Furthermore, Bakeman suggested that reporting ES in addition to *p* value allows for comparison across studies of the strength of the intervention and that ES should be given equal—if not greater—emphasis than *p* values. Cohen's *d* and the odds ratio were two measures of ES noted. He also advocated shared data representation in which a visual depiction of the data includes both the group mean and each individual data point. He characterized such representations as offering full disclosure and enabling skew in the data to be detected quite readily. He concluded by emphasizing that studies reporting significant and ES facilitate meta-analysis.

David Francis discussed the contributions of group randomized trials, which tend to carry greater status than other designs as they purport to demonstrate causal impact. Francis warned that these designs might not be superior for the purpose of understanding the mechanism of communication intervention with the target population because the model employed in most randomized control designs estimates average causal effects (e.g., what one might expect on average for an individual assigned to treatment compared with what would be expected for that person on average if assigned to the control condition). When there is no average by virtue of the extreme heterogeneity of the population, average causal impacts tell researchers very little about how to tailor intervention to the strengths and limitations of each individual. A more useful approach would give researchers data that help them understand whether an individual with a particular profile is likely to benefit from a treatment. The field needs a taxonomy of profiles, a taxonomy of treatments, and an understanding of which dimensions of treatment are most relevant in order to accomplish this. Francis went so far as to suggest that the field would benefit far more from improved characterization of participants and treatments than from 10 years of randomized trials characterized by unspecified treatments with unspecified populations. He also amplified Burchinal's concerns about the limitations of standardized measures, suggesting that language monitoring—such as that afforded using systems such as Lena—enabled construction of much more sensitive outcome measures.

MEASUREMENT ISSUES PANEL

Richard Serna, Julie Washington, Howard Goldstein, and Billy Ogletree

Richard Serna spoke about the potential role played by behavioral technologies, which allow for precise evaluation and characterization of client skills when standardized testing is not appropriate and/or gives little useful information. Serna also noted that the techniques of behavior analysis are particularly well suited to people with severe disabilities because it has a long-standing history of adapting testing procedures for individuals who are not able to understand spoken directions. Serna described well-established procedures that are already available to probe clients' ability to tell the difference between augmentative and alternative communication (AAC) symbols and to match AAC symbols (e.g., line drawings) to real-world referents (e.g., objects). Also available are techniques for establishing these skills in individuals who appear to have difficulty with discrimination or relational learning. Serna also discussed a line of research on auditory discrimination of speech sounds (i.e., methods for determining whether an individual can tell the difference between phonemes and/or syllables or words). Such auditory discrimination may lay the groundwork for comprehension of spoken language, a skill that has been demonstrated to be important in AAC (e.g., Romski & Sevcik, 1996; Sevcik & Romski, 2002). In summary, this presentation reflected an emphasis on integrating tools of behavior analysis as important supports in assessment and intervention measurement.

Julie Washington discussed cultural and linguistic diversity as it applies to individuals with severe disabilities. She highlighted that although these issues can be difficult to talk about, it is imperative to consider how cultural and ethnic characteristics influence what researchers do. As she noted, if these difficult discussions cannot occur in science, then they cannot occur anywhere. In terms of applications to communication in severe disabilities, Washington reminded the group that the goal was about much more than increasing the racial or ethnic diversity in research samples; it is about understanding how race and ethnicity affect assessment, intervention, participation, compliance, retention, and interpretation. The language skills of children are affected by cultural and linguistic differences, and the perspective of families regarding what their children need is essential. The targets of intervention need to be consistent with the communication practices of the family and their culture. There is great risk of developing assessment procedures that do not apply to a large segment of the population when measures are developed that ignore practices across communities.

Howard Goldstein turned to issues of social validity in assessment and how it relates to evidence-based practice. Goldstein identified three dimensions of social validity—consumer satisfaction and the desirability or feasibility of treatment, whether changes resulting from intervention are either perceptible or valued, and the degree to which changes resulting from intervention are comparable with an appropriate normative group. Studies in the domain of interest rarely evaluate consumer satisfaction and/or social validity. Goldstein presented the idea of including not only group-design studies as part of evidence-based practice but also strong single-case research designs and measuring any given study based on its individual design characteristics, external validity, measurement methods, and evaluation of treatment effects. A taxonomy by which individual studies might be judged on these dimensions was introduced, and an example of its application to a series of studies concerning social skills intervention with children with autism spectrum disorder was shared. Goldstein identified numerous benefits arising from inclusion of social validity measures in research. The value of their perspective is affirmed by measuring what matters to families, peers, and research participants. A focus on normative comparison helps clarify the goals of the intervention, and social validity measures help to contextualize the other findings (e.g., there may be small effect sizes [ES] although stakeholders report meaningful behavior change). In summary, Goldstein emphasized the value of external validity, especially social validity, as assessment tools and intervention strategies for individuals with severe communication disabilities are developed.

Billy Ogletree offered the final presentation, which centered on the measurement of receptive and expressive communication. He cited a study by Snell et al. (2010) and noted how infrequently comprehension was included as a dependent measure in research examining the communication behaviors of those with significant communication challenges. Although 94 of 116 studies (81%) measured production in some way, only 20 studies (17%) measured or reported on receptive skills, suggesting that although production is being measured, less is being done to measure receptive skills. He noted that a variety of means for assessing production was described, including criterion-referenced tests, norm-referenced tests, observation, and informants; yet, only informants, observation, and skill-based probes were used for receptive skills. Ogletree suggested that any assessment of language should consider the learner, the partner, and the environment. In terms of the learner, subjective measures are often relied on, in part because many individuals with severe disabilities may not have reliable and/or conventional means of expressive communication. Challenges associated with the partners and environments include ensuring that the systems that surround the learner and how the supports interact with performance in comprehension and production, including cultural and linguistic diversity as well as other contextual dimensions, are examined. Measurement has to extend beyond the spoken modality to include other symbolic and nonsymbolic forms, and it has to look beyond form and function to socially valid outcomes attained.

PROMINENT DISCUSSION THEMES

Theme 1: Do Researchers Adapt Existing Measurement Tools or Create New Ones?

The relative value of using existing tools (with adjustments or accommodations as necessary) and developing tools that are specifically tailored to the unique needs and profiles of the population was one of the major points of discussion. Arguments in favor of adjusting existing tools reflect the value professionals put on being able to modify something that has already been established. The challenges, however, are the well-known threats to validity that are posed by making changes to standardized procedures. It may be useful to explore established methods in educational assessment, which has a science of adaptation of instruments, which are intended to reveal the ways in which different kinds of accommodations affect validity. Systematic delineation of the ways in which different accommodations affect validity would afford guidance as interventionists seek to adapt existing procedures.

Arguments in favor of developing population-specific tools reflect the concern that existing tools do not measure the kinds of skills that are most essential for this particular population and/or are not good reflections of those skills. An analogy was made to the state of assessment related to autism 20 years ago, in which there was no systematic diagnostic tool available; when autism experts moved toward developing a specialized tool. The result was The Autism Diagnostic Observation Schedule (ADOS) and the Autism Diagnostic Interview- Revised (ADI-R; Lord et al., 2012), which are the current gold standards. Similarly, in the period prior to the development of tools that specifically differentiated true language disorder from language difference associated with minority dialects, children who spoke a dialect such as African American English were being overidentified for special education and communication services and thus erroneously placed in language intervention. It may be necessary to develop a specialized tool for assessing skills in individuals with significant communication limitations; yet, it is likely that existing measures, adapted measures, and new measures all have the potential to help interventionists understand communicator, partner, and environmental characteristics.

Theme 2: What Are the Main Issues Related to Existing Tools?

The limitations of standardized norm-referenced tests with this population are well recognized, as are their limitations for measuring change after intervention. Panel members were asked to discuss the strengths and limitations of parent report, and they noted a variety of considerations concerning the merits of this particular type of measure. Parent report provides an insider's perspective on the child that other instruments simply cannot offer, most particularly with regard to family and cultural insights. Some existing instruments that rely on parent report are excellent and provide relevant sources of information; however, if a parent/caregiver questionnaire of any sort is to be used, then it is critically important to be sure that the questions on that questionnaire are appropriate in terms of the cultural or linguistic background of the client and/or informant, as well as in terms of their social validity and meaningfulness to those individuals. The same issues arise with other informant-based data collection mechanisms such as focus groups.

The possibility of bias is another consideration that engendered some debate. Although Goldstein pointed out that there is a body of literature suggesting that parents are reliable informants, there are clear risks of bias in parent report. Washington noted that some parents may focus on aspirations for their child (what they would like their child to be able to do) rather than current ability.

Two primary conclusions resulted from this discussion. From an immediate standpoint, one conclusion was that informant-oriented tools can be quite valuable when paired with more objective measures. The second conclusion was that this issue of reliability of parent report warrants further attention. In particular, if there are systematic differences in reporting within or across groups, then it becomes critically important to document those differences and delineate how to interpret such reports.

Theme 3: What Should Researchers Be Trying to Measure?

The panel was asked whether there are considerations unique to this population that will bear on the decision to adjust an existing tool versus create a client-specific tool. The discussants agreed that the heterogeneity makes it difficult to identify one specific characteristic that could be considered unique to people with severe disabilities. Rather, it was suggested that interventionists should be seeking to assess common underlying constructs that can describe clients or participants across studies despite etiological, contextual, or other differences. In pursuit of this goal, it will be important to work with teams and brainstorm with colleagues from other disciplines to uncover these underlying constructs.

This point naturally led to a discussion about how to determine what to measure and how to measure that same construct across time and experience. One option would be to develop a systematic inventory of constructs that all researchers could consider as they characterize personal profiles or behaviors before, during, or after intervention. Such a taxonomy would allow for a better understanding of how those constructs relate to intervention both from the perspective of proximal (immediate) teaching effects as well as distal effects and social validity outcomes.

Even with a proposed taxonomy, however, the measurement of these constructs across an intervention period is complicated by the need to understand the relation of a measure taken early to a later outcome, when the individual will have matured, experienced other interventions, made the transition to new places, and so forth. There is a tension between the assumption of a fairly universal developmental trajectory (i.e., a similar order of acquisition, even if there are developmental or chronological lags) and the reality that there might be very different patterns of trajectory from a norm within certain disorders. Consequently, any taxonomy would have to take these two dimensions into account so that researchers would be able to ask whether any given child might be expected to follow a developmental trajectory or, instead, follow a different path to learning. The answer might have important implications for both assessment and intervention.

Another discussion thread concerned the World Health Organization's (WHO) International Classification of Functioning, Disability and Health (ICF) framework for characterizing functioning (WHO, 2001). The ICF framework focuses on participation and supports and, therefore, might be useful both as a means to identify critical underlying constructs and provide guidance for the development of new population-specific tools as well as the use of existing or adapted tools. The adoption of an ICF-based framework is currently an emphasis within the discipline of physical therapy and could make an excellent model for efforts in communication intervention as well.

Theme 4: How Do Researchers Maintain Experimental Control While Choosing Clinically Relevant Intervention Goals and Adapting to Heterogeneity?

One of the main points highlighted in the panel presentations was that the outcomes researchers might be interested in measuring must have social, clinical, and cultural relevance for clients and their families. It was noted during the discussion afterward that the outcomes and dependent measures of research are more nuanced today than they were in the past; that is, researchers have moved beyond basic skill-based measures to more sophisticated and sensitive assessments of socially and ecologically valid outcomes. Nuanced and contextualized dependent measures can sometimes be problematic, however, particularly given the heterogeneity of the population. When there is variability either in the participant sample or in the implementation of an intervention (to respond to the heterogeneity), it can pose challenges to reporting and replication. The very considerations that customize an intervention to improve its impact can interfere with the integrity of the research design.

This issue of balancing heterogeneity and individualization with experimental control arises in intervention studies in particular because the goal is to effect socially valid change in natural settings and contexts. It is more difficult to control aspects of the naturalistic contexts, relative to the laboratory. Although providing an environment in which it is easier to control extraneous variables, studies in the laboratory likely have less external validity. Is there a means to determine which context is more appropriate for any given study, outcome, or set of outcomes?

Although no single answer to this question may exist, the panelists suggested looking at a convergence of measures, rather than at isolated outcome measures. This approach allows for the possibility of identifying a highly relevant dimension that is not typically considered. Moreover, there may be some powerful statistical metrics, including latent variables that incorporate multiple related measures as dependent measures. These approaches represent potentially important future directions for highlighting effects that might otherwise be masked by the variability inherent in naturalistic contexts.

PROMINENT DISCUSSION THEMES

Theme 1: What Are the Issues in Moving from Demonstration Through the Phases of Efficacy and on to Effectiveness?

The discussion began with a question as to how interventions that have been primarily tested in constrained settings or with a limited number of participants get scaled up. This led to a fruitful discussion of the various stages of translational research, from initial demonstration or determination of the mechanism of change related to an intervention (Phase 1), to initial efficacy testing and verification of no adverse impact (Phase 2), through full-blown efficacy testing within a controlled environment and/or implemented by trained research personnel (Phase 3), to the study of effectiveness in which the treatment is disseminated or delivered to and/or by the population at large (Phase 4).

The ensuing discussion began to disentangle some of the key issues facing the discipline, in particular when moving from efficacy phases to the effectiveness phase. One main point was there is little reason to move to evaluation of effectiveness without strong evidence of efficacy (i.e., unambiguous demonstration of an effect under more controlled conditions). Therefore, it is critical in designing efficacy research to so thoroughly characterize the treatment that a manual detailing how it is to be delivered can be used to train those responsible for its implementation. The design not only must specify the population for whom it is expected that this treatment would be effective but also some sense of who might not benefit from the intervention. Clear delineation of which measures are expected to change and which are unlikely to be affected by the treatment is also needed.

A related issue concerned the distinction between effectiveness research in which the effectiveness of the disseminated treatment is studied intentionally versus broad dissemination of information tested only to the level of efficacy without the step of effectiveness evaluation. Both of these reflect situations in which the implementation of the treatment is no longer fully within the control of the investigators. The interpretation of implementation can be complicated by a multitude of factors, however, without specific effectiveness research. For instance, an intervention that has been demonstrated to be efficacious within laboratory or controlled conditions would be one with known parameters (participants, methods, mechanisms of change), including demonstrated efficacy. To move or scale this intervention into widespread use requires a delivery system that is committed to fidelity of implementation, even when that implementation is occurring outside of a controlled setting and/or is being implemented by a wide range of individuals. Evaluation of effectiveness is necessary to determine the ability of the intervention to operate in the larger environment and to assess the quality of the delivery/dissemination system.

Theme 2: What Are the Advantages and Disadvantages of Different Research Methods for Studying Efficacy and Effectiveness, Particularly with Low-Incidence and Heterogeneous Populations?

A lively discussion considered the relative contributions of different types of research methods for evaluating interventions, either in terms of their mechanisms of change and appropriate populations (efficacy) or in terms of the potential scalability to widespread usage (effectiveness). The panel presenters discussed a range of approaches from single-case designs through growth curve modeling and randomized controlled trials (RCTs), elaborating the benefits and drawbacks of each approach.

This discussion thread was prompted by a question about whether single-case research designs could satisfy the criteria identified for efficacy studies (e.g., thoroughly characterized treatment, details about how it is to be delivered, specific information about the populations expected to benefit as well as those likely not to benefit, which measures are expected to change after treatment). There was general agreement that single-case designs can be useful in demonstrating mechanisms of change associated with the provision or withdrawal of treatment and helping to define fidelity measures, as well as promixal, medial, and distal outcome measures, to be incorporated into large-scale studies. The potential contributions of single-case and large-group studies to determine efficacy as well as effectiveness was the subject of some debate.

One consideration was how generalization to a larger population might occur. Generalization to larger populations is limited because single-case research designs are by definition characterized by small sample size. A panelist expressed concern about how well findings "from a single-subject study where everything is so individualized" would apply beyond the initial participants studied. This argument suggests that the results obtained from larger group studies—typically, an average—are more likely to represent a generalized conclusion about a given intervention and, thus, more likely to apply across the population.

A competing viewpoint argued against the aggregation inherent in large-group designs. One panelist lacked confidence in the extent to which any group design captures or reflects the behavior or characteristics of any single member within the group. This panelist pointed out that obtaining an average across a large set of individuals risks an outcome "where [the] group average doesn't touch anybody that's in the group." Single-case research methods, however, allow examination of impact at the individual level and provide a sense of the proportion of individuals for whom the treatment leads to the targeted outcomes. One important suggestion was that the key to assessing potential generalization to the population was not the method itself, but rather the "concatenation of data," irrespective of how that concatenation occurs. Although concatenation of data in large-group designs occurs by sampling large numbers of participants, several discussants noted that concatenation of data in single-case designs occurs through the systematic and repeated replication of an effect over time, participants, behaviors, studies, and so forth.

From this discussion came acknowledgement of the potential complementary contributions of the two types of design and the importance of matching the design to the question being asked. A panelist used the example of growth curve modeling and noted that its usefulness depends on the question being asked and the extent to which a growth curve that is aggregated to a group level answers that question. Issues of sample size are also important because it can be questionable to use certain analytical techniques if the sample is too small; this practical issue is quite important with low-incidence populations. As one panelist put it: "I see those as different tools, and many of us need both of those tools."

Theme 3: How Do Researchers Balance the Experimental Constraints of Careful Scientific Approaches with the Practical Constraints of Clinicians and Other Stakeholders Who Provide Services to Individual Children?

The distinction was made earlier between effectiveness research and broad dissemination/implementation of treatment that has been tested for efficacy under controlled conditions but not yet evaluated in actual implementation. Concern was expressed that many treatments may be disseminated and implemented prematurely (i.e., without direct research on this final step). It was noted that the practical issues of service delivery are not trivial and that the relation to the scientific process is complicated. Many stakeholders have varying needs, from the children who need immediate treatment supports, to insurance companies that make decisions about service coverage, to administrators who insist that only evidence-based treatments can be provided. One panelist acknowledged that this is a cost-benefit world in which schools and insurers are demanding evidence derived from RCTs, but it is appropriate to say that researchers just do not have that kind of evidence in some cases. There is pressure to scale up from policy makers, but doing so may be contraindicated because the foundational evidence justifying an effectiveness study simply is not available. It can take years of iterative investigation to amass sufficient efficacy data to warrant a randomized trial study, particularly with small *n* research.

No definitive solution to this challenge emerged in the discussion. This very fact may highlight the critical need to develop closer links between the research and service delivery communities to enable greater appreciation for and alignment of the goals and needs of each.

Theme 4: How Do Publication Standards and Expectations Influence the Maturation of the Field?

It was widely acknowledged that standards by which research on communication interventions is evaluated have delayed the emergence of the taxonomies (of participant profiles, of interventions) that are so critical in determining what works for whom and under what conditions. One discussant noted that communication behavior falls along a continuum, yet the vast majority of studies in the field examine a narrow slice of communication behavior, leaving researchers with the impossible task of trying to obtain coherence in their knowledge base by piecing together results obtained from disparate participant groups working to achieve isolated communication targets.

It also was suggested that researchers in this arena need to be better advocates for their work with regard to publication. Journals are not in the business of publishing failures, and it is not fashionable to talk about what did not work. Editors and authors alike need to be resolute in supporting the publication of manuscripts that provide candid accounts of the messy and sometimes unsuccessful research undertaken with individuals who experience the greatest communication challenges. For example, it is not common practice to report attrition among participants, yet attrition can at times be a proxy for mismatch between participant characteristics and the features of the intervention. If researchers do not keep, analyze, and report the entire participant sample, then it is impossible to say for whom the treatment works and does not work, which in turn robs researchers of the opportunity to speculate as to why. In addition, the statistical management of the data—or the lack thereof—can be a barrier to publication of research findings. Finally, research reports published in peer-reviewed journals often do not contain the depth of information about participants and methods necessary to enable replication. Until the expectation for thorough explication of these details becomes the norm, researchers working in this low-incidence arena may be better able to mount valid replications of small *n* studies through a network of collaborators than by relying on the presence of adequate detail supporting replication in the literature.

CONCLUDING OBSERVATIONS

The two panels were characterized by diverse membership, and the insightful perspectives of the members converged to underscore the challenges facing researchers who seek to improve the communicative competence of individuals with severe disabilities. Although the first panel was tasked with exploring design challenges and the second with exploring measurement challenges, they catalyzed discussion that yielded an agenda capable of driving research for many years to come.

There was widespread agreement that research with this population is challenging, owing to considerations related to sample size, heterogeneity, assessment, and methods. Decades of iterative work is necessary in some cases to innovate and refine assessment or intervention approaches that are appropriately deployed across the full spectrum of those with the most significant disabilities. There was a clear sense that a multitude of design approaches can and should contribute to the knowledge base. In fact, a uniting theme across the panel presentations and ensuing discussion was that single-subject designs, small *n* designs, large *n* designs, and RCTs all contribute to the identification and refinement of intervention that enhance the communication success of individuals with the most significant communication challenges. Regardless of the scope of the design, the integrity of the design is paramount, and this includes appropriate specification of the participants, the procedures, and the measures.

There was strong support for the development of taxonomies by which researchers can characterize participant profiles as well as intervention elements; such taxonomies would help to systematize how design considerations and research findings are structured and reported, leading to greater coherence in an evidence base that is currently distressingly fragmented. There was also support for the creation of new assessment technologies and the refinement of existing ones to reflect important underlying constructs of communication. Woven together, these constructs provide a framework for understanding, describing, and measuring the universe of factors relevant to communication status; among them are individual characteristics, characteristics of the communication environment (including linguistic and cultural dimensions), and characteristics of the prevalent communication opportunities and expectations in the individual's environments. At the same time, distinctions among the developmental trajectories of those with significant communication challenges may require flexible application of the construct framework in order to accurately represent a given individual's communication profile.

Although RCTs are widely regarded as the gold standard with regard to research design, it is essential to have control of the independent variables that influence behavior prior to undertaking an RCT; otherwise, one risks spending a lot of money for relatively little good information. It is with regard to achievement of experimental control that the field has both excelled and continues to be challenged. Single-subject and small *n* designs have often been the default design given the heterogeneous and low-incidence nature of the target population, yet they also can serve as the steppingstones to more large-scale investigations. Replications of well-specified single-subject studies can yield data that is aggregable and amenable to more traditional data analysis. Single-subject and small *n* studies inform the development of fidelity measures that can be extended to large-scale studies. This is particularly important when conducting cross-site trials because there needs to be consistency in the way in which participants are selected and interventions are deployed in order to aggregate the data. Large-scale studies are expected to include proximal, medial, and distal measures, and the selection of these measures can be informed by—and piloted in—small-scale studies. A standardized assessment is not sufficiently sensitive to be used as an outcome measure in many cases, and it is prudent to identify measures that are going to behave well in a large-scale analysis.

At the same time, researchers must be prepared to balance the demands of experimental control with the need to respond to the clinical variability across individuals; this can be accomplished both with methodologies that anticipate the need for some flexibility within participants and through the application of powerful statistical means to extract information from complex data. It was clear from the panel discussions that there are viable approaches to empirical investigation that lie between the extremes of single-subject design and RCTs, and some approaches marry the best features of small-scale and large-scale designs. Statistical analysis can be undertaken at all levels, and there are a multitude of compelling reasons for the field to more consistently employ statistical methods, even in small *n* circumstances. Regardless of the design selected, the methods must be sufficiently manualized so they can be replicated with integrity across sites and across intervention agents.

REFERENCES

Cohen, J. (1990). Things I have learned (so far). *American Psychologist, 45*(12), 1304–1312.

Lord, C., Rutter, M., DiLavore, P., Risi, S., Gotham, K., & Bishop, S.L. (2012) *Autism diagnostic observation schedule. Second edition (ADOS-2).* Los Angeles, CA: Western Psychological Services.

Romski, M.A., & Sevcik, R.A. (1996). *Breaking the speech barrier: Language development through augmented means.* Baltimore, MD: Paul H. Brookes Publishing Co.

Sevcik, R.A., & Romski, M.A. (2002). The role of language comprehension in establishing early augmented conversations. In J. Reichle, D. Beukelman, & J. Light (Eds.), *Exemplary practices for beginning communicators: Implications for AAC* (pp. 453–474). Baltimore, MD: Paul H. Brookes Publishing Co.

Snell, M.E., Brady, N., McLean, L., Ogletree, W., Siegel, E., Sylvester, L., Sevcik, R. (2010). Twenty years of intervention research on the communication interaction of individuals who have severe disabilities. *American Journal on Intellectual and Developmental Disabilities, 115,* 363–380.

World Health Organization. (2001). *International classification of functioning, disability and health.* Geneva, Switzerland: Author.

IV

The Future

17

Communication Interventions for Individuals with Severe Disabilities

Research and Practice Gaps, Opportunities, and Future Directions

Rose A. Sevcik and MaryAnn Romski

Jane

Introducing a speech-generating device (SGD) can offer a tool by which new opportunities for communication may be offered for adults with intellectual disabilities (ID) and very limited expressive language, despite the fact that professionals may consider them beyond the developmental window for language and communication acquisition. Jane, a 30-year-old woman with a diagnosis of moderate ID and severe expressive communication disorder, communicated infrequently and typically relied on her mother to speak for her in conversational interactions. Jane's communication profile dramatically changed following the introduction of a SGD. She was able to communicate her thoughts and feelings in a more complex way with both familiar and unfamiliar partners. She gained confidence in her ability to express her emotions and needs with the aid of her SGD (see Cheslock, Barton-Hulsey, Romski, & Sevcik, 2008, for details of her development/experience during adulthood). Today, she has developed independent skills, including creating stunning paintings that people commission.

This volume is focused on communication intervention and individuals with severe disabilities because everyone has the right to communicate (Brady et al., in press), and the ability to communicate opens up the world to an individual. Individuals with severe disabilities include children and adults with a range of developmental disorders including autism spectrum disorder, intellectual and developmental disability (IDD), cerebral palsy, traumatic brain injury, stroke, and a

This chapter is adapted from Sevcik and Romski's (2011) Executive Summary of the NJC Conference on Research Challenges and Future Directions in Evidence-Based Communication Interventions for Individuals with Severe Disabilities. The research conference was funded by the National Institute on Deafness and Other Communication Disorders (NIDCD) grant 1R13 DC-011495.

range of genetic disorders (e.g., Down syndrome [DS], fragile X syndrome) as well as individuals who present with unknown etiologies (Beukelman & Mirenda, 2013). Individuals evidence a continuum of language and communication skills, and only a small percentage of individuals within each etiology fall into the severe disability range. The U.S. Census Bureau (2012) reported that the prevalence of severe disability in the United States population is 4.2% in children under 15 years old and 5.3% in individuals 15–24 years old. The percentage continues to increase to more than 20% as people age. The American Speech-Language-Hearing Association (ASHA; 2015) indicated that more than 2 million people in the United States have a severe communication disorder that affects the ability to speak. These individuals traditionally require ongoing, extensive support in more than one major life activity in order to participate in integrated community settings and to enjoy the quality of life available to people with fewer or no disabilities. They frequently have additional disabilities, including movement difficulties, sensory losses, and problem behaviors. Limited communication skills affect the life-course of all children and adults with severe disabilities (Romski & Sevcik, 2000).

The National Joint Committee Conference on Research Challenges and Future Directions in Evidence-Based Communication Interventions for Individuals with Severe Disabilities, however, was not about what makes these individuals different (e.g., etiology) but what they have in common—a severe communication disability that requires extensive communication intervention services and supports beginning very early in life. Severe communication disabilities compromise an individual's ability to interact with others, be educated, gain employment, participate in community life, and secure an overall good quality of life. Although communication interventions have been developed to address a range of communication needs such as self-expression, comprehension, social interaction, literacy, and the replacement of problem behavior (e.g., Reichle, Beukelman, & Light, 2001; Romski & Sevcik, 2005), empirically validated interventions across individual need(s) are somewhat limited and are still being developed in several domains (see Chapters 1–7). Many factors have contributed to the modest evidence base for communication interventions for people with severe disabilities. Individuals needing these services present varied profiles of etiologies, skills, strengths, and weaknesses as well as preferences. Differences in sensory abilities, cognitive functioning, and physical and motor capacities affect the design and implementation of communication interventions. Designing and implementing systematic communication interventions that accommodate individuals who may or may not speak make these complex communication needs particularly challenging. Although people with severe disabilities historically have been considered a low-incidence population, medical advances and public awareness have led to a significant increase in the identification of these individuals early in their development and an awareness of the communication challenges they face across the life span. Consumers and third-party payers today are asking about the evidence base for any proposed communication intervention, especially if payment is requested to cover the cost of that intervention. Evidence-based practice offers both criteria and approaches for rigorous evaluation of these difficult issues surrounding intervention efforts for people with significant communication disorders (ASHA, 2004).

The conference provided a stimulating and far-reaching analysis of the state of the knowledge base as well as the research design, methodology, and measurement challenges faced by the field. It resulted in an exciting conversation that sets the stage for researchers to enhance intervention science so that they can further positively affect the lives of individuals with severe disabilities. A number of research and training gaps were identified, and some innovative solutions were offered to address them. The purpose of this final chapter is to provide an overall synopsis of the conference outcomes and suggest future directions for the field.

THE EVIDENCE ABOUT COMMUNICATION INTERVENTIONS FOR INDIVIDUALS WITH SEVERE DISABILITIES: RESEARCH GAPS AND OPPORTUNITIES

Chapters 1–7 focused on research about interventions directed to the communication needs of individuals with severe disabilities. The topics provide a characterization of communication intervention studies, including participants with severe disabilities, interventions focused on prelinguistic communication, challenging behaviors, joint attention, augmentative and alternative communication (AAC), and parent training as well as intervention research targeted to individuals with autism, DS, and deafblindness. Five consistent themes emerged from these presentations and comprised much of the discussion during the conference—characterizing participants, developing an intervention continuum, assessing intervention outcomes, integrating rapidly advancing technologies, and implementing communication interventions in clinical and educational settings.

Characterizing Participants

The variability with which individuals with severe disabilities were described in intervention study reports was the first theme that was clear throughout the presentations. This variability makes it difficult to determine how similar or different participants were across studies and to draw strong conclusions regarding who benefits from what type of intervention. Presenters specifically highlighted the wide variability across studies in describing information about the individuals' chronological age, adaptive functioning, and the services and supports they were receiving. Few standardized assessment measures fully capture the skill sets of individuals with severe disabilities, thus making comparisons based on standardized assessments difficult. There also was a lack of detail about the participants' existing receptive and expressive language skills, including how many natural spoken words and sentences were understood as well as how many spoken words an individual had in his or her repertoire. They also noted the need to describe speech imitation abilities and spontaneous communication skills.

In particular, a great deal of variability exists about how researchers describe children and adults who encounter great difficulty using natural speech. Historically, *nonverbal* was the term of choice and is still used a great deal today. Nonverbal has been used to describe a broad range of children and adults who encounter a significant degree of difficulty producing speech from individuals who have motor speech disorders such as dysarthria but understand speech to individuals who have difficulty understanding as well as producing speech and language. This term unfortunately creates a substantial degree of confusion about the language, communication, and intellectual abilities of these children and adults. *Verbal* is defined in the Merriam-Webster dictionary as "of, relating to, or consisting of words" or "spoken rather than written" (http://www.merriam-webster.com). *Nonverbal* is defined as "not verbal: as being other than verbal nonverbal factors, involving minimal use of language nonverbal tests, or ranking low in verbal skill a nonverbal child." Nonverbal also has been used to describe messages that are conveyed in other ways, including paralinguistics and proxemics (Beukelman & Mirenda, 2013). *Nonspeaking* and *having complex communication needs* are other descriptive terms that have been used to characterize individuals who encounter great difficulty using speech. These terms have been variably defined in studies as using fewer than 30, 20, 10, 5, 1, or no intelligible single spoken words (e.g., Drager et al., 2006; Romski et al., 2010). The autism spectrum disorder community has begun using the term *minimally verbal* to describe individuals with autism who have difficulty with speech (Kasari, Brady, Lord, & Tager-Flusberg, 2013). This term, however, also suffers from the same issues as the other terms—how it is defined. These terms are all based on the premise that natural speech, not communication, is the only viable goal. Communication includes being the speaker and the listener in an interaction. Thus, it reflects understanding or receptive language skills and productive or expressive language skills. The inclusion of both receptive and expressive language skills is particularly important in determining the individual's communication profile as well as the most appropriate communication intervention approach to employ.

Two measures have been developed to assess the earliest stages of expressive communication. The Communication Matrix documents the communicative intents and modes (both typical and alternative) that an individual uses for expressive purposes (see Chapter 4; Rowland & Fried-Oken, 2010). Brady and her colleagues (2012) designed and tested the Communication Complexity Scale (CCS). The CCS assesses expressive communication and provides a summary score for interpretation that can be applied across populations of children and adults with limited (often presymbolic) communication forms. These two assessment tools provide optimism that standard ways to describe the expressive communication skill set of individuals with severe disabilities are now available. Using a standard measure, rather than using terms that do not have a consistent definition, will permit researchers to make comparisons across studies, enhance the empirical knowledge base, and ultimately support consistent clinical practice.

Tools to measure receptive language skills during the earliest stages of language development are still lacking. Many tools use parent/caregiver report to gain information about the individual's understanding of individual spoken words (e.g., *MacArthur-Bates Communication Development Inventory,* Fenson et al, 2007) when the individual is not able to provide a consistent pointing response to measures such as the *Peabody Picture Vocabulary Test* (Dunn & Dunn, 2007). Some promising tools deserve further exploration. Miller and Paul (1995) provided a beginning point with the Emerging Language Section of the *Clinical Assessment of Language Comprehension,* although it does not provide a consistent way to measure performance. This section of their measure provides seven tasks (i.e., familiar routines, joint references, object and person names, actions words, absent people and objects, two-word relations, turn-taking in discourse) that assess various developmental aspects of early language comprehension individualized to the person being assessed with words that are found with the individual's daily environment. Brady, Anderson, Hahn, Obermeier, and Kapa (2014) explored the use of eye-tracking tools to measure the receptive language skills of individuals with autism who do not otherwise provide a clear response to the task.

Clear descriptive information that is presented in each study is needed in future studies. It must include information about the general characteristics of the participants (i.e., age, ethnicity, developmental level, history of services and supports) as well as detailed information about the individuals' speech-language profile. This characterization must include not only expressive skills but also receptive skills that can provide insight about the individual's understanding of language and communication (Sevcik & Romski, 2002). These language skills must be described in terms of number of natural spoken words, signs, and gestures; phrases (including length); morphological and syntactic skills; and pragmatic skills (i.e., communication interaction skills such as turn-taking). Including a description of the partners (adults and children) with whom the individual communicates and the environments in which the individual communicates is also important.

The next step is for the field to adopt a measure or profile that becomes the gold standard for the characterization of the communication skills of individuals with severe disabilities. What is needed is similar to what has been accomplished in the area of autism. The Autism Diagnostic Observation Schedule (Lord & Rutter, 2010), a standardized protocol for observation of social-communicative behavior associated with autism, has become this instrument and is expected to be utilized in research studies to report children's autism diagnosis. The World Health Organization's (WHO) International Classification of Functioning, Disability and Health (ICF; http://www.who.int/classifications/icf/en) was discussed at the conference, and its application to individuals with severe disabilities has been considered (Bornman, 2004). Rowland and her colleagues (2012) suggested an adaptation for children who use AAC. Determining and implementing a gold standard for describing the broadly conceived communication profiles of children and adults with severe communication disabilities is still needed.

Developing an Intervention Continuum

The breadth of the interventions themselves was a second theme that emerged. Although there is a substantial history of information about communication interventions in general, the evidence base including individuals with severe disabilities is somewhat fragmented in terms of focused areas of intervention along the language continuum. Treatments are not always well specified as to content or protocol, treatment fidelity, intensity, or duration, which makes replication and clinical adaptation challenging. The most consistent intervention data for this population is in the area of requesting, which is the earliest communication function to emerge (see Chapter 1; Snell et al., 2010). Most of the research has been conducted with school-age children who have made little progress learning to communicate. Sample sizes in these studies vary greatly but are typically very small. The intervention continuum must be expanded beyond single words to include combinatorial utterances and sentences (e.g., Binger, Kent-Walsh, Ewing, & Taylor, 2010). There is also a need to ensure that caregivers, families, peers, educators, and other community partners are included in information about the targeted interventions because they are the partners with whom the individual is communicating.

AAC is one area that requires particular development. Research suggests that AAC may play an important role in communication development for individuals with severe disabilities. Myths still exist, however, that suggest AAC is considered a secondary intervention used with older rather than younger individuals (Romski & Sevcik, 2005). A recent systematic review of the literature on AAC and early language intervention suggests that AAC can be a primary intervention and provide a transition to spoken communication for some young children (Romski, Sevcik, Barton-Hulsey, & Whitmore, 2015). Intervention data also support that AAC does not hinder natural speech development for young children but actually facilitates it (Romski et al., 2010). Including AAC interventions within the context of emerging language intervention is important so that individuals may be served with a range of options beginning with a transitional communication system, if needed, to a permanent communication system appropriate to an individual's age and skill set.

Assessing Intervention Outcomes

How investigators assess intervention outcomes was a third theme raised by many of the presentations. There are two issues—the heterogeneity of the population and how to measure change in outcome. The heterogeneity of the population raises many questions about the types of research designs that should be incorporated into intervention research. Barker and Francis argued that an average effect might not be what researchers are looking for because of the heterogeneity of the population (see Chapter 10). Instead, researchers might need to incorporate mixed models using group and single-subject designs that can be replicated to accomplish their goals (see Chapter 9). Burchinal (2011) encouraged the field to move beyond exploratory studies into investigations that control variables and, thus, strongly argued for randomized controlled trials. Alternate methodological approaches, such as SMART designs (Kasari et al., 2014) and growth curve analyses, need to be considered to maximize power related to relatively small sample sizes. Bakeman strongly suggested that researchers should accept the reality of relatively small sample sizes and use methods and analytic techniques to address the questions they ask with the data they have (see Chapter 11).

Although there is a range of views about the types of research designs to employ, studies must report successes and failures as well as include rates of participant attrition to better understand interventions' outcomes. Ensuring that future studies can replicate successful intervention approaches is also critical. To do so, studies must clearly articulate the intervention protocols that are employed. These replications must mirror the characterization of the study participants and include facets such as the duration and intensity of implemented interventions. Furthermore, comparing different interventions within a single study, in a systematic review, or in a meta-analysis will advance the research base.

The types of outcomes desired is the second issue. Is it a language outcome or a social-communication outcome? Is the targeted goal a change in the perceptions of communication partners such as parents, peers, or co-workers? Are maintenance and generalization being assessed along with the initial acquisition of skills? Articulating the outcome goal(s) of the intervention is essential. Standardized measurement tools do not capture what the individuals are learning from the different interventions in which they participate. Using such tools may actually underestimate the individuals' success in the intervention. Standardized assessments have limitations because they are not normed on this population, and individuals often do not obtain a basal score on these tests. The need to develop and utilize new assessment tools that are sensitive to the skills associated with intervention outcomes and detect meaningful change over time is of critical importance to advancing the field. Language skills are a critical component of the primary outcomes of communication intervention research. It is critical to include detailed receptive and expressive language measures including the range of elicited and spontaneous language skills across environments and partners as well as change over time. These assessments also must incorporate responses that do not require spoken language skills and are culturally appropriate. Tools and techniques that have been used in other fields of study can offer new methods of measurement for individuals with severe disabilities. Eye-tracking measurement tools are one example (e.g., Brady et al., 2014). Other examples are incorporating the use of neuroimaging (e.g., Wilkinson, Stutzman, & Seisler, 2015) or auditory evoked potentials (Molfese, Morris, & Romski, 1990) as tools that can be paired with behavioral measures to identify relationships between changes in an individual's brain and behavior so that researchers can begin to understand why specific language and communication interventions are effective. Social validation is an often overlooked area in communication intervention research (see Chapter 15). The need to socially validate intervention findings that take the perceptions of others, including families, peers, and employers, into account is essential. The importance of ensuring a diverse sample and differentiating the effects of intervention across cultures is lacking in empirical studies as well (see Chapter 13). Results cannot readily be generalized beyond the sample when the sample of individuals with severe disabilities is not ethnically and linguistically diverse. Assessments also must be conducted in a culturally and linguistically appropriate fashion (ASHA, 2005). Adaptations of assessments for individuals with multilingual histories and severe disabilities are needed (Bornman, Sevcik, Romski, & Pae, 2010). Attention to the perceptions of families and how people view the skills of the individuals are important to include as well (Romski et al., 2011).

There is much to be learned from studies of individuals from higher incidence etiology groups (e.g., subtypes of learning disabilities) about subtypes individuals based on their response to intervention. For example, Romski and Sevcik (1996) described two achievement patterns in their intervention study with school-age youth with significant ID (beginning and advanced). Although exploratory in nature, this distinction appeared to be tied to the individual's speech comprehension skills at the onset of intervention and suggested further delineation of the intervention to address the particular needs of the beginning achievers. Describing individual patterns of intervention achievements linked to the individual's intervention onset profile may be a way to better link intervention type to individual for optimal outcomes.

Integrating Rapidly Advancing Technologies

The rapid advancement of technologies and the need to consider how these technologies can advance intervention science was the fourth theme in some of the presentations. The technologies described included readily available smartphones and tablet computers (e.g., iPad with applications) as well as innovative software packages (e.g., LENA). Their widespread use by the general public results in two important opportunities. First, they are available off the shelf at a relatively reasonable cost. Second, their use does not make the person with a severe disability look different but rather just like everyone else.

Researchers are at the very beginning of the integration of these emerging technologies into communication assessments and interventions, and the potential is great. The integration of computerized technologies into assessment approaches will permit greater flexibility and access for individuals with severe disabilities. These adaptations may include, but are not limited to, the use of assistive technology devices (e.g., mouse, joystick), time adaptations, and size/color of stimuli adaptations. They are a critical component of intervention development because researchers may not be able to gain access to individuals' learning without them. A number of opportunities exist to expand assessment, and LENA is a recently developed application in this category.

> LENA Pro is an integrated processing and display software package that enables researchers, speech-language pathologists (SLPs), audiologists, and pediatricians to collect, manage, and analyze multiple recordings of children ages 2 months to 48 months. LENA Pro reports include count and percentile data on speech-language measurements such as estimates of adult words spoken to and around the key child (the child wearing the LENA recorder), adult–child conversational interactions, and child vocalizations. (http://www.lenafoundation.org/lena-pro)

Mobile technologies (MTs) include smartphones and tablet computers equipped with applications (apps). Apps are pieces of specialized software loaded onto MTs to provide a broad range of specialized functions, including intervention. They have been used to provide a range of health services, from monitoring drug treatment to reminding parents to talk to their children. These apps can assist interventionists in providing 24-hour, 7-days-a-week support to parents and caregivers who are communicating with individuals with severe disabilities (Romski, Bornman, & Sevcik, 2015). These applications can create a novel approach to intervention by enhancing the standard intervention protocol with home caregiver strategies monitored and coached by clinicians via the MTs. These technologies have the potential to deliver communication interventions to individuals across a range of communities. Finally, although not discussed at the conference, brain–computer interfaces (BCIs) are being employed as environmental controls and communication output for adults with significant motor impairments (e.g., amyotrophic lateral sclerosis) (Fried-Oken, 2015). As BCI technologies evolve, their utility for communication assessment and intervention for individuals with severe disabilities may open heretofore unanticipated possibilities (Fried-Oken, 2015; Romski, 2015).

Researchers must be vigilant and open to the potential for these new technologies to affect communication intervention services and supports for individuals with severe disabilities. The limits of their application are unknown at this point in time. Researchers must not make the mistake they made when people with severe disabilities were deemed ineligible for AAC devices because they were thought not to have what were arbitrary prerequisites (National Joint Committee [NJC], 2003).

Implementing Communication Interventions in Clinical and Educational Settings

The need to develop and test interventions that can be implemented by professionals in clinical and educational settings was the final theme echoed in many of the presentations. This issue speaks to the need to conduct clinical trials and move interventions forward to the point that knowledge can be translated and implemented in real-world settings (Grimshaw, Eccles, Lavis, Hill, & Squires, 2012). Communication interventions are not the only research and practice area to face this ongoing challenge. Grimshaw et al. (2012) reported that a failure to translate research into practice and policy is very common in health professions. What needs to be done for such translations to be successful? Eccles and Mittman defined *implementation science* as "the scientific study of methods to promote the systematic uptake of research findings and other evidence-based practices into routine practice" (2006, p. 1) with the goal of improving how new and successful interventions are implemented into practices. Grimshaw et al. suggested that the basic unit of knowledge translation should be "up to date systematic reviews or other syntheses of research findings" (p. 1). Systematic translational procedures need to be developed in order that the experimentally derived communication interventions can be applied to clinical and educational settings. Translators need to identify the key messages to be conveyed as well as the target audiences or stakeholders (e.g., clinicians, educators, parents, policy makers). The NJC has actively attended to this issue across its lifetime. It published guidelines for serving the communication needs of people with severe disabilities (NJC, 1992) and in an upcoming publication provides updated guidance for the field about communication assessment and intervention practices derived from contemporary research (Brady et al., 2016). The guidance document includes a revised and updated Communication Bill of Rights that serves as an overarching policy statement affirming the importance of communication for all.

OPPORTUNITIES MOVING FORWARD

In summary, these five themes offer areas for an approach forward. There is no one way or one approach that will address all the issues, but there must be an integrated approach. A broad national research agenda that includes the support of professional and consumer organizations, scientific journals, and federal agencies is needed. This plan must utilize the themes emerging from this conference to seed research areas. A collaborative network of interdisciplinary researchers focused on communication intervention and individuals with severe disabilities needs to be established. Such a network must include investing in and supporting a new generation of junior investigators who will spearhead the area well into the future.

Cross-site collaborative projects that can yield larger sample sizes and permit the development and scaling up of communication interventions for people with severe disabilities are needed as a part of this plan. Several dimensions for future research studies were specified, including the development of a gold standard consistent characterization of the individual with a severe disability who participates in a communication intervention research study. This characterization must include a standard set of demographic (e.g., chronological age, sensory skills, individual abilities, family information, educational and intervention experiences) along with language and communication (e.g., receptive and expressive language skills, including vocabulary size, the use of phrases or sentences) information. Ensuring the inclusion of individuals and their families from diverse ethnic, socioeconomic, and linguistic backgrounds is essential to expanding research with individuals with severe disabilities. The development of a continuum of communication intervention strategies, using a common terminology that includes measures of the fidelity of their implementation, is necessary. This product should illustrate the types of interventions that are available along the range of language and communication development and the data (or lack thereof) to support them. This continuum may include the identification of extant knowledge of effective interventions along with the areas that require development and additional specification.

Creating a database that serves as a repository for the data from language and communication intervention studies should be a priority. It would be available for secondary data analyses and potentially spur new studies. In addition, such a resource would afford the opportunity to disseminate intervention findings to both the scientific and professional communities, including offering access to the public.

In conclusion, there is optimism about the development of communication interventions for individuals with severe disabilities. Researchers and practitioners alike must ensure that individuals with severe disabilities consistently receive the communication services and supports they need to enhance their quality of life and facilitate their contributions to society. Having the power of communication will facilitate the full and meaningful inclusion of individuals with severe disabilities into society, as Jane's profile illustrates at the beginning of the chapter.

REFERENCES

American Speech-Language-Hearing Association. (2004). *Report of the joint coordinating committee on evidence-based practice.* Retrieved from www.asha.org/njc

American Speech-Language-Hearing Association. (2005). *Roles and responsibilities of speech-language pathologists serving persons with mental retardation/developmental disabilities.* Retrieved from www.asha.org/njc

American Speech-Language-Hearing Association. (2015). *Information for AAC users.* Retrieved from http://www.asha.org/public/speech/disorders/InfoAACUsers.htm

Beukelman, D.R., & Mirenda, P. (2013). *Augmentative and alternative communication: Supporting children and adults with complex communication needs* (4th ed.). Baltimore, MD: Paul H. Brookes Publishing Co.

Binger, C., Kent-Walsh, J., Ewing, C., & Taylor, S. (2010). Teaching educational assistants to facilitate the multisymbol message productions of young students who require augmentative and alternative communication. *American Journal of Speech-Language Pathology, 19,* 108–120.

Bornman, J. (2004). The World Health Organisation's terminology and classification: Application to severe disability. *Disability and Rehabilitation, 26,* 182–188.

Bornman, J., Sevcik, R.A., Romski, M.A., & Pae, H.K. (2010). Successfully translating language and culture when adapting assessment measures. *Journal of Policy and Practice in Intellectual Disabilities, 7,* 111–118.

Brady, N., Anderson, C., Hahn, L., Obermeier, S., & Kapa, L. (2014). Eye tracking as a measure of receptive vocabulary with autism spectrum disorders. *Augmentative and Alternative Communication, 30,* 147–159.

Brady, N.C., Bruce, S., Goldman, A., Erickson, K., Mineo, B., Ogletree, B.T., Wilkinson, K. (in press). Communication services and supports for individuals with severe disabilities: Guidance for assessment and intervention. *American Journal on Intellectual and Developmental Disabilities.*

Brady, N., Fleming, K., Thiemann-Bourque, K., Olswang, L., Dowden, P., Saunders, M., & Marquis, J. (2012). Development of the communication complexity scale. *American Journal of Speech-Language Pathology, 21,* 16–28. doi:10.1044/1058-0360

Burchinal, P. (2011, June). *Options for research designs: Integrating group and single subject designs.* Discussion paper presented at the NJC Conference on Research Challenges and Future Directions in Evidence-Based Communication Interventions for Individuals with Severe Disabilities, Atlanta, GA.

Cheslock, M., Barton-Hulsey, A., Romski, M.A., & Sevcik, R.A. (2008). Using a speech generating device to enhance communicative abilities and interactions for an adult with moderate intellectual disability: A case report. *Intellectual and Developmental Disabilities, 46,* 376–386.

Drager, K., Postal, V.J., Carrolus, L., Castellano, M., Gagliano, C., & Glynn, J. (2006). The effect of aided language modeling on symbol comprehension and production in 2 preschoolers with autism. *American Journal of Speech-Language Pathology, 15,* 112–125.

Dunn, L.M., & Dunn, D.M. (2007). *Peabody Picture Vocabulary Test–4th Edition.* San Antonio, TX: Pearson..

Eccles, M., & Mittman, B. (2006). Welcome to implementation science. *Implementation Science, 1,* 1–3.

Fenson, L., Marchman, V.A., Thal, D., Dale, P., Reznick, J.S., & Bates, E. (2007). The *MacArthur-Bates Communicative Development Inventories: User's Guide and Technical Manual.* (2nd Edition) Baltimore, MD: Paul H. Brookes Publishing Co.

Fried-Oken, M. (2015, September). *The state of the field for AAC-BCI synergy.* Paper presented in L. Shekim & M. Fried-Oken NIDCD Virtual Workshop "Towards AAC-BCI Syngery."

Grimshaw, J., Eccles, M., Lavis, J., Hill, S., & Squires, J. (2012). Knowledge translation of research findings. *Implementation Science, 7,* 1–17.

Kasari, C., Brady, N., Lord, C., & Tager-Flusberg, H. (2013). Assessing the minimally verbal school-aged child with autism spectrum disorder. *Autism Research, 6,* 479–493.

Kasari, C., Kaiser, A., Goods, K., Nietfeld, J., Mathy, P., Landa, R., Almirall, D. (2014). Communication interventions for minimally verbal children with autism: A sequential multiple assignment randomized trial. *Journal of the American Academy of Child and Adolescent Psychiatry, 53,* 635–646.

Lord, C., & Rutter, M. (2010). *Autism Diagnostic Observation Schedule.* New York, NY: Pearson.

Miller, J., & Paul, R. (1995). *Clinical Assessment of Language Comprehension.* Baltimore, MD: Paul H. Brookes Publishing Co.

Molfese, D., Morris, R., & Romski, M.A. (1990). Semantic discrimination in non-speaking youngsters with moderate or severe retardation: Electrophysiological correlates. *Brain and Language, 38,* 61–74.

National Joint Committee for the Communication Needs of Persons with Severe Disabilities. (1992). *Guidelines for meeting the communication needs of persons with severe disabilities.* Retrieved from www.asha.org/policy or www.asha.org/njc

National Joint Committee for the Communication Needs of Persons with Severe Disabilities. (2003). *Position statement on access to communication services and supports: Concerns regarding the application of restrictive "eligibility" policies.* Retrieved from www.asha.org/njc

Reichle, J., Beukelman, D., & Light J. (Eds.). (2001). *Implementing an augmentative communication system: Exemplary strategies for beginning communicators.* Baltimore, MD: Paul H. Brookes Publishing Co.

Romski, M.A. (2015, September). *Entering uncharted waters: Clinical issues in AAC and BCI for the pediatric population* Paper presented in L. Shekim & M. Fried-Oken NIDCD Virtual Workshop "Towards AAC-BCI Syngery."

Romski, M.A., Bornman, J., & Sevcik, R.A. (2015). *Using mobile health technology to optimize communication outcomes for south african children with developmental disorders.* Working paper.

Romski, M.A., & Sevcik, R.A. (1996). *Breaking the speech barrier: Language development through augmented means.* Baltimore, MD: Paul H. Brookes Publishing Co.

Romski, M.A., & Sevcik, R.A. (2000). Communication, technology, and disability. In M. Wehmeyer & J.R. Patton (Eds.), *Mental retardation in the 21st century* (pp. 299–313). Austin, TX: PRO-ED.

Romski, M.A., & Sevcik, R.A. (2005). Early intervention and augmentative communication: Myths and realities. *Infants and Young Children, 18,* 174–185.

Romski, M.A., Sevcik, R.A., Adamson, L.B., Cheslock, M.A., Smith, A., Barker, R.M., & Bakeman, R. (2010). Randomized comparison of parent-implemented augmented and non-augmented language intervention on vocabulary development of toddlers with developmental delays.

Journal of Speech, Language, and Hearing Research, 53, 350–364.

Romski, M.A., Sevcik, R.A., Adamson, L.B., Smith, A., Cheslock, M., & Bakeman, R. (2011). Parent perceptions of the language development of toddlers with developmental delays before and after participation in parent-coached language interventions. *American Journal of Speech-Language Pathology, 20,* 111–118.

Romski, M.A., Sevcik, R.A., Barton-Hulsey, A., & Whitmore, A. (2015). AAC and early intervention: What a difference thirty years makes. *Augmentative and Alternative Communication, 31,* 1–22.

Rowland, C., & Fried-Oken, M. (2010). Communication Matrix: A clinical and research assessment tool targeting children with severe communication disorders, *Journal of Pediatric Rehabilitation Medicine, 3,* 319–329.

Rowland, C., Fried-Oken, M., Steiner, S., Lollar, D., Phelps, R., Simeonsson, R., & Granlund, M. (2012). Developing the ICF-CY for AAC profile and code set for children who rely on AAC. *Augmentative and Alternative Communication, 31,* 21–32.

Sevcik, R.A., & Romski, M.A. (2002). The role of language comprehension in establishing early augmented conversations. In J. Reichle, D. Beukelman, & J. Light (Eds.) *Implementing an augmentative communication system: Exemplary strategies for beginning communicators* (pp. 453–474) Baltimore, MD: Paul H. Brookes Publishing Co.

Snell, M., Brady, N., McLean, L., Ogletree, B., Siegel, E., Sylvester, L., Sevcik, R. (2010). Twenty years of communication intervention research with individuals who have severe intellectual and developmental disabilities. *American Journal on Intellectual and Developmental Disabilities, 115,* 364–380.

U.S Census Bureau (2012). Americans with Disabilities: 2010. Retrieved from http://www.census.gov/prod/2012pubs/p70-131.pdf

Wilkinson, K., Stutzman, A., & Seisler, A. (2015). N400 brain responses to spoken phrases paired with photographs of scenes: Implications for visual scene displays in AAC systems. *Augmentative and Alternative Communication, 31,* 51–62.

Index

Page numbers followed by *b*, *f*, and *t* indicate boxes, figures, and tables, respectively.